CHRISTIC
PATRISTIC BAPTISM

CHRISTIC BAPTISM AND PATRISTIC BAPTISM

ΒΑΠΤΙΖΩ

AN INQUIRY INTO THE
MEANING OF THE WORD
AS DETERMINED BY THE USAGE OF
THE HOLY SCRIPTURES
AND PATRISTIC WRITINGS

BY

James W. Dale

NEW INTRODUCTION
BY
Robert H. Countess

Bolchazy-Carducci Publishers

P&R Publishing Company

Loewe Belfort Projects, Inc.

Cover design
Cynthia Henderson

Reprint of
the Second Edition, 1874, Philadelphia
Presbyterian Board of Publication

© Copyright 1995
Robert H. Countess, Introduction

Published by:

BOLCHAZY-CARDUCCI   P&R
PUBLISHERS   PUBLISHING
1000 Brown Street   P.O. Box 817
Wauconda, IL 60084   Phillipsburg, NJ 08865

ISBN 0-86516-263-8   ISBN 0-87552-234-3

LOEWE BELFORT
PROJECTS, INC.
28755 Sagewood Circle
Toney, AL 35773

Printed in the United States of America

Library of Congress Cataloging-in-Publication Data

Dale, James W. (James Wilkinson), 1812–1881.
     [Inquiry into the usage of [baptizō] and the nature of christic and
patristic baptism, as exhibited in the Holy Scriptures]
     Christic and patristic baptism : [baptizō] : an inquiry into the
meaning of the word as determined by the usage of christic and
patristic writers / by James W. Dale : new introduction by Robert H.
Countess.
          p.   cm.
     Originally published: An inquiry into the usage of [baptizō] and the
nature of christic and patristic baptism, as exhibited in the Holy
Scriptures. Philadelphia : Presbyterian Board of Publication and
Sabbath-School Work, 1874. With new introd.
     Includes bibliographical references and index.
     ISBN 0-86516-263-8 (Bolchazy)—ISBN 0-87552-234-3 (P&R)
     1. Baptism—History of doctrines. 2. Baptism—Biblical teaching.
3. Baptizein (The Greek word) 4. Bible. N.T.—Criticism, interpretation, etc. 5. Jesus Christ—Baptism. I. Title.
BV811.D34 1995
234'.161'09015—dc20   94–44997

INTRODUCTION.

Robert H. Countess

Dale's monumental four-volume work on *baptizo* is a master-piece of lexicographical scholarship. Although written in part as a response to mid-nineteenth-century dogmatism, Dale's conclusions are directed neither at Baptists nor at Presbyterians but should be of interest to both. For according to Dale, the literal and metaphorical senses of *baptizo* refer to general, not specific, actions. Thus it is as incorrect for Presbyterians to assert that *baptizo* means "sprinkle" or "pour" as it is for Baptists to assert that it means "immerse" or "dip."

Thus I wrote on page 3 of my Introduction to *Classic Baptism* in 1989, the first reprint volume of this massive work by the pastor and Greek-Latin Classics scholar, Dr. James Wilkinson Dale (1812–81). Readers are encouraged to read carefully this Introduction since it provides an overview of the entire scope of the argument. Dale's basic argument was:

> Whatever is capable of thoroughly changing the character, state, or condition of any object, is capable of baptizing that object; and by such change of character, state, or condition does, in fact, baptize it.

So simple and yet so forcefully supported by the evidence of hundreds of contexts, this argument deserves continued publicizing to the Christian church so that petty wranglings over "the how" (= mode) may cease.

My aim stands firm and clear: these volumes can bring peace to the church. And this final two-volume-bound-as-one reprint is, as it were, "the icing on the cake."

Christic Baptism was published in 1874, and Dale defined Christic baptism as "Christ's baptism in its various aspects." It was (1) that baptism which Jesus Christ personally received; (2) the immediate baptism administered by Jesus Christ personally upon sinners; (3) the ritual baptism on these believing sinners authorized by Jesus Christ to be performed by others; and (4) the everlasting baptism He secured redemptively for these redeemed sinners.

Christic baptism is twofold: (1) real and (2) ritual. The real baptism is that thorough moral change of condition of the soul by the Holy Spirit's uniting one by faith to the Savior. Ritual baptism is declared by word but exhibited by pure water applied to the body and symbolizing the atoning blood of the crucified Christ.

Patristic Baptism was also published in 1874 and its pagination continued that of *Christic Baptism*. Thus the reader may understand why the Dale set is variously called sometimes a four-volume, but at other times a five-volume, set. *Patristic Baptism* is only 159 pages, whereas *Christic Baptism* is some 470 in length. Dale wrote that *Patristic Baptism* was *Christic Baptism* "as exhibited in the truth and error of Patristic writers."

What is particularly significant, according to Dr. Dale, is that the church fathers he cited displayed a confusing unification of water and Holy Spirit, by which confusion "they are made coactive in effecting an exclusively spiritual baptism, and the symbol baptism of Scripture by pure water destroyed." Along with this there arose ritualistic, even superstitious, ingredients such as exorcism, turning toward both West and East, and the use of oil, salt, and spittle.

Patristic Baptism citations by Dale reach as far as the fifth century.

By enumeration of volumes, they appeared in first edition as follows:

> Classic Baptism 1867
> Judaic Baptism 1869
> Johannic Baptism 1871
> Christic Baptism 1874
> Patristic Baptism 1874

And excerpts from various journals and church newspapers appeared widely both praising and criticizing Dale's work. These comments themselves make for fascinating reading for both their content and their timeliness.

Recently, I discovered a 416-page book attempting to rebut the Dale volumes. It is *Studies on the Baptismal Question; Including a*

Review of Dr. Dale's "Inquiry into the Usage of Baptizo." Its author
was a Rev. David B. Ford, and the work was published in Boston by
H. A. Young & Co. and in New York by Ward & Drummong in 1879.

Thus, Ford's rebuttal came only five years after the last Dale
volume was published and must be considered carefully for its timely
criticisms.

Ford acknowledges that Dale's work was "the hugest work that
has ever appeared on this subject" (p. 5). He praised Dr. Dale for his
originality, ingenuity, intellectual sharpness, unwearied diligence,
and vast research. He criticized Dale for putting forth certain data
and suppressing others—in ways useful to his thesis. Dale also was
guilty of repetition even to the point of overkill, wrote Ford.

Ford's commitment to *baptizo* as immersion or dipping is everywhere in evidence and he argues that lexicographers ought to be
followed when they equate, or virtually equate, immersing with dipping.

Ford then—amazingly!—writes:

> The work of Dr. Dale we regard as, on the whole, essentially
> and strongly Baptistic; and *we are glad* (in one sense) *that he
> has written theses volumes.* In his apology for undertaking this
> *"Inquiry into the Usage of Baptizo"* he says, "The treatment of
> the subject, as heretofore conducted, left the merits of the case,
> in some respects at least, clouded with uncertainty, and em-
> barrassed with perplexity." (p. 7)

Ford's pleasure is bound up with, I suggest, a fundamental misunderstanding of Dale's discussion of the primary usage of *baptizo*
(what I called *Baptizo*[1] in "Figure One" on page 12 of my Introduction to *Classic Baptism).* Dale extensively proved that this primary
usage was a literal envelopment of an object by something, perhaps
a fluid such as water.

Thus, I can understand Ford's joy; however, it is a joy based on
his missing the main point, and his book is written on this erroneous premise he posits at the outset (p. 8). Space, of course, does not
permit extensive rebuttal of Ford's book, but the diligent reader can
readily see where Ford erred.

Ford also erred greatly—in the company of many religious dog-
matists—by insisting upon lexicographers' entries as being capable
of determining word meanings. Dale deserves to be consulted again
and again on this matter, because the careful Bible student is ever
near the precipice into which he falls when he relies too heavily

upon dictionary entries for authoritative resolution of doctrinal issues. Lexicographers fundamentally record usage by authors, and since usage varies it can only be descriptive, never prescriptive—that is, it can never govern what a text must mean. Interpretation is too complex for such a simplistic approach, which allows dictionaries to have such power.

What Ford's detailed critique does afford, however, is an exceptional opportunity for the advanced student of Greek philology regarding *baptizo* to engage in what may have been the best critical effort to counter Dr. Dale's twenty years of research and writing. In my opinion, Ford failed abjectly. Dale triumphed.

Over the years of reprinting these volumes I have sought endorsements by Protestant, Catholic, and Jewish scholars and students. This ecumenical approach has been a deliberate effort toward realizing my goal of effecting peace on the subject of water baptismal mode. On a lecture tour in Australia in 1988, I spoke at a Baptist college one day about *Classic Baptism* and a few days later to a Presbyterian seminary on the same. Both audiences were clearly receptive and not threatened as I emphasized that Dale demonstrates that water mode must come from a Scripture context but not from *baptizo* itself, since over forty different English verbs are required to translate *baptizo* just in the classical Greek contexts.

Over the centuries a *pox* has been on the church when the matter of water baptism arises. I conclude this reprint effort with the greatest appreciation for Bryce Craig and Lou Bolchazy, my co-publishers, and especially for the most capable editor Thom Notaro, but I also conclude with the offer of *pax* (Latin: peace) to the church in hope that it will mitigate—better, cancel—the *pox*.

The Dutch theologian of missions Herman Bavinck placed at the beginning of one of his books the Latin sentence, *"Ecclesia reformata est ecclesia reformanda"* (A Reformed church is a reforming church).

I completely agree. This final volume goes forth with this hope as paramount.

"Sed malumus in Scripturis minus si forte sapere, quam contra. Proinde sensum Domini custodire debemus atque præceptum. Non est levior transgressio in interpretatione, quam in conversatione."—TERTULLIAN.

"Right exposition is at variance with all heresy ; and a fuller and more literal apprehension of Scripture is, at the same time, a shield against doctrinal error."—PUSEY.

COURSE OF ARGUMENT.

I. What is Christic Baptism?

1. Real; 2. Ritual. A modern theory. Objections to this theory: Philological, Chronological, Symbological, Exegetical, ... 17-26

1. *Baptism of Jesus by John.* A covenant baptism. Not " the baptism of John." A formal covenant, with ritual symbol, " to fulfil all righteousness," 27-31

2. *Baptism of Jesus by the Holy Ghost.* Real Baptism. Qualifying to fulfil the covenant assumed, ... 31-34

3. *Baptism of Jesus into Penal Death.* Emblemized as a drinking from a cup. Drank through life, in Gethsemane, on Calvary. Not martyr baptism. The ground baptism of Christianity. Baptism by drinking from a cup, a common baptism among the Classics. Baptism " into Christ" by the Holy Spirit secures the blessings obtained by Christ through his personal baptism into an atoning death, ... 34-52

II. Christ, the Baptizer by the Holy Ghost.

The Holy Ghost abides in Christ as his divine anointing. Christ abides in the Holy Ghost and in the fulness of his influence lives, overcomes Satan, preaches his gospel, works his miracles, offers up himself upon the Cross, rises from the dead, ascends on high, and baptizes the souls of his people, 52-58

1. *The Apostles Baptized for the Apostleship.* A baptism, admittedly, without a dipping or a covering. By " pouring," language based on actual baptism by pouring. " Baptism = subjection to full influence." Cloven tongues the emblem in this baptism as water in ordinary baptism, and as the Dove in the Saviour's personal baptism. The importance of this baptism, ... 58-95

2. *Cornelius and other Gentiles baptized by the Holy Ghost.* " A higher baptism than with water," 95-98

3. *Saul's Baptism by the Holy Ghost.* No evidence of a ritual baptism. Real baptism for the apostleship, ... 98-112

4. *Baptism of the Samaritans by the Holy Ghost.* Why such baptism, 112-117

5. *Baptism of the Corinthians by the Holy Ghost.* Translation. Admission. " Baptism = participation in influence." All share in it, 117-129

III. Christian Baptism Preached.

1. *To Jews and Proselytes.* Translation. Interpretation ; Campbell, Pusey, Baptists. Nature of the baptism, spiritual, " into the remission of sins " through repentance and faith " upon " the Name of the Lord Jesus. Baptist Quarterly, ... 129-153

2. *The Baptism received by the Gladly Hearing.* " Baptized " used absolutely. Difficulties of water dipping. Reasons for Real baptism, . 153-162

(xi)

IV. Baptism Preached incorporated in a Rite.

1. *Ritual Baptism of* Samaritans. The formula declarative of the Real baptism symbolized in the rite. "Into the Name of the Lord Jesus." Import. But "one baptism," realized in the soul by the power of the Holy Ghost, symbolized in the rite by the nature of pure water, applied to the body, ... 162–181

2. *Ritual Baptism of the* Eunuch. The only case under Christianity appealed to by the theory. "Some Water." The Chariot. Went down. Came up. Into. Out of. "The rack." 182–201

3. *Ritual Baptism of* Gentiles. Perpetuity of ritual baptism. "The water." Observance of the rite commanded "in the Name of the Lord." The use of "water," not quantity, ordained, ... 202–209

4. *Ritual Baptism of* John's *Ephesian* Disciples. "Into the Name of the Lord Jesus," 209–216

5. *Ritual Baptism of* Crispus *and* Gaius. "Into the name of Paul?" 216–218

V. Ritual Baptism of Households.

1. Lydia and *her* Household. 2. The Jailer and all his. 3. Stephanas and *his* Household. The family a divine institution. Family unity. Family headship. Individualism, ... 219–240

VI. Doctrinal Truth grounded in Real Baptism.

1. *Real Baptism begets* Holy Living. "Baptism into Jesus Christ = into his death" is not ritual baptism with water, but real baptism by the Holy Ghost, Carson, Ripley, Errett, Fee. Wilson, Halley, Beecher, Stuart. Dr. Pusey, Patrists, ... 241–275

2. *Real Baptism makes* Full *in Christ.* "Baptized into Christ," the equivalent of "made full in Christ," 275–282

3. *Real Baptism makes* Christlike. "Baptized into Christ," the equivalent of "put on Christ." Ritual baptism not the equivalent of the one or the other, ... 282–293

4. *Real Baptism into* Christ, *antitype of the type baptism "into* Moses." The Hebrew of Moses and the Greek of Paul. Israel "baptized into Moses" = *made fully subject*, ... 293–310

5. *Real Baptism into* Christ *inconsistent with Baptism into* Paul. Subjection to two Masters impossible, ... 310–315

6. *Real Baptism into Christ secures* Resurrection unto Life. Baptism for the dead, what? Historical facts uncertain, ... 316–317

7. *Real Baptism into Christ makes* "one body." The work of the Holy Ghost. All members of the body of Christ so baptized, . . 318–323

8. *Real Baptism beyond comparison with* ritual *baptism.* Not the opinion of all. Ritual = Real. Ritual same relation to salvation as Repentance and Faith. Ritual magnified, Pepper, Curtis, ... 324–328

9. *Real Baptism is by* Repentance *and* Faith *through the Holy Ghost.* Repentance and Faith can baptize. Baptizings. Baptism into unchastity by *teaching*, ... 328–335

10. *Real Baptism is saving* Antitype *baptism.* The Ark type of salvation, 335–343

11. *Real Baptism is the "* one baptism *" of Christianity.* Ritual baptism is not a second, diverse baptism, but is the same one baptism declared by words and shadowed in a symbol, ... 344–351

VII. SUPPOSED ALLUSIONS TO RITUAL BAPTISM.

1. John 3:25, *A question about* PURIFYING. 2. John 3:5, *Born of* WATER *and the* SPIRIT. 3. 1 Cor. 6:11, WASHED, *sanctified, justified.* 4. Ephes. 5:26, *Cleansing it with the* WASHING OF WATER 5. Titus 3:5, *Saved us by the* WASHING OF REGENERATION. 6. Heb. 10:22, *Our* BODIES WASHED *with pure water,* 352–384

VIII. REAL BAPTISM INTO THE NAME OF THE FATHER, AND OF THE SON, AND OF THE HOLY GHOST, THROUGH DISCIPLESHIP INTO CHRIST.

1. John 20:21–23. 2. Luke 24:44–50. 3 Acts 26:17, 18. 4. Mark 16:15, 16. 5. Matt. 28:19, 20. Discordant translations. Diversified interpretations. Unsatisfactory. Exposition. Syriac Version. " Baptize into " is the equivalent of the Syriac *Stand firm,* and of the Hebrew *Lean upon, Believe in.* Import, *subjection, reconciliation,* and *affiliation* with the fully revealed Deity through " the fulfilment of all righteousness " in the incarnation, obedience, death, and mediation of the SON OF GOD, ... 385–469

PATRISTIC BAPTISM.

I. ΒΑΠΤΙΖΩ IN GENERAL USAGE.

Agreement with Classic usage. Differences as compared with Inspired writers. Use of analogous words. Ideal element. Spiritual in religious sphere, ... 473–487

II. ΒΑΠΤΙΣΜΑ.

This word in Patristic and in Inspired writings expresses a *spiritual* and not a physical condition. Diverse names. Λουτρόν, spiritual washing. Diverse baptisms; *blood, tears, fire, clinic, sprinkling, pouring.* Without dipping, pouring, or sprinkling, ... 488–543

III. ΥΔΑΤΙ καὶ ΠΝΕΥΜΑΤΙ.

Water and Spirit conjoint *agencies* in Patristic baptism. Special quality and power given to water on which its power to baptize exclusively depends, 544–565

IV. ΣΥΝΘΑΠΤΩ.

Water dipping neither Christian nor Patristic baptism. Symbol of burial with Christ in his rock sepulchre. Burial applied to sin drowned and left in the water, ... 566–580

V. ΒΑΠΤΙΖΩ IN SPECIAL USAGE.

In religious usage neither expresses a dipping nor a *physical* baptism of any kind. Other words to express covering and uncovering in water. These words do not appear in Scripture baptisms because there was no covering and uncovering in water known to them. Proof. Another class of words expressive of *washing, cleansing, purification,* (spiritual) represent βαπτίζω. Proof. Usage of TINGO. Its special character; susceptibility of double use. Tertullian's usage of tingo as a substitute for βαπτίζω. Complementary relations of βαπτίζω *ideal.* Proof. No physical use in religious sphere. Proof, ... 581–622

CONCLUSION.

Origin of Inquiry. Results in brief; special, final, . . . 623–630

PASSAGES OF SCRIPTURE EXPOUNDED.

	PAGE
MATT. 3 : 15, Baptism of Jesus by John,	27
JOHN 1 : 32, Baptism of Jesus by the Holy Ghost,	31
MARK 10 : 38, 39, Baptism of Jesus through a Cup,	34
JOHN 1 : 33, Jesus, baptizer by the Holy Ghost,	52
ACTS 1 : 5, Apostles baptized by the Holy Ghost,	58
ACTS 11 : 15, 16, Cornelius baptized by the Holy Ghost,	95
ACTS 9 : 17, 18; 22 : 13, 16; 26 : 14–18, Baptism of Saul,	98
ACTS 8 : 15, 16, Baptism of Samaritans,	113
ACTS 19 : 6, Baptism of John's disciples,	114
1 COR. 12 : 13, Baptism by special gifts,	117
ACTS 2 : 38, Baptism through Repentance and Faith, commanded,	130
ACTS 2 : 41, Baptism through Repentance and Faith, received,	153
ACTS 8 : 12–16, Ritual baptism of Samaritans,	163
ACTS 8 : 35–38, Ritual baptism of the Eunuch,	182
ACTS 10 : 47, 48, Ritual baptism of the Gentiles,	202
ACTS 19 : 3–5, Ritual baptism of John's disciples,	209
1 COR. 1 : 13–15, Ritual baptism of Crispus and Gaius,	216
ACTS 16 : 15, Ritual baptism of Lydia and her household,	219
ACTS 16 : 33, Ritual baptism of the Jailer and all his,	219
1 COR. 1 : 16, Ritual baptism of Stephanas and his household,	219
ROM. 6 : 2–4, Real baptism into Christ,	241
COLOSS. 2 : 9–13, Real baptism into Christ,	275
GAL. 3 : 26, 27, Real baptism into Christ,	282
1 COR. 10 : 2, Real baptism into Moses, type of Real baptism into Christ,	294
1 COR. 1 : 13, 15, Real baptism into Paul destructive of Real baptism into Christ,	310
1 COR. 15 : 29, " Baptism for the dead,"	316
1 COR. 12 : 13, Real baptism makes Christians " one body,"	318
1 COR. 1 : 17, Real baptism is not Ritual baptism,	324
HEB. 6 : 2, Real baptism through Repentance and Faith,	328
1 PETER 3 : 21, Real baptism is Antitype baptism,	335
EPHES. 4 : 5, Real baptism is the " One baptism,"	344
JOHN 3 : 25, About purifying,	352
JOHN 3 : 5. Born of water and the Spirit,	355
1 COR. 6 : 11, Washed, sanctified, justified,	366
EPHES. 5 : 26, Washing of water by the word,	369
TITUS 3 : 5, Washing of regeneration and renewing of the Holy Ghost,	375
HEB. 10 : 22, Heart sprinkled, body washed,	381
JOHN 20 : 21–23, The Commission,	385
LUKE 24 : 44–50, The Commission,	386
ACTS 26 : 17, 18, Saul's Commission,	389
MARK 16 : 15, 16, The Commission,	390
MATT. 28 : 19, 20, The Commission,	403

CHRISTIC BAPTISM.

AUTHORS AND WORKS REFERRED TO

Æsop.
Achilles, Tatius.
Alcibiades.
Alexander, Prof. J. A.
Alford.
Ambrose.
Apostol. Canons.
Arnold, Prof., Bapt. Th. Sem., Chicago.
Athanasius.
Athenæus.
Augustine.
Baptist Bib. Vers.
Baptist Manual.
Baptist Quarterly.
Barclay.
Basil, of Cæsarea.
Basil M.
Beecher, Presid. E.
Bengel.
Bloomfield.
Booth.
Brantley, Rev. Dr.
Brentius.
Brunner, Presid.
Calvin.
Campbell, Alex. (Beth. Coll.)
Carson, Alex., LL.D.
Cathcart, Rev. Dr.
Chase, Prof., Newton Th. Sem.
Chrysostom.
Clarke, Adam.
Clemens, Alex.
Clemens, Rom.
Codex Sinaiticus.
Conant, J. T.
Conon.
Cox, F. A. (London).
Cremer. Prof. Hermann.
Curtis, Prof.
Cyprian.

Cyril, of Jerus.
Dagg, Prof. J. L.
De Wette.
Didymus, Alex.
Ebrard.
Ellicott.
Ernesti.
Errett, Isaac.
Evenus.
Ewing, Prof. (Glasgow).
Fairbairn.
Fee, Prof. J. G.
Firmilian.
Fuller, R., D.D.
Gale.
Gil, Dr.
Godwin, Prof. (London).
Greg. Naz.
Hackett, H., Prof., Roch. Th. Sem.
Halley, Presid. R. (England).
Harrison, Prof., Univ. of Va.
Herodotus.
Hilary.
Hodge.
Homer.
Ignatius.
Ingham (London).
Irenæus.
Jelf.
Jerome.
Josephus.
Jewett, M. P., Prof.
J. M. R. (Western Recorder).
John of Damascus.
Judson, Dr. A.
Justin, M.
Krehl.
Kühner.
Kuinoel.
Lange.

Lightfoot.
Lloyd, J. T. (Rel. Herald).
Lucian.
Luther.
Marcus Eremita.
Matthies.
Methodius.
Meyer.
Middleton.
Morell (Edinburgh).
Murdock, J., Prof.
Neander.
Newcome, Archbishop.
Olshausen.
Origen.
Owen, Rev. John.
Pearce, Rt. Rev.
Pengilly.
Pepper, Prof., Crozer Th. Sem.
Plato.
Plutarch.
Pusey, Prof. E. B.
Ripley, Prof., Newton Theol. Sem.
Rosenmüller.
Schaaf, Prof.
Stier.
Stovel, C. (London).
Stuart.
Tertullian.
Turretin.
Venema.
Vitringa.
Wardlaw.
Wayland, Presid.
Wesley, John.
Wickham.
Wilson, Prof. (Belfast)
Winer.
Xenophon.
Zuingle.

CHRISTIC BAPTISM.

WHAT IS ITS NATURE AND HOW DOES IT ILLUSTRATE THE
USAGE OF

$B A \Pi T I Z \Omega$?

WHAT IS CHRISTIC BAPTISM?

CHRISTIC BAPTISM is Christ's baptism in its various aspects:
1. The baptism received by Christ personally; 2. The immediate
baptism of sinners administered by Christ personally; 3. The
ritual baptism of such authorized by Christ to be administered by
others; 4. The everlasting baptism secured by Christ for the redeemed. Christic baptism as established by Christ has a twofold
character: 1. Real; 2. Ritual. REAL Christic baptism is a thorough change in the moral condition of the soul effected by the
Holy Ghost and uniting to Christ by repentance and faith, and
through Christ re-establishing filial and everlasting relation with
the living God—Father, Son and Holy Ghost. RITUAL Christic
baptism is not another and diverse baptism, but is one and the
same baptism declared by word, and exhibited (as to its purifying nature) by pure water applied to the body; symbolizing the
cleansing of the soul through the atoning blood of Christ by the
Holy Ghost.

Every symbol is necessarily imperfect as compared with the
wholeness of that which is symbolized. No symbol can exhibit
everything which enters into the object symbolized. A symbol,
ordinarily if not necessarily, exhibits one thing and not many
things. The type lamb slain on Abel's altar exhibited one thing—
the *death* of the Antitype Lamb slain on Calvary. The Bread and
the Wine in the Lord's Supper as *sources of life to the body* sym-

2   (17)

bolize one thing—the body and the blood of Christ as *sources of life to the soul*. The antecedent type (the Lamb slain) sets forth substitutionary death; the consequent symbols (Bread and Wine) set forth life proceeding from that death. Water has by universal acknowledgment a physically purifying quality, and hence, has been accepted in all ages as a symbol of purity, in religious rites. The fundamental characteristic of baptism by the Holy Ghost (*Real* Christic baptism) is moral purification. This characteristic is selected by divine wisdom for symbolization by water in *ritual* Christic baptism. And having performed this one duty, we say that the symbolizing function of the water is exhausted. It is a matter of universal admission, that if this be the sole office of the water then, neither quantity nor mode of use has any place for consideration. But such sole office is denied.

A modern theory respecting ritual Christian baptism throws into deepest shadow this idea of purification, and declares, that another and diverse baptism, namely, a dipping into water (not found in and not possible to the real baptism), constitutes both the spirit and the substance of the rite; and, that in it is exhibited a *death*, a *burial*, a *resurrection*, a *grave*, a *womb*, a *pollution*, and somewhere, somehow, a *purification*. This theory is so unique in the complexity and perplexity of its symbolism, and is so grievous (as declared by them) to its friends in compelling a separation from all God's people who receive but " one baptism " (the real Christic baptism by the Holy Ghost and its ritual Christic baptism by water), that it becomes necessary to draw out its details for a rational judgment and a Scriptural determination. This I will endeavor to do by briefly adducing the statements of those who are of acknowledged authority among its friends.

1. This theory says: God commands, in baptism, a definite act to be done, which act is expressed by the word Βαπτίζω, " a word which has but one meaning, to dip and nothing but dip, through all Greek literature." *Evidence:* " In baptism we are commanded to perform THE ACT *represented by* the word baptize." *Prof. M. P. Jewett* (*p.* 46). " The word *baptize* is perfectly sufficient for me why baptism implies immersion without a particle of evidence from any other thing." *Carson* (*p.* 144). " The action which Jesus Christ commanded in the word Βαπτίζω calls for exact obedience; this word indicates a *specific* action, and can have but one meaning; it derives its meaning and immutable form from Βάπτω, and therefore inherits the proper meaning of the *bap*, which

is *dip.*" *Alex. Campbell* (*pp.* 116–120). " The text (Matt. 28 : 19) shows the appointment of immersion in water." *Stovel* (*p.* 479). " As soon as the convert goes down into the water to obey Jesus . . . cease to resist the truth. . . . Can you trifle with baptism ? . . . 'Arise and be baptized and wash away thy sins.' These are the words of God himself, and take care how you slight them. It is a plain duty which you may not evade without insult to the Saviour and peril to your soul. . . . I warn you that the gospel " (dipping into water) "is to be *obeyed* as well as *believed.* . . . 'He that believeth and is baptized shall be saved, he that believeth not shall be damned.' Saved or damned ? " *Fuller* (*pp.* 9, 104).

2. The theory says : The water in baptism represents a *grave.* *Evidence :* " In baptism we are figuratively put into the grave along with him. In our baptism we are emblematically laid in the grave with Christ." *Carson* (*p.* 143).

3. The theory says : Death precedes the baptism or takes place in and by the baptism. *Evidence :* " The external ordinance represents a burial and supposes, of course, a death to have taken place. . . . We do not believe in death by drowning as being *represented* in this ordinance, although this appears to have been the belief of a few Baptists." *Ingham, London* (*p.* 258).

4. The theory says : The burial in this symbol water-grave is of varied significance. *Evidence :* 1. It refers to a burial in Jordan. " The baptismal water reminds of the *Jordan* when Jesus went down into the water and was buried." *Prof. Pepper, The Relation of Baptism and Communion* (*p.* 16). 2. It refers to a burial in the rock sepulchre of Joseph. " As Jesus was buried in the *tomb of Joseph,* so we are buried by baptism. We are buried with Christ." *Ingham* (*p.* 251). 3. It refers to a burial of the old man. " In our baptismal burial we emblematically deposit *our moral corruption.*" *Prof. Ripley, Reply to Stuart* (*p.* 94).

5. The theory says : The lifting out of this water-grave is a symbol of the resurrection. *Evidence :* " Baptism might have a reference to burial without resurrection. These two things are quite distinct." *Carson* (*p.* 140). This resurrection, like the burial, is multiple in character. 1. It refers to the resurrection of Christ. " The *resurrection* of Christ is set forth in baptism." *Prof. Pepper* (*p.* 16). 2. The resurrection of *the baptized.* " The central prophecy of baptism is the believer's glorious resurrection at the Lord's second coming." *Prof. Pepper* (*p.* 19). 3. The resurrection of *the new man.* " The external act of baptism is a

symbol of the burying of the old man and the rising up of the new man." *Christian* (*C. B.*) *Quarterly* (*July*, 1872, *p.* 405).

6. The theory says: The acts in baptism which make up a dipping (putting into and taking out of) are of a symbol character. *Evidence:* "It is possible that an ordinance performed by immersion might have had no instruction in the mode. It might have been all in the water. Had not the Apostle explained this ordinance we should have had no right so to do." *Carson* (*p.* 456). "In scriptural baptism there is a literal going down into the water and there is a literal rising up from the water. The literal action included in baptism represents spiritual and important truth. This is the Divine arrangement and purpose in connection with this ordinance, as it is also with the breaking of bread, &c., in the Lord's Supper." *Ingham* (*p.* 252).

7. The theory says: The water in baptism is a womb. *Evidence:* "To be born of water most evidently implies, that water is *the womb* out of which the person who is born proceeds. To be born of water is that birth which is represented by being immersed in water. To emerge out of the water is like a birth." *Carson* (*p.* 476).

8. The theory says: The grave of baptism is a place for the deposit of pollution. *Evidence:* "Baptism proclaims the sinner's pollution." *Pengilly* (*p.* 113). "When we rise from this grave we leave our moral loathsomeness behind, and rise to a new and holy life." *Prof. Ripley* (*p.* 94).

9. The theory says: The water in baptism is an emblem of purification. *Evidence:* "The water in baptism must be an emblem, not a means. The purification of the heart is by faith. This washing takes place before baptism. Baptism is an emblem of this washing and regeneration." *Carson* (*p.* 479). "If in baptism there be a perfect emblem of purification, immersion must be the mode." *Ingham* (*p.* 260). This washing must be of the entire body, because depravity is entire. "There is good reason for employing so much water as to immerse the body. If the Christian felt his entire depravity, his utter defilement from the crown of his head to the sole of his foot, and desired to be *thoroughly* washed from his iniquity, he might crave the entire immersion of his body in the waters of baptism, as symbolic of the universal cleansing which he sought by the influence of the Holy Ghost." *Prof. M. P. Jewett* (*p.* 99).

10. The theory says: Baptism is emblematic of suffering. *Evi-*

dence : " Baptism is a figure of our Lord's *overwhelming suffer-ings.*" *Pengilly (p.* 114).

11. The logic of this theory as declared by its friends is this: Outside of this theory there is no baptism, no Lord's Supper, no Christian ministry, no Christian church—and by the same inex-orable logic, no Christian man. *Evidence :* " Christian baptism is immersion of a believer in water, in the name of the Father, Son and Holy Ghost—nothing else is. Baptist churches are the only Christian churches in existence. Pedobaptists have no right to the Lord's Supper. Whenever they partake of the Lord's Sup-per they partake unworthily and eat and drink damnation to them-selves." *J. T. Lloyd (Religious Herald).* " For Baptists to call Pedobaptist bodies churches having the right to administer the Lord's Supper is logical insanity and idiocy." *J. M. R. (Western Recorder).*

Which is the more curious, the theory itself or these logical deductions, it would be difficult to estimate. This however is certain : All who accept the one, or the other, or both, have a just claim on our deepest sympathy, because of that intellectual and moral burden which they have unwittingly assumed, and which they declare to be " grievous and hard to be borne." Conscience is a sacred thing. It is still venerable in its root even while re-volting in its fruit in verily thinking, that it does God service by filling Saul with threatenings and slaughter, and sprinkling his garments with martyr blood, or in prompting the theory to exclude from the body and blood of Christ his redeemed ones when the memorial ordinance is spread by its friends, and declaring that they act a lie—an unintelligent lie*—when they venture to sit down at the Lord's table among themselves.

Every high priest taken from among men should be one " who

---

* " A believer, acting as a believer, cannot act a lie. But if one with full knowledge of the import of the rites begin with the Communion, he does act a lie. He says in act, in a most solemn, formal act, 'I have a spiritual life which did not begin.' If he be baptized after he has communed, he lies, for he solemnly, sacramentally affirms, I now first begin a life, which yet he has long declared to be his. He comes into Christ for the first time, though he has been already abiding in him. In declaring such acts to be lies, it is *only* on the supposition that the acts are performed intelligently, with an understanding of their true nature. Our argument requires the considera-tion of no other cases." *G. D. B. Pepper, Prof. of Theol., Crozer Sem. Bap-tism and Communion (p.* 34).

can have compassion on the ignorant and on them that are out of the way; for that he himself also is compassed with infirmity." We should be mindful of this "infirmity," and be emulous of this high priestly spirit in dealing with this most remarkable theory, "speaking the truth in love" fully persuaded, that the theory and its logic are alike held "in all good conscience," even when, in their characteristic vocabulary, they stigmatize God's people as Communion Table liars.

OBJECTIONS TO THIS THEORY.

There are some objections to this theory which appear on its face, that it may be well to state briefly before entering on a more detailed prosecution of our inquiry.

1. *Philological.* This inquiry has advanced sufficiently far to warrant the statement, that the philological basis of the theory neither has nor ever had any existence. The corner-stone of the theory (not the stone supporting one corner, but every corner and all between the four corners) is the word $Ba\pi\tau i\zeta\omega$. Now, if anything out of mathematics was ever proved, it has been proved that this word does not mean *to dip;* that it never did, that it never can so mean, without there be first an utter metamorphosis as to its essential character. That which above all other things discriminates and puts a great gulf between $Ba\pi\tau i\zeta\omega$ and "dip" is the time of intusposition demanded, respectively, for their objects. "Dip" puts its object in a condition of intusposition *momentarily;* it puts in and draws out; $Ba\pi\tau i\zeta\omega$ demands a condition of intusposition for its object without any limitation as to the time of continuance in such condition, but allows it to remain for ages or an eternity. There are no writings in which these discriminating characteristics are more essential or more boldly presented than in the Scriptures. It is obvious, that under these meanings no one can be baptized *into water,* for death must follow, and therefore, the theory apologetically introduces "dip" and says: "The command of God to *baptize* Christians into water cannot be obeyed, therefore *dipping* into water must be substituted." But might it not be well to review the theory and inquire, whether God ever gave any command to baptize his people into water? In fact, there is not a particle of evidence for any such command. Inasmuch as there is no element in $Ba\pi\tau i\zeta\omega$ for withdrawing its object from the water, there is nothing in Christian baptism to play the part of "resurrection from a grave," or

of " birth from a womb." And if there is no provision for taking
out of this grave and womb, it will be hard to find any one who
will be willing to go into this water-grave-womb. As the theory
cannot exist without a *dipping*, and as Βαπτίζω makes no provision
for a dipping, its philological foundation falls out bodily.

2. *Chronological.* A second difficulty confronting the theory
is chronological. Dr. Pepper, Prof. of Theology in Crozer Baptist
Theological Seminary, says (Baptism and Communion, p. 26),
" Turn now to the two ordinances, and note the times of their
institution. The puerile inquiry, raised in defence of Rantism,
whether John's Baptism was Christian Baptism, we may assume,
can have only one answer, and that affirmative. The time of the
institution of Baptism is thus fixed at the beginning of John's
ministry." Not caring, just now, to engage " in defence of
Rantism" (whatever that may be), nor to intermeddle in any
" puerile inquiry," I propose a chronological inquiry in relation
to burial and resurrection as entering into a baptism by dipping
into water. The inquiry is this: Where from the beginning to
the ending of John's ministry is there one word said about
" burial and resurrection" being elements in baptism? Extending the chronological range I would inquire: Where in all the
ministry of Peter, beginning at the baptism of Pentecost among
the Jews, and extending through the baptism at Cæsarea among
the Gentiles, to the Bible close of his Apostolic work, where does
a burial or a resurrection appear in his baptizing? Extend the
period through the entire history of the Church as given in the
book of Acts, and where among its many recorded baptisms do
we find a record of burials and resurrections? It is not until
more than a quarter of hundred years after " the institution of
Baptism" that such terms are found in connection with the word
baptize, and then not in the administration of ritual baptism, not
in the exposition of ritual baptism, and not in connection with
ritual baptism in any way. " Buried with Christ *by baptism into*
HIS DEATH " is no more burial with Christ *by baptism into* WATER,
than George the Third of England is George Washington of
America, because " George" appears in both names. " The Third
of England" expounds the first George, and " Washington of
America" expounds the second George; so, " into *his death*"
expounds the first " baptism," and " into *water*" expounds the
second " baptism." And these baptisms are as diverse from each
other as the George of England is diverse from the George of

America. It is an embarrassment which confronts those who
make burial and resurrection the grand features of ritual baptism,
that from the time of John until the time of Paul's epistle to the
Romans, more than a quarter of a century, there is not one word
of Scripture on which they can hang their theory.

But there is a longer chronological period which claims attention. It extends through a thousand years. And what I would
ask of the friends of the theory is this: What is the name
of one man who during a thousand years after the institution
of baptism wrote or said or believed that dipping into water
was Christian baptism? In other words, tell us of one man
among the millions of ten centuries who believed the theory, or
would have thought it worthy of consideration. Do not mistake
my demand. The inquiry is not, for one who practiced the
covering of the body in water in ritual baptism; nor is it, for one
who interpreted such baptism as a burial and resurrection; there
is not only one such, but one legion; but what is sought is quite
other than this, to wit: one who believed that *this covering with
water* was Christian Baptism.

If this theory of baptism is so alien from the teaching of the
Holy Scriptures, that no one for some thousand and a half thousand years ever found it there, then, there is a portentous chronological difficulty in the way of its acceptance in these latter days,
so long as we have the Bible in our hands.

If it should be asked, Why these ancient worthies " covered
with water" in baptism? I answer: For the same reason that
they baptized men and women naked. And precisely here (in
the absolute nudity of the ancients and in the water-tight India-
rubber vestments of the moderns) is revealed the antipodal character of these baptisms. The ancients believed, that there was
a *vis baptismatis* in the water which applied to the body reached
to the soul, and thus effected Christian Baptism; therefore this
water was applied to the whole body naked for the better development of its baptizing power. The friends of the modern
theory adopt the empty water covering of the ancients while they
reject their soul baptism, substituting for it the unknown, unscriptural, impossible baptism—*dipping* into water.

3. *Symbological.* Another difficulty of the theory is its very
remarkable symbology. Symbols, like words, have one definite
meaning. If words in the same utterance cannot have many and
diverse meanings, neither can symbols. The Bible is full of sym-

bols, types, and emblems, from the Tree of Life in Eden to the River of Life flowing out of the throne of God and the Lamb in heaven; but in no one through all these intervening ages can there be found many and diverse meanings. A false interpretation once taught, that the words of Scripture meant all that could be put into them; the theory adopts this principle in its interpretation of ritual Baptism. Out of the elements entering into this ordinance are selected as symbolic, the water, the believer, and the double action putting into and taking out of. The administrator is not used in the interpretation, only his eliminated acts; neither is any use made of those great words (the very soul of the ordinance) "*into* Christ," "*into* the Name of the Father, and of the Son, and of the Holy Ghost," save in a jejune and destructive interpretation, " by the authority of." What is left out, however, has its compensation in the quantity of that which is put in. The water appears in three offices : 1, of a grave; 2, of a womb; 3, of the blood of Christ. As a grave the living "believer" is put into it; (1.) As dead with Christ; (2.) As dead, by natural death; (3.) As "the old man" dead, to be buried and to be left in the grave. And he is taken out of the grave, (1.) As risen with Christ; (2.) As risen at Christ's second coming; (3.) As risen "a new man" to holy living. This would seem to be enough of symbolization for one transaction. It is, however, only the beginning. The water must, again, appear in a wholly new office, that of a womb. The interpretation, here, is not so complex but is more perplexed; since the putting into the water and the taking out of the water are both represented as a birth. In its third office the water appears as the blood of Christ. And Professor Jewett tells us (with a humanism which responds to the naked baptism of old), that total depravity calls for a total covering in this symbol blood. Into this symbol blood the " believer" is dipped, and under it he leaves his pollution, being drawn out washed and without spot.

It is hardly necessary to say, that such exposition is no more grounded in the Scripture than it is in common sense. It is vain to plead, that burial with Christ, and resurrection, and new birth, and cleansing by the blood of the Lamb, are in the Scriptures. They are there; but they are not there impossibly and absurdly piled up upon the ritual water whose one and sole office it is to symbolize the purification of the soul by the blood of Christ, through the Holy Ghost. If the theory did not lose every element of life under its absolute repudiation by philology, if it could find a better status in the chronology of ages, still, such symbolization must constitute a monument under which it must be forever buried.

4. *Exegetical.* The theory which makes Christian Baptism to consist in a dipping into water in the name (" by the authority") of the Father, the Son, and the Holy Ghost, is as absolutely rejected by a just exegesis of the Word of God, as it is by philology, chronology, and the law of Symbols. This it is now our business to establish. The result will, we think, show beyond any question, that this modern theory teaches a baptism which is not only not commanded in the Scriptures, not only imperfect in its nature, but is a pure and absolute abandonment of that baptism which God has ordained in his word.

We will now proceed to a consideration of individual cases under Christic Baptism.

CHRISTIC BAPTISM: BAPTISM RECEIVED BY CHRIST.

BAPTISM OF JESUS BY JOHN.

Matthew 3 : 15.

Οὕτω γὰρ πρέπον ἐστὶν ἡμῖν πληρῶσαι πᾶσαν δικαιοσύνην.
" Thus it becometh us to fulfil all righteousness."

WHAT BAPTISM DID JESUS RECEIVE FROM JOHN?

A Covenant Baptism.

JOHANNIC BAPTISM concluded with a consideration of the place where the Lord Jesus was baptized by his Forerunner. The nature of the baptism then received was not considered, because it did not pertain to "John's baptism," but was grounded in that peculiar work for the accomplishment of which the Son of God was made manifest in the flesh—"the fulfilment of all righteousness." It is one thing to be baptized by John and quite another thing to receive the "baptism of John." Therefore, while the Scriptures teach us that Jesus came to the Jordan to be baptized by John, they do not teach us that he came to receive John's baptism. Indeed it is impossible, in any just aspect of the case, that he could have received it. Whatever involves an absurdity must be impossible and untrue. That an absurdity is involved in such a supposition is thus shown: "The baptism of John" was for sinners; demanding "repentance," "fruits meet for repentance," and promising "the remission of sins." But the Lord Jesus Christ was not a sinner, could not repent of sin, could not bring forth fruit meet for repentance on account of sin, could not receive the remission of sin. Therefore the reception of "the baptism of John" by Jesus is impossible, untrue, and absurd. Again: The baptism of John was "to prepare a people for the Lord." But to address such a baptism to the Lord (preparing the Lord for himself) is absurd. Therefore the reception of John's baptism by the Lord Jesus is impossible, untrue, and

(27)

absurd. It is just as absurd to suppose that he received this bap
tism formally but not substantially. A baptism exists only while
its essence exists. The essence of John's ritual baptism is found
in its symbolization of purification in the soul through repentance and remission of sin. But in the Lord Jesus there was no
basis for such symbolization, and consequently there was no basis
for the baptism of John. The idea that John's baptism could be
received representatively is just as impossible. To the glory of
God in the highest, the Lord Jesus did "bear our iniquities," was
"made sin for us;" but he was not hereby the more qualified to
receive John's baptism. The Lord Jesus did not represent penitent sinners, nor sinners whose iniquities were remitted. He
came as the Friend of publicans and sinners, to call sinners to
repentance, to give repentance to Israel; there was no adaptation
in the baptism of John to such Sin-Bearer. He must accomplish
a baptism for himself; it must be of blood and not of water;
"without the shedding of blood there is no remission of sin" such
as Jesus bore. In his character as Bearer of the sins of others, he
neither had nor could have anything to do with John's baptism.

The Bearer of Sin must be baptized; but it is with a baptism
which none other can share. It must be the baptism of one who
is able "to fulfil all righteousness," and to bear the penalty of a
broken law, in order to the redemption of the guilty. This baptism, this "one baptism," may form the basis for John's baptism;
but to suppose that the Originator of the baptism by atoning
blood could enter personally or representatively into the baptism
of John, is as absurd as to suppose that the foundation of a house
can rest upon the house which is builded on it, or that a fountain
can be supplied by the stream which flows from it, or that a rock
can enter into the shadow which it casts for the weary. The
Lord Jesus never baptized any with water symbolizing spiritual
blessings. It was as unsuitable for the Dispenser of all spiritual
blessings to do so, as to give *symbols* of healing to the blind, and
deaf, and dumb, and lame, and sick. And it was just as unsuitable for him to receive from John not merely the symbol involving
the impossibilities of repentance and remission, but the symbol of
any spiritual blessing, he himself being the source of all spiritual
good. But if it were not too grossly earthy to suppose that our
Divine Sin-bearer could go through the fiction of confessing sin,
declaring repentance, and receiving remission, he would know,
and John would know, and all would know, that such service

was no administration of "John's baptism." All who came to
John's baptism were exposed to, and "warned to flee from the
wrath to come." From what wrath to come could Jesus flee?
There is no aspect in which the ministry (preaching or baptism)
of John can be considered which will allow of the Coming One to
be made subject to it. John himself recognizes this truth, and
promptly declares it when Jesus comes to him. And it is not
until an explanation is given, reminding him of the peculiar relation in which they stand to each other, and indicating the nature
of the baptism sought, that John's embarrassment is removed.
This is effectually accomplished through those brief but most significant words—"thus it becometh us to fulfil all righteousness."

This language cannot apply to the ritual baptism of John.
That was not a thing of law. One confessing himself a sinner,
and fleeing from the wrath to come, could hardly claim for himself the doing a work of righteousness. David did not imagine
that he was doing a work of righteousness when he presented
before God "a broken heart and a contrite spirit." An act of
righteousness and godly sorrow for sin do not belong to the same
category. It cannot be claimed that the Lord Jesus was under
obligation to undergo this baptism as a part of "all righteousness;" 1. Because there is no righteousness in it; 2. Because
what there is in it is just that which he did not come to do. He
did not come to repent for sinners, nor to exercise faith for
sinners. These things do not enter into that "all righteousness"
which he came to fulfil. And he did not come to receive John's
baptism; which is just as far removed from the wondrous work
which he came to do. These words must be received at their full,
normal, scriptural value. They describe with divine brevity, fulness, and force, the work which the Mightier than John came into
the world to do—"TO FULFIL ALL RIGHTEOUSNESS." Never was
there a time more suitable for its announcement. They are the
first words of his public life. To no person could they be more
suitably spoken. The Forerunner is hereby notified that the
Coming One has met him. Nothing could be more appropriate
to the amazing mission which brought him into our world, than
some expressive and visible covenant declaration and act. No
one could share in such inauguration with a fitness comparable
with that of his great Forerunner. And to this fitness of relationship reference is had in the words—"thus it becometh us "—
"thus," by baptism; "us," administered by thee, my Forerunner,

to me, the Coming One proclaimed by thee; "now," entering
upon my covenant work which I now declare and am ready to
begin—"to fulfil all righteousness." Can there be, in view of the
persons, the time, and the circumstances, any other satisfactory
interpretation of these great words?

Stier (Words of the Lord Jesus, I, 30–33) recognizes this baptism, although not always with accurate discrimination, as far different from that of John's baptism. "'For thus it becometh us
to fulfil all righteousness.' First of all we cannot but be profoundly impressed by the lofty contrast between *this* avowal of
righteousness, and the *confession of sin* of all the others, who
came to be baptized. And it is strange that Theologians in their
search for testimonies of the sinlessness of Jesus, do not find here
the first and most luminous *dictum probans* from his own mouth.
This was the decisive declaration which set John perfectly at rest.
. . . Here at the very first does the Lord openly announce to
John: Placing myself in the likeness of sinners, *taking their sins
upon me*, I shall and will fulfil righteousness for them. . . . This
baptism is truly and essentially the true *beginning point* of that
Obedience, the consummation of which, in the death of the Cross
in order to the Resurrection, it pretypifies; '*thus*,' not *herein* nor
hereby, is an expression of comparison, which points forward to
the thing compared. This baptism is his anointing to that sacrifice of himself for sinners which now first properly begins. He
afterwards was baptized with the baptism of death, in which he,
as the Lamb of God, bore our guilt; which was not to him the
wages of sin, but the highest meritorious righteousness for us all.
. . . He presents himself, saying—Behold I come to do thy will;
the Father responds—This is my beloved Son! This acceptance
and obligation is to him what the confession of sin is to the sinner.
Therein our sins are confessed as done away in his righteousness,
and *the future baptism* for the true forgiveness of sins, which
should be ours by virtue of his baptism, is foreannounced."

These extracts show a great gulf separating this baptism of the
Lord Jesus by John from "the baptism of John."

Venema says: "The water of baptism denotes the *punishing
justice* of God. Into this justice Christ was immersed. This is
the *baptism* of Christ concerning which he speaks, Matt. 20 : 22 ;
and this was represented by the baptism of water which was administered to him by John." Such views, as just as profound,
preclude our accepting the barren and superficial conception, that

this baptism of Jesus is to be swallowed up in myriads of like bap·tisms received by the people of Jerusalem and Judea! It is not a like baptism. It stands solitary and alone. But one could re·ceive it. In it there is an announcement of the work of redemp·tion and a covenant engagement by the Son of God to accomplish it. This announcement and assumption of covenant obligation the Father accepts and declares himself " well pleased." The Holy Ghost makes like declaration by descending upon and bap·tizing the covenanting Son for his amazing work now assumed at Jordan, but "finished" only on Calvary.

Bengel (Matt. 3 : 15) speaks with characteristic wisdom and penetration: " It becomes *me*, as the principal; *thee*, as the min·ister. In the mind of Jesus it might also have this sense, ' It becomes me and my Father that I should fulfil all righteousness.' This (all righteousness) is effected not by John and Jesus, but by Jesus alone, who undertook that very thing in his baptism; whence the appellation ' baptism ' is transferred also to his passion, Luke 12 : 50. Jesus uttered the words here recorded instead of that which others who were baptized, being sinners, confessed concern·ing their *sins*. Such a speech suited none but the Messiah him·self." . . . 1 John 5 : 6 ; " He not only undertook, when he came to *baptism*, the task of fulfilling all righteousness, Matt. 3 : 15, but he also completed it by pouring out *his blood*," John 19 : 30. And Ambrose (IV, 680) says: " It was becoming that the precepts of the Law which he had established, he should fulfil, as he says else·where, ' I have not come to destroy the Law, but to fulfil.' " Also, Hilary (I, 927): " All righteousness must be fulfilled by him, by whom only the Law could be fulfilled."

This baptism is a covenant " to fulfil all righteousness."

JOHN 1: 32.

Ὅτι τεθέαμαι τὸ Πνεῦμα καταβαῖνον ὡσεὶ περιστερὰν ἐξ οὐρανοῦ, καὶ ἔμεινεν ἐπ' αὐτόν.

" I saw the Spirit descending from heaven like a dove, and it abode upon him."—*John* 1 : 32 (*Matt.* 3 : 16; *Mark* 1 : 10; *Luke* 3 : 22.)

BAPTISM OF THE LORD JESUS BY THE HOLY GHOST.

The term baptism is not immediately applied to this transac·tion. It is, however, very clearly involved in the words immedi·ately following—" Upon whom thou shalt see the Spirit descend·ing, and remaining on him, the same is ὁ Βαπτίζων ἐν Πνεύματι Ἁγίῳ."

This title, " The Baptizer by (ἐν) the Holy Ghost," is predicated on the previous personal baptism of our Lord by the Holy Ghost as none other had been or could be (illimitably) and therefore wielding all the power of this Divine person in baptizing others. But apart from this statement there is no want of evidence for authorizing this transaction being called a baptism. Evidence, to excess, has been furnished for the existence of baptisms where no envelopment was to be found in fact, or could rationally be conceived. The usage, under such circumstances, being based on a similarity of condition with that produced on a class of bodies susceptible of being penetrated, pervaded, and so receiving quality from some enveloping element. Therefore this descent of the Holy Ghost and his abiding upon our Lord is called a baptism, and not because of any irrational and impossible external envelopment. That the whole being of " the Christ " was henceforth under the influence of this *anointing* the Scriptures abundantly testify : 1. By declaring through the Forerunner (John 3 : 34) that " the Spirit is not given by measure unto him," and therefore the farther statement, " Jesus being full of the Holy Ghost." That such a gift would have a controlling influence, we are not left to infer ; but it is expressly declared by John—" He whom God hath sent speaketh the words of God, *for* God giveth not the Spirit by measure unto him." 2. This gift was as unlimited in continuance as it was in measure—" I saw the Spirit descending from heaven like a dove and it *abode* upon him " (John 1 : 32). 3. Under this influence he preached—" The Spirit of the Lord is upon me, because he hath anointed me to preach the gospel to the poor, . . . to preach the acceptable year of the Lord. And he began to say unto them, This day is this Scripture fulfilled in your ears " (Luke 4 : 18, 21) ; " God anointed Jesus of Nazareth with the Holy Ghost and with power " (Acts 10 : 38). 4. His miracles were wrought by this power—" If I by (ἐν) the Spirit of God cast out devils then the kingdom of God has come unto you " (Matt. 12 : 28). 5. The offering up of himself as the Lamb of God was through the same Spirit—" Who through the eternal Spirit offered himself without spot to God " (Heb. 9 : 14). This offering was the consummation of that covenant assumed at his baptism by John when he engaged " to fulfil all righteousness." And it was the triumphant ending of that work in loving sympathy with which the Holy Ghost descended and abode upon him until the sacrificial offering was " finished."

It was conclusive evidence of the pervading and controlling influence of a baptism, that the Saviour immediately after such baptism is represented as being under the full influence of the divine Spirit—"Then was Jesus led up by (ἐν) the Spirit into the wilderness" (Luke 4 : 1). And when he came out of the wilderness he came invested with all the singular potency of this Divine agent—"Jesus returned in the power of the Spirit" (Luke 4 : 14). And in this condition of baptism did our most blessed Lord continue during all the period in which he was engaged in accomplishing his covenant " to fulfil all righteousness."

All must be struck with the irreconcilableness between this baptism and the theory. The theory requires a dipping; where is the dipping in this baptism? The theory requires a covering; where is the covering in this baptism? The theory requires momentary continuance; where is the momentariness in this life-long baptism? On the other hand, the identity between the conclusions reached in Classic baptism, illustrated in Judaic baptism, and confirmed by Johannic baptism, and the features of the baptism before us, is obvious. Here, as everywhere, we find the presence of a controlling influence, a thorough change of condition, and no limitation of time. It is as impossible for the theory to expound the baptisms in the Bible or out of the Bible as it is impossible for a sieve to hold water.

It is not without practical value to notice the harmony between this baptism of our Lord, on entering upon his office work, and that baptism of the Apostles at Pentecost, when entering upon their office work. Both baptisms were by the Spirit. Both baptisms were, in their nature, qualifying for office. Both baptisms were distinct from, while essentially related to the "one baptism." Both baptisms were of life-long continuance. Neither baptism was connected with a water symbolization. The "like as a dove" well betokened the Holy Ghost and not a particular gift; while the "like as of fire" tongues, aptly set forth the more specific endowments conferred upon the Apostles. The Saviour was not covered over in the "like as a dove" appearance; nor were the Apostles covered over in the "like as of fire" tongues; yet both were as much covered in the one or the other as men and women were covered in the symbol water of their baptism.

While there are harmonies between the baptisms of our Lord and of his Apostles by the Holy Ghost, there is also diversity which separates them measurelessly and precludes the use of the

3

phraseology ("immersed in the Holy Ghost") insisted on by the theory. The New Testament proffers to men a " baptism into' repentance—into the remission of sins—into Christ." Did any one ever imagine that if a myriad should receive either of these baptisms that they would not receive identically the same baptism? Is it not absurd to suppose that those who should be "baptized in the Holy Ghost" would receive diverse baptisms? And yet the Lord Jesus, the Apostles, and Cornelius, received essentially diverse baptisms, while all are declared by the theory to be alike "immersed in the Holy Ghost!" It is not true, therefore, that there is any baptism *in* the Holy Ghost taught in the Scriptures, but a baptism *by* the Holy Ghost leaving this Divine Agent to " divide to each severally as he will."

BLOOMFIELD, Acts 10 : 38, says : " 'Anointed,' by a metaphor taken from the mode of inaugurating kings, signifies *invested* and *endued*, namely, at his baptism. And in Πνεύματι Ἁγίω καὶ δύναμει there is a hendiadys. The sense is, With the powerful influence of the Holy Spirit."

REV. ISAAC ERRETT (Campb.), Christian Standard (Campb. Bapt.), Aug. 9, 1873, thus acknowledges a peculiarity in the baptism of Christ : " Now, not to speak of the *peculiar* design of the baptism of Jesus—as peculiar to himself as was all else that made up his mediatorial mission—which unfits it to set forth the design of baptism to a penitent sinner." . . . .

This baptism is not a dipping, but an *abiding* "without measure" of the Spirit, in order to "fulfil all righteousness."

BAPTISM BY DRINKING FROM A SYMBOL CUP.

MARK 10 : 38, 39.

Δύνασθε πιεῖν τὸ ποτήριον ὃ ἐγὼ πίνω καὶ τὸ βάπτισμα ὃ ἐγὼ βαπτίζομαι βαπτισθῆναι; Οἱ δὲ εἶπον αὐτῷ, Δυνάμεθα. ὁ δὲ Ἰησοῦς εἶπεν αὐτοῖς, Τὸ μὲν ποτήριον ὃ ἐγὼ πίνω, πίεσθε καὶ τὸ βάπτισμα ὃ ἐγὼ βαπτίζομαι, βαπτισθήσεσθε.

"Can ye drink of the cup that I drink of and be baptized with the baptism that I am baptized with? And they say unto him, We can. And Jesus said unto them, Ye shall indeed drink of the cup that I drink of ; and with the baptism that I am baptized withal shall ye be baptized."

BAPTISM INTO PENAL DEATH.

The theory which makes Christian baptism to consist in a dipping into water, in the name (" by the authority ") of the Father, the Son, and the Holy Ghost, appears to regard the use of the term baptism to describe the transaction announced in this passage as a matter of rhetoric, and applied somewhat irregularly to a case standing out of the line of true baptisms, and with which as baptisms they have no concern. By such a view the theory shows itself (as under every other crucial test) to be a pure error from centre to circumference.

This baptism, so far from being out of the line of Bible baptisms and bearing a common title with them *e gratia* only, is the very centre of all Bible baptisms, and reflects upon them its own great claim to be the "one baptism" of the Scriptures, in which all other baptisms are grounded and from which they derive their character and worth.

This baptism was singularly Divine. The Subject of the baptism was God the Son, manifest in the flesh to this very end; the Upholder of the Divine-human Subject of this unutterable baptism was God the Holy Ghost, Sympathizer and Comforter, descending and abiding upon him; and the Executor of this baptism is God the Father, who holds the cup full of penal woe to the lips of his "forsaken" (Matt. 27:46) but "beloved Son." As that cup is drunk "the just dies for the unjust"—baptized into penal and thus made atoning death.

In this baptism are grounded all the typical baptisms of Judaism with their power for ceremonial purification; the baptism of John with its spiritual but imperfectly unfolded baptism "into repentance"—"into the remission of sins;" the fully developed baptism of Christianity "into Christ"—"into his death;" and the remoter, yet from the beginning purposed, baptism of all the redeemed "into the name of the Father, Son, and Holy Ghost." But among all these baptisms we look in vain, in the Bible or out of the Bible, for that baptism bearing the self-contradicting title—"dipping into water;" this can be found only in the theory. Its ambiguous life can find nurture in no other atmosphere.

Although this baptism is stated absolutely, without any defining adjuncts, still there has been a universal agreement in referring it to the atoning death and fulfilment of all righteousness, by the Lord Jesus.

The evidence in support of this conclusion is abundant: 1. There is a suggestion of difficulty and suffering. This is plainly involved in the questions, "Can ye drink?" "Can ye be baptized?" A Cup may be used to express what is productive

of gladness and life, but here evidently it points to sorrow, if not
to death. What gives character to the contents of the cup, must
give character to the baptism also. 2. Allusion to this same
baptism, on another occasion, confirms this view; Luke 12:50,
" I have a baptism to be baptized with, and how am I straitened
until it be accomplished." This language is indicative of distress
and oppression. It shows, also, that the baptism was exclusive
in its character, bearing only on the Saviour himself. And we
are farther led to the conviction that this baptism was familiar to
his mind, and that he was now passing through it while on his
way to Calvary, where it was to be "finished." 3. The context
develops suffering and death distinctly; Mark 10:33, 34, " The
Son of man shall be delivered unto the chief priests and unto
the scribes; and they shall condemn him *to death*, and shall
deliver him to the Gentiles : And they shall mock him, and
scourge him, and shall spit upon him, and *shall kill him.*" Matt.
20:28, " The Son of man came *to give his life* a ransom for
many." 4. Parallel passages abound in which this baptism, in
its elements of suffering and death, is brought to view; Matt.
16:21, " Jesus began to show to his disciples, that he must go
unto Jerusalem and *suffer* many things of the elders, and chief
priests, and scribes, *and be killed ;*" Matt. 17:22, " Jesus said
unto them, The Son of man shall be betrayed into the hands of
men ; *and they shall kill him ;*" Luke 9:22, "Jesus said, The Son
of man must *suffer* many things, and be rejected by the elders,
and chief priests, and scribes, *and be slain ;*" Luke 9:30, " Moses
and Elias talked with Jesus amid the glory of the Transfiguration
of his *decease* which he should accomplish at Jerusalem." These
and like passages show unmistakably the nature of this cup and
its baptism. 5. The repeated use of the same figure as the baptism draws nigh its accomplishment, removes all doubt; Matt.
26:39, " O my Father, if it be possible let *this* CUP pass from
me ;" v. 42, " O my Father, if *this* CUP may not pass from me
except I drink it, thy will be done ;" Luke 22:44, " And being
in an agony he prayed more earnestly ; and his sweat was as it
were great drops of blood falling down to the ground." At a
later hour of the same night he says: " The CUP which my
FATHER hath given me shall I not drink it?" John 18:11. That
CUP was at his lips, upturned by his Father's hand, the last drop
of penal woe passing from its brim when in untold woe he cried,

" Eli! Eli! lama sabachthani ?" and gave up the ghost, baptized into death!

This baptism of course does not suit the theory. What true baptism ever did? The Cup (that only source of his baptismal sorrows recognized by our Lord) must be got rid of. It is too small for the theory. More, shall I say, more penal woe than the Father could put into that Cup for the baptism into death of his beloved Son must be secured? no, not more penal woe, but more *Water*. So Dr. Carson says: " This figure represents the sufferings of Christ as an immersion in water" (!). It is in vain to quote the poetry of David in vindication of a " dipping." What is there of a " dipping" in Ps. 42 : 7—" Deep calleth unto deep at the noise of thy water-spouts; all thy waves and thy billows are gone over me;" or Ps. 69 : 1, 2 —" Save me, O God; for the waters are come in unto my soul. I sink in deep mire, where there is no standing; I am come into deep waters, where the floods overflow me ;" or Ps. 88 : 6, 7—" Thou hast laid me in the lowest pit, in darkness, in the deeps. Thy wrath lieth hard upon me, and thou hast afflicted me with all thy waves." To make a " dipping" the measure of these poetical outbursts is only to give another illustration of the truth that the sublime and the ridiculous are separated but by a single step. A dipping with its essential triviality constitutes the baptism of the theory. Neither dipping nor triviality ever made up any true baptism. Sprinklings and pourings have, as baptisms, been abundantly ridiculed. Whenever we say, that the conception in a baptism is measured in its height and depth and breadth by a sprinkling or a pouring, we will not object to any who will, saying *ne teneatis risum;* but when we say that a certain class of baptisms (Jewish) may be *effected* by a sprinkling or a pouring, or when we say that another class of baptisms (Christian) may be *symbolized* as to their spiritually purifying character, by a sprinkling or a pouring, and are so ordained of God to be ritually celebrated, then we give kindly notice to all indulgers in merriment, that " As the crackling of thorns under a pot, so is the laughter of the man who is not a son of Solomon."

It is not a mark of interpretative wisdom to take the glowing poetical forms of the Psalms and incorporate them in the calmer prosaic statements of the Gospels. Nothing could more justly and more vividly delineate persistent and oppressive sorrows than the language of David; but there is no approach to any such

picturing by Matthew, Mark, Luke, or John, when they speak of
the sufferings of their Lord.   David might fitly so write as a poet.
The writers of the gospels were not poets; they were historians.
There is neither statement nor implication in any language used
by them of "waves," "billows," "water-spouts," or "waters."
The unutterable woes of the Redeemer of a lost world are expressed under the simplest and quietest of figures, the drinking
from a cup, while the result of that drinking penetrating and
pervading his whole being "even unto death," is expressed as a
baptisma; a term never employed either in profane or sacred
writings to express a *covering in water*. It would be a "blunder"
perhaps "worse than a crime" to displace the sublimely simple
language of the Gospels in order to make room for the "waves,"
and "billows," and "water-spouts" of the Psalms, so illy accordant with the narrative of Gethsemane and the calmly self-con-
tained spirit of the Lamb of God in his death hour.   But if such
things should be introduced, they will only serve to make (under
the shadow of this cross baptism) more boldly erroneous the
notion, that *a dipping* can be a baptism.

PATRISTIC BLOOD BAPTISM.

Patristic writers speak of baptisms by blood and by water,
equally, as baptisms.   The differences as to the quantity, or as to
the manner of using the blood or the water, are never considered as
having anything to do with the matter.   A true baptism because
of *a dipping;* a false baptism because of *no dipping;* are things
unheard of.   The origin and coequal value of these baptisms is
thus declared by a writer in Tertull. III, 1198: "'I have another
baptism to be baptized with' (Luke 12:50); 'Can ye drink the
cup which I drink; or be baptized with the baptism that I am
baptized with' (Mark 10:38)? quod sciret homines non solum
aqua, verum, etiam sanguine suo proprio habere baptizari: ita ut
et solo hoc Baptismate baptizati fidem integram et dignationem
sinceram lavacri possint adipisci et utroque modo baptizari, æque
tamen unum, baptisma solutis et honoris pariter et æqualiter
consequi. Quod enim dictum est a Domino, 'I have another baptism to be baptized with;' hoc in loco non ut secundum Baptisma,
ac si sint duo Baptismata, significat, sed alterius quoque specici
Baptisma ad eamdem salutem concurrens donatum nobis esse
demonstrat. Because he would teach men to be baptized not only

by water, but, also, by their own blood : so that baptized by this baptism only they may secure a true faith and pure cleansing, and baptized in the one way or in the other equally to secure one baptism of salvation and honor. Because the Lord says, ' I have another baptism to be baptized with,' he does not mean a second baptism, as though there may be two baptisms, but he shows that Baptism has been conferred upon us issuing, under the one species or the other, in the same salvation." This passage (as well as other writings in these days) shows, that a dipping baptism was an unknown baptism, and blood baptism and water baptism are declared to be " one baptism " and *not two* baptisms. But this latter statement is an absolute falsehood stated in the most naked terms, if baptism is *a dipping*.

Cyril of Jerusalem, 440 : " If any one should not receive baptism, he has not salvation, except martyrs only, who may receive the kingdom even without the water. For the Saviour who redeemed the world by the cross, being wounded in the side, poured out blood and water; that some in times of peace (ἐν ὕδατι βαπτίς- θωσιν, οἱ δὲ ἐν καιροῖς διωγμῶν ἐν οἰκείοις αἵμασι βαπτίσθωσὶ) might be baptized with water, but others in times of persecution, might be baptized with their own blood. For the Saviour called martyrdom baptism, saying, ' Can ye drink the cup that I drink ?' " In this baptism, as in the preceding, whatever diversity there may be in " water" and " blood " as " species," and whatever diversity there may be in quantity of the one or the other, and whatever diversity there may be in the application of either to the body, their applicability as agencies in baptism is of Divine authority; each equally effects a baptism, and each effects *identically the same baptism*. It is a matter of indifference whether it be ἐν ὕδατι or ἐν αἵματι; in either case the issue is εἰς ἄφεσιν ἁμαρτιων as the " ONE BAPTISM."

Cyprian, 1123, 4 : " But if (Baptisma publicæ confessionis et sanguinis) the Baptism of public confession and of blood cannot profit a heretic to salvation, because salvation is not out of the Church, by how much more will it not profit him, if in the dens and caves of robbers (adulteræ aquæ contagione tinctus) he be contaminated with the pollution of impure water. . . . They, catechumens (baptizentur gloriosissimo et maximo sanguinis baptismo), may be baptized by that most illustrious and greatest baptism of blood concerning which the Lord said, that he had another baptism to be baptized with."

Augustine, IX, 276 : Petilianus rebuts the charge of baptizing twice, by saying, that those who put them to death as heretics baptize twice also, because they in slaying them baptize them by their blood, and adds, "But so the Saviour himself, also, having been first baptized by John, declared that he must be baptized a second time (non jam aqua, nec spiritu, sed sanguinis baptismo, cruce passionis) not now by water, nor by Spirit, but by the bap· tism of blood, by the Cross of his passion; as it is written—'and with the baptism with which I am baptized'—Blush! blush! O persecutors, ye make martyrs like unto Christ (quos post aquam veri baptismatis sanguis baptista perfundit) whom after the water of true baptism, baptizing blood sprinkles." Augustine replies: "If all who are slain are baptized by their blood, all robbers, unjust, accursed, and impious persons who are put to death, must be reckoned martyrs, because they are baptized by their own blood. But if none are baptized by their own blood, but those who are slain for righteousness, 'for of such is the kingdom of heaven' (Matt. 5 : 10). . . . If you make schism you are impious; if you are impious you will die as a sacrilegious person punished for impiety; if you die as a sacrilegious person how are you bap tized with your blood?"

It will be observed, that it never enters into the mind, much less into the discussion between Petilianus and Augustine, to inquire into the quantity of blood in a man's veins to determine whether a robber or a martyr could be dipped into it. These men did not deal in nor conceive of the rhetorical elegance by which a lake was to be put into the blood of a frog, or a dying man to be dipped into his own blood. It is not only rhetorical nonsense to talk of a figurative dipping of a man into his own blood, but it is a logical impertinence to raise such a question in these blood baptisms. The blood is not the receptive element, but the agency. And the same is true of the water used in bap· tism by water; *no matter what may be the quantity* of the water or *what may be the manner of the use*, the water is used as an AGENCY. If the water be used by sprinkling, or pouring, or covering the whole body, the baptism is no more effected by it than in the case of a blood baptism when the crimson current flows through wounds made in the hands by driven nails, or through the broader wound made by the spear cleaving the heart, or from spouting arteries when the head is stricken from the body. There is no baptism in the direction toward which the face of the theory

is "set as a flint." But one must be had. And so one is made,
by the most marvellous rhetoric, in the martyr's blood; and again
in the water, by a scarcely less remarkable philology.

These baptisms were to these Greek writers not rhetorical fic-
tions, but most practical realities, thoroughly changing the condition of the soul. There is a *vis baptismatis* in martyr blood,
with which quantity has nothing to do, which effects the baptism.
It is the absence of this, and not because of diminished quantity,
which leaves the impious unbaptized.

Origen, II, 980: "Christ, whom we follow, shed his blood for
our redemption, that we may depart washed by our own blood
(Baptisma enim sanguinis solum est quod nos puriores reddat,
quam aquæ baptismus reddit). For it is the Baptism of blood
only which can make us more pure than the baptism of water has
made us. And this I do not assume, but the Scripture declares,
the Lord saying to his disciples, 'I have a baptism to be baptized
with that ye know not of. And how am I straitened until it be
accomplished.' You see, therefore (quia profusionem sanguinis
sui baptisma nominavit), that he called the shedding of his blood
baptism. If God should grant to me that I might be washed by
my own blood so that I might receive a second baptism, dying
for Christ, I would leave this world satisfied."

Origen longed for a blood baptism as more perfect than a water
baptism. Covering, then, did not enter into his idea of a baptism; for in the water baptism of his day there was a covering,
while in blood baptism there was none; and yet the latter was a
more perfect baptism than the former. Again, the *profusio sanguinis* by our crucified Lord, Origen declares to be the *baptisma*
he was to endure. Then it was not an "immersion in water" as
some would have us believe. This most learned Greek also believed that the death baptism of our most blessed Lord was "the
perfect Baptism"—τὸ τελεῖον βάπτισμα—"perfect," not by some
marvellous introduction of water, but—διὰ τοῦ μυστηρίου πάθος—as
effected "through his mysterious passion." Yes; it was the
mystery of his passion which perfected the baptism. It was "the
mystery of the passion" which filled that Cup which the Father
gave him. And floating all through the mystery of that passion
was death—and in that death, *the death of* DEATH!

Origen, I, 600: "Let us remember our transgressions; and
that remission of sins cannot be received without baptism; and
that it is not possible according to gospel laws to be baptized

again by water and spirit into the remission of sins (αὖθις βαπτί-
σασθαι ὕδατι καὶ Πνεύματι εἰς ἄφεσιν ἁμαρτημάτων), and that the baptism of martyrdom is given to us ; for so it is called as is evident—
' Can ye drink the cup which I drink ?' or ' Be baptized with the
baptism that I am baptized with ?' Elsewhere it is also said,
' I have a baptism to be baptized with.' "

In this passage we have the agencies "Water and Spirit " (ὕδατι
καὶ Πνεύματι) stated most clearly by the instrumental Dative, and
the ideal element (εἰς ἄφεσιν ἁμαρτιων) no less clearly stated. There
is no room left for doubt either as to the nature of the baptism,
or as to the relation of the elements to each other. This baptism
(ὕδατι καὶ Πνεύματι εἰς ἄφεσιν ἁμαρτημάτων) cannot be repeated, but
another baptism (βάπτισμα τὸ τοῦ μαρτηρίου) which is (αἵματι εἰς
ἄφεσιν ἁμαρτημάτων) "the baptism of martyrdom," which is " by
blood into the remission of sins." These agencies differ ; in the
one case we have ὕδατι καὶ Πνεύματι ; in the other we have αἵματι ;
but the baptism effected in the one case or the other, is identically
the same—εἰς ἄφεσιν ἁμαρτημάτων. It is essential to understand
the great diversity, both in nature and form, of *the agencies* recognized by these writers, as well as *the perfect unity* of *the baptism*
effected by them.

Gregory Nazianzen, Orat. xxxix: " I know a fourth baptism
(βάπτισμα τὸ διὰ μαρτυρίου καὶ αἵματος, ὁ καὶ αὐτος Χριστὸς ἐβαπτίζετο)
that through martyrdom 'and blood, with which Christ himself
was baptized, and much more sacred than the others, because it
is not defiled by any subsequent pollution." Attention is again
called to what is so vital in the interpretation of these baptisms,
to the agency as **expressed** in the most unequivocal manner by
the Genitive διὰ.

Athanasius, Quæst. ad Antioch. lxxii: " God hath granted to
the nature of man three baptisms purifying from all manner of
sin ; I refer to that (τὸ ὕδατος, καὶ πάλιν τὸ διὰ μαρτυρίας τοῦ ἰδίου
αἵματος, καὶ τρίτον τὸ διὰ δακρύων) which is through water; and again
that which is through our own martyr blood, and third, that which
is through tears." Another agency (" tears ") is here added to
" martyr blood " as divinely appointed and made divinely compe·
tent, equally with " water," to baptize "into the remission of
sins." Some, misunderstanding the relation of " tears " to the
baptism, would subject them to hyperbolic inflation until a pool
deep enough to receive the penitent should be constructed. This
task is as gratuitous as it is extravagant. The " tears " are the

agency, not the receiving element, in this baptism. The "water" used in the ordinary ecclesiastical baptism occupies precisely the same relation to baptism. It is no more the receiving element than is martyr blood and penitential tears; but like them is an agency possessed of the *vis baptismatis* which baptizes (εἰς ἄφεσιν ἁμαρτιων) *into* THE REMISSION OF SINS. It is true, that "water" being more abundant than "blood," or "tears," there was no need of hyperbole to find enough of it to cover the whole body; and the body was covered. But this covering of the body was not the end sought; but only a means to that end. And in order that the means might have fuller development of its power all clothing was taken from the body. The idea that these men who baptized men and women naked believed that baptism was "a dipping into water" is on its face absurd, as well as in absolute contradiction to their statement, that baptism is δὶ ὕδατος—δὶ αἵμα-τος—διὰ δαχρύων The water was believed by them to be an agency; and that agency was believed to operate more properly and more effectively on the naked body; and hence the violence to natural modesty and Christian decency in order to secure an assured baptism (εἰς ἄφεσιν ἁμαρτιων) into the remission of sins.

CALVARY BAPTISM AND MARTYR BAPTISM.

While the baptism by martyr blood is grounded in the blood shed by Christ on the Cross, we are not to suppose that these baptisms were believed to be of the same precise nature. The likeness is exhausted in a common purifying character. Martyr baptism was to purify the martyr. The baptism of Christ was the sacrificial death of "the Lamb of God that taketh away the sins of the world." So, John of Damascus speaks of (Τὸ βάπτισμα δὶ αἵματος καὶ μαρτυριου ὅ καὶ ὁ Χριστὸς ὑπερ ἡμων ἐβαπτίσατο) "The baptism through blood and martyrdom with which Christ was baptized for us." Here is declared the vicarious character of the Saviour's baptism "by the Cross of his passion." And it was by virtue of the atoning blood shed in that passion, constituting a baptism into penal death under the demand of broken Law, which constituted martyr blood a baptism into the remission of sins. Thus the words of the loving Redeemer were verified, and the disciples became partakers of the baptism of their Lord—"baptized with the baptism with which he was baptized." "Without the shedding of blood" (not of any blood, not of martyr blood, but of atoning blood) " there is no remission of sins." " He who knew no sin was made sin for us, that we might be made the righteousness of God in him." " Behold the Lamb of God that taketh away the sins of the world." " This cup is the New Testament in my blood which is shed for many for the remission of sins." These passages and a thousand others are steeped in this blood baptism of the Lamb. No wonder that he should exclaim as he presses on toward this baptism and through this baptism—" How am I straitened until it be finished."

Origen, IV, 1384, in commenting on Mark 10 : 38, speaks instructively on martyr baptism. He says : " Martyrdom has a twofold significance, of which the one is called ($\pi o \tau \acute{\eta} \rho \iota o \nu$ $\sigma \omega \tau \eta \rho \acute{\iota} o \nu$) the cup of salvation, the other baptism ($\beta \acute{a} \pi \tau \iota \sigma \mu a$); so far as one bears sufferings, *a cup is drunk by him who bears whatever is brought upon him*, enduring and as it were drinking sorrows, neither repelling nor rejecting and vomiting them out; but as he who bears these things *obtains the remission of sins*, it is a *baptism.*" In this indication of the application of the terms " Cup" and " Baptism" to martyrdom, Origen speaks in entire harmony with classic writers with whom baptism by drinking from a cup was one of the most common forms of baptism.

CUP BAPTISM.

MATT. 20 : 22.

$\Delta \acute{\upsilon} \nu a \sigma \theta \epsilon \ \pi \iota \epsilon \tilde{\iota} \nu \ \tau \grave{o} \ \pi o \tau \acute{\eta} \rho \iota o \nu \ \grave{o} \ \grave{\epsilon} \gamma \grave{\omega} \ \mu \acute{\epsilon} \lambda \lambda \omega \ \pi \acute{\iota} \nu \epsilon \iota \nu;$
" Are ye able to drink the cup that I shall drink of?"

LUKE 12 : 50.

$B \acute{a} \pi \tau \iota \sigma \mu a \ \delta \grave{\epsilon} \ \grave{\epsilon} \chi \omega \ \beta a \pi \tau \iota \sigma \theta \tilde{\eta} \nu a \iota, \ \kappa a \grave{\iota} \ \pi \tilde{\omega} \varsigma \ \sigma \upsilon \nu \acute{\epsilon} \chi o \mu a \iota \ \grave{\epsilon} \omega \varsigma \ \emph{\"{o}} \tau o \upsilon \ \tau \epsilon \lambda \epsilon \sigma \theta \tilde{\eta}.$
" I have a baptism to be baptized with; and how am I straitened until it be finished."

Matthew, according to the Codex Sinaiticus, speaks only of the Cup to be drunk; while Luke (in another connection however) speaks only of the baptism to be received. Mark, as we have seen, conjoins the Cup and the Baptism. In other words, Matthew includes in the Cup the unstated effect of drinking that Cup, and Luke, reversely, by stating the Baptism would indicate the Cup causative of that Baptism. Mark makes express statement both of the Cup and of the Baptism, of the cause and of the effect.

Dr. Carson objects to a remark of Mr. Ewing of Glasgow— "There is perhaps a more intimate connection between a 'cup' and a 'baptism' as belonging to *one* allusion, than some readers of Scripture have as yet remarked, as shown by Matt. 20:22, &c." Dr. Carson (p. 117) says: "These figures both respect *one* object, but they have not, as Mr. Ewing asserts, *one allusion*. They are figures as independent and distinct, as if one of them was found in Genesis, and the other in Revelation. One of them represents the sufferings of Christ as a cup of bitterness or poison, which he must drink; the other represents the same sufferings as an immersion in water." Here arises the question, What is meant by "an immersion in water"? The error of the theory is shown most clearly by the loose and inconsistent use which it makes of its own select terms. Does "an immersion in water" mean a *dipping* in water? Then the phrase is as incompetent to express intense suffering, much less atoning suffering, as any that could well be invented. Does it mean "an immersion in water" up to the chin? How does that express suffering? Does it mean an entire covering in water? Then we have an expression not of suffering but of death; and how does that accord with a "dipping"? The whole subject of baptisms is, in every aspect, unmanageable by the theory. Dr. Carson adds: "When the Psalmist says, 'The Lord God is a sun and shield,' both the figures represent the same object, but they have a separate and altogether different allusion. The *sun* is one emblem, a shield is another." This is very true; and because it is true proves Dr. Carson to be in error. The sun and the shield are diverse in nature, and must in figure represent diverse things. They do so here; they represent essentially diverse relations in which the Lord God stands toward his people. According to Dr. Carson these diverse things should be taken to express precisely the same thing. For he declares that while a Cup and a baptism are as distinct from each other as is Genesis from Revelation, yet they represent precisely the same thing, namely, "the same sufferings." It is irrational to suppose that a drinking and a dipping would be used in the same sentence to express precisely the same thing. Besides, this interpretation fails to meet the breadth of the unfigured and expository language of our Lord. In the context immediately preceding the cup and the baptism of Mark we

are told : " And he took again the twelve, and began to tell them
what things should happen unto him, saying, Behold, we go up
to Jerusalem ; and the Son of man shall be delivered unto the
chief priests, and unto the scribes; and they shall condemn him
to death, and shall deliver him to the Gentiles : and they shall
mock him, and shall *scourge* him, and shall *spit* upon him, *and
shall kill* him." And again (Matt. 16 : 21), " Jesus began to show
unto his disciples, that he must go unto Jerusalem and *suffer*
many things of the elders, and chief priests, and scribes, *and be
killed;* " (Luke 9 : 22), " The Son of man must *suffer* many things,
and be rejected by the elders, and chief priests, and scribes, *and
be slain.*" And in the context (v. 28) immediately following the
announcement by Matthew of the cup to be drunk, our Lord says,
" The Son of man came *to give his life* a ransom for many "
Thus in all these prophetic teachings *death* stands out in the
boldest relief as the great fact, the one momentous and essential
result in which all antecedent sufferings issue. But " death " is
neither in the cup nor in the baptism of Dr. Carson—" the cup
represents the sufferings of Christ," baptism " represents the
same sufferings." That is to say, the very essence of this prophetic announcement—*an* ATONING DEATH, the theory is unable to
grasp. To admit that baptism has within itself the power of
death, would be to give over to death a dipping baptism. The
death of Christ must be interpreted out of his atoning baptism
in order that the theory may live. We adoringly accept the interpretation by our Lord of his own words as given again and again,
and recognize the cup filled with penal woe such as was never
held to the lips of any other, and the baptism into death consequent upon the drinking of that cup, as meeting the demands of
a broken law—" the end of the law for righteousness to every one
that believeth."

In vindication of this understanding it may be observed : 1. It
is in the most absolute harmony with the representation of Scripture—suffering *and death*, suffering *causative* of death. This is
evident from the quotations already given as well as the whole
tenor of Scripture. 2. It is in no less harmony with the force and
usage of Βαπτίζω and Βάπτισμα, as used in the Classics and in the
Scriptures. The Greek verb is frequently used in Classic writings where it is causative of death — " The dolphin baptizing
killed him" (Æsop); " I baptizing you by sea waves, will *destroy*
you " (Alcibiades); " Baptizing others into the lake," *drowned*

them (Heliodorus); "Whom it were better to baptize," *to drown* (Themistius). We do not find *Βάπτισμα* in Classic writings. Its form is expressive of the action of the verb as a result. Whatever power there may be in the verb to effect death, the same power is in the substantive to express death. Whatever may be the competency of *Βάπτισμα* to express the condition of an object physically baptized, yet as a matter of fact it is never so used in the Scriptures. Its usage there is limited to express baptisms which are verbal or purely ideal in character. It is once used with the verbal form expressed (Rom. 6 : 4) *διὰ τοῦ Βαπτίσματος εἰς τὸν θάνατον*, which is implied in the passage under consideration—"Can ye be baptized with the baptism (into death) with which I am baptized." 3. But the question arises: Although the Scriptures conjoin "suffering and death," and although baptize and baptism be competent to express death, yet is it allowable to speak of a baptism—a baptism into death, as effected by drinking from a cup? In answer to this question it may be replied, that there is no one class of baptisms which is more frequently spoken of by Greek writers than just such baptisms—baptisms by drinking. It is not true that every kind of baptism can be effected by drinking; nor is it true that baptisms which can be effected by drinking, can be effected by drinking any kind of liquid.

Baptisms by drinking are various in character, yet all marked by *a thorough change of condition pervaded and controlled by the* CHARACTERISTIC *of the baptizing liquid.* No liquid which cannot thoroughly change the condition of the drinker and subject him to its characteristic quality, is capable of baptizing. The following are examples of baptism by drinking: 1. "Whom, by the same drug (*καταβαπτίσας*), having baptized," by drinking from a cup (*Achilles Tatius*); 2. "Baptized (*βεβαπτίσθαι*) by unmixed wine," by drinking from a cup (*Athenæus*); 3. "Baptizing (*βαπτίσας*) powerfully," by drinking from a cup (*Athenæus*); 4. "Baptized (*βαπτίσας*) Alexander," by drinking from a cup (*Conon*); 5. "Baptizes (*βαπτίζει*) with sleep, neighbor to death," by drinking from a cup (*Evenus*); 6. "He resembles one baptized (*βεβαπτισμένω*)," by drinking from a cup (*Lucian*); 7. "I am one of those yesterday baptized (*βεβαπτισμένων*)," by drinking from a cup (*Plato*); 8. "Baptizing (*βαπτίζοντες*) out of large wine jars, they drank to one another" out of cups; 9. "Baptized (*βεβαπτισμένοις*) by yesterday's debauch," by drinking from a cup (*Plutarch*); 10. "The body not yet baptized (*βεβαπτισμένον*)," by drinking from a cup (*Plutarch*). These cases from classic Greek writings show not only that a baptism may be effected by drinking from a cup, but that this was one of the most familiar methods of effecting a baptism with which they were acquainted. These baptisms were not specifically of the same character. Some were baptisms of drunkenness, in which there was a thorough change of condition in the baptized by the pervading and controlling influence of the intoxicating quality characterizing the liquid drunk. Some were baptisms of opiate stupor, because the characteristic of the liquid drunk was soporific in its nature, and consequently, so thoroughly changed the condition of the baptized as to bring them under the controlling influence of that characteristic. It is an error of the most primary character to call in question a baptism because it is effected by drinking from a cup. It is a matter of infinite indifference what is the nature or form of an act, or what is the character or mode of applying any influence; if the result is a thorough change of condition by envelopment without limitation of time, or without envelopment by a penetrating and controlling influence, a baptism is effected. 4. As the way is clear for a baptism by drinking, so the case itself demands such interpretation. To make two figures each limited to suffering is beyond justification. Any exposition which does not include death is equally without justification. The drinking of a cup is not an end, but a means to an end. What that end is must be determined by the contents of the cup. This cup is full of suffering, of penal suffering, demanding and only to be satisfied by death. The drinking of this cup, then, has as its issue not suffering but death. The import of a *baptism* is the opposite of a drinking. It is not a means, but an end. It is a result reached through some antecedent action. The natural relation, therefore, of a drinking and of a baptism is that of cause and effect. Such is the representation here—" Can ye drink of the cup of penal woe of which I drink, and thereby be baptized with the baptism into an atoning death with which I am baptized?" All this was in the mind of the Redeemer, and constituted the ground of impossibility which was involved in the inquiry; but it was not in the minds of the disciples, and hence their mistaken reply, which their Lord does not attempt to correct but accepts, in so far as it was susceptible of a true interpretation, namely, their full participation in the benefits of his baptism. 5. The usage of Scripture in parallel cases vindicates this interpretation: " For thus saith the Lord God of Israel unto me:

Take the wine cup of this fury at my hand, and cause all the nations, to whom I send thee, to drink it. And they shall drink, and be moved, and be mad, because of the sword that I will send among them. Thus saith the Lord of hosts, the God of Israel: Drink ye, and be drunken, and spew, and fall, and rise no more, because of the sword that I will send among you. And the slain of the Lord shall be at that day from one end of the earth even unto the other end of the earth." (Jerem. 25 : 15–38.) "Thus saith the Lord God: Thou shalt drink of thy sister's cup deep and large; thou shalt be laughed to scorn and had in derision; it containeth much. Thou shalt be filled with drunkenness and sorrow, with the cup of astonishment and desolation, with the cup of thy sister Samaria. For thus saith the Lord God: I will bring up a company upon them, and will give them to be removed and spoiled. And the company shall stone them with stones, and dispatch them with their swords; and they shall slay their sons and their daughters, and burn up their houses with fire." (Ezek. 23 : 32–47.) These passages are sufficient to show that in the Scriptures the drinking from a cup is a means to an end, and that in these cases that end was death. They drank, and were baptized into death. 6. This figure of a cup is preserved until its resultant baptism is finished: "O my Father, if it be possible, let *this* Cup pass from me;" "O my Father, if *this* CUP may not pass from me except I drink it, thy will be done." (Matt. 26 : 39, 42.) "Father, if thou be willing, remove THIS CUP from me; nevertheless, not my will but thine be done." (Luke 22 : 42.) "Abba, Father, all things are possible unto thee; take away *this* CUP from me: nevertheless, not what I will, but what thou wilt." (Mark 14 : 36). "*The* CUP which my Father hath given me shall I not drink it?" (John 18 : 11.) In these allusions to "the Cup," there is no omission of the baptism. The baptism is in the Cup. That Cup was upturned, and the last drop of penal woe passed those pale lips as they opened to cry "Eli, Eli, lama sabachthani?" and with it "he gave up the ghost," and the baptism into death— that death which a broken law demanded, that death which only "the just for the unjust" could die, that death which made the dying One "the Lamb of God which taketh away the sins of the world," and "the Lord our Righteousness," that death which was the death of Death, was "finished." Finally, this baptism of our Lord is the only baptism of the New Testament which is represented as effected by drinking from a cup. There is no other

A

baptism which could fitly be so represented. This baptism stands all alone. It was no ordinary death baptism, it was no martyr death baptism, it was an atoning death baptism. The ordinary baptisms, agencies, and symbols, are out of place. What so fit, so tenderly beautiful, as a Cup held to his lips by his Father's hand? In that Cup, melted down by the mighty menstruum of the Law, are the Incarnation, the manger, the temptations of the Wilderness, the contradiction of sinners, the scoff, the derision, the blaspheming, the buffeting, the thorn, the nail, the spear, the forsaking by his Father! and He drank it all, and was baptized into death, "that whosoever believeth on him might not perish but have everlasting life." The believer in Christ drinks of the cup of which he drank, but not until it is emptied by his Lord of its penal woe, and is made unto him a "cup of salvation;" he is "baptized with the baptism with which he is baptized," but not until its death issue is exhausted, and life springs up in its stead. The sinner who comes to Christ, penitent and believing, is baptized into Christ, "who is made sin for us that we might be made the righteousness of God in him." This baptism of soul purification could not be represented by the drinking from a cup; this might represent the gift of life, but not the remission of sin; therefore Christian baptism, the purification of the soul by the blood of Christ, through the Holy Ghost, is fitly symbolized by pure water, not drunk, but applied to the body.

THREEFOLD CHARACTER OF THE BAPTISM RECEIVED BY CHRIST.

The personal baptism of Christ is presented by Scripture in a threefold form: 1. As a covenant baptism engaging to the fulfilment of all righteousness; received from his Forerunner on his public assumption of that work which he came into the world to do. 2. As a baptism by the Holy Ghost, the third Person of the Godhead, descending upon him and abiding with him in loving sympathy with the covenant baptism, and purposed co-operation by measureless influence, in order to its perfect accomplishment. In this baptism (ἐν Πνεύματι Ἁγίῳ) (*he was never taken out of it*) the Saviour ever lived; under its power he ever spake and wrought his miracles of power; and finally, "through the eternal Spirit offering himself without spot to God," he did on Calvary redeem the covenant made on Jordan, "fulfilling all righteousness," and by his blood shed purging the conscience from dead works to serve the living God. (Heb. 9 : 14.) 3. As a baptism into penal and atoning death. By this baptism, endured as "a ransom for many," the Lord Jesus Christ becomes "the Lamb of God that taketh away the sin of the world." He is possessed of this power in the most absolute degree. The characteristic quality of any liquid substance is developed by and communicated in the fullest measure to an object baptized into it. Any suitable object (fruit) baptized (not *dipped*) into vinegar, becomes pervaded with its acid quality and is thoroughly changed as to its condition, is converted into a *pickle*. If the liquid be melted sugar, the saccharine quality pervades the fruit; it is thoroughly changed as to its condition, and becomes a *preserve*. If the fluid be alcoholic in character, the fruit is pervaded by this alcoholic characteristic, becomes assimilated to it, and thoroughly changed in condition, as *brandied fruit*. These unquestionable facts furnish the basis for the following twofold usage: 1. Where a characteristic quality is communicated, in any way, so as to pervade, assimilate, and thoroughly change the condition, to wit, as by drinking an opiate, or by the descent, indwelling, and filling of the Holy Ghost, those who receive such communication are declared, alike by heathen and by inspired writers, to be baptized. 2. Where it is desired to express the communication of a characteristic pervading, assimilating, and thoroughly changing the condition, but where, in the nature of the case, there can be no intusposition for this purpose, a verbal form (εἰς with the impossible receptive element) suggests such communication in the clearest and strongest possible manner, and is employed to express a verbal or ideal baptism. This form of phraseology does not appear in the Classics. It originates in the Scriptures. It abounds there; sometimes expressing essentially diverse baptisms, but generally, under diversified phraseology, conveying the same substantial truth. The design of the phraseology appears to be to express the truth taught in the strongest, most explicit, and most impressive manner possible. Concurrent with this design may have been another, namely, to separate in the most marked manner the New Testament baptisms, real and ritual, from physical intuspositions, of which the New Testament knows absolutely nothing.

Corollary. If the characteristic of the Lord Jesus Christ, as "THE LAMB OF GOD THAT TAKETH AWAY THE SIN OF THE WORLD," be expressed as developed in the fullest, the clearest, and the most impressive manner, it will be by phraseology expressive of a *Baptism* INTO CHRIST.

CHRISTIC BAPTISM: BAPTISM ADMINISTERED BY CHRIST.

BAPTISM BY THE HOLY GHOST.

JOHN 1 : 33.

Οὗτός ἐστιν ὁ βαπτίζων ἐν Πνεύματι Ἁγίῳ.

"This is he that baptizeth by the Holy Ghost."

This passage might be translated, "This is THE BAPTIZER who is *in*"—full of, invested with the power of—"the Holy Ghost."

The translation—"This is he that baptizeth (=immerseth, dippeth?) in the Holy Ghost" (Baptist version), making the Holy Ghost *the receiving element* of the baptized object, is an impossible translation whether we consider grammatical law, Greek (Classic and Hellenistic) usage, or New Testament doctrine.

The translation—"This is the Baptizer who is in the Holy Ghost," is one which is unquestionably possible, quite probable, and not without many and strong reasons to vindicate as the true translation. The following are some of the reasons which sustain it: 1. It is generally admitted (Stuart, Hodge, Ellicott, Olshausen, Winer) that such phraseology may be explained by the supply of the participle (ὤν) *being*, or its equivalent. Winer (p. 389) says: "In Rom. 15 : 16 ἐν Πνεύματι Ἁγίῳ is employed designedly, *in* the Holy Spirit (an internal principle). Least of all does ἐν Χριστῷ ever signify *per* Christum; but this phrase invariably refers, for the most part in an abbreviated way, to the *being in* Christ, εἶναι ἐν Χριστῷ. So, likewise, in 1 Cor. 12 : 3, ἐν πνεύματι θεοῦ is to be rendered quite literally, speaking *in the Spirit of God*, the element in which the speaker lives. The preposition in ἐν ὀνόματι τινος simply means *in*. And something takes place 'in a person's name,' when it is to be set down to *his personal activity*, cf. Acts 4 : 7, Ἐν ποίᾳ δυνάμει ἢ ἐν ποίῳ ὀνόματι ἐποιήσατε τοῦτο ὑμεῖς; In what power or in what name have ye done this?" Olshausen (Rom. 9 : 1) says: "After these words, ἐν Χριστῷ, *in Christ*, ἐν Πνεύματι Ἁγίῳ, *in the Holy Ghost*, we ought rather to understand ὤν." Under this principle of interpretation the phrase ὁ βαπτίζων ἐν Πνεύματι

Ἁγίῳ represents the condition of ὁ βαπτίζων as "*in* the Holy Ghost."
With this should be associated the principle stated by Bishop
Ellicott, Ephes. 5 : 18, ἐν Πνεύματι. There would seem to have been
an intentional inclusiveness in the use of this preposition, as Matthies suggests : "The Spirit is not the bare instrument *by* which,
but that *in* which and *by* which the true Christian is fully filled."
So in the phrase under consideration, ἐν Πνεύματι Ἁγίῳ does not
denote merely instrumentality or inness of condition, but has an
inclusiveness which embraces both ideas ; ὁ βαπτίζων is *in* the Holy
Ghost, and is thereby invested with power to baptize *by* the Holy
Ghost. And according as the one idea or the other may be predominant in a particular case of usage, the translation should be
"*in* the Holy Ghost" or "by the Holy Ghost." 2. This view is
clearly and strongly sustained by the context. The ὁ βαπτίζων ἐν
Πνεύματι Ἁγίῳ was to be identified by this evidence, namely, "Upon
whom thou shalt see the Spirit descending, and remaining on him,
the same is ὁ βαπτίζων ἐν Πνεύματι Ἁγίῳ." Now such descent of
the Holy Ghost is always indicative of spiritual endowment and
qualification for office or special work. It was so in this case by
special declaration. He on whom the Holy Ghost descended and
on whom he remained, "without measure," was thus qualified for
his amazing work, and qualified to be ὁ βαπτίζων ἐν Πνεύματι Ἁγίῳ—
the Baptizer who was himself *in* the Holy Ghost, and being in the
Holy Ghost was thereby invested with power to baptize *by* the Holy
Ghost. 3. Other passages of Scripture sustain the same view. As
a consequence of the Holy Ghost descending and remaining on
him, "Jesus was full of the Holy Ghost, and was led *in* the
Spirit (ἐν Πνεύματι) into the wilderness" (Luke 4 : 1). This statement of Luke is not to be confounded with that of Matthew 4 : 1,
"Then was Jesus led up of the Spirit (ὑπὸ τοῦ Πνεύματος) into the
wilderness." The statements are different but harmonious. Luke
states directly the condition, ἐν Πνεύματι, in which Jesus was, and
thus, indirectly, the influence under which he acted; Matthew
omits the condition in which Jesus was, and states the Divine
influence by which he was guided. This distinction is overlooked
by Middleton, and his suggestion that ἐν is put for ὑπὸ falls under
the condemnation of Winer (p. 362), pronounced against "an
arbitrary interchange of prepositions (upheld in part by an abuse
of parallel passages) . . . . Luke (4 : 14) farther says: "And Jesus
returned (ἐν τῇ δυνάμει τοῦ Πνεύματος) *in* the power of the Spirit."
Thus we have expressly stated the double truth, that Jesus was

"in the Spirit," and as a consequence, he was invested with "the *power* of the Spirit." We are farther told (v. 18), that by "the Spirit upon him" he was anointed to preach the gospel and (v. 32) "his word was with power." 4. As the preaching of Jesus was ἐν Πνεύματι, so also were his miracles wrought ἐν Πνεύματι Θεοῦ. We have in Matt. 12: 24–28 a parallel usage of this preposition— "Οὗτος οὐκ ἐκβάλλει τὰ δαιμόνια εἰ μή ἐν τῷ βεελζεβοὺλ: This fellow doth not cast out devils, but by Beelzebub." This might with as much propriety be translated, "He casts out devils in Beelzebub" (making Beelzebub the recipient of the devils cast out) as Αὐτος ὑμᾶς βαπτίσει ἐν Πνεύματι ʽΑγίω be translated, "He shall baptize you *in* the Holy Ghost," making the Holy Ghost the recipient of the baptized. Neither translation can be tolerated. The Baptist version expounding the use of ἐν, says: "ʼΕν with *dative* of *person* denotes the one *in* whom resides the power or authority, by which a thing is done; hence *by* or *through*." But this explanation is inadequate. It does not cover the case. The connection between the Caster out of devils and Beelzebub is not accounted for. How does he become possessed of that power which is in Beelzebub? This is naturally and clearly expounded by placing Οὗτος and ἐν in their proper relation to each other; "this fellow" is then declared to be "*in* Beelzebub," and thus becomes invested with his power. This clearly is the statement made, as shown by the words of Jesus (v. 27): "If I (ἐν βεελζε- βοὺλ) in Beelzebub cast out devils;" where the relation of ἐγὼ and ἐν cannot be mistaken. This point is farther established by the statement of Mark 3: 23, "Ὅτι βεελζεβοὺλ εχει, καὶ ὅτι ἐν τῷ ἄρχοντι τῶν δαιμονίων . . . Because he hath Beelzebub and because he is *in* the Prince of the devils he casts out the devils." Here a demon power is expressly declared to be possessed by Jesus, and he is declared to be "*in* the Prince of demons" whence this demon power proceeds. The relation of ἐν, then, is with Οὗτος, and "this fellow" is declared to be ἐν βεελζεβοὺλ, and thus invested with his power. This view is conclusively established by the repudiation of this singularly wicked charge and the claim by the Lord Jesus, that he was *in* the Spirit of God—"Εἰ δὲ ἐγὼ ἐν Πνεύματι Θεοῦ. If I *in* (and therefore invested *with* the power of) the Spirit of God cast out devils;" and Luke 11 : 20, "Εἰ δὲ ἐν δακτύλῳ Θεοῦ. But if *in* (therefore *by*) the finger of God I cast out devils" . . . . Throughout this narrative the preposition ἐν has most evidently its instrumental force, grounded in its primary meaning, as bearing upon Οὗτος. The same is true as to ἐν and its relation with ὁ βαπτίζων in the passage under consideration. "The Baptizer" is represented as being *in*, and hence baptizing *by* the Holy Ghost. 5. The prophetic declaration of John, Matt. 3 : 11, "He shall baptize you (ἐν Πνεύματι Ἁγίῳ) being *in* (and therefore *by*) the Holy Ghost." The translation of this passage by the Baptist version —"He shall immerse (dip?) you in the Holy Ghost," is untenable in every point of view: (1.) It cannot be vindicated under the theory held as to the meaning of βαπτίζω. (2.) The conjunction of βαπτίζω ἐν to express the transition of an object out of one medium into another medium cannot be vindicated by any Classic usage. (3.) The prophecy put into the mouth of John declaring, that the great characteristic of the mission of the Lord Jesus Christ should be "to immerse (dip) in the Holy Ghost" is without a word of Scripture to support the declaration, and without a fact to evidence its fulfilment. We accept therefore the great announcement of John, that his Lord should be in and baptize by the Holy Ghost; a declaration made ages before by the Prophets, proclaimed as a fact by the Evangelists, and exemplified with power and great glory in the history of the church. 6. This interpretation is confirmed by a contrasted parallelism with the personal condition and power ascribed by the Scriptures to the Forerunner. In Luke 1 : 17 it is said : "And he shall go before him (ἐν πνεύματι καὶ δυνάμει Ἡλίου) in the spirit and power of Elias." No one, so far as I know, ever questioned, that by this language John was foretold as coming *in* (therefore invested *with* and qualified *by*) the spirit and power of Elias for the great work before him. When now it was foretold by Isaiah, that the anointing spirit of the Lord should be upon Jesus ; when it was foretold to John that the Holy Ghost should descend and remain upon him ; when it was foretold by John that he should baptize being ἐν Πνεύματι Ἁγίῳ; when John declares he saw the prophetic sign verified with his own eyes, and on that foundation immediately declares Jesus as Οὗτος εστιν ὁ βαπτίζων ἐν Πνεύματι Ἁγίῳ ; why shall we hesitate to accept this multiplied testimony to the personal condition and power of the divine Baptizer, and recognize the truth, that because John came " ἐν πνεύματι καὶ δυνάμει Ἡλίου," while his Lord came " ἐν Πνεύματι Ἁγίῳ—ἐν δυνάμει καὶ Πνεύματι Θεοῦ " —*therefore* the Forerunner was " unworthy to bear the shoes " of the Coming One ?

The interpretation of this passage will remind us of the rules of Winer (p. 353): The present participle (with the article) is often used substantively, and then as a noun, excludes all indication of time. In Eph. 4 : 28 ὁ κλέπτων is *the stealer;* Matt. 27 : 40 ὁ καταλύων *the destroyer;* Gal. 1 : 23 ὁ διώκων *the persecutor;* and (p. 135) " When an adjunct (consisting of a noun and preposition) which in reality forms with the substantive but one leading idea, is to be linked to the preceding noun simply by the voice, the grammatical connective of the written language (*i. e.* the article) is wanting, *e. g.* Col. 1 : 8, τὴν ὑμῶν ἀγάπην ἐν Πνεύματι, *your love in the Spirit.* This takes place especially in the oft-recurring apostolic phrase, ἐν Χριστῷ, ἐν κυρίῳ, (ἐν Πνεύματι), as 1 Thess. 4 : 16 οἱ νεκροὶ ἐν Χριστῷ *the dead in Christ,* with which is contrasted (v. 17) οἱ ζῶντες (ἐν Χριστῷ) *the living in Christ;* Eph. 4 : 1 δέσμιος ἐν κυρίῳ *the prisoner in the Lord.*" On this last passage Ellicott quotes Fritz. Rom. 8 : 1, ἐν Κυρίῳ ὢν vinctus est *he was bound being in the Lord.* The Lord Jesus Christ—ὁ βαπτίζων ἐν Πνεύματι Ἁγίῳ —is " the Divine baptizer *being in* the Holy Ghost."

The interpretation which does not recognize Christ as " in the Holy Ghost," but represents him as " immersing (dipping) in holy spirit," " in the essence of holy spirit," " in abstract holy spirit," " in a holy spirit," shows how an initial error leads on to other and more portentous error. The translators of the Baptist Bible have no difficulty in seeing a personal Beelzebub in ἐν τῷ Βεελζεβοὺλ, but they see no personal Holy Ghost in ἐν Πνεύματι Ἁγίῳ, John 1 : 33, Matt. 3 : 11, although indissolubly connected with Matt. 3 : 16, 4 : 1; Luke 4 : 1, 14; Matt. 12 : 28; Acts 1 : 2, 5; Heb. 9 : 14 . . . . This statement is illustrated by the following quotations from the notes on the Baptist version : " Matt. 3 : 11, ' He will immerse you in holy spirit ;' note, *In holy spirit.* By this is meant that divine influence, so often expressed by the Greek words . . . The omission of the article, in this and similar cases, will enable the English reader to make the distinction intended by the sacred writer." " ' John 1 : 33, he it is that immerseth in the Holy Spirit.' *Note:* I would greatly prefer to render these words literally, *Holy Spirit,* without the article. I do not consider the πνευμα ἅγιον here spoken of to be *the personal spirit,* contemplated as such, but, simply, *divine essence,* abstracted, in the mind of the writer, from all ideas of personal attribution or relations." Dr. Conant does not appear to approve of this translation as interpreted. In his Dissert. p. 67, while he repeats the translation of Matt. 3 : 11, " he will immerse you *in holy spirit,*"

he translates John 1 : 33, " this is he that immerses *in the Holy
Spirit* "

The translator of Acts does not seem to agree with either of his
fellow-laborers in the interpretation of this phrase: "' Acts 1 : 5,
You shall be immersed in the Holy Spirit.' *Note :* The Book of
the Acts is not inappropriately called ' The Gospel of the Holy
Spirit.' His personal attributes, mission and work, are more fully
developed. . . . Speculative theologians have been much perplexed in their versions and criticisms upon the anarthrous forms
of this Divine person. . . . We judge it expedient to take a critical and full view of this *third personal* manifestation of Jehovah.
. . . Thus πνεύμα becomes definite, because specific, by the adjunct
ἅγιον. There is no room for mistake. So far from the article being
necessary to give definiteness or individuality to πνευμα ἁγιον, *it is
its very definite and individual character that enables it to stand
without the article.* It is a great mistake to suppose that πνευμα
ἁγιον is an *abstract noun.* Πνευμα alone may be used as an abstract
noun, but surely not with the qualifying and specific adjunct ἁγιον.
. . . The Holy Spirit is set forth in his individual, personal, and
specific character, as πνευμα ἁγιον; not as an influence of something
else, but a concurring and self-acting personal divine agent in
consummating and completing the work of redemption. . . . Here
there can be no mistake. The τὸ Πνεύμα τὸ ʿΑγιον promised in John
14 : 26 is the πνευμα ἁγιον in which the Harbinger promised they
should be immersed, the same πνευμα ἁγιον for which the Saviour
bid them tarry at Jerusalem, and the το ἁγιον πνευμα which was to
come upon them in order to endue them with power, &c., as found
in v. 8. The identity of the subject as indicated by the several
expressions, πνευμα ἁγιον, το πνευμα το αγιον, and το αγιον πνευμα, cannot be doubted.''

This is sufficiently decided as against an immersion (= dipping)
" in holy spirit," " in divine essence," " in abstract spirit," " in *a*
holy spirit " (Stovel); but how such great office work of the Holy
Ghost in a world's redemption accords with a representation of
the third Person in the Godhead, being a *quiescent medium* into
which the souls of men are to be introduced by the Lord Jesus
Christ, remains to be explained.

The passage is to be understood as announcing the peculiar
character of the Lord Jesus Christ as a Baptizer. This is done
by exhibiting him in a twofold aspect: 1. As being personally
ἐν Πνεύματι ʿΑγίῳ. 2. As a consequence of being ἐν Πνεύματι ʿΑγίῳ,

being invested with the power of baptizing *by* the Holy Ghost. In the use of this phraseology the Scriptures are self-interpretative: Acts 4 : 7, "'Εν ποίᾳ δυνάμει ἢ ἐν ποίῳ ὀνόματι, being *in* (therefore working *by*) what power, or being *in* (therefore working *by*) what name?" v. 9, " ἐν τινι, in (therefore *by*) whom;" v. 10, " ἐν ὀνόματι I. X., in (therefore *by*) the name of Jesus Christ;" v. 12, " ἐν ἄλλῳ οὐδενὶ, in (therefore *by*) no other;" " ἐν ᾧ, in (therefore *by*) whom we must be saved;" v. 30, ἐν τῷ, in (the Lord (v. 29) being *in*) therefore healing *by* his hand; " διὰ τοῦ ὀνόματος, *through* the name (by those being ἐν τω ὀνόματι) of thy holy child Jesus." The Lord Jesus being ἐν Π. 'A. did " διὰ Π. 'A. give commands" (Acts 1 : 2), and " διὰ Π. 'A. offered himself without spot to God." (Heb. 9 : 14.) John " coming *in* the spirit and power of Elias" was qualified to do his work *through* that spirit and power. John's Lord coming " *in* the Spirit and power of God" was qualified to do his work *through* that Spirit and power.

Some may prefer interpreting ἐν Πνεύματι 'Αγίῳ as qualifying ὁ βαπτίζων as expressing an act rather than in a purely substantive use. Such interpretation will affect the form only of the argument

---

ACTS 1 : 5.

Ὑμεις δὲ βαπτισθήσεσθε ἐν Πνεύματι 'Αγίῳ.
"But ye shall be baptized by the Holy Ghost."

THE BAPTISM OF THE APOSTLES FOR THEIR APOSTLESHIP.

This great baptism is a worthy illustration of that divine investiture publicly received by the incarnate Redeemer in entering on his covenant work by the descent of the Holy Ghost, and by reason of which he was proclaimed by his Forerunner to be— " ὁ βαπτίζων ἐν Πνεύματι 'Αγίῳ—the Baptizer who being *in* the Holy Ghost baptizes *by* the Holy Ghost." It is also a very clear and striking illustration of the diversity in baptisms. The theory does not and cannot consistently recognize diversity in baptisms. The argument is—" A dipping is a dipping and a baptism (= dipping) is a baptism (= dipping)." There may be a dipping of diverse objects into diverse elements with diverse results, but the dipping remains unchanged and unchangeable. To baptize is to perform " a definite act," *to dip;* and this is its meaning they say always, never being used to express the *result* of an act, laying aside definite form. That is to say, the friends of the theory still make their argument as to βαπτίζω as formerly in relation to βάπτω, to turn on a modal act, exclusive, invariable, and always present in fact or in imagination. Those who do not accept this theory deny the foundation (modal action) on which it rests, affirming that βαπτίζω does not belong to the class of verbs expressing modal action, but to that class which makes demand for condition. They farther affirm, that the condition (intusposition) demanded for its object by βαπτίζω does invariably, from the necessity of the case, result in a complete change of condition of the object, and ordinarily in a farther change of condition in consequence of the object being penetrated, pervaded, and thus assimilated to the characteristic quality of the encompassing element. And, grounded in this unquestionable fact, it is still farther affirmed, that βαπτίζω has a secondary usage in which the condition of intusposition does not appear, but a condition identically the same as or analogous to that resulting from intusposition (namely, interpenetration and assimilation), but effected in any way or by any means. The friends of the theory having been confronted by Dr. Carson with the rhetorical enormity of " dipping a lake in the blood of a frog," they abandoned the doctrine that βάπτω means " to dip and nothing but dip," and accepted a secondary meaning based upon the *effect* of dipping under certain conditions, namely, into a dyeing liquid an object fit to receive by interpenetration and assimilation the characteristic quality of the dye, so that *dipping in* blood (ἐβάπτετο δ'αἵματι) became transformed into " *dyed by* blood," the modal act utterly disappearing. The " fantastic tricks " of rhetoric resorted to in order to save modal act to βάπτω are a trifle compared with those which have been found necessary (not to save for it never was there, but) to give, *de novo*, modal act to βαπτίζω. Many of these rich imaginings we have already met with, and shall meet with more, and with one (not the least remarkable) in the passage now to be considered.

Dr. Carson and the Theory.

There is a propriety in giving prominence to the views of Dr. Carson on this subject, because he is regarded in Great Britain as without a peer among his fellows; and in America his writings are issued by the Baptist Board of Publication as of standard authority. All must acknowledge that the writings of Dr. Carson have unusual power. This arises in part from the element of truth which is obvious; but still more by the boldest statements declaring that to be true which is untrue (he honestly believing his statement to be true) and the ordinary reader being unable to detect its falsity. Dr. Carson is also a man of the profoundest convictions, of the most daring courage, of imperious will, and an utter stranger to veneration for any human name that stands opposed to him. He sees difficulties only to trample them under foot. He meets opposing suggestions only to fling them behind his back. He writes with the unreserved force of a man who claims that what he writes is "demonstration" and for "eternity." With such characteristics associated with respectable learning, and special study of language in some of its departments, the writings of Dr. Carson could not but be impressive. Other writers are more learned, as Gale; more critical, as Ripley; more broad and judicious, as Conant; more refined and candid, as Morrell; but no writer of his class has the power which belongs to Carson. I am happy to say, farther, that whatever of amenity and polish may be obviously lacking in the author of these writings, there is no less of evidence that he is a truly honest and Christian man. Some of his friends may think that it was a sad illogicism which led this earnest defender of a "dipping into the water" not to refuse to others "a crumb dropping from the children's table," and even to allow them to sit down with him and eat of the same "bread" and drink of the same "cup." But this sin surely was not remembered against him when in death he passed into the presence of the Master who gave of the children's bread even to a Syrophenician.

If the views of Dr. Carson as to the baptism under consideration appear to be such as no rational man could entertain, it must be remembered that their very extravagance is proof that Dr. Carson was no ordinary man. A common man, one of an everyday courage, self-confidence, and faith in a theory, would have shrunk back from their promulgation; it required the nerve and faith of Carson to follow theory into self-contradiction and absurdity with a triumphant step. But let us look at his interpretation of this baptism of the Apostles by the Holy Ghost, as a dipping.

"Baptism of the Holy Spirit."

The section which introduces the discussion bears the heading, "Baptism of the Holy Spirit." This phraseology exemplifies the

deceptive and (in view of his fundamental principles) the inconsistent use of language which so largely characterizes and vitiates
the entire book. No friend of the theory has a right to speak of
"the baptism *of* the Spirit." Such language implies either that
"the Spirit" is to be the object dipped, or is to be the agent who
is to dip some one else; but the theory rejects both these views,
and insists upon a dipping of somebody by somebody "*in* the
Spirit." Then stand by this position. Do not tacitly disavow it
by going into the camp of the enemy to borrow their banner.
"Baptism *of* the Holy Spirit" is our legend. Let those who
believe in "a dipping *in* the Holy Spirit" manfully avow it, boldly
display it, and if they can triumphantly defend it.

The statements of Dr. Carson under this heading will now be
given and followed by needful criticisms.

"*Figure*"—"*Immersion*"—"*Dipping*"—"*Sanctification.*"

"The baptism of the Spirit is a figurative expression, explicable
on the principle of a reference to immersion. This represents the
abundance of the gifts and influences of the Spirit of God in the
enlightening and sanctifying of believers. That which is immersed in a liquid, is completely subjected to its influence and
imbued with its virtues; so, to be *immersed in the Spirit*, represents the subjection of soul, body, and spirit to his influence.
The whole man is sanctified."

"Believers are said to be immersed into the Spirit, not because
there is anything like *immersion* in the manner of the reception
of the Spirit, but from the resemblance between an object immersed in a fluid and the sanctification of all the members of the
body and faculties of the soul."

"But though the baptism of the Holy Spirit is a figurative
baptism to which there cannot be a likeness in the literal baptism;
yet, as respects the transaction on the day Pentecost, there was
a real baptism *in the emblems of the Spirit*. The disciples were
immersed into the Holy Spirit by the abundance of his gifts; but
they were literally covered with the appearance of wind and
fire." . . .

"Now though there was no dipping of them, yet, as they were
completely surrounded by the wind and fire, by the catachrestic
mode of speech which I before explained, they are said to be
immersed." . . .

"Air and fire were elements of the baptism that took place on the day of Pentecost, but they are not the elements in the standing ordinance of Christ. . . . . They who were baptized on that day in wind and fire, had been baptized before." . . .

" 'A dry baptism!' exclaims Dr. Wardlaw. Be patient, Dr. Wardlaw; was not the Pentecost baptism a dry baptism? Christian baptism is not a dry baptism; but the baptism of Pentecost, and of the Israelites in the Red Sea, were dry baptisms."

"The baptism did not consist in the mode of the coming of the flame, but in the being *under* it. They were surrounded by the wind and covered by the fire above. They were therefore buried in wind and fire " (pp. 104–114).

Criticism.

1. "The baptism of the Spirit is a figurative expression, ex plicable on the principle of a reference to immersion." The term "figurative" is without well-defined boundaries. Its use is oftentimes vague and unsatisfactory. A figurative expression is, most naturally, one which is designed to point the mind to the "figure," form, outline, of something physical, as having some element in common with and expository of something which does not pertain to physics. "A wave of trouble rolled over the land " suggests a resemblance between "trouble" and "the land," such as is found in a wave of water rolling broadly and resistlessly over the ocean. "He has dipped into mathematics " suggests an object put into a fluid for a moment and withdrawn. What is momentary and superficial is necessarily limited in effect. A physical dipping, therefore, expounds a dipping *into mathematics* as a study limited in time and attainment. "He is immersed in thought " suggests an object completely covered. How covered, or with what covered, the allusion has nothing to do; the covering is unlimited in extent and in time. We learn, therefore, that "immersion *in thought*" is complete engagedness in (not *assimilation to*) thinking to the exclusion of everything else. Such usage is plainly and designedly figurative. The mind is unavoidably led to the physical allusion, and without effort apprehends the reason of it.

But there are other phrases which by some are called figurative with less obvious propriety. "The people are enlightened;" "The man is debased;" "Imbued with love;" "Endued with wisdom;" such phrases are very questionably called figurative.

They may be all traced to a physical origin, but not one in ten thousand does so trace them in their use or in hearing them used. Indeed "debase," "imbue," "endue," have no physical use in our language, and a merely English scholar could not refer to their use in physics to aid him in the understanding of their actual use. In the Greek language βάπτισμα has as little use in physics as "imbue," "endue," have in English. It is never so used in the New Testament. I do not remember any such usage in Christian Greek writers; and it does not appear at all in classic writings. It is of course traceable to physics through the verb, and its value is clearly deducible from such source; but when it is said to be used "figuratively," the term is too loose, in such application, without some defining explanation.

The phrase, "baptism of the Spirit," does not occur in Scripture. "The baptism of John" is of frequent occurrence, and always means the baptism proceeding from John as preacher or administrator. "The baptism of repentance" is also met with, and always indicates that baptism proceeding from repentance as its source. "The baptism of the Spirit," interpreted by parallel phraseology of Scripture, must mean that baptism of which the Spirit is the teacher or the executive; but the Scriptures do not represent the Spirit as a teacher of a baptism, while it does represent him as the executor of baptism. This phrase, therefore, can only represent the Spirit as the executor of baptism. But the theory teaches a baptism *in* the Spirit as the receiving element, and not *by* the Spirit as the executor; it therefore teaches a doctrine unknown to the Scripture, and which precludes their use of the phrase " baptism *of* the Spirit."

The language of Dr. Carson, made consistent with the theory, would read thus: "The dipping in the Spirit is a figurative expression, explicable on the principle of a reference to dipping." This, as Carsonism, is plain enough. It refers us to the dipping (therefore momentary and superficial introduction) of an object into water with trivial effect; therefore it teaches us that Christians are momentarily, superficially, and trivially, brought under the influence of the Spirit. Such baptism may suit those who believe in the theory; it will not suit those who believe in the Bible.

2. " This " (baptism = immersion = dipping) " represents the abundance of the gifts and influences of the Spirit of God." A dipping never was used in figure and never can rationally be so

used to express "abundance of gifts and influences." Its import
is the right opposite. And if immersion is so used, in figure, it
is an unusual use. It may express covering, and so quantity
sufficient for such purpose; but this is a very different conception
from "abundance of gifts and influences." But however this may
be it is of no help to the theory, for in its vocabulary "immersion"
is not *immersion*, but a dipping. Baptism is never used to express "abundance;" its idea is always that of *power*. A cup of
wine will baptize by its intoxicating power; a draught of an opiate
will baptize by its soporific power; a dove-like appearance has
power symbolly to baptize; cloven tongues as of fire have power
symbolly to baptize; drops of water have power symbolly to baptize. A baptism has nothing to do with abundance, but is a
resultant condition effected by some pervading, assimilating, and
controlling influence. "Abundance" belongs to *pouring*, and not
to dipping or baptism. And in this connection the idea originates in, and is borrowed from, the "*pouring out* of the Spirit."

3. " That which is immersed in a liquid is completely subjected
to its influence and imbued with its virtues; so to be *immersed
in the Spirit* represents the subjection of soul, body, and spirit to
his influence."

If Dr. Carson used language at its true value, and used it consistently, and there was any such statement in the Scripture as
" immersed in the Spirit," then this language would express important truth, and the theory would be rejected as " Nehushtan."
But unhappily none of these things are true. The opportunity, however, is given for bringing into relief some things
which are true. (1.) The radical difference between dip and immerse precluding their interchangeability. Dr. Carson says:
" That which is immersed in a liquid is completely subjected to
its influence and imbued with its virtues." This is perfectly true
using "immersed" at its proper value = within a fluid without
limitation of time, and the object being of a nature adapted to
that influence or virtue belonging to the liquid. But now substitute for "immersed" *dipped*, and how will the statement appear?
" That which is *dipped* in a liquid is completely subjected to its
influence and imbued with its virtues." Could a statement be
more utterly devoid of truth? A vegetable "immersed" (by the
force of the word without limitation of time) in vinegar becomes
completely subjected to its influence and imbued with its virtues,
and is thoroughly changed in condition—converted into *a pickle.*

Is this true of a vegetable *dipped* (by the force of the word limited to momentary continuance) in vinegar? Is it completely subject to the influence of the vinegar, imbued with its virtues, and transformed into *a pickle?* (2.) The shifting in argument from immerse to dip, and from dip to immerse, using them respectively in their distinctive value as the exigency of the case may demand, and again interchanging them as though they had no distinctive value, is a wrong to truth, is destructive to argumentation, and is proof of the falsity of the cause which demands such support. But such shifting runs through Dr. Carson's writings, and constitutes his club of Hercules. (3.) But this statement of Dr. Carson has special value as vindicating a radical principle in this Inquiry. It has been insisted upon that βαπτίζω did not mean *to dip*, that it did make demand for intusposition without limitation in the time of continuance. It has farther been insisted upon that the effect of such intusposition on suitable objects was to bring them under the controlling influence of the investing element interpenetrating, pervading, assimilating, and controlling, or (to use Dr. Carson's words) "completely subjecting them to influence of the liquid and imbuing them with its virtues." And proof has been adduced that on this basis was grounded a secondary usage of βαπτίζω in which the investing element disappeared, and a condition (the result of some pervading and assimilating influence) was directly expressed. Dr. Carson now admits (to the destruction of a dipping) that "complete subjection to influence and imbuing with virtues" is the result of a baptized condition, and he expounds the baptism under consideration as *one in which no dipping, no immersion, is to be found.* Thus the radical truths developed in Classic Baptism, and revealed throughout this Inquiry, are vindicated by the admissions of Dr. Carson, and *a secondary usage grounded in the* EFFECT *of the primary is established.*

4. " To be immersed in the Spirit represents the subjection of soul, body, and spirit to his influence. The whole man is sanctified."

This interpretation again subverts the theory: (1.) A dipping cannot subject the soul, body, and spirit to any influence. (2.) If " *immersion* in the Spirit " accomplishes this profound, abiding, and assimilative change, then the word which expresses " *immersion* in the Spirit " cannot express *dipping* in water. (3.)

While the Scriptures do not teach an "immersion in the Spirit," they do teach a "baptism *into repentance*" (εἰς μετανόιαν), and if Dr. Carson will apply his exegesis as above, he will find all so baptized (not *dipped*) "completely subjected to the influence of repentance and imbued with its virtues." The Scriptures also teach a baptism (not a *dipping*) "into *the remission of sins*" (εἰς ἀφεσιν ἁμαρτιων) by which the baptized (not the *dipped*) are "completely subjected to the influence of the remission of sins and imbued with its virtues." The Scriptures also teach a baptism "into Christ" (εἰς Χριστὸν), by which the baptized (not *dipped*) are " completely subjected to the influence of Christ our Redeemer, and imbued with his virtues " as the Lord our Righteousness. These baptisms should compensate for the taking away from the friends of the theory the error respecting a baptism "*in* the Spirit," especially as these baptisms "into repentance"—"into the remission of sins"—"into Christ"—are all baptisms *of* the Spirit, so that instead of being a quiescent medium in which souls should be baptized by some baptizer, he is himself the active, mighty, and divine Agent by whom the souls of men are baptized "into repentance," "into the remission of sins," "into Christ."

The error of the theory is still farther shown by the statement that the one result of "immersion in the Spirit" is "Sanctification." If there were such a thing as "immersion *in* the Holy Spirit" the natural result would be (from complete subjection to such influence) "Sanctification." And what would be the result in one case must of necessity be the result in every case. If one vegetable immersed in vinegar becomes a pickle, then every vegetable immersed in vinegar becomes a pickle. If one soul baptized into the remission of sins receives forgiveness, then every soul baptized into the remission of sins will receive forgiveness. In like manner if one soul is baptized "in the Holy Spirit" and the result is "Sanctification," so every soul baptized "in the Holy Spirit" must receive "Sanctification." But this again destroys the theory; (1.) In general; because the office of the Holy Spirit in redemption is not limited to Sanctification, but is most comprehensive and varied, "dividing to every man, severally, as he will," and therefore his work cannot be represented as an "immersion *in* the Spirit." (2.) In particular; because in the baptism before us, which Dr. Carson says was an "immersion *in* the Spirit," the result was not Sanctification, but "power" *for the Apostleship* and (immediately) the power "to speak with tongues." The theory is not only erroneous, but it is pure error through and through. It is no less erroneous in the application of true principles than it is in the making of false definitions.

5. " Believers are said to be immersed *into* the Spirit, not because there is anything like *immersion* in the manner of the reception of the Spirit, but from the resemblance between an object immersed in a fluid and the Sanctification of all the members of the body and the faculties of the soul."

Observe (1.): The shifting from " immersed *in* the Spirit " to " immersed *into* the Spirit." This is far from being a trivial matter. It is not only erring in translation (which all may do), but it is a usurpation of that language which the Holy Spirit has established as a barrier against the error of the theory. There is no such language in the history of the work of redemption as baptism "*into* the Holy Spirit." The prepositions εἰς and ἐν, in connection with baptism throughout the New Testament, are used with a severe discrimination which has no exception. The former (εἰς) is invariably employed to designate the receptive element (which is always ideal), and the latter (ἐν), or the dative alone, is always used to denote the agency, whether efficient that of the Holy Spirit, or symbol that of water. This discrimination is a silent but impressive warning against confounding what God has distinguished. But the theory has not only converted the Holy Spirit into a receptive medium under the plea that ἐν means *in*, but having done this is dissatisfied that her self-created baptism should stand alone bearing a mark alien from all divine baptisms, and so has displaced ἐν (the divine mark of agency) and of her own will has substituted εἰς, thus taking away from and adding unto the word of God in most vital points. Observe (2.): In this unhappily entitled " immersion *into* the Spirit," there is " not anything like *immersion* in the manner of the reception of the Spirit;" the baptism consists solely in the *effect* produced, a thorough change of condition, namely, " the Sanctification of all the members of the body and the faculties of the soul." If Dr. Carson had grasped this truth and followed its guidance in the interpretation of Classic baptisms, it would have saved him and his friends from whole seas of bad rhetoric of the lake-frog-blood class. It is a master-key truth, that in Classic, and Jewish, and Christian baptisms there is a large proportion of baptisms in which " there is not anything like immersion," but solely *a thorough change of condition* analogous to *the effect* produced on a class of objects by

immersion without limit of time. And the settled establishment
of this point will be an adequate issue to this Inquiry. But observe (3.): The explanation of Dr. Carson lacks both correctness
and congruity. If " believers are immersed into the Spirit," then
it is neither correct nor congruous to speak of the manner in which
they " *receive* the Spirit." Whatever a man is " immersed into "
receives him, not he it. Blot out this " immersion into " (and *in*
also) which is not in the Scriptures and which is a burden heavy
to be borne by the theory, and then the way will be clear to speak
of " the manner of the reception of the Spirit " when baptized *by*
the Spirit. There is a farther error and incongruity when " believers are said to be immersed in the Spirit because of the resemblance between an object immersed in a fluid and the Sanctification
of body and soul." That is to say, the baptism of the Spirit con
sists in the Sanctification of the body and the soul without having
anything to do with or with anything like dipping or immersing,
and yet this is called baptism because of its resemblance to an object immersed in a fluid. Is not this on its face incorrect and hopelessly incongruous? How can what is not ("there is not anything
like an immersion ") resemble that which is = "an *immersed* object "? Or, is the baptism (= Sanctification) like " the object "
(a rock) apart from the immersion? This is impossible. What
then is meant? Is it this, Dr. Carson has severely condemned
his friends for admitting that an *effect* could be called a baptism ;
but here he is brought face to face with such a baptism, and in
his extremity he shrinks from acknowledging "effect" (so destructive in its bearings) and writes in its stead " immersion," logically
meaning *the effect* of immersion? Whether Dr. Carson so meant
or not such is the truth. It is impossible for a sane man to talk
of a resemblance between " Sanctification of body and soul " and
an " *immersed* object." Suppose that object to be a flint rock or
a mass of iron, what is the resemblance to a Sanctified body and
soul? Who has the courage to attempt an answer? Resemblance
to an "*immersed* object" must be abandoned. Try now an object
which is capable of receiving influence, of being changed in condition, made assimilant to the characteristic of the enveloping
element; for example, take some fruit put into melted sugar a
year ago; what is its condition now? Is it not penetrated, pervaded, and assimilated to the saccharine characteristic of the
element in which it has been immersed? Is not its condition as
fruit thoroughly changed? Does any one hesitate to recognize

the resemblance between such an *effect* produced upon the fruit (thoroughly changing its condition by an influence pervading and controlling it by its own characteristic) and the *effect* produced upon the soul, thoroughly changing its condition by an influence of the Holy Spirit pervading and controlling all its faculties, and making them subject to its own holy characteristic? The baptism of the Spirit, then, is an *effect* produced in the soul without a dipping, without an immersing, without anything like either; but which is like *the* EFFECT produced on certain objects by baptism in a fluid having a special characteristic, and which thus receive and are made assimilant to such characteristic. In other words, it is admitted that the terms baptize and baptism have ceased to express dipping, or immersing, or "anything like" them, and does directly express an effect like to the effect of physical baptism, *in whatever way* such effect may be produced. By this admission βαπτίζω and βάπτω are placed side by side as to the ground of their secondary usage. The former lays aside its modal condition of intusposition, and adopts the effect of such intusposition on a certain class of objects as a secondary meaning; the latter lays aside its modal action of dipping, and adopts the effect of such dipping on a certain class of objects as a secondary meaning. As Dr. Carson's protest against the rhetoric of his friends which would dip a lake into drops of blood was triumphantly successful, inducing its prompt and universal abandonment and the establishment of a secondary meaning for βάπτω in which there was no dipping, so may his repudiation of " anything like immersion " in the baptism of the Spirit prove to be no less happy in its results, and relieving his friends of their singular rhetoric, establish among them a secondary meaning for βαπτίζω in which "anything like immersion " shall forever pass away.

6. " But though the baptism of the Holy Spirit is a figurative baptism to which there cannot be a likeness in the literal baptism, yet as respects the transaction on the day of Pentecost, there was a real baptism *in the emblems of the Spirit*. The disciples were immersed into the Holy Spirit by the abundance of his gifts; but they were literally covered with the appearance of wind and fire."

(1.) Dr. Carson has admitted that the baptism of the Spirit is not a " figure " of dipping or immersing, for there is not anything like these things in it; but it is called a baptism because it produces *an effect which resembles the* EFFECT produced by physical baptism. These effects have individual differences, yet have this common feature, namely, a thorough change of condition assimilant to the characteristic of that which effects such change. Now of such *effect* the baptism of the Spirit is not a " figure," but is an exemplification. It is therefore a real baptism—not changing the condition of an object by introducing it within a physical covering, nor (what is a very different thing) the condition of an object through an influence operating by means of a physical envelopment, but changing the condition of an object in like *character* as an influence operating through envelopment changes it, developing its influence, however, in other ways than by envelopment. Denying therefore that any envelopment, real or imaginary, exists in these baptisms (the correctness of which denial Dr. Carson admits), and affirming that the name applied to them (baptism) is derived from that class of baptisms in which the envelopment is only a means to an end, namely, assimilative change, we farther affirm, that this mode (by covering) for effecting such changes ceases to be exclusive, and ANY *act or influence competent to effect like change* is accepted as effecting a baptism. The thorough change in the condition of the soul, effected by the Holy Spirit assimilating it to itself, is therefore a real baptism, and is not "the figure " of a dipping, or an immersion, or a covering.

(2.) " The disciples were immersed into the Holy Spirit by the abundance of his gifts."

As there is no baptism " into the Holy Spirit " in his official working in the scheme of redemption, and the nature of his relation to the scheme of redemption as the great Worker in the souls of men, does not allow of his being regarded as a quiescent medium out of which some one else is to extract virtue by putting the souls of men into it, this statement is erroneous. But who confers " the abundance of his gifts "? Is it the Holy Spirit? Then the Holy Spirit " immerses into the Holy Spirit," for this immersion is "*by* the abundance of his gifts." This is not the wisdom of the Scriptures. Does some one else bestow " the abundance of his gifts "? Then what becomes of the office of the Holy Spirit? In this statement Dr. Carson is leading us in a circle. He has already told us that " immersion in the Spirit " confers " abundance of gifts " and " sanctifies body, soul, and spirit." We are now told that " abundance of gifts " previously conferred has a power to " immerse into the Spirit." Error cannot square with the truth.

(3.) " There was a real baptism *in the emblems of the Spirit.* . . They were literally covered with the appearance of wind and fire."

(*a.*) " A real baptism " (!) no " figure " here. (*b.*) " In the emblems of the Spirit." There were no " emblems of the Spirit " present at Pentecost. The Spirit does not baptize " in emblems." All baptisms of the Holy Spirit are real baptisms of the soul, not coverings of the body in " sound " and " cloven tongues." The " sound as of a mighty rushing wind " proclaimed the presence of the Deity; and the " cloven tongues as of fire " symbolized the gift conferred to speak in other languages. The " appearance as of a dove " descending and remaining on the " beloved Son " when he was baptized " without measure " by the Spirit, was an emblem of the Holy Ghost; wind-sound and cleft tongues are not. (*c.*) " They were literally covered with the appearance of wind and fire." If there had been but one Bible in the world, and that under lock and key in Dr. Carson's study, this statement might have received some credence, or, if there were but one intellect (though erratic) in the world, and from its supreme wisdom had come such announcement, the remainder of a witless race might have accepted this " *real* baptism " in " the *appearance* of wind and fire." As, however, there are other copies of the Scriptures in the world, and happily so written that " a fool may not err " in such a case, we withhold our faith from this " real " " appearance " baptism.

7. " Now, though there was no dipping of them, yet as they were completely surrounded by the wind and fire, by the catachrestic mode of speech which I before explained, they are said to be immersed."

On reading such a statement there is a natural impulse to ask: Was it propounded in a lunatic asylum? Solomon in one of his Proverbs unites with the common sense of all ages to forbid a formal answer to such extravagance. One element in it, however, may be noticed. It is this: *Dipping*, as a modal act, is the theoretic *sine quâ non* of baptism with Dr. Carson. That this is so, is placed beyond all doubt by the necessity felt by Dr. Carson to make out a modal dipping in a " real baptism " where there was claimed to be an unquestionable " surrounding " and " covering." With some this would have been sufficient to vindicate a baptism, but not so with Dr. Carson; he insists that " to baptize " is " to *dip* and nothing but *dip* through all Greek literature," and there-

fore he undertakes to make out a dipping where there is confessedly none, and this he does by his old and trusty friend Catachresis, whom we have heretofore met with as "the Old Guard,"
reserved for dire exigencies.   We call attention to the fact, that
it is out of the bowels of *dip* that Dr. Carson has drawn the fila-
ment with which he has woven his theory, because this little word
has suddenly fallen into such disrepute that the *Baptist Quarterly*
denounces it, and enters a denial that Dr. Carson ever believed
in it.   The reed on which we once leaned when breaking and
piercing our hand is condemned and rejected as worthless.   It is
not well, however, in discarding a trusted friend to say—We never
leaned upon you.   There is another point hardly second in importance to this, which is developed in this same sentence.   It is
this: the use of dip and immerse as equivalents, having precisely
the same meaning.   We are told, "though there was no dipping
yet, by *Catachresis*, they are said to be immersed " = dipped.   A
dipping was what was lacking; a dipping was what Dr. Carson
set out to find, and under the guidance of *Catachresis* he finds it
in "immersed."   But in a previous sentence Dr. Carson has used
"immersed in the Spirit" not in the sense of dipping (= momentary introduction and withdrawal), but in the sense of unlimited
continuance.   Thus a claim is set up for a word to mean both
momentariness and continuance unlimited only by the eternal
ages.   The legs of such a theory are too unequal to allow it to
walk erect.

8. "The baptism did not consist in the mode of the coming
of the flame, but in the being *under* it.   They were surrounded
by the wind, and covered by the fire above.   They were therefore buried in wind and fire."

Dr. Carson was certainly something more than an extraordinary
man.   If there is a second friend of the theory in the Old World or
the New who would venture to write these three sentences it would
be a pity, for no wonder would be left to be expended on him.
Times without number we have been told by Dr. Carson and his
friends, that we show the greatest stupidity in talking about "the
mode" of baptism.   With a knowledge exhaustive of all truth
upon the subject we have been informed, that baptism itself is
mode and nothing but mode; and to talk about the mode of baptism is as witless as to talk about "the mode of dipping."   But
our Instructors now tell us, that they have discovered a "baptism
which does not consist in the mode of the coming of the flame,

but in the being *under* it." Well; may a disciple inquire about "the dipping"? That, I believe, does not mean "being *under* a flame." Oh! "Catachresis" will attend to that.

"They were surrounded by the wind," although there was no "wind;" "and covered by the fire above," although there was just as little "fire" as there was wind, "THEREFORE they were *buried in* WIND *and* FIRE"!!! Well, no doubt just as the nakedness of an African prince is "buried" out of sight when he goes abroad regally attired in a "covering of wind" and "under" a flaming umbrella. The baptism is remarkable as Dr. Carson puts it; it would be still more remarkable if it was found in the Bible; but happily neither it nor any element as an apology for it is to be found there. This peerless advocate of the theory asks permission of none in heaven or on earth to mould the language of Scripture to suit his necessities any more than to call on "Catachresis" to help his theory out of difficulties.

I conclude this examination by a quotation from President Halley, equally accomplished as a writer and a scholar. "Dr. Carson continues (p. 110): 'The wind descended to fill the house, that when the house was filled with the wind, the disciples might be baptized with it.' This philosophy of a house full of wind is not of Scripture, but of Dr. Carson, I would have skeptics take notice, lest they should profanely ask, was it ever empty of wind? or if there was more than usual, what kept the building together? 'Their baptism consisted in their being totally surrounded with the wind, not in *the manner* in which the wind came.' Of course he means came upon them. Will you believe me, gentle reader, that his book is written to prove that to baptize is a modal verb, referring exclusively to *the manner* in which the action is performed; the manner in which the wind, or water, or baptizing fluid incloses a person, by his being *put into it*, and not by its coming upon him?"

The lake-dipping into a frog's blood by Dr. Gale is hard, round common sense compared with this chaffy, catachrestic dipping of the Apostles into "sound and cloven tongues" by Dr. Carson.

Translation.

"John truly baptized (ὕδατι) with water; but ye shall be baptized (ἐν Πνεύματι Ἁγίῳ) by the Holy Ghost."

The translation of ἐν Πνεύματι Ἁγίῳ cannot be baptized "*in* the Holy Ghost" (making this Divine person the figurative recipient of the Apostles), because: 1. It is not the grammatical form to express such idea. In Classic Greek, when an object not already in a condition of baptism is spoken of as to be baptized, the receiving element is invariably expressed in the Accusative with εἰς. 2. When ἐν with the encompassing element in the Dative, is used by the Classics, it invariably expresses that the object is already in a baptized condition, and so continues without limitation of time. 3. When the Dative without a preposition is used by the Classics (they never use a preposition) it invariably expresses the agency by which the baptism is effected, and not the receiving element into which the baptized object passes. 4. In the New Testament when the agency (symbol or real) and the receiving element (which is never physical) are both stated, the agency is invariably expressed by the Dative (with or without ἐν), and the receiving element by the Accusative with εἰς. 5. When the Dative (with or without ἐν) appears in the New Testament without the Accusative and its preposition, it *of necessity must* (both by Classic and New Testament usage) express the agency effecting the baptism or symbolizing the baptism effected. Where the receiving element has been previously stated, we are under obligation to supply, by ellipsis, such element as stated, with the Accusative and its preposition, in all like baptisms; but when the baptism is special in its character, and the Dative only appears, we are not under obligation or necessity to construct any receiving element by supplying a verbal form in the Accusative with εἰς, because the agency and the attending circumstances will always indicate the nature of the baptism. The Classics never supply a receiving element with the Dative. They use this case in connection with baptisms of the second class, expressing thorough change of condition without envelopment. The Scriptures so use it. It is the Dative only (ἐν ὕδατι, ὕδατι, supplied by ellipsis, John could baptize in no other way but symbolly) which appears in the baptism of Jesus by John. The nature of the case and positive statement showing that it was a rite exhibiting a covenant baptism engaging " to fulfil all righteousness." In the baptism of Christ by the Holy Ghost, this Divine agent appears in the Nominative (= instrumental Dative) and the nature of the baptism is indicated by the nature of the case and by positive statement, showing it to be a measureless Divine influence qualifying for the wondrous work of redemption. So, in the baptism under consideration there is no receptive element stated, nor is any needed; the agency expressed in ἐν Πνεύματι Ἁγίῳ, the persons to be baptized, the end in view, leaves not the shadow of a doubt as to the nature of the baptism; it was a thorough change of condition by the Holy Ghost *qualifying them for the Apostleship.* 6. This phrase cannot denote a receptive element "in" which souls are to be baptized; because in that case there could be no diverse baptisms of the Spirit. All baptized in the same element must receive the same baptism, just as all vegetables baptized in vinegar must receive the same baptism, and all fruit baptized in melted sugar must receive the same baptism. But the baptisms of the Holy Spirit are diverse in their nature; as, for example, the baptism of "the beloved Son" was diverse in its nature from that baptism received by publicans and sinners; and the baptism received by the Apostles was widely diverse from both; and the baptism of all Christ's people (ἐν ἑνὶ Πνεύματι εἰς ἓν σῶμα) "by one Spirit into one body" has diversity as its very essence. Therefore ἐν Πνεύματι Ἁγίῳ cannot possibly be the element in which the souls of men are baptized. 7. This cannot be so, because it subverts the revealed economy of redemption. The third Person in the Godhead is everywhere in Scripture represented as, emphatically, the Agent. It is through his constant, universal, and mighty working in the wondrous incarnation itself (Matt. 1 : 18, Luke 1 : 35), through all the life and death of the incarnate Redeemer, and among the souls of men, that the fruits of the incarnation are secured. All this teaching of the Scriptures is swept away by the idea that the Holy Ghost is a Bethesda's pool awaiting some one to bring into it the spiritually halt, and lame, and blind, and who without such helper must remain a long, long time "in that case." 8. The translation cannot be "*in* the Holy Ghost" and accord with the principle recognized in the Baptist translation of Matt. 9 : 34, ἐν τῷ ἄρχοντι *through* the prince of the devils, with this *note:* "'Εν with *dative* of *person* denotes the one *in* whom resides the power or authority *by* which a thing is done; hence *by* or *through;*" and Matt. 12 : 27, " ἐν Βεελζεβοὺλ, *through* Beelzebub;" and v. 28, " ἐν Πνεύματι Θεοῦ, *through* the Spirit of God," referring for vindication to the above-quoted note on Matt. 9 : 34. The translator of Luke 11 : 15, in a note quotes these passages and says, "they should all be translated *by.*" This principle must be abandoned, or the Personality of the Holy Ghost must be denied by translating " ἐν Πνεύματι Ἁγίῳ *in* the Holy Ghost." And in denying the personality of the Holy Ghost, here, there must be a reconciliation with the affirmation of their associate translator of Acts, that "the Holy Ghost, the third Person in the Trinity, is here designated," as well as the multiplied translations of the same phrase ("*by* the Holy Ghost") throughout their New Testament.

We adoringly recognize the third Person of the Godhead in this great work, and translate in accordance herewith and with all other related considerations—"Ye shall be baptized *by the* HOLY GHOST."

The Baptizer.

The original author of this baptism is the Lord Jesus Christ; the executive agent is the Holy Ghost; the giver of the Holy Ghost is the Father; so that, in varying relations, the entire deity, Father, Son, and Holy Ghost, is engaged in this baptism, which is to "endue with power" these men to lay the foundations of that kingdom which is an everlasting kingdom, and to the dominion of which there shall be no end. This truth is evolved by the following passages: Luke 24:49, "I send (ἐξαποστέλλω) the promise of my Father upon (ἐπὶ) you, but tarry ye in the city of Jerusalem until ye be endued with power from on high." This promise is repeated by this same writer in Acts 1:4, 5: "He commanded them that they should not depart from Jerusalem, but wait for the promise of the Father which ye have heard of me; for . . . ye shall be baptized (ἐν Πνεύματι Ἁγίῳ) with the Holy Ghost not many days hence;" v. 8, "Ye shall receive (δύναμιν) power after that the Holy Ghost (τοῦ Ἁγίου Πνεύματος) has come upon you;" 2:4, "And they were all filled (Πνεύματος Ἁγίου) with the Holy Ghost, and began to speak as (τὸ Πνεῦμα) the Holy Ghost gave them utterance;" v. 33, "This Jesus . . . at the right hand of God being exalted, and the promise (τοῦ Ἁγίου Πνεύματος) of the Holy Ghost being received, from " (παρὰ *by the side of*, where Jesus stands, Acts 7:55; see Harrison, Greek Prepos., pp. 372–4) "the Father" (τοῦ πατρὸς, Gen., whence the Holy Ghost proceeds), "he hath shed forth this, which ye now see and hear." In view of such statements, how can the personality of the Father and of the Son be retained while that of the Holy Ghost is converted into "abstract spirit," "essence of spirit," "holy spirit," "a holy spirit," "influence?" Does not the Nominative announce the Agent having power to baptize? Does not the Genitive announce the Agent whence the power to baptize proceeds? Does not the

Dative and ἐν announce the Agent in whom the power to baptize resides? Does not the article abound? Is not its absence in the presence of a preposition just as it ought to be? Does not Ἁγίου demonstrate the presence of Him of whom Jesus said, "There is none good (Holy) but one, *that is* GOD?" What objection can there be to the interchange, or to the use as equivalents, of "the promise," "the gift," "the power," and "the Holy Ghost," in whom they meet, on whom they depend, and without whom they cannot exist?

An ancient oracle, it is said, promised to a defeated people that if they would ask a Leader from a neighboring state they would receive power to conquer. The request was made, a Leader was given, and power to conquer was secured. What, now, hinders "promise," "power," "gift," "Leader," from being interchanged, or used as equivalents, in speaking of this transaction? Why not say "the promise" (= the Leader) came? "the gift" (= the Leader) endued them with power? "the power" (= the Leader) secured the victory? Do not promise, gift, and power, meet in the Leader, go out from the Leader, perish apart from the Leader? And what is "the promise" of Christ, or "the gift" of the Father, or "the power" of the Apostles, apart from the living, divine Holy Ghost who works in all, through all, over all, and without whom we can do nothing?

Ὕδατι—Ἐν Πνεύματι Ἁγίῳ.

The use of the preposition ἐν with Πνεύματι Ἁγίῳ in connection with baptisms by the Holy Ghost is invariable, while the use of ἐν with ὕδατι in symbol-water baptisms is variable. Can any reason be assigned for such varying usage? This may be said: The relation between John (the usage only appears in connection with John, although the truth applies to all others) and "water," and the relation between Jesus and "the Holy Ghost" is not the same. John's qualification for his ministry was in no wise dependent upon ἐν ὕδατι; this was derived from his being "ἐν πνεύματι καὶ δυνάμει Ἠλίου in the spirit and power of Elias." John was always "in" this spiritual condition, and *by* it he fulfilled his ministry. The omission of (ἐν) the preposition making the statement, "he shall go before Him *by* the spirit and power of Elias," would be quite another statement from that of the Bible, "he shall go before Him *in*" (and thus invested with) "the spirit and

power of Elias." The preposition cannot be omitted. But the
use of the preposition (ἐν), in connection with water, rests on
quite another basis. It is simply a Hebraistic (also, limitedly,
Classical) use expressive of instrumentality. This usage is so
common, that the Baptist Bible translators recognize it and so
translate it nearly forty times in the single Gospel of Matthew.
There is, then, nothing to require a uniform use of ἐν ὕδατι; on
the contrary, we would look for its abandonment by a more
Greekly writer. And such is the fact. Luke, less affected by
Hebraism, never uses the preposition, in this connection, in his
Gospel or in the Acts. Thus the use and the disuse is fully
accounted for, and under such circumstances that both use and
disuse establishes the instrumental sense. But the Lord Jesus
has nothing to do with "water," and his ministry has no concern
with ἐν as used in that relation; but the fulfilment of his ministry
begins and ends with ἐν Πνεύματι Ἁγίῳ; the relation, therefore,
of this preposition is with the usage developed in ἐν πνεύματι καὶ
δυνάμει Ἡλίου, and not with the very different usage in ἐν ὕδατι,
where symbol agency is directly expressed, and in no wise dependent on the idea of antecedent inness. For a reason, then,
as obvious as that which allows the disuse of ἐν in connection with
ὕδατι, the persistent use of this preposition is demanded in connection with Πνεύματι Ἁγίῳ, as it is demanded in connection with
ἐν πνεύματι καὶ δυνάμει Ἡλίου. But inasmuch as this phrase suggests
inness with a view to a consequent investiture with power, it will
follow, that under diverse circumstances, the one idea or the other
will emerge into greater prominence, and the translation be fitly
with, by, or in. This is exemplified in Luke 4:14, "Jesus returned (ἐν τῇ δυνάμει τοῦ Πνεύματος) in the power of the Spirit," as
compared with the passage before us, "Ye shall be baptized (ἐν
Πνεύματι Ἁγίῳ) by the Holy Ghost, in whom Jesus is, and by whom
therefore he accomplishes his work."

The Baptism—Its Emblem.

The specific character of this baptism is not indicated by the
statement that it was " (ἐν Πνεύματι Ἁγίῳ) by the Holy Ghost." The
Holy Ghost is an Agent most mighty, most wise, and of infinite
resources. Therefore his baptisms (thorough changes of spiritual
condition assimilated to his own wisdom, or power, or other characteristic entering into his holy nature) are greatly varied. This

phrase can only, of itself, give some general character to the baptism. It was not the ordinary Christian baptism. This is a matter of universal admission. The friends of the theory not only do not claim the presence of a dipping into water, but admit that there was not anything like it. Dr. Carson will not even invoke the aid of Catachresis to make this something out of nothing. He admits (what this Inquiry has proved times without number) that it was nothing more nor less than a baptism consisting in *a thorough change of condition* resulting from " subjection to influence and imbuing with its virtues." Those who reject the theory declare that it could not be an initiatory baptism, because that is entirely unsuitable to the position of those who had not only been long the disciples of Christ, but also his chosen Apostles. Dr. Carson says it was a baptism of Sanctification, "thoroughly Sanctifying body, soul, and spirit." This he grounds on the idea that there was a baptism " in " and " into the Holy Spirit." This has been shown not to be true, and with the foundation destroyed that which is built upon it must fall. But this is farther disproved as being entirely inadequate to fit for the Apostleship. No man by mere sanctification could be fitted to be an Apostle. Stephen was a man " full of the Holy Ghost ;" but he was not an Apostle, nor is there any evidence to show that he was fitted to be one.

The specialty of this baptism consisted in the fitting those who received it for the Apostleship. This is evident from the promise made to those chosen for this office—Luke 24 : 49, " Behold I send the promise of my Father upon you ; but tarry ye in the city of Jerusalem, until ye be endued with power from on high ;" from the express statement in Acts 1 : 2, 4, 5, that these words contained a command addressed to the Apostles, and a promise of baptism by the Holy Ghost, which (v. 8) was to endue them with " power " for their wonderful work. Farther evidence is found in the accomplished facts ; they did wait at Jerusalem, they did "receive the promise of the Father," that promise was " sent " by Jesus, they were " baptized by the Holy Ghost," they were " endued with power," they did enter upon their work, and from that hour *they were thoroughly changed in their spiritual condition* as qualified Witnesses for Christ, and endowed with every requisite necessary to discharge the high duties of the Apostleship.

Emblem. This interpretation of the specialty of this baptism is confirmed by the emblem of it. Dr. Carson speaks of more than one emblem—the emblems of this baptism = " wind and fire."

But who ever heard of diverse emblems being employed to denote the same baptism ?   This is like the drinking from a cup and the dipping into water so incongruously introduced into the baptism of the Redeemer.   There could be no dipping in a " cup," and so water is introduced to make up the deficiency.   But if Dr. Carson had remembered his present admission as to this Pentecostal baptism, he would have understood that no dipping was necessary to a baptism, and that drinking from a cup had a potency "to subject to influence and imbue with the virtue " of its contents.   But there is reluctance to part with an old friend.   And as " nothing like dipping " could be found in the baptism of the Spirit it must be found in something related to it.   But " the fire " (?) is no larger than a cup and will not answer   The " wind " (?) then must be introduced as " sound " is too unsubstantial.   It is made to fill all the house.   This is enough (much wind) for a dipping, at least by Catachresis, for there is none in fact; but it will not answer for the human addendum emblem wholly to exclude that of divine provision, therefore " the fire " (?) rather ornamental than useful, for the dipping by Catachresis is already complete in the house full of " wind" (?), is made quite superfluously to rest above the top of the head.   This richness of invention, however, must fail after all.   There is no " wind ;" there is no " fire."   We must, therefore, be what most persons have been, content with a single emblem for a single thing, even such as the divine wisdom has provided, namely, "cloven tongues like as of fire."   If no dipping of the Apostles can be accomplished in these " tongues," then we must bear the disappointment in the case of the emblem as we have already had to do in the case of the reality.   We dismiss, then, this " Curiosity of Literature " for something of more practical value. The instruction which is furnished by this divinely appointed emblem is of no small value: 1. It teaches us in the clearest manner that this baptism was one qualifying for the Apostleship, because it emblemizes (" cloven tongues ") one of the principal requisites for that office (the power to speak in other languages) and one which was immediately brought into requisition—" We do every man hear in his own tongue in which he was born."   2. It teaches us that the symbol or emblem used in baptism has no part or lot in a dipping, or immersing, or covering, or bigness, or muchness, or with any part of the body except the touching of the head.   In harmony with this teaching is that of the sweet emblem of a Saviour's baptism, " the appearance as of a dove " descending and remaining upon him ; also, that of " the cup " full of penal woe held to his lips by a Father's hand ; also, the " water," simple and simply abstract " water," ordained of God as the emblem of cleansing by a Saviour's blood, all unite to teach that the addition of *wind* to a cloven tongue, or of a *feather* to the pinions of the Dove, or of *enlargement* to the Redeemer's Cup, or of *one drop* to " *water* " in symbol baptism for dipping, or immersing, or covering, *adds to the word of God.* 3. It teaches that the emblem of a baptism is representative of one thing and not of many things. As " the cloven tongues " represent one characteristic gift—the power to speak in diverse languages—in this many-sided baptism, and as " the Dove " represents the sympathy of the living Spirit in the wholeness of his Deity and the measurelessness of his power, with the work of Redemption on which the incarnate Son was entering, and as " the Cup " represents the deadly suffering which enters into redemption, so " *water* " represents the purification effected in the soul by the Holy Ghost, and not a grave, a burial, a resurrection, a womb, a birth, a washing all over (of *clothes* in these latter days) for "total depravity " and—I know not what. If the theory can carry all these things, well ; but let the Bible, as a revelation from God, be saved from being overwhelmed by such a heap of things so evidently of the earth earthy.

Corollary. If there is no dipping into the " cloven tongues," the divine symbol *by* which the Apostles were baptized ; if there is no dipping into " the Dove," the divine symbol by which the covenanting Redeemer was baptized ; if there is no dipping into " the Cup," the divine symbol by which the atoning Lamb of God is baptized ; then there is no dipping in " water," the divine symbol by which sinners are baptized.

Professor Ripley—Professor Hackett.

Professor Ripley, of the Newton Baptist Theological Seminary, presents the following views bearing upon this subject in his Commentary on Acts 1 : 2. *After that he* (διὰ Πνεύματος Ἁγίου) *through the Holy Ghost had given commandments.* " Jesus is represented in the Bible as having been abundantly furnished with spiritual influences, or as acting by the special aid of the Holy Spirit. Hence he is said in 10 : 38 to have been anointed with the Holy Spirit ; and in Luke 4 : 1 to have been full of the

Holy Spirit; and in John 3:34, it is said, the Father giveth not the Spirit *by measure*, that is, in any limited degree, to him. It was under this divine impulse that he instructed and commissioned his apostles; v. 4, *Wait for the promise of the Father.* God the Father had promised the gift of the Holy Spirit, by which the apostles of Jesus should be fully and finally qualified for their office; v. 5, *Ye shall be baptized with the Holy Ghost.* The word baptize primarily signifies to *immerse*. And as a person who has been immersed in water has received it most copiously, this word is well used to express the idea of *great abundance* or *plentifulness*. Compare Matt. 20:22, 23, where the words *baptize* and *baptism* evidently convey the idea of *overwhelm* and *overwhelming*. To be baptized *with the Holy Spirit*, then, means *to receive the influences of the Holy Spirit in great abundance.* The apostles were to be most plenteously endued with divine influence. The copious influences of the Spirit would qualify them for their office as apostles, by correcting all their erroneous views, and leading them into all Christian truth, by greatly promoting their piety and zeal, and by endowing them with miraculous powers. . . . The promised effusion of the Holy Spirit took place about ten days from this declaration; v. 8, *Ye shall receive power.* Ye shall receive all needed ability for the office to which ye are called. The apostles were to be endowed by the Holy Spirit, *After that the Holy Ghost is come upon you.* It was by the Holy Spirit's agency that the apostles were to be fully prepared for their office; 2:2, *A sound from heaven as of a rushing mighty wind.* A noise like wind. That the sound was actually that of a violent wind, Luke does not say, but that it *resembled* such a noise. It was altogether of a supernatural character. *It filled all the house.* The noise was heard throughout the house. . . . The apostles held themselves ready for some immediate manifestation of his (the Holy Spirit's) presence and agency; v. 4, *And they were all filled with the Holy Ghost.* The tokens of the Spirit's descent were connected with the immediate enjoyment of his influence, and the outward manifestation of it. The Spirit was imparted so copiously, that the disciples are said to have been filled with it. New and unusual mental power was possessed by them. Their religious views became clearer, and their religious fervor was greatly increased. *As the Spirit (τὸ Πνεῦμα) gave them utterance.* As the Spirit enabled them to express themselves. The gift of tongues was a miraculous endowment by the Holy

Spirit. The Holy Spirit miraculously bestowed on the apostles the power to use foreign languages; v. 14, *Peter standing up with the eleven.* What a change had taken place in Peter since the night in the high priest's palace! He was evidently now endued with power from on high; v. 17, *I will pour out of my Spirit.* The idea is, I will impart a copious supply of my Spirit's influences; v. 33, *Having received of the Father the promise of the Holy Ghost.* That is, having received of the Father the promised Holy Spirit. The disciples had kept themselves in expectation of the Spirit's coming. *He hath shed forth this which ye now see and hear.* What you now see and hear, as resulting from the Spirit's power, has been shed forth by Jesus. . . . All this was to be traced to Jesus."

In these comments Professor Ripley recognizes as true the following positions: 1. This baptism of the Apostles by the Holy Ghost, and the baptism of the Lord Jesus by the Holy Ghost, were of the same generic character, with differences inseparable from the need and the nature of the parties. In neither case was there a physical element into which a dipping, or immersing, or covering took place; nor was there any such thing to be supplied by the imagination. In both cases there was a physical symbol present by which the nature of the baptism effected was betokened. Both baptisms were effected by the Holy Ghost. In both cases there was a thorough change of condition, bringing the baptized under the influence of the baptizer, and investing with his power. This change in the case of Jesus is indicated by being " abundantly furnished with spiritual influences;" by "acting under the special aid of the Holy Spirit;" being "anointed by the Holy Spirit;" being "full of the Holy Spirit;" "the Father giving him the Spirit without measure;" "under this divine impulse instructing and commissioning the apostles." "What a change in Peter!" is language which may be applied to all the apostles. This change is indicated by "the correction of error," the bestowal of "mental power," of "miraculous power," of "religious fervor," of "needed ability for the apostleship." This *change of condition* is represented by Prof. Ripley *as constituting the baptism* received. He is right in doing so. All baptisms of this class consist in a thorough change of condition assimilating to the characteristic of the baptizing power.

2. There was no " wind;" there was no " fire;" there was a "noise" heard throughout the house. There was consequently

no " dry baptism " in wind, and no " catachrestic " dipping into wind. The apostles were not baptized in the cloven tongues, nor dipped into them by catachresis when they sat upon their heads. There is no connection whatever between the act of βαπτίζω and the fire-like tongues. The office of this symbol is simply to point out the nature of this baptism by a visible indication of one of the gifts entering into it.

3. The baptism consisted simply and solely in the thorough change in the condition of the apostles effected by the Holy Ghost through varied gifts " enduing with power " for the apostleship. The modal action (not actual, but verbally expressed) in effecting this baptism was, as Prof. Ripley says, " effusion," *pouring.* But we do not say, on this account, that βαπτίζω expresses the modal act *to pour.* This we deny. Proof has been furnished all through this Inquiry that this word never had, and from its very nature cannot have, anything to do with modal action. But this trans-action does prove that a baptism may be by pouring, and that the end of the pouring is not a covering, but a thorough change of condition in which there is no dipping, and its introduction, by catachresis, begets a broad smile.

4. The personality of the Holy Ghost as a divine Agent, oper-ating through all this transaction, is fully recognized by Prof. Ripley. " The Holy Spirit descends," " bestows," " qualifies." It is " HIS presence," " HIS influence," " HIS agency," that does the work. At the same time there is a no less clear acknowledg-ment that Jesus is the author of this baptism. It is Jesus who announces " the promise of the Father;" it is Jesus who receives that " promise from the Father ;" it is Jesus who " sheds forth," " pours out," this " promised Spirit ;" and all that relates to this baptism is " traceable to Jesus." This relation between Jesus and the Holy Ghost, and of both to baptism, is the development of the declaration of John— " He shall baptize you ἐν Πνεύματι Ἁγίῳ (being *in* and therefore) *by* the Holy Ghost," and " ὁ Βαπτίζων ἐν Πνεύματι Ἁγίῳ this is the Baptizer who is in the Holy Ghost." And the fitness of the force of ἐν, as expounding the personal relation of Jesus to the Holy Ghost, is exhibited by that transaction in which " the Holy Ghost descended and remained upon him ;" while its relation to others, through this new condition of Jesus, is exhibited by his baptizing the apostles (ἐν Πνεύματι Ἁγίῳ) *by* the Holy Ghost.

5. Prof. Ripley says, " The word baptize primarily signifies

to *immerse*. And as a person who has been immersed in water
has received it most copiously, this word is well used to express
the idea of great *abundance* or *plentifulness*." This is the only
point in these comments which needs amendment. The difficulty
arises from the want of accurate discrimination. Prof. Ripley
has in view a person who is dipped (momentarily immersed) in
water and with the clothing on. In such case there must be a
sufficient abundance of water to effect a covering; but, to receive
water in an abundance adequate to cover momentarily, and to be
immersed in water so as to secure the effect distinctive of such
immersion, are things which are as diverse as any two things can
well be. Clothing from its porous nature will be made quite wet
by a dipping, and will be saturated by an immersion. A person
divested of clothing does not receive the water, as does his clothing, when dipped into it. A flint rock and india-rubber vestments may be covered in water, but they do not "receive it
abundantly" as a means of influence; it cannot penetrate beyond
their surface. Wetness is not the distinctive character of an immersion any more than of a pouring or of rain-droppings. The
result to a clothed living person of an immersion in water is,
that his clothes are saturated and he is suffocated. Therefore
the Greeks used βαπτίζω to express the condition of a man not
dipped into water, but who had been brought under the distinctive power of water by immersion and thus drowned. It is
on the fact that immersion develops the power of the covering
element over the baptized object that baptize is used to express
such like *power*, not "abundance," where there is no immersion.
There is no "abundance" in a cup of wine, yet the Greeks said
it had a *power* to baptize. There is no "abundance" in a few
opiate drops, yet the Greeks said they had a *power* to baptize.
There is no abundance in a half dozen bewildering questions,
yet the Greeks said they had the *power* to baptize. The reference to Matt. 20 : 22, 23, sustains the view here presented, namely,
that of *power*, not that of "abundance." The statement that in
this passage "the words *baptize* and *baptism* evidently convey
the idea of *overwhelm* and *overwhelming*" is, in general, correct,
with a correct meaning attached to those words. "Overwhelm"
is rarely used in the simple sense of its elements *whelm, over*.
In this it resembles overcome (come, over), overthrow (throw,
over), overbear (bear, over), and countless other words which lay
aside the form of conception in their elements and adopt some

involved result. Now in *whelming over* there is always present
a resistless power, and the whelming over of waters is generally
connected with a destructive issue, and the compound "overwhelm" adopts these ideas, namely, *resistless power*, commonly,
hurtful in its nature. The idea of "abundance" is not involved
in this usage; a word, a look, a poisonous drop, may "overwhelm," when it could not *whelm over.* This is the usage (if
these words be applied here) in Matt. 20 : 22, 23; the cup is full
of penal woe, and in the drinking of it the Friend of sinners is
"overwhelmed" by a resistless, deadly *power;* and hence the
fitness of using βαπτίζω and βάπτισμα in this case, as expressive
of limitless power. The same usage precisely obtains in the
baptism under consideration. However many in number, however varied in character, however rich in measure, may have been
the gifts received by the apostles, their *baptism* had no essential
connection with "abundance," but consisted in their being "endued with *power*" by the Holy Ghost for the apostleship. In this
point (amid the most marvellous extravagances) Dr. Carson is
more correct than Professor Ripley, when he says, "That which
is immersed in a liquid is *completely subjected to its influence and
imbued with its virtues;* so to be immersed in the Spirit represents the *subjection* of soul, body, and spirit *to his influence.*"
The idea of "abundance" springs out of "pouring," not out of
immersion. "Immersed in thought;" "immersed in study;"
"immersed in the books;" are phrases which have no connection
with abundance. " I will POUR you *out* a blessing so that there
shall not be room enough to receive it;" "I will POUR OUT my
Spirit on all flesh," are phrases which have no intelligent meaning except under the idea of *abundance.*

Professor Hackett, of Rochester Baptist Theological Seminary,
presents similar views in his Commentary on this passage. 1.
Christ is both personally baptized, and is baptizer by the Holy
Ghost: Acts 1 : 2. Gave commandment διὰ Πνεύματος Ἁγίου, *through
the Holy Spirit*, his influence, guidance. This noun as so used
may omit the article or receive it, at the option of the writer,
since it has the force of a proper name. This passage, in accordance with other passages, represents the Saviour as having been
endued abundantly with the influences of the Spirit, and as having acted always in conformity with its dictates: see Luke 4 : 1,
"Jesus being full of the Holy Ghost was led up (ἐν τῷ Πνεύματι)
by the Spirit:" John 3 : 34, "For God giveth not (τὸ Πνεῦμα) the

Spirit by measure unto him." 2:33, "Having received of the Father the promise of the Holy Ghost," *i. e.*, the Holy Spirit promised. "He hath shed forth this." The effusion of the Spirit which is ascribed to God in v. 17 is ascribed here to Christ.

2. The personal divine Spirit was the Agent. Acts 2:6, "Now when this sound"—that of the descending Spirit; v. 18, "The effusion of the Spirit was to be universal as to classes. . . . The modes of divine revelation and of the Spirit's operation, which are specified in this passage; . . . It portrays the character of the entire dispensation. Those special manifestations of the Spirit marked the economy as one that was to be eminently distinguished by the Spirit's agency."

3. The baptism of the apostles was not a dipping into or covering over with anything, but qualification for their work. "1:8, Ye shall receive power after the Holy Ghost has come upon you; δύναμιν efficiency, *i. e.*, every needful qualification to render them efficient in their apostolic spheres; *come upon you*, designates the time when they should receive this power, as well as the source of it."

4. There was no wind. "2:2, *As if a mighty wind, filled*, to wit, ἦχος, sound, which is the only natural subject furnished by the context."

5. The Cloven tongues were symbols of the baptism. "2:3, The fire-like appearance may have assumed the appearance of tongues as a symbol of the miraculous gift which accompanied the wonder."

The eminent scholarship of Prof. Hackett is excelled only by his unassuming Christian character.

Booth—Morrell.

"The venerable Booth" says (I, 101): "The extraordinary gifts and influence received at Pentecost is called the *baptism* of the Holy Spirit. . . . Our brethren will, I think, allow that a person may be *so* surrounded by subtle effluvia; that a liquid may be *so* poured, or it may *so* distil upon him, that he may be *as if* immersed in it. A writer speaking of electricity says, ' The first is the electrical *bath;* so called because it surrounds the patient with an atmosphere of the electrical fluid, in which he is *plunged*, and receives positive electricity.' This reminds me of the language, '*there came a sound from heaven as of a rushing*

mighty wind, and it FILLED ALL THE HOUSE WHERE THEY WERE
SITTING.' Was the Holy Spirit *poured out*, did the Holy Spirit
fall upon, the Apostles and others, at that memorable time? it
was in such a manner, and to such a degree, that they were, like
a patient in the electric bath, *as if immersed in it.*"

It is useless for " Rantists " to protest against such wild talk
being called interpretation; but as Professor Ripley and Professor Hackett are not " Ranters," their friends may be willing to
learn from them, through this Pentecost baptism, a broader and
a truer usage of βαπτίζω, even as they learned a broader and a
truer usage of βάπτω, from Dr. Carson, at the shore of the
Homeric lake.

Morell (Reply to Dr. Halley, Edinburgh, p. 170) says: "As it
regards the baptism of the Pentecost, the wind and the fire had
no modal signification whatever. When we read of the Holy
Ghost 'coming upon the disciples,' of its being 'poured out,' and
'poured down,' these phrases denote simply the bestowment or
the abundance of the gifts and influences of the Spirit. The Pedobaptist interpretation, which derives an argument for a particular
mode of baptism, viz., affusion, as best resembling the supposed
mode in which the soul is baptized by the Spirit, is to materialize
a divine influence, and to construct a baseless argument upon a
mere figurative expression. The occurrences at Pentecost are
generally considered as fulfilling the language of John, 'He shall
baptize you with the Holy Ghost and with fire.' When Jesus
apprises his disciples of the Pentecost baptism, he says nothing
about the fire. . . . The lambent flames, like cloven tongues, which
came and sat upon the disciples' heads, while they were very expressively emblematical of the most distinguished gift of the Spirit
on that day, viz., the power of speaking in other tongues, had no
allusion to baptism whatever. . . . While the *Rantists* say, 'The
wind came upon them;' the *Baptists* may say, 'The wind completely surrounded them, so that they were symbolically immersed
in it.' But the Scripture does not say that there was not any
wind. All we can learn is, that there was a *loud mysterious noise*
which filled the house. A noise, surely, cannot symbolize sprink
ling or immersing. The baptism of Pentecost consisted in the
minds of the disciples being entirely absorbed by the Spirit, and
all their powers and faculties wholly subjected to its influence."

Morell writes with the courtesy and candor which indicate the
refined man, as well as the cultivated scholar. In the style which

prevails among writers on his side, the use of the term "Rantists" would pass unnoticed amid harsher expletives; but on his page it is a snag which we encounter with a shock. We make no complaint of the use of such terms. If opponents can afford to use them they will neither harm nor annoy us. The objection of Morell against "the Rantists" grounding a claim *to pour* in ritual baptism on the use of "pour out," "pour down," to express the manner in which the Spirit was given to effect the Pentecost baptism, is without value, because it is without any foundation laid by "the Rantists." Their reasoning is turned upside down and wrong end foremost. Their argument is not, "The Holy Ghost is 'poured out' to effect baptism, therefore water should, in like manner, be 'poured out' to effect ritual baptism," but this: "The Holy Ghost is figuratively said to be poured out to effect a baptism, THEREFORE *this figurative appropriation of* POURING OUT *must be grounded in a previous physical use* of 'pouring out' to effect baptism." We do not deduce authority to pour water in baptizing from the use of "pouring" in the baptizing by the Spirit, but reversely we say, that authority to use pouring figuratively in the baptism of the Spirit is deduced from the previous physical use of pouring in ritual baptism. If this be "a baseless argument materializing a divine influence," we will abandon it when the evidence shall have been adduced. But between us and such evidence stands the altar of Carmel, on which *water is being poured* in order to its baptism, without dipping, immersing, or covering, thoroughly changing its condition from ceremonial impurity to ceremonial purity. On such antecedent physical practice is based the subsequent figurative use. Morell is right in separating these "as of fire" tongues from the "baptism by fire" spoken of by John. They have nothing to do with each other. He is also right in saying, that "they had no allusion whatever to baptism," using "baptism" in the sense of dipping, immersing, covering; but using it in the only sense in which it is used in the New Testament (thorough change of condition), and in which confessedly it is used here, then, these cloven tongues have not only some "allusion" to the baptism, but are a most vital element in its exposition. The apostles were really baptized by the Holy Ghost "giving them power to speak in other tongues;" they were symbolly baptized by tongues as of fire, indicative of the nature of the real baptism which had been received. This is the precise value of the admission by Morell—"The cloven tongues were very expressively emblematical of the most distinguished gift of the Spirit on that day, viz., the power of speaking in other tongues." And precisely the same relation which these "cloven tongues" have to this extraordinary baptism does the pure water have in the ordinary Christian baptism. As the "cloven tongues" do by their nature symbolize and expound the nature of *this* baptism by the Holy Ghost, so does the pure water by its nature symbolize and expound the nature of *that* baptism by the Holy Ghost. And if it would be regarded as a singular perversity which should connect these "tongues" with βαπτίζω, and insist on the Apostles being *dipped into them*, so it is a like logical and grammatical perversity which insists that men and women should be dipped into the symbol water betokening the nature of the baptism in the soul by the Holy Ghost. The verb βαπτίζω has no more to do with the symbol water than it has to do with the symbol tongues, and it has no more to do with either than Chang Eng of the Celestial Empire has to do with the succession to the Presidency over this "Flowery Kingdom" of America.

Irenæus—Cyril of Jerusalem—Gregory Nazianzen.

Irenæus (844) characterizes the baptism of the Apostles as "being endued with power from on high, by the Holy Spirit coming upon them, being filled with all official requisites, and having complete knowledge." That is, he believed that it was a complete change of condition qualifying them for their high office.

The representation given of the baptism of Jesus is of the same character; (900) "God anointed Jesus of Nazareth with the Holy Ghost and power;" (871) "Matthew says concerning his baptism: The heavens were opened to him, and he saw the Spirit of God, as a dove, coming upon him. And behold a voice from heaven, saying, 'This is my beloved Son, in whom I am well pleased.' For Christ did not then descend into Jesus; nor is Christ one and Jesus another; but the Word of God, who is the Saviour of all, and Lord of heaven and earth, who is Jesus, who also assumed flesh, and was anointed by the Spirit from the Father, was made Jesus Christ. And as Isaiah says: 'The Spirit of the Lord shall rest upon him, the spirit of wisdom and understanding, the spirit of counsel and might, the spirit of knowledge and of the fear of the Lord, and the spirit of the fear of the Lord shall fill him.' And again Isaiah, foretelling his anointing and for what he was anointed, says: 'The Spirit of God is upon me, wherefore he has anointed me; he hath sent me to preach good tidings to the lowly, to bind up the broken-hearted, to proclaim pardon to the captives, and sight to the blind, to proclaim the acceptable year of the Lord, and the day of vengeance, to comfort all who mourn.' For the reason that the Word of God was man, out of the root of Jesse and Son of Abraham, therefore the Spirit of God rested upon him, and he was anointed to preach good tidings to the lowly."

It is obvious that Irenæus regarded the baptism of the Word of God as to his manhood, by the Holy Ghost descending and remaining upon him, as identical, in general character, with that of the Apostles by the Holy Ghost coming down upon them; that is to say, the baptism in either case was a meet preparation for the fulfilment of official duty on which they were just entering. The personality and the distinctive character of the work in the two cases differed measurelessly; and the baptism was "without measure" in the one case, and by measure in the other. And because the baptisms differ while they agree, the baptism could not be by dipping, nor by honest immersion *in* the Holy Ghost, as a receiving element, because then the baptisms must be the same. The baptism was by an intelligent Divine agent, "who divides to every one severally as He will."

Cyril of Jerusalem (440) says, "The Baptizer (*ὁ βαπτίζων*) with water is good, but what is he to the Baptizer with the Holy Ghost and fire? The Saviour baptized the Apostles (*Πνεύματι Ἁγίῳ καὶ πυρὶ*) by the Holy Ghost and fire when cloven tongues as of fire appeared to them, and sat upon each one of them, and they were filled of the Holy Ghost." Here Cyril by dropping ἐν in connection with *Πνεύματι Ἁγίῳ* shows that he understands that phrase to express agency. The same conclusion is reached by the conjunction of *πυρὶ* with this phrase in this baptism where in the nature of things there could be no dipping in the " tongues," and therefore there could be none designed in its associate *Πνεύματι Ἁγίῳ.*

978. " But John, who was filled with the Holy Ghost from his mother's womb, was sanctified for this purpose, that he might baptize the Lord; but he did not confer the Spirit, only announcing him who did confer the Spirit. 'He saw the Spirit of God descending as a dove and coming upon him.' It was necessary, as some interpret, that the first fruits and first gifts of the Holy Ghost to be baptized be furnished to the humanity of the Saviour

who gives like grace." The Saviour is represented both as being baptized and himself baptizing by the Holy Ghost.

986. "Pentecost being come the Paraclete descended from heaven. He descended that he might endue with power and baptize the Apostles. The grace was not divided, but the power complete. . . . For as one inclosed with waters and baptized is surrounded on all sides by the waters, so also they were completely baptized (ὑπὸ) by the Spirit. But the water is poured around (περιχεῖται) externally, but (τὸ Πνεῦμα) the Spirit baptizes the soul within completely. And why do you wonder? Take a physical illustration, slight and simple, but useful to the more uninstructed. If fire penetrating within the density of iron makes the whole fire; and the cold becomes hot and the black becomes bright; if fire being a substance penetrating within the substance of iron works so without hindrance; why dost thou wonder if the Holy Spirit enters into the innermost parts of the soul?"

Cyril had a very fair opportunity here to say that βαπτίζω means *to dip*, but he declines to adopt so un-Greekly a doctrine, and ranks himself with those who declare that it makes demand for condition. His exposition of baptisms based on effect without covering as illustrated by the mass of iron penetrated by fire and communicating its own quality to it, changing its condition of coldness to hotness, and of darkness to brightness, is identical with the doctrine developed in this Inquiry, to wit: a thorough change of condition by penetrating, pervading, and assimilating to the characteristic of the baptizing power. If Cyril had set out to illustrate this definition he could not have done it in a more complete manner.

Origen (III, 1864), "He shall baptize you by the Holy Ghost and fire." "When does Jesus baptize (Spiritu sancto) by the Holy Ghost, and again, when does he baptize (igne) by fire? Does he baptize at one and the same time (Spiritu et igne) by the Spirit and fire, or separately and diversely? The Apostles were baptized after his ascension to heaven (Spiritu sancto) 'by the Holy Ghost,' but that they were baptized (igne) 'by fire' the Scripture does not relate."

Throughout this passage the preposition is omitted, and "Spiritu sancto" and "igne" appear as agencies. The interpretation which connects John's declaration, "He shall baptize by the Holy Ghost and fire," with the Pentecostal "tongues as of fire," is rejected, and properly so.

The Importance of this Baptism.

The importance of the narrative of this baptism in its relations to Christian baptism and the usage of βαπτίζω can hardly be over-estimated. This importance is both intrinsic and incidental. The narrative has intrinsic value: 1. Because of its fulness; no other baptism in the New Testament is related with equal detail. The time (Pentecost), the place (a house), the persons (a limited class, Apostles), to be baptized; the baptizer, more remote its divine Author, more immediate its divine Agent; the baptism, its nature spiritual, its mode " coming upon," in figure as to the Agent, *in fact as to the symbol ;* its emblem " cloven tongues;" its proof as an accomplished fact " speaking in other tongues;" nothing is lacking to completeness. 2. Because of its clearness; hereby is established the personality of the Holy Ghost as *an active* AGENT in effecting baptism; the union and the relation in union of Christ and the Holy Ghost in the work of baptism; the " wind " is no symbol of baptism and is not present in this baptism; the "cloven tongues " are a symbol of this baptism and are present to illustrate its nature; the quantity of a tongue does not enter into its power of symbolization; the symbol of a baptism has no other relation to baptism than *its power by its own* NATURE to symbolize the *nature of the* BAPTISM; these truths are radical helps in the right interpretation of Christian baptism. 3. Because of agreement induced : (1.) It is agreed in view of this transaction, that there may be a baptism in which there is no dipping, or immersing, or covering, in fact, and into which it cannot allowably be introduced, by Catachresis or otherwise; but the use of the word must be traced to the result of immersion on a penetrable body placed within an element having some definite characteristic which it thus imparts to the baptized object, the mode of effecting such result disappearing in the secondary usage and giving place, without limit, to any mode of operation or influence capable of effecting a like result. (2.) It is farther agreed, that the true expression for this baptism is " the subjection of an object to some definite influence and the consequent imbuing of it with its virtue," or the equivalent—the penetrating and pervading of any object by any power assimilating such object to its own characteristic, as iron penetrated and pervaded by fire becomes subject to its characteristic heat and is made fire-like. (3.) It is agreed, that this baptism was spiritual, the work of the divine Spirit on the human spirit, subjecting it to his influence, imbuing it with his own characteristics, and enduing them with consequent "power." (4.) It is agreed, that with this spiritual baptism there was a physical symbol in which there was no baptism, but its sole office was, *by its own nature*, to indicate *the nature of the baptism.*

These agreements, consistently carried out, will establish unity of interpretation in every baptism of the New Testament.

The narrative of this baptism has incidental importance : 1. Because it is the first baptism under Christianity. For that reason it is made resplendent with the glory of the Father who gives, with the glory of the Son who pours out, and with the glory of the Holy Ghost who executes this baptism. That this baptism (as introductory to kindred baptisms running down through long ages) might be thoroughly understood, we have its full and clear record for our study. 2. Because it throws light on Christian baptism. This baptism is not technical Christian baptism. The baptism of Christ into the covenant fulfilment of all righteousness, with water fitly symbolizing its nature, was not Christian baptism. The baptism of Christ by the Holy Ghost, fitly symbolized by the Dove, enduing his humanity with every requisite for the accomplishment of his covenant, was not Christian baptism. The baptism of Christ into penal death by a broken Law (fitly symbolized by a cup filled with deadly woe) was not Christian baptism. But all these baptisms constituted a basis on which Christian baptism was to rest, and without which it could not exist. The baptism of the Apostles was not Christian baptism, but it was a basis divinely laid, on which as Christ's ministers that baptism might be proclaimed, and without which they could not have done so. As this was a spiritual baptism, the work of the Holy Spirit, so it teaches us that Christian baptism, for which it was preparative, must be a spiritual baptism, and the work of the Holy Spirit. It farther teaches us, that Christian baptism as a *spiritual* baptism may be accompanied with and *illustrated as to its nature* by a *physical* symbol. And this is true in fact ; Christian baptism, the work of the Holy Ghost, has its divinely appointed symbol (water), which *by its nature* fitly illustrates *the purifying nature* of the work of the Divine Spirit in the sinner's soul, as the " cloven tongues " with divine perfectness symbolized the work of that same Spirit in the souls of the Apostles. It teaches us that the symbol of Christian baptism is perverted from its divinely appointed office when there is an attempt to effect a baptism in it, and that such attempt is stamped with the guilty folly of placing a usurping fiction alongside of, or rather in the stead of, the baptism by the Holy Ghost.

Acts 11: 15, 16.

'Επέπεσε τὸ Πνεῦμα τὸ ῞Αγίον ἐπ' αὐτοὺς ὥσπερ καὶ ἐφ' ἡμᾶς ἐν ἀρχῇ. 'Εμνή-
ςθη 'Ιωαννης μὲν ἐβάπτισεν ὕδατι, ὑμεις δὲ βαπτισθήσεσθε ἐν Πνεύματι 'Αγίῳ.

"And as I began to speak, the Holy Ghost fell on them, as on us in the beginning. Then remembered I the word of the Lord, how that he said, John indeed baptized with water; but ye shall be baptized with the Holy Ghost."

Christ the Baptizer by the Holy Ghost.

This baptism belongs to the same class of baptisms as that of Pentecost. It has the same divine Author the Lord Jesus Christ, the same divine executive Agent the Holy Ghost, it had the same outward development speaking with tongues, and their oneness is declared by Peter—" the Holy Ghost fell on them, as on us at the beginning." But while these baptisms belong to the same class there is between them essential diversity. The baptism at Pentecost was a baptism qualifying for the Apostleship; this baptism was a baptism qualifying for Christian life, with such special endowment as should convince Peter and others, that Gentiles were to be received even as Jews into the Christian church. No one can imagine for a moment that there was sameness of gifts conferred on Peter and his associates, and on Cornelius and his associates. Sameness in some respects there undoubtedly was; but even where there was sameness in kind, there was not necessarily or probably sameness of measure. The gift of tongues was common to both baptisms; but it does not follow that they spake the same languages or the same number of languages. The baptism of the Lord Jesus Christ by the Holy Ghost belongs to the same class of baptisms with that of the Apostles; while in its discriminating character as qualifying him for his wondrous mission, it is essentially diverse; so, the baptism of the Apostles by the Holy Ghost belongs to the same class of baptisms with that of these Gentiles, while in its discriminating character as qualifying them for the Apostleship, it was essentially diverse. And by this diversity in sameness of baptism, the theory is again overturned. The life of the theory centres, legitimately, in modal action ; but this being found at every turn pierced through and through by the sharp spearing of facts, retreat is sought in " covering," however induced ; but when the covering is not induced in any way " however," what then ? " Covering " must be *covering*, as surely as " dipping " must be *dipping*, and when a baptism is developed in which there is no " covering," then, in that moment, the theory dies. But here there is confessedly a baptism without a " dipping," and without a " covering," the theory then perishes. The theory is too short for the facts to stretch themselves in, and too narrow to wrap themselves in. Baptisms are diverse ; and at the touch of diversity the theory is shattered into fragments. It is in vain to attempt to retrieve this ruin by referring to a covering in immersion, and saying that this baptism is founded on the covering in an immersion. This is not true, and to rest in it is only a self-deception. It is the same as saying that *to dye* (βάπτω *second*) is founded in the modal act *to dip* (βάπτω *first*). This is clearly an error. The foundation of the secondary meaning is grounded *not in the form of the act* but *in the effect* resultant upon the dipping of certain objects into certain (*dyeing*) liquids. The modal act is an accident which makes no appearance in the secondary meaning. The modal act of *dipping* might be repeated forever and a day into an un-colored liquid, and it would never become the foundation for the meaning *to dye*. Precisely so is it with the secondary meaning of βαπτίζω, which is grounded in *the effect* produced upon certain objects (permeable) mersed in certain fluids (having definite qualities). With the covering as causative of the effect, the secondary meaning (*thorough change of condition with assimilation*) has nothing to do, and it never enters into that meaning ; but on the contrary is expressly repudiated by it, and its very life depends upon such repudiation. Now, while the theory is dumfounded in the presence of diverse baptisms, all such baptisms join in declaring—" Our diversity is in unity *under a thorough change of condition assimilated to the characteristic of the power effecting* such change of condition."

Professor Ripley—Professor Hackett—Baptist Version.

The views of this baptism presented in the Commentaries of Professors Ripley and Hackett, and in the Baptist Bible Version of Acts, will now be presented.

In 10 . 45 it is said : " On the Gentiles also was *poured* out the gift of the Holy Ghost." The relation of " pouring " to baptism is thus presented by Prof. Ripley in his comment on v. 38 of this chapter—" ' God anointed Jesus of Nazareth with the Holy Ghost and with power.' As, in a literal anointing, the oil was poured on a person, so the Holy Spirit is said to be poured forth on Jesus ; that is, it was abundantly bestowed on him, that he might perform his holy work. . . . The term *anoint* was figuratively used, even when there was not a literal anointing, to signify *setting apart* and *qualifying* for a certain office. Jesus was *set apart* as the Messiah, and abundantly *qualified* for his office by receiving the Holy Spirit and power from on high." On 11 : 15, " ' *The Holy Ghost fell on them, as on us at the beginning.*' The Spirit shed forth the extraordinary gifts . . . as at the beginning of the Lord's imparting these extraordinary gifts on the day of Pentecost, when the promise of the miraculous gifts of the Spirit began to be fulfilled." ANOINTED is here the substitute for baptized.

The transaction at Cæsarea is identified by Prof. Ripley with that at Jerusalem, so far as sameness of baptizer, generic sameness of baptism, and sameness in representation as to the mode of accomplishment, " pouring," are concerned.

Professor Hackett says, 10 : 44, " ' *The Holy Ghost* (τὸ Πνεῦμα τὸ ʿAγίον) *fell on all them that heard the word,*' τὸ Πνεῦμα, *i. e.*, the author of the gifts mentioned in v. 46. 11 : 46, ' I remembered the declaration of the Lord, *John indeed baptized with water, but ye shall be baptized with the Holy Ghost ;*' *i. e.*, had it brought to mind with a new sense of its meaning and application. The Saviour had promised to bestow on his disciples a higher baptism than that of water, and the result proved that he designed to extend the benefit of that promise to the heathen who should believe on him, as well as to the Jews."

Professor Hackett not only thinks that this was a baptism, but, with that of Pentecost, " a higher baptism " than with water.

The translator (anonymous) of the Baptist Version of Acts says in a note on 10 : 44, " ' *The Holy Ghost* (τὸ Πνεῦμα τὸ ʿAγίον) *fell upon all.*' The Holy Spirit represents not a spirit of God, nor an angel of God, but all Divinity, and, Divinity, too, in all its grandeur. . . . We thank God that we can have the full assurance of understanding that Πνεῦμα ʿAγίον, like Jesus Christ, is the divinely established designation of the Christian's Advocate and Sanctifier. . . . In the Christian currency Πνεῦμα ʿAγίον, τὸ Πνεῦμα τὸ ʿAγίον, and τὸ ʿAγίον

Πνεῦμα, are like ὁ Ἰησοῦς, Ἰησοῦς Χριστός, and ὁ Ἰησοῦς ὁ Χριστός. . .
That which is ascribed to Πνεῦμα is ascribed to τὸ Πνεῦμα, and to
Πνεῦμα Ἅγιον, and to τὸ Ἅγιον Πνεῦμα, and to make it superlative to
τὸ Πνεῦμα τὸ Ἅγιον, which caps the climax of grammatical precision
and of exegetical development; v. 47, 'Who have received the
Holy Ghost as well as we.' They had received τὸ Πνεῦμα τὸ Ἅγιον,
that same τὸ Πνεῦμα τὸ Ἅγιον of which he had spoken, and they had
witnessed."

11 : 15. " 'The Holy Ghost fell on them, as on us at the beginning.' . . . The interval between the day of Pentecost and the
calling of the Gentiles at Cæsarea, is about seven or eight years.
. . . This scene in Cæsarea and that in Jerusalem are called—
and they are the only scenes that in Holy Scripture are called—
the Baptism or immersion of the Holy Spirit. They spoke as
fluently in foreign tongues as in their vernacular. The display
was sensible, visible."

This translator insists in the strongest terms on the divine
personality of the Holy Ghost, and that He is the executive Agent
in effecting this baptism, whence these conclusions follow: 1. The
preposition in the phrase, " He shall baptize you ἐν Πνεύματι Ἁγίῳ,"
should be translated by; 2. The executive Agent in effecting a
baptism cannot be the quiescent element in which such baptism
is effected by somebody else. For this double reason, therefore,
there is no such thing in Scripture as a " Baptism in the Holy
Ghost." The Lord Jesus Christ is—ὁ Βαπτίζων ἐν Πνεύματι Ἁγίῳ—
invested measurelessly with, and therefore baptizes by, the Holy
Ghost.

SAUL'S BAPTISM.

ACTS 9 : 17, 18; 22 : 13-16; 26 : 14-18.

Ὁ Κύριος ἀπέσταλκέ με, . . . ὅπως ἀναβλέψῃς καὶ πλησθῇς Πνεύματος Ἁγίου.
. . . ἀνέβλεψέ τε παραχρῆμα, καὶ ἀναστὰς ἐβαπτίσθη.

Ἀναστὰς βάπτισαι καὶ ἀπόλουσαι τὰς ἁμαρτίας σου, ἐπικαλεσάμενος τὸ ὄνομα
τοῦ Κυρίου.

Εἰς οὓς νῦν σε ἀποστέλλω.

"The Lord hath sent me . . . that thou mightest receive thy sight and
be filled with the Holy Ghost. . . . And he received sight forthwith, and
rising was baptized."

" Brother Saul, look up! And the same hour I looked up upon him. . . .
Rising baptize thyself and wash away thy sins, calling on the name of the
Lord."

" Delivering thee from the Gentiles unto whom now I send thee."

What was Saul's baptism?   Who was his baptizer?

This baptism presents some peculiarities which render its right interpretation a matter of special interest while it is attended with more than ordinary difficulty.   The conversion of the individual baptized separates his case from that of all others.   The narrative of the baptism is given by different persons with difference in circumstance and in language; and not only so, but in terms differing from those used in any other baptism.   The immediate call of this individual by the Head of the church while a Persecutor of himself (through his people) to fill the Apostleship, takes him not only out of the ranks of ordinary Christians and ordinary gospel agencies, but makes him stand alone among the Apostles. These peculiarities extend, I think, to his baptism.   Whenever God departs from his ordinary ways in providence or in grace, there is always a reason for it and instruction to be derived from its study.   And whenever there is a departure from the accustomed language of Scripture there is a reason for it, and it should not be slurred over but should be made the subject of special study, with the assurance that there is "hid treasure" in it.

So far as I am able to understand this baptism it was a baptism for the Apostleship and was substantially the same as that received by the other Apostles at Pentecost, incidentals (growing out of the peculiarities of that case) not being introduced.   It is usually supposed to be an ordinary ritual baptism.   Were the purpose of this Inquiry no higher than to make points against the theory this baptism might be allowed to stand as it is, a thorn hedge against all rational progress toward a dipping, but wishing to know what is truth, as developed by usage on this subject, I will endeavor to examine this case as presented by divine inspiration and submit it to the judgment of others wiser than myself.

Was this a case of dipping into Water?

" I see nothing in Paul's case to prevent his immediate immersion " (Carson, p. 357). " For immersion he must go to the water " (Campbell, p. 170).   To maintain the view that this baptism of Saul was a "dipping into water," there is no claim made for any such express statement, nor is it claimed that water is expressly mentioned, nor is it claimed that the place (a house) necessarily implies the presence of water suitable for dipping; but it is said: 1. The word means *to dip;* 2. Water essentially be-longs to ritual Christian baptism ; 3. Therefore, although no statement is made of a dipping *into water,* and although no appliances for such dipping are suggested by the circumstances, still, the water must be supplied by ellipsis and so supplied that there may be a dipping into it.

To this it may be replied: 1. The word does not mean "to dip." The shore of the sea is not dipped into the rising tide, but it is "baptized" by it. 2. It does not mean to cover momentarily. The ships "baptized at the mouth of the Tiber" have been under cover two thousand years. 3. It does not always require a covering. The altar on Carmel was "baptized" by water poured upon it, yet was not covered. 4. A fluid may be employed in a baptism and not be used for dipping into it. Men are "baptized" by wine without being dipped into it. 5. Therefore the use of the word in any case of baptism does not necessitate a dipping or a covering.

In reference to the necessary presence of water for ritual baptism, it may be said ; 1. The necessary presence of water in ritual Christian baptism is admitted; 2. The presence of water in ritual baptism for dipping the person to be baptized into it, is denied ; 3. There are other baptisms in the New Testament than ritual baptisms and in them water is not present ; 4. The Apostles were baptized without the presence of water ; 5. This was the baptism of an Apostle; 6. It may have been a baptism like that of the other Apostles by the Holy Ghost, without water; 7. A ritual baptism must be proved not assumed ; and when this is proved, it must farther be proved (against philology, and grammar, and facts), not assumed, that the water is present in ritual baptism *for a dipping* and not as a symbol.

On the supposition that this was not ritual baptism the way is open for one of two conclusions : 1. Ritual baptism may have been received at some after time; 2. One called into the kingdom of God, and introduced into the Apostleship "not of man nor by man" but personally by the Lord Jesus Christ, did not need and could not suitably receive a symbol rite from man, but needed only (as John the Baptist) to be baptized "by the Holy Ghost."

Was Saul now called to be an Apostle?

This is a radical question in determining the nature of this baptism. If Saul was not now called to the Apostleship then he could not receive the baptism of an Apostle; but if he was so called then the question arises, Was this a baptism by the Holy Ghost to qualify him for his life mission, or was it a rite introducing him as a private member into the visible church?

The evidence that Saul was already called to the Apostleship is of the most explicit and positive character. Luke testifies, Acts 9 : 15, " The Lord said, he is a·chosen vessel unto me, to bear my name before the Gentiles, and kings, and the children of Israel." Ananias says, Acts 22 : 14, "The God of our fathers hath chosen thee, that thou shouldst know his will, and see that Just One, and shouldst hear the voice of his mouth. For thou shalt be his witness unto all men of what thou hast seen and heard." Paul testifies, Acts 26 : 16, 17, " I have appeared unto thee for this purpose, to make thee a minister and a witness both of these things which thou hast seen, and of those things in the which I will appear unto thee; delivering thee from the people, and from the Gentiles, unto whom now I send thee (ἀποστέλλω)" = make thee an Apostle.

This point is then settled beyond question—Saul was now called by the Lord Jesus Christ to the Apostleship.

Was this baptism by the Holy Ghost to qualify for the Apostleship?

The way is now fairly open for the question, Did Saul now receive the ordinary ritual baptism of Christianity or the extraordinary and real baptism by the Holy Ghost already received by his fellow Apostles? Those who think that they can find the materials for a dipping into water in this narrative will bring forth their hidden treasures; as I see none I will pass on to adduce the evidence for that " higher baptism " which Professor Hackett says had been promised to the Apostles.

In the prosecution of this purpose let us inquire for what object Ananias was sent to Saul. This information is given us by Ananias himself in 9 : 17, " Brother Saul, the Lord, even Jesus, that appeared unto thee in the way as thou camest, hath sent me, that thou mightest receive thy sight, and be filled with the Holy Ghost." The mission of Ananias, then, was definite and limited. It embraced two specific results, the one physical, the other spiritual; 1, the restoration of sight; 2, the being filled with·the Holy Ghost.

These questions now arise: Did Ananias go on his mission? Do we know the results of his mission? Both these questions are expressly answered by the Scriptures in v. 17, " Ananias went his way, and entered into the house, and putting his hands on him . . . immediately there fell from his eyes as it had been scales: and he *received sight* forthwith *and* rising *was baptized.*" Here are two results declared to be consequent on the mission of Ananias: 1. Saul received his sight; 2. Saul was baptized. Are these two things those same two things for which Ananias was sent? There can be no doubt as to the first, for it is stated in precisely the same terms; but how is it as to the second, which is not stated in the same terms? Why, clearly, if this baptism which Saul received was a *dipping into water*, then it was not being " filled with the Holy Ghost;" and if it was not being " filled with the Holy Ghost," then a second thing *which did not enter into the mission of this messenger* was done by him, and that second thing *which did enter into his mission was left undone.*

But do the Scriptures say that this baptism was a ritual baptism? Do they intimate that there was water adequate for a dipping? Do they say that there was a particle of water touched by Saul or Ananias, or was present in the room or house? They do not. But the theory says, " I do not care; I will find a bath in the room, or I will take him out of the house to some Arbana or Pharpar, and dip him there." This compelled addition to the Scripture narrative reminds us of the fact (almost without exception), that the theory is unable to interpret baptisms in the Scriptures or out of the Scriptures without addition, or omission, or self-contradiction, or appeal to most irrational figure. Dr. Carson sees no difficulty in the way to Saul's being dipped *instanter* in his chamber. Why not add, that the bath was provided by miracle as the sight was miraculously restored? The President of Bethany College sees as little difficulty in " going to the water" in some river of Damascus, better than all the waters of Judea. Why not keep on to the Jordan? Such absolute additions to the word of God are without justification from *a solitary word* of Scripture saying that " dipping" entered into baptism, or *a solitary fact* showing that a man or woman was ever put under water in baptism. But if Saul was not " dipped into water" when he was " baptized," what was the baptism which he received, and why is it stated, that he " saw and was *baptized*," and not that he " saw and was *filled with the Holy Ghost*"? I answer: the baptism which this newly called Apostle received was the same baptism which his fellow Apostles had already received according to the promise of that Lord who had now called Saul, when he said, " Ye shall be baptized by the Holy Ghost." The accompaniments of the original baptism (sound as of wind, tongues as of fire) were incidentals attendant upon the baptism, and not essentials entering into its execution. Saul (= Paul) in after life is found "endued with power" for all entering into the Apostolic office, "speaking with tongues more than they all," which power he received now, or we are never told by Scripture when he did receive it. It is said that he "saw and was *baptized*," and not that he "saw and was *filled with the Holy Ghost*," simply because the two phrases have the same identical value. To be "*filled* with the Holy Ghost" and to be "*baptized* by the Holy Ghost" squarely cover the same idea, namely, to be *thoroughly under the influence* of the Holy Ghost. If any one should object to the addition "baptized" *by the Holy Ghost*, the justifying answer is this: "baptized" always requires some ellipsis in the New Testament; that ellipsis (so far as agency is concerned) may be ἐν ὕδατι (symbol) or ἐν Πνεύματι Ἁγίῳ (efficient); because baptism *by the Holy Ghost* is just as surely established as baptism *by water*. This is a general justification for the right (under ellipsis) in any absolute use of βαπτίζω, to present the claim of ἐν Πνεύματι Ἁγίῳ for recognition. The special justification in this case is: 1. The Lord Jesus Christ promised that the Apostles should be baptized ἐν Πνεύματι Ἁγίῳ and not ἐν ὕδατι, *and this was the baptism of an Apostle*. 2. The Apostles when *baptized* by the Holy Ghost are said to be "*full* of the Holy Ghost." The phrases are used interchangeably and as of equal value, as shown by Acts 1 : 5; 2 : 4. 3. Saul was to be "filled with the Holy Ghost" by promise, and in the fulfilment he is said to be "baptized"—*with the Holy Ghost*, of necessity; (1) because the right to such ellipsis (as possible) has been established, (2) because the exigencies of the passage demand it, (3) because the introduction of a dipping *into water* sets at naught the promise, and introduces an element wholly foreign to the specialty of the case. The promise to the band of the Apostles was that they should be "*baptized* by the Holy Ghost;" the fulfilment of this promise is not verbally recorded as a *baptism*, but as being "*filled* with the Holy Ghost;" while reversely in the case of this last of the Apostles, the promise was that he should be "*filled* with the Holy Ghost," and the fulfilment of the promise is described as a "baptism." 4. The Apostles were to "receive (δύναμιν) power after the Holy Ghost came upon them." Saul after his baptism, like Peter, "straightway preached Christ" and "he was clothed with power (ἐνεδυναμοῦτο)." How the double promise could be more clearly declared to have had its precise double accomplishment I cannot well imagine. Everything entering into the specialty of the case makes imperative demand for a baptism by the Holy Ghost, and just as imperatively rejects a baptism by dipping into water.

Ἀνέβλεψέ τε παραχρῆμα καὶ ἀναστὰς ἐβαπτίσθη.

The Cod. Sin., the Syriac, the Vulgate, and other versions omit παραχρῆμα. The particles τε . . . καὶ show a unity of relation in the statements with which they are connected. While "he received sight" is accessory and adjunctive (τε) to "there fell from his eyes as it had been scales," the whole statement "there fell from his eyes as it had been scales and he received his sight" is dependent on the statement "putting his hands on him;" and no less the conjunctive (καὶ) statement, "rising he was baptized," is dependent on the same fact, to wit, "the putting his hands on him." If we omit the intervening words explaining the design of the act, namely, that through it the Lord was to give sight and to fill with the Holy Ghost, and bring together the act and its results, it would read thus: "Putting his hands on him, immediately, scales, as it were, fell from his eyes and he saw, *also*" (in addition to this and associated with the same fact) "rising he was baptized," being filled with the Holy Ghost. The relation between ἀναστὰς and ἐβαπτίσθη is not that of an antecedent act after the doing of which some consequent act is done, but the thought in the participle is intimately and coincidently related to the thought in the verb. If ἀναστὰς expresses the physical act of "rising," it does not imply that subsequently to this act another act disconnected with it, to wit, a dipping into water, took place, but that the baptism was coincident with the rising; in other words Saul rose up a baptized man, thoroughly changed in condition by the Holy Ghost. If this participle denotes, as Professor J. Addison Alexander (in loc.) seems to suppose, a mental and moral *rousing* "from his previous prostration and inaction" rather than a physical rising, the coincidence is the same. If the participle be supposed to have an adverbial force, as stated by Winer (p 608) of

Luke 15 : 18, " ἀναστὰς πορεύσομαι, I will *forthwith* go," and we translate " he was *forthwith* baptized " by the Holy Ghost, the same intimacy of relation is preserved, and the sight and the baptism are alike dependent on "the putting on of hands," and "immediately " consequent upon that act. In other words as Saul was commissioned (Acts 26 : 18) " to open the eyes of the Gentiles, and to turn them from darkness to light," so now his own eyes (both of the body and of the soul) were opened to the light of the sun and to the knowledge of God.

Alexander Campbell, President of Bethany College.

The view of this phrase as given by Alexander Campbell is as follows: " In Luke's writings alone we have this idiom eight times. *Anastas*, with an imperative immediately following, and without a conjunction or a comma, is found in Luke 17 : 19; 22 : 46; Acts 9 : 11; 10 : 13, 20; 11 : 7; 22 : 10, 16. In every instance it indicates a command from the Lord in person, or from a supernatural agent acting for him. Nothing expressed by the term *rise* different from the action to be performed. In no instance does the precept *arise* terminate the action. It never means two actions in any one case. It is not arise *and* be baptized. It is an idiom of expressing one immediate action. The idiom always changes when an action different from rising up is intended. Another imperative form, with a copulative of some kind, intimates two actions, as in Acts 8 : 26; 9 : 6, 34; 26 : 16. In all these it is *anasteethi*, followed by a copulative, rise and stand upon thy feet, rise and go into the city, etc. . . . But in this case, *rising* is no more than an adjunct. It is not a distinct precept; therefore it is never rendered stand up. Almost every orator uses the term *Rise* when an erect position, or a mere change of position, is never thought of: Rise, citizens! rise, sinners! and let us do our duty. In this common sense import of the term did Ananias address Saul."

This view strongly sustains the interpretation suggested.

Ἀναστὰς βάπτισαι καὶ ἀπόλουσαι τὰς ἁμαρτίας σου, ἐπικαλεσάμενος τὸ ὄνομα τοῦ Κυρίου.—ACTS 22 : 16.

Acts 22: 12–16 differs from that passage now examined as being more full in statement, and with material variety in phraseology. This applies with special force to the statement of the baptism as given in the two passages. In the first it is condensed in the two words ἀναστὰς ἐβαπτίσθη; in the second it is enlarged into ἀναστὰς βάπτισαι καὶ ἀπόλουσαι τὰς ἁμαρτίας σου, ἐπικαλεσάμενος τὸ ὄνομα τοῦ Κυρίου. The specially new element in the second account is the connection of the baptism with the personal action of Saul; there is nothing in the first account to forbid such an element, but it does not there make any appearance. It is possible that it may be involved in the undeveloped ἀναστὰς, while in the second account the enlargement, by stating what Saul did, is but explicatory of the ἀναστὰς by which the call upon him is made. The baptism in both cases is spiritual. The unification of the narratives is, in general, to be found in the fact that the first states the baptism as a thing accomplished, and the other states the means for such accomplishment. A combination of the two gives the following: "Rising baptize thyself, and wash away thy sins calling on the name of the Lord; and he was baptized." It will be observed that the force of the middle voice is retained in this translation. A discriminating use of words in Scripture has always a reason for it, and our business is not to change the statement to make it accord with some other statement, but to accept it, and seek for the reason of it. This is the only passage where βαπτίζω is so used in the middle voice. There must be a reason for it. The whole transaction is unique. The baptism is entirely removed from ordinary baptisms. There is nothing in the teaching of Scripture, or in its free and frequent use of language, to prevent a call being made on Saul to "baptize himself and to wash away his sins by prayer." This duty laid upon him toward himself rests on precisely the same basis as that duty toward the Gentiles now imposed upon him, "To open their eyes, to turn them from darkness to light, and from the power of Satan unto God to the receiving of the forgiveness of sins" (Acts 26:18). Now Saul might have said (as Paul did say) "Who is sufficient for these things?" I cannot give the Gentiles spiritual sight; I cannot turn their hearts from error to truth; I cannot break the bonds which bind them to Satan and make them subject to the living God. And yet these great duties were made imperative upon him, and he fulfilled them by preaching a crucified Redeemer. Just so, Saul could not "baptize himself," and could not "wash away his sins," and yet could do both by "calling on the name of the Lord." And he did so. He was baptized by the Holy Ghost, and his sins were washed away in answer to prayer in the name of the Lord, who is the Lamb of God that taketh away the sins of the world and baptizes by the Holy Ghost. While it is contrary to all Scripture that Saul should ritually baptize himself, and just as contrary that ritual baptism should wash away sins, it is in the most absolute harmony with all Scripture that the Holy Ghost should be given, and sins should be pardoned in *answer to prayer.*

Structure of the Sentence.

The sentence " Baptize thyself and wash away thy sins, calling on the name of the Lord," is a compound sentence, in which the successive clauses develop and expound the preceding. The first clause is developed and expounded as to its character and effect by the second, from which we learn that the baptism is spiritual in its nature, and possessed of the power to take away sin ; the third clause is expository of the means by which this baptism is secured, and the ground of its efficiency, namely, *by means of prayer and through the Lord Jesus Christ.*

The translation of this passage from the Syriac by Dr. Murdoch is as follows : " Arise, be baptized and be cleansed from thy sins *while* thou invokest his name." Here the baptism and the cleansing from sin are to be secured by prayer, and " while " the prayer is being made.

This baptism is the same as that preached by John the Baptist, who makes " baptism into the remission of sins " the result of " repentance," and therefore the work of the Holy Ghost. It is the same baptism as that preached by Peter, " Repent and be baptized *into the remission of sins* (believing) upon (ἐπὶ) the name of Jesus Christ," where repentance is presented as the means, and the Lord Jesus Christ declared to be the ground cause of the remission of sins. The entire harmony of these statements with that of Ananias, " Baptize thyself and *wash away thy sins calling on* (ἐπὶ) *the name of the Lord,*" is obvious.

Harmony with other commands of Scripture.

Isaiah 1 : 16–18, " Wash you, make you clean, ... Though your sins be as scarlet, they shall be as white as snow; though they be red like crimson, they shall be white as wool."

The parallelism is complete as to the call personally to " wash themselves " spiritually, and to " cleanse themselves " from moral pollution: while the transformation of scarlet and crimson guilt into snowy purity is still to come from God. Again, Ezekiel 18: 30, 31, "Repent and turn yourselves from all your transgressions, so iniquity shall not be your ruin. . . . . Make you a new heart and a new spirit, for why will ye die?" Can sinners "repent" and "turn themselves" from sin, and make themselves a "new heart and a new spirit" any more than David, who declared it to be God's work to "create in him a clean heart, and to renew in him a right spirit"? 1 Peter 1:22, "Ye have purified your souls, by obeying the truth, through the Spirit." Here is a declaration of self-soul purification; but it is "by the truth" and "through the Spirit." And again prayer is the specified medium, as in Acts 2:21, "And it shall come to pass that whosoever shall call on the name of the Lord shall be saved." Salvation involves the washing away of sin and the baptism of the soul by the Holy Ghost, and this is secured by prayer. What, then, can be more fully harmonious with the analogy of Scripture than a call upon Saul to baptize himself and wash away his sins by calling on the name of the Lord (whose name is JESUS, because he takes away the sins of his people), and who is their "Baptizer by the Holy Ghost."

As a Ritual Baptism no just and safe exposition.

Doctor Carson (p. 212) says on this passage: "Here we see baptism figuratively washes away sins, and supposes that they are truly washed away." The passage says nothing of "figurative" washing away sin *by water*. Such addition to Scripture radically changes its character. The removal of sin is real and *by prayer*. Prof. Hackett (*in loc.*) says: "This is the only instance in which this verb occurs in the middle voice, with reference to Christian baptism. *And wash away thy sins.* This clause states a result of the baptism in language derived from the nature of that ordinance. It answers to εἰς ἄφεσιν ἁμαρτιῶν in 2:38, *i.e.*, submit to the rite in order to be forgiven. In both passages baptism is represented as having this importance or efficacy, because it is the sign of the repentance and faith which are the conditions of salvation. *Calling upon the name of the Lord.* This supplies essentially the place of ἐπὶ τῷ ὀνόματι Ἰησοῦ Χριστοῦ in 2:38."

Professor Hackett is probably as far removed as any one from attaching an unscriptural efficacy to ritual baptism ; but some of this language can only be explained by being explained away. If " the washing away of sin " is language which states the result of ritual baptism derived from its nature, what language will state the effect of baptism by the Holy Ghost derived from its nature ? If men are to be told " to submit to THE RITE *in order to be forgiven,*" in what terms shall they be told to submit to CHRIST in order to be forgiven ?

The interpretation is just as applied to baptism by the Holy Ghost and remission of sins through Christ ; but when applied to ritual baptism it shows, that the wisest and the best are compelled to use language which proves that their feet " tread on slippery places."

Alexander Campbell of Bethany (On Baptism, pp. 246–259), says: " The *design* of baptism is the transcendent question in this discussion. John proclaimed ‘the baptism of repentance *for the remission of sins.*’ Were it not for an imaginary incongruity between the means and the end, or the thing done and the alleged purpose or result, no one could, for a moment, doubt that the design of baptism was ‘ for the remission of sins.’ It is the only purpose for which it was ordained, whether in the hands of John or of the twelve Apostles. The death of the Messiah was not more certainly *for the remission of sins,* so far as the expression goes, than was the baptism of John. It does not, however, follow that they are *in the same sense* ‘ for the remission of sins.’ Baptism is ordained for the remission of sins, not as a procuring, or meritorious, or efficient cause, but as an instrumental cause, in which faith and repentance are developed and made fruitful and effectual in the changing of our state and spiritual relations to the Divine Persons whose names are put upon us in the very act. ‘ *He that believeth and is baptized shall be saved.*’ To associate faith and baptism as antecedents, whose consequent is salvation, will always impart to the institution a pre-eminence above all other religious institutions in the world. ‘ Arise, brother Saul, and be baptized, and *wash away thy sins,* invoking the name of the Lord.’ A most unguarded and unjustifiable form of address, under the sanction of a divine mission, if baptism had not for its design the *formal and definite* remission of sins."

President Campbell and Professor Hackett do not differ materially in the language which they employ in the first place to characterize ritual baptism ; but in the after-interpretation of

that language they do differ. When Professor Hackett says:
" *Wash away thy sins* " is " a *result* of ritual baptism," and is
" language grounded in the nature of that ordinance," and that
men are called upon to " submit to the rite in order to be forgiven,"
he says of the " result," and " nature," and the " in order to,"
of the ordinance just what Campbell (initially) says.   In the interpretation of his language the Professor teaches that this remarkable language is not applied to ritual baptism on its essential merits, but " because it is *the sign* of the repentance and faith
which are the conditions of salvation."   This interpretation is
not obvious in the language.   And Campbell denies that it is
there at all.   He affirms that the rite is not a " sign " but a *cause ;*
not illustrative of " repentance and faith as the conditions of salvation " but is itself a condition, side by side with them.   We cordially accept the doctrine reached by the Professor but must as
absolutely reject the terms used to characterize the rite ; and we
accept the interpretation of the President as justified by the terms
used to characterize the rite, while we reject those terms and the
doctrine deduced from them.

Alexander Campbell was originally a Presbyterian minister
but through an error as to the position occupied by water in ritual
baptism his feet slipped, and he became a Baptist.   Accepting
the language which he there found taken from the baptism by the
Holy Ghost and *by a sad error misapplied to baptism by water*,
and giving to it an obvious logical interpretation, his feet further
slipped, and he became the head of a body to whom he taught
that ritual baptism was a " cause " of the forgiveness of sins,
and a " condition " of salvation.   The feet of his followers being
thus placed in positions so slippery, it would have been not merely
marvellous but miraculous if the many had not slipped farther
down into the abandonment of limiting definitions (sometimes
given by their leader), and taken them at their full, popular value.

It is without Scripture justification to say, " *the washing away
of sin* is *a result* of ritual baptism."   Water neither washes away
sin, nor symbolizes the *washing*.   The blood of Christ washes
away sin, and " the result " is *purity*.   This accomplished result
(soul purification) is symbolized by pure water.

It is WITHOUT SCRIPTURE JUSTIFICATION to say, " *the washing
away of sin* is language derived from the nature of ritual baptism."   This language is derived from the cleansing power of the
blood of atonement.   The use of water in ritual baptism is derived

from the same source. The language is not grounded in the ritual shadow, but in the actual blood of the Cross. "These are they which have *washed* their robes and made them white *in the* BLOOD OF THE LAMB " (Rev. 7 : 14).

It is WITHOUT SCRIPTURE JUSTIFICATION to say, that men are called upon "to submit to the rite *in order to* be forgiven." There is no semblance of any such language in Scripture applied to ritual baptism. It is solely due to a confounding of ritual with real baptism.

Doctor Pusey (Scriptural Views of Holy Baptism, p. 174) says : " It is commonly thought that St. Paul, having been miraculously converted, was regenerated, justified by faith, pardoned, had received the Holy Ghost, before he was baptized. Not so, however, Holy Scripture, if we consider it attentively : before his baptism he appears neither to have been pardoned, regenerated, justified, nor enlightened. . . . What took place during those three days and nights we are not told beyond a general intimation. . . . But as yet neither were his sins forgiven, nor had he yet received the Holy Ghost; much less then was he born again of the Spirit, before it was conveyed to him through his Saviour's Sacrament. Ananias says, 'Arise and be baptized and wash away thy sins.' This was done; He arose and was baptized. By baptism he was filled with the Holy Ghost."

There is no material difference among these three interpreters as to the first step in the interpretation of this Scripture. With each of them the baptism is a "ritual" baptism ; the " result " of the baptism is *the washing away of sin ;* the purpose of the baptism is " *in order to* be forgiven." From this common basis Professor Hackett deduces a "sign ;" President Campbell deduces an "instrumental cause ;" and Dr. Pusey deduces *an efficient sacrament* through which is obtained "the Holy Ghost, the forgiveness of sin, the regeneration of the soul, and justification."

That the logic of this last interpreter is less sound than that of those others who stand with him on the same accepted premises, does not clearly appear. The value of the logic, however, is not a primary concern with us, but the value of the premises. These we reject with a peremptory denial, affirming that they are grounded in a fiction ; no ritual baptism having an existence in the case.

We may, however, learn from these variant interpretations this instructive lesson : INITIAL *error is the radiant centre of many errors.*

Irenæus—Chrysostom.

It has been shown from the Scriptures that the phrases " to be *baptized* by the Holy Ghost" and "to be *filled* with the Holy Ghost " are used by them as equivalent expressions. The form of thought as expressed in primary use is not the same ; but the secondary or metaphorical use (indicative of effect and not of form) has an equal value. This is recognized by Irenæus, who, in speaking of this transaction, substitutes βαπτίσθῆναι for " filled with the Holy Ghost " in the announcement of his mission as made by Ananias. This is his language (902): " Paul after the Lord sent Ananias to him (καὶ αναβλέψαι καὶ βαπτισθῆναι) both to receive his sight and to be baptized." The language of Ananias is—" that thou mightest receive thy sight and be *filled with the Holy Ghost*," for this last statement Irenæus substitutes the equivalent phrase—" *be baptized*" (with the Holy Ghost), the single word representing the entire phrase.

Chrysostom very pointedly indicates the distinction between baptism " into the name of Christ," and " baptism by calling upon the name of Christ:" " Hom. 47, ' Rising baptize thyself and wash away thy sins calling upon his name.' Here a great truth was uttered ; for he did not say, ' Baptize thyself *into his name ;*' but ' *calling upon* the name of Christ ;' this shows that he was God." " Baptize thyself into the name of Christ " indicates the nature of the baptism by the ideal element (*into the* NAME OF CHRIST) to which the soul is made subject, and by which it is imbued with its sin-remitting power; while " baptize thyself CALLING UPON *the name of Christ*" indicates the means by which the baptism is attained, namely, by invoking divine power.

This baptism (by its general unity and discriminating differ- ences as compared with the Pentecost baptism) enforces the con- clusion, that it is effected by a wise and discriminating divine Person, and not " in divine essence," or " in abstract spirit," or " *in* the Holy Ghost " (as a receptive medium), which would necessitate one uniform result under all circumstances.

BAPTISM AT SAMARIA.

ACTS 8:15, 16.

Οἴτενες καταβάντες προσηύξαντο περὶ αὐτῶν, ὅπως λάβωσι Πνεῦμα Ἅγιον. Οὔπω γὰρ ἦν ἐπ' οὐδενὶ αὐτων ἐπιπεπτωκὸς, μόνον δὲ βεβαπτισμένοι. . . . .

"Who (Peter and John) when they were come down prayed for them, that they might receive the Holy Ghost. For as yet he was fallen upon none of them, only they were baptized into the name of the Lord Jesus."

Baptism by the Holy Ghost.

1. This is properly designated a baptism: (1.) Because it is inferable from the statement "they were only baptized into the name of the Lord Jesus," and had not been yet baptized by the Holy Ghost enduing them with miraculous gifts. The one baptism "only" having been received the other was sought for them. (2.) Because the same term (ἐπιπεπτωκός) is here used as is used, Acts 8:44, ἐπέπεσε, in describing the like baptism at Cæsarea. (3.) Because "the receiving (v. 17) the Holy Ghost" of necessity effects a baptism="subjecting to his influence and imbuing with his virtue."

2. This Πνεῦμα Ἅγιον (v. 15) for which prayer was made was the personal Divine Spirit. This is certain because (v. 18) in answer to their prayer τὸ Πνεῦμα τὸ Ἅγιον was given.

3. The means to secure this baptism was the same (v. 15) as that used by Saul—prayer.

4. Prayer was accompanied by the symbol laying on of hands, v. 17.

5. The gift and consequent baptism by the Holy Ghost was accompanied by sensible evidence — "When Simon *saw* that through the laying on of hands the Holy Ghost was given." If the baptism had been simply spiritual, without sensible evidence, Simon must have been ignorant of its bestowal.

If objection should be made to this as a baptism because it is not verbally so designated, the insufficiency of the objection is shown: 1. By the fact, that the word has been already used on other like occasions. 2. By the fact, that neither the word nor any correspondent word is used in the narrative of the Red Sea passage, and yet Paul declares there was "a baptism of Israel into Moses" through the influence exerted by the double miracle wrought on that occasion, namely, "the division of the sea," and the illumination "by the cloud."

ACTS 19 : 6.

Καὶ ἐπιθέντος αὐτοῖς τοῦ Παύλου τὰς χεῖρας, ἦλθε τὸ Πνεῦμα τὸ 'Αγίον ἐπ' αὐτοὺς, ἐλάλουν τε γλώσσαις καὶ προεφήτευον.

"And when Paul had laid his hands upon them, the Holy Ghost came on them, and they both spake with tongues and prophesied."

Speaking with Tongues and Prophesying.

1. *When Paul had laid his hands on them.* It is not stated that he prayed, but doubtless he did as is stated in Acts 8 : 15, and Acts 22 : 16, in the case of his own baptism.

2. *The Holy Ghost came upon them.* This τὸ Πνεῦμα τὸ 'Αγίον was undoubtedly the personal Divine Spirit. It is the fullest and most precise form by which such announcement could be made.

3. *They spake both with tongues and prophesied.* (1.) The thorough change in their spiritual condition hereby announced is absolute proof of the propriety of designating such change as a baptism; (2.) The power to speak with tongues is neither an exclusive evidence nor necessary in order to evidence a baptism by the Holy Ghost. The twelve baptized at Pentecost spake with tongues; these twelve baptized at Ephesus, also, spake with tongues, and in addition "prophesied." Saul, baptized at Damascus, neither spake with tongues nor prophesied (at the time, though "endued with power" so to do when necessary); the scales falling from his eyes was a sensible token of the Spirit of God resting upon him. (3.) The double result of the Holy Ghost coming upon these twelve is stated in a manner (ἐλάλουν τε γλώσσαις καὶ προεφήτευον) so similar in form with the result of the Holy Ghost coming upon Saul (ἀνέβλεψε τε καὶ ἐβαπτίσθη), as to give renewed proof that this restored sight and spiritual baptism was also a double result of the work of the Holy Ghost.

4. The introduction of this new element of "prophesying" is fresh evidence that baptism is by a Divine Person who wisely, as sovereignly, discriminates in his gifts. And if this be so, then the representation that ἐν Πνεύματι 'Αγίῳ is a quiescent, receptive element is not true.

That the laying on of the hand upon the head was believed to

be adequate to effect a baptism is a matter susceptible of unquestionable proof.   It was the common faith of the Patrists that they
could baptize with the Holy Ghost by the laying on of hands.   In
Cyprian (1061) Successus ab Abbir says: "If heretics cannot
baptize, they cannot give the Holy Ghost; but if they cannot
give the Holy Ghost, because they have not the Holy Ghost,
neither can they spiritually baptize."   This spiritual baptism was
effected by laying the hand upon the head and prayer.   In connection with a discussion, respecting the baptism of heretics, by
the Council of Carthage, the following judgments are expressed:
Cyprian, 1122. Januarius a Lambese, "I judge that all heretics
must be baptized (pænitentiæ manu) by the hand of repentance;"
Secundinus a Cedias, "They who fly to the Church must be baptized by repentance" (through the laying on of hands); Januarius a Vico Cæsaris, "Those whom the Church has not baptized
(per pænitentiam baptizemus) we must baptize by repentance;"
Felix, "Purged by the sanctification (lavacri pænitentiæ) of the
washing of repentance;" Adelphius, "Since the Church may not
rebaptize heretics, but (per manum baptizet) may baptize by the
hand;" Marcus a Mactari, "Since we have decreed that heretics
(per manus impositionem) must be baptized by imposition of the
hand;" Aurelius ab Utica, "I think that they should be baptized
(in manu) by the hand of repentance, that they may receive the
remission of sins;" Lucianus, "I think that heretics should be
baptized by imposition of the hand;" Felix, "That they may
receive, where it is lawful, the grace of baptism by imposition of
the hand."

So John of Damascus (T. 261) says: "John was baptized
(ἐβαπτίσθη) by putting his hand upon the divine head of his
Master."   And in the *Acti Sancti Thomæ* it is said: "And putting his hand upon her head he sealed her into the name of the
Father, and of the Son, and of the Holy Ghost.   And many others
were sealed with her.   But the Apostle ordered his deacon to
spread a table" for the administration of the Lord's Supper, as
was common after baptism.   The editor remarks, "Sealing" was
"a most ancient and most frequent designation of baptism."
Firmilian says, "Paul baptized again with spiritual baptism
(baptizavit denuo spiritali Baptismo) those who had been baptized by John, and put his hand upon them that they might receive the Holy Ghost."

In the third volume of Tertullian (1195), *Anonymi Liber*, it is said : "All the disciples having been baptized by water, were baptized again, after the resurrection, by the Holy Spirit; and others also may be baptized again ' with Spiritual baptism, that is, by the imposition of hands and conferring the Holy Ghost '— (Baptismate spiritale, id est manus impositione episcopi, et Spiritus Sancti subministratione"). Also, 1162, "The blessed apostle Paul baptized again with spiritual baptism those who had been baptized by John before the Holy Spirit had been sent by the Lord (baptizavit denuo spiritali Baptismo), and so laid his hand upon them that they might receive the Holy Spirit."

These quotations place beyond question the belief in "a baptism (*per manum, in manu, manu*) by the hand." They did unquestionably believe that baptisms of the Holy Ghost, giving "repentance" and "remission of sin," were effected by the laying of the hand upon the head. They did, undoubtedly, believe that baptisms were effected by the laying on of the hands of Ananias, of Peter, of John, and of Paul. They saw nothing in the nature of a baptism inconsistent with its being effected by the touch of the hand. Their practice was grounded in this Scripture practice. Whether their interpretation of these Scripture facts as to their purport was right, or whether their perpetuation of such practice was just, are not questions now to be examined; what concerns us now is this,—men who had every opportunity to know the essential character of a baptism did claim to baptize (*manu, in manu, per manum*) by the hand laid upon the head; and farther claimed that the baptism so effected was (*baptizare spiritaliter*) a spiritual baptism. We may, then, stand unhesitatingly on this foundation and affirm, that there is no objection which can lie against the interpretation of the laying on of hands with prayer, by the Apostles, as effecting baptisms by the gift of the Holy Ghost. And these baptisms were real baptisms, and not a meaningless use of words. They effected a thorough change in the condition of the recipient. In these baptisms by the hand, the hand occupies the same grammatical position and logical relation to the baptism effected as does *the water* in the ritual baptism of Christianity, namely, of agency; in the case of water a symbol agency; in the case of "the hand" just what character of agency (symbol or efficient, it makes no matter to the argument) it may please the Patrists to attribute to it. Hence it follows, that if it be a grammatical or logical absurdity to regard "the hand" as the receptive element within which the baptism takes place, it is just as absurd grammatically and logically (the nature of the hand or the water is not concerned in the argument) to make *water* the receptive element within which the baptism takes place. These baptisms by *touching* with the hand are entirely parallel, in principle, with the Classic baptisms effected by *drinking* a cup of wine, *eating* indigestible food, *hearing* bewildering questions. How much of dipping, immersing, covering, there is in them, "a child can understand."

In view of such usage and such facts, may it not be well to reconsider the order which sends "the angel Gabriel to school," because he demurs at the dictum—"βαπτίζω means dip, and nothing but dip, through all Greek literature."

BAPTISM ἐν Πνεύματι Ἁγίῳ AT CORINTH.

SPECIAL GIFTS.

1 COR. 12: 13.

Καὶ γὰρ ἐν ἑνὶ Πνεύματι ἡμεῖς πάντες εἰς ἓν σῶμα ἐβαπτίσθημεν.
" For by one Spirit are we all baptized into one body."

Other Readings.

No other readings of this passage are met with except such as are found among some of the Patristic writers. Basil (IV, 117) quotes the text thus: Πάντες γὰρ ἐν ἕνι σώματι εἰς ἓν Πνεῦμα ἐβαπτίσ-θημεν. Whether the change in the phraseology was designed or not we cannot tell; but this is certain, the course of Basil's argument required a baptism *into* the Holy Ghost, and he got it in the form as quoted when he could not have got it as it stands in the text. No one would think of making ἐν ἑνὶ σώματι, as presented by Basil, the receiving element in this baptism. No one would hesitate to assign this duty to εἰς ἓν Πνεῦμα. By parity of reasoning ἐν ἑνὶ Πνεύματι, in the received text, cannot be the receiving element, but εἰς ἓν σῶμα must be.

Didymus Alexandrinus (717), carrying out a special line of argument, quotes the passage as does Basil, reversing, by an interchange of cases, the respective relations ascribed by the inspired text to ἓν Πνεῦμα and ἓν σῶμα in this baptism. The entire revolutio of sentiment by this exchange of preposition and case

is instructive. The double presence of the Dative and Accusative cases in New Testament baptisms (expressed or implied) is
the rule; extraordinary baptisms are the exception. The law,
that the Accusative with εἰς denotes the receiving element, has no
exceptions. By such designation the nature of the baptism is
made as definite as language can express it. In the New Testament, WATER *never has such designation*—εἰς ὕδωρ.

Clemens Alex. (I, 288) quotes the passage as we have it except
by the omission of the preposition before Ἑνὶ Πνεύματί; thus
strengthening the idea of agency which so clearly belongs to the
Holy Spirit.

Translation.

The translation of this passage by the Baptist version is as
follows: " For by one Spirit we were all immersed into one
body." And in the version circulating among the Disciples
(" Campbellites "), by H. T. Anderson, the translation is the same,
" For by one Spirit we all were immersed into one body." Both
of these versions translate the same grammatical forms diversely
in other passages, *e. g.*, Matt. 3 : 11, "I immerse you (ἐν ὕδατι
εἰς μετάνοιαν) *in* water *unto* repentance. . . . He will immerse you
in the Holy Spirit" (Baptist version); "I immerse you *in* water
in order to repentance. . . . He will immerse you (ἐν Πνεύματι
Ἁγίῳ) in the Holy Spirit" (Disciples' version); John 1 : 33, "The
same is he who immerses in the Holy Spirit (ὁ βαπτίζων ἐν Πνεύματι
Ἁγίῳ") (Baptist version); "This is he that immerses *in* the
Holy Spirit" (Disciples' version); Acts 1 : 5, " For John, indeed,
immersed (ὕδατι) *in* water; but ye shall be immersed (ἐν Πνεύματι
Ἁγίῳ) *in* the Holy Ghost" (Baptist version); " For John, indeed,
immersed in water, but you shall be immersed *in* the Holy Spirit"
(Disciples' version). The grammatical form (βαπτίζω with the
Dative and the Accusative, expressed or implied) in all these
cases is the same; but the translation, as compared with the
translation of 1 Cor. 12 : 13, works a complete revolution in the
grammatical and logical relations of the elements entering into
the baptisms.

In Matt. 3 : 11, the preposition with its regimen, water (ἐν ὕδατι)
is made the receiving element of the baptized object, while the
preposition and its regimen in the Accusative (εἰς μετάνοιαν), is
wholly dissevered from the baptism strictly speaking, and is
appended to it as an end " unto" which it tends but never reaches,

according to the Baptists; and "in order to" which it is ex-ecuted, but which it never effects, according to the Disciples. But when this last preposition and its regimen take the form of εἰς ἄφεσιν ἁμαρτιῶν, the Baptist version still, consistently, says, this phrase does not enter into the baptism, but is something apart from it, pointed to by it yet never reached through it; while the Disciples' version, adhering to the same verbal form ("in order to") declares, that while "immersion in water *in order to* REPENTANCE" is a worthless fiction, yet, "immersion in water *in order to* REMISSION OF SINS" is the very power of God, and as truly a cause (instrumental) of the remission of sins as the blood of the incarnate Redeemer. That is to say, the same grammatical form, in the same grammatical and logical relation to "immersion in water," finds that relation worthless "in order to *repentance*," but priceless "in order to *the remission of sins*." To declare that inspiration says, "immersion in water" is "*un*-TO repentance," when it is not so; and "*un*-TO the remis-sion of sins," when it is not so; and "*in order* TO repentance," and "*in order* TO the remission of sins," when it is not in order to the former, but is in order to the latter, is assertion the burden of which must be taken from inspiration and laid, where it be-longs, on human infirmity.

But all this is changed when we come to the baptism in 1 Cor. 12:13. The same grammatical forms, in the same grammatical relations, undergo a complete revolution as to the offices they are to sustain. Now, ἐν ἑνὶ Πνεύματι instead of being as ἐν ὕδατι, ἐν Πνεύματι Ἁγίῳ, the receiving element *in which* the baptized object is to be received, is transformed into the baptizing agency *by which* the baptism is to be effected; and εἰς ἓν σῶμα, instead of being as εἰς μετάνοιαν an end "unto" which, or "in order to" which, immersion is powerless, or as εἰς ἄφεσιν ἁμαρτιῶν an end which (whether attained or not attained, according to the one or the other phase of the theory) is outside of the baptism, is in-troduced within the baptism, and becomes so vital to it that there can be no baptism without it; in a word it is transformed into the receiving element within which "all are immersed."

In the previous volumes will be found the evidence in proof that the translations "*in* water *unto, in order to*, repentance," "*in* water *unto, in order to*, the remission of sins" are fatally erroneous; as also, "immersion *in* the Holy Ghost *unto, in order to*, repentance and the remission of sins." The true translation in every case is that which the translator (Baptist and Disciple alike) has given in the passage under consideration, "by" with with the Dative, and "into" with the Accusative.

The translation of ἐν by, with Πνεύματι and its variations, which has been persistently refused up to the present, is at last accepted, and now comes by the handful, as we have it so translated, in a little more than half a page, no less than *five* times—ἐν Πνεύματι Θεοῦ, by the Spirit of God, ἐν Πνεύματι Ἁγίῳ by the Holy Spirit, twice ἐν τῷ αὐτῷ Πνεύματι by the same Spirit, ἐν ἑνὶ Πνεύματι by one Spirit.

This translation, reached in the responsible task of translating the Scriptures by two branches of the Baptist body, five times on one page, should arrest hard speeches against others when they venture to translate ἐν "by," especially when they translate ἐν Πνεύματι, ἐν Πνεύματι Ἁγίῳ by the Spirit, by the Holy Spirit, and yet more especially in connection with baptism, as so fully indicated in the passage before us. Also, while we have before us so encouraging an example in εἰς ἓν σῶμα *into one body*, we might be held scathless for translating εἰς μετάνοιαν *into* repentance, and εἰς ἄφεσιν ἁμαρτιῶν *into* the remission of sins. And with the conjoined translation "*by* one Spirit *into* one body," we may enter a plea for gentle dealing with our "*by* water (symbolly) *into* repentance," "*by* the Holy Ghost (really) *into* repentance," "*by* water (symbolly) *into* the remission of sins," "*by* the Holy Ghost (really) *into* the remission of sins."

While we accept with great pleasure the change of "in" for *by;* and of "unto," "in order to," for INTO; we must decline accepting the old "immerse." We do so for these reasons: 1. It violates the theory which says, "βαπτίζω means dip and nothing but dip." Immerse does not mean *to dip*. No word can by any possibility mean distinctively *to immerse* and also mean distinctively *to dip*, because these words do not belong to the same class; the one makes demand for condition to be effected in any way and without limitation as to the time of its continuance, the other makes demand for an act definite in character and limited in duration. 2. A burden is laid upon the word too heavy for it to bear. The theory cannot get along without a dipping. It must have a dipping into water (a putting in and taking out) necessarily limited as to duration; but none of these elements are found in βαπτίζω, and to force it to such duty is not to extract from it such meaning, but to commit word-murder. But a dipping is not all that the theory needs. It needs just as much the right opposite. There is a " baptism into repentance." But to say that Christianity inculcates a *dipping* " into repentance " is to utter lukewarm nonsense which the Author of Christianity will " spew out of his mouth." The same is true of a *dipping* " into the remission of sins," a *dipping* " into Christ," a *dipping* " into the name of the Father, and of the Son, and of the Holy Ghost," and (as in the passage before us) a *dipping* " by the Holy Spirit into one body." The theory will find that " a dipping " is one of those sorry auxiliaries which to keep or to dismiss is alike ruinous. 3. This word, immerse, has no usage correspondent with and therefore no power to express the characteristic usage of the Greek word in the New Testament. It is admitted, that in the baptism of the Apostles at Pentecost by the Holy Ghost there was no dipping, or immersing, or covering, or anything like the one or the other; but the baptism consisted in " being subjected to a controlling influence and imbued with its virtue." Now, where is the single instance in all English literature in which " immerse " means " to be subject to an influence so as to be imbued with its virtue "? To say that I know of no such case is to say but little; but who will supplement my lack of knowledge? If the Pentecost usage stood alone the defect would be of comparatively small consequence; but this is only a representative case of that which prevails through all the New Testament. A baptism into repentance is " a subjection to influence and imbuing with virtue;" a baptism into the remission of sins is " a subjection to influence and imbuing with virtue;" a baptism into Christ is " a subjection to influence and imbuing with virtue;" a baptism into one body is " a subjection to influence and imbuing with virtue;" a baptism into water (if such a thing could be found in the New Testament, which happily or unhappily cannot be) would be " a subjection to its influence and imbuing (the lungs at least) with its virtue;" but the theory escapes such a baptism, while insisting upon it, by the substitution of a dipping. 4. Any such use of *the foreign* immerse is precluded by the older indigenous words, *drench*, *soak*, *steep*, etc., which enter into that usage. 5. Another remark, not so important yet pertinent as showing that " immerse " does not measure the Greek word, is this: In English immerse is rarely, if ever, used with the preposition *into*, while this is emphatically the New Testament usage of βαπτίζω. *Immersed in* does not differ from " baptized into " merely in failing to extract and to communicate quality to its object, as does the latter, but it farther differs, in failing to express complete as well as thorough change of condition. To be immersed in business, in pleasure, in study, does not imply, that one has not been before a man of business, or pleasure, or study, but gives emphasis to their prosecution. But it is not so with "baptized into repent- ance," "into the remission of sins," "into Christ;" these phrases imply, that one has not been before in a state of repentance, or of remission, or relation to Christ, but passes *out of* a contrary state *into* these wholly new conditions.

For these, among other reasons, we reject *immerse* as the rep- resentative of βάπτιζω, and, also, immerse *in* as the representative of baptized *into*. We will adhere to the conceded Pentecost meaning for the Greek word, and will add to it the concession, that in baptism ἐν is indicative of the agency *by which* it is effected, and that εἰς points out the receiving element *into which* the baptized object (suggestively) passes. This, I believe, is about all that we need by way of concession on the part of the friends of the theory to secure (in good time) their utter aban- donment of it.

Interpretation.

Dr. Charles Hodge, of Princeton (Comm. *in loc.*), says: "To be baptized ἐν Πνεύματι cannot mean to be immersed in the Spirit any more than to be immersed ὕδατι, Luke 3 : 16, Acts 1 : 5, can by possibility mean to be immersed in water." This judgment of Dr. Hodge as to the force of the nude Dative is sustained by the general judgment of scholars.

Dr. Pusey (On Baptism, p. 166) says: "To the Galatians St. Paul inculcated their actual unity as derived from having been baptized into one Christ; so here again, to the Corinthians from their having been baptized in One Spirit; thereby showing that to be baptized into Christ is to be baptized in the One Spirit; and neither is the baptism of Christ without the Spirit, nor is there a baptism of the Spirit without the baptism instituted by Christ."

Dr. Pusey has as good ground for saying that the passage under consideration teaches a baptism "*in* One Spirit" as the friends of the theory have for saying that Matt. 3 : 11 or Acts 1 : 5 teaches a baptism "*in* the Spirit." There is no foundation for either statement. There is no " baptism *in the* SPIRIT" known to the New Testament. A baptism *in* the Spirit can by no rational possibility be the same or the equivalent of a "baptism *into* CHRIST." John the Forerunner (John 1 : 29–31) says, that baptism by water was divinely appointed in order that "JESUS, *as the Lamb of God that taketh away the sin of the world*, should be made manifest." Now a baptism into Christ, as an atoning redeemer (= "making subject to his influence and imbuing with his virtue") can have no other issue than "the remission of sins;" but a "baptism in the Spirit," who is *not* an atoning Redeemer, can by no possibility issue in "the remission of sins." Baptism into Christ and baptism in the Spirit must then, of necessity, be two essentially diverse baptisms. But there is only "one baptism" which is distinctive of Christianity, and that is *baptism into* CHRIST, the Lamb of God, the Crucified of Calvary ; therefore, baptism in the Spirit (if there were any such thing) could not be Christian baptism. But there is no such thing known to the word of God as "baptism in the Spirit;" it is purely a human invention, as also is the idea of a "baptism *in* water."

The true and sole relation of the Holy Spirit to Christian baptism is that of executive Agent. Thus Dr. Pusey subsequently, though not consistently, says: "For in baptism the Spirit is the Agent. It is not any outward or visible incorporation into any mere visible body (since for a mere visible union there needed not an Invisible Agent), but an invisible ingrafting into Christ, by the invisible working of the Spirit. What St. Chrysostom says is this: 'That which caused us to be one body, and regenerated us, is One Spirit: for the one was not baptized by the One Spirit, the other by another; and not only was that which baptized us One, but that also into which He baptized was One.'" Now, all this as said and quoted by Dr. Pusey is true to the letter. If there was any ritual water in his mind (there is none in his words, there is none in the Scriptures) when he speaks of "baptism," it is a foreign element of which he must dispose himself, we have no concern with it, and he should have none according to his own reasoning, for as "an Invisible Agent is not needed to incorporate in the visible church," so a visible element is not needed to incorporate in the invisible church.

Professor Ripley.

Professor Ripley (Christian Baptism, p. 52) says on this passage: "The same Spirit has baptized us all, so that we have all been made members of the same body; that is, *we have all most copiously participated* in the same Spirit's *influences;* an idea *very naturally flowing* from the *radical* meaning of Βαπτίζω." In a note he adds : " In such passages, reference is made to the *abundant* communications of the Spirit; an idea *very happily conveyed* by the use of the word *baptize.* The *manner* of the communication is not regarded ; only the *copiousness.* Hence, so far as the *administration* is concerned, no argument can be drawn against immersion as being the only baptism, from the fact that the Spirit is elsewhere said to be *poured out.*"

These statements recognize : 1. The Spirit as THE AGENT in baptism. Then, the baptism is spiritual. Then, the Spirit is not *a receiving element in which* men are baptized ; 2. "All are baptized by the Spirit." Then, if all at Corinth, so, all everywhere, in all ages (who are of the body of Christ) are baptized " by the Spirit." Then, the notion of such friends of the theory as limit baptism by the Spirit to such extraordinary occasions as Pentecost, is foundationless ; 3. The result of baptism by the Spirit is membership in the invisible church—"so, all are made members of the same body." Then, in the real church of Christ "all" are received into membership by *baptism*, without one being "immersed." These statements claim, 1. That baptism by the Spirit imports "a copious participation in the Spirit's influences." This is a mistake. Baptism has no necessary relation to copiousness. Its relation is, as already stated, to *power*, competency to produce an effect. Copiousness may be associated with baptism, yet never proceeding from the fact of a baptism, but from outside causes, as the "pouring out" of the Spirit. 2. "Copious participation is happily conveyed by *baptize*." Baptize does not involve, by its own force, "participation" in influence in any measure. A flint rock cast into the sea is baptized ; but, as a mass, it participates neither in the wetness, nor in the saltness of sea-water. If the whole Mediterranean had been poured through the pitchers of Elijah upon the altar on Mount Carmel there would have been a wonderful copiousness but no baptism according to the theory. A *certain class* of bodies when enveloped by a fluid are penetrated and pervaded and so assimilated to the quality which may be characteristic of the encompassing fluid. This is a result which is due, not to copiousness, but to the power of the liquid to bring the object subjected to its influence under the control of its characteristic. This effect produced on a certain class of bodies becomes the basis of a secondary use of *baptize* in which suchl'ke effect, *however induced*, is called a baptism. It is this usage which is illustrated at Pentecost and throughout the New Testament in which, without exception, baptism contemplates EFFECT *without covering.* The four water pitchers emptied by Elijah on Carmel's altar had no relation by copiousness to the baptism, one would have sufficed for that; but the thrice four pourings were necessary to extinguish all suspicion that "fire had been put under" the sacrifice. The copious outpouring of the Spirit at Pentecost had no special relation to the baptism that day effected, but to the promise—" It shall come to pass in the last days that I will pour out my Spirit on all flesh," which promise is declarative of profusion not in one case, but relatively, throughout the entire Christian dispensation as compared with those which had preceded it. Power not quantity is the essential element in Christian baptism and in every kindred baptism.

3. " The manner (pouring out) of the communication is to be disregarded." If Professor Ripley means, that we are to disregard this language as proof that there was, in fact, a pouring out, we assent. If he means, that we are to disregard this language as proof that *to pour* is the meaning of Βαπτίζω, we assent. If he means, that we are to disregard this language as proof that *pouring upon* is a just means and of divine authority for effecting a true baptism without covering, then we say, this is "kicking against the pricks." And, as words cannot make the case plainer, we must patiently wait until the deep shadow of the theory shall have passed away and the mental eclipse which it has occasioned shall have terminated. Then it will be found that *pouring upon* does baptize.

4. " No argument against immersion as the only mode." That is to say: a baptism declared to be effected by " pouring out," is of no consequence! And a baptism in which there is, confessedly, "no immersion nor anything like it," does not disprove " immersion is the ONLY mode " (!) These are just the persons to " send the Angel Gabriel to school."

The Baptizer.

It is admitted on all hands, that the executive Agent in this baptism is the Holy Spirit. How does this settled point bear on the unsettled relation of the Holy Spirit to other baptisms? We say, that there is essentially but " one baptism " pertaining to Christianity (which is stated with verbal differences but exhibits one truth), and that the uniform relation of the Holy Spirit to this baptism is that of executive Agent. In support of this position it may be said: 1. That it is unreasonable to suppose that the Holy Spirit would occupy two relations to baptism so alien from each other as that of executive Agent and a receiving medium. 2. The quiescence of a receiving medium is inconsistent with the ceaseless activity ascribed to the Holy Spirit in the office of redemption. 3. It is inconsistent with the " one baptism " of Christianity that there should be a baptism in the Holy Spirit and a baptism " into Christ." 4. It is inconsistent with a two-fold relation to baptism that the same phraseology which is admitted to teach executive Agency, should be used to describe the relation in those cases where agency is denied and receptive medium is affirmed. 5. The interpretation of ἐν Πνεύματι, ἐν Πνεύματι Ἁγίῳ, as expressive of agency, harmonizes with other facts and teaching of Scripture. It is in harmony with the declaration of John that Christ should be the Baptizer. He and the Holy Spirit are not announced as two independent Baptizers, but as most intimately united. John proclaims the coming One as "ὁ βαπτίζων ἐν Πνεύματι Ἁγίῳ the Baptizer (who is) in the Holy Spirit," and, therefore, baptizes under the influence of = by the Holy Spirit. The facts at Pentecost are harmonious with this view. That baptism is ascribed both to Christ and to the Holy Spirit. It is a divine interpretation of ὁ βαπτίζων ἐν πνεύματι Ἁγίῳ. The Holy Spirit is the Agent in that baptism, proceeding from Christ, and is the farthest possible removed from a quiescent receptive medium. This relation of Christ and the Holy Ghost, developed in baptism, is in harmony with all other Scripture representations of this relation. The Baptist Version (Luke 4 : 1) says: "Jesus being full of the Holy Spirit . . . was led (ἐν τῷ Πνεύματι) in the Spirit;" v. 14, " Jesus returned (ἐν τῇ δυνάμει τοῦ Πνεύματος) in the power of the Spirit;" 10 : 21, " He rejoiced (ἐν τῷ Πνεύματι τῷ Ἁγίῳ, Cod. Sin., Tisch.) in the Holy Spirit." " Jesus exulted in the Holy Spirit" (Syriac, Murdock). If in the phrase ἠγαλλιάσατο ἐν τῷ Πνεύματι τῷ Ἁγίῳ the state and influence under which he that rejoices is indicated by ἐν τῷ Πνεύματι τῷ Ἁγίῳ, why in the phrase βαπτίσει ἐν Πνεύματι Ἁγίῳ does not the state and influence under which he who baptizes, find indication in ἐν Πνεύματι Ἁγίῳ? David (Bapt. Version, Mark 12 : 36) speaks, being " in the Holy Spirit." Why does not David's Lord baptize, being " in the Holy Spirit?" Simeon (Bapt. Version, Luke 2 : 27), " came ἐν

Πνεύματι, *by* the Spirit into the temple;" Jesus (Luke 4:1), *ἐν Πνεύματι*, *in* the Spirit "was led into the wilderness." The state of both was the same. 6. This interpretation is in harmony with the classical use of the Dative to designate the agency in baptism. It also shuns the discordant application of *ἐν* in baptism, now to indicate the agency and now to indicate the receptive element. Being limited to express the agency, it leaves *εἰς*, as exclusively, to fulfil its admitted function to point out the medium, real or ideal, which gives specific character to the baptism.

The Subjects of this Baptism.

The " all" who receive this baptism are not limited to membership in the church of Corinth. Paul was not a member of the church of Corinth, yet he claims a place (" *we* all ") among those " baptized into one body." The " Jew and the Gentile, the bond and the free," partake of this baptism not because they are members of the church at Corinth, but because they " drink of the same spirit " with them. The Galatians were partakers of this same baptism (3: 27, 28) not surely because they were members of the church of Corinth, nor yet because they were members of the church of Galatia, but because they were members of the " one body " by baptism into Christ, "in whom (v. 28) there is neither Jew nor Greek ; in whom there is neither bond nor free; in whom there is neither male nor female ; for ye are ALL *one* in Christ Jesus." That this "all" embraces every believer in Christ, of every place and in every age, is farther proved by the prayer of " the Head of the Church, which is his body " (John 17 : 21). " Neither pray I for these alone, but for them also which shall believe on me through their word; that they ALL *may be one; as* thou Father art in me and I in thee, that they also may be one in us ; that THE WORLD may believe that thou hast sent me." They who believe that the unity prayed for by Christ is the unity effected by the Holy Spirit, will also believe that the "all" includes every believer in Christ among all the generations of men throughout all the ages of time. And if this be true, then the prophecy of Joel (2 : 28) of the " pouring out of the Spirit, in the last days, upon all flesh" did not contemplate an occasional, rare, and transitory transaction, nor did the prophecy of John (Matt. 3 : 11), " He shall baptize by the Holy Ghost " (a great truth taught by inspiration and (John 1 : 33) confirmed by miraculous sign), exhaust itself at Pentecost or at Cæsarea, nor did the gifts which the Redeemer (Ephes. 4 : 8) ascended on high to give unto men, fail because of profusion bestowed upon the Corinthians, but until "the last days" shall come to an end, and "all flesh" shall cease to need to be baptized by the Holy Spirit, and the Church shall no longer require gifts from on high, Jesus Christ will continue to bear the title ὁ Βαπτίζων ἐν Πνεύματι Ἁγίῳ, and its illustration will be found in the never-ceasing office work of the Holy Spirit, executive of this baptism.

The Nature of this Baptism.

1. The nature of this baptism, in general, is spiritual: (1.) Because the Agent in the baptism is the Holy Spirit, who neither effects physical baptisms, nor uses symbol baptisms, which are but the shadow of real, spiritual baptisms. (2.) Because the verbal receptive medium (εἰς ἓν σῶμα) is a spiritual body, the body of Christ, the invisible church, the members of which are "in Christ" by faith, which is the gift of God. (3.) Because there is no such thing as a physical baptism in the New Testament. There is such a baptism (in word) according to the theory; but in practice (*desinat in piscem*) it ends in a *dipping*. 2. More particularly, this baptism of "all" is a baptism ulterior to that of the *individual*. It is a unifying of the diverse members of the body by "diversities of gifts" so that "all," members one of another, shall make "one body." In some respects the baptism εἰς ἓν σῶμα, and the baptism (Galat. 3 : 27, 8) εἰς Χριστὸν, are the same or equivalent baptisms; but not in every respect. The baptism "into Christ" confronts the sinner as he "arises to go to his Father." He can only go through that baptism which "cleanses from all sin," as received by the Holy Spirit. The baptism "into one body" does not so immediately express the baptism of the sinner, as a baptism by "diversity of gifts" for "the perfecting of the saints;" as in Eph. 4 : 8. . . . "When he ascended on high and gave gifts unto men. . . . He gave some, apostles; and some, prophets; and some, evangelists; and some, pastors and teachers; for the perfecting of the saints, for the work of the ministry; for the edifying of *the body* of Christ. Till we all come in the unity of the faith . . . unto a perfect man . . . may grow up into him in all things, which is the head, even Christ, from whom *the whole body fitly joined together* and compacted by that which every joint supplieth, maketh increase of

the body unto the edifying of itself in love." This is a development of the baptism "into one body." The office of the Holy Spirit has a diverse bearing on the impenitent sinner and upon the regenerate Christian. With the one he "strives" and "convinces of sin," and when the sinner is made "subject to his power" (truly penitent) and "imbued with his virtue" (sincerely believing) he is, yes, he is hereby (through repentance and faith, the work of the Holy Spirit) baptized "into Christ" = "into the remission of sins." With the Christian the office of the Holy Spirit is "to sanctify," "leading into all truth," begetting "growth in grace and increase in knowledge," and thus, baptizing (as a perfected member) "into the one body." This twofold work and baptism of the Holy Ghost is indicated in Titus 3 : 5, 6, "He saved us by the washing of regeneration and renewing of the Holy Ghost, which (ἐξέχεεν πλουσίως) he poured out abundantly upon us through Jesus Christ our Saviour." Here is the baptism in which we find Jesus Christ and the Holy Ghost indissolubly united and co-operating; the sinner by "the washing of regeneration" baptized into Christ, and the Christian "renewed" day by day (2 Cor. 4 : 16) and perfected by baptism "into one body."

The nature of this baptism, then, is the unification of the individual members of the body of Christ, by diversity of gifts and graces, supplementary of each other, so that the whole shall form one complete body governed by one Head, moved by one Spirit, each member satisfied with his own gifts (received under the distribution made "to every man severally as He will"), and rejoicing in the complementary fulness found in the gifts conferred upon others. In a word this baptism "of all by one Spirit into one body" is the answer, through the ages, to the prayer offered up by the Head of his people on his way to Calvary—"Father! I pray that they ALL *may be* ONE."

CHRISTIC BAPTISM: BAPTISM COMMANDED TO BE PREACHED.

BAPTISM INTO THE REMISSION OF SINS THROUGH REPENTANCE AND FAITH.

CHRISTIAN BAPTISM PREACHED.

ACTS 2: 38.

Μετανοήσατε καὶ βαπτισθήτω ἕκαστος ὑμῶν, ἐπὶ τῷ ὀνόματι Ἰησοῦ Χριστοῦ εἰς ἄφεσιν ἁμαρτιῶν.

" Then said Peter unto them, Repent and be baptized, every one of you, (believing) upon the name of Jesus Christ, into the remission of sins."

THE BAPTISM OF CHRISTIANITY FIRST PREACHED.

THIS baptism cannot be John's baptism. The mission of the Forerunner has passed away. The Mightier One has come. His title " Baptizer by the Holy Ghost" (so entitled because he himself is in the Holy Ghost invested with the power of the Holy Ghost, and pours out the Holy Ghost from on high upon the souls of men, and not because he puts others in the Holy Ghost), has been vindicated by his thus baptizing the Apostles and endowing them with spiritual gifts and graces for their peculiar and most responsible office. If baptism by the Holy Ghost was simple and single in its nature, not admitting of diversity, then that nature would be determined and bounded by this baptism of the Apostles. This, however, has been proved not to be true, by the diversified baptisms which have been already considered and by their universal application to the entire membership of the body of Christ.

The baptism under consideration has peculiarities of time and relation that give it an importance which can hardly be overestimated. It is the first baptism preached under Christianity. It is preached by one down on whom the baptism from the skies has scarcely ceased to be poured. It is addressed to men in or near the temple on Mount Zion cut to the heart by convictions of sin, the work of the Holy Ghost (John 16 : 9), and crying out, " What must we do?" In answer to this cry a baptism is announced. What was this báptism? Was it Jewish baptism, a ceremonial cleansing of the body merely? Was it John's baptism, a spiritual baptism (βάπτισμα μετανοίας) in which no Holy Ghost was yet "poured out," no *crucified* Redeemer was yet revealed? Was it Christian baptism, the baptism of CHRIST, the Crucified, the Risen, the Ascended, the Pourer out of the Holy Ghost? If it be a new baptism, or if it be a fuller development of an old baptism, now, here at its first announcement, we are above all other times to look for a full and distinct statement of its peculiarities. When John preached his divinely appointed baptism (radically diverse in nature from that baptism practiced by the Jews), he at once announced that diversity in the most distinct terms. He preached a βάπτισμα μετανοίας, a βάπτισμα εἰς μετάνοιαν, a βάπτισμα μετανοίας εἰς ἄφεσιν ἁμαρτιων, language so express, and so explicit, that no one can have a good reason for failing to understand. It presented a baptism in the most direct and absolute antagonism to the prevalent Jewish baptism, which was a ceremonial purification by the agency of water. Having preached this baptism—soul repentance, preparation to receive the coming One, he announced (it is nowhere said that he preached) his commission to administer a rite in which water applied to the body should symbolize this baptism received by the soul. The Jews well understood, they could not do otherwise, both this soul baptism and its ritual symbol. This is evident from the statement of Josephus (Jud. Bapt., p. 389), that "the purification of the body would only be acceptable to God when the soul had been previously thoroughly purged by righteousness." If John was so careful to give in his first preaching (stated in briefer form afterwards) a full and explicit statement of his baptism, we may reasonably look for the same thing by Peter, when appointed by God to make announcement for the first time of the baptism of Christianity. He has done so in fact. His language is full and clear. They who first heard it had not a shadow of doubt as to its purport. We must guard against the misconception of words and phrases, and the darkling shadow from mistaken human usage. The importance of a right interpretation of this passage cannot be overestimated. To err here is to err in every after case of Christian baptism. We cannot, then, give to it too close attention. It will well repay all our labor. Let us then give to it full consideration.

Translations and various Views.

A translation which is seriously defective must necessarily beget an interpretation just as defective. The translations of this passage are not uniform. The diversity relates mainly to the prepositions ἐπί and εἰς. The common English version reads thus: "Repent and be baptized, every one of you, *in* the name of Jesus Christ, for the remission of sins."

The Baptist version was made to correct the errors of our English Bible. In the quarto form this passage is thus rendered: "Reform and be immersed, every one of you, *in* the name of Jesus Christ, *for* the remission of sins." The following is the *note* on Ἐπὶ τῷ ὀνόματι: "This indicates authority, and in such cases is well represented by our prepositions *in* or *upon*—in the name, or upon the name of the Lord be immersed, every one of you; εἰς, immediately following, intimates transition into a new state or relation, such as matrimony, citizenship, servitude, or freedom." The note given on Acts 4 : 18 contradicts both the value attached to the phrase ἐπὶ τῷ ὀνόματι and the translation given of it. The note is as follows: "Ἐπὶ τῷ ὀνόματι." Inasmuch as we have in the original Scriptures three forms of expression connected with ονομα Ιησου Χριστου, of very different import, it seems to me not merely expedient, but obligatory, that we should give to an English reader three corresponding formulæ in our language, such as "*in the name of*," "*upon the name of*," and "*into the name of*." These three formulæ are as distinct in sense as in form. The first indicates authority, viz., "*in the name of* the king or commonwealth." Then ἐπὶ τῷ ὀνόματι in Acts 2 : 38 does not (as we were told) "indicate authority," nor is the translation "*in* the name" accordant with the "sense" or with the "obligation" resting upon the translator. The note on εἰς is this: "Εἰς ἄφεσιν. We enter into contracts, states, conditions, into marriage, into servitude, into freedom, into Christ, into the church, into heaven. Εἰς and ἐν can never be substituted the one for the other. As any one *in* any state cannot enter *into* it, so he that is commanded to repent, or to reform, or to be baptized—εἰς *for, in order to,* or into any state, condition, or relation—cannot be supposed to be already in that state, condition, or relation, into which he is commanded to enter. Hence those immersed by Peter were immersed into Christ, into a relation, and into privileges not secured to them before. Εἰς, immediately following, and indicating trans

ition, not rest, like ἐν, intimates an important change, if not in
character, at least in the *state* of the proper subject of this Divine
Law or Ordinance of admission." Observe here not only the
admission, but the strong assertion (as made through all this
Inquiry) that βαπτίζω εἰς makes demand for a *thorough change of
condition* on the part of the baptized person. This demanded
condition is *travestied* when converted into a "dipping." Is entrance into marriage, into partnership, into citizenship, expressed
by *dipping* into marriage, *dipping* into partnership, *dipping* into
citizenship? Does "dipping" introduce any one into a *state?*
But the baptism of Christianity makes imperative demand for a
state expressive of a thorough change of condition, unlimited in
duration, and which can no more be expressed by a dipping than
a command to see can be expressed by a direction to close the
eyes. Observe also the statement that εἰς and ἐν, *into* and *in*,
cannot be interchanged on this subject, and their distinctive
usage must be maintained. But that is just what the theory does
not do. The distinctive use and force of these prepositions, as
exhibited in Scripture in connection with baptism, is disregarded,
and one is lawlessly made to take the place of the other. Observe
farther that the translation given of both ἐπὶ and εἰς is the right
opposite of the principles laid down ; ἐπὶ τῷ ὀνόματι is confounded
with ἐν τῷ ὀνόματι, and εἰς ἄφεσιν passing *into* a state of remission,
is confounded with doing something "*for*" remission, and *entrance into* marriage evaporates in *preparation for* marriage. The
final Baptist revision modifies this translation thus: "Repent,
and be each of you immersed, *upon* the name of Jesus Christ,
unto remission of sins." "Immersed" is interpreted as having
"in water" understood, and is introduced on the assumption that
Peter is preaching a ritual baptism to souls in anguish under the
convicting power of the Holy Ghost, which assumption is sustained by adding interpretatively (ἐν ὕδατι) to the words of inspiration, and thereby introducing another gospel into this divine
exposition of Christianity and the way of salvation, thus begetting
the necessity for a metamorphosis of what the Holy Spirit has
said, by changing *into* the remission of sins for "*unto* the remission of sins," in contradiction of acknowledged principles.

Professor Ripley (*in loc.*) says: "To be baptized *in the name
of Jesus Christ* is to receive baptism in token of faith in him, and
subjection to him." If the statement was "Repent and be baptized *in the Holy Ghost*," would the interpretation then be "*in*

token of faith in him, and of subjection to him?" Baptist translations and interpretations lack harmony. An interpretation (if
it were correct) of "IN *the name* of Jesus Christ" is not an interpretation of ἐπὶ τῷ ὀνόματι.

For the remission of sins. "Pardon would be bestowed on
those who should truly repent and be baptized through regard to
his authority. . . . . It should here be carefully borne in mind
that the apostle did not direct his hearers merely *to be baptized*
in order to receive the forgiveness of their sins; but he directed
them *to repent* and *be baptized.* Baptism without repentance
would be of no avail, and sincere repentance would be" (*of no avail
without* BAPTISM; we would expect to follow from their co-ordina-
tion, but Prof. Ripley does not say so, but) "would be necessarily, from its very nature, accompanied with a spirit of obedience to Christ. . . . It was, therefore, to repentance and faith in
Jesus, *as manifested in baptism*, that forgiveness of sins, strictly
speaking, was promised." Prof. Ripley does not mean, I am sure,
to make ritual baptism the turning-point for the forgiveness of
sins; but what else on its face means "forgiveness of sins,
strictly speaking, is promised to repentance and faith in Jesus,
as manifested in baptism" in WATER? It is impossible to introduce a ritual baptism into this exposition of the way of salvation
to guilty sinners, pressing around the opening gates of Christianity, without blotting the gospel. All attempts at an evangelical interpretation are but vain attempts to wash out the stain.

Professor Hackett with characteristic accuracy and discretion
translates and interprets thus: "*Upon the name of Jesus Christ*
as the foundation of the baptism, *i. e.*, with an acknowledgment
of him in that act as being what his name imports, to wit, the
sinner's only hope, his Redeemer, Justifier, Lord, final Judge.
The usual formula in relation to baptism is εἰς τὸ ὄνομα. It may
have been avoided here as a matter of euphony as εἰς follows in
the next clause,—*in order to the forgiveness of sins*, we connect
naturally with both the preceding verbs. This clause states the
motive or object which should induce them to repent and be baptized. It enforces the entire exhortation, not one part of it to
the exclusion of the other."

Nothing could be said to improve the translation—"UPON *the
name of Jesus Christ*," or to make more just the general interpretation of this phrase. But the remark, that "the usual formula
in baptism" is εἰς τὸ ὄνομα, implying that ἐπὶ τῷ ὀνόματι here takes

the place of that formula, is a mistake. That formula is represented in the passage with its usual and necessary preposition εἰς ἄφεσιν ἁμαρτιων. This phrase βάπτισμα μετανοίας εἰς ἄφεσιν ἁμαρτιῶν expressing the baptism of John, Peter now connects with the baptism of Christianity. This phraseology of Peter is (as will be seen hereafter) the equivalent for εἰς Ἰησοῦν Χριστὸν. Nor does Professor Hackett, with all his eminent evangelical feeling, find a remedy against ritual baptism when introduced into the terms of salvation. Relief is sought by connecting "forgiveness of sins" with "both verbs," i. e., *Repent and baptize.* But the remedy does not master the disease. Without raising the question as to a necessity (beyond theological) for this double connection, still it remains true, that repentance and baptism *in water* are made co-ordinate terms of salvation. And no one knows better than Professor Hackett whither such doctrine as, " It enforces the entire exhortation, not one part of it " (repent), " to the exclusion of the other " (be baptized *in water*), IN ORDER TO *the forgiveness of sins,* has led and must ever tend to lead.

Alexander Campbell.

Alexander Campbell (President of Bethany College), and his large following are an illustration of the sure, if not logical, sequence to the incorporation of a ritual baptism in the terms of salvation. This man of unusual ability and of wide influence accepted the "unto" of the Baptist critical version, and the "for" of the revised version, and the "in order to" of Professor Hackett, and, refusing to allow their force to be annulled or diluted by more remote theological considerations, declared his faith in water baptism as *designed for* the remission of sins, and operating as a condition *in order to* their remission, on the same level with repentance and faith, and as truly a cause of the remission of sins ("though not in the same sense") as the atoning blood of Christ.

He declares that " the design " of baptism in water is the transcendent question which out-tops the question " Who should baptize?" or " Who should be baptized?" or " What is the *action* in baptism?" He seeks by many quotations to prove the force of " for ;" and declares, that any one who shall say that in connection with the remission of sins, it has not the same meaning, " he is regardless of his reputation, and as unsafe as unworthy to be reasoned with on any question of morality." "John and the Apostles clearly affirm a connection between baptism" (in water?) "and the remission of sins—must it not follow that the *only divinely instituted baptism*" (in water) "*is* FOR *the remission of sins?*"

Rev. ISAAC ERRETT, who ably expounds (with evangelical sympathies) Alexander Campbell's views, says : " Peter told them what to do *to be forgiven:* 1. To repent; 2. To be baptized. The promise of remission of sins was not theirs until they repented *and were baptized.* Although baptism cannot *procure* forgiveness, as the death of Christ procured it, it is nevertheless '*for* the remission of sins.' . . . How dare any man keep back this part (baptism) of the counsel of God, stopping with repentance and faith?" If it were a part of my faith (as it is of Baptists), that " *immersion in water* " was incorporated by Peter with repentance, and faith in Jesus Christ, *in order to, unto, for,* "the remission of sins," I should expect such faith to be derisively flung in my face whenever I did battle against " Campbellism "—and what to answer I should not know.

Dr. Pusey.

There is another aspect in which this error, incorporating a ritual baptism with the ground elements of salvation, works itself out. Dr. Pusey (Holy Baptism, p. 170), says: " If men would observe all the indications in Acts, they would find a stress laid upon Baptism which would surprise them, and thereby evince that there was something faulty in their previous notions. . . . Baptism is not urged upon converts as a proof of sincerity, or a test of faith, but for its own benefits, in and for itself. Let any one think what would have been his answer to the multitude who pricked in heart asked Peter and the rest, ' Men and brethren, what shall we do ?' I doubt that their answer would *not* have been, ' Repent and be *baptized*, every one of you, in the Name of Jesus Christ, for the remission of sins.' I cannot but think that very many of us would have omitted all mention of Baptism, and insisted prominently on some other portion of the Gospel message. Such was the first conversion. . . . It was by Baptism that the disciples enlarged their Lord's church. It was by Baptism that men were saved."

The views of Dr. Pusey and Alexander Campbell differ very materially in their specialties; but they agree, in being rooted in a common error in supposing that a ritual baptism is here spoken of. They differ, also, very materially as to what enters into a ritual baptism and the details which follow its administration. Both, however, believe that it lies imbedded in the fundamentals of our religion and that its physical administration is accompanied with singular spiritual effects.

And now, of how much practical value is it to determine whether the specialty of Alexander Campbell or that of Dr. Pusey be the more true, so long as both systems have a common root? The worth or worthlessness of a tree does not depend on its trunk or its branch, but on its root. As is the root so will be the fruit. If the nature of the fruit be deadly, what matters its color or its form? If Peter, on this momentous occasion, announces repentance and faith as the web, and ritual baptism as the woof of Christianity, then, both these systems are legitimate issues, and they or others like them will be, must be, and ought to be, the result. Then, the question for us to determine is not, the comparative merits or demerits of these or related systems, but this—Has Peter here announced a *ritual* baptism which stands intermediate between Repentance toward God on the one hand and Faith in Jesus Christ on the other hand as a coequal ground cause with them, or beyond them, *for the remission of sin* and *the salvation of the soul?* If a rite be there at all, the time, the circumstances, and the language, unite to say: It cannot be there in any other position than as a fundamental element in the redemption of Christianity. To this point, then, let us give attention.

The True Translation.

The only translation which can be vindicated by general usage or by the particular usage of the New Testament is this: "Repent and be baptized—every one of you—(believing) UPON the name of Jesus Christ—INTO the remission of sins."

This translation is sustained by the fact that every word has its normal, primary value; and by the further fact that the relation in which any questionable word stands makes special demand for such meaning. The translation of *baptized* by "immersed" is declined: 1. Because it is, by its friends, confessed to be inadequate to follow the usage of the Greek word; 2. Because in physics, where its introduction would find the best apology, the mersion of the baptized object is without limitation of time, and as the same word cannot be used to express a sharp limitation of time and time without limit, it is impossible for this Greek word or any just representative to express the dipping of men and women into water, if there were any such thing belonging to Christianity; 3. The distinctive usage of *baptize* in the New Testament is to give thorough development to an ideal element over its object, for which use " immerse " has no counterpart. In particular, such is the usage of "baptized" in the passage under consideration, and therefore *immersed* must be rejected.

The translation of ἐπὶ *upon* has, in general, a universal sanction. Professor Harrison (Greek Prepositions, p. 266) gives "on, upon" as the primary meaning, with six " figurative " meanings growing out of it, among which (with the Dative, as here) is " *upon* (ground, reason)." There is a special " reason " in New Testament use with " Jesus Christ," because he is represented as a " rock " *upon* which the Church is built; also " upon " whom the troubled soul may rest, as in Acts 16 : 30, " What must I do to be saved?   Believe (ἐπὶ) *upon* the Lord Jesus Christ and thou shalt be saved." Could anguished feeling and the cry bursting out from it, be more identical than that of the Jailor at Philippi and that of the three thousand at Jerusalem?   Unless Peter preached another gospel from that preached by Paul, ἐπὶ in his mouth has the same value as in the mouth of his fellow-Apostle.   But both preached as their Lord commanded, Luke 24 : 47, " Repentance and remission of sins should be preached (ἐπὶ) UPON *his name* among all nations."   There is yet another reason why " upon " should be carved deep, just then, in Jesus Christ.   He is at Pentecost for the first time revealed as a crucified Redeemer, and proclaimed as the Corner-stone, elect, precious, the sure Foundation-stone, " upon " which the guilty and the perishing of Jerusalem and of all lands and of all ages must build their hopes for the forgiveness of sins and everlasting redemption.   No chisel has yet been tempered in the fire adequate to erase from the rock of God's truth that divine lettering—" UPON *the name of* JESUS CHRIST."   This and this only is the new element that enters into Peter's preaching.   It had no place in the preaching of John.   He did preach repentance.   He did preach remission of sins through repentance. He did announce Jesus as " the Lamb of God that taketh away the sin of the world."   But that John, himself, had any clear knowledge of Calvary and its Cross there is no evidence. That he did not preach a crucified Redeemer is absolutely certain. Yet it is just as certain that the Repentance and the Remission of sins preached by John rests, both for their existence and their worth, on the yet unrevealed Cross. It was for Peter to announce that uncovered Cross, and bid the guilty lay their sins upon the Guiltless One. This he does, not by preaching repentance merely, nor by announcing the remission of sins merely, but by declaring that in their exercise of repentance and in their reception of remission they must rest only and wholly *upon* JESUS CHRIST. Thus is laid across the threshold of the opening door of the Christian dispensation that "foundation other than which no man can lay, which is JESUS CHRIST." (1 Cor. 3 : 11.) To build "upon" this foundation faith in the foundation is essential. Therefore *believing* is necessarily involved in ἐπὶ, and is supplied in the translation given.

The translation of εἰς by *into* needs, in itself, no vindication; but as against other meanings admitted to belong to this word, it does. Professor Harrison (p. 210) says : "The proper signification of εἰς is *within, in,* with the idea of the being within a space having boundaries. The other seemingly derivative meanings, as *for,* etc., are really due to the Accusative case with which the preposition is conjoined, or to the character of the action which it qualifies."

The only meaning which is offered in opposition to "into" is *for, unto, in order to,* derived from the *telic* use of the preposition. To what is this *telic* use due ? It must be to "Repent" or "Baptized" considered independently or jointly. "Repent" might (theologically) have "*for* (εἰς) the remission of sins," as its expressed subordinate end; but I know of no such grammatical construction as μετανοήσατε εἰς ἄφεσιν ἁμαρτιῶν, nor of any such bald appeal as "Repent *for* the remission of sins." The Scripture does not place repentance in immediate relation with remission, but with difficulties to be taken up out of the way, upon which being done, remission of sins, from Christ, flows in upon the soul. John preached "Repent!" *to prepare the way of the Lord,* the Lamb of God that taketh away sin. But it is impossible for εἰς to reach over "baptized" and receive a *telic* character from "Repent" exclusively. It is as impossible to ground such idea in "baptized" exclusively. There is no basis for it either in the language or the doctrine of Scripture. No such statement as "immersed *in water* for the remission of sins" can be found; and no such appendage

can be attached to the word "baptized" without assuming the right to "add to the words" which the Holy Ghost teacheth. John says, "I baptize ἐν ὕδατι εἰς μετάνοιαν," but no one ventures to say that this is *for* securing "repentance;" the hesitancy to do so is not, however, for any grammatical or theological reasons, but because the exposure of the error by continued impenitence after "dipping in water" is too patent. If the issue of remitted sin by ritual water were as open to inspection as penitence or impenitence is, we would hear as little of εἰς ἄφεσιν ἁμαρτιῶν being "*for* the remission of sins" as of ἐις μετάνοιαν being "*for* repentance." Whenever facts can be adduced in proof that *dipping in water* issues in effecting "godly sorrow for sin," then we will cease to object to "the remission of sins" being made *telic* of baptized *in water*.

This preposition cannot receive a *telic* character from the two verbs conjointly. The conjunction of "Repent" and "dipped in water" to a common end, viz., εἰς ἄφεσιν ἁμαρτιῶν, puts both on the same level and precludes a discrimination as to essential efficiency "for" that end. But it has been shown that "dipping in water" has no Scriptural recognition as having any causative power "for" the remission of sin; it cannot, then, be lawfully conjoined with Repentance "for" such a result, nor if unlawfully conjoined can it receive any power to aid in such result. Finally, this preposition cannot have the character attributed to it, because it has grammatical relations which require its service in its primary meaning and thus excludes every other. The indication of this position will require us to enter upon the general interpretation of the passage.

The Interpretation.

Repent. Repentance occupies a well-defined position, and has a determined value in the Christian system.

1. *Repentance is the gift of God:* 2. Tim. 2:25, "If God peradventure will *give them repentance;*" Acts 5:31, "Him hath God exalted with his right hand to be a Prince and a Saviour, *to give repentance* to Israel and remission of sins."

2. *Repentance is essential to salvation:* Luke 13:5, "*Except ye repent* ye shall all likewise perish;" 2 Cor. 7:10, "Godly sorrow worketh *repentance to salvation.*"

3. *Repentance is the proximate cause of the remission of sins:* Luke 24:47, "It was necessary that Christ suffer, and that *re-*

pentance and remission of sins be preached upon (ἐπί) his name;" Acts 5:31, "Jesus, whom ye slew and hanged on a tree, him hath God exalted . . . to give *repentance and the remission of sins;*" Acts 3:19, "*Repent* therefore and turn, *that your sins may be blotted out.*"

4. *Repentance is itself a baptism:* Matt. 3:11, "I baptize you" (symbolly) "with water" (εἰς μετάνοιαν) "into repentance." This implies that John had preached a baptism into repentance to be received in reality by the soul. It is also involved in what he says immediately after, "But he shall baptize you by the Holy Ghost" (into repentance). Inasmuch as Repentance is a thorough change in the condition of the soul exercising a controlling influence over the life, it cannot but be a baptism of the soul. And a βάπτισμα εἰς μετάνοιαν is the obvious expression for the preaching of John.

5. *Repentance also effects a baptism:* John (Luke 1:77) was commissioned "to give *knowledge of salvation* to the people of the Lord *by the remission of their sins.*" This knowledge he gave by preaching a baptism "into repentance" (εἰς μετάνοιαν), a "baptism of repentance" (βάπτισμα μετανοίας), and a "baptism of repentance into the remission of sins" (βάπτισμα μετανοίας εἰς ἄφεσιν ἁμαρτιῶν). These statements form as plain a statement as can be put into words, that repentance (which is the work of the Holy Ghost) is causative of a "baptism into the remission of sins." And this is only another form of stating the relation between repentance and the remission of sins to be found everywhere in the Scriptures, as in passages above quoted: "*Repent* and turn, *that your sins may be blotted out*"—"That repentance and remission of sins" (as its consequence) "be preached"— "Exalted to give *repentance and the remission of sins,*" in the relation (subordinate) of cause and effect.

Baptized. "Repent and be baptized:" In the last statement we see the reason for the conjunction of these two terms as well as the nature and purport of their relation. Repentance and the remission of sins are, in the gracious system of the Gospel, indissolubly connected. Repentance cannot exist for a moment without the remission of sins any more than the lightning flash without the thunder peal. To be repentant is "to be baptized into the remission of sins." The Holy Ghost who gives repentance does, therewith, confer baptism, εἰς ἄφεσιν ἁμαρτιῶν. Therefore Peter preaches, "Repent and (as its inseparable accompani ment) be baptized *into the remission of sins*." There is no ellipsis to be supplied to make out the import of "baptized." The occasion is too momentous for enigmatic speech. The way of salvation for souls "cut to the heart" cannot be left for human supplement. Therefore the *sine qua non* condition, "Repent!" is made to ring upon the ear; therefore, its inseparable and cheering accompaniment, "and" (thereby) "be baptized into the remission of sins" is fully stated. There is no place for the *telic* use of εἰς. Its service is demanded in its primary signification. And its power is exhausted in bearing the penitent sinner out of a state of guilt *into* a new state of remission. The phraseology, "Repent and be baptized into the remission of sins" is, in sentiment, nothing else than, *Repent and be forgiven;* but the sentiment is intensified by the form of expression, which teaches us, that as an object put into a fluid having some marked characteristic and remaining there is penetrated, pervaded, and imbued through every pore with such characteristic, thoroughly changing its former condition, so, a guilty soul is by repentance brought into a new state or condition, the characteristic of which ("the remission of sins") penetrates and pervades the soul in every part, subjecting it to its sweet influence.

That the construction "Repent and be baptized" does not indicate two things independent of each other (as repent and *be immersed in water*), but have the gracious relation of cause and effect, is shown by the parallel construction in Acts 3:19, "Repent and be converted (turn), that your sins may be blotted out (to the blotting out of your sins)." No one will say, that "Repent" and "be converted" (turn) represent two independent acts, or will deny, that the latter is embraced in and proceeds from the former, as an effect is embraced in and proceeds from its cause. No man ever repented of sin with godly sorrow without turning from it; and no man ever turned from sin as required by Scripture, without being penitent, and being moved thereunto by repentance. These two passages serve not merely to illustrate this construction, but, no less, the baptism. The statement, "Repent and be baptized into the remission of sins," is reflected both in sentiment and in power (with difference of form) by that other statement (both made by the same speaker), "Repent to the blotting out of your sins" (εἰς τὸ ἐξαλειφθῆναι) "obliterated from the book or tablet where they are recorded" (Hackett). This figure of "blotting out" has a power of expression not less (of its kind) than "baptizing into," and both are used for the same purpose, namely, to express in the strongest manner that language will allow, absolute forgiveness to the repenting sinner. If one seeking admission into the church should be required to make out a list of his sins, and then the admission should be consummated by "blotting them out" by turning the ink-bottle over them, and no one be allowed to come to the communion table without this, the error would not be so great, nor the perversion of the figure so absolute, as in receiving a man into the church by dipping him into water, and excluding others because such blotting out would be conformable to the letter of the figure, while the conversion of a "baptism" into a *dipping* is an utter abandonment of the letter and of the spirit.

The *telic* use of εἰς in the phrases βαπτίζειν εἰς τὴν θάλασσαν, εἰς ἄφεσιν ἁμαρτιῶν, is unnatural, if not impossible, by reason of the essential nature both of the verb and the preposition. It is contradictory to universal Classic usage. It is as incongruous as to say, the ship entered *unto, in order to, for* the sea; or, the tiger penetrated *unto, in order to, for* the jungle. To enter, to penetrate, requires something *into* which entrance or penetration shall be effected. In the phrase, "The horse entered *for* the cup," there is an ellipsis, *into the race,* for the cup. In the phrase, Be baptized εἰς ἄφεσιν there can be no rational ellipsis, because "baptized *into* remission" meets the demand naturally and exhaustively both of verb and preposition; it gives a true meaning harmonious with all the teaching of Scripture. If, however, an ellipsis should be insisted upon, it must be such as expresses that *into which* the object of the verb passes. No ellipsis will meet the case in which *in* appears as a substitute for "into." "He *entered* the house" has not the force of the verb expressed by "He entered *in* the house." That form says nothing of the power of the verb; it only declares position after the action of the verb has terminated; it leaves *into* still to be supplied—"He entered *into,* and so was *in* the house." The ellipsis, therefore, cannot here be ἐν ὕδατι—"Be baptized (*in* water) *for* the remission of sins"—because the force of the verb, as applied to an object in one condition, and to be brought out of such condition into a diverse condition, has no expression in ἐν, which is expressive simply of *rest.* Such phrase can only mean, an object being "*in* water" was baptized *into* something else, or an object having been baptized into something else is left "*in* water." It is a philological impossibility for βαπτίζω ἐν ὕδατι to express the power of the verb as demanding the transference of its object out of one state into another state. But the *alpha* and the *omega* of the demand of Scripture baptism is, that the sinner *shall pass* OUT OF *a state of impenitence* INTO *a state of penitence, out of* a condition of guilt *into* a condition of remission. To express this thought βαπτίζω is used, and in its use the nature of the verb is carefully met by εἰς, and the nature of the resultant condition is explicitly stated by the regimen of the preposition—βαπτίζω ἐν ὕδατι εἰς μετανοίαν. We are thus guarded by divine wisdom (both by philology and grammatical law) against the error which should attribute to ἐν ὕδατι the office of expressing the demand of the verb to the displacement of εἰς μετανοίαν. To guard against a farther error, which would give to ἐν ὕδατι a power (where assigned to its own sphere of symbol agency) which did not belong to it, John is taught by the Holy Ghost to say, instructively and warningly, "*I* baptize *into* repentance, ἐν ὕδατι; this is all that I can do, but there cometh one after me mightier than I, he shall baptize *into* repentance, ἐν Πνεύματι Ἁγίῳ." In view of such express statement, and such explicit instruction, might not the Author of inspiration well ask, "What more could I have done for the true interpretation of this passage than that I have done?"

To supply by ellipsis ἐν Πνεύματι Ἁγίῳ as expressing the grammatical demand of the verb, is as objectionable as is ἐν ὕδατι; but, so far as agency (adequate to fulfil the demand of the verb carrying its object εἰς ἄφεσιν ἁμαρτιῶν) is concerned, it is not only unobjectionable, but must be supplied, except as it may be regarded as already comprehended in repentance, which is "the gift of God" and the work of the Holy Ghost, therefore properly made representative of the power which bears the soul *out of* its guilt *into* the remission of its sins.

The *telic* use of εἰς with βαπτίζω may, very confidently, be declared to have no existence, whether in the Scriptures or out of the Scriptures. The full form (expressed or understood) is that given by Clement of Alexandria (II, 1212): "'Εκ σωφροσύνης εἰς πορνείαν βαπτίζουσι, they baptize *out of* chastity *into* fornication." Who would think of translating this phrase, "They baptize out of temperance *unto, for, in order to,* fornication?" Professor Wilson, of Belfast (On Baptism, page 341) says: "The rendering of εἰς after βαπτίζω, or any of its derivatives by 'for,' as in 'I baptize εἰς μετανοίαν,' and 'Baptism of repentance εἰς ἄφεσιν ἁμαρτιῶν,' we consider wholly unauthorized. The correct translation is *into*."

'Επὶ τῷ ὀνόματι 'Ιησοῦ Χριστοῦ. *Upon the name of Jesus Christ.* Alexander Campbell (On Baptism, p. 154) says: "βαπτίζω and ἐπί so perfectly disagree as never to be found construed in amity in any Greek author, sacred or profane." This verb and preposition are not unfrequently conjoined, although the preposition does not appear as an exponent of the verb. The usage is instructive as bearing on the present passage, and therefore some examples will be presented. Judith (12:7): "ἐβαπτίζετο ἐπὶ τῆς πηγῆς baptized herself *upon* the fountain." The preposition expresses that *upon* which Judith rested when she baptized herself. Every "fountain" has "a lip," an edge, on which one can stand and be baptized. Clement of Alexandria (I, 1352) says: "It is a custom of the Jews ἐπὶ κοίτῃ βαπτίζεσθαι to be baptized *upon* a couch." The preposition points out that *upon* which the Jew rested when he received baptism; he *rested upon* a couch. Matt. 3:13. "Jesus comes from Galilee ἐπὶ τὸν 'Ιορδάνην βαπτισθῆναι." He comes from Galilee toward the Jordan, and when he reached it he *rests upon* it (every river, like every fountain, has "a lip," an edge, a bank, *upon* which one can stand) to be baptized. These examples present a physical basis on which the baptized rested. The case under consideration exhibits the moral basis upon which the soul must rest in receiving the baptism into the remission of sins. The Jew may rest upon the edge of a fountain, or upon the edge of a couch, in being baptized *out of* ceremonial impurity *into* ceremonial purity; but the soul to be baptized *out of* guilt *into* the remission of sins must rest, not upon repentance (as any meritorious or ultimate ground), but must *rest upon that* NAME, "which is the only name given under heaven whereby we must be saved," JESUS CHRIST. It was faith in the fountain's edge as able, physically, to sustain her, that led Judith to rest confidently upon it; for like reason the Jew rested confidently upon his couch as able, physically, to sustain him; and the soul believing that Jesus Christ is able, morally, to sustain all who rest upon him, does confidently accept the preaching of Peter, declaring that every penitent sinner, *resting upon* JESUS CHRIST, as an atoning Redeemer, shall thereby be baptized into the remission of sins.

This is the one exclusive doctrine of Christianity. It is the sole doctrine of salvation, more or less fully unfolded from the first page to the last page of the Bible. It is the clear and only doctrine of Peter under the severest interpretation. And any other doctrine, directing the sinner " cut to the heart " to look for a " baptism into the remission of sins " from any other source save repentance toward God and faith upon the Lord Jesus Christ, is " another " Gospel.

Alexander Campbell and Dr. Pusey are alike mistaken when they suppose that the evangelical preacher would rather turn "to some other teaching of Scripture than this " when answering the cry, " What must we do to be saved?" No Scripture is more full of condensed evangelical truth. It illuminates, as with the light of seven suns, the way of salvation. It is the light of the knowledge of the glory of God in the face of JESUS CHRIST which shines through it all. It is an inscription worthy to be written not in gold, but in the more precious blood of the Lamb, upon the posts and lintel of the doorway into the new and perfect dispensation. And any preacher who cannot preach the faithfully interpreted preaching of Peter, but will substitute for it—be dipped in water or be ritually baptized in any form, may some day understand that it would have been better for him had his tongue cleaved to the roof of his mouth than that it should ever have uttered such things.

Baptist Quarterly.

The following article on this passage appeared as an " Exegetical Study," in the Baptist Quarterly, October, 1871 :

" Βαπτισθῆτω ἐις ἄφεσιν ἁμαρτιῶν. What is the meaning and force of the preposition εἰς in connection with βαπτίζειν ? Does the *usus loquendi* of the New Testament justify or allow such a rendering as be baptized *for* or *in order to?* The proper way to determine this is to marshal all the passages in which the preposition εἰς is used in connection with *baptize.* They are not very numerous, and below will be found an example of every case in the New Testament, omitting duplicate passages for the sake of brevity." Here follows a quotation, from the common English Bible, of the following passages—Matt. 3 : 11, Matt. 28 : 19, Mark 1 : 9, Luke 3 : 2, 3, Acts 2 : 38, Rom. 6 : 3, 4, 1 Cor. 10 : 2, 1 Cor. 12 : 13, Galat. 3 : 27—with a remark, " Our English translators " (and Baptist Bible also) " have given us as a rendering of one Greek preposition, four words, *for, in, into, unto;* and so greatly obscured the Greek simplicity." The same passages are then repeated, in the same form, with the exception of the introduction of εἰς, untranslated. He then remarks, "If the correct rendering of Acts 2:38 is be baptized *in order to* remission, it will be useful to put this translation in all the passages, and see if it will make good sense." The quotations are again repeated with the substitution of *in order to.* The judgment pronounced is this: "It is obvious that nonsense is made by this translation in nearly every passage. If *in order to* be the translation of Acts 2:38 it is plainly an exception to almost every other passage; and thus we are presented with the absurd postulate that Peter on the Day of Pentecost used an expression conveying a meaning entirely different from the common *usus loquendi* of the words employed; and this, too, when he was laying down the fundamental demands of Jesus Christ for participation in the blessings of the Reign of Heaven. The conclusion, therefore, follows that IN ORDER TO is not the proper translation here. Let the reader put the word FOR in the place of IN ORDER TO, and it makes as much nonsense as the other in most of the passages given.

"But, now, suppose we translate εἰς in all these passages by the English preposition *into,* which is its nearest representative, and see what is the result. In every case it makes good sense, and gives us the key out of this doctrinal labyrinth. Peter said to the penitent Jews, on the Day of Pentecost, 'Repent, and be baptized every one of you, in the name of Jesus Christ INTO the remission of sins.' In this he gives an inspired model for all gospel preachers. We all may and must direct all truly penitent and believing souls to be baptized INTO the pardon of sins; but not *for* or *in order to* pardon.

"And now, having a word which gives us the meaning of the original Greek, let us ascertain its doctrinal value. What is the doctrinal value of being baptized INTO the forgiveness of sins? It is clear that it does not mean that these people were to receive pardon by being baptized. Look, now, at all the passages again, and see whether in any case the noun which follows the preposition εἰς refers to anything the subjects of baptism were to receive. John's converts did not receive repentance by being baptized INTO it. When John dipped penitents INTO the Jordan it was not for the purpose of swallowing a portion of the stream. When the Great Commission directs that all believers shall be baptized" (= dipped?) "INTO the name of the Triune God, it is not something they are to receive. When the Jews were baptized" (= dipped?) "INTO Moses, just as when Christians are now baptized"

(= dipped?) "INTO Christ, INTO his death, into his body, in no case does it express as the *terminus ad quem* some personal favor which the baptized receive in the act.

"So Acts 2:38 does not teach that the believing Jews should be baptized" (= dipped?) "IN ORDER TO be pardoned of their sins. Nothing, indeed, is said of their individual sins. They were to be baptized" (= dipped?) "INTO the remission of sins; and the *usus loquendi* demands that we give no more personal application to the words than in the kindred phrases, baptism" (= dipping?) "INTO repentance; INTO the name of the Father, Son, and Holy Spirit; INTO the Jordan; INTO Christ; INTO his death; INTO his body; INTO Moses in the cloud and in the sea. Therefore we conclude that Christian baptism" (= dipping?) "is INTO Christ, INTO his death, INTO his body, INTO forgiveness; but it is not IN ORDER THAT the baptized may receive any one of these.

"But this is merely *negative.* If our view be correct, it is wrong to regard this text as teaching baptism" (= dipping?) "as a condition of forgiveness. What, then, is the affirmative idea involved in the expression, 'Be baptized INTO the forgiveness of sins?' We answer: *It is a highly tropical expression, designed to set forth the teaching of baptism, its doctrinal relation to the Trinity, to Christ, to his death, to the forgiveness of sins.* When John the Baptist is said historically to have baptized his converts INTO the Jordan, *literally dipped* them into Jordan, we have the bare and literal fact. When he is said to baptize" (= dip?) "INTO repentance, we have a tropical use of the very same language. So when baptism" (= dipping?) "is said to be INTO Christ, INTO pardon, there is the tropical use of language which literally means *to dip into* a substance. To dip a child into the sea conveys to us a plain and literal image; to dip a penitent man INTO Christ, INTO his death, INTO the body, INTO the pardon of sins, is undoubtedly highly poetic and figurative language, but its tropical use ought to convey no idea radically different from its literal. It must never be forgotten that the radical idea of baptism is *a dipping into.* Hence its relations to Christ, to his death, to pardon, to his body, would naturally find expression in such expressions as baptizing" (= dipping?) "into these."—T. J. M.

This "exegetical study" is given at length, because it is desirable to know the views held by those represented by the BAPTIST QUARTERLY on this most important passage.

From this "study" we learn: 1. The *telic* use of εἰς with βαπτίζω, whether in this passage or in any other is rejected as "nonsense." Whether this is the best term to characterize the "for" of the Baptist Quarto version, or the "in order to" of Professor Hackett, in his Commentary, is doubtful. Some things are erroneous in their nature, and pernicious in their tendency, while they are not "nonsensical" in their logic. Whoever believes that Peter preached, "Repent and be immersed in or (as T. J. M. says it should be) *dipped into* WATER *for* the remission of sins" believes, I think, an error most unscriptural in its nature and most pernicious in its tendency; and if the Baptist Quarterly can prove, in addition to this, that it is "nonsense," no one need complain.

2. The "study" says, this preposition, with the verb, can only be truly translated by "into" in every passage of the New Testament. In this conclusion we cordially concur, as to every case in which the preposition originates in the verb, and has in regimen the complement of the verb. In this judgment, however, T. J. M. is against the Baptist Bible Translators generally, and against Dr. Conant in particular, as arguing against the translation of βαπτίζειν εἰς by " baptized *into* " in Matt. 28 : 19.

3. "The doctrinal value of baptized INTO the forgiveness of sins:" (1.) Negatively: "It does not mean that these people were to receive pardon by being baptized." Proof: "John's converts did not receive repentance by being baptized INTO it." "John's converts" were made by the Holy Ghost and every convert by the Holy Ghost was "baptized *into* repentance" and did so receive from that Divine Agent godly sorrow for sin. "When John dipped penitents INTO the Jordan, it was not for the purpose of swallowing a portion of the stream." No, nor did John "dip penitents INTO the Jordan" on any better authority than that of T. J. M. The phrase εἰς Ἰορδανην never occurs in connection with the "dipping," or the immersing, or the baptizing of "penitents." It occurs only in connection with the baptism of Christ, and then the preposition does not originate in βαπτίζω but in the verb of motion which brings the Saviour from Galilee. To say, that "baptism INTO repentance," "baptism INTO the remission of sins," "baptism INTO Christ," conveys nothing to the baptized, is not "nonsense," it is absurd-sense; it is a contradiction in terms. It is also an express contradiction of Scripture, which declares that "as many have been baptized INTO Christ *have put on Christ.*" It makes Peter's preaching a farce. Men charged with "taking THE CHRIST of God and by wicked hands crucify-

ing and slaying him," cut to the heart, cry out, "What must we do " to wash our hands and souls of blood. And Peter's answer, " Repent and be baptized INTO *the remission of sins*," we are told, means nothing! They receive nothing—no, not so much as " swallowing a portion of Jordan's stream." And when Alci- biades threatened to baptize Eupolis *into the sea*, did his threat mean that he was "to receive nothing," no, not so much as a mouthful of salt water, by such baptism? And when Josephus says: " Gedaliah was baptized *into insensibility*," does he mean that he " received nothing " by such baptism? And when Clem- ent speaks of men "baptized into fornication," does he mean that they " received nothing " by such baptism? And when the Holy Ghost teaches us that the end of the provision of the gospel is, that the guilty and the perishing may be baptized " *into* CHRIST," is it that they may " receive nothing" by such baptism? And when, as the consummation of all, a redeemed world shall have been baptized " into the name of the Father, and of the Son, and of the Holy Ghost," will it be that in their emptiness they may take up the cry, " We have received nothing "? The theory can no more master the language of Scripture, than a newborn babe can wield the sword of Philistia's Giant. (2.) " But this is merely *negative*. What, affirmatively, does ' Be baptized into the forgiveness of sins' teach? We answer: *It is a highly tropical expression, designed to set forth the teaching of baptism, its doc- trinal relation to the Trinity, to Christ, to his death, to the forgive- ness of sins.*"

I give the passage, as it appears, in wording, in punctuation, and in underscoring, and if as an answer to the self-proposed question, it be not the purest " nonsense " (empty and void of all sense) it is at least the truest illustration of " a stone given to the hungry for bread, and a serpent given for a fish."

4. But T. J. M. enters a plea, that while there is but an empty void out of which nothing is to be received in a dipping into Christ, and into the forgiveness of sins, through his redeeming blood, still, the language has this to commend it—" it is highly poetic and figurative " (!). Perhaps Peter was a poet. T. J. M. says, he is "highly poetic " at Pentecost. Perishing sinners crying out for redemption, are answered in " poetry and figure," out of which they can " receive nothing."

5. " It must never be forgotten that the radical idea of baptism is *a dipping into*." The doctrine in this statement is no novelty.

It was the faith of Roger Williams two hundred and fifty years ago, as shown by a treatise entitled "Dipping is Baptizing and Baptizing is Dipping," then circulated by him. In the year 1645 "A Treatise on Dipping" was issued by A. Barber, London. In 1611 Gale says: "Dipping only is Baptism." And in the same year "the venerable Booth" says: "Jehovah makes use of a term which properly signifies *dipping*." F. A. Cox, London, 1824, says: "The idea of *dipping is in every instance*." Dr. Carson, Philadelphia Baptist Board of Publication, 1853, says: "My position is that it always signifies *to dip*, and nothing but *dip*, through all Greek literature." The translator of the Baptist Version of Mark and Luke says: "It has been settled that there is no difference, as to signification, between βάπτω and βαπτίζω." The translator of the Baptist Version of Acts says: "Being words of *action* and not of *mode, they can have but one literal and proper meaning*." He adds, "βάπτω occurs in the New Testament three times, always translated by *dip*." These statements are identical with those of T. J. M., as to the signification of the word—"the idea of baptism is *a dipping into*," and consequently this "idea" has been broached by a historical succession of writers from Gale, 1611, to T. J. M., 1871, through a period of *two hundred and sixty years*. This "idea" of *dipping* has not been loosely and inconsiderately introduced, but as "radical to baptism." It has been specifically defended as "the only literal and proper meaning," on the ground that the verb expressed "action," and therefore could not have any second, literal meaning. That the distinctive meaning of "dip" and nothing else was the "idea," is conclusively established by the fact that the notion of a resurrection in baptism is grounded in that feature of *dip* which brings its object out of a fluid after a momentary introduction into it. *Sink* does not bring its object out of a fluid, *plunge* does not bring its object out of a fluid, *overwhelm* does not bring its object out of a fluid, *immerse* does not bring its object out of a fluid, but "dip" does, and consequently neither *sink*, nor *plunge*, nor *overwhelm*, nor *immerse* can furnish a basis for a resurrection. It follows therefore, that neither of these words can express the Greek verb, or there is no resurrection in baptism. But there is another historical aspect of this matter. After "the idea of baptism as a dipping" has been insisted upon as "the meaning," "the only meaning that can be," it is thenceforward treated as an intruder and cast out of nearly every translation, while the right opposites (as to characteristic meaning) *sink, plunge, overwhelm, immerse,* fill its place. The evidence of this is found in the fact that Dr. Dagg in fifty cases of the usage of the Greek verb never once translates it *dip*. Dr. Conant in a hundred like cases translates it so rarely by *dip*, that the number could be counted on the fingers of your hand. And in the Baptist Version of the New Testament, while βάπτω is always translated *dip*, βαπτίζω (with the exception of Mark 10 : 38, 39, translated *endure*) is always translated *immerse*.

This conflict between principle and practice can have no rational reconciliation. Dip and immerse can never be equivalents in primary meaning until definite action becomes the equivalent of indefinite action, or limited time becomes the equivalent of unlimited time, or feebleness becomes the equivalent of power. In the figurative and secondary use of the Greek verb there is not the faintest shadow from *dip* falling on that usage. It is invariably expressive of power and not feebleness.

This exhibit receives confirmation from the Baptist Quarterly itself. In the April number, 1869, p. 143, we read thus: "We repeat with emphasis for the consideration of our Baptist brethren: Christian baptism is no mere literal and senseless 'dipping,' assuring the frightened candidate of a safe exit from the water; it is a symbolical *immersion.*" Thus under the hard pressure of condemning usage, *dipping* (that once priceless pearl which has adorned the brow of the theory for two centuries and a half) is cast away into the very sharpest acid as a " senseless " thing, and dissolves into an " immersion." But this same Quarterly (October, 1871, p. 488) says: "It must never be forgotten that the radical idea of baptism is *a dipping into.*" Now, what shall we conclude when this learned periodical declares through one of its writers, that a dipping baptism is " senseless," and through another, pronounces " dipping " the very thing which lies at the root of baptism? The only answer to be given is this: The usage of the Greek word compelled, in the first case, the abandonment of *dipping* as " senseless," while the iron demand of the theory that " John's converts should be *dipped into* the Jordan " required, in the second case, that the outcast and " senseless" dipping should (for the occasion at least) be again taken into favor.

In applying the doctrine of the Baptist Quarterly of 1869, p. 142—" The law of God in Revelation sends the Baptist down into the waters of immersion ; the equally imperative law of God in

nature brings him safely out "—to the baptism under consideration, this question arises: "If the God of Revelation sent these
sinners of Pentecost down into the remission of sins for an 'immersion,' did the God in nature imperatively bring them out"?
If brought out did they come out in a state of nature ("not having
swallowed so much as a mouthful" of remission) or in a state of
grace? If in a state of nature, what benefit comes from this "immersion" any more than from T. J. M.'s dipping, which "gives
nothing"? If the sinner is baptized by the Holy Ghost into a
condition of remitted sin, why should he by any "imperative law
of nature" be brought out of that condition? Why not let him
stay in that condition in which the God of Revelation and the
Greek βαπτίζω put him?

There is nothing in this "Exegetical Study" to win us to "Repent and be *dipped into water in* the name of Jesus Christ *into*
the remission of sins." We prefer the wisdom and grace of God
as in the great announcement—"Repent and be baptized, *upon*
the name of Jesus Christ, into the remission of sins." *Repentance*, the work of the Holy Ghost, being the immediate cause of
the baptism; "upon" involving *faith* which unites to Christ the
meritorious foundation, and "remission of sins" the state of
gracious pardon *into which* we are introduced by "the God of
Revelation," and *out of which* no "God of nature" will ever withdraw us.

THE BAPTISM RECEIVED.

ACTS 2:41.

Οἱ μὲν οὖν ἀσμένως ἀποδεξάμενοι τὸν λόγον αὐτοῦ ἐβαπτίσθησαν καὶ προσετέθησαν
τῇ ἡμέρᾳ ἐκείνῃ, ψυχαὶ ὡσεὶ τρισχίλιαι.

"Then they that gladly received his word were baptized, and were added
(to the Lord) that day about three thousand souls."

THE BAPTISM PREACHED BY PETER RECEIVED BY THE
REPENTING AND BELIEVING.

In this passage "baptized" stands without association with
any word immediately explanatory of its nature. In such case
the word itself, in consequence of varied use, is incompetent for
any specific self-explanation.

Plutarch (see Classic Baptism, p. 306) gives, without explana-tion, the following quotation: " *Ὅτι τοὺς ταμίας ἐβάπτισεν, Because he baptized the stewards, being not stewards, but sharks.*" In such case, not having any context to enlighten, we must be in the dark as to the specific character of the baptism. It may be a physical baptism, drowning them in the sea making them food for sharks, as they like sharks had fed on others. It might be a baptism in kind with their rapacity, stripping them of their rapacious gains, and bringing them into poverty. It might be a mental or moral baptism, by the open exposure of their unjust greed. Either of these baptisms would suit the case, and they are all, and many others, Classic baptisms; but which, if either, is the baptism in fact, none can tell. Now in the Scriptures we have diverse bap-tisms, and more especially we have the intimately related, yet, in value, the infinitely diverse baptisms by the Spirit, thoroughly changing the condition of the soul, and by water symbolizing the nature of such change. In all ordinary cases it is necessary that every penitent sinner believing upon the Lord Jesus Christ should receive both of these baptisms, viz., the real baptism by the Holy Ghost, which is exhibited by repentance and faith, and the sym-bol baptism by water, which betokens that changed, purified con-dition of soul out of which repentance and faith do flow. From the obligation upon all Christians to receive both these baptisms (the invisible reality and the visible symbol of that reality) and their ordinary coexistence, there is an essential difficulty in deter-mining to which baptism reference is made when it is said of any one or of any number of penitent sinners—" they were baptized." Such language may refer directly and exclusively to baptism by the Holy Ghost " into repentance," " into the remission of sins," " into Christ," leaving unstated the reception of the rite which symbolizes such baptism; or this language may refer directly and exclusively to the symbol baptism, and leave unstated the anterior spiritual baptism. In such case we must learn the nature of the baptism from the context, and supply, accordingly, the ellipsis from other fuller statements of Scripture, or we must forever re-main in ignorance as to the definite character of the baptism.

An illustration of this possible difficulty is furnished by 1 Cor. 15:29: " What shall they do who are baptized for the dead, *οἱ βαπτιζόμενοι ὑπὲρ τῶν νεκρῶν.*" Whether this baptism be a ritual baptism, or whether it be a baptism of a wholly different character into which the reception of a rite does not enter, never has been definitely determined among commentators, and probably never will be, any more than the baptism in Plutarch.

No one can say, that the language in Acts 2 : 41 is self-determining as to the nature of the baptism. It may, so far as its own terms are concerned, refer exclusively to the baptism of the soul by the Holy Spirit, or the baptism of the body by symbol water. The context must determine between the two, or we must remain in ignorance.

Was it a dipping into Water?

All who reject the theory which teaches that Christian baptism is a dipping into water, might be well content to allow this statement to pass without questioning for a ritual baptism, if their aim were merely to embarrass an opponent and not to attain and vindicate the truth. For never had any theory difficulties, as mountain upon mountain piled up upon it, like that which burdens itself with the necessity for dipping these three thousand into water, "that day."

1. Among the difficulties of the case is the fact that water is neither mentioned in the passage nor in the context. This is not met by saying it is implied in "baptized;" because the context speaks of a baptism without water in contrast with a baptism with water—"John baptized with water, but ye shall be baptized with the Holy Ghost." The baptism without water is that of which the context speaks as executed. Water cannot be put into "baptized" by assumption. 2. No one ever suggested that there was water in the house or around the house into which these thousands could be dipped. And the assumption that they went somewhere else for the dipping may be very convenient to meet an exigency, but it would be worth more as evidence, if it could be found in the record. 3. It being admitted, that somewhere in or around Jerusalem there was "much water," is no help to this dipping. It is an assumption without evidence and against evidence, that reservoirs of water gathered for city purposes would have been available for dipping three thousand men into them. 4. If the enemies of the Lord Jesus Christ who seven weeks before planted his Cross on Calvary, and in less time took these very men and imprisoned and scourged them, are now ready to put the city water-pools at their disposal for the administration of the distinctive rite of this hated sect, still, it remains to be

shown, that Peter and the people were in a condition to avail themselves of this the most extraordinary courtesy from deadly enemies the world ever knew. There is no evidence that a man or woman had ever received ritual baptism in Jerusalem. There is no evidence that the Apostles sought a public exercise of their ministry during the days of their tarrying at Jerusalem. The Apostles came together without the remotest idea of baptizing any one. The people came together with, if possible, still less idea of being baptized. We ask proof that the disciples and people were in a condition to avail themselves of this assumed marvellous change upon the part of their enemies. 5. Supposing that the enemies of the Cross of Christ put the city reservoirs at the disposal of the men whom to-morrow they will imprison and scourge, and "straitly charge no more to speak" in that hated name, and that the Apostles are ready to enter upon the work leading three thousand men into the drinking reservoirs (some or all) of the city, what is to be done in the matter of dress?

In a dipping into water this is as necessary to be provided for as the water. In later times Jews and Christians put their converts into the water naked. This would be one way of solving the dress question. Were they dipped into water in the same dress with which they came to the meeting? If so, did they go home through the streets in their dripping apparel? Did they go home to get a change of apparel? Where did they go through the process of disrobing and enrobing? Were there any females among these three thousand? Did the enemies of Christianity make special provision for their privacy? 6. If the Jerusalemites who yesterday cried "Crucify" the Master, do to-day put their city reservoirs at the service of his disciples, and do open their public rooms or their private houses to three thousand dripping men and women to go into their chambers, still, who are to be the baptizers? The record does not say that the Apostles baptized one. Who will say that they could baptize all? But where the inspired record is silent human utterances are loud. We are told, that "the seventy" could help; and if that were not enough, where were the "one hundred and twenty"? I have not heard it suggested that the angel who "went down into the pool of Bethesda" was doubtless close at hand, and as it is not said that the Apostles, or the Seventy, or the One hundred and twenty, performed the dipping, it may have been all done by this strong Angel, alone. But this addition to the text may be held as a reserve force. It is, no doubt, worth quite as much as the other *addenda*. 7. But supposing that "the Twelve," and "the Seventy," and "the One hundred and twenty" were enough to dip three thousand men, I ask, if they were adequate to the public dipping into water of one woman, if there was so much as one woman among these thousands? Where is the evidence that such a thing was ever done by divine authority under Judaism, or was ever inculcated under Christianity? It will not do to cover over this very serious point by saying, all disciples are to be dipped into water, women are disciples, and therefore women must be dipped into water. We deny the dipping altogether; and sustain the denial by the absence of fact, and precept, and the pronounced impropriety by the age as to the dipping of females into water, publicly, by men. It will as little do to say, that those who practice the public dipping of females by men into water see no impropriety in it. Females were dipped naked into water for a thousand years, and they who did it "saw no impropriety in it." All see the impropriety now. And the feeling of the million, to-day, is against the becomingness of the public dipping of women into water by men. And this feeling, with solid evidence, we put as a difficulty in the way of the dipping into water of the females among the three thousand. 8. As a final difficulty, in making all these *de novo* arrangements, the dipping into water of these thousands was to be consummated "that day." The record is express and explicit on this point, as to the baptism announced, whatever that baptism may be. The baptism and the addition was (ἐν, Cod. Sin.) within "that day."

The attempt to sustain the dipping into water of these three thousand, as disciples of the rejected Christ, in the city reservoirs of Jerusalem, dependent upon its Cross-hating citizens for privacy to change their dripping apparel, or walking up and down the streets to find a thousand "bath-tubs" to meet the exigency, seems to me one of the most irrational things that men ever undertook. And this without one word, in text or context, of evidence to sustain the mad endeavor. If it had been said, that these persons were baptized in the Mediterranean, that they were transported thither as Philip was transported to Azotus after the baptism of the Eunuch, and that the baptism was performed by "the angel that went down into the pool and troubled the water," it would have been just as well sustained by Scripture, and quite as readily believed (with half the training) by those who now believe that three thousand men and women were that day dipped into water in Jerusalem.

Was it a Ritual Baptism in any form?

In attempting to show that this was not a ritual baptism in any form we are under no temptation to make a point against dipping, but the reverse. If the attempt should be successful, we might expect the warm thanks of the friends of the theory for relieving them from the dire necessity of maintaining one of the most flagrant violations of probability, not to say possibility, ever undertaken by rational men. While the reception of these thousands, that day, into the church by dipping into water, is improbable to absurdity, for reasons both moral and physical, their reception by any ritual form whatever is, for moral considerations mainly, not without embarrassment. These thousands were all personally strangers to the Apostles, mostly from foreign lands, Parthians, Medes, Elamites, Mesopotamians, Cretes, Arabians, etc., etc. An hour before they were mockers of the work of the Holy Ghost, and declared the Apostles to be drunk. Now, is there moral fitness in the reception of such men into the church by a rite without any personal intercourse to learn their moral condition? But the passage states that the baptism was grounded in the "glad reception of the word" preached. If the baptism was the work of the Apostles, then this knowledge must also be the knowledge of the Apostles; and if so, then it must have been obtained either by divine illumination or by personal intercourse; but if by a personal intercourse touching repentance and faith, the knowledge of Christ and the duty of baptism, then, how could the addition of three thousand be made "that day"? If it be said, that the knowledge was by divine illumination, then, it is an addition to the inspired record to meet a difficulty which may be as human in its origin as is the addition. Again; while Alexander Campbell, believing that dipping into water is *for* the forgiveness of sins on the same plane with Repentance and faith, and Dr. Pusey, believing that ritual baptism is for the regeneration of the soul, may feel the need of introducing this rite under any the most adverse circumstances, yet, the evangelical world, which has no such faith, must feel that the crowding of a ritual baptism into "that day" is something remarkable, if not inexplicable.

Let us, then, inquire whether this baptism may not be that

other baptism which is by the Holy Ghost, and whether it may not better adjust itself to the words and to the facts of the case.

Was this Baptism by the Holy Spirit?

1. *They were baptized.* It is unnecessary to say a word in proof that this language *may* express a baptism by the Holy Spirit. It is a matter of universal admission that there is a baptism by the Holy Spirit, and that this baptism is designated by the same word as is used in the case of a ritual baptism. Such baptism, therefore, *may* be expressed here, and the inquiry is legitimate, whether what may be true is not true in fact. The affirmative is sustained: 1. By the negative evidence that neither in the text nor in the context is baptism by water mentioned. 2. By the positive evidence that in the context (1 : 5) baptism by the Holy Ghost is spoken of to the express exclusion of baptism by water—" John baptized with water, but ye shall be baptized with the Holy Ghost not many days hence." It is a matter of universal admission that this promised baptism was received "that day." If it should be said, " This promise has direct and special reference to the Apostles," the answer is: This is true, the Apostles did receive a first and special baptism of the Holy Ghost " that day," qualifying them for their office; but in discharging the duties of that office, the first words of Peter are a declaration that this baptism was not to be limited to the Apostles. This statement is sustained by quoting (2 : 17) the prophet Joel—" It shall come to pass in the last days, I will pour out of my Spirit upon all flesh, and your sons and your daughters shall prophesy . . . and on my servants and my handmaidens I will pour out of my Spirit . . . and whosoever shall call on the name of the Lord shall be saved." The promise, then, of the Lord Jesus Christ to be fulfilled " not many days " hence, was a republication and special application of the promise through Joel a half thousand years before of the baptism of " all flesh " by the Holy Spirit, which had a primary and special fulfilment in the case of these thousands. It is, then, a settled point, that, not only was a baptism by the Holy Spirit promised and received **that** day, but it was promised unto and received by these thousands; v. 39, " For the promise is *unto you* and to your children." Unless, now, there can be positive evidence, that there was another baptism, wholly diverse from this, namely, by water, this baptism (which is in evidence by the most explicit

testimony) must stand as the baptism and the only baptism, of "that day."

They that gladly received his word. This states *who* were baptized, and *why* they were baptized. They were the three thousand; and the reason of their baptism was the "glad reception of Peter's word." The question now arises, Is there any connection between the "glad reception of the word" and baptism by the Holy Ghost? The answer is, this is the very means by which the Holy Ghost convinces of sin, gives repentance, begets faith, regenerates the soul, baptizes "into Christ." Therefore "the word" is preached. And "the word of God" is, by the Holy Ghost, made "quick and powerful, sharper than any two-edged sword, piercing even to the dividing asunder of soul and spirit." "The word of God," on this occasion, "cut to the heart" these thousands. And when thus convinced of sin, Peter uttered that cheering word—"Repent and you shall be baptized, through faith upon Jesus Christ, into the remission of sins." This baptism cleansing from sin, is "the washing of regeneration and renewing of the Holy Ghost" (Titus 3 : 5). "The word" of Peter calling to Repentance and faith being "gladly received," the promise, grounded in that repentance and faith, was also received—"*they were baptized.*" We have, then, a statement of the means, adequate and ordained, through baptism by the Holy Ghost, and that means bearing with divine energy upon these three thousand. Did "the word gone out of the mouth of God return unto him void," or did it "accomplish that whereunto it was sent"?

And were added. Ἐβαπτίσθησαν καὶ προσετέθησαν "were baptized and were added." "Whoever baptized," also "added." Whatever, in kind, was the baptism, such, in kind, was the addition. If the Apostles baptized ritually, the addition was to the Church visible. If the Holy Ghost baptized really, the addition was to the Church invisible, and to its adorable Head. Have we any means of knowing the character of this *addition?* To whom or to what was it? The passage does not directly state. But light may be gathered from other passages close at hand. In this same chapter (v. 47) it is said, "The Lord added to the Church daily such as should be saved." If "the LORD added" these, then we may believe it was "the Lord," and not the Apostles, who "added" those three thousand. If the Lord added "those" or "these," *he added them by the baptism of the Holy Ghost.* Acts 5 : 14, "And believers" (upon the name of Jesus Christ) "were the more added to the Lord." If these believers upon the Lord were "added *to the Lord*," then they were added to the invisible church through its adorable Head, by baptism of the Holy Ghost. And if these "multitudes both of men and women" were added to the Lord, then why not those three thousand? But if they were "added *to the Lord*," then they were not added by the Apostles through ritual baptism, but by the baptism of the Holy Ghost. Acts 11 : 24, "And much people was added unto the Lord." In all these passages the Greek word for "added" is the same. In every passage where the author of the addition is stated, that author is Divine. In every passage where that to which the addition is made is stated, it is to the Lord himself, or by the Lord to the church, necessitating a spiritual union with the invisible church.

Having proved that souls are "added" *by the Lord* to the church through the Holy Ghost, and that souls are "added" *to the Lord* by the Holy Ghost, we claim, that these three thousand "were baptized" by the Holy Ghost, and "were added" TO THE LORD by the same divine Agent.

"*The same day.*" This limitation of time is a trouble to those who insist on three thousand being dipped into water without preparation on their part, or on that of any one else. Therefore Professor M. P. Jewett feels pressed to say (p. 42): "We are not informed whether *fifty*, or *five hundred*, or *more*, were *baptized* on this occasion. . . . 'The same day were *added—not were baptized*—about three thousand souls.'" Prof. Jewett is uncertain about "fifty" being baptized; he, probably, is pretty certain that so many as *two* were "baptized," inasmuch as the verb is in the plural number. A more searching exegesis would reveal a happier line of retreat from the troubles of dipping those who were "BAPTIZED and added *that day*."

Others, not believing in baptism by dipping, yet believing that it was *ritual*, have also felt embarrassed by the severe limitation, "that day." Bishop Wilson says: "*The same day, i. e.*, at that time, on account of that sermon; though they might not all be baptized in one day, but were at that time converted." Bossuet says: "Nothing obliges us to say that they were all baptized on the same day." It is an unpleasant position to be in when, to maintain our views we are compelled to say, that we are not 'obliged" to conform to the clear statement of Scripture.

In the interpretation suggested we have given every word its

11

scriptural value, and, in doing so, we find ourselves without the shadow of embarrassment, and the three thousand baptized and added (to the Lord) without asking for the extension of time one moment beyond "that day."

It hardly needs to be added, that this baptism by the Holy Spirit in that house or around that house, and the addition hereby made by the Lord to that church "which is his body" on that day, does not preclude their being received by ritual baptism into the visible church some other day.

Our concern is to give interpretation to the baptism here announced, not to make provision for some other which is not announced.

We have a cheerful confidence that a just consideration of this passage will lead to the conclusion that *the* BAPTISM *which Peter preached*—"into the remission of sins"—(not a baptism with water, nor a dipping into water) was precisely THAT *baptism which these three thousand received.*

To those who suppose that these thousands were added to the visible church by ritual baptism, these questions may be proposed: Was there a visible Christian church in existence at Pentecost? Was there any one competent to organize a Christian church before Pentecost? Did not the divine Head of the church himself furnish the materials for a church organization, officers and members, "that day"? Was there a Christian organization effected, as well as tri-millenary baptism administered, "that day"? Were they organized and then baptized, or baptized and then organized?

These are practical questions which arise out of the exigencies of the case, and which must receive satisfactory answers.

CHRISTIC BAPTISM: THE BAPTISM PREACHED INCORPORATED IN A RITE.

BAPTISM, WITH WATER, INTO THE NAME OF THE LORD JESUS.

RITUAL BAPTISM OF THE SAMARITANS.

ACTS 8 : 12–16.

—μόνον δὲ βεβαπτισμένοι ὑπῆρχον εἰς τὸ ὄνομα τοῦ Κυρίου Ἰησοῦ.

"But when they believed Philip, preaching the things concerning the kingdom of God, and the name of Jesus Christ, they were baptized (ἐβαπτίζοντο) both men and women.

"Then Simon himself believed also; and when he was baptized (βαπτισθείς), he continued with Philip, and wondered, beholding the miracles and signs which were done. . . . *Only they were baptized* (βεβαπτισμένοι) *into the name of the Lord Jesus.*"

THE FIRST STATED RITUAL BAPTISM UNDER CHRISTIANITY.

THE baptism just considered, originally announced by Joel, reannounced as close at hand by Christ, interpreted and held forth in cheering promise by Peter, and now exhibited for the first time under Christianity, and revealed as endowing the Apostles for their wondrous work and extending remission of sin to the guilty and the perishing through repentance and faith upon Christ, has demanded special attention, because it is the baptism of the Holy Ghost and THE BAPTISM OF CHRISTIANITY. It stands forth, in the divine wisdom, not only as first in the order of time, but solitary and unapproachable in power and in excellence. The baptism now about to be considered justly claims special attention, because it is the first *ritual* baptism under Christianity. Such attention is demanded not so much for considerations intrinsic, as extrinsic; not so much for the inherent truth, as for the adherent error; not so much for that which is in its own substance, as that of which its substance is the shadow. The ritual baptism of Christianity has no independent existence as a bap

(163)

tism. It is solely the adumbration of the baptism by the Holy Ghost. They are not two baptisms, the one spiritual and the other physical, but "one baptism," the former real, the latter ritual, symbol of the real. They are no more two baptisms, diverse in nature, than a rock and the shadow of that rock are two rocks, diverse in nature. Ritual baptism with water is not the effecting of a physical baptism by water as a fluid, but it is the symbolization of the real and purifying baptism in the soul by the nature of water as a pure and purifying element. Ritual baptism, therefore, is the incorporation and visible exhibition of the "one baptism" of Christianity which is proclaimed in its preaching as essential to salvation and effected through the Holy Ghost, purifying the soul by the atoning blood of the Lamb of God, and investing it with his spotless righteousness.

This ritual baptism we will now consider as presented before us in the words of inspiration.

BAPTISM INTO THE NAME OF THE LORD JESUS.

The point of supremest importance in this passage of Scripture is the express and clear statement that the baptism was "*into the Name of the* LORD JESUS."

The essential character of any baptism is made known in the clearest and most exhaustive manner when the receptive element (that into which the baptized object really or verbally passes) is declared. Thus, when I am told that a living man is baptized *into* WATER, I know that he is put into a condition which, by its terms, has no self-limitation, and which subjects to the full influence of water as destructive to the function of the lungs, and therefore issues, of necessity, in the destruction of life by suffocation. If the baptism is *into* FIRE, I know, by like reasoning, that the issue is the destruction of life by burning. So, if the baptism is *into* INSENSIBILITY, the issue declared is a condition of complete unconsciousness; or, if *into* IMPURITY, a condition of complete pollution. No form of language can be clearer or more exhaustively expressive of a designed thought.

There is neither change of principle nor obscurity of thought induced by a *person* being introduced as the receptive element. Who would stumble at the statement, "I have dipped into *Aristotle*," any more than at the statement, "I have dipped into the *writings* of Aristotle?" He is "imbued with *Plato*," rather than "imbued with the *philosophy* of Plato?"   "He is immersed in *Shakspeare*," rather than "immersed in the *dramas* of Shakspeare?"   "He is steeped in *Voltaire*," rather than "steeped in the *infidelity* of Voltaire?"   As the names of Aristotle, Plato, Shakspeare, and Voltaire, are so intimately associated with certain distinctive conceptions that the names alone are suggestive and representative of them, so the Name of the Lord Jesus is indissolubly and solely connected with the sacrificial atonement for sin, and it is therefore a difference in form and not in thought when sinners are said to be baptized "into the remission of sins," or "into the name of the Lord Jesus," from whom the remission of sins alone proceeds—"Unto him that loved us and *washed us from our sins by his blood* be glory forever and ever."

IMPORT OF BAPTISM INTO THE NAME OF THE LORD JESUS.

As Greek Classic writers leave no room to doubt that a baptism "εἰς θάλασσαν" expresses a condition issuing in drowning, and Jewish uninspired writers do as explicitly use a baptism εἰς ἀναισθησίαν to express a condition of complete unconsciousness, so the inspired writers of the New Testament do not leave a shadow of doubt as to the meaning in which they use a baptism "into *the Name of the Lord Jesus.*"

1. Evidence of this meaning is found in the language expressing the baptism preached and ritually administered by John the Forerunner.   John, as preparing the way of the coming Messiah, preached "Repentance" = godly sorrow for sin, and to those who "brought forth fruit meet for repentance," he administered a rite in which water applied to the body was a symbol of the purification of the soul consequent upon repentance.   The repentance demanded and professed was expressed in the ritual formula, "I baptize thee, with water, into Repentance."   A baptism "into repentance," that is to say, a condition of the soul completely under the influence of godly sorrow for sin, was demanded by the preaching, and this same condition was set forth by word and by symbol in the rite.   In order that men might be encouraged to hear and obey the call to a baptism into repentance, John preached another baptism, namely, "the baptism *of repentance* INTO THE REMISSION OF SINS;" hereby teaching the people that the baptism "*into Repentance*" was not the sole or ultimate baptism to be received, but was only antecedent to another baptism inseparable

from it, namely, a baptism "into the remission of sins," the strongest possible expression declarative of a condition in which there was complete pardon of all sin. While repentance is indicated by John as the immediate agency in the baptism "into the remission of sin," he teaches that its primary and worthy source is in "the LAMB OF GOD *that taketh away the sin* of the world," and it is in order to his manifestation that he had come baptizing with water (John 1 : 29–31).

2. This phrase receives farther elucidation from the preaching of Peter at Pentecost. To sinners under deep conviction of their guilt and righteous exposure to condemnation inquiring—"What must we do?" he answers by demanding, as did John, *Repentance*, and cheering, as did he, with the promise of a baptism thereupon "into the remission of sins," basing this promise more vividly than the Forerunner could do, UPON the Name of Jesus Christ "whom ye have crucified." Here are the same elements in the preaching, and the same characteristics in the baptisms, of John and of Peter. They have the same issue—remission of sin through Jesus Christ "the Lamb of God that taketh away the sin of the world."

3. This formula is also brought into very clear light by those words of our Lord, "Ye shall indeed be baptized with the baptism that I am baptized with" (Mark 10 : 39). This baptism was "into an atoning death" on Calvary. By undergoing this baptism He secured to himself the power to remit sin, so that all who are baptized *into* HIM partake of his baptism in its sin-remitting power.

These sources of evidence bring us to this clear issue : As it was a matter of ultimate indifference under the ministry of John whether it was said, that the soul was baptized "into repentance," or baptized "into the remission of sins," inasmuch as under the economy of grace these baptisms were inseparable, so, under the ministry of Peter and Philip it was a matter of verbal and not real difference, when the soul was said to be baptized into the remission of sin or "into the Name of the Lord Jesus," because the one could have no existence without the other. But as the cause is nobler than the effect, it is becoming that under Christianity, when we have a full revelation of the source whence comes the remission, the baptism should be proclaimed not as into the effect, but as into the source of that effect, which is Jesus Christ, without the shedding of whose blood there would be no remission of sin.

WAS THE BAPTISM RITUAL OR REAL?

Thus 1ar we have only spoken, in general, of the force of the terms in this formula. Their practical value must be determined by another question, namely, Was the baptism real or ritual? The baptism of Christianity, which is the purification of the soul by the blood of atonement, has a twofold exhibition in Scripture: 1. *As a* REALITY, in the complete change in the condition of the soul effected by the power of the Holy Ghost. 2. *As a* RITE, in which this changed condition of the soul is declared as a necessity, and its nature exhibited by an appropriate symbol. The former of these baptisms is necessary to salvation; the latter is obligatory, as of divine appointment, based in divine wisdom and goodness as well as divine sovereignty. The difference of inherent value between the two is infinite. The one is the power of God unto salvation; the other is the power of a symbol. The one is spiritual, is designed for a spiritual result, and has inherent power (that of the Spirit of God) to produce such result; the other is not spiritual, is not designed in itself for a spiritual result, and has not inherent power (it is simple water) to produce any spiritual result. It is obvious, then, that the value of baptism as spoken of in Scripture can never be rightly apprehended until a true answer be given to the inquiry—Was it a real or a symbol baptism? And it should be well understood, that this inquiry is by no means equivalent to this other—"Was it a spiritual or a physical baptism?" *There is no such thing in Scripture as a* PHYSICAL *baptism.* The *baptism* SYMBOLIZED by water is not another baptism, but *the very baptism* ACTUALIZED by the Holy Ghost *declared* by the ritual words and *illustrated* by the ritual symbol. In answer to the question—What baptism did the Samaritans receive? it must be answered: They were generally baptized by the Holy Ghost, regenerating the soul, remitting sin, giving repentance, uniting by faith to the Lord Jesus Christ, and also were baptized "into the Name of the Lord Jesus" with the visible ritual symbol of this baptism. A ritual baptism is not expressly stated, but the evidence for it leaves the fact beyond question. The evidence is as follows: 1. It is stated in v. 12 that the baptism was subsequent to the believing. If the baptism were ritual it would of necessity, in the case of these Samaritans, be sequent to the believing. But if the baptism were by the Holy Ghost, then the believing and the baptism would be coincident and in-

separable. Certainly the soul is not baptized by the Holy Ghost
" into the Name of the Lord Jesus " subsequently to its believing
upon the name of the Lord Jesus ; still, as " believing " is a mani
festation of the baptism of the soul by the Holy Ghost, it might
be spoken of as subsequent in the order of time. 2. Evidence
for a ritual baptism may be found in the statement, that " both
men and women " were baptized. In a baptism by the Holy
Ghost it would be unnecessary to specify " women," because from
the nature of the case they are equally with men the subjects of
this baptism. This, however, is not true as to religious rites. It
was not true, certainly, under Judaism. There is no scriptural
statement or fact showing, with any certainty, that " women "
were included in the ritual baptism of John. There is much, beyond this negative element, to throw doubt upon it. (1.) John's
ministry was temporary. It lasted but for a few months. Completeness, therefore, did not belong to it. " Women," as a class,
were not necessarily included in its rite. (2.) John's ministry
was specific. While his preaching " Repent," was as applicable
to " women " as to men, still, that repentance had an immediate
issue, namely, " to prepare the way of the Lord," that when " he
came to his own " he might be " received by his own." This
rational reception depended upon the active ruling classes rather
than upon the " women." The " daughters of Jerusalem " wept
for him when the priest and the ruler rejected him. (3.) John's
ministry was not a ministry of organization. He organized nothing. He addressed individuals. He did not say, " The promise
is to you *and to your children*." Peter did so say. He did not
" take up *little children* in his arms and bless them." Christ did
so do. He did not visit homes to preach. His ministry was in
the wilderness. As the Scriptures do not say, that " both men
and women " received John's ritual baptism, while it does say
that they, in common, received Christian baptism, so, the general
features of his ministry give emphasis to that silence, and point
to the conclusion, that neither women, nor children, nor the family,
as such, were embraced in the ritual baptism of John. While,
therefore, the substance of his ministry and baptism was the same
as that under the gospel, we must not confound or measure his
temporary, limited, and inorganic ministry with the permanent,
universal, and organizing ministry of Christianity.

We may set down the statement, that " both men and women "
were baptized by Philip (" children " had already (Acts 2 : 39)

been taken to the bosom of Christianity by Peter) as referring to their ritual baptism. 3. Farther evidence to this conclusion may be found in v. 16, " Only they were baptized into the NAME of the Lord Jesus." This is conclusive against a baptism *into* WATER, unless two utterly diverse things can be shown to be one and the same thing. It does not, however, determine in favor of a baptism with symbol water " into the Name of the Lord Jesus," as against the real baptism by the Holy Ghost.

Nor is such determination established by the statement, that the Apostles " prayed for them that they might receive the Holy Ghost, for as yet he was fallen upon none of them," only they were baptized " into the Name of the Lord Jesus." This statement is conclusive against the doctrine of a baptism *in* the Holy Ghost, and establishes the doctrine that baptism is by the Holy Ghost; but it is not conclusive against but rather implies, that they had already been baptized by the Holy Ghost " into the Name of the Lord Jesus." There is nothing more certain than that the baptism by the Holy Ghost is not limited to a single species, namely, to that which regenerates, uniting to Christ by repentance and faith, with the remission of sins. The baptism of the Apostles at Pentecost did not belong to this species of baptism. That, surely, was not a regenerative baptism. That baptism of the Holy Ghost received by Cornelius and his friends at Cæsarea was not, or not merely, a regenerative baptism. And this baptism at Samaria, by the laying on of the Apostles' hands and prayer, was not a regenerative baptism. The baptisms at Jerusalem, and Cæsarea, and Samaria, belong to the same species, namely, of miraculous endowment for special ends, and are wholly diverse from that species of baptism which regenerates the soul, remits sin, and unites to Christ. This distinction is clearly taught in the passage before us, where baptism " into the Name of the Lord Jesus " is broadly separated from that baptism of miraculous gifts which was obvious to the senses, and which (v. 18) " Simon saw," and the multitude of Pentecost, and " the circumcision " at Cæsarea, " heard." This baptism of the Holy Ghost, therefore (received subsequent to the arrival of Peter and John), does not show that they had not received that baptism of the Holy Ghost, which is " into Christ," before their arrival. While, therefore, we may believe that the statement of a baptism " into the Name of the Lord Jesus " refers especially to a symbol baptism, yet the proof is not hereby made absolute, much less that the real baptism is excluded.

4. There is, however, one other source of evidence, which must end all doubt. It is found in the baptism of Simon. We are told in v. 13, that "Simon was baptized;" and in vv. 21-23 we are farther told, that " he had neither part nor lot in Christ," that " his heart was not right in the sight of God," and that " he was in the gall of bitterness." Now, no man was ever baptized by the Holy Ghost " into the Name of the Lord Jesus," and remained " without part or lot " in him, having " a heart not right in the sight of God," and "in the gall of bitterness and bonds of iniquity." It follows, therefore, of necessity, that Simon had not received that real baptism of the Holy Ghost which regenerates the soul and unites to Christ. But baptism, with symbol water, "into the Name of the Lord Jesus " has no power to regenerate the soul, or to change its relations to God, or iniquity; and as Simon, after baptism, remained unregenerate, out of Christ, and in iniquity, it follows of necessity, that his baptism must have been by symbol, and by symbol only.

WATER NOT MENTIONED.

It being made certain that there was a ritual baptism at Samaria, it is no less certain that symbol water was used in the administration, for this is the element and the only element of divine appointment. As there is no express statement of the presence of water, so, of course, there is no express statement of the manner of its use. We must, therefore, supply the ellipsis from other passages where water is mentioned, and as it is mentioned. There is, happily, no embarrassment in so doing, for this element never appears in the administration of baptism except in one form, that of the Dative. In Matthew and John, the form ἐν ὕδατι appears; in Mark (Cod. Sin.) and Luke, ὕδατι, without a preposition. As Luke is the writer of Acts, the ellipsis can only be supplied in that form invariably used by him, both in his Gospel and in the Acts. The passage would then read thus : ὕδατι βεβαπτισμένοι εἰς τὸ ὄνομα, or βεβαπτισμένοι ὕδατι εἰς τὸ ὄνομα, the first order appearing in the Gospel by Luke (3 : 16), the second in the Acts (1 : 5). As to the translation of these words, I doubt whether there is a scholar living who, meeting in Classic Greek with βαπτίζω thus associated with the Dative and the Accusative, would think of any other translation than one which would make the Dative to express agency, and the Accusative to express the receiving element. As a matter of fact, there is no Baptist scholar who has ever translated εἰς with its case thus associated with βαπτίζω outside of the Scriptures, by any other word than *into*, and under like circumstances they have (with wellnigh the same undeviating uniformity) translated the Dative as indicating the instrument. There is no just reason for abandoning this uniformity when we come to the Scriptures. The only allowable translation, then, must be " *with* water, baptized *into* the Name of the Lord Jesus," or, " were baptized, with water, into the Name of the Lord Jesus." The only matter left to choice is the order of words ; for the translation itself, in view of the whole range of usage, there is no choice. The syntax thus developed is identically the same with that in John's baptism—βαπτίζω ἐν ὕδατι, ὕδατι, εἰς μετάνοιαν—here the *water* occupies the position of symbol agency, and *repentance* (verbally) that of receiving element. The fact that the symbol agency remains the same, both under John's ministry and under the Christian ministry, while the verbally receiving element *which denotes the nature of the baptism* is changed (in conformity with the distinctive characteristics of the one and the other ministry) is a demonstrative confirmation of the interpretation demanded by the syntax. John's ministry demands a baptism " into repentance ;" and we have it. The Christian ministry demands a baptism " into Christ ;" and we have it. No other defensible and rational translation can be given.

This is the view of all Patristic writers. They universally regard the water as occupying the position of agency, and " Repentance," " Remission of sins," " Christ," etc., as the verbal element giving character to the baptism. This is true in whatever form the water is used by them, whether by covering, or pouring, or sprinkling. The water ever had, in their estimation, a divine energy as an agency in baptism, and never occupied in their view the position of a mere receptacle.

CONFIRMATORY PATRISTIC QUOTATIONS.

The evidence that early Christian writers regarded water in baptism as agency, and the receptive element as verbal and ideal only, is complete, as the following quotations (a few out of a number without number) will show :

Clemens Romanus, 885 : *Βαπτισθέντες γὰρ εἰς τὸν τοῦ Κυρίου θάνατον, καὶ εἰς τὴν ἀνάστασιν αὐτοῦ.*

"Having been baptized *into* THE DEATH of the Lord and *into his* RESURRECTION."

"Into" brings under the full influence of "the death and resurrection of the Lord." *Unto, for, in order to*, subvert the divinely taught baptism of the Scriptures.

Apostolical Canons. 42 (Gale, 191); *τρία βαπτίσματα . . ἓν βάπτισμα τὸ εἰς τὸν θάνατον τοῦ Κυρίου.*

"Three baptisms" (into the name of the Father—and of the Son—and of the Holy Ghost), "one baptism which is *into* THE DEATH of the Lord."

Among the errors now introduced was a "*three-one*" (trinity) baptism, baptizing, distinctively, into each Name of the Trinity. "One baptism into the Name of the Lord" was condemned. Under this error stands out the truth, that the several persons of the Trinity (in the one case) and "the death of the Lord" (in the other case) constitute the ideal element of the baptism.

Cyprian, 1112 : "In nomine Jesu Christi baptizati esse—Baptized in the name of Jesus Christ." " In nomine " is an improper translation of *εἰς τὸ ὄνομα.* It shows, however, a rejection of the translation of *εἰς* by *unto, for, in order to.* " In nomine " does not admit of such translation. It does, however, admit of *inness*, which is expressed by *εἰς*, and must be so interpreted. While " in nomine " corrects the error which would translate the preposition by *for, unto, in order to*, it has given origin to a new error, expressed by the wholly foreign conception *by the authority of.* The Greek *εἰς τὸ ὄνομα*, and the proper Latin form " *in nomen*," and the only just English expression *into the name*, do all imperatively reject any such interpretation.

Methodius, 149 : " *Εἰς Χριστὸν βεβαπτισμένοι.*—' Touch not my christs (anointed ones), and do my prophets no harm.' As if those baptized *into* CHRIST (the Anointed) were made *christs* (anointed ones) by partaking of the Spirit " (by which Christ was anointed).

Here, in addition to the syntax, we have an argument drawn from the import of the name " Christ " (= Anointed), showing, that those baptized *into* " the Anointed One " become thereby " anointed ones," just as any object put into ointment becomes, thereby, anointed. They who are baptized into *water* will never thereby become " *anointed* ones."

Origen, III, 1855: "Fluvius Dei Salvator noster Dom.nus, in quo baptizamur—Our Lord and Saviour is the river of God, in which we are baptized."

Here, as in the preceding case, we have, in addition to the syntax, the most indubitable evidence (by the likening of the Saviour to a river), that Origen believed that the baptism of the Bible was not *unto*, nor *for*, nor *in order to*, nor *by the authority of*, but "*into* CHRIST."

These quotations might be indefinitely multiplied. Early Christian writers present but one aspect of Christian baptism. It is never into a physical element, but always "*into* CHRIST" or its equivalent. This statement has no reference to the manner in which the water in early ages was used; that is a different matter and will be noticed in its place.

CHANGE OF FORMULA.

Having seen that the baptism administered by Philip was a baptism εἰς τὸ ὄνομα τοῦ Κυρίου Ἰησοῦ, it is necessary to call attention, at least briefly, to its apparent want of accord with the formula announced in Matt. 28:19 and which at an early period superseded that formula which appears in this baptism at Samaria; but which is the only formula that appears throughout the New Testament in connection with the administration of Christian baptism. The fact of such change is quite remarkable, and calls for a strict inquiry into the essential value of each formula and their relations to each other. This will be done when we come to consider Matt. 28:19. At present it will be sufficient to call attention to the fact, that the formula used throughout the New Testament in the administration of ritual baptism is not that which appears in Matthew; to the fact, that this departure from the supposed commanded formula was recognized by early Christian writers; and, to the attempt made by them and others to unify the two.

Basil of Cæsarea and others.

The following quotation is from Basil of Cæsarea, IV, 116: "Let no one be deceived by the fact of the Apostle frequently omitting, in mentioning baptism, the name of the Father and of the Holy Ghost, nor imagine, on this account, that the invocation of these names is unimportant. 'As many,' says he, 'as have been baptized into Christ have put on Christ.' And again, ' As many as have been baptized into Christ have been baptized into his death.' For the naming of Christ is the confession of every one; for it reveals God who anoints, and Christ who is anointed, and the Spirit who is the ointment, as we are taught by Peter in the Acts, ' Jesus of Nazareth whom God anointed with the Holy Ghost.' And in Isaiah 61 : 1, and the Psalmist, 44 : 8. The Apostle, however, sometimes seems to make mention only of the Spirit, on the subject of baptism; ' For,' says he, ' we are all baptized by one body into one Spirit' (1 Cor. 12 : 13). And with this agrees the passage, ' But ye shall be baptized by the Holy Ghost;' and that, ' He shall baptize you by the Holy Ghost.' But not on this account would any one say, that baptism was complete in which the name of the Spirit only was invoked."

It is unnecessary to give the Greek of this passage as there is nothing dependent upon its form. The force of the sentiment turns on the form of the Scripture quotations, especially Gal. 3 : 27, εἰς Χριστὸν ἐβαπτίσθητε; Rom. 6 : 3, ἐβαπτίσθημεν εἰς Χριστὸν 'Ιησοῦν; εἰς τὸν θάνατον; 1 Cor. 12 : 13, ἐν ἑνὶ Πνεύματι εἰς ἓν σῶμα ἐβαπτίσθημεν.

In this last quotation Basil (designedly or undesignedly) reverses the grammatical form and sentiment, making it ἐν ἑνὶ σώματι εἰς ἓν Πνεῦμα, by one body into one Spirit, instead of " by one Spirit into one body." There is no foundation, however, for the remark of Basil—that there is even a semblance of " the Spirit " being mentioned alone in any baptism in a form parallel to εἰς τὸ ὄνομα Χριστοῦ. The Dative in which " the Spirit" always appears expresses the agency in effecting the baptism, while the Accusative in which " Christ" (or its equivalent) always appears expresses the receiving element.

Cyprian, 1120, grounds the distinctive use of the formula of baptism in the diverse position occupied by the Jew and the Gentile: " Alia enim fuit Judæorum sub Apostolis ratio, alia est gentilium conditio. Illi, quia jam legis et Moysi antiquissimum baptisma fuerint adepti, in nomine quoque Jesu Christi erant baptizandi, secundum quod in Actis Apostolorum Petrus ad eos loquitur et dicit, *Pœnitemini, et baptizetur unusquisque vestrum in nomine Domini Jesu Christi in remissionem peccatorum.* Jesu Christi mentionem Petrus facit, non quasi Pater omiteretur, sed ut Patri quoque Filius adjungeretur. Denique ubi post resurrectionem a Domino Apostoli ad gentes mittuntur in nomine Patris, et Filii, et Spiritus Sancti baptizare gentiles jubentur.

" The condition of the Jews and of the Gentiles is different. The Jews, because they had already received the most ancient baptism of the Law and of Moses, were baptized also in the name of Jesus Christ, as Peter says, Acts 2 : 38, ' Repent and be baptized, every one of you, in the name of Jesus Christ into the remission of sins.' Peter makes mention of Jesus Christ, not as if the Father should be omitted, but that the Son should be conjoined with the Father. Finally, when after the resurrection the Apostles are sent by the Lord to the nations, they are commanded to baptize the Gentiles in the name of the Father, and of the Son, and of the Holy Ghost."

The explanation of Cyprian cannot be received, because it does not square with the facts of the case. It has no adequate historical basis.

Didymus Alex., 1660, commenting on Acts 2 : 38, says : " The Saviour having commanded the perfected to be baptized ' into the name of the Father, and Son, and Holy Ghost,' some, unwisely interpreting the Scriptures, having heard Peter exhorting every one to be baptized (ἐν τῷ ὀνόματι τοῦ Χριστοῦ) in the name of Christ, imagine the one equal to the three names. But the Church, believing the Trinity indivisible and inseparable, declares the Father to be of the Son, and the Son of the Father, and the Holy Ghost to be of the Father and the Son. So, through this unity (τὸν βαπτιζόμενον εἰς ὄνομα Χριστοῦ, κατὰ τὴν Τριάδα βαπτίζεσθαι) he who is baptized into the name of Christ, is baptized into the entire Trinity."

There are insuperable difficulties (of which more will be said hereafter) in the way of such interpretation.

Hilary, II, 538, alluding to passages of Scripture apparently contradictory, or capable of an unscriptural interpretation, urges that such passages of Scripture are not to be rejected or disesteemed by us, presenting this consideration : " Ne postremo apostoli reperiantur in crimine, qui baptizare in nomine Patris, et Filii, et Spiritus Sancti, jussi, tantum in Jesu nomine baptizaverunt. Lest, finally, the Apostles may be found guilty, who, having been commanded to baptize in the name of the Father, and of the Son, and of the Holy Ghost, baptized only in the name of Jesus." Hilary points out the difficulty which arises on the as-

sumption that the Apostles were commanded to baptize ritually
into the name of the Father, Son, and Holy Ghost, by reason of
the fact, that they never did so baptize, but baptized into something else; but he suggests no solution of the difficulty. A commentator on Hilary makes the following suggestion : " Baptismus
in nomine Jesu dici possit, qui non ut prius Joannes, sed Jesu
Christi auctoritate institutus sit, quamvis dandus in nomine Patris,
et Filii, et Spiritus Sancti—Baptism may be said to be in the
name of Jesus, which is instituted, not as the former of John, but
by the authority of Jesus Christ, although administered in the
name of the Father, and of the Son, and of the Holy Ghost."
This interpretation is precluded from consideration by the fact,
that its idea of " authority " is derived from " in nomine," which
is an erroneous translation of εἰς τὸ ὄνομα, which does not admit of the idea of being established " by the authority " of any
one.

Origen IV, 1039: The Greek of Origen is wanting. It exists
only in a Latin translation. He says : " Perhaps, also, you may
ask this : Since the Lord himself said to his disciples, that they
should ' baptize all nations into the name of the Father, and of
the Son, and of the Holy Ghost,' why does the Apostle here use
the name of Christ only, in baptism, saying, ' Whosoever of us
have been baptized into Christ,' since it is not regarded as legitimate baptism unless under the name of the Trinity ? But see the
discretion of Paul, since, in the present passage, he did not desire so much to discuss the subject of baptism, as that of the
death of Christ, through the likeness of which he would, also,
persuade us that we ought to die to sin and be buried together
with Christ. And it was not suitable that when he spake of death,
that He should mention either the Father or the Holy Ghost.
For ' the Word was made flesh,' and properly, where the flesh is,
there death is treated of. Nor was it proper to say, ' Whosoever
of us have been baptized ' into the name of the Father, or of the
Holy Ghost, ' have been baptized into his death.' "

This interpretation looks in the direction where the truth lies,
but does not fully uncover it. It does indicate an essential difference between εἰς Χριστὸν and εἰς τὸ ὄνομα τοῦ Πατρὸς, καὶ τοῦ Υἱοῦ, καὶ
τοῦ Πνεύματος Ἁγίου, which entirely precludes their interchange as
equivalents. The former phrase indicates the second Person of
the Trinity, and points to his distinctive work as " God manifest
in the flesh," and its fruits toward his redeemed people; while the

latter phrase indicates the Deity simply in his Trinity, with such several distinctive relations to man as the Scriptures unfold.

Until the whole scheme of redemption as made known in the Scriptures is confounded, it is impossible that the one of these baptisms can stand for the other.

Matthies and others.

Matthies (Baptismatis Expositio, pp. 121–133) presents the facts in the case very clearly. " The Apostles are commanded by Christ, to bind by baptism every one about to embrace the Christian religion to faith into God the Father, Son, and Holy Ghost. But the baptism which is said to have been administered by the Apostles not into the name (*in nomen*) of the Father, Son, and Holy Ghost, but into the name (*in nomen*) of Christ, seems to oppose the very command of Christ (Acts 2 : 38; 8 : 12, 16; 10 : 48; 19 : 3, 4, 5; Rom. 6 : 3; Gal. 3 : 27; 1 Cor. 1 : 13, 15; cfr. 1 Cor. 10 : 2). . . . Luke, although he frequently relates the administration of baptism in the Acts of the Apostles, yet never mentions the words used by Christ in the institution of baptism; nor is there less silence in all the other books of the New Testament respecting the use of the formula of the Trinity in the administration of baptism. Why this is, very many conjectures are proposed, which indeed are easy of suggestion, but which are very far from being established by sound arguments derived either from Scripture or from history. Sacred Scripture clearly teaches us that the Apostles, although they were commanded by Christ to baptize ('in triunum deum') into the Triune God, nevertheless, did actually baptize εἰς ὄνομα Χριστοῦ. Were the Apostles regardless of the command of Christ? Or, did Christ himself hold in light esteem his own commandment? Very many who have treated of this subject have freely inclined to the one view or the other, although there is no evidence by which it can be proved either that the Apostles neglected the commands of Christ, or that Christ lightly esteemed his own teaching. Since it is necessary that we have faith in those things concerning the administration of baptism, which are related in the books of the New Testament, we cannot doubt, but that the Apostles did truly baptize (*in nomen Christi seu in Christum*) into the name of Christ or into Christ. . . . From those things stated concerning the **import of the formula** εἰς τὸ ὄνομα Χριστοῦ, it can readily be seen, how it could happen

12

that, although it is frequently stated in the books of the New
Testament that the Apostles baptized only (*in nomen Christi*)
into the name of Christ, yet from the time of Justin Martyr baptism was administered (*in triunum deum*) into the triune God.
Nor did the Apostles baptize contrary to the command of Christ,
nor did the ecclesiastical Fathers essentially change the baptism
of the Apostles, but the same idea of baptism belongs to both.
Christ, to state the whole thing briefly, instituted baptism into
the Father, Son, and Holy Ghost, which triune God is manifested
in that eternal Logos who was made man; but the Apostles administered baptism (*in æternum λογον*) into the eternal Logos,
who has his truth in the triune God, or in the idea of the Trinity;
if you regard the essence of each, it is the same."

The facts are well stated by Matthies. The statement of the
relation between the eternal Logos and the Triune God is, no
doubt, substantially true. But because that is true of the eternal
Logos, and *not of the eternal Logos* "*made man*," it entirely fails
to explain and to unify these two baptisms. The baptism administered by the Apostles was not *into the eternal Logos*, but
"into the name of the Lord Jesus," and "into Christ." Now,
no one will say, that there is not an amazing difference between
"the eternal Logos" considered simply as such, and "the eternal
Logos *made flesh*." It is just because of this difference, qualifying him to become "the Lamb of God which taketh away the
sin of the world," that the baptism of the guilty is into Him =
the Lord Jesus, and not "into the Father," nor "into the Holy
Ghost," neither of which (whatever their divine unity with the
eternal Logos), is "the lamb of God *slain from the foundation
of the world*," and, in the fulness of time "Christ *crucified*" on
Calvary. Matthies assumes that there must be not only absolute
accord between these baptisms, but unity of import. He assumes, also, that Matt. 28 : 19 is the institution of and formula
for ritual baptism. Both these assumptions may be erroneous.
They both need to be proved. We may always assume a real
harmony between apparently incongruous statements of Scripture; but we must prove and not assume a particular explanation
of the incongruity. There may be harmony where there is not
sameness. There may be harmony and interchange of statement
between cause and effect; while the attempt to prove, that the
harmony was grounded in unity, and that the capability of interchange was due to sameness of nature would be a great failure

The explanation of the relation between these baptisms, while recognizing that wondrous element in which they agree (the eternal Logos present in both), must turn on that in which they *differ*, namely, the presence in one, and not in the other, of the man JESUS who dies, and whose blood baptism "cleanses from all sin." And just in this great difference will these baptisms be found to have their real agreement and unification.

Neander (P. and T., 275) says : "Baptism in the name of Christ is equally baptism in the name of the Father and of the Holy Spirit."

The question which concerns us is not, Whether these two baptisms have, historically, been used in the administration of ritual baptism in the church, but, 1. Whether they were so used in the New Testament church; and 2. Whether they do, by their terms, express the same or an equivalent baptism. Neander does not say why these verbally diverse formulæ are equal to each other; but his explanation would probably be in substantial accord with that given by Matthies.

Calvin, Comm. I, Cor. 1 : 13, speaks on this point with characteristic penetration and force.

" It is asked : What it is to be baptized in the name of Christ? I answer, that by this expression it is not simply intimated that baptism is founded on the authority of Christ, but depends, also, on his influence, and does, in a manner, consist in it; and, in fine, that the whole effect depends on this—that the name of Christ is therein invoked. It is asked further: Why it is that Paul says, that the Corinthians were baptized in the name of Christ, while Christ himself commanded (Matt. 28 : 19) the Apostles to baptize in the name of the Father, and of the Son, and of the Holy Spirit? I answer, that in baptism the first thing to be considered is, that God the Father, by planting us in his church in unmerited goodness, receives us by adoption into the number of his Sons. Secondly, As we cannot have any connection with him except by means of reconciliation, we have need of Christ to restore us to the Father's favor, by his blood. Thirdly, As we are by baptism consecrated to God, we need also the interposition of the Holy Spirit, whose office it is to make us new creatures. Nay, farther, our being washed in the blood of Christ is peculiarly his work; but as we do not obtain the mercy of the Father, or the grace of the Spirit, otherwise than through Christ alone, it is on good grounds that we speak of him as the peculiar object in view in baptism, and more particularly inscribe his name on baptism. At the same time this does not by any means exclude the name of the Father and of the Spirit; for when we wish to sum up in short compass the efficacy of baptism, we make mention of the name of Christ alone ; but when we are disposed to speak with greater minuteness, the name of the Father, and that of the Spirit require to be expressly introduced."

This explanation of Calvin proceeds on a basis essentially different from that of any other yet adduced. Its hinge is not the Deity of Christ, and therefore the essential unity between one person of the triune God and the entire Godhead, but it is that in which Christ is distinct, namely, in his incarnation, in order to redemption and reconciliation. It is in this character and by this work, that it becomes possible for the guilty to be baptized by the Holy Ghost " into Christ," and thus to be made regenerate, to receive remission of sins, to be clothed with righteousness, and then, and thus, to be made meet for reconciliation with and subjection unto (= baptism into) the full and essential Godhead, " Father, Son, and Holy Ghost."

The interpretation of Calvin is made under the light of the scope of Scripture teaching rather than under the specific guidance of the force of the terms entering into the formula. If the latter had been fully apprehended he would have seen, that there was no need nor propriety in the introduction of the name of the Father, or of the Holy Ghost, into a baptism *which belonged to the distinctive work* of Christ. Baptism " into Christ " makes meet for baptism " into Father, Son, and Holy Ghost." See Calvin's " Secondly."

Prof. J. Addison Alexander (Comm. Acts 8 : 12, 16) says : " The other subject of his preaching was the name of Jesus Christ, *i. e.*, all denoted by these names, one of which means the Saviour of his people (Matt. 1 : 21), and the other their Messiah, or Anointed Prophet, Priest, and King. Into this name, *i. e.*, into union with Christ and subjection to him, in all these characters, the Samaritan believers were introduced by the initiatory rite of baptism, which, unlike that of Judaism, was administered alike to both men and women. . . . ' Into the name,' *i. e.*, into union with him and subjection to him, as their Sovereign and their Saviour."

The interpretation thus given by this princely scholar admits, as a compendious statement, of no improvement. The spirit of it is identical with that of Calvin ; but as it is derived not from the light of general truth, but from the specific force of terms employed, it is more nicely accurate and more absolutely true. And the harmony of both with the twofold baptism of Scripture, viz., the primary baptism into the name of the Lord Jesus, and the ulterior baptism into the name of the Father and of the Son and of the Holy Ghost is, that *the former baptism is causative of the latter baptism.*

IMPORT OF FORMULA BY FORCE OF TERMS.

The results of this Inquiry teach: 1. That εἰς, with βαπτίζω, points to its regimen as complementary to the idea of the verb; 2. That the regimen of this preposition is the element (real or ideal) into which the baptized object passes without return; 3. That such phraseology is the most distinct and absolute statement as to a baptism of which language is capable; 4. That whether the complement of the verb be real or ideal it does equally express a complete change of condition in the baptized object, the general nature of which as penetrating, pervading, and assimilating, is indicated by the verb, and the specific character of which is shown by the preposition and its regimen, whose characteristic always gives character to the baptism. Guided by these determined results, the formula " Baptized into the name of the Lord Jesus " can only mean a complete change of condition by being made fully subject to the distinctive influence which characterizes " the name of the Lord Jesus " = a SOVEREIGN *and a* SAVIOUR *from sin.* Whether this change of condition be real or ritual depends upon which of those twofold agencies, the Holy Spirit or symbol water, is the executive of the baptism. In the baptism immediately under consideration, it is a ritual service; the condition, therefore, expressed in the formula is not one which is actually effected, but only symbolly exhibited.

The account of this baptism at Samaria has claimed a more special and detailed consideration, because it is the first ritual baptism clearly stated under Christianity. This fulness of examination will enable us to pass over others more briefly.

I only now add, that it is through the real baptism of the souls of men " into the name of the Lord Jesus " = *the crucified* REDEEMER *of his people, that they become qualified for* that ulterior baptism into the only living and true God—the Father, Son, and Holy Ghost.

RITUAL BAPTISM OF THE EUNUCH.

ACTS 8 : 35, 36, 38.

'Ως δὲ ἐπορεύοντο κατὰ τὴν ὁδὸν, ἦλθον ἐπὶ τι ὕδωρ καὶ φησιν ὁ εὐνοῦχος· 'Ιδοὺ
ὕδωρ· τὶ κωλύει με βαπτισθῆναι ;

Καὶ ἐκέλευσε στῆναι τὸ ἅρμα· καὶ κατέβησαν ἀμφότεροι εἰς τὸ ὕδωρ, ὅτε Φίλιππος
καὶ ὁ εὐνοῦχος· καὶ ἐβάπτισεν αὐτὸν Ὅτε δὲ ἀνέβησαν ἐκ τοῦ ὕδατος, Πνεῦμα Κυρίου
ἥρπασε τον Φίλιππον·.

"And preached unto him Jesus." . . .

"And as they went on their way, they came upon some water; and the
Eunuch said, See! water; what doth hinder me to be baptized?" . . .

"And he commanded the chariot to stand still; and they alighted, both,
at the water, Philip and the Eunuch, and he baptized him."

"But when they remounted from the water, the Spirit of the Lord caught
away Philip; and the Eunuch saw him no more, for he went on his way
rejoicing."

THE SOLE TRUST OF THE THEORISTS.

This is the solitary case under Christianity to which appeal is
made to prove the dipping into water theory.

The baptism of the three thousand in or around an upper room
at Jerusalem; the baptism of Saul in a chamber at Damascus;
the baptism of Cornelius and his friends in his own home at
Cæsarea; the baptism of Lydia, away from her home and from
change of raiment, at Philippi; the baptism of the Jailor, at mid-
night, in a prison; the baptism of "the twelve" without warning
or preparation at Ephesus; nor any other ritual baptism under
Christianity (except that now before us) has presented a single
circumstance to which appeal could be made, even by despair, to
prove a dipping into water. In no instance do those crutches
(*river* and *much water*) upon which the theory leans in the baptism of John, appear in the baptisms of Christianity. Whenever
these baptisms are cited against the theory, its friends are compelled to seize the oars and row against wind and tide, argue
against time and circumstance (as well as the true meaning of
the word), to save their dipping from hopeless destruction.

Carson.

Dr. Carson has given this case special attention. He says
(pp. 128–140): "I have written some hundreds of pages concern-

ing the mode of this ordinance, yet to a mind thirsting to know the will of God, and uninfluenced by prejudice, this passage without comment is, in my view, amply sufficient.

" The man who can read it, and not see *immersion* in it, must have something in his mind unfavorable to the investigation of truth. As long as I fear God, I cannot, for all the kingdoms of this world, resist the evidence of this single document. Nay; had I no more conscience than Satan himself, I could not, as a scholar, attempt to'expel immersion from this account. All the ingenuity of all the critics in Europe could not silence the evidence of this single passage. Amidst the most violent perversion that it can sustain on the rack, it will still cry out *immersion, immersion !*"

" When they came to the water, instead of sending down one of the retinue to bring up a little water, they went down to the water. But they not only went down to the water; they went *into* the water. It is not only said, 'they went into the water,' our attention is fixed on the fact that they *both* went into the water. Had the water been deep enough at the edge, the Eunuch only might have been in the water. Now this determines that the preposition εἰς must be rendered *into* and not *unto*."

" Their return is called a coming up out of the water. This is more precise than the account of our Lord's baptism. There it is said, He came up *from* the water. Here it is *out of* the water. I am far from denying that εἰς sometimes signifies *unto*. It is not of itself, therefore, definite. *Εἰς* might be used if the advance was only to the margin. But I utterly deny any such indefiniteness in ἐκ. I say it always signifies *out of*. *Εκ* as signifying the point of departure or motion from one point to another is more definite than ἀπὸ, since it always implies that the point of departure is within the object and not without it. From this there is not only no exception, but there is no color of exception."

" I conclude, then, with all the authority of demonstration, that Philip and the Eunuch were *within* the water because they came *out of* it."

The above is a condensed statement of Dr. Carson's exposition of this baptism. This exposition opens with the declaration that a " Satanic conscience " must be appalled by an attempt to repel the evidence of this document for " immersion " (= *dipping* into water). It closes with a " demonstration " that Philip and the Eunuch were *within the water*, because they came out of it. Dr.

Carson does not laugh (loud enough to be heard) when he adduces Philip and the Eunuch *wiihin* the water, as "demonstrating" that Philip *dipped* the Eunuch *into the water.* Perhaps he would do so if any one should adduce Ireland (and Dr. Carson upon it) *within* the Atlantic Ocean, as demonstrating that Dr. Carson *dipped* IRELAND *into* the Atlantic Ocean. To appeal to βαπτίζω is to appeal to a broken reed: 1. Because βαπτίζω does not *dip.* 2. Because " into water " is taken out of the theory and not out of the Bible.

If it is any pleasure to Dr. Carson and friends to put Philip and the Eunuch *within* the water, we assure them that such pleasure of theirs is no special displeasure to us. But when they make the water " shallow at the edge," and cause the parties to walk out into " two feet nine inches " depth, in order " to make it convenient" for Philip to dip the Eunuch into water (or so much as the Eunuch has not already, himself, put under water), instead of conforming to the Scripture, and baptizing him " *with* water *into* the name of the Lord Jesus," then, we are just so far displeased as we ought to be whenever human conceit is substituted for divine inspiration. That this has been done in Dr. Carson's interpretation will appear by a detailed consideration of all the elements which enter into a solution of the case.

Some Water.

It is a matter of vital moment to the friends of dipping that they should show that this " some water " was sufficient in quantity to admit of the body of a man being dipped into it. Such proof has never been presented. Such proof it is impossible to present. There is the most utter absence of all material so to do. The Eunuch saw " water ;" the chariot came " upon (ἐπί) some water ;" they stepped " to, or into, this water ;" the Eunuch was " baptized " *with* this water; they came up " from, or out of, this water." Such statements exhaust all that is said about the water, and there is nothing about adequacy for a dipping.

If it should be objected, that it is not *said* that the baptism was " *with* water," I answer: Although it is not so stated here, it is so stated elsewhere, and always by Luke, the writer of this passage, with the simple instrumental Dative, ὕδατι, and never by εἰς ὕδωρ, and consequently the statement is here, by ellipsis, just as certainly as if it had been expressed, " *with* water."

Other reasons join with these to show, that this water was small in quantity. Among these are: 1. The expression τὶ ὕδωρ; "not a *certain* water, which might seem to mean a well-known lake or stream, of which the region seems to have been wholly destitute, but, as the Greek words properly denote, *some* water; the indefinite expression (like that in 5 : 2) suggesting naturally the idea of a small degree or quantity." (Alexander *in loc.*) 2. The nature of the country through which they were passing; "this is desert." Whether "desert" apply to the region or to the road, it shows a want of water. "Arrian speaks of a road desert for want of water." 3. The Eunuch was surprised to see water, as shown by his exclamation "See! water," "where it might have been least expected." (Alexander.) 4. The promptitude and urgency for baptism; implying that if this spot should be passed by no other such spot might be found on the road. Everything said and implied points to a limited quantity of water. There is nothing which indicates "two feet nine inches" at the edge or anywhere else.

The Chariot.

Dr. Carson has nothing to say of *the chariot* as an element to be considered as explanatory of the terms entering into this baptism. It is an element which appears in no other New Testament baptism. It is the determining interpretative element in important phraseology of this baptism in which it does appear. These are the facts: 1. Philip and the Eunuch riding in a chariot (ἦλθον ἐπὶ τὶ ὕδωρ) "came *upon* some water," and there the chariot was stopped. The position of the chariot in relation to the water is of vital importance. This must, primarily, be determined by ἐπὶ. The chariot stands wherever ἐπὶ τὶ ὕδωρ puts it. This may be either *upon*, *over*, the water (the wheels in the water of a streamlet running across the road), or immediately adjacent to the water. Winer says, ἐπὶ means *upon*, *above*, *on* the shore; *beside*, *near*, in local sense is not established. 2. The movement of the parties in the chariot. This is expressed by κατέβησαν. What is the import of this word? A few cases closely parallel will sufficiently answer this question: Matt. 14 : 29, "Peter having *stepped down* (καταβάς) from the boat walked (ἐπὶ τὰ ὕδατα) upon the water." The walking (περιεπάτησεν) is expressed by another word. Xen. Eq. 11, 7, uses this word to express the *dismounting* from a horse (ἵππος καταβαίνεται). Judges 4 : 15 (Septuagint), "And Sisera (κατέβη) *stepped down* from his chariot."

In all these cases καταβαινω is used to express precisely the same act which it was necessary, from the nature of the case, that Philip and the Eunuch should do, namely, " step down" from the chariot. Now, whether it be due to a " Satanic conscience " or not, we say, that κατέβησαν expresses neither more nor less than that the occupants of the chariot *stepped down* out of it. The interpretation which would make this word express *a walk* from " a shallow edge down a declining channel into slowly deepening water " may be worth preserving as a curiosity, but its fitness is only for a museum of abnormal developments.

Went Down into the Water.

The position of the chariot may, farther, be determined by the statement κατέβησαν εἰς ὕδωρ, "they stepped down *to or into the water.*" This additional fact is in the most absolute accord with the declaration, that the chariot came and stopped (ἐπὶ τι ὕδωρ) "*upon, over,* or *in immediate contiguity with,* some water." Whether the chariot wheels were in the water or on the edge of the water, they who " stepped down " must step down "*to or into* the water." But this fact, again, confirms what everything points to, namely, the limited quantity of the water. The implication is, if they stepped down "*into* the water " that it was so trifling in depth as to make it unnecessary to change the position of the chariot; certainly no one would step down out of a chariot into water *two feet nine inches* in depth; which they must have done, if at all, at one step, for there is no second step in the record beyond that which brought them down out of the chariot. Going down, step by step, from shallower into deeper water, is the purest fiction.

It is unnecessary to prove that κατέβησαν εἰς τὸ ὕδωρ does not necessarily require the stepping down *into* the water, because this is admitted by Dr. Carson; and, farther, because I do not mean to insist upon any such point. I cheerfully admit that they may have stepped down from the chariot *into* the water under circumstances above indicated, which are the farthest possible removed from what the theory desires and demands. That κατέβησαν εἰς τὸ ὕδωρ does not require entrance *into* the water is clearly established by Luke 8 : 23 (κατέβη λαῖλαψ ἀνέμου εἰς τὴν λίμνην), " a storm of wind came down " (*not*) "*into* the lake." The proof is no less clear that when καταβαινω carries down into water, it does not induce a *walking* "from shallower into deeper water." So John 5 : 4: " An angel (χατέβαινεν) went down into the pool; " but no one, I presume, ever imagined that this taught, that "the angel walked from the water shallow at the edge down, step by step, into deeper water." In the same verse it is said, " Whosoever first (ἐμβάς) *stepped in* was made whole." Many have written touching this troubled water and its healing, but I never heard of any one who supposed that ἐμβαίνω required a second step to be taken within the water. This phase of the argument for a dipping (which is the only novelty deduced from this transaction) may be dismissed without fear of awakening qualms in any conscience, even though it should be much more sensitive than "that of Satan."

Came Up.

The movement of Philip will not receive just consideration unless we look at the reverse movement indicated by (ἀνέβησαν) "they *came up*." Those who would "order the angel Gabriel to school" if he should question that βαπτίζω means *to dip*, affirm that this movement is "the walking up out of deeper water into shallower water at the edge." Others, who prefer the anathema which brands with a "Satanic conscience" (when such conscience brings into school fellowship with Gabriel) think, that if χατέβησαν means *to step down*, ἀνέβησαν must mean *to step up*. This conclusion, however obvious, from the verb being the same in both cases, and the compounding preposition being in the one case "*down*" and in the other "*up*," does not rest merely upon the verb and its composition, but upon established usage, as shown by the following references : Josephus (12 : 4, 3) uses this word (ἀναβῆναι) to express the mounting or stepping up into a chariot— "Ptolemy desired him *to step up* into his chariot." Homer, Herodotus, Plato, Xenophon, use this same word to express the mounting or stepping up upon a vessel, a camel, a staging, a horse, etc. And in this very chapter we have ἀναβάντα (v. 31) used to express the stepping up by Philip into the chariot of the Eunuch, as Joseph stepped up into the chariot of Ptolemy. Thus, as it is in express evidence that ἀναβαίνω takes Philip up into the chariot, so the evidence is clear for χαταβαίνω to bring him down from the chariot. But Professor Hackett objects, saying "the Eunuch only, returned to the chariot." This, however, is a mistake. The Scripture says, the Eunuch, only, pursued his journey in the chariot; but it does not say, "the Eunuch, only, returned to the chariot." If the Eunuch dismounted from the chariot and afterward pursued his journey in the chariot, he must have re-mounted into the chariot. Now, this dismounting is either not expressed at all or it is expressed by κατέβησαν; and if by this word, then it includes Philip, for it is plural; so, the remounting of the Eunuch is either not expressed at all, or it is expressed by ἀνέβησαν; and in that case it, again, includes Philip, for the verb is plural. If it be asked, Why did the Spirit of the Lord wait until Philip had gone up into the chariot before He carried him away? I answer by asking, Why did the Spirit of the Lord wait until he "came up out of the water"? Why not carry Philip away out of a chariot, as well as carry away Elijah in a chariot?

The case stands thus: Philip and the Eunuch came in a chariot upon some water; they dismounted from the chariot, stepping down at or into the water; a word is used which is employed both by Greeks and Jews to express stepping down from a chariot, and we say it is so used here; but the friends of a dipping say: " It is not so used, it is used to express ' walking down from shal-lower into deeper water ' " (not a word of which appears in Scrip-ture) " and the dismounting is not expressed at all." Again: it is admitted that the Eunuch did remount into his chariot, and a word is used which is employed by Greeks and Jews to express mounting up into a chariot, and which is employed in this same narrative to express Philip's mounting up into the chariot with the Eunuch, and which we say is here, again, employed to ex-press the remounting of the Eunuch (including Philip, the verb being plural) into the chariot from which he had dismounted; but the friends of dipping interpose and say, " No; the word means to walk back again from deeper water into shallower " (making an absolute addition to Scripture), " and there is nothing to ex-press the remounting of the Eunuch." Which interpretation has the greatest appearance of verisimilitude, that of those who, like Dr. Carson, " thirst to know the will of God," or that of those who " have no more conscience than Satan himself," the thought-ful will determine.

Baptized Him.

Professor Ripley complains that Professor Stuart argues against immersion based on " going down into the water," and says, " going down into the water is no part of the baptism." This position is at the expense of the postulation which requires,

1. That the whole and not the part of an object must be baptized; 2. Self-baptism is not Christian baptism; a duly qualified minister must be the baptizer; 3. "To modify a command of God for the sake of convenience is rebellion." If the Eunuch "baptized" one half of his body he had no authority to do it. If Philip "baptized" only so much of the body of the Eunuch as he left uncovered by "walking into the water," then he did not baptize "the whole," but a part only. The walking into the water is not claimed to be a divine command, but a human addition to avoid a very great inconvenience. The walking into the water by the Eunuch is, also, a purely human addition.

The language of Scripture, unquestionably, may express stepping down *into* the water, and just as unquestionably this may have been due to the position of the chariot when suddenly arrested, and because the limited quantity of water made such action a matter of indifference.

The assumption that the baptism of a person standing in water necessitates a dipping into water is an assumption "as unstable as water." It is certain, that $\beta a\pi\tau i\zeta\omega$ does not mean *to dip*. It is certain, that Greek baptisms without number were effected by a fluid without a fluid covering. It is certain, that early Christian writers represent baptism as effected in a variety of ways, and, among others, by stepping into water without being dipped into it. Thus Dionysius Alexandrinus (708), declares, that the pool of Bethesda was ($\varepsilon i\varkappa\grave{\omega}\nu\ \beta a\pi\tau i\sigma\mu a\tau o\varsigma$) the image of baptism, not because one was dipped into the water, but because he *stepped into it and* WAS HEALED. So Ambrose (III, 426) says: "Habes quartum genus baptismatis in piscina—Thou hast a fourth kind of baptism in the pool (Bethesda)." These writers neither believed that a dipping into water was necessary to a baptism, nor effected a baptism at all. They believed that he who stepped into the troubled water of Bethesda was baptized, not because "the body was immersed after the Jewish manner; namely, by walking into the water to the proper depth, and then sinking down till the whole body was immersed" (Conant, 58), but because the water had the power of healing by stepping into it, just as they believed that the water of Christian baptism, impregnated by the Spirit, had power to heal the soul, when applied to the body by them. It is so certain that baptism may be without covering the body in water, that Morell frankly admits that profuse superfusion is baptism. Fuller admits it in the case of the altar on Carmel.

And Professor Arnold (admitting that it is the practice, mcre or less frequently, in the Eastern Churches, to baptize one when in the water by pouring water from the hand upon the head) says, the lack of a covering in such case is but " a punctilio " (!). As we are ready to admit, that the Eunuch *may* have stepped down from the chariot into the water, will not Prof. Arnold and friends admit, that water *may* have been poured from the hand of Philip upon his head, and being so "baptized" any one who should complain of a lack of *covering* in water, must be condemned as standing on "a punctilio"? It is as certain as anything within the range of human knowledge, that baptisms are freely spoken of by early Christian writers without the slightest regard to the dipping or covering of the baptized object (see Judaic Baptism).

We conclude, therefore, with Prof. Ripley, that the stepping down into the water was no part of the baptism, and taking the pouring or the sprinkling of Professor Arnold (without the " punctilio "), we say with Luke, that the Eunuch was baptized " *with* water" (ὕδατι), and not *into* water (εἰς ὕδωρ), but "into the Name of the Lord Jesus." The baptizer was the same Philip who had just baptized the Samaritans "into the Name of the Lord Jesus ;" and the historian is the same who expresses the water used in baptism (whether in Gospel or in Acts) by ὕδατι, which precludes a dipping into water; and to say that the Eunuch was baptized in any other way than " ὕδατι εἰς τὸ ὄνομα τοῦ Κυρίου Ἰησοῦ, *with water* INTO THE NAME OF THE LORD JESUS," is to contradict the word of God.

᾽EK.

Dr. Carson insists, "that ἐκ has no indefiniteness in its meaning. It always signifies *out of*. It always begins at a point within, and not without, the place of departure. To this there is no exception and no color of exception." For this reason he insists that Philip and the Eunuch must have been within the water, and, *therefore*, the Eunuch was *dipped* into water. This has already been shown to be a *non sequitur;* but as another exhibition of that error of " one meaning and but one meaning " so characteristic of the theory, it may be well to inquire of usage as to this unvarying meaning.

A quotation from Sir William Hamilton (Classic Baptism, pp. 23, 24) was given to show, that the doctrine of a cast-iron definitism in βαπτίζω was in conflict with the laws of language. The same doctrine now urged for ἐκ is also shown to be at war with language development as stated by Marsh (Origin and History of the English Language) : " So, too, he refutes a current notion, that words individually and independently of syntactical relations, and of phraseological combinations, have one or more inherent, fixed and limited meanings, which are capable of logical definition. Words live and breathe only in mutual combination and interdependence with other words."

The correctness of this statement will be manifest by a limited exhibition of the usage of this preposition.

Harrison (Professor in the University of Virginia) has written a standard work on the Greek prepositions. His view of the meaning of this preposition (ἐκ) is thus stated:

" 1. OUT, WITHOUT; that is on the outside.

" 2. *Out of, from out;* = out + motion from. *a.* Of space; *out of; from out. b.* Of a number of objects; *out of, from* (out). *c.* Of origin, parentage, source, cause, agent, material; *of, from. d.* Of that from which an action, motion, event, etc., begins; *from:* (1.) Of space, and generally ; *from.* (2.) Of time ; *from.* (3.) Of the point of attachment; *from.* (4.) Of the space to which an object is referred for its position ; *on, in.*"

Jelf (§ 621). Primary meaning, *out*, opposed to ἐν, *in.*

Kühner (Gram., § 288) gives substantially the same view : " 1. In a local relation: *a. removal* either from within a place or object, or from immediate participation or connection with a place or object, with verbs of motion ; *b. distance* with verbs of rest: *without, beyond;* 2. Of time, *immediate* outgoing, development, or succession ; 3. In a causal and figurative sense: *a.* Of *origin; b.* Of the *whole* in relation to its parts; *c.* Of the *author; d.* the *occasion* or *cause; e.* the *material; f.* the *means* and *instrument; g. conformity.*"

Winer (366) makes the original meaning of ἐκ issuing *from within.* He says, it is antithetic to εἰς. Harrison says, " it is just the opposite of ἐν." Jelf and Kühner make the same statement. Harrison farther says: " The common signification of ἐκ, not in composition, is *out of, from out*, with the idea of proceeding from out of a circumscribed space. This meaning, being due partly to the action or motion of which it is the qualification, is not to be considered as simple and proper to ἐκ; the sense contained in the preposition itself is no more than that of *out, without.*" While all of these grammarians recognize ἐκ as related to

movement beginning within circumscribed space, none of them
consider *depth* as entering into the idea of this preposition.
They all recognize action *proceeding from the surface* of any
object, or from within any circumscribed space (without penetration) as fully meeting the demand of this preposition.

That ἐκ is used where there is neither depth nor superficial
withinness, Harrison gives the following among other evidences:
" 1. The derivative ἔξω, *without*, the opposite of within; 2. ἐκκαθεύδειν,
to sleep out of doors ; 3. παῖς ἐκκείμενος, *a child lying out, exposed;*
4. ἐκκλεῖσαι τῆς πόλεως, *to shut out from the city ;* 5. ἐκλείπειν, *to
leave out ;* 6. ἐκ βελέων εἶναι, *to be out of the reach of darts.* . . .
ἐκ with the genitive case occurs in some instances with the primary and simple meaning *without, out :* e. g., ἐκ καπνοῦ κατέθηχ', I
deposited the weapons out of, without the smoke ; that is, on the
outside with respect to the smoke. Odys. XIX, 7; ἐκ τόξου ῥύματος,
a foot soldier out of bowshot. Xen. Anab. III, 3, 15; that is,
without, on the outside, with respect to a bowshot; ἐκ τοῦ μέσου,
sat down out from their midst. Herod. III, 83 ; out, on the outside, in respect to the midst of them. The compound ἐκποδών,
out, or *without*, with respect to the feet, belongs here together
with a number besides in which ἐκ retains its proper sense, on
which the genitive depends."

This doctrine that ἐκ signifies *out, without*, simply, and also
proceeding from within a boundary line, or from superficial contact, together with other derived and related meanings, is sustained by Scripture usage: Matt. 27 : 38, " Two thieves were crucified with him, one (ἐκ δεξιῶν) out from the right, and one (ἐξ
εὐωνύμων) out from the left." Here we have the meaning " *out*,"
with respect to the right, " out," with respect to the left, without
any antecedent withinness. 1 John 2: 19, " They went (ἐξ ἡμῶν)
out from us, but they were not (ἐξ ἡμῶν) of us." Here is a diversity of usage in the same sentence. In the first case, there is
reference to position within a company of persons and movement
thence carrying without the company ; in the second case, there
is no reference to position or movement, but to unity of character
and continued sympathy as a consequence. A parallel passage is
found in I Maccab., XIII, 49, " But they who were (ἐκ τῆς ἄκρας)
of the citadel in Jerusalem were hindered (ἐκπορεύεσθαι) from
going out." The first use of ἐκ has lost all idea of separation
and expresses *belonging to*, while the second ἐκ (in composition)
turns wholly on the idea of separation. So, in Herodotus I, 62,

"Those Athenians who were (ἐκ ἄστεος) of the city." And Josephus XIII, 2, 1, "The impious and deserters (ἐκ τῆς ἀκροπολεως) of (= belonging to) the citadel, feared greatly." Another usage is shown in Matt. 12 : 33, "A tree is known (ἐκ τοῦ καρποῦ) *by means of* its fruit." A similar usage, with one diverse, is seen in Rev. 9 : 18, 19, "And out of (ἐκ) their mouths issued fire, and smoke, and brimstone. The third part of men were killed (ὑπὸ) by these three, namely (ἐκ τοῦ πυρός), by means of the fire, and (ἐκ τοῦ καπνοῦ) by means of the smoke, and (ἐκ τοῦ θείου) by means of the brimstone, which issued (ἐκ) out of their mouths." Here, in the same sentence ἐκ represents both agency and movement, beginning at a point indefinitely deep within the mouth.

Inness inappreciable ; superficial ; no contact.

Luke 7 : 38, "And began to wash his feet with tears and (ἐξέμασσε) *wiped* them *off* with the hairs of her head ;" John 11 : 2, "Anointed the Lord with ointment, and (ἐκμάξασα) *wiped off* his feet with her hair ;" Matt. 10 : 14, "When ye depart out of that house or city (ἐκτινάξατε) *shake off* the dust of your feet ;" John 6 : 37, "And him that cometh (πρὸς) to me, I will in nowise (ἐκβάλω) *cast out ;*" Matt. 12 : 13, "He said (ἔκτεινον) *stretch out* thy hand. And (ἐξέτεινε) he *stretched* it *out ;*" Acts 27 : 32, "Then the soldiers cut off the ropes of the boat, and let her (ἐκπεσεῖν) *fall off.*"

In these passages we have dust shaken *off from*, and tears and ointment wiped *off from* the feet. Does the shaking or wiping, in such cases, begin *within* the feet? When the hand is stretched out from the body, *within* what does the movement begin? The sinner is invited to come *to* Jesus ; could the casting out of such a one begin at a point *within* Jesus to which the sinner had never attained?

The rope which holds a boat, not within a vessel nor in contact with a vessel but floating in the water, is cut, and it falls *off*, floating away. Does this floating movement begin at a point *within* the vessel? Prof. Hackett (Comm.) says, "The ropes of the boat which fastened it to the vessel; not those by which they were lowering it, as that was already done; *let it fall off (i. e.,* from the side or stern of the vessel), go adrift."

This justly esteemed scholar (*primus inter pares* from earliest

13

student life it gives me pleasure as a fellow-student to testify) knows nothing of the absolutism of Dr. Carson's doctrine.

As many of these examples present the preposition in composition it may be well to adduce others of simple form.

Acts 28: 3–5, "There came a viper (ἐκ τῆς θέρμης) out of the heat and fastened on his hand. And when the barbarians saw the venomous beast hang (ἐκ τῆς χειρός) off from his hand. . . . And he (ἀποτινάξας) shook off the beast into the fire."

Prof. Hackett (Comm.), says, " ἐκ τῆς θέρμης, *from* the heat, the *effect* of it. . . . This is the common view of the expression, to which De Wette also adheres. It may also mean *from* the heat, the *place* of it, as explained by Winer, Meyer, and others; ἐκ is kept nearer in this way to its ordinary force. . . . ἐκ τῆς χειρός, *from his hand*, to which it clung by its mouth."

This case of the viper all can understand. Whether it had fastened on his hand by coiling around it, or by a tooth struck into it, is a matter of no conseqence. If Dr. Carson is satisfied that the motion of the viper's fall began within the hand because a tooth may have been stuck into the flesh, we will make no earnest objection. He will no doubt in turn admit, if the toe of the sandal of Philip or the Eunuch touched the water's edge, it will justify the statement that the action of mounting up into the chariot began within the water.

Acts 12: 7, " And his chains (ἐξέπεσον) fell off (ἐκ τῶν χειρῶν) from his hands."

Prof. Hackett translates, " His chains fell *off from* his hands or wrists. They were fastened to the wrist in the Roman mode." The Baptist Version translates, " His chains fell *off from* his hands." In a note, it is said, ἐκ τῶν χειρῶν, not *out of*, but *from* his hands. They could not have fallen *out of*, unless he had held them in his hands."

We have then, here, the most absolute and admitted evidence that Dr. Carson's doctrine respecting this preposition is erroneous. It may be possible to have even a little more conscience than the devil, and still question whether ἐκ by its essential force proves that the Eunuch was dipped into the water or even that he was within the water at all. So far from Dr. Carson's friends accepting the doctrine that ἐκ " always means *out of*, implying that the point of departure is within the object, to which there is no color of exception," they expressly deny that it can have, in this case, the meaning " out of," and must have the meaning *from*. As it is admitted by Dr. Carson himself that εἰς may mean *unto*, it necessarily follows, so far as the force of terms is concerned, that Philip and the Eunuch may have stepped down from the chariot *to* the water and stepped up into the chariot *from* the water. While we claim that this *may be* the translation, we do not claim that it *must* be. There is no need for our doing so. It is in proof, that the position of the chariot *may* have been such as to necessitate stepping into the water in stepping down from the chariot; and it is in proof, that the quantity of water *may* have been so limited as to make it unnecessary to change the position of the chariot on this account. These points being proved, as possible, the extremest definitions of εἰς and ἐκ do not militate against our view; while such proof is an absolute arrest to the (accustomed) assumption of a dipping.

John 12 : 32, "If I be lifted up (ἐκ τῆς γῆς) from the earth; . . . This he said signifying what death he should die." This case shows, again, exterior position with respect to the earth, without the possibility of movement to secure such position beginning within the earth. Thucyd. IV, 31, "Which was (ἐκ θαλάσσης) from the sea steep, and (ἐκ τῆς γῆς) from the land difficult of assault." The preposition here does not indicate that the promontory came "out of the sea" on one side, and "out of the earth" on the other side; but where it stood *out*, with respect to the sea, it was steep, and where it stood *out*, with respect to the land, it was hard to be assailed. "The Genitive case, with ἐκ, has uniformly the meaning *with respect to*" (Harrison). Lycophron, lin. 844, "Who forming men (ἐξ ἄκρου ποδος) from the extremity of the foot, making a statue." A statue is not formed "out of" the extremity of the foot.

The association of this preposition with εἰς does not change its character.

Homer, Iliad XVI, 639, "Covered with darts, and blood, and dust (ἐκ κεφαλῆς ἐς πόδας ἄκρους) *from* the head *to* the extremities of the feet." If εἰς does not carry the darts, and blood, and dust, *into* "the extremities of the feet," why must ἐκ bring them *out of* "the head"? Achilles Tat. IV, 18, "Stooping forward (ἐκ τῆς νεὼς) *from* the vessel, he directs his face (εἰς τὸν ποταμὸν) *towards* the stream." This is Dr. Conant's translation. If we translate the passage under consideration in the same way, it will read, "They stepped down *towards* the water, and stepped up *from* the water," and then what becomes of the "Satan" argument for immersion?

Is it said, "Circumstances modify the meanings of words"? We answer, This is common sense; but what then becomes of the postulation which makes βαπτίζω mean "one thing and only one thing," and ἐκ to mean "movement beginning within an object, to which there is no color of exception"? If the position of the Egyptian must be considered, namely, sailing in a boat on a river; and if his object must be considered, namely, to get a drink of water by making a cup of his hand; so the position of Philip and the Eunuch must be considered, namely, travelling in a chariot and arrival ἐπὶ τὶ ὕδωρ; and their object must be considered, namely, to administer *Christian* baptism (ὕδατι εἰς τὸ ὄνομα τοῦ Κυρίου ʼΙησοῦ) "*with* water *into* the Name of the Lord Jesus." And when this has been done, the dipping of the Eunuch into water has far more absolutely disappeared than has the dipping of the boatman's face into the river Nile.

Πρὸς, ἐπὶ, εἰς, ἐκ μνημείου.

There is a transaction related in Scripture where ἐκ occurs, which is stated with so much of detail and precision, that it may be well to consider it. I refer to the rolling away of the stone from the sepulchre of our blessed Lord.

Mark 15 : 46, "And laid him in a sepulchre which was hewn (ἐκ πέτρας) *of* rock." This use of ἐκ indicates the material of which the sepulchre was made, viz., "of rock." Matthew (27 : 60) expresses the same idea in another form, "hewn (ἐν) in the rock;" Luke uses yet another form (23 : 53), "in a rock-hewn sepulchre (ἐν μνήματι λαξευτῷ)."

This use of ἐκ, indicating material of which something is formed, and consequently sameness with that which is formed, is quite common, and is illustrated in John 3 : 6, "That which is born (ἐκ τῆς σαρκὸς) of the flesh, is flesh;" and John 4 : 31 "(ὁ ὢν ἐκ τῆς γῆς, ἐκ τῆς γῆς ἐστι, καὶ ἐκ τῆς γῆς λαλεῖ) He that is of the earth, is of the earth (= earth-like), and speaketh of the earth (= earth-like)."

Closely allied to this usage is that in which ἐκ indicates not the material of which anything is made, but the agency by which it exists or from which it receives character. 1 John 5, "Whosoever is born (ἐκ τοῦ Θεοῦ) of God sinneth not " = is like the Author of his life in character, who does not sin; John 3 : 6, "That which is born (ἐκ τοῦ Πνεύματος) of the Spirit, is spirit " = is like the Spirit by whom the change expressed by "born" has been effected; John 3 : 5, "Except a man be born (ἐκ ὕδατος) of water." *Birth*

here, and in the preceding cases, has of necessity, a modified meaning. It expresses, in general, a radical change. The specific
character of this change will depend upon its cause. The change
produced by simple water applied to a filthy person is very radical
but purely physical. This cannot be the birth of water held out
to Nicodemus. It must refer to that water with which he was
familiar as a Jew, and especially as a "Pharisee." This water
had nothing to do with physical cleansing. It had the power to
cleanse from ceremonial impurity and to typify spiritual cleansing.
Therefore Nicodemus is taught the insufficiency of such change
as water effects in a man's religious condition, and the necessity
for such other change as is "of the Spirit," in order to see the
kingdom of God.

This usage of ἐκ, with the agency, is strikingly illustrated in the
interpretation of this passage as given by the change of a word in
the Apostolical Constitutions VI, 15, "Whosoever is unwilling (ἐκ)
of contempt to be baptized, shall be condemned and reprobated as
ungrateful and foolish. For the Lord says, Ἐὰν μή τις βαπτισθῇ
ἐξ ὕδατος καὶ Πνεύματος, 'Except a man be BAPTIZED of water and
the Spirit, he cannot enter into the kingdom of God.'" The syntax makes it impossible to translate βαπτισθῇ by *dipping* or *immersing*. "To be dipped *of* or *out of* water and the Spirit," and
"to be immersed *of* or *out of* water and the Spirit," are absurd
statements. "To be baptized (in the sense *to be made regenerate*)
of water and of the Spirit" is facile syntax and as good theology
according to the Apostol. Const's. This passage, therefore, overturns the univocal theory of Dr. Carson both as to βαπτίζω and as
to ἐκ. This passage is, also, confirmatory of the interpretation of
one parallel as to syntax mentioned in Classic Baptism, p. 335,
"βαπτίζοντες ἐκ πίθων," where ἐκ is indicative of agency, "*Baptizing
of cups*," *i. e., making drunk* BY wine in the cups. "Baptism (ἐκ)
of the Spirit" is *regeneration* BY the Spirit. And "Baptism (ἐκ)
of the wine cup" is *intoxication* BY the wine cup. This use of ἐκ,
as expressive of agency, is recognized by the Baptist translation
of John 3 : 34, "God giveth not the Spirit (ἐκ μέτρου) *by* measure
unto him."

Out Of.

JOHN 20 : 2. "They have taken away the Lord (ἐκ τοῦ μνημείου)
out of the sepulchre." This is a clear case in which the action connected with ἐκ "begins at a point within the object." This point

of beginning, however, is not due to any essential force of this preposition, but 1. To the nature of the case. The place for a dead body is within a sepulchre. 2. We are expressly told that the body was *within* the sepulchre, as in Matt. 27 : 60, "Joseph laid the body (ἐν) *in* his own new tomb;" Mark 15 : 46, "And laid him (ἐν) *in* a sepulchre;" Luke 23 : 53, "And laid it (ἐν) *in* a rock-hewn sepulchre." If, under these circumstances, the body is "taken away," it is impossible for the movement to begin at any other point .than that where the body is, to wit, *within* the sepulchre.

The case proves, as stated by Harrison, and Kühner, and Jelf, that " ἐκ is the opposite of ἐν." It does not, however, prove that ἐκ requires for its object a preceding interior position such as that of the body within the sepulchre. The essential element is an exterior position in contrast with an interior position. How such position is secured, whether originally occupied without move-ment, or whether by movement from within the related object, or from within a superficial space, or from contact at any point, or by the dissolution of some intermediate bond, ἐκ does not deter-mine. This is shown by another use of this preposition in con-nection with this same transaction.

Out From.

JOHN 20 : 1. " Mary Magdalene cometh (εἰς μνημεῖον) to the sep-ulchre, and seeth the stone taken away (ἐκ τοῦ μνημείου) *out from* the sepulchre."

A "stone," unlike a buried body, may or may not be within a sepulchre. Do we know from other sources what was the char-acter and position of this stone? The information on both these points is full and precise : Matthew (27 : 60) says, " He rolled a great stone (προσκυλίσας τῇ θύρᾳ τοῦ μνημείου) *to* the door of the sepulchre, and departed;" Mark (15 : 46) says, "And rolled a stone (ἐπὶ τὴν θύραν) *upon* the door of the sepulchre." This stone was " a great stone," and its office was to close the entrance of the sepulchre. Matthew indicates the position of the stone as " rolled (πρός) *to, against* the door;" and Mark as " rolled to and (ἐπὶ) *upon* the door." Now, observe the contrast between the natu-ral relations of a buried body and of this stone to a sepulchre. A buried body is of necessity within the sepulchre, and the stone which closes the entrance to a sepulchre is of necessity precluded from being within the sepulchre. In accordance with this, Matthew, Mark, and Luke testify that the body of our Lord was *within* the sepulchre, and Matthew and Mark testify that the stone was without the sepulchre, rolled *against* and *upon* the door Could contrast be broader as to the position, with respect to the sepulchre, occupied by this buried body and this protecting stone? This testimony which puts the stone in position is confirmed by that which states its removal: Matt. 28 : 2, " The angel of the Lord descended from heaven and (προσελθών) came *to* and rolled away the stone (ἀπό) *from* the door, and sat upon it." Here we are told the angel came, not into the sepulchre, but *to* the stone, which was exterior to the sepulchre, and " rolled it away (ἀπό) *from* the door." That this stone was not *within* the sepulchre is farther proved by the statement of Mark (16 : 3, 4), in which he uses ἐκ, " Who shall roll (ἀπό) away the stone for us (ἐκ) *out from* the door? And when they looked they saw the stone (ἀποκεκύλισ-ται) was rolled away."

Here ἀπό and ἐκ are associated in the removal of the stone; but the relation of ἐκ is more specific, it is OUT *from* the *door*, and not *out of* the sepulchre. The statement that an object is *in* a door is very diverse from the statement that it is *within* the door. And the statement that a body is in the *door* of a sepulchre is very diverse from the statement that it is in the *sepulchre*. This "very great stone" was *against* the door, *upon* the door, and limitedly (probably) *in* the door; it was in no sense *within* the sepulchre.

Notwithstanding the relations of this stone to the sepulchre, purely external; and notwithstanding the express statements of Matthew, Mark, and Luke, declaring the external position necessary to the fulfilment of its office; and notwithstanding the statement that the angel came to the stone, rolled it away, and sat upon it without entering into the sepulchre; and notwithstanding the absurdity of leaving the entrance to the sepulchre without any protection, when they were to " make it as secure as ye can ; " still the translator of the Baptist Version (John 20 : 1) contends, in an elaborate note, that this " very great stone" was *within* the sepulchre and attached to an inner crypt! He also insists that εἰς here means *into*, and Mary Magdalene came (εἰς μνημεῖον) *into* the sepulchre before she saw that the stone was rolled away from the sepulchre.

When Jesus came εἰς τὸ μνημεῖον of Lazarus did he come " *into* the sepulchre " before he saw that the stone was *not* taken away?

When Jesus commanded the stone which ($ἐπίχειτο ἐπ’ αὐτῷ$) "lay *upon* the sepulchre" of Lazarus to be taken away, was the stone *within* the sepulchre? When "the stone was put upon the entrance of the lion's den ($ἐπέθηχαν ἐπὶ τὸ στόμα τοῦ λάχχου$)" and "sealed" with the signet of king and lord, was it put, not on the outside of but, *within* the den? Theory, as well as "much learning," doth make men "mad."

The stone was rolled away *from* and *out*, with respect to the door and the sepulchre.

The Postulate.

We can now judge of the value of Dr. Carson's postulate. Does the wiping off of "dust," "tears," "ointment," *begin within* the object? Does the stretching out of the arm from the body *begin within* the body? Does the falling off of a chain, or of a viper from the hand, *begin within* the hand? Does the falling off of a boat in the sea, from a vessel (by reason of the cutting of a rope), *begin within* the vessel? Does the rolling away of a stone from the door of a sepulchre *begin within* the sepulchre?

If these questions should be answered by the friends of the theory in the affirmative, and they are willing to take a tear-drop resting upon the foot, or a chain resting upon the wrist, or a stone resting against a rock, as expressive of the depth of withinness demanded by $ἐx$, I do not know that any one need object to allowing both Philip and the Eunuch to step into the water, and step out of the water, having entered to a depth quite equal to the profoundest of either of these cases.

"The Rack."

Dr. Carson says, "Amid the most violent perversion that this passage can sustain on the rack, it will still cry out immersion, immersion!" It is quite possible that on the rack the cry of "immersion" will be emitted, for under the torture of "the thumbscrew" and "the boot" falsehood has oftentimes been uttered for truth; but if these words of the Holy Ghost are allowed to speak under no other pressure than that of truth, they will evermore proclaim—"baptism into the Name of the Lord Jesus," "baptism into the Name of the Lord Jesus!" And this they will do, *to* what or *into* what, *from* what or *out of* what, Philip and the Eunuch may have stepped down or stepped up.

The interpretation thus given takes every word and every circumstance in its natural order and at its proper value. The interpretation of the theory does neither : 1. It arrests the chariot before it comes " (ἐπὶ τὶ ὕδωρ) *upon* some water ; " 2. It creates a space between the chariot and the water ; 3. It converts this space into a declivity ; 4. It takes the word which expresses stepping down from the chariot (leaving its occupants to dismount the best way they can), and conducts them (by the help of this borrowed word) down the created declivity to the water ; 5. At the water εἰς is used farther to conduct into "two feet nine inches" water for the convenience of dipping ; 6. The force of τι is rejected, and a limited quantity of water is converted into unlimited quantity ; 7. The meaning of βαπτίζω (as a farther convenience) is converted into dipping ; 8. As a necessity, εἰς ὕδωρ into water, is supplied from the theory, while " εἰς τὸ ὄνομα τοῦ Κυρίου ᾿Ιησοῦ, into the Name of the Lord Jesus" (supplied by inspiration in this same chapter 8 : 16, under the ministry of this same Philip) and ὕδατι *with* water, the uniform term used by the narrator of this transaction, are rejected ; 9. The word appropriate to express (and so used in this same chapter 8 : 31) the stepping up into the chariot, is rejected from such use and compelled to do service in bringing up out of deeper water into "shallower at the edge ;" 10. Having deprived Philip and the Eunuch of the means for remounting into the chariot, Philip is dismissed without obtaining a seat at all, and the Eunuch is sent on his way having entered his chariot *no one can tell how.*

Such is the detail of *the* ONLY CASE of RITUAL *baptism under Christianity, to which the friends of dipping ever ventured to appeal as lending any possible countenance to their practice during* THE ENTIRE HISTORY OF THE NEW TESTAMENT CHURCH.

To those who "thirst to know the will of God" we leave it, that they may gather from it its teachings. Should their conclusions differ from ours, we will not on that account declare, that they have "no more conscience than Satan," however much we may believe them to be mistaken.

RITUAL BAPTISM OF THE GENTILES.

"BY THE AUTHORITY OF THE LORD,"
WITH WATER, INTO THE NAME OF THE LORD JESUS.

ACTS 10 : 47, 48.

Μήτι τὸ ὕδωρ κωλῦσαι δύναται τις τοῦ μὴ βαπτισθῆναι τούτους, ὅιτινες τὸ Πνεῦμα τὸ ῞Αγιον ἔλαβον καθὼς καὶ ἡμεῖς; Προσέταξέ τε αὐτοὺς βαπτισθῆναι ἐν τῷ ὀνοματ τοῦ Κυρίου.

" Can any man forbid the water, that these should not be baptized, which have received the Holy Ghost as well as we?

" And he commanded them, in the name of the Lord, to be baptized ?"

POINTS OF SPECIAL INTEREST.

This case of ritual baptism has points of special interest: 1. The Gentiles are now, for the first time, welcomed into the Christian church by ritual baptism, under the special authority of the Lord, having previously been baptized by the Holy Ghost, both with that baptism which regenerates the soul, and with that baptism which invests with miraculous endowments; 2. Water is expressly stated as entering into Christian ritual baptism, now, for the second time only, and for the last time ; 3. The use of the phrase ἐν τῷ ὀνόματι τοῦ Κυρίου so as to raise the grammatical question, What is its syntactical relation ? and, thus, answer another question, What is its logical value ? 4. The Gentiles received the same baptism as did the Jews.

These are all points not merely of theoretic interest but of great practical value.

Ritual Baptism to be Perpetuated.

This ritual baptism of Gentiles, by special divine authorization, proves, that this rite enters, essentially and permanently, into the constitution of the Christian church. And the fact, that these Gentiles were baptized first by the Holy Ghost and subsequently by water, proves, that Christian baptism is not a result effected by conjoint and co-operative agencies, viz., the Holy Ghost *and* water ; but that these agencies are distinct, disjoined, and diverse in nature, power, and office, *while related to one and the same baptism* (= the remission of sin, and the regeneration of the soul) which is effected by the Holy Ghost and is symbolized by water. This disjunction of the Holy Ghost and Water as co-operative agencies or as conjoint agency, and their conjunction as efficient agency and sequent symbol agency showing forth visibly the work of the Holy Ghost, is of the last importance in view of the early development of doctrine upon this point, which has been, more or less, perpetuated to this day.

"The Water."

WATER, whenever spoken of in Scripture as entering into the administration of baptism, is invariably spoken of in the abstract, and without regard to quantity.

In the administration of baptism by John quantity was present; but this quantity was an accident belonging to the locality of John's ministry, not an essential entering into the rite. Neither the Jordan nor any other river ever afterward appears in the administration of baptism. At Enon (springs) " much water " = many waters, or springs, are spoken of; not, however, to show that there was a quantity of water for baptism, but to explain how it was, that John and the disciples of Jesus could baptize in the same neighborhood without interfering with each other.

That this explanation of the relation of Jordan and of Enon to the administration of baptism is correct, is shown by the fact, that when the singular wilderness ministry of John passes away, the river baptism vanishes from Scripture with it; and when the singular concurrent baptism of John and Jesus ceases, Enon and its " many springs " ceases to be heard of. Farther confirmation is found in the fact, that when John gives the authority for his using water in baptism he says nothing of quantity, but mentions WATER simply and abstractly—John 1 : 33, " He that sent me to baptize with WATER." The translation " baptize *in* water " being an error (*see* Johannic Baptism), the quantity of water, thereby elicited, is also an error. The Saviour, when speaking of the water used by John in baptism, speaks of it in the same abstract manner—Acts 1 : 5, " John indeed baptized (ὕδατι) with WATER." Philip evidently taught the Eunuch that it was *water*, and not quantity of water, which entered into Christian baptism, as shown, when they came " (ἐπί τι ὕδωρ) upon *some* water," by his exclamation, " See! WATER." The passage before us (the only other one in which water is mentioned in connection with the administration of the rite in Scripture) establishes the same point. Peter reiterates the doctrine of John, of John's, and his, Lord, and of the instructed Eunuch, that it is *water*, simple and abstract and not quantity, which characterizes Christian ritual baptism—inquiring, "Who can forbid the WATER?" This question was addressed to those who came with him and were familiar with the use of "the water" in Christian baptism. The use of the definite article (τὸ ὕδωρ) "THE water," would be inappropriate to water in a running stream. It implies water separated from other water and set apart for a special use. Any water may be so separated from other water and from other uses, but it is only after such separation and appropriation, that it becomes "*the* water of baptism." A stream of water is no more "*the* water of baptism" than it is the water of *fishing*, or the water of *sailing*. Water brought in a vessel and so separated from all other water and appropriated to the specific use of the Christian rite, becomes "THE WATER *of baptism*." It might as well be said, that Pilate came down from the judgment-seat and went out to the pool of Siloam to get water to wash his hands, as that Peter and Cornelius went out to some stream for "*the* water."

The language of Scripture is exhausted by ἐν ὕδατι, ὕδατι, τι ὕδωρ, τὸ ὕδωρ, in speaking of ritual baptism, and the addition to it of quantity is an absolute addition to the words of inspiration.

Ἐν τῷ ὀνόματι τοῦ Κυρίου.

It is a very common idea, that this phrase here represents a formula of baptism and as such must be connected with βαπτισ-θῆναι. Olshausen, in answering the question—"Did the Lord intend to establish a fixed formula of baptism in Matt. 28 : 19?" says, "This question would not have been suggested at all, had the other portions of the New Testament shown that the disciples in administering baptism employed these words. But instead of this, we find, that even in the history of the Acts of the Apostles, as often as baptism is mentioned, it is performed only εἰς or ἐπὶ τὸ ὄνομα, ἐν τῷ ὀνόματι Ἰησοῦ or Χριστοῦ." The idea of Olshausen, that ἐπὶ τῷ ὀνόματι Ἰησοῦ Χριστοῦ (Acts 2 : 38), and ἐν τῷ ὀνόματι τοῦ Κυρίου in the passage before us, are formulæ of baptism and indicate, that the baptism takes place "*in* the name, etc.," is shared by Professor Ripley and by Baptist writers generally, as well as by many others.

There are insuperable objections against this view. The fol

lowing are some of these objections: 1. There is no satisfactory evidence of a single case in the New Testament in which ἐν points out the receiving element (real or ideal) in baptism; 2. Cases are frequent in the New Testament where this formula (with a command) expresses the source of authority for such command; e. g., Acts 3 : 6, "In the name of Jesus Christ (ἐν τῷ ὀνόματι 'Ιησοῦ Χριστοῦ) rise up and walk;" Acts 16 : 18, "I command thee (ἐν τῷ ὀνόματι 'Ιησοῦ Χριστοῦ) in the name of Jesus Christ to come out of her." This last command is by Paul; the first is by Peter, the same who issues the command in the passage under consideration. Both refer their authority to Jesus Christ, and claim to derive authority from him by being " in his name " and thus invested with his authority. There was no occasion in all Peter's ministry when he more needed to be invested with divine authority, than when the door of the Christian church was to be opened to the Gentile world. He here claims to be " in the name of the Lord," while he commands these Gentiles to be baptized. If objection should be made to this interpretation on the ground of the order of the words, it may be answered: That the order of sequence does not necessarily determine the grammatical or logical order. The order of ὕδατι in Matt. 3 : 11 is after βαπτίζω, and in Luke 3 : 16 is before it; yet in both cases the grammatical and logical relations of ὕδατι to the baptism remains unchanged. It may be farther answered; Cyril of Jerusalem (432) quotes this passage giving another order, thus; "Peter commanded them (ἐν τῷ ὀνόματι I. X. βαπτισθῆναι) in the name of Jesus Christ, to be baptized." It is highly probable, that this was the order and the phraseology of the text used by Cyril, as it is also that of the Codex Sinaiticus. Objection from the order is therefore not only annulled, but whatever of weight belongs to it is thrown heavily on the other side.

3. The plea for disjoining βαπτισθῆναι and ἐν τῷ ὀνόματι is greatly strengthened by the quite unlooked-for approval of the translator of the Baptist Version, who, retaining the order of the common text and translating "he commanded them to be immersed in the name of the Lord," still, in a note, says, "'Εν τῷ ὀνόματι, in the name, or by the authority of the Lord, he *commanded* them to be immersed. 'Εις τὸ ὀνομα, and ἐν τῷ ὀνόματι, are never substituted in Sacred, or Classic literature, as synonyms. The authority by which any act is performed must never be confounded with the meaning, or intention of it."

There are some points developed in this note which have special value as coming from a Baptist scholar. Among them are these: 1. Ἐν τῷ ὀνόματι although immediately sequent to βαπτίζω has not, thereby, a complementary relation to it as expressive of the element within which the baptized object is received.

Dr. Conant in translating Matt. 3 : 11, "βαπτίζω ὑμᾶς ἐν ὕδατι, I immerse you *in* water," says in a note : " This is the only sense in which ἐν can be used in connection with βαπτίζω." If the " connection " between βαπτίζω and ἐν referred to by Dr. Conant is that of simple sequence, then his position is contradictory to that of his associate translator. But if a connection between these words requiring the translation " immersed *in* " be not established by mere sequence, then it should be proved and not assumed that in Matt. 3 : 11 there is beyond sequence such a connection between βαπτίζω and ἐν ὕδατι as requires that ἐν ὕδατι should be taken as the complement of βαπτίζω. And this proof must confront and nullify, 1. The fact, that such complementary relation *drowns;* 2. The fact, that in the parallel passage (Luke 3 : 16, ὕδατι βαπτίζω) there is no ἐν present, and its regimen in Matthew (ὕδατι) does not follow but precedes the verb ; and also 3. The fact, that Matthew offers another claimant (εἰς μετάνοιαν) of far better right to this complementary relation.

2. The translator of Acts says, "βαπτίζω ἐν τῷ ὀνόματι and βαπτίζω εἰς τὸ ὄνομα are not synonymous phrases, are not interchanged either in Classic or in Sacred literature, and require a discriminating translation."

This view antagonizes that of Dr. Conant presented in his translation of Matt. 28 : 19, where he says, " *in* the name is the proper English expression of εἰς τὸ ὄνομα." And this antagonism is made farther manifest by the translation of Acts 8 : 16, "Only they had been immersed (εἰς τὸ ὄνομα) *into* the name of the Lord Jesus," which translation (as to the preposition) is made emphatic in a note, " They had only been immersed *into* the name of the Lord Jesus." But against this translation and sentiment Dr. Conant says : " *Into the name* is not an English phrase, and though the literal form of the Greek does not give the sense."

Dr. Conant, as the final reviser of the Baptist Version, has prevailed over his fellow-translator, and in Matt. 28 : 19, Acts 8 : 16, he has made εἰς τὸ ὄνομα " *in* the name ;" and in Acts 10 : 48 he has made ἐν τῷ ὀνόματι, also, " *in* the name," thus confounding diverse forms, as his associate says is never done either " in

Classic or Sacred literature." Baptist writers have neither unity
nor consistency in their interpretations, whether we have regard
to their relations to one another, to themselves, or to the principles of language.

3. The translator of Acts teaches, that the difference between
βαπτίζω εἰς and βαπτίζω ἐν is not merely verbal, but of essential and
unalterable value among Classic and Sacred writers. This doctrine is correct. And it is of vital importance in the translation
and interpretation of the Scriptures. Both forms are there found,
and their use is discriminating in their relation to each other, but
uniform in the sphere appropriate to each. This diversity is
ignored and the different forms are confounded by Dr. Conant in
his Baptist Version, which merges βαπτίζω εἰς in βαπτίζω ἐν, so that
a reader of the Baptist Bible would never know that a baptism
(εἰς τὸ ὄνομα) "into the Name of the Father and of the Son and of
the Holy Ghost " was commanded, or that a baptism (εἰς τὸ ὄνομα)
"into the Name of the Lord Jesus " was administered by the
Apostles. The baptism announced by the Holy Ghost is blotted
out.

On this point hear, farther, the associate translator of Dr.
Conant. In a note on Acts 4 : 18 he says : "Inasmuch as we
have in the original Scriptures three forms of expression connected
with ονομα του Ιησου Χριστου, of very different import, it seems to
me not merely expedient, but obligatory, that we should give to
an English reader three corresponding formulæ in our language,
such as—in (ἐν) the name of—upon (ἐπὶ) the name of—into (εἰς)
the name of. These three formulæ are as distinct in sense as in
form. The first indicates authority, viz., in the name of the king
or commonwealth. The second indicates the subject on which
the authority terminates, the citizens of the commonwealth ; and
the third the reason why, or the object for which, the action is
performed." This translator is hardly consistent with the principles thus laid down when, in Acts 2 : 28, he translates "immersed
(ἐπὶ) in the name of the Lord Jesus (εἰς) for the remission of
sins ;" consistency requires the translation—"baptized upon the
name of Jesus Christ into the remission of sins." He adds: "εἰς,
immediately following, intimates transition into a new state of
relat*on, such as matrimony, citizenship, servitude, or freedom "—
or (let me add with Peter) into THE REMISSION OF SINS. Dr. Conant agrees with this sentiment (p. 104): " The word BAPTIZEIN
. . . by analogy expressed *the coming into a new state of life or*

experience, in which one was as it were inclosed and swallowed up, so that, temporarily or permanently, he belonged wholly to it. . . . The change in the character and state of the believer was total, comparable to death, as separating entirely from the former spiritual life and condition." Now this is precisely the baptism which the Scripture declares, and it is precisely the baptism which Dr. Conant rejects. How could language express "the coming into a new state of life or experience—total change in the character and state of the believer, separating entirely from the former spiritual life and condition "—more clearly and absolutely than does *baptism into* REPENTANCE, *baptism into* THE REMISSION OF SINS, *baptism into* THE NAME OF THE LORD JESUS, *baptism into* THE DEATH OF CHRIST, *baptism into* THE NAME OF THE FATHER, and OF THE SON, and OF THE HOLY GHOST? These are the baptisms of the Bible, and they are all rejected by the friends of the theory; *they are eliminated from the* BAPTIST *Bible*, and *in their stead is substituted a dipping* INTO WATER, "*in* the name," etc.; neither the "dipping," nor the "into water," nor the "in the name of," being found in Revelation anywhere as an element entering into its baptism.

4. This translator teaches, that ἐν τῷ ὀνόματι τοῦ Κυρίου although immediately following βαπτίζω is not logically connected with it, but is expository of the condition of Peter, who is represented as being "in the name of the Lord," and hence deriving authority to speak and to represent the Lord—" ἐν τῷ ὀνόματι, in the name, or by the authority of the Lord he *commanded* them to be baptized."

By parity of reasoning ἐν Πνεύματι Ἁγίῳ following βαπτίζω in Matt. 3:11 must be expository of the condition of αὐτὸς (= CHRIST), who being "*in* the Holy Ghost " is invested with his power to baptize the soul into repentance and the remission of sins ; as he is also "*in* fire " = *invested with the power of condemning judgment* toward the impenitent and the unbelieving.

On the other hand, by ἐν ὕδατι, John declares that he is neither invested with the power of the Holy Ghost, nor with that of divine judgment; but merely with such power as belongs to simple water, which is a symbol power = to set forth the purifying nature of that baptism which is by the Holy Ghost.

RESULTS.

This narrative of the introduction of Christian baptism among the Gentiles proves 1. That ritual baptism is to be perpetuated; 2. That the element and the only element to be used in this rite is WATER; 3. That the relation of water to the baptism is that of a symbol instrument, as expressed by the nude dative (ὕδατι), the only form in which water is expressed by the historian of the Acts and of the baptisms by the Apostles; 4. The baptism of these Gentiles was the same as that of the Samaritans (8:16) "into the Name of the Lord Jesus;" 5. To add quantity to the element (water) is to add to the words of the Holy Ghost.

As the facts and the terms, divinely descriptive of this baptism of the Gentiles ἐν Πνεύματι Ἁγίῳ, prove, that this baptism was not "*in* the Holy Ghost," and consequently that such interpretation of these words is unscriptural and false, so, the facts and terms, expressed or supplied by necessary ellipsis, prove, that there neither was nor could be any baptism *into water* under the divine instruction, that the rite was to be administered "ὕδατι, εἰς τὸ ὄνομα τοῦ Κυρίου Ἰησοῦ, *with* water *into* THE NAME OF THE LORD JESUS."

RITUAL BAPTISM OF JOHN'S DISCIPLES WITH WATER, INTO THE NAME OF THE LORD JESUS.

ACTS 19: 3-5.

Εἰς τί οὖν ἐβαπτίσθητε; Οἱ δὲ εἶπον· Εἰς τὸ Ἰωάννου βάπτισμα. Εἶπε δὲ Παῦλος· Ἰωάννης, μὲν, ἐβάπτισε βάπτισμα μεταονοίας . . . Ἀκούσαντες δὲ ἐβαπτίσθησαν εἰς τὸ ὄνομα τοῦ Κυρίου Ἰησοῦ.

"Into what, then, were ye baptized? And they said, Into the baptism of John. Then said Paul, John verily baptized the baptism of repentance, saying unto the people, that they should believe on him which should come after him, that is, on Christ Jesus."

FACTS.

Paul finds at Ephesus a company of John's disciples apparently living apart from heathenism, Judaism, and Christianity. These persons remained (some score of years subsequent to the ministry of John) uninformed respecting the development of Christianity. They were especially without knowledge of Jesus as the Lord Messiah, and of the gift of the Holy Ghost consequent upon his ascension to heaven.

Apparently because of their long-isolated position and lack of

14

knowledge, they are both instructed in the knowledge of Jesus and of the gift of the Holy Ghost, and are baptized with water into the name of the Lord Jesus, and also by miraculous endowments from the Holy Ghost shed down upon them.

A deduction from a case so special in its character, affirming the re-baptism of all John's disciples under widely diverse circumstances, would be unsafe. The disciples of John were " baptized, with water, into repentance," and they were taught that real repentance-baptism insured " baptism into the remission of sins," and they were yet farther taught, that this remission of sins came through " the Coming One " whom John pointed out in the person of Jesus, saying, " Behold! the Lamb of God that taketh away the sins of the world." That they who immediately believed on Jesus, and passed from the ministry of John into his discipleship were a second time baptized with water " into repentance," " into remission of sins," or " into the Name of the Lord Jesus," there is no Scriptural evidence.

The farther deduction from this case, that all who were ritually baptized were also miraculously baptized by the Holy Ghost with prophetic gifts and power to speak with tongues, would be wanting in any adequate Scripture evidence.

That the reference in this transaction is to the special manifestation of the Holy Ghost under Christianity, and not to the mere existence of the Holy Ghost, is evident 1. From the nature of the case, every Jew knew of the existence of the Holy Spirit; 2. From the teaching of Christ—John 7 : 39, " This spake he of the Spirit which they that believe on him should receive; for the Holy Ghost was not yet given;" 3. From the facts at Pentecost, Cæsarea, and Samaria; 4. From such bestowal on this occasion of the Holy Ghost.

Translation—Εἰς.

The position occupied by εἰς in relation to Christian baptism, is one of supreme importance, and must determine the real nature of that baptism. That such determination may be truly made, it is essential that its true value, as in the mind of the Holy Spirit, should be clearly attained and maintained. The diversity of translation which characterizes this preposition, as related to the subject of baptism, is remarkable. We have *in, into, unto, for, in order to, with reference to,* as a part of the list. This varying translation of a preposition, in the same relation, shows that there must be some aspect of the case not yet fully brought into the light. The passage before us affords some special help toward a right translation and conception of Christian baptism, and yet there is no uniformity.

The Baptist translator of Acts translates thus: "*Into* what, then, were you immersed? And they said, *Into* John's immersion. Then said Paul, John indeed administered an immersion of reformation. . . . They were immersed *into* the name of the Lord Jesus." The preposition is here translated *into*, and "baptized" by *immersed*, except where "administered" is substituted for it in what would otherwise be, "*immersed* an immersion of reformation." To some this translation may be intelligible, but to others it will remain "Greek" still. In a note, this translator says, "*Εἰς* ought never to be translated *in*. The Greeks having ἐν *in*, as well as εἰς *into*."

Dr. Conant, as final reviser of the Baptist Version, rejects this translation and the doctrine of the *note*, and substitutes this: "*Unto* what, then, were ye immersed? And they said, *Unto* John's immersion. Then said Paul, John indeed immersed *with* the immersion of repentance. They were immersed *in* the name of the Lord Jesus."

Dr. Conant translates εἰς by *unto* and *in*, and introduces *with* (as his associate substituted "administered") to smooth over immersed an immersion.

Prof. Hackett translates *unto*. But a writer in the "Baptist Quarterly" advocates a uniform translation of this preposition in connection with baptism, by *into;* while another writer, in the "National Baptist," says: "I have felt a serious objection to *into* the name after baptize or immerse, because that construction seems to me to indicate the element in or into which, literally or metaphorically, the person is placed by the act. . . . But rather that we are immersed *in*, or, if you please, *into* water *with reference to* the name of, etc." Thus, this writer prefers *in* to *into*, but thinks *with reference to* would be an improvement over both. He thinks, too, that it might be well to translate ἐν ὕδατι *into* water ("or, if you please, *into* water"). I suppose for a like reason that he thinks it would *not* be well to translate εἰς τὸ ὄνομα *into the Name*, to wit, "because that construction seems to indicate *water* as NOT the element into which the person is placed." There is a beautiful childlike simplicity in this statement. When the Holy Ghost teaches a baptism of the soul "(εἰς) *into* Repentance," "(εἰς) *into* the remission of sin," "(εἰς) *into* the Name of the Lord Jesus," "(εἰς) *into* the Name of the Father, and of the Son, and of the Holy Ghost," and indicates the use of the element, solely by ἐν ὕδατι, ὕδατι, *by* water, *with* water, it is not strange that *into* should indicate the new condition *into which* the soul must pass, and that there should be a willingness that *by* water, *with* water, should be metamorphosed so as to take the shape *into* water, and thus win the appearance of "indicating the element *into* which the person passes." But as this is not our Bible of inspiration, the "indication" had better remain as it is. And if the friends of the theory reject this confessed "indication" of the Holy Spirit, and make a substitute of their own, the responsibility is theirs. We will have none of it. We accept what is acknowledged to be an "indication" as much more than an indication, even as a clear, express, and uniform declaration of the Divine will, enforced as such by just principles of interpretation, and sure doctrines of inspiration.

Prof. J. Addison Alexander may stand as a representative of a large number who believe that εἰς, in this relation, should be and must be translated at its normal value, "into." In his commentary on the passage, he says: "*Unto*, in both clauses, should be *into*, as the usual and strict sense of the Greek word, and as more expressive of the main idea here suggested, namely, that of initiation, union, and incorporation. . . . They were baptized *into* the name of the Lord Jesus, *i.e.*, into union with him as the only Saviour."

Into What?

To translate, εἰς τί ἐβαπτίσθητε, "Into what *water* (fresh or salt, river or spring, hot or cold) were you baptized?" is a translation not yet, I believe, proposed by those who insist that Christian baptism is a dipping into water. But such should be Paul's inquiry if the theory be true. There is no room for the inquiry, "Into what—water, or *milk*, or *oil*, or *wine*—were you baptized? for neither John nor Christianity has anything to do with aught but water in baptism.

Whatever translation of εἰς may be possible in its varied relations, there is no possible translation when it relates to a real or verbal baptism, but *into*.

To translate "unto what," or "for what," is at best a bungle, for the moment we are told into *what* any one is baptized, we are

thereby informed "unto" what and "for" what he is baptized.
When Timon or Alcibiades proposes to baptize a man "into *the
river*," or "into *the sea*," we know that it is a baptism "unto"
death, and "*for*" the purpose of killing. When Ishmael baptizes
Gedaliah into *drunken stupor*, we know that it is "unto" profound insensibility, and "for" facilitating murder.

When we are told that John preached baptism "into *repentance*," we know that it was "unto" godly sorrow for sin, and
"for" preparing the way of the Lord. But the translation *unto*
repentance, *for* repentance repudiates the form of statement by
the Holy Spirit in order to repudiate the statement itself; for such
translators deny that there is any baptism *into* REPENTANCE at all.
But those to whom Paul addressed the question εἰς τὶ ἐβαπτίσθητε ;
understood him, as Bloomfield suggests, to ask, εἰς τὶ βάπτισμα ;
as shown by their answer, εἰς τὸ Ἰωάννου βάπτισμα, "into
the *baptism of John*." This abbreviated statement was perfectly
plain to Paul, because he was familiar with the nature of John's
baptism as a βάπτισμα μετανοίας. He, also, knew that a baptism
εἰς μετάνοιαν, *preparing for* the Coming One, was essentially diverse
in its nature, and in the knowledge communicated by it, from a
baptism εἰς τὸ ὄνομα τοῦ Κυρίου Ἰησοῦ, "into the Name of the Lord
Jesus" come and *crucified*, risen and ascended. Dr. Carson says,
"What is baptism in one case is baptism in another. Between the
baptism of Christ and the baptism of John there could be no difference in the mode." It would hardly be possible to put a greater
amount of error into the same number of words. *There is no
mode of action essential to any baptism.* Baptism expresses a
condition under some controlling influence. A drowned man at
the bottom of the sea is in a state of baptism; a drunken man in
the highway is in a state of baptism; and a man in a deep sleep
on his bed is in a state of baptism. If now "what is baptism in
one case is baptism in another," then a baptism in the sea, is the
same as a baptism in the highway, or in a feather bed!

In like manner a baptism into repentance is the same thing as
a baptism into the remission of sins; and a baptism into the name
of Paul is the same thing as a baptism into the name of the Lord
Jesus; and a baptism into Moses is the same thing as a baptism
into the name of the Father, and of the Son, and of the Holy
Ghost. Dr. Carson's idea of a baptism is as far removed from the
truth as the idea of a Hindoo respecting this round globe, when
he pronounces it a broad plain.

Baptize a Baptism.

Paul says, " John baptized the baptism of repentance." The
Baptist Version feeling that the phrase " immersed the immersion of repentance" was impracticable, introduces *with*—" immersed *with* the immersion of repentance ;" how much better this
is I cannot say as I do not understand it. Some might be disposed to think, that it would be truer to the theory to translate
"dipped the dipping of repentance," or " dipped *with* the dipping
of repentance ; " but to all except to the initiated these translations will need to be translated. The phraseology of Luke seems
to be parallel to the Classic phrase βάψω βάμμα Σαρδιανιχόν (Aristophanes), which does not declare, " I will immerse a Sardian
immersion," or, " I will dip a Sardian dip," but, " I will *dye* a
Sardian *dye*." And as the phrase from Aristophanes indicates a
secondary meaning of βάπτω, so the phrase used by Paul points
to a secondary meaning of βαπτίζω. As βάμμα Σαρδιανιχόν does not
express a *dip* of Sardis, but a dyed condition (purple) such as
Sardis was famous for, so βάπτισμα μετανοίας does not express a
dip of repentance, but a condition such as repentance effects,
which condition is a spiritually purified condition, as the Scriptures expressly declare, that the βάπτισμα of repentance is (εἰς
ἀφεσιν ἁμαρτιων) into the remission of sins, leaving the soul which
has received this baptism in a condition of unsullied purity. Just
as βάπτω received its *colored* character from use among dyes, so
βαπτίζω receives its *uncolored* character by use among purifications. Just as Σαρδιανιχόν defines βάμμα, so μετανοίας answers Paul's
inquiry Εἰς τὶ βάπτισμα; and defines τὸ βάπτισμα 'Ιωάννου. Βάμμα,
used among dyes, expressed a thorough change of condition by
some influence capable of coloring. This general idea was limited
and defined by an adjunct; in the case before us by Σαρδιανιχόν =
a *purple* (Βάμμα) color. Βάπτισμα, used among purifications, expresses a thorough change of condition by some influence capable
of purifying. This general idea was limited and defined by adjuncts; thus there was a βάπτισμα 'Ιουδαιχον, a Jewish baptism,
which was by heifer ashes, etc., which was a real ceremonial purification and a type of spiritual purification; also, a βάπτισμα ἐν
Πνεύματι 'Αγίῳ, a Holy Spirit baptism, which was a real spiritual
purification of the soul by Divine power; also, a βάπτισμα 'Ιωαννου,
a Johannic baptism, which was a symbol purification giving ritual
visibility to the real purification of the soul by the Holy Ghost

a βάπτισμα ἐπὶ τῷ ὀνόματι Ἰησοῦ Χριστοῦ = εἰς τὸ ὄνομα τοῦ Κυρίου Ἰησοῦ, a purification from sin by faith resting (as a foundation) *upon* the name of Jesus Christ as "the Lamb of God that taketh away the sin of the world," or (the same idea expressed under another form), by entering *into* the Lord Jesus, the atoning Redeemer, and thus becoming penetrated and pervaded with his sin-remitting power; and, still farther, a βάπτισμα ἐξ ὕδατος καὶ Πνεύματος, a baptism by water and Spirit, which is a purification of body and soul by water impregnated with the power of the Holy Ghost. *This baptism is unknown to the Scriptures.* It is of Patristic origin and pervades their writings and theology. We will meet with it hereafter.

This glance at the various relations of βάπτισμα makes it obvious, that to the inquiry Εἰς τὶ βάπτισμα ἐβαπτίσθητε; the reply, "Εἰς τὸ Ἰωαννου βαπτισμα, into the baptism *of John*," gives an answer equally precise, with the reply to the question Εἰς τὶ βάμμα ἐβάφθητε; into what dye were you dipped? We were dipped into *Sardian* dye. Βάπτω with εἰς τὶ βάμμα must, I think, express the primary meaning of the verb (to dip), and with βάμμα Σαρδιανικόν it must express its acquired meaning (to dye), the effect of dipping into a dye. How absolutely the primary meaning (to dip) is lost, is shown by the fact that this Sardian dye was effected *by beating with the fists.* In like manner βαπτίζω with εἰς τί βαπτίσμα must be understood as related to this ideal baptism in its primary meaning; while in the very diverse construction ἐβάπτισε βάπτισμα μετανοίας, it must be understood in a secondary sense (to purify) secured from the effect of the ideal baptism of repentance, which is (εἰς ἀφεσιν ἁμαρτιων) into the remission of sins, and therefore, of necessity, purifying in its nature.

This parallel usage shows that the affinity between βαπτίζω and βάπτω is not through the stem which *dips;* but through that which *dyes* = thoroughly changes condition by imparting *color;* while βαπτίζω thoroughly changes condition by imparting some other (uncolored) influential characteristic; under Christianity such characteristic as belongs to repentance, remission of sins, and a crucified Redeemer.

THE BAPTISM RECEIVED BY "THE TWELVE."

Water is not mentioned in this investigation respecting the baptism received by these Ephesian twelve. It is, however, excluded again and again from the position of receiving element, by the express declaration that this position was filled by a wholly different element. It was unnecessary that water should be mentioned. It had already been stated; it was uniformly presented under one and the same aspect, that of instrumental symbol agency, and would, as such, be necessarily supplied; indeed, this is all that can be supplied; every other element is present, the administrator, the subject, the ideal element; what is lacking is the agency; and this Luke supplies for us by statement elsewhere; and thus fully equipped these twelve " (ἐβαπτίςθησαν ὕδατι εἰς τὸ ὄνομα του Κυρίου Ἰησοῦ) were baptized *with water* INTO the Name of the Lord Jesus."

RITUAL BAPTISM OF CRISPUS AND GAIUS *not* "INTO THE NAME OF PAUL."

1 CORINTHIANS 1 : 13–15.

Εἰς τὸ ὄνομα Παῦλου ἐβαπτίσθητε ; . . . οὐδενα ὑμῶν ἐβάπτισα, εἰ μὴ Κρίσπον καὶ Γάϊον: Ἱνα μή εἴπη τις ὅτι τὸ εἰς εμὸν ὄνομα ἐβάπτισα.

"I am of Paul. . . Was Paul crucified for you? or were ye baptized into the name of Paul? I thank God that I baptized none of you, but Crispus and Gaius: Lest any should say that I had baptized into mine own name."

" INTO THE NAME OF PAUL."

This is the last case of ritual baptism mentioned in the New Testament with any adjuncts calculated to throw light upon the nature of the baptism. It gives instruction on the following points: 1. This was ritual baptism. It could not be a baptism conferring miraculous gifts; for then Paul could not have thanked God that he had not conferred such baptism. It was not regenerative baptism; for this was beyond the power of Paul to bestow. It must then have been, what all the facts show that it was, ritual baptism.

2. Ritual baptism was extended and perpetuated. The place where this rite was administered was Corinth, a city of Greece; the time of its administration was twenty or more years after the death of Christ.

3. The persistent and sole formula expressive of Christian

baptism was (εἰς τὸ ὄνομα τοῦ Κυρίου 'Ιησοῦ), "into the Name of the Lord Jesus." Peter, in the first sermon preached under Christianity, announced the baptism (εἰς ἄφεσιν ἁμαρτιων ἐπὶ τῷ ὀνοματι *I. X.*), "into the remission of sins grounded upon the Name of Jesus Christ;" and in the first ritual baptism this sentiment is condensed into the formula " (εἰς τὸ ὄνομα τοῦ Κυρίου 'Ιησοῦ), into the Name of the Lord Jesus." The subsequent use of this formula is expressly stated (Acts 19 : 5), and no other is so stated at any time. This formula was clearly before the mind of Paul as shown by the condemnatory substitution of his own name for the name of the Lord Jesus.

4. As to the meaning of this formula. To be baptized (really or ideally) into anything, expresses the fact that the baptized object is made subject to the controlling power or assimilating influence of such thing, whatever it may be. Baptism "into the name of Paul," therefore, expresses subjection to Paul's influence as a Leader and Teacher. In other words, induces that cry heard at Corinth—"I am of PAUL!" Baptism into the Name of the Lord Jesus, expresses subjection to his power and influence as " Lord," to rule over, and as " Jesus," to save from sins.

5. The ellipsis of water. The doctrine of ellipsis is, that that which is the most essential requisite in any transaction may be omitted, on the ground that it cannot but be missed, and therefore will not fail to be supplied. The most essential requisite in the administration of Christian ritual baptism is *water*. Without this the Christian rite cannot be administered. Therefore whenever it is stated, that ritual baptism has been administered in any case, as for example by Paul to Crispus and Gaius, we know that water was used, although there is no mention of it. When Christian baptism was first instituted, it was necessary to make express statement of its distinctive character, so far as it differed from that of John and of the disciples of Jesus (John 4 : 1, 2). And this was done by declaring, that this baptism was no longer εἰς μετανοίαν, nor εἰς ἄφεσιν ἁμαρτιων—" into repentance " —" into the remission of sins;" but that these antecedent baptisms were merged in that to which they owed their origin, and from which they derived all their value, namely, baptism " into the Name of the Lord Jesus." It was not necessary that in the announcement of Christian baptism there should be a renewed mention of *water*, because in this respect there was no change; and, therefore, water is never formally mentioned as entering

into the Christian rite; although it is mentioned, incidentally, twice—Acts 8 : 36 ; 10 : 46.

The same imperative necessity which makes the supply of the elliptically absent water necessary, makes it necessary, that it should be supplied in precisely that form and in such relation, as it is furnished to us by inspiration. That form is without exception in the dative, with or without a preposition, and associated with an accusative and εἰς. These cases do, in Classic Greek, invariably express *the agency by which* a baptism is effected, and *the element into which* the baptized object passes. We so interpret them and with the same invariableness, in Scripture. We know negatively, that Crispus and Gaius were not baptized (εἰς ὕδωρ) *into* water, because there is no such statement to be found anywhere in Scripture ; and we know affirmatively, that they were baptized " (ὕδατι εἰς τὸ ὄνομα τοῦ *K. I.*) *with* water *into* the Name of the Lord Jesus," because this is the distinct and exclusive statement of the Holy Spirit in the case of such like baptisms.

6. *The comparative value of ritual baptism.* Paul neither believed that ritual baptism had power to regenerate the soul, nor that the manner of using the water in the rite constituted the *sine qua non* of church membership, and of the right to sit down at the Lord's table, nor, a discriminating test of obedience to God, else he never could have said—" Christ sent me not to baptize, but to preach the Gospel."

COROLLARY. To preach a ritual baptism is not to preach the Gospel ; and, *a fortiori*, to preach a modal use of water is not to preach the Gospel.

All the cases of ritual baptism, which could throw light upon its nature or administration, have now been passed in review. The result is, that there is not one fact which exemplifies, not one word which inculcates, a dipping into water; but on the contrary, to teach and to practice *a dipping into* WATER as Christian baptism is an abandonment of the baptism taught in the word of God, which is, "WITH *water*, INTO *the Name of the* LORD JESUS."

CHRISTIC BAPTISM: RITUAL BAPTISM OF HOUSE-HOLDS WITH THEIR FAMILY HEAD.

RITUAL BAPTISM OF HOUSEHOLDS WITH WATER INTO THE NAME OF THE LORD JESUS.

ACTS 16 : 15.

'Ὡς δὲ ἐβαπτίσθη, καὶ ὁ οἶκος αὐτῆς.

" And when she was baptized and her household."

ACTS 16 : 33.

Καὶ ἐβαπτίσθη αὐτὸς καὶ οἱ αὐτοῦ πάντες παραχρῆμα.

" And was baptized, he and all his, straightway."

1 COR. 1 : 16.

'Εβάπτισα δὲ καὶ τὸν Στεφανᾶ οἶκον.

" And I baptized, also, the household of Stephanas."

HOUSEHOLD BAPTISM.

THE peculiarity of these baptisms, as compared with the bap-tisms previously considered, is, that the household is baptized with the believing Family head.

This fact is so distinctly and so repeatedly stated as to admit of no question. The reason for this fact, namely, the baptism of a household with its family Head, is questioned. Some say the reason of this baptism is stated as well as the fact, in that it is declared to be "*his* household," "*her* household." They say there was a necessity from the nature of the case, that in recognizing the sovereignty of God over him and his, and the grace of God in Christ toward him and his, he should make recognition of such sovereignty and grace, both as an individual and as a family Head, in the way appointed by God. The same condition of things which makes it fit and necessary that he should, by Christian baptism, acknowledge his subjection to the divine sovereignty and his need of divine grace, made it imperative that he should make like acknowledgment for " all his." It is undeniable, that the rights of God as a sovereign extend over an infant child ; it is equally

(219)

undeniable, that the redemption of Christ is needed by an infant child; but an infant child is unable personally to make acknowledgment of these great truths and their correspondent duties; and if there be none whose duty it is to make such acknowledgment, and assume such responsibilities as grow out of this acknowledgment, then the rights of God and the spiritual interests of this child must pass into abeyance. But neither the claim of divine sovereignty, nor the efficacy of Christ's redemption, becomes inoperative through infancy. That sovereignty which an infant cannot recognize, the parent is bound to recognize as it extends over *his* child; and whatever is necessary to qualify that child to understand this divine claim, and to respond to its obligations, is an imperative duty for the parent to perform. God makes this claim and requires this duty: " As the soul of the father, so, also, the soul of the son is mine." These truths underlie the language of these baptisms, "*her* household," " all *his*," and constitute the underlying reason, why households were baptized with their family Heads. The relation between the household and the family Head, (making *one* family) and of both (in their *unity*) to God, is the reason, on the face of these Scripture statements, for household baptism. These are divine reasons, and are confirmed by a broader view of the family as historically presented in the Scriptures.

The Family is a Divine Institution.

The origin, character, and true value of the Family are elements of essential value in determining the ground and obligation of Household baptism. Fortunately those who are interested in this question admit, that the Family is a divine institution. They also admit, that the Family is from the beginning, and that the whole human race is one vast outgrowth of a single Family head. Within this world family there are a thousand times ten thousand other families of miniature dimension, but with identically the same constitution. These families, more or less conformed to their divine original, fill the earth. It is obvious, that this world is founded on a family constitution. Its constitutional unit is not an independent, dissociate individuality, but a conjunct and associate individuality in and under the Family constitution.

Family Unity.

The rights, duties, and obligations of the individual man or woman are essentially modified and controlled by their entering upon that relation of twain-unity divinely established in marriage. These, also, are modified, varied, and deepened by the establishment of parental relations, the existence and nature of which are of God. The child belongs, in a profound and wonderful sense, to the father who has begotten it and to the mother of whom it has been born. And they are jointly and severally responsible, in the same profound and wonderful sense, for the unfolding of that life in holiness and to the glory of God. It is a multiplication of their own life; and God gives to them a vast, if not an absolute, control over it, and holds them responsible for the exercise of such control. There is a unit life as well as a multiplied life in the family; and there is an immeasurable responsibility for that life of "*her* household," and of "all *his*," resting on every family Head. The idea, that the claims of God as a Sovereign and the grace of Christ as a Saviour, come to a family Head with the same limitations to naked individuality as they come to one who stands alone in the world, is ineffably absurd.

God has always dealt with the family as a unity in its Head. Therefore, the whole human family is what it is to-day—" As by one man sin entered into the world and death by sin;" "As by the offence of one judgment came upon all men to condemnation." God covenants with the family Head including "his" as a unity— "Noah was a just man and walked with God. With thee will I establish my covenant; and thou shalt come into the ark, thou, and thy sons, and thy wife, and thy son's wives, with thee. And the Lord said unto Noah, Come thou and all THY *house* into the ark; for thee have I seen to be righteous before me in this generation." Thus "his house" was saved through its family Head. Again, God covenants with Noah as the second head of the human family, and with his sons as subordinate family Heads—"And God spake unto Noah, and to his sons with him, saying, And I, behold I, will establish my covenant with you *and with* YOUR *seed after you*." God includes in his family covenant children before they are born.

The angels said unto Lot, "Hast thou here any besides? son-in-law, and thy sons, and thy daughters, and whatsoever thou hast in the city, bring them out of this place." The salvation of Lot's family turns solely on their being "HIS." They may have no immediate personal-covenant relation with God, yet they are beloved for their father's sake, and embraced in covenant blessings with the Family head.

Family Headship.

Authority is committed by God to the family Head—Gen. 18 : 19, "I know Abraham that *he will command* HIS *children* and HIS *household* after him." Deut. 32 : 46, "Ye shall *command* YOUR *children* to observe to do all the words of this law."

Obligation is laid upon children to respect this authority—Exod. 20 : 12, "*Honor* thy father and thy mother." Ephes. 6 : 1, "Chil dren, *obey* your parents in the Lord."

Responsibility accompanies this authority—Deut. 4 : 9, "*Teach* them to thy sons and thy son's sons." Prov. 22 : 6, "*Train up* a child in the way he should go." Ephes. 6 : 4, "Ye fathers, *bring up* your children in the nurture and admonition of the Lord."

Parents must enforce God's law in their households—Exod. 20 : 8, "Remember the Sabbath day to keep it holy; Six days shalt thou labor and do all thy work: But the seventh day is the Sabbath of the Lord thy God: in it thou shalt not do any work, THOU, nor THY *son*, nor THY *daughter*."

The authority vested in a family Head and the responsibility under it is grandly announced by Joshua to all the family heads of Israel when they were called upon to choose whom they would worship as their God—"As for me and MY *house* WE will serve the Lord." Joshua was a ruler over God's people and a ruler, in God's name and for God's glory, over his own house. "A bishop must be one that ruleth well HIS OWN *house*, having HIS CHILDREN *in subjection*" (1 Tim. 3 : 4).

Promises are given to encourage in the fulfilment of the duties of family Headship—Genesis 17 : 7, "I will establish my covenant between me and THEE *and* THY *seed* after thee . . . *to be a* GOD *unto* THEE *and to* THY SEED after thee."

Peter introduces Christianity by a reiteration of this promise embracing the family Head and household—Acts 2 : 39, "The promise is to YOU *and to* YOUR CHILDREN."

Paul renews it to the Jailer—"Believe and *thou* shalt be saved *and* THY *house*." "By faith Noah prepared an ark to the saving of HIS *house*" (Heb. 11 : 7). And every head of a family who does by faith receive the Lord Jesus Christ, does thereby lay hold of promises full of salvation to his house. Therefore the Lord Jesus says of the believing Zaccheus, "To-day is salvation come to *this house forasmuch as* HE also is a son of Abraham" (Luke 19 : 9).

For these and suchlike reasons we believe, that the language in which these household baptisms is expressed does declare, not merely the historical fact that such baptisms did take place, but also, expressly and pointedly, the ground on which they do divinely rest; namely, *the unity of life between the family Head and its members* making it obligatory upon the Head to receive God's commands and promises ALIKE *for his* FAMILY *as for* HIMSELF; and to recognize the obligation, to consecrate that unity of family life to the glory of God laboring for its unfolding under the promises, in the beauty of holiness.

Another view.

Another view of these baptisms declares, that the statement of family Headship on the one part, and of Household membership on the other part, is a mere record of historical facts wholly outside of the baptism, and in no wise entering into the character of the baptism or affecting its administration. Baptism is declared to be limited to an individual personality in the exercise of repentance and faith, and therefore restricted to an adult, acting with independent individuality. This theory denies family unity under the Law of God, and rejects family life from the kingdom of God.

We object to this view as grounded in a misconception of scriptural baptism; as presenting a fundamentally erroneous view of the relations of the human race to God the Creator and to God in Christ the Redeemer; and also as dividing the kingdom of God against itself, making God's constitution of the church antagonistic to God's constitution of the human race.

1. Baptism with water is grounded in the blood baptism of Christ. The blood of Christ secures through the Holy Ghost the regeneration of the soul, the remission of sins, and reconciliation with God. Infants need these blessings as truly as adults need them. Infants can receive these blessings as truly as adults can receive them. Whenever infant or adult receives them, they are the gift of God. In the bestowal of these gifts God may be moved solely by his own sovereign grace, or by the prayer of faith in the name of his Son. This **prayer** of faith may be offered by the adult for himself; the infant cannot offer such prayer for himself. Is the infant therefore excluded from the Cross of Christ (in its power through the Holy Ghost to regenerate, to remit sin, and to reconcile to God) by hopeless exclusion from the prayer of faith?

By no means. *All the blessings of the prayer of faith are open to the new-born babe.* The parent (whose life has passed into that infant life) may and is under infinite obligation to pray for that new-born soul *as for his own soul.* "As the soul of the father so also the soul of the son is mine." He may and he is bound to pray for the second birth of that infant soul, for the remission of that sin which proceeds from being born of his flesh, and for the eternal reconciliation with God in his holiness of this new-born babe, in the Name and for the sake of the babe of Bethlehem, the holy child Jesus, the crucified of Calvary! What a parent *may pray for* to be given to his child, *may be granted to* a child, in answer to a parent's prayer. Now if the water in baptism be the seal of blessings promised in answer to faith in the promises of God in Christ, and if those blessings are available for infants, and if parents are required of God to offer prayer, believing in those promises, for their infant children, then the seal of those promises belongs to infant children through parental faith. When the Bible shuts out infants from the richest blessings of the Cross, and precludes parents from praying in their behalf for those blessings, then, but not till then, men may shut them out from the seal of those blessings which belong through covenant grace alike to parents and their children.

Household relation to God.

The idea that the human race stands related to God as an aggregation of individuals, on an exclusive basis of personal responsibility, is an error absolute and profound. Every page of Scripture and of history condemns it; every man's observation and experience refutes it. It is doubly disproved by the Bible declaration—"As in ADAM all die, so in CHRIST shall all be made alive." Personal responsibility is a truth most real and oppressive by reason of the responsibilities which gather around it. But personal responsibility, as that of mere individualism, is not the only responsibility in our world. The whole human race, by reason of a common life and death (the web and woof of its universal existence) has a marvellous personality, together with its no less marvellous responsibilities. That there is a common life in every household is a simple fact beyond denial. To deny that that household life has a head, and that in that head vests a household responsibility which includes every living member of such household, is to kick against the pricks sharpened by God's truth, and made rigid by the experience of ages. Individual life and individual personal responsibility are not more truly or more fully taught in the Bible, than are household life and family responsibility under the household head.

Was it in illustration of mere individual responsibility that the sword of the destroying angel was drawn in Egypt to smite the first-born of every house? What was the personal act of impenitence or unbelief which gave individual responsibility to that first-born babe whose birth-cry was merged in its death-wail on that fearful night? Or, did that Messenger of wrath cross the family thresholds of Egypt slaying the first-born (and wounding in that deathstroke every heart of the household) *without responsibility for sin against God resting anywhere*? Was it in illustration of that mere individual responsibility which knows no father, no mother, no son, no daughter, that the command was given to *the household* HEADS of Israel to sprinkle their FAMILY *door-posts* with the blood of the Lamb *in order that the* FIRST-BORN OF THE HOUSE might be saved from death? Where is the personal faith and obedience of *that* BABE *resting on its Mother's bosom* developed in that act of blood-sprinkling? Is the responsibility of that act (on which life and death are suspended) laid over upon that unconscious *babe* or upon the FAMILY HEAD?

Can such cases (abounding everywhere in the Bible and superabounding in every age under the providential rule of God) be met by the doctrine of a naked individual responsibility? The wailings of the households of Egypt over their dead children, and the joy in the households of Israel that the blood of the Lamb, *sprinkled by the obedience and faith of their Household Heads*, HAS SAVED THEIR CHILDREN *who could, personally, neither obey nor believe*, alike reject the doctrine. This doctrine is repudiated, and the doctrine of household life, and the responsibility of household Headship to hear the command and promise of God for those who are sharers of this life, is established as an abiding and universal truth by the command—"Ye shall observe this thing for an ordinance to thee and to thy sons forever. And it shall come to pass, when your children shall say unto you, What mean ye by this service? that ye shall say, It is the sacrifice of the Lord's passover, who passed over *the houses* of the children of Israel in Egypt, when he smote the Egyptians, and delivered OUR *houses*" (Exod. 12 : 24–27).

Little children of the household SYMBOLLY *redeemed by the blood of sprinkling* THROUGH THE FAITH AND OBEDIENCE OF THE FAMILY HEAD, *was the truth written in blood and taught in every household of Israel for a* THOUSAND AND A HALF THOUSAND YEARS, even until the typified Lamb came and by the shedding of his own blood, *confirmed this great truth of the past and commanded that it should be preached* at Pentecost and thenceforward, forever, *that* " THE PROMISE IS TO YOU AND YOUR CHILDREN."

Another illustrative case is found in the baptism of all the families of Israel (parents and children together) " into MOSES." The demand made of Pharaoh was, that Israel should go out of Egypt by families. He was willing that the adults should go, but not with the " little ones." But the God of the family constrained him to grant, at last, the permission. Now, on whom did the responsibility of this great movement, carrying these families out of the kingdom of Pharaoh into the kingdom of God, rest? Was it the act of these " little ones," or of their family Heads?

Never was there such a procession of FAMILIES *going* (as Paul (1 Cor. 10 : 2) tells us) *on their way to baptism.* There were a half million, more or less, families. It is not doubtful, I presume, whether there were any children in these families or not. There was quite a number of " little ones." And just as Lydia and her household, and the Jailer and all his, were baptized together, so these parents and their households received one and the same baptism. It is true, that while they " went down to the water " (and there was so " much water " that a thousand Jordans and Enons might have been swallowed up in it) still, it was not used for dipping. And while we reject the theory's conceit of a " dry baptism " in the Red Sea, we are happy (so long as there are any who like Pharaoh would send parents out to baptism without their " little ones ") to remind them, that God would not allow that to be separated which He had joined together, and would gently indicate the *argumentum ad hominem* which this *cobaptism of a* HALF MILLION PARENTS AND CHILDREN " into Moses " (type of " the Coming One ") puts into our hands. When God would establish a visible kingdom and church he rejects the Pharaonic individualism and demands his own Family constitution. A brief glance at one more fact, and I pass from this phase of the error which destroys family life and repudiates family Headship as ordained of God with authoritative and responsible action under divine command and promise. When the antitype Passover Lamb had come, and his precious blood was freely offered for the salvation of parents and their children (not less broadly efficacious surely than the blood of the type lamb) Jewish parents refused it—" All the people said, His blood be on us *and on our children.*" Parents rejected " Christ our Passover " for themselves and their children. Was there any efficacious power in that rejection by parents? Has there not been a drawn sword (reddened with blood) over the houses of those " parents and their children " these eighteen hundred years in consequence of that rejecting imprecation? Are not they presumptuously bold who in view of such facts (a few among others numerous as the stars) do deny, that there is a Family life immediately and responsibly related through the Family Head to God in his commandments and promises, ordinances and judgments? Are they who refuse the Symbol of the blood of the Lamb for their children, wiser than would have been the Parents of Israel had they said, " This sprinkling *by* us can do our CHILDREN no good; they cannot repent, they cannot believe, they cannot obey, they cannot understand anything about it; WE WILL NOT OBSERVE SUCH A SERVICE"? If Israel's parents had said, " OUR *act,* OUR *obedience,* OUR *faith,* can do *our* CHILDREN no good," would there not have been lamentation and weeping *over the* DEAD *in all such homes* on the morrow?

The Family rejected from the kingdom of God.

The doctrine that the kingdom of God = the Church, is made up solely of individuals on the basis of a personal repentance and faith, without recognition or provision for the relation of parent and child in family unity, any more than for the relation of a lawyer to his clients, of a physician to his patients, or a merchant to his customers, is a doctrine, which the Lord of that kingdom rejects on the ground of that folly and ruin which must be the portion of " a kingdom divided against itself."

That the constitution of this world is divine, will be admitted by all who believe that there is a God. That the constitution of the human race has its fundamental element in the Family Institution and not in the individual man will be admitted by every rational being. That the strongest, the tenderest, and the most influential ties bind parent and offspring together under divine constitution, the brute creation would testify, if men should deny. That moral duties and responsibilities inhere in the relation of parent and child, making the parent responsible (who shall fix the limits?) for the moral wellbeing of the child, none can rationally deny, who admit the moral nature of the new-born babe and the claim of God—" all *souls* are mine."

Now, from this kingdom, under a Family constitution, God has by sin been rejected. And he has declared his purpose to overthrow his enemies and to re-establish his kingdom—" Every knee shall bow to me;" " Out of the mouth of babes and sucklings thou hast ordained praise." The doctrine under consideration declares, that God will not re-establish this kingdom; but will set up another kingdom under a radically diverse constitution, from which family life shall be rejected and a solitary individualism be substituted. There would, thus, be two kingdoms of God in the world; the one having the Family Institution as its controlling feature, and the other refusing to give the Family institution any admission. " If Satan cast out Satan, Satan's kingdom cannot stand." If God's Family be cast out of God's kingdom the result remains to be developed. There has been no trial of such evisceration. The church for five thousand years has accepted this as the divine Constitution of the human race, nor has she ever supposed that God has set up another kingdom radically antagonistic to his own original kingdom. It does not, however, remain to be shown, that no nation or community organized on a basis rejecting or subverting the divine Institution of the Family, can stand. This has abundantly been proved. Throughout heathenism generally the family is in ruins; and the moral ruin is as abounding. China has a singular history both as to permanence *and as to regard for the family.* Mohammedanism has substituted the harem for the family. France, at her influential centres, is largely destitute of family life; history declares the result. Romanism receives individual men and women into her monasteries, and nunneries, and priesthood, and rejects the family; the result is on record. Communism, Fourierism, Shakerism, Mormonism, reject or subvert the family; and the balance-wheel of permanence, and the germ of development and moral blessing is gone.

They who are attempting to build up a kingdom in God's name of individual men and women, rejecting from it the Family Institution, have been engaged in the task too short a time and their piety is too much better than their logic, to show the natural and fully developed fruit.

Should a father and mother, with their newly born babe, appear before the custodians of such an organization, and ask admission into the Church, the visible kingdom of God, the answer must be: "You can be received because you can repent and believe; but there is no provision for the impenitent and the unbelieving." But our babe has not performed one act of impenitence or originated one act of unbelief. "That is true; but he must personally repent and believe or he cannot come into the kingdom of the gospel; 'Repent and be baptized every one of you;' 'He that believeth and is baptized shall be saved, he that believeth not shall be damned.' Your child is a child of the Devil." Is our babe under the curse of the Law without any personal act of his but solely by the act of his parents and his birth from them, and yet incapable of being received into the kingdom of the gospel by their act, acknowledging the sovereign right of God in him, the commands of God laid upon us for him, confessing his need of cleansing by the blood of Christ the Redeemer, and accepting with adoring faith the promises "made unto parents and their children," and holding him forth by the prayer of faith to be received into a Saviour's arms? "Your child is under *the covenant of* DEATH as your child; but he is *not under the covenant of* LIFE as your child. *No provision is made in the gospel for the salvation of children with their parents.*" Will you, then, receive us *as* PARENTS? "No, we cannot. When we reject *your child as your child* received from God to be nurtured, trained, taught in his kingdom for his glory, *we reject* THE FAMILY *in all its elements* and therefore cannot receive you into the kingdom of God as Parents, Father and Mother. We have no fathers and mothers, or sons and daughters, in our kingdom. And if your child (now unprovided for and left out in the kingdom of Satan because he cannot repent and believe) should live long enough to repent and believe, he could not come into the kingdom *as your child;* and when in it, *he could not be related to you as your child* under the laws of the kingdom, but only as any other individual believer." Well, then, we will enter the kingdom of God as HUSBAND *and* WIFE. In God's name, and by God's ordinance, we twain have been made one. Marriage, no doubt, is a part of the law of God's kingdom. "No, it is not. The only elements which can be considered in receiving into the kingdom of God is individualism, not twain-unity any more than family unity. We cannot recognize you in your relation as husband and wife, any more than we can recog nize Richard Roe and John Doe as partners in business, when they come together to be received into the kingdom. Beside, if we were to recognize **Marriage** as an element in the kingdom of God, and you entering that kingdom as husband and wife should have a child born to you, *what could we do with it?* We would be placed in the dilemma of recognizing Marriage, and Husband and Wife, as belonging to the kingdom of God, *and casting 'the fruit of the womb which is His reward' out of his kingdom, as unholy!"* When your members intermarry do they marry in the kingdom? "No; Marriage is God's institution, it is celebrated by God's minister, it is performed in God's house, it is sanctified by prayer in God's name, *but it is all* OUT *of His kingdom*, and in the world" (Satan's kingdom?) "to which MARRIAGE *and* THE FAMILY BELONG (!). In the kingdom of God there is nothing but naked individualism (man, woman), repenting and believing."

Does not the Bible address Husbands and Wives as in the kingdom and as having duties to perform toward each other? "That is an accident not entering into the constitution of the kingdom any more than when it addresses rich men and poor men, and enjoins just weights and equal balances. Marriage no more enters into the kingdom of God than does a commercial partnership; nor the Family with its parents and children, any more than an Orphan Asylum with its Steward and Matron and orphan waifs."

Thus rejected, Father and Mother *bear away their babe*, saying, "O my soul, come not thou into their secret; unto their assembly, mine honor, be not thou united."

And let all who fear God and keep his commandments say— AMEN.

Results.

1. The Rev. Dr. Brantley is reported, at a meeting of Baptist ministers in Philadelphia, as saying: "The nation has no God, and the Family has no God; individuals only have a God." How much better is this destructive logic than that of the child who destroys his watch in quest of the individual action of wheel and spring, or than that of the daughters of Pelias who anatomize the body of their parent into its individual members in search of a higher life, I do not know. Why this logic does not repudiate the reasoning of the heathen Menenius Agrippa and of the christian Paul in establishing a common life (with its peculiar duties

and responsibilities) as belonging, severally, to the nation and to the church, I cannot tell. Why duty and responsibility should attach to the whole man (body, soul, and spirit) and not rather a primitive code be established on the basis of the act of Scævola and of Cranmer in committing *the guilty* HAND to the flames, the friends of this logic must show. And in their labors must be included a vindication of the denial, *that* THE CHURCH has any God, any more than the Nation or the Family—the baptism of all individuals "into one body" with Christ as its head, being only a pretty rhetorical conceit to be resolved into the plain prose of a naked individualism. And when this shall have been all done it will only remain to show, that as the Family has no life but in its individual members (and on each separately and distinctively rests duty and responsibility without duties and responsibilities from community of organic life), and as the same is true of the Nation, and of the Church, so, it is true of the Godhead itself, that in it *there is no common divine life constituting the One God*, JEHOVAH, but merely three distinct "individuals," the Father, the Son, and the Holy Ghost. This chemical logic which resolves all forms of life into inorganic, irresponsible, independent individualism, has a broad application, and is but illy adapted to that sexual and family life under which it has pleased God to give life to the human race; and just as illy adapted to the constitution of his church and kingdom as revealed through all his Word.

2. The terms in which these baptisms are expressed indicate ownership and partnership of life, with all consequent share in duties and responsibilities. Lydia was baptized and " hers ;" the Jailer was baptized and " his." The nature of the ownership is indicated by the object; it was " her *household*," " all his *house*." Parental ownership in children is of universal acknowledgment. This ownership is subordinate only to the divine claim—" all souls are mine." The rights invested in parents over their children are bounded and enforced by the inculcation of duty, by the imposition of command, and by the holding forth of promises all through the revelation of God. This language, expressive of parental right in and over their children, which is from God, and involves eternal responsibilities toward God, the doctrine of individualism repudiates. It does, also, repudiate the language addressed to parents for their encouragement—(" The promise is to *you and to* YOUR *children*")—declaring that there is no union hereby established between parents and their children any more

than between those who are not parents and any other children. In other words, that the promise "to parents and their children," has in it nothing distinctive for parents and *their* CHILDREN, but it means, indifferently, *anybody and everybody.* If such interpretation of the language of revelation be just, then we have no revelation. If this doctrine of individualism requires such interpretation, then it does hereby involve itself in a *reductio ad absurdum* = its Revelation is in words of concealment and contradiction.

3. The necessity in which this doctrine is involved of rejecting from the Gospel kingdom, the family, which God has ordained to be the integral and vital element of the human race, so, evoking the contradiction both of sustaining and rejecting the family under the same general economy, is, if possible, still more absurd.

4. But the idea that the kingdom of God and its embodiment, the visible church, is founded in a bare individualism, with its repentance and faith, must confront another absurdity, which is the greatest of all, namely, that the kingdom of God was established for the recovery of a lost race in which *countless millions of little children* were an essential and ever-present element, yet, in that kingdom *there was no provision for so much as one new-born child to be received into it*, but, on the contrary, *was* SO CONSTITUTED *as designedly and necessarily* TO EXCLUDE *them.*

The human imagination never conceived an incredibility more incredible, nor an absurdity more absurd. If the Shaster of Brahma, or the Koran of Mohammed, or the Book of Mormon, claimed to be a revelation from God designed to mould the human race after the will of God, and we should find, that the one suffered men and women to herd together as individuals, and the other converted the Family into a seraglio, and the third substituted polygamy for monogamy, we would at once say, "This alone stamps the claim to be of God *a fiction;* and the work to be done *preposterous;* BECAUSE God's Family Institution is rejected."

Any nation which shall attempt to develop a national life in purity, blessing, and abiding prosperity on the theory of individualism (rejecting the family and its little ones as integral and vital elements of its life) will soon find occasion, with the great Napoleon, to ask, " What is it mars the development of our national life ?" And the answer will be that of the noble woman who replied, " *France wants* MOTHERS !"

Any Lodge of Free Masons. or of Odd Fellows, or of Good

Templars, who should seek *to. mould* THE WORLD by receiving individual men and women into their conclaves, *rejecting* THE
FAMILY, would enter upon a fool's errand.

Any man or body of men who should offer to the human race
a constitution purporting to be that of the kingdom of God and
for the human race, in which there was no Family, no Husband,
no Wife, no Father, no Mother, no Son, no Daughter, but only
individual MEN and WOMEN, would assume a position by which
they placed God in antagonism with Himself; because in antagonism with that constitution which He had from the beginning
given to the human race; and would offer a revolutionary constitution ineffably unadapted to the human race. The claim, that
such a constitution is from God is antagonistic to God's dealings
with our race from the beginning; it is antagonistic to every
page of his revelation in Old Testament and New Testament; it
is as ill-adapted as it must be ineffective to master the human
race, as it is in every respect essentially incredible and absurd.
No amount of proof can make it credible or bring it within the
bounds of what is rational.

This prodigious error the theory has taken into its fellowship.

Incredibilities.

Dr. Carson not only rejects the Family from the constitution
of God's kingdom, but separates the salvation of parents and
children from each other by an impassable gulf. Parents are
saved by the gospel; their children are not saved by the gospel.
He says (p. 215), "They tell us that the covenant of Abraham
was the new covenant. Now, for argument's sake, let it be the
new covenant, and I deny the result that they wish to draw. IN-
FANTS ARE NOT SAVED BY THE NEW COVENANT" (Capitals Dr. Carson's), "and therefore they cannot be connected with it, in any
view that represents them as interested in it. It is a vulgar mistake of theologians to consider, if infants are saved, they must be
saved by the new covenant" (p. 173). "Certainly; if there were
no way of saving children but by the Gospel, this conclusion
(that a person must actually believe, else he cannot be saved)
would be inevitable. The Gospel saves none but by faith. But
the Gospel has nothing to do with infants, nor have Gospel ordinances any respect to them. It is good news; but to infants it
is no news at all. They know nothing of it. The salvation of
the Gospel is as much confined to believers, as the baptism of the

Gospel is. None can ever be saved by the Gospel who do no-
believe it. Consequently, by the Gospel no infant can be saved.
. . . Infants are saved by the death of Christ, but not by the
Gospel."

Had-the sword of Solomon divided the babe, it would not have
been more murderous to the child or more pitiless to the mother,
than is this theory which divides Christ and his Gospel separating
parents and their children. It is a sadly erring theory which
attempts to hammer out the promises of salvation to the believing
to the full breadth of the Gospel, leaving it too short and too narrow to wrap little children in. Was it something else than the
Gospel which was announced to "the Mother of all living," saying, "The seed of the woman shall bruise the Serpent's head?"
Or, were little children excluded from this great work of "the
holy child Jesus?" Was it the Gospel which was proclaimed by
the Angel messenger—"Behold I bring you good tidings of great
joy, which shall be to all people?" Gospel to the Shepherds because "they could hear it," but no "Gospel" to new-born babes
(like unto the Babe of Bethlehem that day born and laid in his
manger cradle) because they could not hear it! Was it the Gospel
which that other Angel announced—"His name shall be called
JESUS, for he shall save his people from their sins?" or, was it
something else, because little children may be included among
his people redeemed from their sins? Was it the Gospel that
Christ announced when he said—"Except any one be born again
he cannot see the kingdom of God?" or something else, because
little children may be "born again of the Spirit," and then, the
Gospel would have to be widened, so as to save all made regenerate by the Holy Ghost, whether it can be manifested by repentance and faith or not? Was it of the fruits of the Gospel that
the Saviour said, "All that thou hast given me shall come unto
me?" or of something else, lest "little children" should be regarded as given by the Father unto his Beloved Son when they
could not personally repent and believe? Should not the friends
of a theory which excludes little children from the kingdom of
God, ponder that utterance of astonishment from the lips of that
kingdom's Lord—"Have ye never read, 'Out of the mouth of
babes and sucklings thou hast perfected praise?'" And that other
like utterance, "Suffer little children to come unto me and forbid
them not, for of such is the kingdom of heaven?"

Are there two bands in heaven, one of which says, "Unto him

that loved us and washed us from our sins in his own blood, be glory and dominion forever," saying nothing of being old enough to hear, and repent, and believe, and therefore, " *not saved by the Gospel;*" while another band shall say, " Unto him that ' saved us by the Gospel,' *because* we were old enough to hear it, and repent of sin, and believe the promises, be glory forever !"

Is this the Gospel of individualism ?

But Dr. Carson cannot away with such a theory. Having defended the rejection of little children from salvation by the Gospel by a most groundless limitation of the term Gospel and its covenant promises, he is compelled to acknowledge the existence of a covenant which does embrace the babe and the suckling as well as the adult; which does bless "the senseless and the faithless babe," notwithstanding that it cannot "hear" or understand "the glad tidings" of such a covenant being made in its behalf. He says (p. 216), "Theologians justly considering that infants have sinned in Adam, have also justly considered that they must be washed in the blood of the Saviour." The parts of this statement are not harmonious. " Theologians justly considering *that infants having been included in the covenant of obedience with their family head* (although they could not hear the Law, and could not obey the Law) and were thus brought into an estate of sin and condemnation," is a statement which should find its counterpart thus : Therefore theologians have also justly considered *that infants being included in the covenant of grace with their family head* (although they cannot hear the Gospel or believe the Gospel) are thus, by a faithful observance of that covenant on the part of believing parents, brought into an estate of gracious covenant relation with God in Christ. But Dr. Carson while finding the want of knowledge and incapability of obedience no difficulty *in placing infants under a covenant of* DEATH, finds these things insuperable barriers *against placing infants under a covenant of* LIFE. " The legs of the lame are not equal." The attempt to make the Gospel an exclusive covenant with individuals capable of believing, and excluding all covenant with believing parents for their children, is in flat contradiction to the declaration, "the promise is to you and your children ;" to the fact, that Christ gave his blessing in response to the faith of parents to their little children brought to him ; and to the truth, that pardon of sin and reception into the kingdom of God are not grounded in repentance and faith as ultimate reasons, but as expository of what is essential—*a regenerate nature*, the work of the Holy Ghost alike in infant and adult. So, it is not true, that there is a diverse ultimate ground on which the adult or infant receives the highest blessings of the covenant of redemption. When Dr. Carson says, " The new covenant knows nothing of any salvation but through faith. Such a covenant cannot save an infant, who believes nothing," he contradicts Christ teaching, that the ultimate requisite to salvation is REGENERATION *by the Holy Ghost* and of which faith is a fruit. *Infant children may be made regenerate by the Holy Ghost.* The infant son of Zacharias and Elizabeth was so made regenerate—" filled with the Holy Ghost, even from his mother's womb." There is no other rational explanation of the prayer and blessing of the Lord Jesus Christ granted to the infants brought to him. A common covenant embracing infants and adults is acknowledged by Dr. Carson when he says, " But there is a covenant in which they are included, and which will save as many as are included in it—the covenant of redemption between the Father and the Son, in which he engaged to lay down his life, as a ransom, for his chosen, whether infants or adults." With such an admission what folly to deny, that infants are saved by the Gospel ; or to affirm, that adults are saved in any essentially different way from infants = by grace, through the blood of Christ and the renewing of the Holy Ghost.

Alexander Campbell.

A Baptist writer (Christian Standard, June 28, 1873) quotes Alexander Campbell (President of Bethany College) thus : " He did not admit, 'that infant children were depraved in any sense which makes it necessary to regenerate them, either with or without the Word, in order to their salvation.' "

The editor, in commenting on this statement, says : " Point us to a single text concerning the work of the Spirit that is fulfilled in the case of 'a speechless and faithless babe.' A babe without knowledge, without faith, without love or hate, without the least idea of sin or righteousness, God or man, heaven or hell—regenerated ! . . . It is the merest assumption without one particle of direct proof ; and an exceedingly nonsensical assumption at that. There is nothing more at war with reason or common sense in the Roman Catholic doctrine of Transubstantiation than in this of infant regeneration — a miracle transcending all our conceptions and at war with all we know of human nature."

Thus, the error which begins with contemptuous sneering at "senseless and faithless babes" as an apology for excluding the Family and its children from the kingdom of God, progresses to the exclusion of these little ones from the salvation of "the Gospel," by Carson, and culminates in a denial, that they can be or that they need to be made regenerate by the Holy Ghost, by Alexander Campbell.

Error carried out to its logical issues has, sometimes, the happy effect of frightening back to the truth those who had taken the first step, all unconscious of the end toward which their faces were set.

A writer in the National Baptist (June 26, 1873) is shocked at the doctrine of individualism as it is applied to the nation and progresses to a denial of the Family, or the Nation, having any God. He refers to sentiments advanced at a meeting of Baptist ministers, held a short time previously, in Philadelphia. This is his language: "This argument is good only on the assumption that the *unit* of society is the *individual, one* person, either man or woman. But this is the boldest of absurdities. A man alone or a woman alone, is but half a unit, hardly that. It takes the two in conjugal union, and having around them the fruits of such union, to make up the true unit. In a word the *family*, not the individual, is the true unit of society, and of the state. . . . *Husband* is *houseband*, the one who by his authority (in its legitimate exercise) orders and *binds* together in one organic whole the different parts of the *one* family. . . . Let Dr. Cathcart and every other Doctor who teaches the apostolic theory of the state, take note of it. And before again quoting this country as an example of the successful working of that theory, let them wait a modest century or two, until the real drift of it can be seen. ' The mills of God grind slowly, but they grind exceedingly fine ;' and if this nation tries the mad experiment of ignoring God, it will be ground to powder. God has never said that he is *not* the God of nations and states, and hence that they are *not* to serve him ; but he said, 'The nation and kingdom (not merely the individual, not an unorganized mob of individuals, but the *nation* and the kingdom) that will not serve thee shall perish.' "

Here the idea, that the individual only stands in responsible and covenant relation to God under law and grace is logically carried out to the denial, *that the nation or the Family has any God*, and to the rejection of the Family as the integral element

of national life, so as to shock this writer who accepts the doctrine *in its application to the kingdom of God and the household
of faith.*

It cannot be but that, sooner or later, all good and wise men
will be shocked by any system which places the kingdom of God
in antagonism with the Family constitution of the human race,
and with the whole structure of revelation in which Family unity
is ingráined, and with the attributes of the Deity as making provision for a race without providing for a class of that race made
up of untold millions, and *with the nature of the Deity itself revealed in* TRI-UNE and not *in* TRI-INDIVIDUAL *life.*

We believe that the constitution of God's gospel kingdom is in
harmony with God's constitution of the human race. We do,
therefore, accept the statements — " Lydia *and* HER *household*,"
" the Jailer *and* HIS *household*," " Stephanas *and* HIS *household*,"
at the normal value of their terms, and as declaring that " households" are received into the kingdom of God as embraced in a
covenant relation established between the Family head and the
God of the Family. And we do reject as the profoundest of
errors, essentially vitiating the constitution of Christ's kingdom,
and as antagonizing every covenant formed by God with the
human race from the beginning of time until now, the idea, that
individualism has supplanted and excluded THE FAMILY as an
organic element in the kingdom of God and in the covenant of
Redemption.

ALL RITUAL BAPTISMS EXAMINED ; THE RESULTS.

All the cases of ritual baptism in the New Testament which
can throw any light upon the meaning of βαπτίζω have now been
examined. The result is clear. The full formula of New Testament baptism embraces: 1. The verb in the active voice; 2. The
symbol agency in the dative, with or without ἐν; 3. The complement of the verb, the verbal or ideal receiving element, in the
accusative with εἰς.

This full formula appears in Matt. 3 : 11, βαπτίζω ἐν ὕδατι εἰς
μετάνοιαν; and in an abbreviated form (also with the omission of ἐν
and a change of order), in Luke 3 : 16, ὕδατι βαπτίζω. *No abbreviated form can be made the basis of interpretation.* It must first
be completed by a supply of the ellipsis.

In the full form the active voice expresses the transition of the object from one condition into another; the dative expresses the symbol agency by which this change is effected; the accusative with εἰς denotes the ideal element into which the object baptized passes, thus becoming thoroughly subject to its influence. That in this full formula *the agency* is represented by *the dative* is certain: 1. From the office of the dative; 2. From the universal Classic usage with the verb in the active voice; 3. From the nature of the case, which forbids a living person to be put into water without withdrawal, which the meaning of the verb demands.

It is no less certain, that in this full formula εἰς with its regimen represents the complement of the verb (the ideal element into which the baptized object verbally passes), and is thus represented as coming under its full influence. This is certain: 1. From the separate, and especially from the combined, power of βαπτίζω εἰς; 2. From the accepted force of such combination without exception, in Classic, Jewish, and Patristic usage; 3. From the fact that the full force of the verb can be and the teaching of Scripture requires, that it should be expended in this direction; 4. From the fact that whenever a diversity in the baptism (= the controlling influence to which the baptized object is to be subjected) is designed, *it is this regimen of* εἰς *which is changed to meet the demand.* Thus the εἰς μετανοιαν expressive of the baptism of John is changed to the εἰς το ὄνομα τοῦ Κυρίου Ἰησοῦ, to express the baptism of Christians; and this is changed by the Apostle for εἰς τὸν Μωσῆν, to express the baptism of the Israelites; and again (to express and to condemn a suggested baptism of the Corinthians) we have εἰς τὸ ὄνομα Παύλου; while to express a special baptism common to all Christians, we have εἰς ἐν σῶμα; and the ultimate and eternal baptism of all the redeemed, εἰς τὸ ὄνομα τοῦ Πατρὸς καὶ τοῦ Υἱοῦ καὶ τοῦ Ἁγίου Πνεύματος; and finally, as a universal phrase covering every case of baptism, we have εἰς τὶ ἐβαπτίσθητε.

Few things, in the whole circle of revelation, are established on more full, varied, and unquestionable evidence than the statement, *that the complement of* βαπτίζω *in the New Testament is invariably an* IDEAL *element,* suggestive of the most controlling spiritual influence, realized or symbolized.

COROLLARY. To attempt the establishment of a system on the idea, that the Scriptures teach a complementary relation between βαπτίζω and *water*, is to build on a most absolute and impracticable error which can never be reduced to practice ; but necessitates the abandonment of *a* BAPTISM for the composite action of *walking* and DIPPING, as also a division of administrative function between the baptizer and the baptized, and still farther and worst of all, the substitution of a *dipping into* WATER (which is scripturally *a nonentity*) for that most precious symbol baptism " WITH *water* INTO *the Name of the Lord Jesus.*"

CHRISTIC BAPTISM:

DOCTRINAL TRUTH GROUNDED IN OR EXPOUNDED BY REAL BAPTISM BY THE HOLY GHOST.

HOLY LIVING THE FRUIT OF REAL BAPTISM.

ROMANS 6 : 2-4.

Ἢ ἀγνοεῖτε, ὅτι ὅσοι ἐβαπτίσθημέν ἐις Χριστὸν Ἰησοῦν εἰς τὸν θάνανον αὐτοῦ ἐβαπτίσθημεν ;
Συνετάφημεν οὖν αὐτῷ διὰ τοῦ βαπτίσματος εἰς τὸν θάνατον.

" How shall we that are dead to sin, live any longer therein ?

" Know ye not, that so many of us as were baptized into Jesus Christ were baptized into his death ?

" Therefore we are buried with him by baptism into his death : that like as Christ was raised up from the dead by the glory of the Father, even so we also should walk in newness of life."

Baptism into the death of Christ, not ritual Baptism.

THOSE who believe, that ritual baptism should be administered by the candidate walking into the water " to a convenient depth," and the administrator dipping into the water so much of the body as the candidate may not himself have put under the water by walking, attach a supreme importance to this passage for the vindication of their practice.

This is done notwithstanding there is no administration of the rite in the passage ; notwithstanding there is no proposed exposition of the rite ; notwithstanding there is no declared allusion to the rite ; notwithstanding there is no mention of water ; and notwithstanding that the subject under discussion—holy living essential to every true Christian—excludes a ritual ordinance as the basis of the argument.

The idea, that a ritual baptism is referred to in this passage is grounded on the most absolute assumption. That assumption is twofold : 1. That the ruling baptism of the New Testament is (not the superior and real baptism by the Holy Ghost, but the

16   (241)

CHRISTIC BAPTISM.

inferior and ritual baptism with water); 2. That where baptism is spoken of in the New Testament absolutely, reference is made to the inferior and ritual baptism, and not to the superior, and real baptism of which the rite is but the symbol.

This assumption is erroneous in both its parts. The proof is this: 1. It is an error of principle to give precedence to the in ferior over the superior ; 2. It is impossible to reduce the assumption to practice : (1.) If it be ritual baptism which is spoken of, then, the ellipsis must be supplied and the phraseology completed and interpreted on that basis. This being done, it would read thus : "As many of us as were dipped in water into Christ, were dipped in water into his death ; Therefore we are buried with him by dipping in water into his death." Such translation and construction is untenable, because the substitution of *dipped* for "baptized" is the erasure of a most important word of inspiration and the insertion of its right opposite in meaning; and because it destroys the integrity and the momentous truth in the phrases, "baptized *into* CHRIST," baptized "*into his* DEATH;" and because neither Paul nor any other rational man ever wrote or reasoned after the style of this ritually completed phraseology; (2.) A *baptism* into WATER (not taking out) is impossible; a *baptism* into CHRIST (*not taking out*) is the very demand of Salvation.

Baptism into Christ, Real Baptism.

1. The presumption in every case of the absolute use of baptism in the New Testament is, that the reference is to real baptism. It is universally admitted, that the New Testament speaks of baptism by the Holy Ghost, which is most real in its operation and in its spiritual effect, thoroughly changing the condition of the soul from the love of sin to the love of holiness; it is also of universal admission, that the New Testament announces a baptism of water, which is believed (so far as the parties immediately involved in this Inquiry are concerned) to have no essential spiritual power, but to serve as a rite to symbolize the purifying power and effect in the soul of the real baptism by the Holy Ghost. This real baptism is as abiding in the Church as is the atonement on which it is grounded, and as universal in its application as is the blood of the Lamb which cleanseth from all sin. It was preached by John ("He shall baptize you by the Holy Ghost") as the distinguishing characteristic of the coming and kingdom of the Mightier

One. It was declared by the Lord Jesus (" Ye shall be baptized by the Holy Ghost ") when he was about to ascend to his throne. It was proclaimed by Peter at Pentecost, " I will pour out of my Spirit upon all flesh." It was republished at Cæsarea, when on the Gentiles also was poured out the gift of the Holy Ghost, and Peter " remembered the word of the Lord, ' Ye shall be baptized by the Holy Ghost.' " It was declared by Paul to the Corinthians, to characterize every soul united to Christ, " We are all baptized by one Spirit into one body." And it is this same baptism of the Spirit, received by every Christian, which Paul declares to the Romans when he says, " So many of us as have been baptized into Christ have received newness of life." This real baptism vindicates its claim by the ability to meet in the most absolute manner all the exigencies of the argument. A symbol baptism presents its plea in vain, because it does as absolutely fail to meet such exigencies. The demand for a real, regenerative baptism of the Spirit is imperative. This necessity Patristic writers recognized and accepted. While groundlessly deducing from the passage the idea of a symbol *burial* in water, they earnestly believed that *the baptism* was not a dipping in water. This no Patristic writer believed. Whatever error attached to their view it preserved that vital element in the argument of the Apostle, to wit, every one baptized into Christ must die to sin and live to holiness ; because every such person has, by such baptism, received newness of life. But the modern advocates of a burial in water, rejecting the idea that the Spirit does really baptize the soul in the rite, and introducing the novelty that dipping into water is Christian baptism, do eviscerate the argument of the Apostle of all its life.

2. That this baptism is real, by the Spirit, and not ritual, by water, is farther conclusively shown by the fact, that εἰς with its regimen related to βαπτίζω declares definitely and finally the baptism and the nature of the baptism.

This is true without exception of Classic usage. In such phrases as βαπτίζω εἰς θάλασσαν, εἰς λίμνην, εἰς ποταμόν, no one ever thought of any other translation or interpretation than that which makes the baptized object pass *into the* SEA, *into the* LAKE, *into the* RIVER, without any purpose or power of the verb to bring out ; therefore, subjecting the object to the unlimited influence of sea, lake, or river. The same is true of Jewish writings. When Josephus speaks of a baptism εἰς ἀναισθησίαν an intelligent translation pre

cludes any other than a baptism "*into* INSENSIBILITY," the verbal
form being modelled after that of a physical baptism; but inasmuch as a physical passing "into *insensibility*" as an element is
impossible, this idea is rejected; and that other idea of unlimited
influence consequent upon an object being introduced, without
withdrawal, into a physical element, is accepted as the idea designed to be conveyed by such phrase. The same form, with the
same power of expression, is used by Patristic writers. Clemens
Alex. speaks of a baptism εἰς ὕπνον *into* SLEEP; where, again, we
reject the impossible idea of a passage "into sleep" as an element,
and accept the associate and inseparable idea, unlimited influence
of sleep. Now, unless the Greek of the New Testament be under
essentially different laws from all other Greek (Classic, Jewish,
and Patristic), then baptism "*into* CHRIST" is modelled after the
form of a physical baptism which represents an object passing
into a physical element, and thus subjected to the fullest influence
of such element; but inasmuch as the redeemed souls of a world
cannot, in fact, pass "into *Christ*," we reject this idea (except as
suggestive) and take the inseparable, consequent idea of unlimited
influence exerted by Christ over his redeemed people = taking
away the guilt of sin, and giving "newness of life" through the
regenerating power of his Spirit. The same explanation applies
to baptism "*into* HIS DEATH," which is only a more precise statement as to *the source* of that influence exercised by Christ over
his people. Christ is what he is to his people by reason of his
atoning death; therefore, "so many of us as have been baptized
into CHRIST, have been baptized into his DEATH."

3. There is no just ground for error or doubt as to the import
of εἰς and its regimen in relation with βαπτίζω. The principle of
interpretation is clear and fixed. It is found in the influence
exerted over an object in physical baptism. The nature of such
influence is no less clear and fixed. It is the most unlimited =
penetrating, controlling, and assimilating influence which the
nature of the case allows. The variable quantities in such baptism are found in the nature of the element and the nature of the
object. If water or oil be the element into which a fleece of wool
is baptized the effect upon the wool will be diverse, according to
the diverse nature of water and oil. If a vessel and its crew be
baptized together into the sea, the effect of this common baptism
on vessel and crew will be diverse, according to the nature of life-
less wood and of living men. A baptism "into insensibility"

differs from a baptism "into repentance" just as *insensibility* differs from *repentance*. And a baptism "*into* MOSES," "*into* PAUL," "*into* CHRIST," differs the one from the other just as Moses and Paul and Christ differ the one from the other.

If these things be true, then, when in the statement of any baptism εἰς and its regimen appears, *the baptism is thereby definitely and absolutely declared*, and all farther inquiry is concluded.

In the passage before us the baptism spoken of is declared to be "*into* CHRIST" and (its equivalent baptism) "*into* HIS DEATH;" and this it must be for all with whom the word of God expressly declared is the end of all controversy. And as we can only be made partakers of the blessings which belong to Christ and his death, by the grace and power of the Holy Ghost, this baptism can only be the real and regenerative baptism of the Divine Spirit.

Dr. Carson.

The following is a summary of the views of Dr. Carson on this passage:

"All eminent scholars will confess, as plainly as prudence will permit them, that we have both the meaning of the word and the inspired explanation of the mode in our favor. . . . But the thing is so plain in itself, that if all the men on earth should deny it, I could not think otherwise of it than I do. . . . Any one who understands the words, will be able to understand the assertion as clearly as Newton or Locke. *Buried with Christ by baptism* must mean that baptism has a resemblance to Christ's burial. Were the angel Gabriel to hesitate, I would order him to school. In many cases of error I can see the plausible ground on which it rests; but here I can perceive no *den* in which deception can be concealed. . . . Believers are buried with Christ by baptism, and it is by baptism, also, they die with him. Death, burial, and resurrection are all expressly in the emblem. . . . There are two distinct emblems in baptism: one of purification by water, another of death, burial, and resurrection, by immersion. . . . But the fact is that baptism, as far as it is here expounded, refers to death, burial, and resurrection, without any mention of purification, or any allusion to it. Baptism is here spoken of, not with respect to the water, but with respect to the mode. In this there are death, burial, and resurrection" (pp. 383–386).

"They are literally immersed, but the burial is equally figurative as the death; and they die in baptism as well as they are buried in baptism. Indeed it is *by being buried* that they die. That this figurative burial is *under water* is not in the passage: this is known from the rite, and is here supplied by ellipsis" (p. 411).

" Here is a burial by or through the means of baptism. What buries us into death? It is baptism. But the death into which baptism buries us must be a figurative death. It is faith that buries us truly into Christ's death. But the death and burial here spoken of are effected not by faith, but by baptism. . . . Nay, it is by burial we die. We are supposed to be *buried into death.* To immerse a living man affords an emblem of death as well as of burial. The baptized person dies under the water, and for a moment lies buried with Christ. Christ's own death was spoken of under the figure of a baptism " (p. 157).

" Twist and twist as you will, still there is burial in baptism. Believers are *buried into death.* It is not they die and are buried, but they are buried and die. Mode is the point at issue, and is the only thing signified by the word itself. Some Baptists it seems do not see the force of the argument on Rom. 6 : 3, 4. At the very worst this is only the loss of a single argument, an argument, however, which I would hold were an angel to reject it " (p. 420).

" To be baptized into Jesus Christ imports the being baptized into the faith of his death as our substitute; but to be baptized into his death imports that by baptism we are exhibited as dying with him " (p. 159).

" The death, burial, and resurrection which are ascribed to baptism, take place *in baptism*, and *by means of baptism.* The washing away of sins, ascribed to baptism, is effected by baptism. This washing, this death, this burial, and this resurrection, then, cannot be the washing, death, burial, and resurrection which are effected by faith, and *which take place before baptism.* If the washing away of sins, the death, burial, and resurrection, ascribed to baptism, were effected previously, and by other means, the Scriptures are not true that speak of them as effected *in* baptism and by baptism. The reality has already taken place, but it is represented in figure, as taking place in the ordinance, and by means of the ordinance " (p. 161).

Criticism.

1. "All eminent scholars will confess, as plainly as prudence will permit them, that we have both the meaning of the word and the inspired explanation of the mode in our favor." *Answer:* The result of this Inquiry shows that Dr. Carson and his friends have fatally mistaken the meaning of the word, having substituted the meaning of βάπτω for βαπτίζω. Whether there be any "inspired explanation of the mode " in this passage, the examination of it, in which we are engaged, will determine.

2. "Any one who understands the words will be able to understand the assertion as well as Newton or Locke." *Answer:* A right understanding of words is oftentimes adequate to develop truth; but the mere understanding of individual words in organic phraseological combination is oftentimes worthless to elicit the truth. The passage before us is, to a remarkable degree, made up of phrases which cannot be broken up into disjunct words without the destruction of their life.

3. "*Buried with Christ by baptism* must mean that baptism has a resemblance to Christ's burial. I would order the angel Gabriel to school. I can perceive no den in which deception can be concealed." *Answer:* To give the statement "buried with Christ by baptism " as the statement of Paul, is as untrue as for Herod to give the detruncated body of John to his disciples, and declare that it was the Forerunner of Jesus. The headless trunk of John cries out "Murder!" and "buried with Christ by baptism " *is but a murdered trunk;* its head ("into his death ") having been decapitated by the sharp sword of the theory. It is only by the death of its slain victim that the theory has any hope of life. This is an illustration of the death dismemberment of an organic phrase. Dr. Carson might as well quote for Bible truth, "There is no God," leaving out "The fool hath said in his heart." And if the angel Gabriel, under the "order " of Dr. Carson, were to go to school where the heads of organic phrases were lopped off, as is here done by this lordly Imperator, he would be but little wiser at the end of his schooling than at its beginning.

4. "Death, burial, and resurrection, are all expressly in the emblem." *Answer:* This is the purest assumption and assertion. It is the purest assumption to talk of any emblem being in the passage; and it is the purest assertion, to say that there is death, burial, and resurrection in baptism here or anywhere else in

Scripture. Sirius is as truly in the solar system as resurrection
is in baptism.

5. " There are two distinct emblems in baptism : one of purification by water, another of death, burial, and resurrection, by
immersion." *Answer :* That there should be " two distinct" emblems in one emblematic rite is unnatural and incredible, if not
impossible and absurd. It savors strongly of humanism, which
" has sought out many inventions," and not of divine simplicity.
Whatever may be the essential merits of this statement, two
things are certain : 1. There is not one word of Scripture for its
support ; 2. Dr. Carson is at fault in his arithmetic. Instead of
" *two* distinct emblems," a correct summing up furnishes us with
four (1.) Purification ; (2.) Death ; (3.) Burial ; (4.) Resurrection. And why a dipping into water should be limited to giving
birth to this quartette group, I do not know ; but the paternity,
as it stands, must be set down to a prolific theory and not to
Christian baptism.

6. " But the fact is that baptism, as far as it is here expounded,
refers to death, burial, and resurrection, without any mention
of purification, or any allusion to it." *Answer :* That is to say,
when Paul undertakes to establish the essential purity of Christian character, he frames an argument " without any mention of
or allusion to purification," but does so clearly establish the mode
of a rite (!) that " the angel Gabriel must be ordered to school "
if he should have the shadow of a doubt on so vital a point, as
compared with the minor issue of soul purification through union
with Christ in his wondrous work of redemption !

7. " Baptism is here spoken of, not with respect to the water,
but with respect to the mode. In this, there are death, burial,
and resurrection." *Answer :* Then, why these remarkable things
should be unrevealed and unsuggested for more than a quarter
of a hundred years after baptism was instituted, taught, and
practiced, must remain among " the hidden things," until resolved
by the theory.

8. " They die in baptism, as well as they are buried in baptism.
Indeed it is by being buried that they die." *Answer :* These are
three conceptions to be credited to a rich imagination, but for which
divine inspiration refuses to accept the slightest responsibility.

9. " That the figurative burial is *under water* is not in the
passage : this is known from the rite, and is here supplied by
ellipsis." *Answer :* Dr. Carson is always honest in his intention

even when most profoundly erroneous in his conviction. " There is no water and no burial under water in the passage." Then here is an admitted fixed point. And on it we stand and sternly refuse that either " water or burial under water " shall be assumed or asserted into a passage from which they have been excluded by the Holy Spirit. But it is said, that we know that they should be there "from the rite." First *prove* (don't assume and assert) that " the rite " is there. " It is supplied by ellipsis." Then prove (as the law of ellipsis demands) that " burial under water " appears in any other antecedent passage. When such proof is given we will lift our foot from the concession and stand back; but not till then.

10. " Here is a burial by or through the means of baptism. What buries us into death? It is baptism. But the death into which baptism buries us must be a figurative death." *Answer:* To say that there is any burial by *ritual* baptism, in the passage, is as untrue as to say that the headless body of John is the living Forerunner. Both the question, " What buries us into death?" and the answer, " It is baptism," is as far removed from express-ing anything in the passage, as the west is from the east. There is not a syllable in the passage about Christians being " *buried* into death " by baptism or anything else. The statement of in-spiration is, " We are buried *with him* (Christ) by baptism (not into *water*, nor yet into *death*, but) into HIS death." The article, τὸν θάνατον, shows that it is not death in the abstract that is spoken of, but as concrete in the crucified Christ. And the state-ment of a " *burial* into death by baptism " as representing the text is the most absolute perversion and contradiction of the text. The burial is not "into death," but co-burial " with Christ," and this co-burial with Christ is not by baptism *in water*, but " by baptism *into his death*."

11. " It is *faith* that buries us truly into Christ's death." *Answer:* Truth and error are here mixed together. The error consists in the substitution of bury for *baptize*. The Scriptures know nothing of a " *burial* into Christ's death." They do teach a " *baptism* into Christ's death." " *Burial* into Christ's death " is nonsense; " Baptism into Christ's death " is the wisdom of God and the power of God, as well as the love of God, and the grace of God, bringing life from the dead. The truth of the statement is in the declaration, " It is FAITH that *baptizes* us truly into the death of Christ." And if Dr. Carson and his friends

will be satisfied with the double truth which he has stated; (1.) "There is no water nor burial under water in the passage;" (2.) "Faith baptizes us, truly, into the death of Christ;" we will rejoice together in having attained unto the mind of the Spirit. And abandoning the remarkable reading, "As many as have been dipped in water into Christ, have been dipped in water into his death; buried with him by the dipping in water into death," we will accept the better reading, "As many as have been baptized by faith into Christ, have been baptized by faith into his death; buried with him through baptism by faith into his death." This is the simple and exhaustive truth of the passage. "Water," "burial under water," "death in water," "resurrection out of water," are all finger-marks of human improvements (?) of the inspired text.

12. "We are supposed to be buried into death. To immerse a living man, affords an emblem of death as well as of burial. The baptized person dies under the water, and for a moment lies buried with Christ." *Answer :* These statements are nothing but successive shocks to the good sense and right feeling of thoughtful minds. It has already been stated, that "burial into death" has no existence in the passage. And there has been occasion, many times, to say, Dr. Carson has no right to use immerse or bury for baptize. He asserts that "dip" is the only and universal meaning of the Greek word; and between the distinctive meanings of *dip* and *immerse* there is as much difference as between light and darkness. "Immersion" will not only furnish an emblem of death and burial for a living man, but will give the reality—

> . . . . . "*dead*
> By cold *submersion*, razor, rope or lead."

> . . . . . "*immersed*
> Deep in the flood, found, when he sought it not
> The *death* he had deserved, and *died* alone."

If ever (apart from the remarkable interpretation of this passage) the avowed momentary dipping of a living man (or the upper part of his body after he had walked into the water) was ever considered by any people as indicative of a death, and burial, and resurrection, it might be worth while to indicate when, or where, or among whom, this singularity has made and revealed itself. As to the conceit, that "the baptized person dies under the water," I respond with Origen, "No living person is ever buried." And as for "lying buried with Christ, for a moment, under the water," the Bible doctrine will be more acceptable to his people who are "crucified with him," that they lie buried with him in his rock sepulchre, not for a moment, but through all the time that he lies there, even as he himself taught in that only Bible type of his burial—"As Jonah was three days and three nights in the whale's belly: so shall the Son of man be three days and three nights in the heart of the earth," and so long his people are co-buried with him. So long as this miracle type of Christ's burial remains of divine authority, we cannot accept its right opposite (momentary dipping) as a substitute, however earnestly men may plead for it.

13. "Christ's own death was spoken of under the figure of a baptism." *Answer:* Yes; it was. Christ was baptized into death, into penal death, into that death which was demanded by the broken law. And how was he baptized into death? Was it by being dipped into water? Or, *by drinking the cup* held to his lips by a Father's hand, in which were melted down, the humiliation of "taking upon him the form of a servant," the bearing of the name of "Nazarene" and Beelzebub, the endurance of buffetings and stripes, the nails, and the thorns, and the spear, and the averted face of his ever-loving Father? All this he drank, and *by it was baptized into penal and atoning death.* And now, having endured this penal death satisfying the demands of the Law, his death becomes impregnated with a sin-remitting and life-giving power, so that all who are baptized "into HIS death" become fully partakers of these wondrous virtues, and THEREFORE Paul teaches, "So many of us as have been baptized into Christ, *have been baptized into* HIS *death*," not into DEATH, which would make the death of Christ of no effect; not into *penal* death, which would supersede the death of Christ as the propitiation for our sins; but "into HIS death," that we might be brought fully under its sin-remitting and life-giving power. How vain to appeal to the baptism of Christ into penal death to buttress up that marvel of a "baptism into death"—a dipping into water!

14. "Twist and twist as you will, still, there is burial in baptism." *Answer:* This ever-echoing refrain of a "*burial* in baptism," as extracted from the statement, "buried *with him by baptism into his death*," is an error so patent that it would be inexcusable in a Sabbath-school child, or in "a wayfaring man

though a fool," whatever excuse may be found for it in one who "orders the angel Gabriel to school." Burial and Baptism have nothing common.

15. " Mode is the point at issue, and is the only thing signified by the word itself." *Answer:* The word never signifies a modal or definite act of any kind, much less "dip and nothing but dip."

16. " To be baptized into Jesus Christ imports, the being baptized into the faith of his death as our substitute; but to be baptized into his death imports, that by baptism we are exhibited as dying along with him." *Answer:* Whistling to the wind, is as much an interpretation of these Scripture phrases as this fancy exposition of Dr. Carson—" Baptized into Jesus Christ" means " to be dipped in water into the faith of his death as our substitute" (!). Yes, just as truly as "baptized into insensibility" means to be dipped in water into the faith of obliviousness to all sublunary things! And " baptized into his death" means, by dipping in water we are exhibited as dying along with him (!). But whence these diversities of interpretation? Why have we " faith" introduced into one exposition, and an "exhibition" introduced into another? Must we interpret "baptized into sleep" as a dipping in water exhibiting us as going to sleep? There is just as much authority for introducing a dipping in water into the interpretation of " baptized into insensibility," and " baptized into sleep," as into " baptized into Jesus Christ," and "baptized into his death." These phrases have an absolute completeness within themselves, as have those other phrases, " baptized into repentance," " baptized into the remission of sins," and must all be interpreted on the same principle, namely, the baptized object is declared to come under the full influence of " insensibility," " sleep," " repentance," " remission of sins," "Jesus Christ," and " his death." The statement in every case is direct and without intervening ellipsis of any kind whatever, and to introduce water is to murder the truth. While these phrases are complete in themselves they may be enlarged by a statement of the agency by which they are effected; but, in the present case, we have nothing to do with the agency effecting these baptisms, but simply with the baptisms declared to be effected. And these are as destitute of water as is " Jesus Christ" and " his death."

17. " The reality has already taken place, but it is represented in figure as taking place in the ordinance and by the ordinance."

Answer: This admitted distinction between the real baptism and the symbolization of that baptism in a rite, covers radical truth. It is the real baptism received by every true Christian of which Paul speaks and not of its shadowy symbol. The Christian is really " baptized into Christ," " into his death" (which are equivalent baptisms), that is, he is brought under the full influence of Christ as Lord and atoning Redeemer, by the Holy Ghost working in him faith and repentance, and thus made partaker of remission of sin and newness of life. There is in all this, no death of the Christian, that can be exhibited, it is Christ that dies ; there is no burial of the Christian that can be exhibited, it is Christ that is buried ; there is no resurrection of the Christian that can be exhibited, it is Christ that rises from the dead and from the grave. There is but one thing pertaining to Christian life which can be exhibited by symbol, and that is its purifying nature ; this is done by the pure water of the rite. And this is that which God has ordained to be done.

Dr. Carson (p. 279) says, " I arraign our opponents as estab lishing innumerable false principles of interpretation, and as trampling on many of the clearest laws of language. Here, then, let me be met." I have endeavored to plead to this arraignment.

Professor Ripley and other Baptist Commentators.

1. Professor Ripley, of Newton Baptist Theological Seminary (Christian Baptism, pp. 83–97), has given this passage an extended examination. If this examination has not yielded such results as fairly belong to the language of the Holy Spirit, the failure can be attributed neither to the want of a Christian spirit, nor of ample learning on the part of this christian Scholar. In addition to what has been already said a few points only need claim attention. The translation of v. 4 is important both doctrinally and critically. The translation given by Prof. Ripley is, " buried with him by baptism into *his* death." The translation in the Baptist Version is the same, " buried with him by the immersion into *his* death." Stuart, Bloomfield, Alford, and others, give the same translation. The incalculable difference between baptism into simple *death* and " baptism into *his* death " is shown by the following passage from Irenæus, 975, " Quemadmodum Serpens Evam seduxit . . . sic et hi in mortem demergunt sibi credentes." Baptism into death = *dying thou shalt die.* " Baptism into *his*

death" = release from sin and its death penalty. The definite article with βάπτισμα indicates a particular baptism; as does the definite article with θάνατον indicate a particular death; "We are buried with Christ by *the* baptism which is into *the* death of Christ." This is, no doubt, the true translation. It is doctrinally important, because it teaches, that all the blessings of Christian life are concentred in Christ's death; and are appropriated, not by a dipping into water, nor by a baptism into death (real or emblematic) but by *the* baptism which is into Christ's death, effected not by man through a rite, but by the Holy Ghost uniting to Christ and making participant in all the blessings of his sacrificial death. This real baptism of the soul into Christ, and into his death, by the Holy Ghost, is set forth as to its purifying nature in a rite by symbol water.

This translation is important, critically, because it gives clear and bold relief to the *nexus* of the Christian's burial with Christ. The qualifying antecedent for burial with the slain Lamb of God in his rock sepulchre is, *baptism* INTO HIS ATONING DEATH *upon the Cross.*

This precludes, in the most absolute manner, the connection of burial with Christ with a dipping in water. It also arrests the removal of the body of Christ from its rock sepulchre to be deposited at the botton of a pool of water, that the baptized may there lie buried with him "for a moment" (Carson), or, be "buried with HIM by baptism, by being plunged into the water" (Gale).

2. Prof. Ripley loses the benefit of his just translation by eliding it from his argument, and constructing a new basis on which he plants himself. This basis is as foreign in its nature from that furnished by the Holy Spirit as any two things can be. His argument is this: "The burying is performed *by baptism*, an external rite. . . . It is διὰ τοῦ βαπτίσματος BY *baptism* that we are buried. . . . Baptism is here represented as *the very thing, the very instrument*, or more properly, *the very act*, BY which, or BY MEANS of which we are buried." The italics and capitals are as given by Prof. Ripley.

In a note we are told: "It is important to bear in mind that the burying is performed *by baptism*, and thus refers to an external act."

The *sine qua non* in the argument of Prof. Ripley, and which he tells us is "important to bear in mind," is, that the baptism in

the passage is " an external act." But where is the authority for
this statement? There is none attempted to be given. It is
opposed to every feature of the passage. The word for burial
(συνετάφημεν) is unfavorable to it. Its meaning, as approved by
Prof. Ripley, " we were interred, or covered up in a grave, or laid
in a tomb " is not appropriate to a dipping in *water*. The preposition in composition shows that there is no reference to water,
but to the rock within which Christ was buried, *not* BAPTIZED (!).
It was only in that rock sepulchre that we could be buried-*with*
him. The argument of the Apostle is made as worthless as a
broken reed by making it to lean on an external rite. Paul would
never undertake to prove that Christians did not and could not
live in sin, because they had professed through a rite, that they
would not do so. The language of the Holy Spirit excludes " an
external act " as explicitly as it can be done by the Greek language.
It is impossible to baptize the body or the soul " into the death
of Christ " *by an external act*, just as it is impossible *to dip* " into
insensibility " or " into sleep." But the state or condition indicated by " Baptism into insensibility," " Baptism into sleep,"
may be induced by appropriate agencies, and so, that state or
condition indicated by "the baptism of the soul into the death of
Christ" may be effected through the appropriate agency, which is
only and solely the divine power of the Holy Spirit.

The error of converting this baptism into " an external act " is
farther shown by its rendering the passage thoroughly impracticable for intelligible interpretation. Prof. Ripley considers
βαπτίζω to express an " act," what act he does not say. If it expresses any act it must be a *definite* act. Carson says it is dip;
Gale uses *plunge* to expound this passage. But as dip is not
plunge, nor plunge dip, the Greek word, if it expresses the distinctive idea of either, cannot express that of the other. Booth
objects to *plunge*, and the " Baptist Quarterly " objects to *dip*.
The Baptist Version adopts " immerse; " but this does not
express any definite act, nor action embracing varied definite elements, but condition effected by some unexpressed act, which may
be endlessly multiplied and varied within the limits of competency to effect the demanded condition. To abandon act and
adopt condition as the demand of βαπτίζω, requires the revolution and abandonment of Baptist argumentation from the beginning. Beside this, the noun (βάπτισμα) which appears in this
passage (but which does not appear in Classic Greek) has no

physical application in the New Testament. It is a matter of no moment whether "the act" of Prof. Ripley be represented by "dip" or "plunge," or by the "immerse" of the Version, each is alike destructive to all grammar or logic in the passage : where it is completed on that basis—"As many as have been dipped, plunged, or immersed in water into Christ, have been dipped, plunged, or immersed in water into his death ; buried with him by dipping, plunging, or immersing in water into his death." In such a construction a double and impossible *rôle* is assigned to these verbs, and to make a rational construction you must wholly recast it and abandon (not interpret) the words of inspiration. And this Prof. Ripley is constrained to do when his argument is based, as it is, upon the partial quotation, " buried with him by baptism," omitting " into his death " (which the Holy Spirit gives as defining the baptism) and substituting " in water."

And this line of argument, abandoning that portion of the text in which is its pulsating life, is followed by Prof. Chase, Prof. Jewett, Dr. Carson, Dr. Gale, and every other Baptist writer with whom I am acquainted, and has been urged for nearly two cen- turies, from Gale to this hour, as I have just read in the " Western Recorder " " the man whose hands had buried me in baptism."

3. Prof. Ripley says, very justly, " The expressions, *baptized into Jesus Christ*, and *baptized into his death*, require explana- tion." These phrases are the hinges on which the interpretation of the passage turns. As they are understood or misunderstood, the passage will be understood or misunderstood.

Prof. Ripley, in elucidation of these phrases, appeals to Matt. 3 : 11, correcting the translation thus, " I baptize you unto repent- ance (εἰς μετάνοιαν), that is *into* repentance." And adds, " The meaning of this declaration I understand to be this, *I baptize you into an acknowledgment of repentance; so that by this baptism you acknowledge yourselves to be in a state of Repentance;* in other words, by submitting to this baptism you profess repentance and bind yourselves to a life of amendment."

What Prof. Ripley says respecting " acknowledgment " and " profession" is, undoubtedly, involved in the reception of this ritual baptism of John, but the form of his statement is not an interpre- tation of the phrase used by John. The Forerunner came (κηρύσσων βάπτισμα μετανοίας εἰς ἄφεσιν ἁμαρτιῶν) "preaching the baptism of re- pentance into the remission of sins " (Luke 3 : 3). This preaching of John had two elements : 1. Repentance ; 2. Baptism into the remission of sins. He makes Repentance precede the baptism into the remission of sins, and to be immediately causative of it. Repentance is represented as effecting the baptism into the remission of sins; by which phrase is expressed the most thorough and complete remission of sins. This certainly is the doctrine everywhere in the Bible; and that it is the import of this phrase is conclusively shown by that analogous one used by Josephus— ὑπὸ μέθης εἰς ἀναισθησίαν. Here beyond all question drunkenness is represented as precedent and causative of the "baptism into insensibility." Wine baptizes into drunkenness; and drunkenness baptizes into insensibility. The Holy Spirit baptizes into repentance; and repentance baptizes into the remission of sins.

This was the *preaching* of John in which there was *no* WATER. But John observed a rite in which there was water, and of this rite he said (using the order and simple Dative of Luke): Ἐγὼ ὕδατι βαπτίζω εἰς μετάνοιαν "I with water baptize into repentance." This language does not change the baptism from a baptism into repentance to a baptism into water, nor in anywise change the essential value of the phrase baptism into repentance; but the additional statement that John, and not Christ, is the baptizer, and that water, and not the Holy Ghost, is the agency, teaches that the baptism into repentance is not effected as a reality, but only by a symbol. And the office of a symbol exhausts the function and the power of water in this phrase. To give it any other place in the rite than that of an illustrative symbol agency is a destructive perversion of the words of inspiration. There is no authority for introducing "into an acknowledgment of" into this baptism. The baptism is "*into* REPENTANCE" whether in the preaching or in the rite. Its qualification is to be found in the agency. In the preaching of John the agency is that of the Holy Ghost, and therefore "the baptism into repentance" is a real change in the condition of the soul begetting godly sorrow for sin, and issuing into the remission of sins; but in the rite of John the agency is pure water, and consequently it is but a symbolization of the purification induced by the real baptism into repentance = into the remission of sins. When Prof. Ripley says, "By this baptism you acknowledge yourself to be *in a state of repentance,*" he must get "state of repentance," or "state" *in which the soul is thoroughly under the influence of repentance,* from the phrase "baptism into repentance," which is in truth the meaning of the phrase. So "baptized into Christ;" the phrase imports that the soul is

17

brought into "a state " *in which it is thoroughly under the influ-*
ence of CHRIST; and "baptized into the death of Christ" imports
that the soul is brought into "a state " *in which it is thoroughly
under the influence of* THE DEATH *of Christ.* To expound these
phrases by the unauthorized introduction of "*into* THE ACKNOWL-
EDGMENT OF" is destructive criticism.

Further Explanation.

As this point raised by Prof. Ripley enters profoundly into and
controls the interpretation of the baptisms of the New Testament,
it may be well to indicate more fully the sources whence a true
interpretation must be derived.

βάπτω. In the phrase "βάπτων τὸν πέπλον εἰς τὸ χρῶμα dipping
the robe into the dye," all will unite in saying that the robe is
put into the dye *for the purpose of imparting to the* ROBE *the full
distinctive* COLOR *which belongs to the dye,* whatever that may be,
whether *yellow, blue,* or *purple.*

The phrase " ἐνέβαψεν εἰς τὸν κηρὸν τὼ πόδε he dipped the feet
into the wax," shows that the feet were put into the wax in order
that they might be *brought fully under the distinctive* (adherent)
quality of wax.

This communication of a distinctive quality by dipping into
something which has such quality and can thus impart it to the
object dipped into it, is denoted when neither the object receiving
the quality, nor that which communicates the quality, admits of a
dipping in fact. Thus, "βάπτεται ὑπὸ τῶν φαντασίων ἡ ψυχή the soul
is imbued by the thoughts." In this phrase *the soul* is represented
as brought under *the distinctive quality of the thoughts* by the same
verb as was used in the previous phrases. The end secured is of
the same general nature, but the process is wholly diverse. The
soul cannot be dipped "into the thoughts," neither can the
thoughts impart their quality in any such way.

In the phrase " διχαιοσύνη βεβαμμένον εἰς βάθος imbued with integrity into the depth of the soul," the distinctive quality of "integrity" is represented (again by the same word) as communicated
to the soul not by dipping the soul into it—in fact that is impossible—but by integrity penetrating and pervading the soul as a
coloring quality, reaching to its innermost depths. The following
passage will illustrate the idea: "Ten years ago I *imbued* myself
with him (Tennyson) thoroughly. Like an animal that is fed

on madder I was *dyed in* HIS *color* to the very bones." *Imbued* = "dyed in his color." These are illustrations of a like generic effect (distinctive quality) communicated, the same verb (*βάπτω*) characterizing the effect, but where the processes by which the effect is secured have nothing in common.

βαπτίζω. The following phrases express the purpose to develop the distinctive quality of the several fluids named over the objects *baptized into* them: 1. "εἰς τὴν λίμνην βαπτίζοντες baptizing them *into* the lake;" the design was to develop the distinctive (suffocating) influence of liquids over human beings baptized into them. 2. "κοντὸν εἰς τὸ ὕδωρ βαπτίζουσι they baptize the pole *into* the water," for the purpose of developing the distinctive (gold-bearing) quality of the water, the pole being thus covered with gold particles. 3. "τῷ βαπτισθέντι εἰς τὸ ὕδωρ everything baptized *into* the water;" thus the distinctive (salt) quality of this water was developed, incrusting with salt whatever was baptized into it. 4. "βαπτίζειν εἰς γάλα γυναικὸς baptize it *into* breast-milk," to develop its distinctive (emollient) quality.

These are sufficient cases to show that *βαπτίζειν εἰς* is familiarly used with the clear design to develop *the distinctive quality* of that into which an object is baptized, with a view to such quality being communicated to or exerted over the baptized object.

This same form is used to denote the development of characteristic quality when neither the object spoken of as baptized, nor the regimen of *εἰς* into which the baptism is (verbally) said to take place, will admit of any baptism in fact.

One case of this kind is found in that passage of Josephus already referred to, " βεβαπτισμένον ὑπὸ μέθης εἰς ἀναισθησίαν baptized by drunkenness *into* insensibility." Here " *baptized into* INSENSIBILITY " is used to denote the insensibility induced by profound drunkenness as bearing upon the drunkard. The same verbal form (baptized into) is used as in the case of physical substances, and the result (development of characteristic quality) is the same, but the processes have nothing in common. The one is effected by actual " baptizing into a lake," or " gold-bearing fountain," or " salt-saturated water," or " emollient milk," while the other is effected by *drinking deeply* of intoxicating liquor. A parallel passage is furnished by Clem. Rom., " παραπεσουσα εἰς μέθην the feast *passing into* DRUNKENNESS ;" and, also, by Clem. Alex., " εἰς ἀναισθησίαν ὑπο φερομένη *carrying down into* INSENSIBILITY." In all these cases the verb expends its force through εἰς upon the regimen of that preposition which can only be translated *into.* Clem. Alex. also speaks of a baptism " εἰς ὕπνον *into* SLEEP," and Clem. Rom. uses a parallel phrase, " εἰς ὕπνον καταπεσόντων *having fallen into* SLEEP." The former of these writers uses a still fuller and if possible a more unmistakable form of baptism, " ἐκ σωφροσύνης εἰς πορνείαν βαπτίζουσι they *baptize out of* chastity *into* UNCHASTITY."

Such passages as these place beyond controversy the use of the phrase βαπτίζω εἰς to develop the influence of *the distinctive quality of the associate regimen over the baptized object.* And in this established truth we have the ποῦ στῶ which must be occupied in order to the only just and intelligible interpretation of the baptisms of the New Testament.

John preaches the " βάπτισμα μετανοίας εἰς ἄφεσιν ἁμαρτιων the *baptism* of repentance *into* THE REMISSION OF SINS," a phrase developing the peculiar power belonging to the remission of sins in relation to the guilty who share in its baptism. John administers a rite in which the baptism which he preached as a spiritual necessity (εἰς μετανοίαν) is declared verbally, and symbolized as to its nature by pure water.

So, in the passage under consideration, " the *baptism* is *into* JESUS CHRIST," developing the characteristics which belong to " Jesus Christ," and applying them in their power to " as many as are *baptized into* HIM ; " and in like manner, " *baptism into* HIS DEATH " develops the characteristic of his atoning death as applied to the guilty and the perishing who share in this baptism.

We are hereby not only furnished with the means of explaining the phrases immediately before us (which Prof. Ripley justly regards as most important), but with a principle which applies to all like baptisms of the New Testament ; and all baptisms of the New Testament do, without exception, belong to this same class. A baptism into water (or any other physical element) is unknown to the New Testament. That a human being should be baptized into water in a religious rite is forbidden by the meaning of βαπτίζω, which never takes out what it puts in. That water should be the element into which the baptized object passes is forbidden by the grammatical construction which always exhibits the water of the rite in the Dative, as a symbol agency. That the element is ideal, and the baptism a spiritual state or condition (realized in the soul and symbolized in the rite), is made as sure and as clear as the express and invariable declaration of the Holy Spirit can make it—"As many as are *baptized into* CHRIST, are *baptized into* HIS DEATH; buried with him by *baptism into* HIS DEATH."

Professor Chase is a colleague of Professor Ripley in Newton Theological Seminary, and appeal is made to him to sustain the statement—"The Apostle himself explains what he means by *burying* when he adds *by baptism.*" The interpretation given by Prof. Chase is this: "'Buried with him by baptism.' The language is figurative. The word συνετάφημεν means *we were interred,* or *covered up in a grave,* or *laid in a tomb,* or *buried with* Christ." There is no figure in the burial of Christ. This is a simple fact. And there is no other burial spoken of in fact or in figure. There is a burial of *other persons,* but no other *burial,* any more than there are other crucifixions when "our old man (συνεσταυρώθη) is crucified with him." The statement is equally explicit in both cases that there is but one burial, and that is Christ's; and there is but one crucifixion, and that is Christ's; but in that one burial and in that one crucifixion his people share, not through some figurative burial or figurative crucifixion, but by that union with Christ, their head, which the Bible, here and everywhere, teaches. The figure is the UNION *with Christ;* a figurative grave is a fiction. That this is so is shown by the answer given by Prof. Chase to the question—"How buried with Christ? *By baptism,* the Apostle adds; and this addition modifies the figure, and makes the sense as clear as it is possible for express words to make it. *In* or *by baptism* Paul and Christians were *buried.*" It is truly marvellous that Prof. Chase could see that "buried with Christ" is modified by "the addition *by baptism,*" and failed to see that he had not given the modifying addition furnished by the Holy Spirit. Prof. Chase elides from the divine addition "into his death," and taking one-half ("*by baptism*") substitutes *into* WATER for the rejected "*into* HIS DEATH."

Prof. Chase must amend his plea and show how "burial with Christ" in his rock sepulchre, is modified "*by baptism into* HIS DEATH," and not by *dipping into* WATER.

Prof. Chase seeks to nullify the objection, that ritual baptism does not furnish any parallelism with the co-crucifixion of Christians and Christ, by saying, "The Apostle does not teach that believers are *crucified* with Christ *by baptism.*" This answer admits the correctness of the objection so far as to there being no resemblance to a crucifixion in the dipping into water, but denies its force on the ground that we are not said to be "crucified with

Christ *by baptism*" = by dipping into water. His answer farthei implies, that from the nature of a dipping into water we could not be said to be "crucified with Christ" by it. This is no doubt true, and therefore the conversion of the baptism of the passage into a dipping into water is not true. The baptism of Christians *into* CHRIST, and thus *into* HIS DEATH, secures their co-crucifixion (συνεσταυρώθη), and co-burial (συνετάφημεν), and co-resurrection (συνηγέρθητε). That we may be "crucified with Christ" *by baptism* (not such as Prof. Chase would put into the text, but by such as the Holy Spirit has put there) is shown by the language of Basil M. (III, 1519), "῞Ουτω καὶ ὁ τῷ Χριστῷ συσταυρωθεὶς διὰ τοῦ βαπτίσματος—So, also, he that is crucified with Christ by the baptism." Here is the very statement, word for word, which Prof. Chase rejects as an impracticable thing. Basil the Great used as much water in the rite as Prof. Chase, and yet his views as to what constituted Christian baptism differed from those of the Professor as much as a "*baptism into the* DEATH of Christ" differs from a *dipping into* WATER. Basil believed, what Prof. Chase does not believe, that by the rite the soul is united to Christ, and by virtue of this union is crucified with him, as well as buried with him, and rises with him. We neither believe with Prof. Chase, that Christian baptism is a dipping into water, nor with Basil, that the soul is united to Christ by a rite; but we do believe, that the soul is united to Christ by the Holy Ghost, which union with its inseparable effects is expressed as a "BAPTISM *into Christ*," and a "BAPTISM *into his death*," involving *ex necessitate rei* co-crucifixion, co-burial, and co-resurrection.

The interpretation of this passage on a ritual basis will not bear examination in any direction save one, and that is—as a moss-covered relic of antiquity. In this respect it is unexceptionable. But as a matter of Scripture authority, or as having the sanction of a just exegesis, it has not the slightest claim to our faith.

Rev. ISAAC ERRETT (editor Christian Standard) says: "In Rom. 6, it is no part of Paul's intention to set forth the design of baptism; anything of that to be gathered from his language is merely incidental. His design is to show, from their death to sin, that they are not to continue in sin that grace may abound."

Professor J. G. Fee, of Berea, Kentucky, in the Christian Standard (Disciple Baptist), Aug. 15, 1874, is disposed to abandon Rom. 6 : 1-4 and Colos. 2 : 12 as cases of physical baptism. He says: "It is true, the leading, underlying thought is death to sin, and spiritual resurrection to newness of life; and in Colos. 2:12 it is true the word baptism is there preceded by circumcision made without hands, which we know was spiritual, and the Apostle may have intended simply to intensify the thought by adding 'buried with him in baptism, wherein ye were raised with him by faith of the power of God who raised him from the dead.' But even with this spiritual view, it is clear to my mind that the thought in the figurative or spiritual, is most manifestly drawn from the ACTION of the *literal* and *material*."

Answer: 1. There is no "*the* ACTION" belonging to βαπτίζω. The acts which meet the demand of this word are diverse and contrary; therefore cannot be expressed in their diversity and contrariness by it; 2. Admitting that the figurative use in Rom. and Colos. arises out of "the *literal* and *material*" use, it is a *non-sequitur* to say, that such literal and material use is to be found in a *religious rite.* Why not taken directly from primary use outside of the religious sphere? 3. It *must* be so derived, (1.) Because βαπτίζω does not take out what it puts in; and a *dipping* (which does do so), is not a baptism; (2.) Because in the baptism of Rom. and Colos., *the* SOUL *is not taken out of the baptism* into which it is baptized; and therefore it cannot be grounded in an imaginary ritual baptism, which is in fact but *a dipping;* but must be grounded in those real baptisms outside of the religious sphere out of which the baptized object is not removed.

Professor Fee quotes Tholuck, Conybeare and Howson, Neander, Schaff, Barnes, Bloomfield, Wesley, Clarke, Nevins, Calvin and Luther as agreeing, substantially, in the language of Tholuck, Rom. 6:4, "In order to understand the figurative use of baptism, we must bear in mind the well-known fact that the candidates in the primitive church were immersed in water and raised out of it again." *Answer:* 1. If "the primitive church" means the post Apostolic church, then it is a sin against chronology to bring a subsequent practice to prove an antecedent practice; 2. When in the post Apostolic church the candidate was "immersed in water and raised out of it again" no one believed such covering and uncovering to be Christian baptism; 3. If by primitive church is meant the Apostolic church, then there is a bald assumption of the question at issue. Such quotations avail nothing to the theory; 4. The figurative use of βαπτίζω and βάπτισμα in the

Scriptures no more rests on ritual baptism for its exposition, than does drunkenness rest for its exposition on the effects of drink ing from the fountain of Silenus as referred to by Lucian (Bac· chus VII)—" When an old man drinks and Silenus takes posses· sion of him immediately he is for a long time silent, and *resembles* one heavy-headed and *drunk* (*Βεβαπτισμένῳ*)." How much wisdom would there be in expounding wine drunkenness (= *baptism*) by this Silenic drunkenness which finds its character dependent upon and expounded by the precedent wine baptism? Just as much wisdom is there in making *ritual* baptism expository of the *figurative* baptism of Scripture, from which it derives its existence and by which it has its character. This is " putting the cart before the horse " in a fashion to make the plainest ploughboy stare. Ritual baptism is but a symbol resemblance to the antecedently declared real (though figurative) baptism of the Holy Spirit. Is the figurative use of *βαπτίζω* by Josephus and Philo based in ritual baptism? The figurative use of Scripture, and Josephus, and Philo have a common origin—the physical use of *βαπτίζω* outside of the Scriptures; *there is no such use in the Scriptures.* *Water* used with *βαπτίζω* no more gives a physical covering use to this word in a ritual baptism, than *wine* used with *βαπτίζω* gives to that word a physical covering use in a drunken baptism.

OTHER COMMENTATORS AND SCHOLARS.

Professor R. Wilson, of Ireland.

Prof. Wilson, of Belfast (On Baptism, pp. 290, 295), asks: " What are we to understand by ' baptism into Jesus Christ?' This point may seem simple or irrelevant, and it has been often overlooked in the discussion; yet we believe it to be so vitally important that a correct answer to this question must regulate and control the interpretation of the entire passage.

" We observe then that there is no emblem whatever indicated when the Apostle speaks of *baptism into Christ.* Whether with Vitringa we understand the words ' into Christ ' as denoting— *into the acknowledgment of Christ*, or with Tholuck, *into participation in Christ*, or with Haldane, *into oneness with Christ*, or, with others, *into the faith of Christ*, still, in none of its patronized or possible varieties is the import symbolically presented in baptism.

"The great fact in the passage is baptism into Christ's death, which does not admit of being symbolized by immersion; and grounded on the fact, is the momentous conclusion, that in this baptism we are joined unto the Lord in his burial and resurrection. From union with Christ in death, union with him in the grave follows by legitimate and necessary deduction."

President R. Halley, of England.

President Halley (The Sacraments, pp. 327, 334) says: "Of what Christian truth is putting into the water a symbol? We are told, Of the burying of the believer with Christ. The burying of a believer with Christ is no more a Christian truth than the going in at the strait gate, or the putting on the helmet of salvation, or the anointing the eyes with eye-salve, but like them a figurative expression of Scripture. The sacraments of Christ are symbols of truth and not of figures.

"If I am dead with Christ, I have been buried with him in my baptism, not into water, but by his Spirit into his death. That baptism is the funeral solemnity of a believer, or his interment in the tomb of Christ, is a doctrine which has no sure warranty in Scripture. If we attempt to unite the ideas of a burial and a purification, we have before us the ludicrous image of a man washing in a grave or dying in a bath. The burial of a believer with Christ, I repeat, being only a figurative expression, cannot be represented in baptism."

Dr. Edward Beecher (On Baptism, p. 113) says: "Not only is it true that external baptism is not meant in Rom. 6 : 3, 4, but it is also true, that there is no reason to think that any part of the language is taken from that rite. The language would have been just as it is, if the rite had been administered by sprinkling, or even if there had been no external rite whatever." This is true beyond any successful impeachment.

Prof. Stuart (Comm. in loc.): "'Baptized into Christ.' The sense of this depends on the meaning of the formula *Baptize into* any one. Here the sense is, 'as many as have become devoted to Christ by baptism.'

"*We have been baptized into his death, i. e.,* We have, as it were, been made partakers of his death by baptism. The being baptized into his death is therefore an internal, moral, spiritual thing.

" *We have been buried with him, then, by baptism into his death,* *i. e.*, We are (by being baptized into his death) buried as he was, συνετάφημεν, where συν means *like,* or *like manner with.*

" Most commentators have maintained that συνετάφημεν has here a necessary reference to the mode of *literal* baptism, which they say was by *immersion ;* and this, they think, affords ground for the employment of the image used by the Apostle, because immersion (under water) may be compared to burial (under the earth). It is difficult, perhaps, to obtain a patient re-hearing for this subject, so long regarded by some as being out of fair dispute. Nevertheless as my own conviction is not, after protracted and repeated examinations, accordant, here, with that of commentators in general, I feel constrained, briefly to state my reasons. . . .

" Indeed what else but a *moral burying* could be meant, when the Apostle goes on to say : *We are buried with him* (not only by baptism, but) *by baptism into his death* ?

" And although the words, *into his death* are not inserted in Colos. 2 : 12, yet, as the following verse shows, they are plainly implied.

" I cannot see, therefore, that there is any more necessary reference, here, to the *modus* of baptism, than there is to the *modus* of resurrection. The one may as well be maintained as the other."

Prof. Charles Hodge (Comm. in loc.): " In the phrase *to be baptized into any one,* the word rendered *into* has its usual force as indicating the object, design, or result, for which anything is done. To be baptized into Jesus Christ, or Moses, or Paul, therefore, means to be baptized in order to be united to Christ, or Moses, or Paul, as their followers, the recipients of their doctrines, and expectants of the blessings which they have to bestow.

" In like manner, in the expression *baptized into his death,* the preposition expresses the design and the result. The meaning, therefore, is, we were baptized in order that we might die with him, *i. e.*, that we should be united to him in his death and partakers of its benefits. Paul uses the expression *baptized into Christ* not for the mere external or formal profession of the religion of the gospel, but for the cordial reception of it, of which the submission to the rite of baptism was the public and appointed expression.

" The meaning, therefore, is, that those who have sincerely embraced Jesus Christ, have done it so as to be united to him, conformed to his image, and the design for which he died. Christ died to save his people from their sins and to purify to himself a peculiar people. Such being the nature and design of the gospel, if we accept of Christ at all, it is that we should die with him, *i. e.*, that we should attain the object for which he died, viz., *deliverance from sin.*

" The words *into death* are evidently to be connected with the word *baptism.*

" It does not seem necessary to suppose, that there is any allusion to the mode of baptism, as though that rite was compared to a burial."

Certainly not; the baptism of Christ and the burial of Christ are as distinct as is the east from the west. And so all Patristic writers believed.

Dr. Pusey.

Dr. Pusey, Regius Professor of Hebrew, Oriel College, on the in terpretation of this passage (Holy Baptism, pp. 78–80) says: " All that a large number of Christians, at the present day, find in this passage, is that Baptism represents (as it does) to us our profession, that we, having been baptized, and having acknowledged Christ as our Lord, are *bound* to lead a new and godly life. This is very true, and is certainly in the passage; but the question is, whether this be all? The Fathers certainly saw herein, not only the death unto sin, which we *were* to die, but that also which in Christ we had died by our having been baptized and incorporated into Christ; not the life only which we *are* to live, but the actual life which by Baptism was infused in us. St. Paul speaks throughout of actual facts, which have taken place in us, and duties consequent upon them. ' We were all baptized into Christ,' *i. e.*, into a participation of Christ, and his most precious death, and union with him; ' we were buried with him by baptism into death, *that we may also walk* in newness of life.' . . . A most intimate communion with the acts in our Lord's own holy life and death is, by the original language, conveyed. It were much, to be buried, to be crucified with him, like him; but it is more to become partakers of his burial and crucifixion; to be (so to speak) co-interred, co-crucified; to be included in, wrapt around, as it were, in his burial and crucifixion, and gathered into his very tomb; and this he says we were by baptism: transfused into his death (συνετάφημεν), implanted or engrafted into it (σύμφυτοι), our old man was thereby nailed to his very cross (συνεσταυρώθη). There is a marked identification with our Lord. . . . These thoughts were prominently in the thoughts of the ancient church, when dwelling on the text; the close connection of what Christ had done for us on the cross, with what he worketh in us by his Spirit in baptism : that this union with him is the power of baptism, and that from this union so imparted is all the Christian's strength to realize Christian duty."

To this interpretation of Dr. Pusey, so far as the interpretation itself is concerned, there is but little exception to be taken. The exception lies against the alliance of the interpretation with ritual baptism, which is not in the passage. " The Fathers" fell into the sad error of unifying the real baptism by the Spirit and the ritual baptism by water. Hence they unhesitatingly ascribed all the results of baptism of the soul by this divine Agent to the ritual use of water; not, however, to the water merely, but as having with it and in it the associated Holy Spirit. Therefore in interpreting a passage which referred, solely, to the work of the Holy Ghost (as in the passage before us) they ascribed it to ritual baptism, not designing, hereby, to exclude the Holy Ghost, but making the ritual water the channel-way through which his divine influence flowed. For this reason their interpretation of a passage, as to its sentiment, might be correct, while the reference of it to the rite might be wholly wrong. This is true of the present passage. They are right in making its baptism efficient in producing a union with Christ, and thus a participation in the fruits of his death, burial, and resurrection. No just interpretation of the words of inspiration, as they stand, can reach any other result. As the words demand it, so the argument of the Apostle requires it. Augustine justly remarks: " It is said, without exception, ' So many of us as were baptized into Jesus Christ, were baptized into his death.' And *this is said to* PROVE, that we are dead to sin." It is no *proof* that any man is dead to sin, because he has *professed* so to be. Christianity demands, that every disciple should be baptized into Christ by the Holy Ghost, which baptism is the remission of sins and regeneration to newness of life, and therefore, Christianity can say, the man who lives in sin and not in newness of life, is not my disciple. The charge is not, that he has violated a ritual profession; but that he is destitute of that life which every true disciple receives from the Holy Ghost by "baptism *into* CHRIST." Dr. Pusey and the Fathers err, not as to the value which they attribute to the baptism of which Paul speaks, but as to the cause of that baptism. They have introduced ritualism where there is nothing but the pure work of the Holy Spirit. There is a failure to accept and to be satisfied with the interpretation of the pure text of inspiration. A very just sentiment of Dr. Pusey may here be applied very forcibly— "RIGHT EXPOSITION *is at variance with all heresy; and a fuller and more literal apprehension of* SCRIPTURE *is, at the same time, a shield against doctrinal error.*"

Patristic Views.

Error never remains alone. The error which so early associated ritual baptism with baptism by the Holy Spirit gave origin to many kindred errors. Patristic writers never adopted the modern error that dipping into water is Christian baptism; but from the error which attributed burial with Christ to baptism with water, instead of "baptism into his death" solely by the Holy Spirit, they adopted the related error of covering the body in water, as well as many others springing from the same seed. Among these errors (closely related to that which sought to establish a resemblance to the burial of Christ by putting the body under the water) was that other error, which sought to work out a resemblance to the "three days and three nights" of burial by putting under the water three times; which thrice dipping became prolific in yet other expositions. Inasmuch as all these errors and additions very early associated with the Christian rite stand or fall together, it may be well to look at the statement of some which are closely related to the passage under consideration.

Cyril of Jerusalem, 1080: "*καὶ κατεδύετε τρίτον εἰς τὸ ὕδωρ, καὶ πάλιν ἀνεδύετε· καὶ ἐνταῦθα, διὰ συμβόλου τὴν τριήμερον τοῦ Χριστοῦ αἰνιττόμενοι ταφήν.*" "And ye were covered over thrice into the water, and again uncovered; and thus you darkly signified by symbol the three days' burial of Christ. For as our Saviour spent three days and three nights in the bowels of the earth; so ye, also, by the first uncovering imitate the first day of Christ in the earth, and by the covering the night. For as one in the night cannot see, but one in the day lives in the light; so in the covering, as in the night, ye saw nothing; but in the uncovering again, ye were as in the day. And in this ye died and were born; and that saving water was to you both grave and mother."

There is just as much scriptural authority for this triple into and out of the water, as there is for one. And there is just as much scriptural authority for the symbolization of day and night by putting under the water and raising above the water, as there is for such symbolization of burial and resurrection. And there is just as much scriptural authority for making the water of Christian baptism " a grave and a mother" as there is for either of the others. And there is just as much scriptural authority for the practice of these early errorists in putting men and women into the water naked to symbolize "naked came I out of my mother's womb," as to make the water "a mother and a womb." That is to say, there is not one word of Scripture to sustain any of these imaginative follies.

Leo (*ad Palæstinos, Ep.* 81) says: "None by his death paid the debt of another, except Christ our Lord, *in* WHOM alone all are *crucified*, all *dead*, *buried*, and *raised* up."

Origen, IV, 1040: "Si mortui sumus peccato, et consepulti sumus Christo, et consurreximus cum eo, necessarium videbitur secundum hanc formam ostendi quomodo etiam cum ipso tres dies et tres noctes in corde terræ sepulti fecerimus. Et vide si possimus tres dies consepulti Christo facere, cum plenam Trinitatis scientiam capimus. . . .

"If we be dead to sin and co-buried with Christ (in his new sepulchre, mentioned just before) and co-risen with him, it will seem necessary, according to this form, to show, how also we are buried with him three days and three nights in the heart of the earth. See, if we can make three days' burial with Christ, when we receive full knowledge of the Trinity. The Father is Light, and in his Light, which is the Son, we see Light, the Holy Spirit. But we make also three nights, when we destroy the father of darkness and ignorance, together with lying, which is born of him ; and in the third place we destroy the spirit of error, which inspires false prophets."

These diverse interpretations of the three days and three nights' burial (equally good and equally bad) nullify each other, just as the marvellous motherhood and nakedness of the one dipping (together with self-incongruity and Scripture contradiction) precludes its acceptance.

IV, 1039: On the page preceding the quotation just made, there is another passage relating to this subject, not without interest: "But some one may ask, why the Apostle in these passages, speaking concerning our baptism and concerning Jesus, should say: 'We have been co-buried with him by baptism into death;' and elsewhere, 'If we die—with him, we shall, also, live —with him;' and, likewise, 'If we suffer—with him, we shall reign — with him;' and never says, We are co-baptized with Christ; since as death is joined to death, and life to life, so, also, it seems baptism ought to be joined with baptism. But see how much caution there is in the words of the Apostle, for he says: 'Whosoever of us have been baptized into Jesus Christ.' He says, therefore, our baptism is into Jesus Christ. But Christ himself is said to have been baptized by John, not with that baptism which is into Christ, but with that which is into the Law. For so he himself says to John: 'Suffer it to be so now; for so it becometh us to fulfil all righteousness.' By which he shows, that the baptism of John was the completion of the old and not the beginning of the new."

Origen, here, repudiates, 1. The idea that dipping into water is baptism of any kind, and especially, it is not Christian baptism, which is "*into* JESUS CHRIST," nor is it the baptism received by Christ from John, which was "*into the* LAW." 2. He declares that the express statement of Scripture distinguishes the baptisms of Christians and of Christ (symbolly received through John) as radically as it distinguishes between grace and law. Origen had no faith in the modern doctrine, "baptism is mode and nothing but mode; what is baptism in one case is baptism in another." Origen believed with Ambrose *multa sunt genera baptismatum;* and that one genus, "into Jesus Christ" (*i. e.*, into the gracious remission of sin through his obedience to the law and dying under the penalty of the Law) was Christian baptism; and that another genus, "into the Law" (*i. e.*, into the voluntary assumption of obedience and fulfilment of all Law demands, in his proper person for the benefit of his people) was Christ's baptism from John. That genus of baptisms which is *into* WATER, and which by the force of its terms drowns human beings, was as unknown to Origen among the *genera* of religious baptisms, as it is unknown to all the writers of the New Testament.

Καταδύσις—Αναδύσις.

In the quotation from Cyril, and in others about to be made, as well as in Patristic baptisms everywhere, we meet with *κατα*

δύω, ἀναδύω, κατάδυσις, ἀναδῦσις; and the question arises, What is
the origin of these terms? The answer to this question may be
of essential importance.

CYRIL of Jerusalem (1080) says: κατεδύετε τρίτον εἰς τὸ ὕδωρ, καὶ
πάλιν ἀνεδύετε. "You were covered over thrice into the water,
and, again, uncovered."

DIDYMUS ALEX., 720: "The Eunomians are rebaptized, because they practice only one (κατάδυσις) covering over, baptizing
'into the death of the Lord;' the Phrygians, also, are rebaptized,
because they do not baptize into three Persons, but believe the
Father, and the Son, and the Holy Ghost, to be one and the same."

ATHANASIUS IV, 1080: "Thou wast baptized . . . by the covering over (τῇ καταδύσει) thou didst imitate the burial of the Lord;
but thou didst arise (ἀνέδυς) thence, again."

DIONYSIUS AREOPAG. I, 404: "The complete covering of the
body by water may be received as a likeness of death and burial.
The baptized by three coverings (καταδύσεσι) in the water imitate
the divine death, and three days and nights burial of Jesus the
giver of life."

These quotations illustrate the constant and abounding use of
καταδύνω, καταδύσις, ἀναδύνω, ἀναδῦσις, in Patristic writings. This
usage as compared with that of the New Testament is remarkable
in several respects: 1. None of these terms appear in the New Testament; 2. Their usage by Patrists is limited to physical relations.
They introduce into and remove out of *water*. And this for the
declared purpose of symbolizing *burial* and *resurrection*. 3. The
offices fulfilled by these terms, and by βαπτίζω and βάπτισμα, are
markedly distinct and not interchanged. Καταδύνω and καταδύσις are never used to introduce "into Christ," "into his death,"
"into repentance," "into the remission of sins," either in the
New Testament or in early Christian writings; while βαπτίζω and
βάπτισμα are invariably and exclusively so used, in both. On the
other hand, while the former terms always introduce (εἰς τὸ ὕδωρ)
"into the water," as stated by Cyril, and for the special purpose
of constituting a symbol of death and resurrection (said to enter
essentially into the rite), the latter terms are never used in the
New Testament to introduce (εἰς τὸ ὕδωρ) "into the water," and
are either never so used in early Christian writings, or, if ever, it
is so unusual as to manifest an exception to the normal usage both
of the New Testament and of Patristic writings.

No thoughtful person will regard the phraseology βαπτίζω ἐν

ὕδατι εἰς μετανόιαν (otherwise stated by Luke, ὕδατι βαπτίζω εἰς μετανόιαν), as opposed to this statement. As little opposed to it is the language of Mark, ἦλθεν ἀπὸ Ναζαρέτ καὶ ἐβαπτίσθη εἰς τ)ν 'Ιορδάνην; (1.) Because εἰς τὸν 'Ιορδάνην is not necessarily the equivalent of εἰς τὸ ὕδωρ; (2.) Because βαπτίζω never appears in the New Testament with εἰς τὸ ὕδωρ, and therefore the authority is wanting to justify changing a phrase which may express locality, into one expressing only fluid element; (3.) The ground of such interpretation (so far as relates to the verb), that βαπτίζω means *to dip* = to put into and take out of, is an error. Therefore, the statement may be made without reserve, that in the New Testament neither βαπτίζω, nor βαπτιστής, nor βάπτισμα is ever used to introduce an object *into* WATER, or to express the condition of being *in* WATER.

Some phrases which appear in early Christian writings might be, and have been, supposed to have such relation to water; but a closer scrutiny of usage will preclude such conclusion. An illustration of the passages referred to may be found in the Apostolical Canon XLIX, "If any bishop or presbyter should not celebrate (τρία βαπτίσματα μιᾶς μυήσεως, ἀλλ' ἐν βάπτισμα εἰς τὸν θάνατον τοῦ Κυρίου διδόμενον, καθαρείσθω) three baptisms of one mystery, but one baptism, given 'into the death of the Lord,' let him be deposed."

A hasty judgment might conclude that these "three baptisms" were three dippings into water, and that βάπτισμα took the place of καταδύσις; but this is not so: 1. Because the evidence of such interchange is wanting; 2. Because the passage expressly declares the one βάπτισμα (opposed to the three βαπτίσματα) to be not into water, but, as always, into a wholly different element—"*into the* DEATH of the Lord;*"* and consequently "the three" must be supposed to be of the same general character. This is confirmed by the subsequent part of the Canon, "for the Lord did not say 'baptize into my death,' but 'into the name of the Father, and of the Son, and of the Holy Ghost.'" The "three baptisms" are clearly into the three, several, Persons of the Trinity, making "the one mystery," and not three dippings *into water*. This is further confirmed by the reason assigned for the rebaptism of the Phrygians, namely, "because they did not baptize into the·*three* PERSONS, but believed the Father, the Son, and the Holy Ghost, to be *one* and the same," and therefore used but one καταδύσις. The orthodox baptism as stated by Clemens Rom. (1045) leads to the same result—"I am baptized into the one Unbegotten, the only true and Almighty God (βαπτίζομαι εἰς ἕνα ἀγένητον), and into the Lord Jesus the Christ, his only begotten Son (καὶ εἰς τὸν Κύριον Ἰησοῦν τὸν Χριστὸν), and I am baptized into the Holy Ghost, that is the Paraclete (βαπτίζομαι καὶ εἰς τὸ Πνεῦμα τὸ Ἅγιον)." Such special evidence (together with that of general usage) renders certain, that these τριὰ βαπτίσματα do not express *dippings into* WATER but, as always, into an ideal element.

Jerome (VI, 1139, Comm. Jonah 3:3) introduces another of these interpretative conceits based on the notion of a three-one baptism: "When our Lord sends the Apostles that they may baptize those who were in Nineveh, in nomine Patris, et Filii, et Spiritus Sancti, hoc est, itinere trium dierum. And this very sacrament of man's salvation (unius diei via) is a journey of one day, that is, it is perfected by the confession of one God. It is to be observed, also, that he does not say (*tribus diebus et noctibus*) three days *and nights*, or one day *and night*, but simply (*diebus et die*), days and day, that he might show that there is *no darkness* in the mystery of the Trinity and the confession of the one God."

The Bible gives no more countenance to three dippings, or one dipping, into water with the attendant feats of imagination which picture a womb and a birth, a death, a burial, and a resurrection, three nights in the grave exhibited by three dippings under the water, and three days in the grave by three liftings out of the water, than it does to the three days' journey around Nineveh to denote the Trinity, and the one day's journey into Nineveh to denote the confession of the one God.

When the simplicity of truth is abandoned we are at once environed by a complicity of errors.

4. In the New Testament we never find καταβαπτίζω, nor ἀναβαπτίζω, καταβαπτισμα, nor ἀναβαπτισμα; while καταδύνω, ἀναδύνω, καταδύσις, ἀναδύσις, abound in Patristic baptizings.

This marked diversity in the use of terms narrating and expounding baptisms between the inspired writers and the uninspired writers coming after them, shows, that there was something in the baptisms of the latter which demanded the introduction of a new phraseology, as compared with the baptisms of the former. And this new after-element introduced into Christian baptism was precisely that which this new phraseology was avowedly used to express, *to wit*, *a burial* and *a resurrection*.

This conclusion is in harmony with the essential meaning of

βαπτίζω (never taking out what it puts in), and its universal ideal relations as to the receiving element.

We therefore say, that the interpretation which introduces into the passage under consideration water, and a baptism into water symbolizing *death*, and *burial*, and a *resurrection* (to say nothing about " womb," " birth," and " mother "), is without the slightest foundation in a just exegesis.

"IN CHRIST" BY BAPTISM INTO CHRIST, FILLS WITH FULNESS OF CHRIST.

COLOSSIANS 2 : 9–13.

Ὅτι ἐν αὐτῷ κατοικεῖ πᾶν τὸ πλήρωμα τῆς θεότητος σωματικῶς.

Καὶ ἐστε ἐν αὐτῷ πεπληρωμένοι· . . . .

Ἐν ᾧ καὶ περιετμήθητε περιτομῇ ἀχειροποιήτῳ, ἐν τῇ ἀπεκδύσει τοῦ σώματος τῶν ἁμαρτιῶν τῆς σαρκὸς ἐν τῇ περιτομῇ τοῦ Χριστοῦ, συνταθέντες αὐτῷ ἐν τῷ βαπτίσματι.

Ἐν ᾧ καὶ συνηγέρθητε διὰ τῆς πίστεως τῆς ἐνεργείας τοῦ Θεοῦ τοῦ ἐγείραντος αὐτὸν ἐκ τῶν νεκρῶν·

. . . συνεζωοίησε σὺν αὐτῷ, χαρισάμενος ὑμῖν πάντα τα παραπτώματα.

" For in him dwelleth all the fulness of the Godhead bodily.

"And ye are made full in him, who is the head of all principality and power;

"In whom, also, ye have been circumcised with the circumcision made without hands, by the putting off the body of the sins of the flesh, by the circumcision of Christ, being buried with him by the baptism (into his death);

"In whom, also, ye have been raised together through faith, the working of God who raised him from the dead;

"And you, being dead in sins and the uncircumcision of your flesh, hath he made to live together with him, having forgiven you all your trespasses."

Translation.

The preposition ἐν throughout this passage (however translated, *in* or *by*) has a causative force, except in the first sentence, where the condition in which Christ is by his divine nature is made the ground cause of the condition of his people who are " *in* HIM."

Since the condition of all who are IN *Christ* is determined by their being " *in* HIM," and they must be what they are because of his relation to them and their relation to him (under the full influence of which they are thus represented as coming) some, as Prof. Ripley, translate "*by* whom," while others, retaining the strong and deeply expressive form "IN *whom*," show its causative power by the translation of ἐν in other phrases dependent upon it. Thus Tyndale translates: "For *in* HIM dwelleth all the fulnes of the godheed boddyly, and *ye are full in* HIM, which is the heed of all rule and power, *in* WHOM *also ye* are circumcised with cir- cumcision made without hondes, *by* putting of the sinfull boddy of the fleshe, *thorowe* the circumcision that is in Christ, in that ye are buryed with him *thorowe* baptism, *in* WHOM *ye are also* rysen agayne thorowe faith, that is wroght by the operacion of god which raysed hym from deeth." It would be difficult to improve this venerable translation. Prof. Ripley, however, does not ac- cept some of its most important features. He proffers this trans- lation of v. 12: "Buried with him *in* baptism, wherein also ye are risen with him through the faith of the operation of God, who hath raised him from the dead; that is by your faith in the power of God who raised up Christ from the dead, ye have IN BAPTISM *been buried with him, and risen with him.* It was IN BAPTISM, then, a physical act, they had been both BURIED and RAISED UP with Christ." Italics and capitals are as quoted.

Prof. Ripley objects to the translation by Prof. Stuart, "Ye are arisen with him by faith WROUGHT BY the power of God;" but says, "That the original is capable of this version, no one can doubt who is acquainted with Hebrew usage, and with that of New Testament Greek, in regard to the Genitive case."

On this point Olshausen (Comm. *in loc.*) remarks: "Faith is here more accurately designated as πίστις τῆς ἐνεργείας τοῦ Θεοῦ. All the later interpreters are unanimous on the point that these words are to be taken thus: 'Faith which the operation of God calls forth,' and not 'Faith in the operation of God.' . . . . This passage is the most decided and open of those in the New Testa- ment in which faith is referred to the operation of God."

The translation of Tyndale, and Stuart, and others, must stand against that of Prof. Ripley. It is greatly to be regretted that the logical connection in the language of the Apostle has been inter- fered with by the division of the vv. 11 and 12, by which that which should have closed v. 11, is made to begin v. 12. The clauses which follow ἐν ᾧ καὶ in v. 11, and precede ἐν ᾧ καὶ in v. 12, are epexegeti- cal of the statement, "In whom also ye are circumcised with a circumcision made without hands," the nature of which circumcision is explained as "the putting off the body of the sins of the flesh;" and the author of the circumcision is explained by the declaration, that it is "the circumcision of Christ;" while the manner of its accomplishment is explained by "being buried with him by baptism" (into his death). The ellipsis being supplied from Rom. 6:4. The sentiment and the construction show that all intervening between the ἐν ᾧ καὶ of v. 11, and the ἐν ᾧ καὶ of v. 12, belongs to the first of these phrases, and consequently makes the baptism into the death of Christ executive of the circumcision of Christ which separates and buries the body of sin, and so regenerates and purifies, and introduces into "newness of life." And as ἐν ᾧ καὶ περιετμήθητε has no concern with a rite, but begins and ends with Christ and his people in union with him; so, also, ἐν ᾧ καὶ συνηγέρθητε has as little to do with a rite, but declares a resurrection in and with Christ, because of union with him, through faith wrought in the soul by the power of God. The conjunction of *resurrection* with the baptism is without justifying authority either in the proper interpretation of this passage, or in the nature of a baptism. The introduction of ritual baptism into this passage can only be effected by violence, and when effected it makes the sentiment unscriptural or an excrescence and a stumbling-block.

Interpretation.

The parallelism between Colos. 2:9–13 and Rom. 6:2–11 is obvious, and is universally admitted. There is, also, a parallelism of equivalence between phrases in these passages (diversely expressed), which claims attention.

Among such passages are the following: 1. Ὅσοι ἐβαπτίσθημεν εἰς Χριστὸν Ἰησοῦν, Rom. 6:3; and ἐστε ἐν αὐτῷ (= Χριστῷ) πεπληρωμένοι, Colos. 2:10.

To be "baptized into Christ," and "to be filled of Christ by being *in* him," are expressions which, under diversity of form, express the same substantial truth. There is no more difference between "*into* Christ" and "*in* Christ," as they appear in these phrases, than there is between *into the river* and *in the river*, as they appear in the statements, "the lead *fell* INTO the river," and "the lead *is* IN the river." "Fell into" expresses, directly, the passing into the river, which necessarily involves, as a consequence, the subsequent *being in* the river. The baptism "into Christ" of

Romans, representing the soul as passing "into Christ," necessarily involves the *being in* Christ of Colossians, for in a baptism
there is no withdrawal of the object baptized.   And the soul which
is "*in* Christ" has, of necessity, previously passed *into* Christ.
And this passing into Christ, without withdrawal, is designated
by the Scriptures as being *baptized* into him.   Therefore, whenever the Scriptures speak of Christians being "in Christ," they
teach a previous baptism "*into* Christ."   Into Christ, and in
Christ, are parts of a whole truth mutually complementary of each
other.   "Ye in Christ are made full," is a universal declaration
applicable to all "in Christ," without exception.   And no one
who is *out of* Christ is or can be partakers of his fulness.   The
statement in Romans, "So many of us as were baptized into Jesus
Christ" is equally universal, and no one who is *not* "baptized into
Jesus Christ" can receive through him "newness of life."   If
dipping into water does not give the soul a place "*in* Christ,"
dipping into water will never "baptize the soul *into* Christ."
Every one who is "in Christ" is so by reason of having been
"baptized into Christ;" and every one who is "baptized into
Christ" does, thereby, become "in Christ."   I am not aware that
the friends of the theory have pressed into service "Ye are in
Christ *made full*" as proof of its truth; and yet the same imaginative logic which finds water with its death and burial, and
womb and mother, in these passages, might readily do so.   An
empty vessel put under water is *made full;* and what better im-
agery is needed to teach that the body, as an empty vessel, is put
under the water to emblemize the soul empty of all good, being
put "in Christ" to be made full of his fulness ?

But before such a plea is entered we make claim to an equivalence of value between "baptism," and being "made full."   Any
vessel which is "made full" has its powers to receive exhausted.
The soul which is "made full" of the fulness of Christ, can receive no more.   *To make full* is consequently used to express
subjection to controlling influence; as by Peter at Pentecost, interpreting the charge, "these men are FULL *of new wine*," replies,
"these men *are not drunken*, as ye suppose."   To be full of wine,
is to be under its controlling influence, to be drunken.   But it
has been proved by scores of facts, that *to be baptized into* anything is expressive of subjection to the controlling influence of
that thing whatever it may be.   A living man baptized into water
is brought under its suffocating influence, and drowned; hot iron

baptized into cold water is brought under its controlling influence, and made cold; a medical prescription baptized into milk is brought under its controlling influence, and made emollient; the soul baptized into Christ, is brought under the controlling of Christ, and is redeemed by his blood.

"Baptized into Christ," and "ye are, in Christ, made full," are varied forms expressive of the same identical truth, namely, the full participation in the blessings of Christ as a Saviour.

In like manner the phrases, "buried with him ($\delta\iota\grave{a}\ \tau\sigma\tilde{\upsilon}\ \beta\alpha\pi\tau\acute{\iota}\sigma\mu\alpha\tau\sigma\varsigma$) *by* the baptism into his death," and, "buried with him ($\grave{\epsilon}\nu\ \tau\tilde{\omega}\ \beta\alpha\pi$-$\tau\acute{\iota}\sigma\mu\alpha\tau\iota$) *in* the baptism (into his death)," are diverse, yet equivalent expressions; they both indicating a consequence of baptism into Christ's death. The first states directly, that union with Christ in his death (expressed by baptism into his death) unites with him in his sepulchre-burial; the second makes the same statement, indirectly, the co-burial with Christ being caused by the influence proceeding from being "*in* the baptism into his death."

So, also, the phrase "he hath made you to live together with him, having forgiven you all your trespasses," finds its equivalent in the phrase descriptive of John's preaching—"the baptism of repentance into the remission of sins." "Repentance" is the evidence of a new life from Christ and with it the "baptism into" (= the full) "remission of all our sins."

This preaching was reiterated by Peter, "Repent, and be *baptized into* the remission of sins," resting by faith "upon the name of Jesus Christ." It is repeated by Paul's, "Whosoever is baptized into Christ is baptized into his death," for without the shedding of blood there is no remission of sins, and baptism into the atoning death of Christ brings under the full influence of its sin-remitting power.

The parallelism of these passages of Paul is far more profound than that which could be exhibited by sameness of words. Where the sameness of words finds no place, the sameness of truth may stand out the more strongly in the diversity. "*In* Christ" declares the baptism of the New Testament as surely as "*Baptized* INTO Christ," and perhaps in terms and under circumstances sufficiently explicit to forbid "*in* CHRIST" from being transformed into *in* WATER.

To Fill.

"Baptize," in Romans, is no more used with a physical application, than is "made full," in Colossians, used in a physical application. It is also true, that when baptize is used with water in the New Testament it is no more used as indicative that some object is to be put into the water, than *fill* when used with bread (as, " whence should we have so much bread in the wilderness, as to fill so great a multitude") is used to express the physical filling of the stomach. This bread was not to be used to fill the stomach as a physical receptacle, but as a physical substance possessed of a quality *to fill* APPETITE, exhaustively satisfy hunger. So, "he would fain have *filled* his belly *with husks*" does not mean, that he was fain to exhaust the containing capacity of the " belly" by putting into it husks, but *to satisfy appetite by eating* husks. And water with baptize is not used as a fluid capable of receiving an object, but as a fluid possessed of a quality capable of symbolizing purity as developed in the phrases " baptized into repentance," " baptized into the remission of sins," " baptized into Christ," " baptized into his death."

The abounding use of " fill " in unphysical relations truly illustrates, and is fairly equivalent in force with that of baptize. In illustration take the following examples: " Thou shalt be FILLED *with drunkenness*" (Ezek. 23 : 33) as compared with Josephus, Jew. Antiq., x, 9, " BAPTIZED *by drunkenness;*" " Be not *drunk* with wine, but FILLED *with the Spirit*" (Eph. 5 : 18) as compared with the Classic Greek " BAPTIZED *by wine*," and the frequent Scripture phrase " BAPTIZED *by the Spirit;*" " Being FILLED *with all unrighteousness* " (Rom. 1 : 29), " Why hath Satan FILLED *thy heart*" (Acts 5 : 3) as compared with the means of recovery, equal in extent, depth, and power, " BAPTIZED *into repentance*" (Matt. 3 : 11); " To FILL UP *their sins*," as compared with " BAPTIZED *into the remission of sins* " (Luke 3 : 3, Acts 2 : 38); " I have FILLED him *with the Spirit of God*," as compared with " *By one Spirit* are we all BAPTIZED " (1 Cor. 12 : 13); " John shall be FILLED *with the Holy Ghost*" (Luke 1 : 15), " Elizabeth was FILLED *with the Holy Ghost* " (v. 41), " Zacharias was FILLED *with the Holy Ghost* " (v. 67), " Peter FILLED *with the Holy Ghost* " (Acts 4 : 8), " That thou mightest be filled with the Holy Ghost " (Acts 9 : 17), " Paul filled with the Holy Ghost " (Acts 13 : 9), as compared with, " He shall BAPTIZE you *with the Holy Ghost* " (Matt.

3 : 11), " Ye shall be BAPTIZED *with the Holy Ghost* " (Acts 1 : 5),
" Then remembered I the word of the Lord," " Ye shall be
BAPTIZED *by the Holy Ghost*" (Acts 11 : 16); and, lastly, "That
ye might be filled" (entering) "into all the fulness of GOD"
(Ephes. 3 : 19), as compared with, " BAPTIZING them *into the
Name of the Father, and of the Son, and of the Holy Ghost.*"

In such usage, " to fill" expresses completeness, exhaustive
satisfaction; the soul that enters, through the love of Christ,
"into all the fulness of GOD" is exhaustively satisfied; and the
soul that is baptized through the redeeming love of Christ into
the TRIUNE GOD (made subject and assimilant to the divine per-
fections) is exhaustively satisfied. *To fill* and *to baptize,* while
diverse, are accordant and equivalent in their diversity when used
in such relations.

Jerome and Others.

Jerome (Comm. *in loc.*) connects what is the beginning of v.
12 in the English Bible with the close of v. 11, as explanatory of
the circumcision of Christ. He also refers the resurrection of
Christians to their relation with Christ (in *quo* et resurrexistis, as
also in the circumcision, in *quo* et circumcisi estis) and not to
ritual baptism. So, also, the Douay Version, " In *whom* also ye
are circumcised." . . . " In *whom* also you are risen again."

Ambrose (III, 498) translates ἐν βαπτίσματι, "*per* baptismum."

Origen (Hom. XIV, on Luke) translated by Jerome (VII, 247)
teaches that the circumcision of Christians is "*in* CHRIST," and
their resurrection, also, is "*in* CHRIST," and not in ritual baptism
by rising out of the water. " Therefore his death, and his resurrection, and circumcision were accomplished for us."

As Paul rejects the Jewish circumcision made with hands, and
takes instead "the circumcision of Christ," which is without
hands (the baptism of the Holy Ghost which unites to him in his
death, burial, and resurrection), so Justin Martyr rejects Jewish
circumcision (which he calls a baptism) on the ground that he has
received the nobler baptism of the Holy Ghost. This is his language (537): " What value to me is circumcision being approved
by the witness of God?" " *Τίς ἐκείνου τοῦ βαπτίσματος χρεία ἁγίῳ
Πνεύματι βεβαπτισμένῳ* What need has he of *that baptism* who has
been baptized by the Holy Ghost?" Justin Martyr was a Greek
of the Greeks, and when he calls circumcision a " baptism " it is
settled that among Greeks baptism meant something else than a
dipping nto water. And when he compares by contrast circum

cision baptism by the exscinding knife, with the soul baptism by
the Holy Ghost, he had another idea of Christ's baptizing by the
Holy Ghost than that of his "dipping *in* the Holy Ghost."

Cyril (513) says: "By the likeness of the faith of Abraham we
come into adoption. And then, after faith, in like manner with
him we receive the spiritual seal, being circumcised by the Holy
Ghost (διὰ τοῦ λουτροῦ) through the washing, not as to the foreskin
of the body but of the heart, as Jeremiah says, ' Circumcise to the
Lord the foreskin of your heart ;' and according to the Apostle, 'By
the circumcision of Christ, being buried with him by baptism.'"

Cyril, in common with Origen and Jerome, identifies the burial
with Christ through baptism into his death, with the circumcision
of Christ ; and like them grounds the resurrection in union with
Christ.

A just interpretation of this passage furnishes no support for
a ritual baptism as giving origin to the form of its language or
sentiment. On the contrary a strict criticism makes this passage
with its parallel in Romans mutually elucidatory and confirmatory
of each other, as teaching a most intimate union between Christ
and his people effected by Divine power, and making them fully
participant of redemption from sin and death through his death,
and of life and immortality through his resurrection. Especially
is there no authority for attaching the notion of a resurrection
from this passage to ritual baptism. The crucifixion, the burial,
and the resurrection are all to be found " in Christ." As additional evidence for this truth, so far as the resurrection is concerned, see 3 : 1, " If ye be risen together with Christ" συνηγέρθητε
τῷ Χριστῷ (Cod. Sin. ἐν Χριστῷ), which proves that the ἐν ᾧ of v. 12
belongs to Christ, as Tyndale has translated it, and not to baptism as in the common version.

BAPTISM INTO CHRIST MAKES CHRISTLIKE.

GALATIANS 3 : 26, 27.

Πάντες γὰρ υἱοί Θεοῦ ἐστὲ διὰ τῆς πίστεως ἐν Χριστῷ Ἰησοῦ·
Ὅσοι γὰρ εἰς Χριστὸν ἐβαπτίσθητε, Χριστὸν ἐνεδύσασθε.

" For ye are all the children of God by faith in Christ Jesus ;
" For as many of you as have been baptized into Christ, have put on
Christ."

Not Ritual Baptism.

In support of the position that this baptism is ritual I know of
nothing which can be adduced except the mere presence of the

word " baptize." But such a position on such a basis is antagonized and nullified by the fact, that this word is used to express
a real baptism by the Holy Spirit as well as a ritual baptism by
water. That the latter is here referred to, therefore, must be
proved and not be assumed. The attempt at proof must begin
with the supply of an ellipsis, namely, " As many as have been
baptized *into water* into Christ, have put on Christ;" which attempt is confronted with these difficulties: 1. Such phraseology
condemns itself; 2. "Baptized into water" destroys life; 3. To
change " baptized " into *dipped* (to save life) is to substitute another word, of essentially diverse meaning, for the word of inspiration; 4. There is no such language in Scripture as "baptized
INTO *water*," and therefore such language cannot be introduced by
ellipsis in the interpretation of any passage of Scripture. It is
neither answer nor contradiction to this to say, βαπτίζω ἐν ὕδατι
occurs in Scripture; because the relation between ἐν ὕδατι and
βαπτίζω (as thus occurring) is not such as is sought to be introduced into the passage under consideration; namely, as complementary of βαπτίζω and as the receptive element into which the
baptized object passes; but expresses the symbol, ritual agency
in the baptism (εἰς μετανοίαν) "into repentance," as is shown in
Johannic Baptism; 5. If this ellipsis should be insisted upon (as
that without which all is lost) this new difficulty emerges, namely,
a baptism *into water* has no power to bring "*into* CHRIST;" and
if this is sought to be met by another ellipsis, " As many as have
been baptized into water *have made a profession of entering* into
Christ," we ask: And what about "putting on Christ"? And,
again, an ellipsis is proffered, "put on Christ *by profession*." Such
helps, to meet the difficulties arising out of a primary error, reminds of the cycle and epicycle introduced to escape the difficulties
induced by the error which made the earth the centre of the solar
system. The cycle and the epicycle failed to change error into
truth, and this ellipsis and epiellipsis equally fails to give truth to
an erroneous interpretation.

This is Real Baptism.

That this baptism spoken of by Paul is a real baptism in which
the condition of the soul is thoroughly changed in its relations to
Christ by Divine power is fully established: 1. By the express
statement of the words of inspiration. The words " baptized

into Christ" do mean, and under the true meaning of βαπτίζω and
the usage without exception of such phrase, can mean nothing
else than, thorough subjection to the controlling influence of
Christ as distinctively distinguished from that of all other beings;
2. That this is the true interpretation of this phrase, is made, if
possible, more certain by the special interpretation of the Holy
Spirit in declaring, that "baptized into Christ" finds its equivalent in "put on Christ." No one ever yet questioned, that the
essential meaning of "putting on any one" was the assumption
in fact of the character of such one, whatever it might be. The
only issue then, is this: Shall we accept this double statement of
truth by the Holy Spirit at its essential value, or shall we eviscerate it of its divine life and substitute for it "profession?"
3. The agency effecting this baptism is not stated in direct connection with the baptism, but is stated in the context, and necessitates a real and not a ritual baptism. This entire chapter presents "faith" as the bond of union between the soul and Christ;
v. 1 exhibits "Christ crucified;" v. 2, "received ye *the* SPIRIT by
the works of the law or by the hearing of *faith?*" v. 3, "having
begun *in the* SPIRIT are ye now made perfect by the flesh?" v. 5,
"he that ministereth to you *the* SPIRIT doeth he it by the law or
by *faith?*" v. 7, "they which are *of faith* are the children of Abraham;" v. 8, "and the Scripture foreseeing that God would justify
the heathen *through faith* preached before the gospel unto Abraham, saying, 'In thee shall all nations be blessed,' so then they
which be *of faith* are blessed with faithful Abraham;" v. 11, "the
just shall live *by faith;*" v. 13, "Christ hath redeemed us from
the curse of the law. . . . Cursed is every one that hangeth on a
tree; that the blessing of Abraham might come on the Gentiles
through JESUS CHRIST; that we might receive *the promise of the*
SPIRIT *through faith;*" v. 22, "that the promise *by faith of* JESUS
CHRIST might be given to them that believe;" v. 26, "Ye are all
the children of God *by faith in* CHRIST JESUS;" v. 27, "For as
many of you as have been *baptized* INTO CHRIST, have put on
Christ;" v. 28, "Ye are all one IN CHRIST JESUS;" v. 29, "And
if ye be Christ's, then are ye Abraham's seed and heirs' according to the promise."

If anything can be made certain it is that the agencies operative
throughout this chapter are "*the* SPIRIT" and "faith," which is
itself the work of the Spirit. This accords with the general teaching of Scripture, that the soul is baptized and made participant

in the blessings of Christ, by the power of the Holy Spirit, and
with the special teaching of Coloss. 2 : 12, " Buried with Christ
by baptism into his death, in whom ye are risen together *through*
FAITH *wrought by God ;*" 4. The entire complexion of the Apostles'
argument imperatively demands a real baptism by the Spirit INTO
CHRIST, thus establishing the soul (v. 28) " IN CHRIST," as in
Colossians, " IN *whom* ye are circumcised;" " IN *whom* ye are
risen together."

Illustration.

The figure by which baptism into Christ is illustrated, that of
putting on a garment as an exhibition of character, is common in
Scripture.   It appears in Isaiah 61 : 10, " I will greatly rejoice in
the Lord, my soul shall be glad in my God ; for he hath *clothed
me with the garments of* SALVATION, he hath *covered me with the
robe of* RIGHTEOUSNESS, as a bridegroom decketh himself with
ornaments, and as a bride adorneth herself with her jewels."
Isaiah 59 : 17, " He *put on the garments of* VENGEANCE for clothing, and was *clad with* ZEAL as a cloak."

Also, in Rom. 13 : 12, 14, " Let us *put off the* WORKS OF DARK-
NESS and *put on the* ARMOR OF LIGHT. . . . But *put ye on the* LORD
JESUS CHRIST;" 1 Cor. 15 : 54, " This corruptible must *put on* IN-
CORRUPTION, and this mortal must *put on* IMMORTALITY.   So when
this corruptible shall have *put on* INCORRUPTION, and this mortal
shall have *put on* IMMORTALITY, then Death shall be *swallowed up*
($\varepsilon i \varsigma$) INTO VICTORY ;" 2 Cor. 5 : 4, " Not for that we would be *un-
clothed* ($\dot{\varepsilon}\varkappa\delta\acute{\upsilon}\sigma\alpha\sigma\theta\alpha\iota$) but *clothed upon* ($\dot{\varepsilon}\pi\varepsilon\nu\delta\acute{\upsilon}\sigma\alpha\sigma\theta\alpha\iota$), that mortality
might be *swallowed up by* LIFE ;" Coloss. 3 : 12, " PUT ON as the
elect of God, holy and beloved, *bowels of mercies, kindness,
humbleness of mind, meekness, long-suffering,* . . . and upon all
these, *charity,* which is the bond of perfectness."

Two things are made certain by these passages : 1. " Put on,"
as a figure *e vestiaria,* is never used in Scripture to express what
is fictitious, unreal, or a mere *profession,* but that which is true
and real ; 2. As the phrases, " put on the armor of light," " put
on incorruption," " put on immortality," " put on charity," express a reality, so " put on the Lord Jesus Christ " (Rom. 13 : 14),
and " put on Christ " (Gal. 3 : 27), express a reality.   And inasmuch as " baptized into Christ " is declared, on divine authority,
to be the equivalent of " put on Christ," then baptized " into
Christ " must express a reality and not a shadow.

These passages have other instructive bearings on our Inquiry. No one doubts that the phrase, "Death is swallowed up into Victory" (*κατεπόθη ὁ θάνατος εἰς νῖκος*) expresses the complete influence of Victory over Death; how, then, can the phrase "As many as have been baptized into Christ," express less, or anything else, than the full influence of Christ over all so baptized? And as the phrase "swallowed up by life" (*καταποθῇ τὸ θνητὸν ὑπὸ τῆς ζωῆς*), expresses "life" to be *the agency* by which the swallowing up and the consequent influence is effected, so, in the phrase of Josephus, "baptized by drunkenness," drunkenness expresses *the agency* by which the baptism is effected and by its nature involves the nature of the baptism, to wit (*εἰς ἀναισθησίαν*) "into insensibility," and so also, in the frequent Scripture phrase "baptism of repentance," repentance expresses *the agency* by which the baptism is effected, and determines the character of the baptism, to wit (*εἰς ἄφεσιν ἁμαρτιων*) "into the remission of sins." And farther, as the phrase "swallowed up with overmuch sorrow" (*τῇ περισσοτέρᾳ λύπῃ καταποθῇ*) 2 Cor. 2 : 7, expresses "sorrow" to be *the agency* (by the Dative), so Luke 3 : 16 expresses, by precisely the same grammatical form (*ὕδατι βαπτίζω*), water to be the symbol agency by which the baptism is effected (*εἰς μετάνοίαν*) "into repentance " = " into the remission of sins." As "sorrow" is the agency by which the swallowing up is accomplished and not the element into which the object swallowed up passes, so, "water" is the agency by which the baptism is symbolly effected and not the element into which the baptized object passes. From all which we draw this conclusion: From the essential meaning of *βαπτίζω* the Scriptures could not, as in fact they do not, teach a baptism into water, while for the same reason they could, and in fact do, teach a baptism "into Christ," "into repentance," " into the remission of sins," and other like, profound, and abiding baptisms.

Interpreters.

The views of Interpreters, both ancient and modern, accord very generally in the belief, that the phrases "baptized into Christ " and " put on Christ " express a real and profound truth, and not one of semblance and profession.

ROSENMÜLLER, on Rom. 13 : 14, "*Put on Christ.* Imitamini Christum, similes illi fieri studete. Sic apud Dionys. Halic. Ant. L., XI. Appius et reliqui decemviri vocantur *οὐκέτι μετριάζοντες* ἀλλὰ τὸν Ταρχύνιον ἐχεῖνον ἐνδυόμενοι non amplius modum servantes, sed Tarquinium illum induentes, *i. e.*, imitantes."

And again, he says : " *To put on*, induere, quum de virtutibus usurpatur, significat, iis summo studio deditum esse, eas diligentissime sectari. Themistius, Orat. 24, hortator. ad philos., ἐπειδήπερ ἀρετὴν ἀντὶ ἱματίων ἠμφίεστο quoniam virtute loco vestium indutus erat. Athenæus L. XIII. c. 2, βουλόμενοι ἐνδύεσθαι αὐτὴν αὐτάχρειαν quum frugalitatem illam induere velitis."

These classical quotations show, that the use of this figure out of the Scriptures, as well as in them, was a strong expression covering a reality.

OLSHAUSEN, Rom. 13 : 14, " *To put on Christ.* The figure is derived from *a robe of righteousness.* Profane writers also use *to put off* and *to put on* in like manner, in the sense of *fashioning one's self unlike or like a person.*" On Galat. 3 : 26, 27 : "*Baptism into Christ* is here conceived of in its profoundest idea. The *putting on Christ* is a description of what happens in the new birth. This expression denotes the most intimate appropriation of Christ. To put on the new man = *being renewed.* To put on immortality denotes the change of the mortal body into the immortal nature of corporeity. But with whomsoever Christ joins himself, to *him* he, the Son of God, also communicates the nature of a child of God."

BLOOMFIELD, Rom. 13 : 14 : " *Put on Christ, i. e.*, Take upon you his dispositions, follow his example. A metaphor *e re vestiariâ*, and found also in the classical writers. So Lucian, Gall. 19, ἀποδυσάμενος δὲ τὸν Πυθαγόραν τίνα μετημφιάσω μετ᾽ αὐτόν. Bengel, Galat. 3 : 27 : *Ye have put on Christ.* Christ is the Son of God, and ye are in Him, the sons of God. Tho. Gataker says, ' *A Christian is one who has put on Christ.*' "

ELLICOTT, Galat. 3 : 27 : " *Into Christ*, not in Christo, but in Christum ; Beza, sed ut Christo addicti essetis. The meaning of εἰς with βαπτίζω appears twofold ; (a) *unto*, object, purpose ; (b) *into*, union and communion with : here and Rom. 6 : 3, the union is of the most complete and mystical nature. Βαπτ. εἰς τὸ ὄνομα is not identical in meaning with βαπτ. ἐν τῷ ὀνόματι, but ever implies a spiritual and mystical **union** with him in whose name the sacrament was administered. The discussion by Fritsche, Rom. 6 : 3, is by no means satisfactory, as he regards εἰς as only implying ethical direction, instead of that mystical incorporation which the passage seems certainly to convey."

" *To put on Christ.* There appears no allusion to *Heathen,* *Jewish,* or *Christian* customs. Wetstein, Rom. 13 : 14, shows *to put on any one,* is a strong expression denoting the complete as-sumption of the nature, etc., of another."

The evidence is conclusive that βαπτ. εἰς always expresses the same radical idea; and βαπτ. εἰς τὸ ὄνομα, and βαπτ. ἐν τῷ ὀνόματι never come in competition, in the same line of thought.

ALFORD says: "As many of you as were 'baptized into Christ,' put on Christ at that time. The aorists make the acts identical." This is true of baptism into Christ by the Holy Ghost; it is not true of ritual baptism into Christ.

Patristic.

Tertullian, III, 1131, " He who was sanctified by baptism, lay-ing aside his sins, and spiritually renewed, was made fit to receive the Holy Spirit, since the Apostle says : ' *As many as have been baptized into Christ have put on Christ,* (Gal. 3 : 27). . . . Christ cannot be put on without the Spirit, nor can the Spirit be sepa-rated from Christ. Mere water, without the Holy Spirit, can neither purge away sins nor sanctify the man. Wherefore it must be admitted, either that the Holy Spirit is there where bap-tism is, or that baptism is not where the Holy Spirit is not; for baptism cannot be without the Holy Spirit."

This extract proves, 1. Tertullian did not believe that " putting on Christ " was a mere profession of Christ, but a regeneration by the Holy Spirit ; 2. Tertullian did not believe that Christian baptism was a dipping into water. This latter point is farther shown by the statement (1166), " If the Apostle does not lie, saying: *Quotquot in Christo tincti estis, Christum induistis* (Gal. 3 : 27) undoubtedly whosoever is there baptized puts on Christ ; but if he puts on Christ, he can, also, receive the Holy Spirit who is sent by Christ."

And in II, 938, " But Jesus, the great High Priest of the Father, clothing us with himself (for (Gal. 3 : 27) *qui in Christo tinguuntur, Christum induerunt*) has made us priests unto his Father." Here " in Christo " is represented as *a* (quasi) *dye* in which whatsoever is placed becomes like the dye in color, so, who-soever is placed "in Christ," becomes like Christ, and as he is the great High Priest, they who are " in Christ " assume a priestly character like him. Also, 991, " Itaque, si exinde quo statum

•ertit, et in Christum tincta, induit Christum (Gal. 3 : 27), Therefore, if thence by which (baptism) he has changed his condition,
and baptized (*tincta*) into Christ, has put on Christ." Such and
suchlike passages preclude any other interpretation except that
which is based in the secondary meaning of tingo, and these
bring it into intimate relation with βαπτίζω. It was the common
opinion of these writers that the water of baptism was not
"*aqua sola*," mere water, but a new "power," or "quality,"
analogous to that of *a dye*, or *medicated* element, was imparted
to it adapting to accomplish those transforming results ascribed
to it.

This idea is referred to by Rigaltius in a note on the passage
as explanatory of the language of Tertullian. He says: "Nor
could sins be washed away before Christ had come; because the
waters themselves had not yet been washed or medicated by the
baptism of Christ (quia scilicet nec ipsæ aquæ adhuc laverant,
nondum baptismo Christi medicatæ fuerant); therefore they were
not yet fit to wash away that kind of uncleanness."

It is in this idea of the "medication" of the waters of baptism
that the usage of *tingo* by Tertullian finds its facile explanation,
as well as its perfect justification. Neither he nor any other early
Christian writer shows the remotest sympathy with the modern
error, that Christian baptism is *a dipping into* WATER. *How* they
used the water has no more concern with the baptism effected,
than how they used the oil or the spittle.

CYRIL *of Jerusalem*, 1078: "Immediately upon entering (ἀπε-
δύεσθε) you put off the tunic; which was an image of despoiling
the old man with his deeds. Having put it off, you were naked,
in this, also, imitating the Christ, naked on the cross. . . . Oh
wonderful thing! you were naked before the eyes of all and not
ashamed." 1088: "Having been baptized into Christ, and having
put on Christ, ye became of like form with the Son of God. Therefore having became partakers of the Christ (Anointed) you are
well called *Christoi* (anointed ones), and concerning you God
says, 'Touch not my (χριστῶν) *anointed* ones.' Ye have become
Christoi, having received the antitype" (the oil in baptism) " of
the Holy Spirit. And everything has been done to you typically,
because you are types of Christ. And he, indeed (λουσάμενος)
having washed in the river Jordan, communicated to its waters
the fragrance of his divinity."

This extract from Cyril shows that he believed Christian bap-

19

tism to be "into *Christ;*" to be productive of a real and powerful effect; that the effect of baptism "into Christ" was to make
Christoi, just as the effect of putting fleeces of wool into a *purple
dye*, is to make *purple fleeces;* and that the water of baptism was
capable of all this, not by its power as *aqua sola*, but as sharing
in that *divine power* communicated to all such water, in common
with those of the Jordan.

BASIL M. III, 1564 : "Being born from above may be deemed
worthy to be baptized in the name of the only begotten Son of
God, and of that great gift announced by the Apostle, saying,
'As many as have been baptized into Christ, have put on Christ.'
It is a necessary consequence that one who is born should be
(ἐνδύσασθαι) clothed.   Then (ἐνδυσάμενος) having been clothed upon
as it were by the Son of God, we become worthy of the perfect
rank, and are baptized into the name of the Father of our Lord
Jesus Christ, who, according to the testimony of John, gave
us power to become the Sons of God" (John 1 : 12).

WICKHAM (Doctrine of Baptism, London), p. 438, quotes and
translates Jerome thus : " Our Lord Jesus Christ, who was not so
much cleansed by the baptism as by his baptism cleansed all
waters. . . . After he was baptized, and by his baptism had sanctified the waters of Jordan. . . . The Apostle shows how we are
born the sons of God by the faith which is in Christ Jesus, saying: ' For as many of you as are baptized into Christ, have put
on Christ.'   Now that Christ is a thing to be put on, is proved
not only from the present passage, but also from another, the
same Paul exhorting us, ' Put ye on our Lord Jesus Christ.' . . .
When a man has once put on Christ, and being passed into the
flame, has been made white with the whiteness of the Holy Spirit,
it is not perceived whether he is gold or silver.   As long as the
heat thus occupies the mass, there is one color of fire, and every
diversity of kind, of condition, and of bodies, is taken away by
a clothing of that sort.   For he is neither Jew nor Greek. . . .
Since all diversity is taken away by the baptism of Christ and by
being clothed with him, we are all one in Christ Jesus."

These views of Jerome as to the reality and power of "baptism
into Christ," and "putting on Christ," accord with those of others
quoted.   This baptism is by the Holy Ghost *into* CHRIST and not
into WATER, bringing all who partake of it under the full influence
of Christ as Lord and Saviour.

Dr. Pusey.

Dr. Pusey accepts these Patristic views not merely as to results, but, also, as to the causes of those results. Quoting (p. 93) Chrysostom X, 704, " *As many as have been baptized into Christ, have put on Christ:* ' And why saith he not, As many as have been baptized into Christ have been born of God? for so had he proved more directly that they were sons. He saith this in a way much more awfully great. For since Christ is the Son of God, and thou hast put him on, having the Son in thyself, and being transformed into his likeness, thou hast been brought into one kindred and one species with him;' he remarks: ' St. Paul speaks then not of duties, but of privileges, inestimable, inconceivable, which no thought can reach unto—our union with God in Christ, wherein we were joined in Holy Baptism,' ' Ye are all one *in* Christ Jesus,' brings out the more clearly how the being ' clothed with Christ,' is the same as being ' *in* Christ Jesus ; ' are *in* Him, by being clothed upon by Him ; . . . for, seeing we are *in* Him, then the putting on Christ is a spiritual reality, the being encompassed, surrounded, invested with him, as a body is with a garment. . . . So, we see the force of those words by which St. Paul so frequently describes our Christian privileges, the being ' *in* Christ.' "

The radical error in this interpretation is the introduction into it of a *ritual* baptism, which has no place in the mind or language of Paul. And while the presence of the Holy Spirit is recognized and declared to be a *sine qua non* in order to the spiritual result, still, the incorporation of the work of the Holy Spirit with the use of the *ritual water*, is a pure error without support here or elsewhere in Scripture.

" In Christ."

Attention has been already called to (what Dr. Pusey says is of so frequent occurrence in Scripture) " *in* CHRIST," as having the most intimate relation to " *baptized into* CHRIST." The phrase " in Christ" is universally regarded as most real, and of the deepest spiritual significance. It occurs in the following passages: Rom. 6 : 11, 8 : 1, 12 : 5, 16 : 7 ; 1 Cor. 1 : 2, 30, 3 : 1, 4 : 15, 15 : 18, 22 ; 2 Cor. 5 : 17, 12 : 2 ; Gal. 1 : 22, 2 : 4, 17, 5 : 6, 6 : 15 ; Eph. 1 : 1, 3–13, 20, 2 : 5, 10, 13 ; Phil. 1 : 1, 4 : 13, 19 ; Colos. 1 : 2,

28; 1 Thess. 2 : 14, 4 : 16; 2 Tim. 3 : 12; 1 Peter 5 : 10, 14; 1 John 5 : 20.

According to the force of βαπτίζω, as shown by this Inquiry, all who are "baptized into Christ," do, thenceforth, remain "*in* Christ," since this word does not take out what it puts in, but leaves its object within what it is placed. And as bearing on this point it is deeply interesting and no less instructive, that the Scriptures do so constantly represent all Christians without exception, both as "baptized INTO *Christ*," and as "IN *Christ*." This is precisely what should be upon our interpretation both of the word and of the phrase; and it is precisely what should *not* be according to the word and the phrase as interpreted by the theory which makes Christian baptism to be "a *dipping into* WATER."

Dr. Carson.

Dr. Carson (p. 213) says: "The Apostle does not state the import of an ordinance of God in Gal. 3 : 27; he does not allege that their submission to baptism was an evidence of putting on Christ, for it is not such; but it is a figure of putting on Christ. Some of them might not turn out to be real believers, but in their baptism they were taken for such."

This exposition is purely contradictory to the inspired text. Dr. Carson says, "The Apostle does not state the import of an ordinance of God." The Apostle does declare the "import" of that of which he speaks, namely, "Baptism into Christ," and declares that it *clothes with Christ,* and if this is not the "import" of an "ordinance of God," then nothing is plainer than that the Apostle is not speaking of "an ordinance of God," but of something which can do what he says it does do. Again; Dr. Carson says, "The Apostle does not allege that submission to baptism was an evidence of putting on Christ; for it is not such." But the Apostle does declare, that to be "baptized into Christ" IS *to put on Christ.* Then why will Dr. Carson insist upon substituting for "baptism into Christ," a "dipping into water," which cannot (according to his confession) *clothe with Christ,* and thus compel himself to contradict the Apostle? Dr. Carson says, "Baptism into Christ" is a ritual ordinance, and nothing but "a figure" of putting on Christ. Paul says, "Baptism into Christ" does, in very truth, *clothe with Christ,* and, therefore, "Baptism into Christ" expresses no figure, but the real work of the Holy Ghost.

Dr. Carson says, "Some 'baptized into Christ' might not turn out to be real believers," which indeed is true enough of "some" *dipped into water*, but applied to those " baptized into Christ," is untrue, and flatly contradicts the Apostle who affirms, " as many as "—" whosoever is baptized into Christ, *puts on* CHRIST."

$$εἰς\ Χριστὸν\ ἐβαπτίσθητε = Χριστὸν\ ἐνεδύσασθε.$$

The language of the Apostle in this passage is complete as it stands. To introduce a ritual ordinance necessitates (as Dr. Carson admits) a revolutionary change in the language and in the sentiment. Any justifiable interpretation of the language as it stands, must affirm what the Apostle affirms, to wit: *All* BAP-TIZED INTO *Christ do* PUT ON *Christ*, and consequently, that this is not ritual baptism, but the baptism by the Holy Ghost.

$$ἐνδύσησθε\ δύναμιν = βαπτισθήσεσθε\ εἰς\ δύναμιν.$$

The entire equivalence of " putting on " (used figuratively) and of " baptizing into " (used figuratively) is farther conclusively shown by a comparison of the parallel passages, Luke 24 : 49, " I send the promise of my Father upon you, tarry . . . until (ἐνδύσησθε δύναμιν) ye be endued with power from on high," and Acts 1 : 4, 5, 8, Wait for the promise of the Father, which ye have heard of me. . . . Ye shall be baptized (βαπτισθήσεσθε) with the Holy Ghost. . . . Ye shall receive (δύναμιν) power after that the Holy Ghost is come upon you.

As the Apostle expounds *baptism into* CHRIST by *putting on* CHRIST, so the Lord Jesus Christ expounds his promise that the Apostles *shall be clothed with* POWER for their Apostleship, by the Holy Ghost (the promise = the Holy Ghost, Acts 2 : 33), by re-peating that promise, through the same inspired writer, in the diverse but equivalent terms, ye *shall be baptized into* POWER for the Apostleship, by the Holy Ghost.

While the main point is thus conclusively established, there is an incidental confirmation of the points : 1. 'Ἐν Πνεύματι 'Αγίῳ used with βαπτίζω (Acts 1 : 5) is expressive of agency: 2.'Ἐν Π. 'Α. must be supplied (Luke 24 : 49) as the investing, clothing, putting on agency, and. also (Gal. 3 : 27), as the baptizing and putting on agency: 3. In this New Testament use βαπτίζω has no more to do with *dipping into water*, than ἐνδύω has to do with *putting on a coat*.

BAPTISM OF ISRAEL INTO MOSES TYPICAL OF BAPTISM OF CHRISTIANS INTO CHRIST.

1 CORINTHIANS 10 : 2.

Καὶ πάντες εἰς τὸν Μωσῆν ἐβαπτίσαντο ἐν τῇ νεφέλῃ καὶ ἐι τη θαλάσσῃ.

"And were all baptized into Moses by the cloud and by the sea."

OLD TESTAMENT AND NEW TESTAMENT.

Translation.

The leading recent writers on the subject of baptism are, generally, agreed as to the translation of the first clause in this passage.

President Halley, President Beecher, Professor Wilson, Professor Stuart, and others, unite in translating, "Baptized *into* Moses;" and, on the other side, Dr. Carson, Professor Ripley, President A. Campbell of Bethany, Ingham of England, and others, offer the same translation, "all were baptized *into* Moses."

There are others, however, who translate, "baptized *unto* Moses." Among these are Dr. Conant, on the one side, and Bishop Ellicott, on the other. Bishop Ellicott (Gal. 3 : 27) says : "βαπτίζω εἰς, has two significations, 1, *unto;* 2, *into;* the context showing whether it means only *object, purpose;* or *union, communion with.*" He thinks that " εἰς Χριστόν, εἰς τὸ ὄνομα, ever implies a spiritual and mystical union ; while εἰς μετανοίαν εἰς ἄφεσιν ἁμαρτιων, and εἰς Μωσῆν, are necessarily less comprehensive and significant." As to the "comprehensiveness" (within their sphere) of these phrases, there is no difference. They all express completeness of influence over their objects. As to "significance," that does not depend upon the preposition, but upon its regimen A baptism εἰς μετάνοιαν cannot lose its character as a baptism (which it does by the translation *unto* repentance), because it differs in significance from a baptism εἰς Χριστὸν ; nor can a baptism εἰς ἄφεσιν ἁμαρτιῶν lose its character by conversion into, *unto* the remission of sins, because it differs immensely in significance from a baptism εἰς τὸ ὄνομα τοῦ Πατρὸς. . . . If a baptism "into repentance," and a baptism "into the remission of sins" be considered verbally and disconnectedly, their significance is widely diverse ; but if they be considered in relation to the gospel system, they have an equivalent value and significance. And so, a baptism εἰς

μετάνοια, becomes a baptism εἰς ἄφεσιν ἁμαρτιῶν; and a baptism εἰς
ἀφεσίν becomes a baptism εἰς Χριστὸν, and a baptism εἰς Χριστὸν
becomes a baptism εἰς τὸ ὄνομα τοῦ Πατρός, καὶ τοῦ Υἱοῦ, καὶ τοῦ Ἁγίου
Πνεύματος.

None of these baptisms requires or allows of a change in the
translation of the preposition. That is a fixed element in such
phrases. The diversity of significance in such verbally stated baptisms must always be found in the regimen of the preposition which
indicates the complement to the idea of the verb. Hence we see,
that the difference between the baptisms εἰς Μωσῆν and εἰς Χριστὸν,
is not to be sought in a modified use of the preposition (making
it in the one case *unto*, and in the other *into*), but in the essential distinction between *Moses* and CHRIST. The proper force of
a baptism *into* MOSES will differ as boundlessly from a baptism
into CHRIST, as Moses *the servant* differs from Christ THE LORD.

The translation of ἐν in the second clause is generally given as
local, " *in* the cloud and *in* the sea," with an application to the
Israelites, as indicating the place where, or that in which, they
were baptized.

There are insuperable difficulties to such a view : 1. It is contradictory to the facts. Granting that, without undue violence,
they might be said to be " in the sea," still, there is no violence
which can locate them " in *the cloud*." The conclusion, then, is
plain ; that the sentiment of the passage cannot turn on the Israelites being " in the sea," for whatever is " *in* the sea," is also " *in*
the cloud ;" 2. This error, which puts the Israelites " in the cloud
and *in* the sea," is grounded in an antecedent error which makes
ἐν expository of the idea of βαπτίζω, while, in truth, ἐν has nothing
to do with such office, which belongs wholly to εἰς through which
the verb exhausts itself. Principle, therefore, joins with fact to
forbid a local idea being attached to this preposition so far as the
Israelites are concerned.

If a local and not instrumental idea be given to ἐν, its relation
must be transferred from the Israelites to the power of Jehovah.
It is a fact, that the power of Jehovah was " *in* the sea," miraculously dividing its waters ; and it is a fact, that the power of
Jehovah was " *in* the cloud," miraculously dividing out to the
Egyptians, darkness from the one side, and to the Israelites, light
from the other side. While the facts forbid that " in the cloud
and in the sea " should be applied to the Israelites ; the facts demand that the power of Jehovah should be recognized as alike

"*in* the cloud and *in* the sea." And herein we have the clear
and unquestionable basis for the instrumental translation of this
preposition. If the power of Jehovah was "in the cloud and in
the sea," miraculously employing them in the accomplishment of
this baptism, then, obviously, they were instrumental agencies;
and nothing can be more conformed to the truth than the translation, "*by* the cloud and *by* the sea." And this is precisely what
the exigency of the case demands; the baptism is declared to be
"*into* Moses," and the agency required for such baptism is now
furnished in the double miracle, wrought by the power of Jehovah
through "the cloud and the sea," which so profoundly impressed
the minds of the Israelites and brought them fully to acknowledge
the often doubted and questioned mission of Moses, so as to justify
the declaration that they were now, and thus, *baptized* into him.

Interpretation.

Ambrose, I, 867, says, "Then we read that, in virtute sua magna
et brachio suo excelso, populum suum de terra Ægypti liberavit,
quando traduxit eum per mare Rubrum, in quo fecit figura baptismatis."

Ambrose, in this passage, uses, "*in* virtute sua magna et brachio
suo excelso," as Paul uses the corresponding Greek preposition
in, ἐν τῇ νεφέλῃ καὶ ἐν τῇ θαλάσσῃ. The Latin "in" becomes instrumental because Jehovah is represented as being "*in* his great
strength and *in* his exalted arm," and therefore, "*by* them he
delivered his people and led them through the sea." The "figure
of baptism" which Ambrose and his associates find in this transaction is very different from that of those who, in these last days,
make Christian baptism *a dipping*, which neither he nor they
knew anything about. The figure, he says, is in the drowning of
the Egypt ans and saving the Hebrews, which is "daily shown
in baptism by the drowning of sin and error, and the saving of
piety and innocence." How the power of Jehovah was in the
divided sea and miraculous cloud Ambrose (III, 393) shows by
quoting, "Thou didst send forth thy Spirit and divided the sea
for them;" and again (424), "The cloud is the Holy Spirit."
"By the Holy Spirit and by the water a type of baptism was exhibited." IV, 827: "The water saved Israel and slew Pharaoh.
Baptism saves the likeness of God and destroys the sins which it
served. The waters, a wall on their right and left, designate our

faith which we receive in baptism; our wall defending us from enemies visible and invisible."

Such interpretation has interest and value as a display of imagination; but as for any exegetical value in expounding the "baptism into Moses," it must be classed with "grave," "burial," "womb," "mother," and "a dry dip," as wood, hay, and stubble, fit only to be burned.

Basil M., IV, 124: "The sea and the cloud, induced at that time, faith through amazement, but as a type, it signified, for the future, the grace that was to come."

Basil makes the sea and the cloud agencies accomplishing their end by the most overpowering influence. This is shown by the additional statement, "The cloud was a shadow of the gift of the Spirit which cools the flame of the passions by mortifying the members." He adds, "*τυπικως εις Μωσην εβαπτισθησαν* they were typically *baptized into* MOSES."

John of Damascus, I, 261 (Paris, 1712), also, speaks of this baptism as accomplished by the sea and the cloud as agencies— *Τό δια τῆς θαλάσσης καὶ τῆς νεφέλης.*

Jerome, XI, 745, thus comments: "*Et omnes in Moyse baptizati sunt.*" "In Moyse, qui Christi typum gerebat—Were baptized into Moses who was a type of Christ." Jerome believed that this baptism was "*into* MOSES" as a type, just as the after-baptism was to be "*into* CHRIST" the antitype.

It is obvious that this interpretation of the baptism "into Moses" by these early writers receives its special coloring from their peculiar views of Christian baptism, which they regarded as herein typified.

They regarded the Israelites as a type of Christ's people, and Moses as a type of Christ; and as they believed that all his people were baptized into Christ through the twofold agency of water and of the Holy Spirit, jointly and simultaneously operating, so, they believed that all the Israelites were baptized "into Moses" through the twofold agency of "the sea and the cloud," representing the water and the Spirit; and as they farther believed that the effect of the conjoint agency of water and Spirit was to destroy sin and to save the soul, so they believed that such effect was represented by the destruction of the Egyptians and the saving of the Hebrews. As they did not believe that *βαπτίζω* expressed a definite act, *to dip*, there is no attempt to discover, with the modern friends of that theory, "a dry dip" (Carson, p. 120):

and as they did not believe that a covering in water was Christian baptism, so, there is no attempt to make a covering out of water walls (one mile or five miles apart), and a cloud roof which had no existence.

This interpretation, so far as it is limited to the elements in the Apostle's statement, is substantially correct: 1. The subjects of this baptism were " all Israel;" 2. The verbal receiving element, into which and under the controlling power of which these subjects of this baptism pass, is Moses; 3. The agency effecting this baptism is the power of Jehovah miraculously operating "in the cloud and in the sea." This exhausts the statement of Paul. What is more than this is Patrism.

Dr. Carson and other Baptist Writers.

Dr. Carson (p. 119) speaks of this baptism and gives the generally received view among his friends. As his views have been presented and considered in Judaic Baptism (pp. 293–301) they will now be only briefly glanced at. He says: " They (the Israelites) are said to have been baptized. Therefore there is in their passage through the sea something that represents the external form and the purpose of Christian baptism. It is, therefore, figuratively called by the name of the Christian ordinance, because of external similarity as well as figuring the same event. The going down into the sea, the being covered by the cloud, the issuing out on the other side, resembled the baptism of believers, attested their faith in Moses as a temporal saviour, and figured the burial and resurrection of Christ and Christians. The baptisms of Pentecost and the Red Sea were dry baptisms."

1. " The Israelites are said to have been baptized." This is a repetition of the *eliding* quotation so frequently met with, and so all-essential to the friends of a dipping *into* WATER. The Israelites are not only said to be " baptized," but they are said to be " baptized *into* MOSES." Now, if " Moses " is *water*, then it makes no difference whether it is said that they were baptized " into water" or " into Moses ;" but so long as the babe in the bulrush cradle differs from the waters in which he floats, it will be better to take the Scripture statement—" The Israelites were baptized *into* MOSES." And with all who understandingly receive this statement of inspiration the theory of a dipping into water perishes as absolutely as Pharaoh in the Red Sea.

2. "Therefore the passage through the sea represents the external form of Christian baptism." This "therefore" is a deduction from the baptism into Moses, and has as much logical connection with it, as, "John Smith is like his father, *therefore* John Smith's horse is like James Jones."

It is Dr. Carson and not Paul who says, that this baptism is to be found in the passage through the sea, and not in the relation established by Jehovah between Israel and Moses. And his reasoning from the baptism into Moses to a resemblance between the agency effecting that baptism and the external form of Christian baptism is the same as if he should say : " Gedaliah was baptized *into drunkenness* by drinking wine ; *therefore*, drinking wine resembles the external form of Christian baptism ; " or, " Satyrus was baptized *into stupor* by swallowing an opiate ; *therefore*, swallowing an opiate is like the external form of Christian baptism."

Dr. Carson's error is a substitution of the agency in effecting a baptism for the baptism effected. Dr. Carson farther errs in assuming that there is any " external form " in Christian baptism arising out of a dipping into water. There is no such language in the New Testament as " baptizing into water," much less *dipping into water*. And in a baptism "*into* CHRIST" there is neither " exterior form " nor interior, but a great spiritual result, just as there was a grand moral result in the baptism of all Israel " into Moses."

3. " It " (the passage) " is therefore figuratively called by the name of the Christian ordinance, because of external similarity."

There is not one word in Scripture, Old Testament or New Testament, which calls the passage through the sea a baptism. There is not one word of Scripture to prove that the term " baptize," as used to express the relation between the Israelites and Moses, after the double miracle wrought to attest his divine mission, was borrowed from " the Christian ordinance." The essential power of the word is its own sufficient vindication. It was used by heathen, by Jews, and by Christians with precisely the same general force (the specific applications being various, and the resultant idea being governed by such specific application) as it is here used by Paul. It is not " the passage " which is the baptism but the condition established in the relation of Israel to Moses.

4. " The going down into the sea, the being covered by the cloud, and the issuing out on the other side, resembled the bap-

tism of believers; attested their faith in Moses as a temporal saviour."

This is an attempt to establish a resemblance between something and nothing, except in so far as it may be found in the theory of Dr. Carson and his friends. Certainly, in Christian baptism there is neither "going down," nor "covering over," nor "issuing out." If such things be sought for through βαπτίζω and its assumed relations and necessities as connected with water, the answer is both short and sharp, namely, this: Neither βαπτίζω, nor βάπτισμα, nor βαπτιστής is ever used in the New Testament in complementary relation with water; therefore the theory which makes Christian baptism a dipping into water, with its going down, covering in, and coming up never had any Scriptural existence.

The idea that this passage exemplified "believers' baptism" and attested "their faith in Moses as a temporal saviour" is, if possible, a more absolute myth than the other. It is in the most absolute contradiction to the statement of Scripture. Never was unbelief in Moses more rampant in Israel, never was their outcry against his leadership more loud than in that hour when they stood on the shore of the Red Sea. It was to crush out this unbelief that Jehovah interposed, and by his power dividing the sea, and by his power pouring light upon them and darkness upon the Egyptians all night long, and by that same power drowning their enemies in the returning waters, he did overthrow their unbelief; but it was not overthrown until the passage was completed, and "they saw their enemies dead upon the shore," then, and not till then, did they believe in Moses as the Servant of the Lord; and then, and not till then, were they baptized into Moses. "And Israel saw that great work which the Lord did upon the Egyptians; and the people feared the Lord, and believed the Lord, and his servant Moses" (Exod. 14 : 31).

There is no distinctive feature in "believer's baptism" which is worth more than this claim for belief on the part of these Israelites who come to the water saying to Moses, "Because there were no graves in Egypt, hast thou taken us away to die in the wilderness? Wherefore hast thou thus dealt with us, to carry us forth out of Egypt? Is not this the word that we did tell thee in Egypt, saying, Let us alone that we may serve the Egyptians? For it had been better for us to serve the Egyptians, than that we should die in the wilderness" (Exod. 14 : 11, 12)

It is amusing to hear Dr. Carson appealing to this baptism, *in which every infant among the millions of Israel shares equally with its parents*, as a "believer's baptism." In conclusion, it should be borne in mind that while this baptism was a type (τύποι 1 Cor. 10 : 6) baptism, it was none the less a real baptism ; and it is only because it was a real baptism that it is suitable to be a type baptism. Moses was a type of Christ, and Israel was a type of the church, and the faith of Israel toward Moses, as their divinely appointed head, was typical of the faith of the church toward her Divine head ; and the faith of Israel begotten by the mighty power of Jehovah, miraculously working through the cloud and the sea as agencies, is a type of the faith of the church begotten by the same Divine power working through appropriate agencies. The baptism of Israel "into Moses" was a real baptism, and directly relates, as a type, to the real baptism "into Christ" by the Holy Spirit working faith in the soul, and has no relation whatever to Ritual baptism.

Prof. Ripley gives a substantially correct interpretation of the phrase "baptized into Moses," but afterward disconnects the baptism from Moses entirely, and attaches it to the passage through the sea as what might, apologetically, be called a baptism. He says (p. 100), "The language is evidently figurative, and is intended to represent the Israelites not as being *literally baptized*, but as submitting themselves to the special authority and guidance of Moses, as Christians, when baptized, submit themselves avowedly to Christ. . . . A time when they made a very signal surrender of themselves to Moses as the servant of God. . . . By baptism Christians avow their confidence in Christ, their choice of him, and their subjection unto him in all the offices which he sustains."

1. "The language is evidently figurative." Certainly "baptized into Moses" is a figurative expression; but figure is neither fiction nor shadow. The profoundest realities may be expressed in figurative phrase. "I am the vine; ye are the branches," is a figurative phrase; but does it any the less express a profound reality? "Put off Pythagoras" is figure; but does it not express reality? "Put on Tarquin" is figure; but does it not express a reality in which the spirit of Tarquin reigns predominant? "Baptized by drunkenness;" "Baptized into insensibility;" "Baptized into impurity," are all figurative phrases; but do they not all express intense realities? How is it, then, that "baptized into Moses"

fails, on the ground of figure, to express that which is most real, and in which reality Moses bears the supremacy? But Prof. Ripley recognizes a reality which this phrase expresses, and which nothing else in the transaction does, to wit, "The language represents the Israelites as *submitting themselves to the special authority and guidance of Moses.*" Now this is the substantial reality which is expressed by the phrase " baptized *into* MOSES;" and if Prof. Ripley would rest in it, and in its logical relations, all would be well; but he does not. He allies this baptism "into Moses" (which is a profound reality effected in the souls of Israel by the power of Jehovah) with a *profession* of submission to Christ made in *ritual* baptism, which profession may be fact or fiction. This cannot be right. This Red Sea baptism is not the type of a ritual baptism which has no such controlling reality, but of that most real baptism which is the work of the Holy Ghost, and baptizes not the body with water nor into water, but the soul " into Jesus Christ," effecting a real change in its condition, shown not by a profession, but by a true " submission to the authority and guidance" *of* JESUS CHRIST. This truth, which is the reality expressed by "baptized into Christ," Prof. Ripley also distinctly expresses when he says : " Christians avow their *confidence* in Christ, their *choice* of him, and their *subjection* to him, *in all the offices which he sustains.*" When this is done in truth, it is done because the soul has been " baptized into Christ " by the Holy Ghost; and the reality consequent upon such baptism is, that the soul has " put on Christ."

If Prof. Ripley would rest in this truth as expository of the baptism " into Moses," and of the baptism " into Christ," and as exhaustive of that baptism, nothing more could be desired ; but he either abandons this sentiment as interpretative of the figuratively expressed phrase, or he makes use of the baptism thus expressed *a second time*, converting it into the sea passage of the Israelites, and a ritual use of water for Christians. This is without authority from Scripture, and is in itself impossible.

Alexander Campbell of Bethany (p. 251) says : " To baptize ' into the remission of sins,' or ' *into what* were you baptized,' intimates that the subject of that act is about passing into a new state, as entering *into* partnership or entering *into* marriage indicates that it is for such purposes the action, whatever it may be. is performed."

This statement is open to two objections : 1. *Ad hominem.* No one who says "βαπτίζω has but one meaning, which is a definite act *to dip*," is justified in saying βαπτίζω εἰς τί carries its object "into a new *state*." If I dip an object into *water*, I do not thereby give to such object a *status* within water. The essential force of "dip" forbids this. It necessitates the prompt withdrawal of the object. If I dip into *mathematics*, I do not enter into a new *state*, whose sphere is "mathematics." Such idea is precluded by the literal meaning of dip, which must always be the basis of metaphorical use. The momentary introduction of an object into a fluid necessarily begets the idea of a trivial impression upon the object dipped. The metaphorical use of dip, consequently, always conveys this idea: If I dip into *mathematics*, into *business*, into *pleasure*, into *politics*, into *vice*, or into *Shakspeare*, the idea expressed is not that I have passed into a new *state* in relation to mathematics, business, pleasure, politics, vice, or Shakspeare, but that I have come under such influences in a very *trivial* degree. Therefore no one who affirms that βαπτίζω means *to dip*, has a right to say "βαπτίζω εἰς τί intimates the passing into *a new* STATE." If such meaning (βαπτίζω = *dip*) be true, then a baptism εἰς ἄφεσιν cannot express *a state* characterized by "remission of sins;" nor can a baptism εἰς Μωσῆν express *a state* characterized by submission to the distinctive claims of Moses as a Leader appointed by Jehovah; nor can a baptism εἰς Χριστόν express *a state* characterized by "subjection to him in all the offices which he sustains." But Campbell and Ripley and Carson and Conant admit that such is the meaning of these phrases; therefore, βαπτίζω cannot mean *to dip*, but must mean what this whole Inquiry from first to last shows that it does mean, namely, to change the state or condition of an object without limitation of time. 1. By *withinness* which does not provide for removal; 2. Without *withinness* by any act or influence competent to effect an analogous change of state or condition.

2. *Ad verum.* The second objection relates to the merits of the statement—"To baptize *into something* (εἰς τί), intimates that the subject of that act is about passing into a new state."

This statement involves a fallacious double use of baptize where it in fact occurs **but** once, and in its second use is introduced in an office alien from the first, and with a meaning contradictory to it. The proof is this: If βαπτίζω εἰς τί, *e. g.*, εἰς μετανοίαν, εἰς ἄφεσιν, εἰς Μωσῆν, εἰς Χριστόν, expresses "the passing into a new state," then it does so by reason of the force of βαπτίζω εἰς, the nature of the state being denoted by the representative τί. This use of βαπτίζω is as exhaustive of its function, as in the phrases, " The cannon-ball was *buried into the* EARTH, or *into the* SAND, or *into the* COTTON BALE*,*" the word " buried " is exhausted by its complementary use with " earth," " sand," " cotton bale." But Campbell, and Ripley, and friends, are not satisfied with such duty; having used βαπτίζω in organic relation with εἰς τι (= εἰς Μωσῆν), it is again introduced, thus: "This phrase intimates that the subject of *that act?*"—what act? That act which is in βαπτίζω εἰς τί (= μετανοίαν, ἄφεσιν, Μωσῆν, Χριστόν)? By no means; but one wholly diverse, as will appear by bringing to light the suppressed phrase βαπτίζω εἰς ὕδωρ which is represented in " *that act* received by the subject." The full statement is this: " The phrase 'baptized into remission' expresses the entrance into a new state of remitted sin, and intimates that the subject of the act of baptizing into " (" remission?" no, but into) " water (!) enters into a new state " (—of what? of water covering? no, but) "of remitted sin." This repetition of βαπτίζω (in wholly new and diverse relations, substituting a baptism into *water* for a baptism into *Moses*, into *Christ*, etc.), is too obviously subversive of truth, to require its being declared to be without foundation in Scripture. It might as well be said, that " buried," in the phrase, " the cannon-ball was buried into the earth," refers to and expounds the manner of " the act " in touching off the cannon. This confounding of the act of baptism, as an agency, with the baptism, the new state or condition resultant from such act, is exhibited in the illustrations of partnership and marriage by which Alexander Campbell seeks to vindicate his position.

He says: " To baptize into remission " (into Moses) " intimates, that the subject of that act is about passing into a new state; as entering *into partnership*, or entering *into marriage*, indicates that it is for such purposes the action, whatever it may be, is performed." Now, " entering into " as related to " partnership " might as well be repeated in " the action," and in doing so, you might as well substitute, *alderman's office*, for " partnership " (covering " partnership " and the surreptitiously introduced *alderman's office* by the same " entering into ") as to make " baptized into " cover both " remission " (Moses, etc.), and a surreptitiously introduced *pool of water*.

The *act* of agreement to enter into partnership, or into marriage, is no more " the new state " of partnership or marriage, than is a means its end, or a cause its effect. The miraculous division of the sea, and shining of the cloud, and destruction of their enemies, were means of baptizing the unbelieving Israelites "into Moses," thoroughly changing their state of unbelief; but these means toward this baptism were not the baptism which Jehovah effected through them.

C. STOVEL (Christian Baptism, London), and writers of his views generally, fall into the same surreptitious double use of βαπτίζω. He says (p. 70): "When the nation was baptized, initiated into Moses, being immersed in cloud and sea, they entered under an authority the exercise of which was destined to secure the glory of God to whom they were subject."

Here "baptized" is first used to express "initiation into"— "entering under the authority of Moses," which is its proper and only function as used by Paul; but after having got such efficient service out of it (quite enough for one word), he uses it a second time for very different work, to wit, "immersing all Israel in *the cloud* and in *the sea*," of which Paul does not say one word and which in itself is most untrue.

PROF. WILSON, of Belfast, in commenting on this statement (p. 275) says: "This comment presents a very unfavorable view of the author's acquaintance with language and of his power of discrimination. He first identifies the baptism of the text with initiation into Moses; and next he proceeds to apply it, in the same occurrence, to a supposed immersion in cloud and sea! In expounding the term *baptized* Mr. Stovel is at liberty to choose between *initiated* and *immersed;* but to represent βαπτίζω as standing for both and doing twofold duty, in the same instance, is arbitrary and apocryphal. Baptism '*into Moses*' clearly implied the acknowledgment of his official claims as a Leader and Lawgiver" (p. 308).

It must be borne in mind that this "acknowledgment of the official claims of Moses" was not a mere formal, verbal, ceremonial acknowledgment; but was *bonâ fide*, real, from convinced intellect and conscience, the result of divine power (not of symbolism) applied to their spiritual life through the miracles wrought before them and for them. It was, therefore, in its nature essentially diverse from, and has no direct relation to, Christian ritual baptism.

The baptism of Israel into Moses, by divine power constraining to the true and profound conviction of his mission, is immediately

20

related (as a type) to the baptism of sinners into Christ, by divine power constraining to the true and profound conviction of his mission as the Redeemer of his people from the bondage of sin and the fear of death.

On the other hand, Christian ritual baptism neither has nor can have any real baptism of its own, but symbolizes that real baptism into Christ, which was typified by the real baptism into Moses. The reality in the baptism into Christ effected by divine power is, the subjection of the soul to Christ and the participation in his peculiar benefits ; the primary one of which is, purification by regeneration and remission of sin, which is, therefore, made the subject of symbolization by the pure water of the rite. And inasmuch as while the phrase baptism into Christ expresses the intensest reality, that reality has no connection with an actual baptism, or with an actual dipping, or pouring, or sprinkling; such things can have no place in the rite save as accidents or as matters of will. And in accordance with the truth, that such things do not enter into the essence of the rite, there is not one word said in Scripture of any of them in the performance of the rite.

DR. CONANT (Meaning and Use of BAPTIZEIN, p. 104) says: " BAPTIZEIN, by analogy, expressed the *coming into a new state of life or experience*, in which one was, as it were, inclosed or swallowed up, so that temporarily or permanently, he belonged wholly to it."

If $\beta\alpha\pi\tau i\zeta\omega$ means *to dip* and has but one meaning, as we are told, then it is as impossible that it should have the meaning here assigned to it, as that a cradled infant should have the strength of the Son of Manoah.

Particular cases of baptism which are given establish the same conclusion : "Baptism *by calamities* = swallowed up by them as by an ingulfing flood."   Is that *a dipping?*   " Baptism *by debts* = owing vast sums and no means of paying them."   Is that *a dipping?*   " Baptism *by wine* = faculties totally overborne and prostrated by it."   Is that *a dipping?*   "Baptism *by sophistries* = mind wholly confounded by them."   Is that *a dipping?*   When the tip of the finger shall cover the breadth of the Universe, then will *dip* cover such usage of $\beta\alpha\pi\tau i\zeta\omega$.

The statements of Dr. Conant are perfectly true, and because they are true, they prove the theory which ascribes to this word " a dipping and nothing but a dipping," to be untrue.

Another statement of Dr. Conant is both true and important: "The relation in which BAPTIZEIN was used associated with it, for the time being, the ideas peculiar to that relation." Thus, when it was associated, in Classic Greek, with human beings and *water*, it secured to itself the idea of *drowning;* when associated with *wine*, that of *drunkenness;* when associated by Jews with their religious rites, that of *ceremonial purification;* and when associated by inspired writers with great doctrinal truths, such as εἰς μετάνοιαν, εἰς ἄφεσιν ἁμαρτιων, εἰς Χριστόν, involving repentance and faith, pardon and salvation, it became, thenceforth, associated through the ages with the ideas of SPIRITUAL PURIFICATION.

Halley and Others.

PRESIDENT HALLEY (p. 371) says: "The baptism was into Moses, the syntax corresponding with the baptism into Christ; and immersion is just as much and as little implied in the one phrase as in the other."

PRESIDENT BEECHER (p. 112) says: "Baptism into Moses neither denotes Christian baptism nor external baptism. The children of Israel were delivered from Pharaoh and united to Moses as a Leader and Saviour, by the cloud and the sea. Moses was a type of Christ, therefore, the name of the antitype is thrown back upon this transaction and it is called a baptism into Moses."

A more comprehensive reason for the use of βαπτίζω to express the relation of Israel to Moses, and one which includes its use in expressing the relation of his people to Christ, as well as every other case of like syntactical use, whether in the Scriptures or out of the Scriptures, is this, namely, the fitness of this word to express the communication of the characteristics of its complementary word in pervading and controlling influence, to the object of the baptism, whatever that may be.

This element of interpretation expounds every case of this usage (inspired or uninspired) as satisfactorily as it does exhaustively.

BISHOP PEARCE (Commentary) says: "They were baptized (not *unto* Moses, as our English version has it, but) *into* Moses, *i.e.*, into that covenant and into those laws which Moses delivered to them from God."

ARCHBISHOP NEWCOME says: "They were figuratively and typically baptized; they were led to acknowledge the divine mission of Moses through those miracles, expressive of baptism."

The Hebrew of Moses and the Greek of Paul.

The statement by Paul, "All our fathers were baptized into Moses by the cloud and by the sea" is evidently the statement of a result effected through the cloud and the sea. Moses, also, makes a statement of the result of this divine interposition through these great agencies. His language (Exod. 14:31) is this: "And Israel saw that great work which the Lord did upon the Egyptians: and the people feared the Lord, and believed the Lord, and his servant Moses."

Are these summings up by Moses and Paul related to each other? Are they related to each other as purposed statements of the final issue of the same facts? If so, do their statements accord with each other?

We take the affirmative of these questions and say, that Moses in Exod. 14:31, and Paul in Corinthians 10:2, refer to the same facts, state the result of those facts, and that the result stated, in both cases, is the same under diversity of words.

The Hebrew word אָמַן in the passage (Exod. 14:31) just quoted, is translated "believed," and is defined by Gesenius as follows: *to prop, to stay, to support—to lean upon, to build upon, to stand firm—to trust—to confide in, to believe.*

These last, *to trust, to confide in, to believe,* are secondary meanings derived from the primary and literal meanings, *to prop, to stay, to support.* So, to influence controllingly, to make thoroughly subject to any influence, penetrating, pervading and assimilating in its nature, to change condition completely by such influence without envelopment, are secondary meanings of βαπτίζω derived from the primary and literal meaning *to merse; to intuspose within any element without limitation of time.*

Now, this Hebrew word evidently teaches us, that the Israelites having been wavering, unstable, and unreliable in their relations to Moses, were made (as a result of the miracles which they had witnessed) *to trust, to confide in, to believe upon him,* with a confidence second only to that cherished toward Jehovah himself, whose minister and representative they now fully believe him to be. In other words we are taught that the moral condition and relation of Israel toward Moses is radically changed, so that his influence over them is thoroughly controlling.

What, now, does the Greek word teach us? Clearly this: the Israelites having been *out of* Moses through unbelief in his mission and thus beyond the control of his influence, they are (by the stupendous miracles wrought by Jehovah in attestation of that mission) thoroughly convinced of its divine origin and authority and submit themselves to it, passing from their outstanding position "*into* Moses," so coming, in the most strongly expressed terms, under his thoroughly controlling influence.

And between these diversely originating conceptions—*firmly standing by* and *thoroughly obedient to* a man through profound conviction of his divine mission, and, *entering into a man* so as to be pervaded by, subjected to, and animated with his spirit—what is the difference?

The Greek word is not a translation of the Hebrew word; but the same independent Spirit, which spake alike through Moses and through Paul, has presented the same substantial truth under phrases widely diverse in their origin and in their individual significance. Which is the more impressive form of statement none will care to inquire while both equally vindicate the truth and the riches of wisdom flowing through all the utterances of " holy men of old who spake as they were moved by the Holy Ghost."

This parallelism of sentiment, developed under diversity of expression, is too remarkably related to another fact related to this Inquiry, not to be reminded of it. I refer to the fact that the Syriac translation of the New Testament (one of the earliest and best) uniformly translates $\beta a\pi\tau i\zeta\omega$ by a word which is closely related (in general significance) to the Hebrew word used by Moses, and is represented with great fidelity by the Hebrew עמד. This last word is thus defined by Gesenius : *to stand, to stand by* or *for* any person, *to stand firm, to stand to it, to stand up, to make stand, to establish.* Dr. Murdoch, the translator of the Syriac New Testament, says, " that the Syriac word used for Baptism properly signifies *to stand up, to stand firm, to stand erect and stable,* like *pillars.*" It is obvious that between this Syriac word which is always used for $\beta a\pi\tau i\zeta\omega$ (and meaning *to stand up, to stand firm*) and the Hebrew word in Exod. 14 : 31 (meaning *to prop, to stand firm*) for which Paul substitutes $\beta a\pi\tau i\zeta\omega$, there is a common element which would well allow their common use to express the same or an equivalent thought. And herein may be the explanation of that deeply interesting fact in the Syriac translation. This point will receive farther attention hereafter.

By the language of Moses, and by every other consideration, the conclusion is established, that the baptism of Israel into Moses expresses their FULL SUBJECTION *to his controlling influence.*

BAPTISM INTO PAUL REJECTS CHRIST CRUCIFIED FOR US.

1 CORINTHIANS 1 : 13, 15.

Εἰς τὸ ὄνομα Παύλου ἐβαπτίσθητε ;
Ἵνα μή τις εἴπη ὅτι εἰς τὸ ἐμὸν ὄνομα ἐβάπτισα.

" Were ye baptized into the name of Paul ?
" Lest any one should say that I had baptized into my own name."

Translation.

Professor Schaff (Revision of N. T., p. xxxi) says : Matt. 28 : 19 "baptizing *in* the name," is an error of translation. So, also, 1 Cor. 1 : 13 "*in* the name of Paul;" and Acts 8 : 16 "*in* the name of the Lord Jesus;" also, Acts 19 : 5 " were baptized *in* the name of the Lord Jesus." This error arises from the translation of the Vulgate " *in* nomine." Tertullian had it correctly "*in* nomen." In other passages, viz., Rom. 6 : 3, 4 *into ;* 1 Cor. 10 : 2 *unto ;* 1 Cor. 12 : 13 *into ;* Gal. 3 : 27 *into ;* Acts 19 : 3 *unto.*

A fuller investigation will, I think, result in making the translation of βαπτίζω εἰς (in all cases where the preposition points to the complement of the verb) uniformly " baptized *into.*" Neither the demands of the verb nor the significance of the phrase can be reached in any other way.

The doctrine of Bloomfield (Ephes. 3 : 19), " *Eἰς* is put for ἐν than which nothing is more frequent in Scripture," once quite prevalent, is now generally abandoned. " It is altogether improbable that in clearly conceived doctrinal statements, the Apostles would have employed ἐν for εἰς or εἰς for ἐν, so as to perplex the reader " (*Winer*, p. 417). This point is of special importance on the subject of New Testament baptism, in treating of which these prepositions are almost exclusively used by the inspired writers, and always used with the most persistent discrimination; εἰς pointing out invariably the receiving element (in the New Testament always ideal) into which the baptized object (verbally) passes ; and ἐν as invariably (when used at all) pointing out the means (efficient or symbol) by which such baptism is effected.

Mark 1 : 9 is no exception to the former statement; because the εἰς of that passage is due to ἦλθεν and not to ἐβαπτίσθη; nor is Acts 10 : 48 an exception to the second statement; the ἐν which there occurs is related to προςέταξέ and not to βαπτισθῆναι. I know of no other cases which have even the appearance of exception.

The statement of this passage, then, by the force of its terms, is, " Were ye baptized *into the name of* PAUL ?"   " Lest any one should say, that I had baptized *into* MY OWN NAME;" and any exposition which would convert these statements into a *dipping into* WATER would establish an expository model such as has not been since exegesis had its birth.

Exposition.

The force of this phrase, " Baptized into the name of Paul," is precisely the same (so far as βαπτίζω εἰς is concerned) as in every other like phrase; the difference of value in such phrases depending always and only upon the word which is complementary of the idea of the verb.   If we take bunches of cotton and put them severally into water and oil and ink (black, red, green, or blue), what constitutes the difference of value in these phrases?   Is it not just the difference which exists between *water*, *oil*, and *ink?* And is not this difference revealed in the different effect produced upon the several bunches of cotton, the one made *wet*, another made *greasy*, and others made *black*, or *red*, or *green*, or *blue?* In precisely the same manner is indicated the difference between the phrases baptized into *sleep*, into *insensibility*, into *repentance*, into *remission of sins*, into *Moses*, into *Paul*, into CHRIST.   " Baptized into " is common to them all, and has precisely the same force in all.   The *differentiæ* are sleep, insensibility, repentance, remission of sins, Moses, Paul, and CHRIST.   And just as these differ from each other, and just as their controlling power over the objects submitted to the full influence of their distinguishing characteristics differ from each other, just so much, no more no less, do these baptisms differ from each other.

Baptism into Menander; into Donatus.

Irenæus (673) says that the impostor Menander, successor to Simon the Magician, represented the benefits flowing from the acceptance of his teachings as a baptism into himself: " Resurrectionem enim per id, quod est in eum baptisma, accipere ejus

discipulos, et ultra non posse mori, sed perseverare non senes-
centes et immortales—For by that baptism which is into him,
his disciples would receive the Resurrection so that they could
not die, but would live without growing old and immortal."

Augustine (IX, 381) charges Petilian and his friends with baptizing into Donatus (in Donati aut in nostro nomine baptizati
sumus); not because they used such formula of words, but because they came so thoroughly under his controlling influence
that they adhered to him and his errors, abandoning the truth
and the church.

Origen (IV, 276) says: "All Israel was baptized *into Joshua*
by the miraculous passage of the Jordan. Paul might say of
this, I do not wish you, brethren, to be ignorant that all our fathers
passed through the Jordan (διὰ τοῦ Ἰορδάνου) and all were baptized
into JOSHUA (εἰς Ἰησοῦν) by the Spirit and the river (ἐν τῷ Πνεύματι
καὶ ποταμῷ)." And in this statement we have conclusive. proof
that the Red Sea baptism was *into* MOSES and *by* the cloud and
sea, and not "a dry dip," since here there is no chance of a dry
dip between water walls and cloud roof. But if this was a baptism of "all Israel into Joshua," by the Spirit and the miraculously
arrested flowing of the river, then the other was a baptism into
Moses by the power of Jehovah exerted through "the cloud and
the sea." Moses and Joshua were divinely appointed leaders of
Israel; each was, in his peculiarity, a type of Christ, and the
thorough submission of Israel to their leadership and influence,
induced by the miraculous intervention of Jehovah, is described
by Paul in the one case, and by Origen in the other, as *a baptism
into* MOSES, and *a baptism into* JOSHUA.

Menander, Donatus, and Paul, were all teachers (although of
widely diverse doctrine), and the reception of them as leaders and
teachers, above all others, is described as *being baptized into
Menander, Donatus,* and PAUL.

AMBROSE (IV, 187) says: "'*Aut in nominine Pauli baptizati
estis?*' If believing (in Christum baptizamur) we are baptized
into Christ, that (in nomine ejus justificemur) we may be justified
by his name, why is it that we make men the authors of this
faith?" Ambrose teaches clearly that it is baptism "into Christ"
which gives a right to his name, and to the righteousness which
comes through that name, and not by a dipping into *water;* and
also that a baptism into Paul, or into Cephas, or into Apollos,
would make these men "the authors" of our hopes.

He farther says (v. 13, Comm.): "The Corinthians began (*subjici*) to be made subject to the names of different heretics, so that men were seen to be venerated in the stead of Christ." Ambrose here uses "subjici" as a substitute for, and the equivalent (measurably) of βαπτίζω εἰς, as expressing subjection = *under controlling influence*. Sub-jacio to *lie under*, to be subject to, and divers other forms of speech, as well as "baptized into," readily develop in forms of expression denoting *controlling influence*.

Analogous Figure.

While the Greek very frequently uses βαπτίζω to express the controlling influence of one thing over another thing by the communication to it of its quality (on the basis of a porous substance put within a fluid having some distinguishing quality, and communicating that quality by penetrating and pervading such substance), it is not common to express by this word the controlling influence of one person over another person by a verbal form suggestive of a like source of influence. There is no reason in the nature of the case why such statement should not be made; but the form of statement has remarkable boldness, while it has, also, an exhaustive power of expression. It appears for the first time in the New Testament, and is there first applied to the return of a revolted world to subjection and allegiance to the living God, which is expressed as *a baptism* "*into* THE NAME *of the* FATHER, *and of the* SON, *and of the* HOLY GHOST." It is afterward applied to sinners, guilty and perishing, as made partakers of remitted sin and a regenerated nature through Christ, stated as *a baptism* "*into the Name of the* LORD JESUS." We have, also, the baptism of Israel *into* MOSES as a type of Christ. We have, also, the statement of a baptism "into the name of Paul," in order to show and to express with the deepest condemnation the sin of the Corinthians in faltering in that sole and supreme dependence which was due to Christ.

While this form of speech is pre-eminent for boldness of conception, and capability for giving expression to the profoundest thought, the same general idea of controlling influence is expressed by other forms of speech originating in a different class of facts Among these is the statement of complete influence grounded in the *filling* a vessel to its utmost capacity: "We will fill ourselves with strong drink" (Is. 56: 12); "I will fill the inhabitants with drunkenness " (Jer. 13 : 13) ; (the same as βεβαπτισμένον ὑπὸ μέθης, *baptized* by drunkenness, *Josephus*) ; " full of wisdom ;" " full of indignation ;" " full of hypocrisy ;" " full of subtilty." The figure is bolder when the filling, and consequent influences, is that of persons. " If first I be somewhat filled with you " (ὑμῶν ἐμπλησθῶ) (Rom. 15 : 24). This figure is so bold that our translation has modified it into " filled with *your company.*" But the same figure, in a more fully sustained form, is presented by Pope, " I am too full of you *not to overflow* upon those I converse with." Here is fulness and its controlling influence. " Why hath Satan filled thy heart to lie to the Holy Ghost ?" (Acts 5 : 3.) " The best commentators seem agreed that ' to fill the heart of any one ' is a Hebrew form of expression signifying *to impel, to incite, to embolden, to persuade* any one " (BLOOMFIELD). " *To take possession of ;* ἐπλήσθην *to be filled with, i. e., to be wholly occupied with,* TO BE WHOLLY UNDER THE INFLUENCE OF anything ; πεπληρωμένους πορνείᾳ 'filled with (= wholly under the influence of) fornication' " (Rom. 1 : 29) (ROBINSON, Lex.). Compare with πεπληρωμένους πορνείᾳ the parallel phrase εἰς πορνείαν βαπτίζουσι (CLEM. ALEX.) ; and can any one doubt that these phrases (starting from the diverse points of *fulness* and *withinness*) do meet together in the same ultimate conception, to wit, " *to be wholly under the influence of* " FORNICATION ? " To be *filled with* fornication," and " to be *baptized into* fornication," is a diversity of form expressive of unity in effect. Hence we have additional proof of the correctness of the " conclusion " in Classic Baptism, that the secondary use of βαπτίζω expresses *to be wholly under the influence of* anything, which conclusion was established in Judaic Baptism, with specific application to ceremonial *purification ;* and exemplified in Johannic Baptism as bearing on *spiritual* purification ; and is now shown to be its exclusive use in Christian Baptism as related to the righteousness, the atonement, and the reconciliation of Christ, in their bearing upon his redeemed people : 1. Really, by the Holy Ghost ; 2. Symbolly, by ritual water. Satan is " the Father of lies," and when he fills the heart his influence is shown by lies. " I have filled him with the Spirit of God " (Exod. 31 : 3) ; " filled with the Spirit " (Ephes. 5 : 18) ; " filled with the Holy Ghost " (Acts 4 : 8) ; " men full of the Holy Ghost " (Acts 6 : 3) = " Completely animated and supported by the influence of the Holy Ghost " (BLOOMFIELD). This figure, by which controlling influence is expressed by *fulness,* is more common and less impressive than that which is derived from putting one thing within another thing, especially one person within another person ; but while differing in their origin, and in shades of significance, as well as the measure of their power, still they are entirely analogous as to their general end, namely, giving expression to a controlling influence. When Peter, at Pentecost, denied that he and his associates were "full of new wine," and thus under its influence = "drunken," declaring that he and they were "full of the Holy Ghost," being "*baptized* by the Holy Ghost," according to the promise of the Saviour and the prophecy of Joel, he admits that he and they are under some controlling influence ; but he denies that it is such as comes from the fulness of wine, and affirms that it is such as comes from the *fulness*, or the *baptism*, of the HOLY GHOST, which terms, as expressive in general of controlling influence, are entirely equivalent expressions.

And as the verb to baptize has here (according to universal admission) nothing to do with effecting a baptism into *water*, so it has just as little to do with any such thing anywhere else in the New Testament. A baptism "into Christ" has no more to do with a baptism into *water*, than has a heart "full of Satan" to do with a heart full of *water*. A baptism "into Paul" has no more to do with a baptism into *water*, than Paul's being "filled with his friends" at Rome has to do with his being *filled with the water* of the Tiber. The water in ritual baptism no more depends for its manner of use upon βαπτίζω, than does the face depend for its reflection from a mirror, upon that mirror being in its form a circle, an oblong, or a square. These two things (βαπτίζω and the manner of using the water) no more stand, in Scripture, conjoined with each other by grammatical or logical relation, than do the earth and the moon stand in creation conjoined by a suspension bridge.

BAPTISM INTO CHRIST INVOLVES THE ASSURED HOPE OF
RESURRECTION AND ETERNAL LIFE.

1 CORINTHIANS 15 : 29.

Τί ποιήσουσιν οἱ βαπτιζόμενοι ὑπὲρ τῶν νεκρῶν, εἰ ὅλως νεκροί οὐκ ἐγείρωνται.

"What shall they do who are baptized over the dead, if the dead rise
not at all? why, then, are they baptized over the dead?"

The Baptism.

The embarrassment in the interpretation of this passage does
not arise so much from difficulty in determining the nature of the
baptism, as in determining the nature of the relation between the
baptism and τῶν νεκρῶν.

There is no reason, so far as I am aware, for referring this
baptism to that which is effected by the Holy Spirit. There is
no aspect in which such baptism brings into relation with "the
dead."

There is no sufficient reason for identifying this baptism with
the baptism of "suffering." Such baptism has no place in the
New Testament except in connection with the atoning sufferings
of Christ. There is, indeed, mention of suffering in the context,
but not so as to identify it with this baptism.

We must accept it as referring to ritual baptism received in a
time of persecution, when, as stated in the immediately succeeding verse, the life of an avowed Christian was "in jeopardy every
hour."

Ὑπὲρ τῶν νεκρῶν.

The precise relation between this baptism and "the dead"
may be due to some local historical fact, not fully stated and
which may, now, be forever beyond our reach. The form of the
phraseology βαπτίζω ὑπὲρ does not originate in the verb and must
be due to some cause independent of it.

The burden of the context, preceding and succeeding, is the
resurrection of the dead and eternal life through the Lord Jesus
Christ as assured doctrines of Christianity; in immediate contact with this baptism ὑπὲρ νεκρῶν we have a statement that Christians are hourly in peril of death; and the last verse of the
chapter exhorts to steadfastness and unmovableness amid encompassing dangers. While the argument of the Apostle de-

velops a great and universal truth of Christianity, still, it is evident that it has a local coloring from facts then existing at Corinth. And our interpretation of the language so far as it is due to those facts cannot be more certain than is our knowledge of those facts. I have no certain, detailed knowledge of them and can, therefore, offer no certain interpretation. So far as the facts appear to be known they seem to justify an interpretation like this: 1. ὑπὲρ τῶν νεχρῶν over the dead; Why are Christians baptized into Christ, who teaches that trials and martyrdom await his disciples, and who have the dead of all generations buried beneath their feet declaring the end of man in this world, unless they believe and have conclusive evidence of a resurrection of the dead and of a blessed immortality through Christ?

The assumption of the badge of Christianity which exposes "every hour" to death reveals a faith in a resurrection which outweighs all appeal to "the dead" as evidence against it; or,

2. τῶν νεχρῶν "the dead;" may refer definitely to some Christians who had been slain at Corinth, and immediately thereupon others had been baptized, if not literally over, yet so as to justify the statement that their baptism was "over the dead" martyrs.

All so baptized could only expect to be slain in like manner; therefore the fitness of the inquiry, "What shall such do, if there be no resurrection?" or,

3. If such interpretation should be thought questionable on the ground of (a generally admitted) exclusive metaphorical use of ὑπὲρ in the New Testament, then, it may be understood as meaning for, in the stead of, "the dead" slain before their eyes, or, day by day, far and wide, because they were Christians.

To join the band of Christians at such a time by baptism, was to step into the place of newly fallen martyrs and to confront that death which they had met.

Such action might well elicit the inquiry, Why do men thus give themselves to death, filling up the places of the slain, unless they believe and do know that in that Christ, into whom they are baptized, they shall have a resurrection from the dead?

Again repeating, that so far as the baptism is concerned, there is no special difficulty; but so far as the relation of the baptism to "the dead" is concerned there is difficulty, because of the want of definite historical knowledge; I offer these interpretations as what may be in the direction of and proximate to the truth.

BAPTISM INTO CHRIST INCLUDES AND CREATES UNITY AMONG
ALL SO BAPTIZED.

1 CORINTHIANS 12 : 13.

’Εν ἑνὶ Πνεύματι ἡμεῖς πάντες εἰς ἓν σῶμα ἐβαπτίσθημεν.

" By one Spirit have we all been baptized into one body."

Translation.

’Εν ἑνὶ Πνεύματι. *By one Spirit* is accepted as the translation
of this phrase by parties of diverse views on the subject of baptism. Not only does Dr. Carson accept the common English
Version, but the Baptist Version, and the Christian (Campbellite)
Baptist Version (by Anderson); it is also accepted by Alexander
Campbell, himself; Luther in his Version translates by *durch;*
Murdoch's Version from the Syriac has "*by* one Spirit;" Commentators and Scholars, generally, agree in this translation. It
is not merely in this passage that ἐν Πνεύματι is translated "*by*
the Spirit," but this accord extends to v. 3 where it appears twice,
" speaking (ἐν) *by* the Spirit of God," " can say (ἐν) *by* the Holy
Ghost;" also, v. 9, twice, " to another (ἐν) *by* the same Spirit;"
thus, in one chapter, we have that phrase which the friends of
dipping in baptism have insisted upon being translated as the
receiving element, and refused to regard as indicative of agency,
acknowledged to be used *five* times instrumentally; and this
when appearing in its accustomed relation to baptism.

It is obvious that such concession bears weightily not to say
controllingly, on the translation and interpretation of this same
phrase in relation to the same subject, elsewhere.

It cannot be said, that a difference is determined here by the
use of διὰ and κατὰ, in connection with ἐν, communicating to it
their distinctive meanings. For each preposition retains its own
peculiarity while uniting in a common issue to which each communicates its own specialty of coloring. Therefore Winer (p.
419) says, " In the parallel clauses in 1 Cor. 12 : 8, 9, spiritual
gifts are referred, by the use of διὰ, κατὰ, ἐν, to the Πνεῦμα from
which they all originate : διὰ, designates the Spirit as mediate
agent; κατὰ, as disposer; ἐν, as container." Thus while each

word has its own distinctive significance, all unite in indicating the *Πνεῦμα* as possessing influential power, and thus lay a basis for the translation "by" as common to them all. Therefore Winer (p. 389) says, "When *ἐν* and *διά* are joined together in the same sentence, *διά* expresses the external means, while *ἐν* points to what was wrought *in* or *on* one's person, and as it were cleaves to him. ... Such passages show that both prepositions are identical as respects the *sense*."

The Ground of the use of ἐν Πνεύματι in Baptism.

It is admitted that *ἐν ἑνὶ Πνεύματι* in this passage, is indicative of agency (as truly as *διά*, or *κατά*) and at the same time indicating such agency as originates in *withinness*. This aspect of agency or influence is profoundly characteristic of the New Testament, especially of that which is divine in its character. It is in this aspect that the Holy Spirit always appears as the Agent in baptism. While Christ is declared to be the Baptizer he is declared so to be on the ground that he, himself, is "*in* the Holy Spirit," and thus invested with the power of the Spirit, does baptize *by* the Spirit. John's prophetic announcement (Matt. 3 : 11) that "He should be *ἐν Πνεύματι Ἁγίῳ* in (= invested with the power of) the Holy Ghost," was verified when (v. 16) the Spirit of God descended upon him ; and John was able to verify his own prophecy : "And John bare record, saying, I saw the Spirit descending from heaven, like a dove, and it abode upon him. He that sent me to baptize with water, the same said unto me, Upon whom thou shalt see the Spirit descending, and remaining on him, the same is he which baptizeth with the Holy Ghost " (John 1 : 32, 33). To convert this statement into a declaration, that Christ should baptize *in* the Holy Ghost, that is, as we are told, should on two occasions (at Pentecost and Cæsarea) confer certain miraculous endowments, is as vapid and incredible in itself, as it is opposed to the whole course of Scripture prophecy, history, and forms of language.

The descent of the Holy Spirit on any one (in Old Testament or New Testament) is invariably to confer some gift and to qualify for some duty. It was so in this case. And from this moment, and in all his utterances and acts even until " he (*διά Πνεύματος αἰωνίος*) through the eternal Spirit offered himself without spot to God " on the Cross, he was ever "*in* the Holy Ghost." That this descent was personal to Christ, and the prophetic anointing for his work (Is. 61 : 1) is evident from the declaration of John, " God giveth not the Spirit by measure unto him " (John 3 : 34), and from his own declaration (Luke 4 : 18), " The Spirit of the Lord is upon me ;" also, from the declaration immediately after the descent of the Spirit (Matt. 4 : 1), " Then was Jesus led up (ὑπὸ) by the Spirit into the wilderness ;" also (Luke 4 : 14), " And Jesus returned from the wilderness (ἐν) *in* the power of the Spirit ;" and, again, from his own declaration (Matt. 12 : 28), " If I (ἐν) *in* the Spirit of God, cast out devils ;" if, now, to this be added the historical narrative of the execution of this baptism in that case related in Acts 2 : 33, " Having received of the Father the promise of the Holy Ghost, he hath shed forth this, which ye now see and hear," the proof is absolute, that ἐν τῷ Πνεύματι relates to the personal condition of the Lord Jesus, as qualifying Him to baptize others by the Holy Ghost imparted unto them.

All of which is grammatically confirmed by the presence (actual or by ellipsis) of both ἐν and εἰς in New Testament baptisms ; under which circumstances no example can be found in which ἐν indicates the complement of βαπτιζω ; nor yet when it stands alone, fulfilling this office with the active form of the verb.

The ground of the use of ἐν τῷ Πνεύματι (as also of ἐν Χριστῷ in CHRIST) " *in* THE SPIRIT," is the influence inseparable from *within-ness*, where one thing is enveloped in another thing. Generally it is the inclosing substance that influences the inclosed ; sometimes it is the reverse, as where " a little leaven is hid in three measures of meal." Both forms of influence are freely used in Scripture. Christians are said to be *in* CHRIST and Christ in *them ;* " There is no condemnation to them that are (ἐν) *in Christ Jesus*" (Rom. 8 : 1) ; " Christ (ἐν) *in you* the hope of glory." So, it is said of the Spirit ; " If the Spirit of God *dwell in you* " (Rom. 8 : 9), " For David said (ἐν τῷ Πνεύματι τῷ Ἁγίῳ) in *the Holy Ghost* " (Mark 12 : 36). This withinness is for the sake of influence. " If *the* SPIRIT of him that raised up Jesus from the dead *dwell in you*, he that raised up Christ from the dead, shall quicken, also, your mortal bodies (διὰ) *by his* SPIRIT that *dwelleth in* you."

There are some who prefer translating " For *in* one Spirit are we all baptized into one body." This is not objectionable so long as ἐν is regarded as pointing out the origin and thus indicating the baptizing power ; but if it should be used to indicate (against εἰς) the ideal element of the baptism, it must be rejected.

Interpretation.

Dr. Pusey (p. 166) says: " 'For in one Spirit were we all baptized into one body,' showing that to be baptized into Christ is to
be baptized in the One Spirit; and neither is the baptism of
Christ without the Spirit, nor is there a baptism of the Spirit
without the baptism instituted by Christ. . . . There is no distinction, as if some were baptized into 'the outward body of professing believers,' as men speak, others into the invisible and
mystical body of Christ, the true Church; some baptized with
water, others with the Spirit; we were *all*, St. Paul says, 'baptized
into one body in One Spirit;' so then, if any had not been baptized in the One Spirit, neither would they have been of the one
body."

Dr. Pusey employs the phrase, "the baptism of Christ" to
denote ritual baptism with water. This is unscriptural. "The
baptism of Christ" can, scripturally, denote nothing but that
baptism which is effected by the Holy Ghost and the administration of which is limited to Christ—"He that cometh after me is
mightier than I, *he* shall baptize you with the Holy Ghost." The
Lord Jesus Christ is especially declared in Scripture never to
have baptized with water. It was wholly foreign from his character to act through shadows and symbols. His acts and his
gifts were realities. The ritual use of water was but a symbol of
the baptism by the Holy Ghost. So John declares by the great
gulf by which he separates them; and so Christ declares by re-
serving to himself the one and committing to his disciples the
other. But these Dr. Pusey confounds; while the teaching of
Scripture and the facts of their administration prove them to be
wholly distinct. While Dr. Pusey conjoins what the Scriptures
separate; he separates what the Scriptures conjoin. He divides
the baptism under consideration into two, by converting the
agency (ἐν ἑνὶ Πνεύματι) into a distinct baptism. There is nothing
said about two baptisms; but "all being in" (= under the influence of) "One Spirit, are," thereby, "baptized into one body."

The introduction of ritual water is without authority by any
word of Scripture, and is, as much, without need from the nature
of the case; the Holy Spirit alone being entirely competent to
effect the baptism announced without any co-operating influence
of water.

21

Dr. Carson says: " In 1 Cor. 12 : 13 it is taken for granted, all who are baptized belong to the body of Christ. They who are baptized are supposed already to belong to the body of Christ; and for this reason they are baptized into it. They are by baptism externally united to that body, to which they are internally united by faith. None are here supposed to be baptized upon the expectation, or probability, or possibility, that they may yet belong to that body. They are baptized into the body."

This may be a very good exposition of Dr. Carson's theory of adult baptism and of the constitution of the church; but it can hardly be called a very good exposition or an exposition of any kind, of 1 Cor. 12 : 13. The idea that a ritual baptism is here spoken of, not only has not so much as a sand grain to rest upon, but is in absolute contradiction to the express statement of the text, to wit, that the baptism is effected by the Divine Spirit. But this most positive statement Dr. Carson and friends cannot accept, because they entertain that marvellous idea which teaches, that the great characteristic of the Messiah's coming and kingdom (baptism by the Holy Ghost) is exhausted by the communication of certain extraordinary gifts on two occasions! Therefore the clear statement of inspiration, that every soul made a member of the body of Christ receives the baptism of the Holy Spirit, must be rejected, and its place supplied by a dipping into water.

Professor Pepper (B. and C., p. 21) seems to admit that this may be *spiritual* baptism; also (p. 28) that *repentance* may be baptism of the Spirit.

R. Ingham (Christian Baptism, London, p. .7) says: " Through the operation, under the guidance, and in the possession of one Spirit, are we all baptized into one body."

Πάντες.

The Apostle makes a universal statement so far as those are concerned who do " by the Holy Ghost call Jesus, Lord." All such are by v. 3 declared to be " ἐν Πνεύματι ‘Αγίῳ, in = under the influence of the Holy Ghost." This use of ἐν Πνεύματι ‘Αγίῳ in v. 3 appears to be the ground of its use in v. 12; if οὐδεὶς, " *no one*, can call Jesus, the Lord, except ἐν Πνεύματι ‘Αγίῳ," then πάντες, *all* who call him the Lord, are *in* = under the influence of the Holy Ghost, and " have been baptized into the name of the Lord Jesus" by this Divine Agent. Now, it is "all" of such individual persons who, being ἐν Πνεύματι ʿΑγίῳ in = under the influence of the Holy Ghost, made subject to the LORDship of Christ, and " saved from their sins" by JESUS; in other words, having been made individually regenerate by the baptism of the Holy Spirit, they are prepared to receive a farther baptism by the distribution of varied and related gifts from " the one and the selfsame Spirit, who divideth to every one severally as He will." By such gifts to all (the one supplementary of the other) a unity, one interdependent whole, is established; and as "all" the individual members are "in" = under the influence of, controlled by, "one Spirit," they are perfected by varied endowments in their relations to one another, and in their common relation to Christ their head, and thus are ἐν ἑνὶ Πνεύματι ἡμεῖς πάντες εἰς ἓν σῶμα ἐβαπτίσθημεν.

This baptism of unification, by the distribution of appropriate and varied gifts to every member of the body of Christ, as distinguished from the baptism of regeneration, which unites the individual soul to Christ and makes participant in his redemption, should cause no surprise; it is as to its nature and end precisely that baptism which the Apostles received at Pentecost. The Apostles had before received that baptism of the Spirit which gives repentance and faith and a regenerate nature; they now receive that baptism of gifts which will fit them for their place, as Apostles, in the "one body of which Christ is the Head."

As the Pentecost baptism of the Apostles was not the baptism of impenitent sinners " into Christ," but a baptism of gifts, conferred upon those who were already ἐν Πνεύματι, " for the edification of the body of Christ," so, also, the baptism announced to the Corinthians was not a baptism for those who (not being ἐν Πνεύματι ʿΑγίῳ) " call Jesus accursed," but a baptism of gifts to all, even the least, in the body of Christ, perfecting all in every one.

This work of double baptism (of the individual " into Christ," and of " all into ONE BODY") will the Holy Spirit carry on among " Jews and Gentiles," until this wondrous work shall be done by the consummating baptism of the redeemed of all ages and of all nations " into the Name of the Father, and of the Son, and of the Holy Ghost."

BAPTISM WITH WATER, THE SHADOW OF ESSENTIAL TRUTH, IS
WORTHLESS IN COMPARISON WITH BAPTISM BY THE
HOLY GHOST, WHICH EFFECTS THAT TRUTH.

1 CORINTHIANS 1:17.

Οὐ γὰρ ἀπέστειλέ με Χριστὸς βαπτίζειν ἀλλ᾽ εὐαγγελίζεσθαι.

"For Christ sent me not to baptize, but to preach the Gospel."

Interpretation.

When Paul says, Christ did not send me to baptize ritually, but to preach the gospel, through which by the Holy Ghost the soul is baptized really, he means to speak comparatively, and to teach: 1. Ritual baptism does not enter as an essential into the gospel; 2. Ritual baptism is an essential appendage to the gospel, but whatever may be its value, it has no value in comparison with the gospel; and must be esteemed as subordinate to the gospel. So that, if ever the gospel and its worth, should come into antagonism with the rite and its worth, the gospel must be acknowledged as having an unapproachable supremacy over the rite. Therefore, while the administration of the rite was included in Paul's commission, it occupied so subordinate a position (consequent and dependent upon the preaching of the gospel) that he could most truthfully say, " My mission is to preach the gospel and not to administer ritual baptism. Which is only a ritual exhibition of the spiritual result of the gospel as blessed by the Holy Ghost in purifying the soul from sin."

This view of Paul concerning the nature of ritual baptism and its relations to the gospel are not, by any means, the views of all others.

There are some (Patrists and others) who believe, that ritual baptism is *the* agency by which the soul is regenerated, its sins washed away, and incorporation is effected in the spiritual body of Christ.

On what grounds these can suppose Paul to deny, that such work did lie within his mission, I cannot imagine.

There are others (Alexander Campbell and friends) who believe, that ritual baptism stands in the same relation to the remission of sins, as does Repentance toward God, and faith toward our Lord Jesus Christ.

Whether this class undertakes to separate remission of sins from "the gospel," or whether they would say, Repentance and faith have nothing more to do with "the gospel" than has ritual baptism, and that Paul might as properly have said, I was not sent to preach repentance and faith, as he said that he was not sent to baptize, I do not know. Or if, when Repentance for sin with its accessories, and faith in the Redeemer, as Lord and God ("my Lord and my God"), and as Jesus (*Saviour*, by righteousness and atonement), and as Christ (*Anointed*, prophet, priest, and king), whether, when these were eliminated from the gospel, they would undertake to declare how much was left of the gospel for Paul to preach, I cannot tell. But if ritual baptism is *for* the remission of sins, how it happened that Paul should be sent to the Gentile world with a commission in which "*for* the remission of sin" was left out, must be a marvel.

There are yet others (Profs. Pepper, Curtis, and friends of the theory generally) who believe, that Christian baptism is a dipping into water, exclusively, imperatively, and divinely appointed, being ordained as the door of the Church, the essential antecedent and prerequisite to the Communion Table, the *sine qua non* to the existence of a regular, true, and lawful church. This dipping into water, we are informed, is unspeakably glorious — "Where through the transparent drapery, the outward garment of profession, shines the rich vesture of a living faith within, the whole assumes a symbolic lustre and magnificence, sufficient fully to justify the warmest eulogium of the Christian. Not too ecstatic to be applied to it is the language of the Prophet when he says, ' I will greatly rejoice in the Lord, my soul shall be joyful in my God; for he hath clothed me with the garments of salvation, he hath covered me with the robe of righteousness, as a bridegroom decketh himself with ornaments, and as a bride adorneth herself with her jewels.' . . . This divinely appointed confession of Christ" (dipping into water), " animated by a true faith, is a garment which well befits all Christians; ' it becomes the crowned monarch better than his crown.' It can make poverty honorable, decrepitude and old age cheerful, sickness and death happy. It suits all ages and gradations of intellect. What sight on earth so beautiful as to behold the *young* and *lovely* descending into the waters of baptism, yielding up their hearts and lives to the service of the Saviour, 'putting on Christ.' . . . It is a garment that never wears out; but like those shawls of

Cashmere that retain their colors brilliant for successive generations, is unfading and resplendent to the last. . . . This garment
is the uniform, divinely appointed for Christians upon earth. It
contains a significance and mystery that angels desire to look
into, and that shall never be unravelled, until Time shall be no
more, and unto all the saints shall be granted everlastingly to be
clothed in fine linen, clean and white " (Prof. Curtis, pp. 69–73).
Any one who attempts to establish a church, or to enter into the
church, or to sit down at the Lord's table, except under the
sanction of this dipping into water, is an " ignorant perverter,"
and " acts a lie," unless he is so " sincere and ignorant " that he
" cannot be made to know" what he is about (Prof. Pepper, pp.
34, 46). Such " ecstatic eulogy " (with its natural anathema) of
" dipping into water," outrivals the most glowing flights of a
Gregory or a Chrysostom. When we turn to the plain prose of
the Bible and hear Paul say, " I was not sent to baptize (' to dip
into water') but to preach the gospel," these waxen wings melt
and the eulogist above the clouds gets a fall. Paul, the Apostle
to the Gentiles and the founder of churches, not sent to open
" the door of the church" or to give a seat at its Communion
table, by " that only way "—*dipping into water!*

Paul's Commission.

It is worth while to look at Paul's commission for more and
for more important reasons than this statement, that he was not
sent to baptize (" to dip into water").

This commission is found in Acts 26 : 16–18 : " I have appeared unto thee for this purpose, to make thee a minister and a
witness . . . delivering thee from the people and (τῶν ἐθνῶν) the Gentiles, unto whom now (ἀποστέλλω) I send thee, to open their eyes,
and to turn them from darkness to light, and from the power of
Satan unto God, that they may receive forgiveness of sins, and
inheritance among them that are sanctified through faith that is
in me.'

With this Commission before his eyes, the most earnest defender of " dipping into water" as the faith delivered unto the
saints, and the warmest eulogist of its " ecstatic" blessings, will
hardly deny the literal accuracy of Paul when he declares, *dipping
into water* makes no appearance in his Commission, and that he
was made an apostle for a very different purpose, namely, "to

preach the gospel." What is in this Commission? We have:
1. The preaching of the truth ("to open their eyes"); 2. Conviction of error and repentance for sin ("to turn them from darkness to light"); 3. Supreme allegiance to the true God ("to turn them from the power of Satan to God"); 4. Forgiveness of sin to the repentant (τοῦ λαβεῖν ἄφεσιν ἁμαρτιων); 5. Salvation through faith in the Lord Jesus Christ ("inheritance among the sanctified by faith in me"). Is this the gospel? Is it the whole of it? Has "dipping into water," that vital element of the gospel, without which no lawful church can exist, no true church membership can be recognized, no right to eat of the broken body and shed blood of a crucified Saviour can be admitted, has this vital element (*stantis vel cadentis ecclesiæ*) been overlooked in the Commission from the adorable Head of the Church to his personally chosen and commissioned Apostle to the Gentiles? Whether it be through oversight or not, it is most certain that no commission to dip into water was given to Paul by the Lord Jesus Christ. The lack of it, however, does not seem to embarrass Paul. He goes forward to preach a gospel of which dipping into water forms no part, and to found churches into the membership of which "dipping into water" does not constitute "the door" (Pepper, 20–23), and to celebrate the dying love of Christ, all unconscious that "a dipping into water" admits or rejects from doing this in remembrance of the Crucified, under the penalty of "acting a lie."

Whether this element entered into the Commission of the other Apostles any more than into that of Paul, will be considered hereafter. Paul fulfilled his Commission (26 : 19, 20) by preaching—"Repent and turn to God through faith in Christ."

Not to Baptize.

Paul does not deny the obligation, or divine authority, of ritual baptism (however much he might do both as to a dipping into water); but he denies its relative worth; he denies that this rite is a primary element in the gospel, or essential to its perfection of power. It is a divine appendage to the gospel as a help to human infirmity, and is dependent upon the gospel for its value. Prof. Pepper (p. 20) says: "The gospel spoken is the interpretation of the gospel embodied in ordinances." This makes ordinances precede the gospel. Paul teaches the reverse of this.

The gospel is antecedent to its symbols, which are but reflectors of its truths and must be interpreted by them. The gospel in the woman's seed was before Abel's slain lamb. The duty of the Patriarchs was not first to slay lambs, but first to preach the promise, and then expound the bleeding victim by that promise. Salvation to the first born was first promised, then came the slaying of the lamb and the sprinkling of the family door-posts in Egypt.

REPENTANCE AND FAITH THOROUGHLY CHANGE THE CONDITION AND DO THEREBY BAPTIZE THE SOUL.

HEBREWS 6: 2.

βαπτισμῶν διδαχῆς.

" Not laying again the foundation of repentance from dead works, and of faith toward God (baptizings of doctrine), and of the laying on of hands, and of the resurrection of the dead, and of eternal judgment."

Translation.

There is no generally accepted translation or interpretation of this passage. Whether what is about to be offered relieves the difficulties heretofore felt, and bears within it the self-evidencing power of truth, others will determine.

The translations which have been proposed are, in general, these: 1. That which makes all the Genitives to depend on *θεμέλιον* (Murdock, Alford); 2. That which makes all after the first two to depend on *διδαχῆς* (Olshausen, Ebrard); 3. That which supplies *διδαχῆς* before *μετανοίας* and *πίστεως* and makes *βαπτισμῶν* the objective Genitive (Stuart, Kuinoel); 4. That which makes *βαπτισῶν διδάχῆς* belong together (*βαπτισμῶν* the governing noun) and depend on *θεμέλιον* (Winer); 5. That which unites *βαπτισμῶν διδαχῆς* making the former the governing noun, and recognizing the peculiarity in the construction of this phrase (by the absence of the conjunction) as compared with other phrases in the sentence (Bengel); 6. That which connects these words as in the preceding case, but with a different grammatical relation, and makes them, with the following phrase, parenthetical and in apposition with the preceding " repentance " and " faith " (Calvin).

The general objection which has been, reciprocally, made to these several interpretations has been—"unjustifiable departure from the construction."

In the translation which we have proposed making "baptizings of doctrine" in apposition with repentance and faith, and parenthetical, the peculiarity of construction which marks these words, is not only regarded but is effectively used; the normal law as to the Genitive in grammatical construction is observed, and made harmonious throughout the sentence; and the use of the plural form βαπτισμῶν, receives explanation. The only point which seems to need elucidation is, the ground on which "baptisms of doctrine" can be placed in expository apposition with repentance and faith. This belongs to the interpretation and the justifying reason will there be offered.

Interpretation.

βαπτισμῶν. If βαπτισμῶν, as used in this passage, refers to Christian baptism, there must be some reason for it and an adequate explanation of it. A reason is required, because the usage is peculiar in applying this term to denote baptisms in connection with Christianity; it being found nowhere else but in this Epistle, and here but in one other place (9 : 10, διαφόροις βαπτισμοῖς) where it plainly refers to Jewish baptisms = purifyings. This word was in use among the Jews before Christianity, and before John's mission. John introduced a new word (βάπτισμα) which was accepted and perpetuated by Christianity. The Jewish form exhibits the executive action of the verb, baptizing, purifying; the Christian form marks the effect of the verb's action, baptism, purification.

John was sent to declare a baptism essentially different in nature from that designated before his coming by βαπτισμός = a ceremonial purification, and therefore (I think we may say) he adopted another word (βάπτισμα), both because of its essential difference and in order to prevent confusion, conjoining it with μετανοίας, to express in the clearest manner that his baptism (required to welcome the Messiah) was a spiritual purification.

The question returns: Why does Paul in this Epistle depart from his practice in other Epistles and here use βαπτισμῶν? I know of no better reasons to give than these: 1. He is writing to "Hebrews" who are familiar with this word; 2. He was writing

concerning the purifyings of the Law to which the distinctive
popular use and meaning of this word was suitable, and to which
he himself (9 : 10) applies it; 3. The essential difference between
βαπτισμα and βαπτισμός was not such as to prevent their interchange when the use was guarded against error, as is done in
this case by the adjunct διδαχῆς, which removes it entirely from its
popular Jewish use; 4. The noble principle ruling Paul's life—
" And unto the Jews I became as a Jew, that I might gain the
Jews." The plural form of this word, as relating to Christian
baptism, has been an embarrassment. This difficulty is factitious,
not real. It is true, that there is but one Christian baptism ; but
it is not true that there is but one form of words, or one form of
thought, by which that baptism can be expressed. John preached
a baptism εἰς μετάνοιαν, and also a baptism εἰς ἄφεσιν ἁμαρτιῶν.
These baptisms, in relation to each other, have distinctive characteristics, and so regarded are *two* baptisms; but in their common relations to salvation, they are *one* baptism, and John conjoins
them in the βάπτισμα μετανοίας εἰς ἄφεσιν ἁμαρτιῶν. Peter introduces
faith as a co-operative element with repentance in this baptism—
" *Repent* and be baptized (ἐπὶ) *believing upon* the name of Jesus
Christ, εἰς ἄφεσιν ἁμαρτιῶν." Here Repentance and Faith, conjointly, baptize " into the remission of sins."

While a baptism εἰς μετάνοιαν, and a baptism εἰς ἄφεσιν, are distinctive baptisms, as between themselves, they are entirely equivalent baptisms in their relation to the baptism εἰς χριστὸν, which
is the " one baptism " of Christianity. There is no difficulty,
therefore, in the plural form of βαπτισμῶν as expressing the discriminating differences between the doctrines of Repentance and
Faith as received into the soul; so regarded they are two baptisms. As to the point—Can Repentance and Faith baptize;
and do the Scriptures teach that they do baptize? An answer
may be gathered from what has been said in explanation of this
plural form, as, also, from the antecedent results developed in
this Inquiry.

There is nothing in Scripture more explicitly stated, than that
the baptism of John's mission was a baptism due to the " doctrine " of Repentance, preached by him. This baptism was
ritualized, not by a second baptism into *water ;* 1. Because there
is no logical congruity between these things ; 2. Because it would
destroy life; 3. Because the proposed substitute for a baptism
(*a dipping* into water) is no *baptism ;* 4. Because the Scriptures

do not say one word about either a baptism or a dipping into water; but this baptism of the soul by repentance was ritualized in a rite wherein this soul baptism was verbally announced, and pure water, as its symbol, was applied to the body.

This same baptism of the soul by the doctrine of Repentance, taught and received, was inculcated under Christianity (Acts 2 : 38); and the baptism of the soul which is by faith in a crucified Redeemer, is announced in those last words of his—" He that believeth and is baptized shall be saved;" in which words there is no incongruous admixture of faith and ritual water as common and equal ground for salvation, but the declaration of a baptism into Christ by faith, when this doctrine of the Scriptures is received into the soul. The clear doctrine of the Bible is, that Repentance baptizes " into the remission of sins," and Faith baptizes " into Jesus Christ." Therefore it is that Paul declares, that Repentance, which so changes the condition of the soul as to separate it (ἀπὸ νεκρῶν ἔργων) " from dead works;" and Faith, which so changes the condition of the soul as to lead it to turn unto and rest (ἐπὶ θεον) " upon God," are " baptisms of DOCTRINE" = baptizing, purifying agencies cleansing through Christ and uniting to God. If these things be so, then, the apposition between " Repentance and Faith," and " Baptisms of Doctrine," is established; while, at the same time, we have the difference characterizing these two words, as compared with the other members of the sentence, accounted for.

This explanation receives confirmation from the form " Repentance (ἀπὸ νεκρῶν ἔργων) *from dead works,*" which corresponds in structure with the Jewish form " βαπτιζομενος ἀπὸ νεκροῦ *baptized from the dead.*" It is impossible to believe, that Paul writing to Jews familiar with the form " baptized from the dead," and using the form " Repentance from dead works," did not refer to the baptism with which they were familiar, and contrast with it the baptism of Christianity, which is not " from the ceremonial pollution incurred by contact with a *dead body,*" but from the soul pollution incurred by doing and trusting in " dead works."

So, the condensed statement, Faith ἐπὶ θεὸν may justly be regarded as grounded in the Christian form—" Be baptized (ἐπὶ) upon the name of Jesus Christ," which issuing (Acts 2 : 38) immediately, in a baptism into the remission of sins through Christ, has its ultimate issue in the baptism, εἰς θεὸν = " Father, Son, and Holy Ghost."

The suggestion as to the structure of the sentence seems to be confirmed by that which is generally admitted to obtain in 9 : 10 " meats, and drinks, and divers baptizings (ordinances of the flesh) until the time of the reformation." " The term ' carnal ordinances ' does not express something additional to the *meats*, and *drinks*, and *baptizings*, but is another name for the same ritual observances." According to the Greek, the " meats and drinks and divers baptizings " go to compose the " carnal ordinances " (Prof. Wilson, of Belfast). The two passages seem to be quite parallel as to the point at issue, namely, explanatory apposition.

There is also a parallelism between the phrases βαπτισμῶν διδαχῆς and βάπτισμα μετανοίας. The one is in general, a *teaching* baptism, and the other is in particular, a *repentance* baptism. The use of the Genitive is the same in both cases.

Commentators.

CALVIN (*Comm.*) : " Some read them separately, ' of baptisms and of doctrines,' but I prefer to connect them, though I explain them differently from others ; for I regard the words as being in apposition, as grammarians say, according to this form, ' Not laying again the foundation of repentance, of faith in God, of the resurrection of the dead, which is the doctrine of baptisms and of the laying on of hands.' If therefore these two clauses, the doctrine of baptisms and of the laying on of hands, be included in a parenthesis, the passage would run better ; for except you read them as in apposition, there would be the absurdity of a repetition. For what is the doctrine of baptism but what he mentions here, faith in God, repentance, judgment, and the like ?"

BENGEL (*Comm.*) : " Καὶ is not put before βαπτισμῶν ; for three pairs of chief particulars are enumerated, and the second particular in every pair has the conjunction ; but only the third pair is similarly connected ; from which it is also evident, that βαπτισμῶν and διδαχῆς must not be separated. Βαπτισμοὶ διδαχῆς were *baptisms* which were received by those who devoted themselves to the sacred *doctrine* of the Jews ; therefore, by the addition of διδαχῆς, they are distinguished from the other Levitical washings."

In a note to this comment, it is said : " Bengel evidently understands these words as *baptisms of* or *into doctrine*, not as Eng. Vers., the *doctrine of baptisms*—ED."

WINER (p. 192): "Heb. 6:2 is a difficult passage; βαπτισμῶν
διδαχῆς (depending on θεμέλιον) certainly belong together, and
διδαχῆς cannot be torn away so strangely and regarded as the
governing noun to all four Genitives, as Ebrard still maintains.
But the question is, whether we should here admit a transposition for διδαχῆς βαπτισμῶν, as most later expositors do. Such a
transposition, however, would be at variance with the whole
structure of the verse; and if βαπτισμοὶ διδαχῆς is translated doctrinal baptisms, baptisms in connection with instruction, to dis-
tinguish them from the legal baptisms (lustrations) of Judaism,
this appellation is confirmed as distinctively Christian by Matt.
28:19 βαπτίσαντες αὐτούς——διδάσκοντες αὐτούς. Ebrard's objection,
that Christian baptism is distinguished from mere lustrations,
not by instruction, but by the forgiveness of sins and regeneration, amounts to nothing, for Matt. 28 says nothing about the forgiveness of sins." Page 551: "As to placing in particular the
Genitive before the governing noun, careful writers avoid such
arrangement if misapprehension could arise from it. Hence in
Heb. 6:2 βαπτισμῶν διδαχῆς is not for διδαχ. βαπτ., especially as in
the other groups the position of the Genitive is in accordance
with the rule."

ZUINGLI (de Baptis.): "The baptism of John *required* a new
life, and pointed to hope in Christ. And this was the baptism
of doctrine (for both equally baptized with water), the baptism
of Christ *required* nothing else, for he began to preach no otherwise than John—'Repent ye.' Since, then, John's teaching and
Christ's teaching was the same, *it follows that if the baptism of
doctrine was the same, that of the water was the same also.*"

BRENTIUS (Hom. 21, in Ev. Luc.): "The baptism of John is
such as is his teaching and his word."

Clemens Alexandrinus.

Clemens Alex. (Stromata III, 18) presents a remarkably full
and clear case of baptism by teaching. It is as follows: "Ἐκ
σωφροσύνης εἰς πορνείαν βαπτίζουσι, ταῖς ἡδοναῖς καὶ τοῖς πάθεσι χαρίζεσθαι
δογματίζοντες—TEACHING *to indulge in pleasure and lust* they baptize *out of* chastity *into* unchastity."

This passage is conclusive as to the following points: 1. A
baptism is a thorough change of condition; 2. This change of
condition will exhibit the evidence of an assimilation to the char-

acteristic of the baptizing influence, whatever that characteristic
may be; 3. This change of condition is without limitation as to
the nature of the influence effecting it, the manner of its exercise,
or the time of its duration; 4. This change of condition may be
expressed under a form of words (ἐκ, εἰς, βαπτίζω) originating in
physics, without requiring a correspondence, in form, to such
physical use; 5. An ideal baptism expresses a profound reality;
6. The presence of water, actual or imaginary, is unnecessary to
a baptism; 7. TEACHING is capable of *baptizing;* and it will *so
baptize as to exhibit its characteristic in its disciples.* Teaching
that inculcates "the indulgence of pleasure and lust" will baptize
its disciples into impurity; and teaching which enjoins "the
observance of all things whatsoever Jesus Christ has commanded," will baptize its disciples into purity and "into the
name of the Father, and of the Son, and of the Holy Ghost."

COROLLARY. All who accept the baptism of Clemens Alexandrinus, εἰς πορνείαν, must accept the Bible baptism εἰς μετάνοιαν, εἰς
ἄφεσιν, εἰς Χριστὸν Ἰησοῦν, εἰς τὸ ὄνομα τοῦ Πατρὸς, καί. . . . . .

The examination of this passage of Scripture shows that the
statement, that baptisms are effected by doctrinal truths, is a
statement in perfect harmony with the entire scope of Scripture,
is confirmed by the results antecedently reached, while it is itself,
in turn, confirmatory of them.

Since writing the above a translation of the Biblico-Theological
Lexicon of New Testament Greek, by Hermann Cremer, Professor
of Theology in the University of Greifswald (Edinburgh, 1872)
has been published. The following quotation s. v. βαπτίζω bears
upon the interpretation above given to the passage before us:
"The baptism of John is styled κατ'. ἐξ. the βάπτισμα μετανοίας; we
might accordingly designate Christian baptism βάπτισμα πίστεως,
coll. Acts 19:45, Acts 8:12, 13. . . . Heb. 6:2, βαπτισμῶν διδαχή
as a constituent of the ὁ τῆς αρχῆς τοῦ Χυ. λόγος. Accordingly it is
less probable that the writer referred to Christian baptism in distinction from O. T. lustrations, than to the difference and relation
between Christian baptism and that of John,—a difference which
would often need to be discussed."

There is no need for introducing the baptism of John, distinctively, since the baptism of Repentance and the baptism of Faith
alike belong to Christianity.

Cremer also says: The *specialty* of a baptism depends upon
the relation into which candidates are brought *as denoted by* εἰς

and its REGIMEN. " *Εἰς is invariably used in an* IDEAL *sense.*" Such is the doctrine of this Inquiry. The acceptance of this doctrine carries with it all the essential results of the Inquiry, when consistently carried out.

ANTITYPE BAPTISM SAVES THE SOUL, AND IS BAPTISM BY THE HOLY GHOST.

1 PETER 3: 21.

Ὃ καὶ ἡμᾶς ἀντίτυπον νῦν σώζει βάπτισμα (οὐ σαρκὸς, ἀπόθεσις ῥύπου, ἀλλὰ συνειδήσεως ἀληθῆς, ἐπερώτημα εἰς Θεὸν), δι' ἀναστάσεως Ἰησοῦ Χριστοῦ.

" By which, also, antitype Baptism now saves us (not of the flesh, the putting away of filth, but of a good conscience, the requirement toward God), through the resurrection of Jesus Christ."

The Text.

The reading of this passage is not settled. Knapp introduces v. 21 with ὃ καὶ, and places ᾦ καὶ, in the margin. Bloomfield reverses this arrangement. The Codex Sinaiticus omits both ὃ and ᾦ, commencing the verse with καὶ.

These diversities are not unimportant. If the reading ὃ be accepted then a relation is established with " water" in the preceding verse and, also (though not with the same facility), with ἀντίτυπον βάπτισμα. If ᾦ καὶ be adopted then its relation is naturally formed with the ἐν ᾦ καὶ of v. 19, and the reference is to the Holy Spirit, and necessarily stamps a' like character on ἀντίτυπον βάπτισμα. The omission of the Codex Sinaiticus throws its whole weight against any reference to " water" in v. 20, and as strongly favors the reference to the Holy Spirit, because with the reading which it presents no connection can be established between ἀντίτυπον βάπτισμα and the flood water ; while its connection with the Holy Spirit, as the baptism effected by Him, becomes imperative.

Translation.

The translation given above (especially that in parenthesis) is not given as that which must be, but which may be, correct. The parenthetic statement is evidently explanatory of the saving power of baptism. It is cautionary against possible error. The Scriptures speak of two baptisms, a symbol baptism of the body, effected by water, and a real baptism of the soul, effected by the Holy Ghost. The Apostle says, antitype baptism which saves, is not that baptism which relates to the body, cleansing from cere-monial or physical defilement, but that baptism which relates to the soul and reaches the accusing or excusing conscience, effect ing what God asks, spiritual purity.

'Επερώτημα is the translation by the Septuagint of the Hebrew *asking* (Eng. " demand") in Dan. 4 : 14, where Gesenius says, " the subject of inquiry," is intended. What God asks for, he requires.

He asks for and requires a good conscience. Paul (Acts 23 : 1) says, " I have lived with all good conscience (τῷ Θεῷ) unto God ;' 24 : 16, " I exercise myself always to have a conscience void of offence toward God ;" and Peter (1, 2 : 19) says, " This is thank-worthy if a man for conscience toward God." These two things are certain : 1. God requires a good conscience; 2. Baptism by the Holy Ghost gives a good conscience, and nothing else does. This lays the foundation for the representation of " a good con-science " as the result of " antitype baptism," and herein meeting the ἐπερώτημα εἰς Θεὸν. Any translation of this passage which makes it to hinge on water (flood water, rite water) is essentially faulty.

Interpretation.

The Baptist Version interprets the water of the flood as the type and the water of rite baptism as the antitype : " Eight souls were saved through water ; which in an antitype, immersion, now saves us also ;" this is, in every aspect, an impossible interpre-tation.

There is no element of congruity between the office of the water of the flood and the office of the water of ritual baptism to con-stitute the one a type of the other. The resemblance can only be in the office, for to make simple water the type of simple water would be absurd. But the office of water in the flood is that of destruction, and to this there is no counterpart in the office of water in baptism. If a saving office for water is sought in its upbearing the ark, and the indication of such function is claimed to be expressed by δι' ὕδατος, the error is twofold : 1. It robs the ark of its saving office to give it to the destroying flood ; and, 2.

It misinterprets δι' ὕδατος which is, properly, expressive of this destructive tendency. The flood did upbear the ark; but this was not its office. Its mission was solely one of death. But the wisdom of God devised a plan whereby safety might be evolved amid destruction. This he did by the introduction of a new and diverse agency having such a quality that it could overcome and rise above the agency for destruction. This was the ark, possessed of a buoyancy which enabled it to overcome the whelming tendency of the waters, and bear in safety " the few " who without its protecting power would have been engulfed in the deadly flood. Was it the Nile water or the bulrush cradle which saved the infant Moses?

The δι' ὕδατος expresses the peril of the waters, and thus magnifies the saving power of the ark. It has in this respect, the same power as διὰ πυρός in 1 Cor. 3 : 15, saved yet so as "through fire ;" that is, " saved with *great difficulty.* That such is the sense of this (as it seems) *adagial* phrase, most Commentators are agreed " (Bloomfield). Peter, in this same epistle (1 Peter 1 : 7–9), illustrates this usage : " Your faith . . . tried (διὰ πυρὸς) through fire . . . the end salvation of your souls." Here " through fire " represents exposure to the extremest perils, while faith has a divine quality able to endure them and save its possessor from them. The ark passed through the extreme and prolonged perils of the flood but saved (δι' ὕδατος) all who were in it, through the goodness, and wisdom, and power of God, who devised it for this very purpose, namely, *to overcome the destructive character* of the waters. If saving power is attributed to the flood water and we ask, Saved from what? this dilemma emerges, namely : *The flood water saved from the flood water.* And if relief is sought by calling on the ark for help, it is a confession that the case, as put, sinks like lead into the waters.

A second radical objection to making the water of the flood a type of the water of ritual baptism, is this : The water in ritual baptism is itself (not *a type,* but) *a symbol,* it cannot therefore be the basis for a type ; nor can it make any claim to the title of an " antitype."

" A type is a symbol appointed by God to adumbrate something higher in the future, which is called antitype. The true type looks forward to the distant future. A pure symbol may represent something which now exists " (Prof. Barrow, Comp. of the Bible, p. 580). If it were possible for so incongruous a thing

22

as a destroying flood to be a type of ritual baptism, still, the mere
ritual, shadow character of this ordinance would preclude it. No
figure can be the basis of a figure.

Type Salvation—Antitype Salvation.

What Peter deduces from his reference to the flood is: 1. *Salvation*—"were saved;" 2. Salvation *by the ark*—"wherein eight
souls were saved;" 3. Salvation in the ark, *by God*—"God
waited" (kept back the destroying waters) "while the ark was a
preparing," as the means of salvation.

Peter says, this *type* salvation of eight souls foreshadows an
antitype salvation: 1. In ANTITYPE *baptism*, "which saves us;"
2. In its adequate and divine method (1) $\varepsilon \iota \varsigma$ $\mu \varepsilon \tau \acute{a} \nu o \iota a \nu$ ("into repentance"); (2) $\varepsilon \iota \varsigma$ $\check{a} \varphi \varepsilon \sigma \iota \nu$ $\acute{a} \mu a \rho \tau \iota \omega \nu$ "into the remission of sins;"
(3) $\varepsilon \iota \varsigma$ $X \rho \iota \sigma \tau \grave{o} \nu$ "into Christ;" which places the souls of the re-
deemed $\dot{\varepsilon} \nu$ $X \rho \iota \sigma \tau \tilde{\omega}$ "*in* CHRIST," as their ark of safety; 3. In its
divine Executor, $\tilde{\omega}$ $\varkappa a \iota$ " by WHOM antitype baptism " (which is the
work of the Holy Spirit) "saves us, through the resurrection of
Jesus Christ," who being put to death in the flesh, but quickened
by *the* SPIRIT ($\tau \tilde{\omega}$ $\Pi \nu \varepsilon \acute{v} \mu a \tau \iota$), through whom ($\delta \iota \grave{a}$ $\Pi \nu \varepsilon \acute{v} \mu a \tau o \varsigma$ $a \iota \omega \nu \acute{\iota} o v$)
he had offered himself without spot to God, this same divine
Spirit having dwelt in Christ living, and watched over his slain
body in the tomb, does now shut up the windows of heaven, close
the fountains of the deep, dry up the imperilling flood waters,
quicken the dead, and bring forth alive again the Ark of our salvation triumphant through the power of God over all perils, and
all his people saved in Him, as attested and sealed "by his resurrection." Therefore, "ANTITYPE BAPTISM, *wrought by the* SPIRIT
of GOD, SAVES *us through the resurrection of* JESUS CHRIST."

Carson and Gill.

Carson (pp. 388–413) says: "Dr. Miller dismisses the argument from 1 Peter 3 : 20, 21, on the ground that there was no
immersion of Noah and his family. With as great propriety the
learned gentleman may deny that a man in a tomb is buried, because he is covered with a coffin. What! Noah not immersed
when buried in the waters of the flood? Are there no bounds to
perverseness? Will men say everything rather than admit the
mode of an ordinance of Christ which is contrary to the commandments of men? What could be a more impressive burial in water,

than to be in the ark when it was floating? As well might it be said that a person is not buried in earth, when lying in his coffin covered with earth. The ordinance of baptism and the salvation of Noah by water, have the most lively resemblance. Noah and his family *were saved by being buried in the water of the flood;* and after the flood *they emerged as rising from the grave.*"

No wonder Dr. Miller, the Princeton Professor, "dismissed *the argument*" (?) contained in words like these. He would have shown that he had lost his senses had he undertaken soberly to listen to the statement, that "Noah and his family were saved by being buried in the water of the flood, and emerging as rising from the grave." I will venture to say, that *one, two, three, four thousand years* rolled away after the flood waters rolled away, before such a conceit ever entered any man's brain.

If Dr. Carson had said, "God saved Noah and his family by converting them into fishes, and burying them in the waters of the flood, whence, on the subsidence of the waters, they emerged as rising from the grave, fully restored to their humanity," he would find just about as many to believe "the argument" (and just about the same persons) as believe the salvation = burial = resurrection "argument."

Dr. Carson is a man of ability, in certain directions of unusual ability, of respectable learning, of honesty, of piety, of deep convictions, of self-confidence which holds a world in arms no worthy match for himself alone, and, for all these reasons combined, a man of power; but on the difficulties of water-dipping, and burial, and resurrection, he is not a sober-minded man. Had he been he would not have written about the *dipping* of Noah and his family by burial in the flood for a year (more or less), followed by a living resurrection; nor of the *dipping* of the millions of Israel by a burial-march and resurrection in the empty space of the Red Sea; nor of the *dipping* of the Apostles "in sound like wind," with burial under cloven tongues (!) and resurrection, I know not how. Sanity never went farther in extravagance.

Gill (Body of Divinity, pp. 642) says: "This dipping into water may be concluded from the various figurative and typical baptisms spoken of in Scripture, as, 1. From the waters of the flood, which Tertullian calls the baptism of the world, and of which the Apostle Peter makes baptism the Antitype, 1 Peter 3:21. The ark in which Noah and his family were saved by water was God's ordinance; it was made according to the pattern he gave to Noah, as baptism is; and as that was the object of the scorn of men, so is the ordinance of baptism rightly administered; and as it is represented a burial when Noah and his family were shut up in it, so baptism; and when the fountains of the great deep were broken up below, and the windows of heaven were opened above, the ark with those in it were, as it were, covered and immersed in water; and so was a figure of baptism by immersion; and as there were none but adult persons in the ark, who were saved by water in it, so none but adult persons are the proper subjects of baptism."

This is a fair specimen of the reasoning which seeks to convert Christian baptism into water-dipping. It is composed of some dozen of lines; let us see how its errors compare with them in number. 1. "This dipping into water." There is not one word of Scripture for a dipping into water as Christian baptism. 2. "The various figurative and typical baptisms spoken of in Scripture." There are no such "various" things in Scripture. Baptism "into Moses" is the only type baptism mentioned in Scripture, and in it must be found all the type dipping, burial, and resurrection, known to inspiration. 3. "Which Tertullian calls the baptism of the world." Tertullian's world baptism is no more like Gill's baptism than is a horse-chestnut like a chestnut horse. 4. "The Apostle Peter makes baptism the antitype of the waters of the flood." This is pure error. 5. "The ark was God's ordinance." Yes, for salvation; then *the waters of the flood were not* God's ordinance for salvation. 6. "The ark was made according to the pattern, as baptism is." The pattern of the ark is in Genesis, cubits and inches; where is the baptism pattern? 7. "As the ark was the scorn of men, so is baptism rightly administered." Of scorn for the ark, I know nothing, as the Bible says nothing. Of the sophistry which declares scorn *for man's inventions*, to be scorn *for God's ordinance*, I know something, for Dr. Gill exhibits it. Dr. Gill and friends say: "For a thousand years baptism was rightly administered;" and yet, through all that time, "babies" were baptized; men and women were baptized naked; oil, and salt, and spittle, were used in baptism; and baptismal regeneration taught, to reject which Dr. Pusey says (p. 39) "is the scarcely disguised contempt of an ordinance of our Saviour;" all which things Dr. Gill "scorns." Does he therefore "*scorn God's ordinance* rightly administered?" When we are told, in vindication of their practice, by those who "administer baptism rightly," that "there is no difference between βάπτω and βαπτίζω;" and also "that βαπτίζω means dip and nothing but dip through all Greek literature," we hold such assertions in light esteem. Do we therefore "scorn God's ordinance?" When we are told ὕδατι βαπτίζω means "to dip into water," but βαπτίζω εἰς μετανοίαν does not mean "to baptize into repentance," we hold such assertions in light esteem. Do we therefore "scorn God's ordinance?" When we are told "*dipping into* water is the door of the church, is necessary to sitting down at the table of the Head of the Church, is essential to the existence of the true church," we hold such assertions in light esteem. Do we therefore "scorn God's ordinance?" When we are told that we "knowingly obscure God's truth," that we "need honesty and not light," that we "act a lie" in sitting down to the Lord's Table, unless "sincerely ignorant" and "incapable of being made to know the truth," we hold such assertions in light esteem. Do we therefore "scorn God's ordinance?"

There are some things which may justly be scorned. Among these are sophistical pleading by raising false issues when true issues cannot be met, and flinging reproaches at character when argument cannot be answered. Is such scorn, also, "scorn at God's ordinance?" 8. "When Noah and his family were shut up in the ark, it is represented as a burial." By Dr. Gill, not by Moses. 9. "So Baptism." Yes, just so; that is, by neither word nor thought. 11. "The ark and those in it *were, as it were*, covered and immersed in water." That is to say by admission, what in the (claimed) antitype is its alpha and omega (*sine qua non*), has no existence in the type, but only a "were as it were." Such a type is fashioned after no other type that ever was. 12. "And so was a figure of baptism by immersion." It might be well to find something that would be a figure of baptism by *dipping*. The ark, not dipped into the waters but rising above them, is not a good figure of "the act commanded" ("the ark was made according to *the pattern*"); nor was the rain sprinkled or poured (without covering or immersing) for forty days and forty nights, a good "figure of baptism by *immersion*." 13. "None but adult persons in the ark who were *saved* by water, in it." Dr. Gill complains that those after whom he patterns in "baptism rightly administered," believed that souls were "saved by water;" and regular Baptists find fault with Campbellite Baptists because they believe that water is necessary "*for* the remission of sins;" and yet he says, *salvation* was "by the type water!" How has this salvation become a vanishing quantity in the Antitype? 14. "So none but adult persons are the proper subjects of baptism." This logic is remarkable. "None but adults *saved* by water; therefore, none but adults *the proper subjects* of water baptism." What has become, in the conclusion, of the "salvation" which was in the premise? But who were these "none but adults in the Ark?" Unbelievers (Noah excepted), if we take the Bible statement (Gen. 7:1). Therefore, as unbelievers were "saved by water," so unbelievers are *the proper subjects* of water baptism. But again: Who were these "none but adults in the ark"? They were a *family*, the Head of which was by faith in covenant relation with God, who, for the father's sake, embraced the children, though unbelieving, within the gracious covenant and "saved them by *water;*" therefore, the children of a believing parent (though themselves unbelieving) are *the proper subjects of water* baptism. Those who handle sharp tools should be careful to note whether they may not have two edges.

This statement of Dr. Gill has an error for every line; and no wonder, for "as is the root so are the branches."

Antitype Baptism is Salvation

GREGORY NAZIANZEN, II, 368, on Baptism, says: "But we being twofold, I mean spiritual and corporeal, the one by nature visible and the other invisible; purification is, also, twofold, by (διά) water and Spirit; the one received visibly and corporeally, the other concurring invisibly and incorporeally; the one (τυπικοῦ) typical, the other (ἀληθινοῦ) real, and purifying the depths." Neither Gregory N. nor any other Patrist believed that there was any *real* ("true") baptism in dipping into water.

DIDYMUS ALEX. XXXIX, 716: Having quoted Ezek. 36:22, "I will *sprinkle* clean water upon you and ye shall be clean from all your sins;" and, also, Ps. 50:8, "*Sprinkle* me with hyssop and I shall be clean; wash me and I shall be whiter than snow;" thus explains: "For the *sprinkling* with hyssop was Judaic purification, which is continued by them to the present time; but 'whiter than snow' denotes Christian illumination, which means baptism. . . . And Peter, that he may show in his first Epistle, that if baptism, which was formerly *in shadow* (ἐν σκιᾷ) saved, much more that which was *in reality* (ἐν ἀληθείᾳ) immortalizes

and deifies us, wrote thus: ' Antitype baptism now saves us.' "
Any one who ventures to say, that Didym. Alex. believed that
dipping into water was antitype baptism ἐν ἀληθεία, thereby for-
feits claim to patristic lore. " *Baptism* in shadow " (type baptism) was effected by *sprinkling* with hyssop. "Baptism in reality " (antitype Baptism) was effected by the Holy Spirit giving
salvation and allying to the Deity.

AMBROSE, *Apol. David*, § 59 : " He who desired to be purified
(*typico*) by *typical baptism was sprinkled* (*adspergebatur*) with
the blood of the lamb by a bunch of hyssop."

Type baptism was by *sprinkled* blood of the lamb of the flock ;
antitype baptism was by the sprinkled blood of the Lamb of
God, which cleanses from sin and saves the soul through the
office work of the Holy Spirit.

It never entered into the imagination of these Greeks and
their disciples, that a type baptism should have in it a dipping,
or an immersing, or a covering ; a " sprinkling " fully met their
Greekly conceptions of a baptism which by its purifying and
saving power was to be a type of that higher purification and
salvation which was to be found in the Antitype baptism, the
work of the Holy Ghost.

The idea of Christian baptism consisting in or being a nullity
without a dipping into water, is a novelty of yesterday, and has
no place in the history of the church until these latter days.
Therefore, those most ludicrously irrational attempts *to bury*
Noah in the ark ; and *to immerse* the ark in the flood ; *to bury*
Israel in the highway opened through the sea ; and *to cover* the
Apostles in " the sound " reverberating through the house, at
Pentecost, in order to find *a baptism*, are extravagances which,
among all the extravagances of the ages, stand unrivalled.

This is said, with the clear perception and full recognition of
the historic fact, that through long centuries, Christian baptism
was administered with the body naked and the water covering
every part. Whether this historic fact conflicts in the slightest
degree with the statement above made, namely, That Christian
baptism as consisting in a dipping into water is a novelty and has
no place in the history of the church for more than a thousand
years after its establishment, will receive consideration in its
place.

CHRISTIANITY HAS BUT ONE DISTINCTIVE BAPTISM WHICH IS
BY THE HOLY GHOST INTO THE LORD JESUS CHRIST.

EPHESIANS 4 : 5.

Εἰς Κύριος, μία πίστις, ἐν βάπτισμα.

"There is one body, and one Spirit, even as ye are called in one hope of
your calling ;
"One Lord, one faith, one baptism,
"One God and Father of all, who is above all, and through all, and in you
all."

"One Baptism."

Professor J. L. Dagg (Manual of Theo., Southern Bapt. Pub.
Soc., p. 16), states the following objection and reply : "Objection.
Paul teaches that there is one baptism. Now, there is a baptism
of the Spirit; and if water baptism is a perpetual ordinance of
Christianity, there are two baptisms instead of one."

"Answer. Paul says, ' One Lord, one faith, one baptism.' As
he uses the words Lord and faith, in their literal sense, so he
uses the word baptism in its literal sense. In this sense there is
but one baptism. John the Baptist foretold that Christ would
baptize with the Holy Spirit: And Jesus said to his disciples,
' Ye shall be baptized with the baptism that I am baptized with.'
Both these baptisms were known to Paul. These figurative baptisms were two in number: while the literal baptism was but one.
He must therefore have intended the latter."

1. This reasoning is not satisfactory. It is a mistake to say: The
baptism by the Holy Ghost foretold by John as characteristic of
the Coming One, is a distinct baptism from that declared by the
Saviour, " Ye shall be baptized with the baptism that I am baptized with." The first statement announces a Divine and efficient
agency in baptism ; the second announces the nature of the baptism which the disciples of Christ in all ages must receive,
namely, the baptism of the Cross, which has a sin-remitting
power and all the virtues of a perfected atonement, which baptism is expressed as a baptism into Christ—" as many as have
been baptized into JESUS CHRIST, have been baptized into HIS
DEATH." This baptism is effected by the Holy Ghost. The statements of John and of Christ, therefore, do not declare two baptisms but the divine Agent, and the "one baptism" of Christianity
effected by that divine Agent.

2. The reasoning is defective, because it assumes that "Lord" and "faith" being spoken of *literally*, therefore "baptism" must be spoken of *physically*. This is an error. "Baptism" represents the phrase "baptism into Christ," and this phrase expresses a *reality* as absolute as does "Lord" or "faith." In the phrase "faith upon Christ" (which is represented by "faith") there is no more of the *physical* than there is in "baptism into Christ" which is condensed into the one word "baptism."

3. A third error is in the assumption of a baptism *into water*. There is no such thing in the New Testament. Baptism, *with water* into Christ, symbolizes the real purification effected in the baptism, *by the Holy Ghost* into Christ. The conclusion falls with the unwarranted assumption on which it rests. And the "objection" remains, namely: According to the theory there are *two* baptisms (the one *in* the Holy Ghost, the other *in* water) which enter (Dr. Dagg seems to admit, although other of his friends do not) into the constitution of Christianity; and thus the theory is placed in opposition to the statement by Paul, that Christianity has but "one baptism."

DR. CARSON (p. 212), adopts another line of argument: "We learn from Ephes. 4 : 5 that there is but one baptism. Now, as the baptism of the Commission cannot possibly extend to infants, if there is such a thing as infant baptism, there must be two baptisms. If then there is but one baptism, there can be no infant baptism."

This logical dart we catch upon our shield and let it drop into the dust, thus: Baptism into Christ by the Holy Ghost (the "one baptism" of Christianity) is essential to salvation; Infants, by the admission of Dr. Carson, receive salvation; therefore, the baptism of the Commission, so far as it is the "one baptism" of Christianity, does apply to infants. Or, *ad hominem;* Baptism of the body in water, cannot possibly identify with baptism of the soul in the Holy Ghost; therefore, since it is affirmed that there is a baptism of the soul in the Holy Ghost, if there be such a thing as a baptism of the body in water, there must be *two* baptisms; but Paul teaches that there is but "one baptism," therefore, there can be no baptism of the body in water.

R. INGHAM (*Christian Baptism*, p. 7, London): "Ephes. 4 : 5; 'One Lord, one faith, one baptism;' we do not believe that the baptism of the Spirit is here meant, from the fact that baptism in or by water was the instituted and well-known ordinance of the church of Christ, and that the divine Spirit had been mentioned in the immediately preceding verse; also because water baptism commanded by Christ, and practiced and enjoined by the apostles, must now have ceased, if the apostle here refers to the baptism of the Spirit; or there must have been two baptisms; or the apostle must have been guilty of an omission, nay, of a misstatement, in saying that there was 'one baptism.' To consider this the baptism of the Spirit is, we think, in opposition to all the candid."

The reasons for this conclusion are: 1. "Water baptism was the instituted and well-known ordinance of the Church." This reason is founded in the error that water baptism constitutes a wholly distinct and diverse baptism from that baptism which is by the Holy Ghost, dislocating "water" from its divinely appointed relation to the baptism as a symbol agency, and convert ing it into (what is every way impossible) a receiving element. 2. " The divine Spirit had been mentioned in the preceding verse." This is most true; and the mention is most adverse to the conclusion. " There is one body, and one Spirit," is the statement; and this statement identifies itself, most unmistakably, with 1 Cor. 12: 13, "We are all *baptized by* ONE SPIRIT into ONE BODY;" and this latter statement declares one universal baptism under Christianity received by all who are received into the body of Christ, which baptism is by the divine Spirit. This must be the " one baptism." 3. " If this be baptism of the Spirit, water baptism must have ceased." This is not an alternative. It is founded on an entire misconception of the rite, as noticed in " 1;" 4. " Or there must have been two baptisms." Nor is this an alternative. There is no second baptism in the rite wholly diverse in purport and *genus* from the baptism effected by the Holy Ghost. This would be absurd. Does the lamb bleeding on the altar of Abel and Noah and Abraham embody truth wholly diverse from that exhibited in the Lamb of God bleeding on the Cross? Do the bread and the wine in the Lord's Supper embody truth wholly diverse from that in the broken body and shed blood of Christ received by faith through the Holy Ghost? Were the purifyings of Judaism or Heathenism *two* purifyings, or sprinklings, or pourings, or dippings, or washings, or *one* purification, effected by essential power attributed to the rite, or symbolizing in shadow what a higher power must effect in reality? A rite must, in its essence, represent a higher kindred reality. But if the essence (that without which it cannot be) of ritual baptism be *a dipping*

ınto water, then there is absolutely nothing in the higher related
truth of baptism by the Holy Ghost, which it can represent. Nor
is there anything in the language of Scripture to justify the idea,
that Christian baptism is a *dipping into* WATER. The Scriptures
teach, that after the Coming One baptism would be by the Holy
Ghost " into repentance," " into the remission of sins," " into
Jesus Christ," and it is a pure absurdity to imagine, that ritual
baptism would be another and diverse baptism, or any other baptism more or less than this same baptism *symbolized*. Therefore
John says, " I (ὕδατι) symbolly, baptize you (εἰς μετάνοιαν) into repentance ;" this is all that I can do ; but there cometh after me a
Mightier One who can and " who will baptize you (ἐν Πνεύματι)
divinely, really, into repentance." As John preached a real baptism into repentance as necessary for the soul, and ritually administered a symbol baptism (with water) into repentance ; so
Christianity preaches the necessity for the real baptism of the
soul into Christ, and administers a symbol baptism (with water)
" into Christ."

This obvious truth is recognized by Dr. Pepper (Prof. of Theol.,
Crozer Bapt. Theo. Sem.) in his work on *Baptism and Communion*,
p. 20 : " The gospel spoken is the interpretation of the gospel embodied in ordinances. Gospel and ordinances are *the same thing
in two forms ;* in the form of words and in the form of deeds."
This precludes " two " baptisms. There may be " one baptism "
under two forms ; but two forms of one baptism can never constitute *two* baptisms. The Scriptures teach " one baptism " into
Christ under two forms, 1. Real, by the Holy Ghost ; 2. Ritual, by
water. The alternative presented " or water baptism must have
ceased," is, therefore, groundless. 5. " Or the apostle must have
been guilty of an omission, nay of a misstatement." This is only
saying, " My notions about baptism are right or the Holy Ghost
by whom the apostle spoke has spoken falsely." Such language
is utterly inexcusable from any man under any circumstances. A
Roman Catholic priest said from the altar, in my hearing, that
what he had been preaching was the truth, and if he were to be
called into the presence of God and God were to say, that he was
in error, he would answer God by declaring—" THOU *art the Author of my error.*" Is not this blasphemy ? Dr. Carson not only
says : " If the angel Gabriel were to differ from him as to the
meaning of a Greek word, he would ' order him to school :' " but,
that *inspired* writers do not tell the truth unless his interpreta-

tions of Greek are true. Any man who thinks, that it invests his
name with honor or his argument with power, to compare, depre-
ciatingly, the scholarship of Gabriel with his own, is welcome to
do it; but when Romish priest, or Dr. Carson, or R. Ingham, declares, under any contingency, " I *am true*, or GOD *is false;*" the
most lenient judgment that can be passed is—*He has lost his head.*

The apostle is neither " guilty of omission or of misstatement."
There is but one distinctive baptism of Christianity which is "*into*
CHRIST," being really accomplished by the divine Agent, the Holy
Ghost, and ritually symbolized by pure water.

Thus the error of Ingham is exposed and the truth of Paul is
vindicated.

ALEXANDER CAMPBELL, *of Bethany* (*Design of Baptism*, p. 252) :
" Ephes. 4 : 5. Now if there be but one baptism, and if it appear
that both the New Testament dispensations of baptism, by John
and by the Apostles, clearly affirm a connection between baptism
and the remission of sins—must it not follow that the *only divinely
instituted baptism is for the remission of sins?* "

The logic of this argumentation may be commended to Dagg,
and Carson, and Ingham, as worthy to be laid by the side of
their own. How they will maintain their logical " one *dipping
into water*," and escape this other logical " one *dipping into
water* FOR the remission of sins," I do not know. For myself,
repudiating the dipping into water as more foundationless than
a dream of the night, I accept as the very truth of God, one
divinely appointed baptism by the Holy Ghost " into Christ" for
the remission of sins, which result is invariably attendant upon
such baptism by the Holy Ghost, and is as invariably symbolized
by the ritual administration of this same baptism.

When the chaff is winnowed from the wheat this logical demonstration evaporates.

Ἐν βάπτισμα.

When Paul says, there is " one baptism" of Christianity, he
cannot mean that there is but one baptism mentioned in connection with Christianity. Such baptisms are, in fact, very many
in number and very various in character. Passing by the mention of Jewish baptisms which appear in the New Testament, and
in which the use of water by sprinkling, or pouring, or otherwise,
was probably the same, while the baptism itself was wholly diverse in character from every baptism under Christianity (being

ceremonial purification, which has no place in Christianity), we
have: 1. Baptism (εἰς μετάνοιαν) into repentance; 2. Baptism (εἰς
ἄφεσιν ἁμαρτιων) into the remission of sins; 3. The personal covenant baptism of Christ, "to fulfil all righteousness;" 4. The
personal baptism of Christ by the Holy Ghost "without measure," in order to the fulfilment of this covenant engagement;
5. The personal baptism of Christ in the actual fulfilment of this
covenant engagement, by baptism into penal death upon the
Cross; 6. The baptism of the Apostles by the Holy Ghost at
Pentecost, endowing them with gifts and power for the Apostleship; 7. The ritual, symbol baptism of the Samaritans "into the
name of the Lord Jesus;" 8. The baptism of Cornelius and
friends by the Holy Ghost endowing with miraculous gifts, but
diverse from the kindred baptizing endowment of the Apostles,
in that these gifts were not such as to qualify for the Apostleship; 9. Baptism into Moses; 10. Baptism into Paul; 11. Baptism "by one Spirit into one body," including regeneration and
endowment, without either of which there can be no membership
in the body of Christ; 12. Baptism "into the name of the Father,
and of the Son, and of the Holy Ghost," which is consequent
upon and the consummation of baptism "into Christ."

Here are twelve baptisms mentioned in connection with Christianity, each differing in some material respect from every other,
and yet all agreeing in one respect, meeting and melting together
in the "one baptism" *into* JESUS CHRIST.

Could proof be more absolute, that while Christianity acknowledges that there are a thousand lords, she teaches that, in the
highest sense, there is but "one Lord" = JESUS CHRIST; and
while she acknowledges, that there are ten thousand objects of
faith, she teaches that there is transcendently above all others,
"one Faith" = *upon* JESUS CHRIST; and while she acknowledges
that there are *multa genera baptismatum*, and does herself present
many species, yet she teaches, that all her promises centre in
"one baptism" = *into* JESUS CHRIST, which sin-remitting and
soul-regenerating baptism is both preparative for and causative
of that ultimate, endless, and amazing baptism into the Name
of the Father, Son, and Holy Ghost. As for this "one baptism"
being *a dipping into water*, there is so little of real evidence to
sustain such idea, that, if put under a microscope of a magnifying power of one million times it would remain still invisible.
Nothing cannot by any multiplication be made something.

Concil. Carthaginens.

Demetrius a Septiminus said: " We guard the one baptism, because we claim for the church catholic that which solely belongs to her. But they who say that heretics do baptize truly and legitimately, they make not one but many baptisms. For since heresies are many, baptisms must be computed according to the number of heresies."

This language could not be used with any propriety if the " one baptism" were *a dipping into water.* The multiplicity of the baptisms turns on the number of the heresies. But no one ever imagined that every heresy had a different way of dipping into water. The different baptisms, then, must be found in the diverse doctrines taught. As " teaching to delight in pleasures and lusts" effected a baptism of its own, so, teaching any particular heresy effected a baptism of its own. These heretical baptisms were not various dippings into water, or connected with water in any way, but with *teaching.* They were " baptisms of doctrine " (Heb. 6 : 2).

JEROME (Comm. in loc.), XI, 831: " *Unum corpus, et unus spiritus. . . . Unus Dominus, una fides, unum baptisma.* Cum omnes in unum corpus baptizati, eumdem Spiritum acceperint: Since all have been baptized into one body, they receive the same Spirit."

Jerome, certainly, did not regard this " one baptism" as a dipping into water; but as that spiritual baptism which all Christians receive being " baptized by one Spirit into one body."

CYRIL of Jerusalem: The creed required of those about to be baptized, under Cyril Archbishop of Jerusalem, has for its ninth article, this: " I believe in (ἐν βάπτισμα μετανοίας εἰς ἄφεσιν ἁμαρτιῶν) one baptism of repentance into the remission of sins ;" the same as in the Nicene Creed.

This creed is not indicative of a faith in dipping into water as the " one baptism." Repentance is the gift of God; and " a baptism into remission of sins," originating in repentance, must be the work of the Holy Spirit.

IGNATIUS (921) says: Ἐν δε καὶ τὸ βάπτισμα, τὸ εἰς τὸν θανατον τοῦ Κυριοῦ διδομενον: " There is also one baptism, that which is given *into the death* of our Lord." This is, by eminence, the one primal baptism of Christianity. Ignatius had no faith in water dipping as the " one baptism."

Dr. Pusey.

PUSEY (*Holy Baptism*, p. 162) says: "'One Lord;' one faith *in Him;* 'one Baptism' *into Him;* and so *into* GOD the Father who is above all, the Author of all; God the Son who is through all, as having been by Him created; God the Holy Ghost, who is in all" . . . (p. 163). And so among the ancient Fathers, St. Gregory of Nazianzen: "One Lord, one faith, one baptism. What say ye, ye destructive baptists, and anabaptists? Can one be spiritual without the Spirit? or honoreth he who is baptized into one created and a fellow-servant? Not so, not so. I will not belie thee, Unoriginated Father; I will not belie thee, Only Begotten Word; I will not belie thee, Holy Spirit. I know whom I have confessed, whom renounced, with whom been united."

In a note it is stated: "The Eunomians rebaptized in the name of the Father uncreated, and the Son created, and the Holy Ghost created by the created Son."

This Eunomian baptism shows, that the "untrue and illegitimate *baptisms* of heretics" did not consist in a departure from a dipping into water, but in a "baptism of doctrine" which abandoned the true baptism "into the name of the Father, and of the Son, and of the Holy Ghost."

Evidence from every legitimate source rejects the idea, that this passage has any reference to a dipping into water, and confirms the position, that it is purely spiritual in all of its elements.

"One Lord," JESUS CHRIST; "One faith," *upon* JESUS CHRIST; "One baptism," *into* JESUS CHRIST.

CHRISTIC BAPTISM:

PASSAGES OF SCRIPTURE IN WHICH THERE IS SUP-
POSED TO BE AN ALLUSION TO BAPTISM.

PURIFICATION.

JOHN 3 : 25.

Περί καθαρίσμοῦ.

"·Then there arose a question between some of John's disciples and the Jews about purifying."

THERE are a few passages of Scripture in which the word baptism does not occur but which have, very generally, been supposed to refer to it. Among these there are some which have exerted a very powerful influence in moulding doctrinal views, as involved in the subject of baptism, and, also, the mode of admin-istering the rite. It is, therefore, desirable to take brief notice of some of these passages.

The passage now to be considered is not one of those deeply influential passages, and yet it has a really important bearing on the subject, and justly claims attention.

Diverse Reading.

There is a diversity of reading (*'Ιουδαίου—'Ιουδαίων*), as to the singular or plural form of the word denoting the party in opposi-tion to the disciples of John. The Baptist translation adopts the singular form ("with a Jew"), and in the Quarto translation with notes, says: "Almost all modern translators and editors regard this as the true reading. All, I believe, reject *'Ιουδαίων*, of the Textus Receptus, as spurious." Whether the singular or the plural of this word be adopted is a matter of no essential moment; but so long as the Codex Sinaiticus presents the plural form the Textus Receptus may be allowed to stand. The translator adds farther: " I confess that I consider the conjectural emendation of Bentley, adopted by Penn (*Ιησου*), sustained by an overwhelming weight of internal evidence; but, as there is, as far as known, no manuscriptal authority for this reading, I dare not recommend its adoption." Markland agrees with Bentley and others, in the change suggested; but the reasons assigned (from internal evidence) is no more satisfactory than that from external evidence, which is confessed to be, nothing.

If the discussion be made to take place between the disciples of John and the disciples of Jesus, the entire statement of the Scripture is revolutionized, and instead of a discussion respecting purification, we have a discussion respecting the comparative personal merits of John and Jesus: "The disciples of John must have felt their vanity wounded while the Jew, probably, gave it as his opinion, that the baptism of Jesus was more effectual than that of John" (Olshausen); "The Jews resorted to Jesus, while the disciples of John were contending, that purifying ought to be sought from John" (Bengel); "The Jews, doubtless, had been baptized by the disciples of Jesus, and preferred that baptism to John's" (Bloomfield). These interpretations depart essentially from the Scripture record in two radical particulars: 1. In changing the discussion from ($\pi\varepsilon\rho\iota$ $\varkappa\alpha\theta\alpha\rho\iota\sigma\mu\sigma\tilde{\upsilon}$) "purification" to the personal merits of John and Jesus, for which there was no ground, as the testimony of John had been clear and profound, from the beginning, on that point; and as to the comparative value of the baptism administered by John and by the disciples of Jesus ("for Jesus himself baptized not") there is no evidence whatever of any diversity existing or being supposed to exist; 2. The conversion of "the Jews," or of "the Jew," into disciples of the Lord Jesus Christ, is destitute of all Scripture warrant. It is incredible that the disciples of Jesus would be designated as "Jews" in contradistinction from the disciples of John. And as for the substitution of *Jesus* for "Jew" in the text (in opposition to all MSS. and construction) this arguing in a circle is presented. The true text is "Jesus," because the discussion was between the disciples of John and of Jesus, and the discussion was between the disciples of John and of Jesus, because the true text is "Jesus."

We must look for something better than this.

"*About Purifying.*"

We take the text as it stands (substantially the same whether

23

" Jews" or *Jew*): " There arose a question from among the disciples of John with some Jews about purifying."

That such a question should arise between these parties was
not only natural, but was one which could by no possibility be
escaped. The Jews had their "purifyings" before John's mission or birth. They had a sharply defined character and met with
universal acceptance. The true nature of Jewish purifyings was
a *ceremonial* purification; but it is very doubtful whether the
popular mind rested in this as its whole value, or did not fail to
see beyond this a higher purification (spiritual) still remaining.
In the midst of this condition of things John came preaching an
exclusively *spiritual* purification, one relating to the soul and not
to the body; to be effected by repentance and not by water. I
say this was an exclusively spiritual purification, because the rite
which was associated with it was not of the nature of Jewish
purifying rites; it purified nothing; it was only a symbol of the
spiritual purification. Jewish purifyings, on the contrary, had
an essential power to effect the purification for which they were
appointed, namely, to remove *ceremonial* defilement and establish *ceremonial* purification. These characteristics seem to be
brought to view by the language of Josephus (Jew. Ant., xviii,
62). " John exhorted the Jews to cultivate virtue and observing
uprightness toward one another, and piety toward God, to come
($\beta\alpha\pi\tau\iota\sigma\mu\tilde{\omega}$) for baptizing; for thus ($\beta\acute{\alpha}\pi\tau\iota\sigma\iota\nu$) the baptizing would
appear acceptable to him, not using it for the remission of sins,
but for purity of the body, provided, that the soul has been pre-
viously ($\pi\rho o\epsilon\kappa\kappa\epsilon\kappa\alpha\theta\alpha\rho\mu\acute{\epsilon}\nu\eta\varsigma$) purified by righteousness."

In this statement Josephus announces very clearly the spiritual
purification with its fruits, as preached by John. He seems to
imply, that John charged the Jews with using their purifyings to
obtain the remission of sins, and taught their unacceptableness
to God for any such purpose; while he declared that the rite he
introduced would be acceptable to God, not for the remission of
sins, but as a symbol of purity, " when the soul had first been
purified ($\delta\iota\kappa\alpha\iota o\sigma\acute{\nu}\nu\eta$) by righteousness," and not by water.

Now, it was precisely this preaching of John which antagonized
Jewish *ceremonial* purification, and which necessitated " a question about purifying" between those Jews who accepted John's
teaching and those Jews who, rejecting it maintained the suffi-
ciency of their old purifyings.

$K\alpha\theta\alpha\rho\iota\sigma\mu o\tilde{\nu}$, has greater breadth than the *$\beta\acute{\alpha}\pi\tau\iota\sigma\mu\upsilon\varsigma$, ceremonial*

purifying, of the Jew, or the βάπτισμα μετανοίας, *spiritual* purification of John; and is therefore, here, properly used, in its generic character, to include both. It is capable, in proper circumstances, of being used when either specific idea is designed to be expressed; and is, as a matter of fact, so used abundantly.

This discussion, then, was as the Scriptures declare, most strictly "about purifying."

REGENERATION.

John 3 : 5.

Ἀμὴν ἀμὴν λέγω σοι, Ἐὰν μὴ τις γεννηθῇ ἐξ ὕδατος καὶ Πνεύματος, οὐ δύναται εἰσελθεῖν εἰς τὴν βασιλείαν τοῦ Θεοῦ.

" Verily, verily, I say unto thee, Except a man be born of water and the Spirit, he cannot enter into the kingdom of God."

Historical Fact.

This passage of Scripture has, by the interpretation given to it, more profoundly moulded the conception of Christian ritual baptism than any or all other passages beside. At a very early period it was quoted as bearing on this rite, and very soon it was accepted as expounding its nature and value. REGENERATION was supposed to be the result of the *co-action* of the water and the Holy Spirit. On this there was a very wide agreement perpetuated through more than a thousand years.

There was but little attempt to make such a view accord with the teaching of other passages of Scripture; or to make a ritual regeneration harmonize with their own oftentimes eminently spiritual views of truth and the way of salvation.

Interpretation.

It is not easy to make a brief statement of baptismal regeneration as the faith of these early Christians without doing injustice to their general faith and Christian life.

The belief, that the SOUL is regenerated and sins remitted *by a* RITE is so wholly alien from the entire spirit of the Christian system, that it seems impossible that the two could be held together. And it is not too much to say, that they cannot, consistently, be so held. And they were not by these Christians. There was so much of truth and duty required before this rite could be received, and there was so much truth coincident with it, and subsequent to it, that the error as to the power of the rite was greatly lost in encompassing truth. To hold such a radical error in connection with the Christian system without constant practical embarrassment and the necessity for adjustment, is no more possible, than to hold that the earth is the centre of the solar system without being compelled to call in aid to meet constantly emerging difficulties.

Repentance and faith were required before baptism; so that they were scripturally regenerated before they were baptismally regenerated. And for sins committed after baptism repentance was necessary or the baptismal regeneration lost its efficacy. Truth under such circumstances largely nullified the error. Still, it is most true, that such an error cannot be held under any circumstances without most pernicious results.

Dr. Pusey.

None can be supposed better qualified to give a just and clear statement as to what is " Baptismal regeneration " than Dr. Pusey. But he says (pp. 21, 39): " While this is easy in some respects, it is not easy in others. The difficulty is twofold: First, from its being a mystery; Secondly, from men being in these days inclined to lower that mystery." But these reasons are not adequate explanations of the facts. The true cause of the difficulty is in the essential impracticability of adjusting so serious an error with the obvious truths of the Christian system. Dr. Pusey adds: " Nicodemus asked, How can these things be? and most of our questions about Baptismal Regeneration are Nicodemus's questions. We know it in its author, God; in its instrument, Baptism; in its end, salvation, union with Christ, sonship to God, resurrection from the dead, and the life of the world to come."

If this can be said, in any rational sense, to be the end secured by ritual baptism, then what need of preaching the gospel, or doing anything else, than to go through the world ritually baptizing men? Any answer to this question which brings in the necessity for the knowledge of the truth, and prayer, and repentance, and faith, is a pure abandonment of the position—" the instrument is Baptism; and its end is union to Christ, and salvation."

It is farther said: " One may then define regeneration to be that act whereby God takes us out of our relation to Adam, and makes us actual members of his Son, and so His sons, and heirs of God through Christ. This is our new birth, an actual birth of God, of water, and of the Spirit, as we were actually born of our natural parents; herein then also are we justified, or both accounted and made righteous, since we are made members of him who is alone righteous; freed from past sin, whether original or actual; have a new principle of life imparted to us, since having been made-members of Christ, we have a portion of his life, or of Him who is our life; herein also we have the hope of the resurrection and of immortality, because we have been made partakers of his resurrection, and have risen again with Him."

" Our birth (when the direct means are spoken of) is attributed to the Baptism of water and of the Spirit, and to that only. Had our new birth in one passage only been connected with Baptism and had it in five hundred passages been spoken of in connection with other causes, still the truth in Holy Scripture is not less God's truth because contained in one passage only. . . . There is no hint that Regeneration can be obtained in any way but by Baptism, or if totally lost could be restored. . . . A commencement of life in Christ after baptism is as little consonant with the general representations of Scripture, as a commencement of physical life long after our natural birth is with the order of his providence. . . . The Christian church uniformly, for fifteen centuries, interpreted these words (John 3:5) of Baptism; on the ground of this text alone they urged the necessity of Baptism; upon it, mainly, they identified regeneration with Baptism. If, then, this be an error, would our Saviour have used words which (since water was already used in the Jews' and John's baptism) must inevitably and did lead his Church into error? One should think that the words ' of water ' (upon which in his immediate converse with Nicodemus the Saviour does not dwell) were added with the very view that his Church should thence learn the truth, which she has transmitted—that ' regeneration ' is the gift of God, in this life, in Baptism only. The misuse of this text has ended in the scarcely disguised indifference or contempt of an ordinance of our Saviour."

Analogy of Faith.

This statement of the doctrine of " Baptismal Regeneration " places it in bold and irreconcilable antagonism with the Analogy of the Christian Faith. A claim is made for water, a physical element, as an efficient cause in the remission of sins and in the spiritual regeneration of the soul. This introduces a foreign element into the otherwise spiritual agencies of the Christian system. And in particular it antagonizes the principle laid down by the Saviour, in this connection, " That which is born of the flesh is flesh; and that which is born of the Spirit is spirit;" according to which principle, that which is born of (receives its existence from) any physical substance, must partake of the characteristics of that substance. But in water there is no quality which could originate the remission of sins or a spiritual regeneration. And in accordance with this principle, John preached *repentance* with the promise of the remission of sins; the Saviour commanded *repentance* and remission of sins to be preached among all people; he himself preached, " Except ye *repent* ye shall all likewise perish;" Peter preached both *repentance* and *faith* as the essential elements requisite for the remission of sins; Paul preached " Believe on the Lord Jesus Christ and thou shalt be saved;" and so, " Being born again of incorruptible seed, by the word of God;" " I have begotten you through the Gospel;" " Of his own will begat he us by the word of truth." These agencies exhibit diversity with unity. They are spiritual and therefore capable of giving birth to spiritual results; but they all differ in this respect from water, and therefore by principle of nature, as well as by the Analogy of Faith, it is excluded from the Christian system as causative of spiritual results.

Baptism.

Dr. Pusey very frequently uses " Baptism " as though it were in the passage. It is not there, and it cannot be put into it; for the question at issue is as to its right to be there. What the Scriptures say directly of baptism forbids any such interpretation of " water " in this passage as is assigned to it under the claim that it represents ritual baptism. John assigns to water a very subordinate place in the ritual baptism into repentance, saying, " I indeed baptize you with water into repentance, but there

cometh one after me mightier than I, He shall baptize you with
the Holy Ghost." He places a great gulf between baptism with
water and baptism with the Holy Ghost. The disciples of Christ
baptized symbolly with water, while he did not, but reserved to
himself the real baptism by the Holy Spirit. When "the promise
of the Spirit had been received," the Lord Jesus Christ baptized
by the Spirit, only, at Pentecost, and not with any commingling
of *water*. Cornelius was baptized by the Spirit, simply, by the
Lord Jesus Christ; and afterward by water, simply, by Peter.
The Samaritans were baptized by Philip with water, simply, and
afterward, through Peter, received special gift of the Holy Ghost.
Simon Magus was baptized with water, and yet he remained unregenerate, "his heart not right in the sight of God," and *Repentance* was held out to him as the only hope of the forgiveness
of sin and the regeneration of his soul. The thief upon the cross
was not baptized with water, but did repent, and did believe, and
was made regenerate, so that he did "enter into the kingdom of
God." Paul said that "he was not sent to baptize with water,
but to preach the Gospel," which he never could have said if
Baptism with water is the way to remit sin, to regenerate the
soul, to ingraft into Christ, and to make sons of God, and not by
the preaching of the Gospel. For Paul declares (Acts 26: 15–18)
that he was sent "To open the eyes of the Gentiles, and to turn
them from darkness to light, and from the power of Satan to God,
that they might receive forgiveness of sins and inheritance among
them that are sanctified through faith in Christ." The baptismal
power ascribed to water in John 3: 5, to remit sins and to regenerate souls, must go down before truths and facts like these.

Elements of Interpretation.

The true interpretation of a passage is oftentimes hopelessly
obscured by its dislocation from the time, and place, and person,
and circumstance, out of which it sprang; and an attempt to adjust it with times, and places, and persons, and circumstances,
which are foreign to its origin. The interpretation of this passage has been thus embarrassed. Its deeply Jewish surroundings
have been ignored; and it has not only been brought into Christianity and its colorings, but is made to utter the profoundest tone
sounding throughout all her teachings and controlling doctrinal
utterances. Let us, then, restore this passage to its divinely

established affiliations and see whether much, if not all, of embarrassment in its interpretation will not be removed.

1. These words were spoken in the midst of Judaism. The
entire life and death of the Lord Jesus Christ were within the
Jewish economy. All of its rites and ceremonies, as divinely appointed, were in legitimate existence. These divinely appointed
rites had greatly suffered both from misinterpretation and by
human additions; through which their worship was made vain,
"teaching for doctrines the commandments of men." In these
circumstances, while teachings that look beyond Judaism may be
expected, yet it is most evidently true, that the Lord Jesus Christ
is singularly reticent as to the future, and slow to lift the veil from
the individual peculiarities of the coming dispensation. As might
be anticipated, our Lord was largely engaged in meeting issues
which were crowding around him, and in so doing establishing
principles for all ages. It would then be most remarkable, if in
the midst of Judaism, and in a private interview with a Jew
steeped in Judaism, the Saviour had, at a bound, passed beyond
this peculiar atmosphere, and announced a truth kept hidden
from the foundation of the world, and which was to reign with
regal supremacy and splendor in another dispensation, to wit:
that WATER was the essential means chosen of God to remit sins,
to regenerate the soul, to reconcile to Himself, and to introduce
into life everlasting! Such announcement, under such circumstances, is not what we would look for. It sounds more like the
projection of Jewish errors intensified to the last degree, into the
new dispensation, rather than a correction of the disposition " to
make clean *the outside* of the cup and the platter."

2. These words were spoken by Him whom John had foreannounced as the Baptizer with the Holy Ghost. John had, by his
ministry, introduced an element in the most absolute antagonism
with the perverted notions of the value of Jewish rites, as well as
with the end for which others had, by superstition, been added to
them. This element was a spiritual baptism purifying the soul
by repentance, without which water washings, with their ceremonial purifications, were worthless. Such teaching could not but
awaken attention, beget discussion, and induce opposition. There
was a widespread and profound movement among the people;
there was " a discussion between the disciples of John and the
Jews about purifying;" there was a rejection of his spiritual baptism and an adherence to their water washings by many, and there

was a rejection by John, of others who came without apprehend-
ing the true nature of this spiritual baptism, and in their old spirit
sought to add another water washing to their already extended
list.

This standard of spiritual baptism, accompanied and illustrated
by symbol water, was lifted up by John in antagonism to the
popular water washings, and as the true exposition of those purifying rites established in the Jewish economy. And this was
done with the declared design to prepare the way for the Coming
One whose baptism was to be exclusively by the Holy Spirit, to
the rejection not only of human water washings (which effected
nothing, but the increase of sin) but, also, of Jewish water rites
which did, by divine appointment, effect ceremonial purification;
for the water under the new dispensation was no longer to effect
a purification of any kind, but merely to be used as a symbol of
that purification effected by a crucified and atoning Redeemer
through the Holy Spirit. And now this divine Baptizer, who was
foretold and whose coming has been thus prepared, has come, and
the text introduces us into his presence, and into that of one
other, who is his sole auditor. Who that auditor is, it is important for us to know.

3. These words of the Baptizer by the Holy Ghost are spoken
to a Jew, to a Ruler of the Jews, to a Teacher of the Jews, to a
Pharisee of the Jews, to a Jew, therefore, of the intensest type.

There is every probability that this Jew had rejected the spiritual
baptism of John, as subordinating Jewish rites and teaching that
they were of no essential spiritual value. This is probable, because he was not merely a Jew, and a Ruler, and a Teacher, but
because he was a Pharisee. The Pharisees were "the straitest
sect" of the Jewish religion (Acts 26 : 5); they were characterized
by the Lord Jesus Christ, himself (Matt. 23 : 25), as "making
clean the *outside* of the cup and of the platter, while *within*
they were full of extortion and excess;" he commanded them
(v. 26), "to cleanse *first that which is within* the cup and platter,
that the outside of them may be clean also." It is certain, that
the Pharisees, as a class, did reject this spiritual baptism, of John
(Luke 7 : 30)—"The Pharisees rejected the counsel of God against
themselves, not being baptized of John." It is morally certain,
that this Jew had not accepted the teaching of John because of
adherence to misunderstood divinely appointed Jewish rites, or
because of the acceptance of such as had been humanly estab-

lished; possibly for both reasons. What, now, to such a Jew would be the teaching of the Lord Jesus Christ? Would he ignore that man's state of mind? Would he repudiate the teaching of John which had prepared the way for his own coming as the Great and exclusively spiritual Baptizer? Would he point to a future dispensation, announcing a truth without any practical bearing upon the case of the earnest inquirer before Him? Do not such questions answer themselves? Suppose it to be true, that under Christianity WATER was to be the means for washing away sin and regenerating the soul, what is that to Nicodemus? He is not under Christianity, nor within the reach of such wonder-working water. It is an anachronism to apply such water of Christianity to the case of this Jew. He wants knowledge for his own case. He wants salvation for his own soul. He wants a passage-way which he can tread and "enter the kingdom of God." If this "water" be that water which is to be impregnated with singular virtues under Christianity, then, it is not the water for the Jew Nicodemus. The exigency of the case requires the dismissal of any such aspect attributed to this water.

Is there a reference to "the water" as used by John? There cannot be: 1. Because those who attach such power to water under Christianity are earnest in their denial of it to the water used by John; 2. Because no such power belonged, in fact, to the water of the baptism of John. He repudiates it himself. He denies to it any spiritual power. He contrasts it with the spiritual baptism of his coming Lord. It is a moral impossibility that the Lord Jesus Christ could associate this water with the divine Spirit, as necessary to salvation.

There remains for consideration but one other religious use of water to which the language of the Saviour could refer,—the divinely appointed Jewish use.

To this every consideration points as alone meeting the demands of the case. Nicodemus lived under the Jewish rites with the full obligation to observe them. He did in fact so observe them. He refused to accept John's spiritual teaching which threw so deep a shadow over the rites he had valued. But his conscience was not at rest; and no multiplicity of his water washings had brought to him peace. In this state of mind he comes for light to Jesus. And Jesus meets him with the evidence that his case is all known to him by the declaration, that he "must be born again," and born again not only by the use

of water (which he acknowledged, but which had power only to
renew *externally* and ceremonially, without reaching to the conscience as stated, Heb. 9 : 9–14, of " divers washings ") but by
the Spirit; which he did not acknowledge, or which was so over-
laid by " water " as to be inoperative, and therefore had led to
the rejection of John's baptism, not as it was a symbol baptism
with water, but as it was a real spiritual baptism by repentance.
The Saviour knowing all hearts, recognizes the mind of Nicodemus resting on " the water of purification " in Judaism, and
passes no condemnation on it ; but he accepts it at its true value,
a necessary Jewish observance to enter the kingdom of God, and
adds : however right and valuable and necessary this may be to
you, *there is another necessity, more absolute,* which you have rejected in rejecting the baptism of John—the βάπτισμα μετανοίας
εἰς ἄφεσιν ἁμαρτιῶν, which is my baptism and which I baptize ἐν
Πνεύματι Ἁγίῳ by the Holy Spirit. This purifies the soul, reconciles to God and introduces into his everlasting kingdom. To be
born of water and Spirit is for Nicodemus to be cleansed externally (Jewishly) and internally (by the Spirit); which means for
all men that they must be *completely* cleansed, body and soul.

Such interpretation meets the specialties of the case of Nicodemus, as a Jew, as a Pharisee, and as troubled in conscience,
after having exhausted the power of ceremonial purifications in
search of peace. It meets the peculiarity of the time as agitated
by that new element thrown into it by the preaching of John.
No element, more alien or more disturbing to the spirit of that
generation, could have been introduced among them than *a repentance* baptism (= internal purification) as contrasted with ceremonial baptisms (= external purification) in preparing for the
kingdom of God. There was a profound agitation among the
people. This visit of Nicodemus was evidence of it. The words
of the Saviour reveal his state of mind far better than his own
words. His case appears, very clearly, to be a specific illustration of the general statement in v. 25, namely, an awakened conscience struggling against the truth, that mere *water washings*
cannot fit for the Messiah's kingdom. Beyond all type or symbol
purifyings there remains the purifying godly sorrow for sin, the
baptism by the Holy Ghost. This interpretation accords with
the mission of John and with the character of the Messiah and
his kingdom, as announced by him. John made no war against
Jewish rites. He gave to them their divinely assigned value and

preached their antitype truth, the purification of the soul by the Holy Spirit. John's Lord did not come to destroy the Law, nor to announce the abrogation of Jewish water washing *as divinely appointed;* but to fulfil by presenting himself as the antitype Lamb, and to confer antitype baptism by the renewing of the Holy Ghost. Therefore, *he does not condemn the Jewish typical use of water,* but teaches, that unless with this there be *associated the antitypical washing by the Holy Spirit* there is no entrance into the kingdom of God. The language of the Saviour does not require that the necessity for Jewish water and for the Holy Spirit, should be the same; but that, however necessary or efficacious ritual water might be to Nicodemus, *it neither fulfilled nor superseded* the work of the Holy Spirit. Having thus met the Jewish difficulties of Nicodemus by granting all that could be justly asked, the Saviour says no more of water as qualifying for entrance into the kingdom of God, but speaks of regeneration by the Spirit, only. And *this phase* of the interview and its teaching looks Christianity-ward. There was a power and a necessity for " water " under the Jewish economy that has no place under Christianity. The Jewish water of purification had by divine ordinance an essential power to purify ceremonially. And without such purification the ceremonially defiled could not enter into the religious assembly. It was therefore, in its place and for its purpose, an imperative necessity. But under Christianity there is no ceremonial defilement and therefore there is no ceremonially purifying water. The water as now used, has only a symbol power; the power to symbolize the purification which is effected by the Holy Spirit; and therefore, it cannot be said under Christianity, as under Judaism, " Except a man be born of water " (which is ordained of God for the outward purification from ceremonial defilement), " and of the Spirit" (by whom alone inward purification from sin, the regeneration to a new life, and sanctification for communion with God, can be effected) " he cannot enter into the kingdom of God." Judaism recognized sources of external defilement and ordained rites for external purification. Christianity does not recognize the one, nor ordain the other.

This language of the Saviour must, therefore, be interpreted under the ruling fact, that it was addressed to *a Jew* on whom the use of ritual water was obligatory and efficacious for the removal of ceremonial impurity; and to *a Pharisee* living under the ministry of John, whose preaching, that the higher and essential purification of the Spirit was necessary in order to welcome the Messiah and to enter into the kingdom of God, he most probably rejected.

'Εξ ΰδατος καὶ Πνεύματος.

Dr. Carson derives an argument for dipping into water from the preposition ἐκ. He says (p. 164), "John 3 : 5 has its explanation most intelligibly in emersion *out of* the water in that ordinance. To emerge *out of* the water, is like a birth. To be born of water most evidently implies, that water is the *womb out of which* the person who is born proceeds " (p. 476). Such interpretation is on a par with that which buries Noah in the Ark, Israel in the highway opened through the Sea, and the Apostles in the Sound like wind. It assumes, that there is an ἐκ which enters into a baptism, *which is not true*, whatever may be true of a dipping; it assumes, that there was a dipping of the body into water required of the Jews, *which is not true;* it assumes, that the preposition here indicates a physical " out of," *which is not true*. The force of the preposition expresses here, agency and the source from which it proceeds, without indicating method or form of proceeding. This is proved by the fact that διὰ is substituted for ἐκ by Patrists. Certainly, if there could be any physical "out of " water, there could be none out of *the Spirit*. In both cases there is the same general indication of agency; while each by its essential nature qualifies and gives character to its several agency. That which is born of water, within the sphere of religion (Jewish) receives a new condition, character, and relations, such as water can effect, namely, one that is external, ceremonial, and ecclesiastical; while that which is born of the Spirit receives a character, condition, and relations in conformity with the nature of the Spirit, namely, such as is essentially pure, spiritual, and divine. Fleshly ordinances produce fleshly results. The Divine Spirit brings forth the image of God. This passage has no direct reference to Christian baptism. It teaches specifically, the necessity for an *outward* and *inward* purification under Judaism, and generically, the necessity in every case for a *complete* purification " to enter into the kingdom of God."

SANCTIFICATION AND JUSTIFICATION.

1 CORINTHIANS 6 : 11.

'Αλλὰ ἀπελούσασθε, ἀλλὰ ἡγιάσθητε, ἀλλ' ἐδικαιώθητε, ἐν τῷ ὀνόματι τοῦ Κυρίου
'Ιησοῦ, καὶ ἐν τῷ Πνεύματι τοῦ Θεοῦ ἡμῶν.

" But ye are washed, but ye are sanctified, but ye are justified, in the
name of the Lord Jesus, and by the Spirit of our God."

Various Views.

Those who refer this and other passages to ritual baptism are
by no means agreed among themselves as to the value that should
be attributed to baptism.

BLOOMFIELD, *in loco :* " I think there can be no question but
that these words have a direct reference to *baptism.* This, indeed, is plain from the turn of expression, which alludes to the
form of baptism; though from the other terms which are sub-
joined, it should seem that the *effects* of baptism are designated.
(᾽Εν τῷ Πνεύματι τοῦ Θεοῦ) must mean by the Holy Spirit proceeding from and imparted to us by the Father."

BENGEL, *in loco :* " You have been entirely set free from *fornication* and sins of impurity, in regard to yourselves ; from *idolatry*
and impiety towards God; from *unrighteousness* against your
neighbor. ᾽Εν τῷ ὀνόματι: From this name we have the forgiveness
of sins. ᾽Εν τῷ Πνεύματι: From this Spirit, we have the new life."

Bengel does not mention ritual baptism.

CALVIN, *in loco :* " Though these three terms have the same
general meaning, there is, nevertheless, great force in their
variety. There is an implied contrast between *washing* and defilement — *sanctification* and pollution — *justification* and guilt.
The term *washing* is metaphorical, Christ's blood being likened
to water. ' *In the name of the Lord Jesus.*' Christ is the source
of all blessings ; but Christ himself with all his blessings is communicated to us by the Spirit. For it is by faith that we receive
Christ, and have his graces applied to us. The Author of faith
is the Spirit."

This washing, according to Calvin and to truth, has no reference to water washing; but is due to spiritual cleansing based on
a metaphorical use of Christ's blood.

OLSHAUSEN, *in loco :* " The three words ἀπελούσασθε, ἡγιάσθητε,

ἐδικαιώθητε comprehend in a climax progressive Christian regeneration. Ἀπελούσασθε exhibits the negative operation of grace,
forgiveness of sins through baptism. Ἐν τῷ ὀνόματι, without doubt
refers to all three particulars. ' *And by the Spirit of our God*,'
refers to the Holy Spirit, who commences his agency where the
work of Christ has made a place."

CARSON, p. 478 : "Faith in Christ is that through which they
are washed ; and the Spirit of our God is the Agent who washes
them by this means. This washing is represented in baptism, to
which this passage refers." Baptism does not represent *a washing*. Βάπτισμα is unsuited for such office. The water in ritual
baptism represents by its nature (pure) the *washed condition* of
the soul through the blood of Christ applied by the Holy Spirit.

It is a radical error to suppose that *the washing* of Christianity,
spoken of by inspired writers, must be referred to the use of
water in ritual baptism as its basis. This use of the word " washing" is grounded primarily in the cleansing quality of water in
general ; and the fitness of such usage in Scripture finds its justification in the real *moral cleansing of the soul by the Holy Spirit,
under the atonement of Christ.* So far from this real moral
washing resting for its title upon the ritual water of baptism (in
which there is no washing, in fact, of any kind) *the use of the
water in the rite is in absolute dependence for its fitness on this
real washing of the soul by the* BLOOD *of* Christ through the Holy
Spirit.

It is also a radical error to conclude, that " the form of ritual
baptism " (covering the body with water) is indicated by the use
of λούω in speaking of this Christian washing.

It is undoubtedly true that λούω is fitly applied to ordinary
physical washings of the entire body ; but it would be a great
mistake to conclude—therefore, in religious washings the whole
body must be covered with water. All that is necessary to the
fullest vindication of the usage is *complete* purification, however
induced. The body of a Jew sprinkled with heifer ashes was
completely cleansed ; and could as properly be said to be washed
(= cleansed), as if any quantity of water to any extent had been
applied to it. What **rational** being would say, that Rev. 1 : 5
" Unto Him that loved us, and washed (λούσαντι) us from our sins
by (ἐν) his blood" meant to teach, that all the redeemed were
covered over in the blood of Christ ? Or, that there was the
slightest difference *as to the completeness* of the washing (= cleans-

ing, purification) as thus indicated and that declared in 1 Peter 1 : 2, "Elect . . . unto obedience and *sprinkling* (ῥαντισμὸν) of the blood of Jesus Christ?" Could error go beyond the idea, that that blood "which cleanses from all sin" was more or less extensively cleansing as it is represented in its application to be a " washing," or a " sprinkling"?

However much *a washing* and *a sprinkling* may differ from each other (in their original and ordinary application) in form and effect, yet, when used to express the application of the blood of Christ to the soul, *the result* (complete purification from sin) is identically the same, in either case. The washing of Christianity is not a physical cleansing. It may be represented as effected by the sprinkling of the blood of Christ, or as symbolized by the sprinkling of pure water, as well as in any other way.

To understand *washed* (" ye are washed ") as applied to the redeemed as meaning, that they were made clean only so far as the blood of Christ may have been superficially applied, and no farther (as, " he washed (ἔλουσεν) their stripes "), would manifest a singular obliviousness both of the nature of the atonement, and of the nature of words by which *a resultant effect* (accomplished in any way), may be expressed, instead of *the form of the act by which* such effect is ordinarily produced.

In the passage before us, the washing must be understood as indicative of an exclusively spiritual condition with which water has nothing to do : 1. Because thus only can it be fitly associated with the purely spiritual condition of " sanctification " and "justification ;" 2. Because this is demanded by the Scriptures which elsewhere ascribe this washing to the spiritual efficacy of the blood of Christ ; 3. Because it is here expressly ascribed to "the name of Christ, and the Spirit of our God," which are adequate to the result; and the introduction of ritual water is alike unnecessary and out of place.

So, Irenæus (1151): "'Abluti estis' credentes 'in nomine Domini,' et accipientes ejus Spiritum. Abluti autem sumus non-substantiam corporis, sed pristinam vanitatis conversationem." He makes the washing spiritual and not physical or ceremonial

THE WASHING OF WATER BY THE WORD.

EPHESIANS 5 : 26.

Ἴνα αὐτὴν ἁγιάσῃ, καθαρίσας τᾷ λουτρῷ τοῦ ὕδατος, ἐν ῥήματι.

"That he might sanctify it, cleansing it with the washing of water, by the word."

Various Views.

DR. PUSEY, p. 160: "St. Paul mentions no other instrument but baptism; for in that he says, 'with the washing of water *by the word*,' he means the Divine word which renders the element of water efficacious to our regeneration, our blessed Saviour's 'word' of consecration."

"By what word? In the name of the Father, and of the Son, and of the Holy Ghost," says Chrysostom; and so Theodoret, "That saying, '*having cleansed in the washing of water, by the word*,' stands for, 'In the name of the Father, and of the Son, and of the Holy Ghost.'"

BLOOMFIELD, *in loco:* "τῷ λουτρῷ τοῦ ὕδατος must be understood of *baptism*, in which the new Christian is washed from the stains of original sin, and which is also a symbol of that purity to which the new professor binds himself. Such appears to be the chief sense. On the sense of ἐν ῥήματι Commentators are not agreed. Some think it adverts to the words of the baptismal form, as accompanied with prayers. *Locke, Beza, Rosenm.*, and others understand by it, *the doctrine of Christ, the Gospel*, as the means of their original conversion and progressive sanctification. This I prefer."

CALVIN, *in loco:* "*That he might sanctify;* that he might separate it to himself. This is accomplished by the forgiveness of sins and the regeneration of the Spirit.

"*Washing it with the washing of water:* Having mentioned the inward sanctification, he now adds the outward symbol, by which it is visibly confirmed. If the *truth* were not connected with baptism, it would be improper to say, that baptism is the washing of the soul. We must not imagine that water cleanses the pollutions of the soul, which nothing but the blood of Christ can accomplish. We must beware of giving any portion of our confidence to the element or to man, but place all our dependence on Christ. The apostle does not say that it is the sign that washes, but God.

24

God employs a sign as the outward means. God acts by the sign
so that its whole efficacy depends on his Spirit. God may bestow
the grace without the aid of the sign. Many receive the sign
without the grace. *In the word.* If the *word* is taken away the
whole power of the sacraments is gone. By the *word* is here
meant the promise, which explains the value and use of the signs.
In the word is equivalent to ' by the word.' "

BENGEL, *in loco:* " *That he might sanctify.* Sanctification is
derived from the blood of Christ; *cleansing* or purification from
baptism and the word. Why did Christ give himself for the
Church? That he might sanctify it. Why did he *cleanse* it?
That he might present it to himself. The former is the new right
acquired by Christ over the Church; the latter shows how he
adorned his bride, as befitted such a bride of such a Husband.
The cleansing power is in the *word,*' and it is put forth through
the *washing. Water* and the *bath* are the vehicle; but the *word*
is a nobler instrumental cause.

" *By the washing with water by the word.* A remarkable testimony for baptism, *in* (by) *the word.* Baptism has the power of
purifying owing to the word, John 15 : 3 ; *in (by)* to be construed
with *cleansing.*

" *That he might present it to himself a glorious church.* We
should derive our estimate of sanctification from the love of
Christ; what bride despises the ornaments offered by her husband? That the Church may be without spot, or wrinkle, or any
such thing, holy and without blemish."

OLSHAUSEN, *in loco:* " In the combination ἵνα αὐτὴν ἁγιάσῃ καθαρίσας we are to take ἁγιάζειν as a consequence of καθαρίζειν : ' that
he might sanctify her, after he had previously purified her by the
bath,' *i. e.,* baptism. But the explanation of ἐν ῥήματι is uncertain.
It can be joined only with λουτρὸν τοῦ ὕδατος. It is in sense equivalent to ἐν Πνεύματι, intimating that baptism is no *mere bath,* but a
bath *in the word, i. e.,* one by which man is born again of water
and the Spirit.

" Ῥῆμα is here, as in Heb. 1 : 3, 11 : 3, a designation of the
Divine power and efficacy, in general, which, from its nature,
must be a spiritual one. But in Christianity the Spirit manifests
itself only in the Word of Truth, which is in Christ.

" As Christ purifies and cleanseth the Church, so likewise a
faithful husband wishes to deliver his wife from every moral
stain."

ELLICOTT, *in loco*: "*That he might sanctify it.* Sanctification of the Church attendant on the remission of sins in baptism. Sanctification and purification are dependent on the atoning death of Christ.

"*Having purified it.* More naturally antecedent to ἁγιάσῃ, but contemporaneous act tenable on grammatical grounds. *By the laver of the water.* The reference to baptism is clear and distinct, and the meaning of λουτρον indisputable, as instrumental object.

"*In the word.* There is great difficulty in determining the exact *meaning* and grammatical *connection* of these words. The meaning is probably *the Gospel;* the word of God preached and taught before baptism. The connection is probably with *the whole expression,* καθ. λουτρ. τοῦ ὕδ. According to this view ἐν ῥήματι has neither a purely instrumental, nor, certainly, a simple modal force, but specifies the necessary *accompaniment,* that *in which* the baptismal purification is vouchsafed and without which it is not granted. *That he might present.* As in 2 Cor. 11 : 2, the presentation of the bride to the bridegroom; Christ permits neither attendants nor paranymphs to present the Bride : He alone presents, He receives."

CARSON, p. 212 : "The bath of baptism is only the figure of that which is done by the word. It is expressly said that the washing of water is by the word. The word is the means by which the believer is washed in the blood of Christ. The believer is washed by the word, even although, through ignorance or want of opportunity, he has never been washed in water."

Unsatisfactory.

None of these views, so far as they make the water of ritual baptism a cause of spiritual purification or place it, in any sense, in living relation with it, are satisfactory. The exposition of Calvin is wisely discriminating. That view which makes ritual baptism a pure *opus operatum,* cleansing from sin and regenerating the soul, is satisfactory in so far as its sentiment is plainly stated and its boundaries are sharply defined; but it cannot be received as a satisfactory exposition of any passage of Scripture, whose general scope and particular statements it contradicts. That view which makes ritual baptism a cause, but not the sole and direct cause, of spiritual purification, does not afford the satisfaction of being either definite or intelligible.

There is a want of accord among its friends as to the co-union of the physical and spiritual element, as well as to the spiritual value of their joint operation. The doctrine is defective as not covering such cases as receive the rite confessedly without spiritual benefit, and such other cases as confessedly receive full spiritual benefit without receiving the rite. It also antagonizes that very teaching of the Saviour out of which it claims to grow, namely, "that which is born of the flesh *is flesh*, and that which is born of the Spirit is spirit." The principle pervading this statement is, "Like begets like;" a principle incorporated in Creation at the beginning and maintained until now. *Physical* agencies beget *kindred physical* results; and Spiritual agencies beget kindred spiritual results. A miracle only can educe spiritual results from physical causes. The Saviour's words establish instead of announcing the overthrow of this law. But the friends of this doctrine *declare it to be a miracle:* " Baptism is so much the more extolled in that it was the end of so many miracles; and *the daily miracle which he worketh in the Baptismal fountain* of our Christian Church receives the more glory, in that the first opening of that 'fountain for sin and uncleanness' was so solemnized; and the daily gift 'of the new birth of the water and the Spirit' in our Gentile church *is greater than that miraculous shedding of the Holy Ghost* which ushered it in and secured it to us " (Dr. Pusey, *Holy Baptism, p.* 180

Others may reject the miracle character of this co-action of water and the Spirit; but they never have made their views intelligible, self-consistent, accordant with facts, or harmonious with the Scriptures. Water regeneration is nothing or it is a miracle.

That view which would make a direct reference to the water of the rite as a "sign" of the higher and sole purification wrought by the Holy Spirit, is in itself possible; but whether there would be any such reference as that, in this passage, to a symbol which does not effect any purification (not physical any more than spiritual) is very questionable.

Suggestion.

All interpreters agree that the purification hinges on ἐν ῥήματι. There is a very general agreement in placing this phrase in close relation with καθαρίσας λουτρῷ τοῦ ὕδατος. There is, also, an expression of decided embarrassment in determining the precise character of this relation. It may be that the embarrassment in adjusting the relation between these phrases arises from the character which is attributed to the former, as representing the water of ritual baptism and purification by it.

The phrase " washing of water," by its own force, denotes a washing which is effected by water.   There is no agency in nature which can effect a more perfect washing of an unclean object. The " washing of water " is capable of use to express *the perfectness of the cleansing* effected by any other agency differing in nature from water, yet purifying in its influence.   That is to say, *the washing which is effected by water becomes the common and supreme standard* among men for purity.   Thus Job (9:30) says: *Snow-water washing* will make " never so clean," and stand any test of purity, *except that of the pureness of God.*   Here moral purity, the result *of holy living*, is likened to that purity of hands which is the result *of snow-water washing.*

The phrase " having cleansed or cleansing by *the washing of* WATER " may express either the cleansing in fact by water, or it may refer to water-cleansing simply as the basis of a comparison with some other cleansing effected by an agency diverse from water, in order to express the completeness of its power to cleanse. Is not this its use in the passage before us?   And is not the relation of ἐν ῥήματι to this phrase (as declaring the diverse cleansing agency) made clear?   The Lord Jesus Christ will sanctify his church (his Bride), cleansing it (*as*) with the washing of water *by the word* through which the Holy Spirit cleanses the souls of his redeemed.   By such reference to the perfect cleansing by water physically, the perfect cleansing "by the word" spiritually is exhibited with both strength and beauty.   And the basis of such reference (the physically cleansing power of water) is precisely the same as that of the symbol use of water in baptism ; but inasmuch as the water in baptism *does not cleanse in fact*, it cannot be the basis of the reference here.   I know of no reason from the phraseology which precludes such interpretation.   It is in the fullest harmony with the teaching of Scripture in general, and with the tenor of this passage in particular.   It relieves of a world of embarrassment which ever has and must gather around any interpretation which takes ritual baptism as its exponent.

If any should wish for more special regard to be had to the article before " water," it may be regarded as indicating *the* water used in Bridal washing, to which, by general admission, reference is made.   " *The* water " furnished for such purpose would (like the "snow-water" of Job) be so pure as to render the object washed "never so clean."

The sentiment of the passage is—The Lord Jesus Christ in preparing the Church for presentation to Himself, "as a Bride adorned for her Husband," will cleanse it from all moral impurity by his word and Spirit, as perfectly as any object can be cleansed from physical impurity by the washing of water, so that the Church can say with David (Ps. 51 : 7), "Purge me with hyssop, and I shall be clean; *wash* me, and I shall be WHITER THAN SNOW." Thus washed it will be "a glorious church, not having spot, or wrinkle, or any such thing; but holy and without blemish."

A quite parallel passage may be found in Ezek. 16 : 8, . . . "I sware unto thee and entered into covenant with thee, saith the Lord God, and thou becamest mine. Then washed I thee with water (ἐλουσάσε ἐν ὕδατι), and cleansed (ἀπέπλυνα) thee from thy blood, and anointed thee with oil (ἐν ἐλαίω), and I clothed thee with broidered work; I decked thee also with ornaments; . . . thy beauty was perfect *through my comeliness, which I had put upon thee,* saith the Lord God." Here "washing with water" is used not to express a thing done by God; but a thing practiced by men *is made the basis to illustrate a kindred result* effected by God, whereby he puts "his own comeliness," in spotless purity, upon his Church. The "washing," and the "broidered work," and the "ornaments," were alike the imparted divine "comeliness."

This washing (λούω) is no more represented as being *in* the water, than is the anointing as being *in* the oil. There is no cleansing by water-washing in fact, any more than there is an anointing with oil; but these things constitute *an allusive basis to expound kindred things* accomplished by God through other agencies.

The Church is sanctified by the Word, and thereby purified as perfectly as the washing by water (the most perfect of all purifying physical agencies) can purify the object washed by it. This appears to be a just paraphrase of the passage. There is no immediate reference to ritual baptism. The point of junction between this passage and ritual baptism is a common basis in the nature of water (pureness) and in the effect of water-washing (purity). Out of these characteristics the use of water in ritual baptism and the language of this passage are equally and independently developed.

THE WASHING OF REGENERATION.

TITUS 3 : 5.

Κατὰ τὸν αὐτοῦ ἔλεον ἔσωσεν ἡμᾶς, διὰ λουτροῦ παλιγγενεσίας καὶ ἀνακαινώσεως Πνεύματος Ἁγίου.

" God our Saviour . . . according to his mercy saved us, by the washing of regeneration and the renewing of the Holy Ghost, which he shed on us abundantly through Jesus Christ our Saviour."

Various Views.

DR. PUSEY, p. 48 : " *The washing of regeneration and renewing of the Holy Ghost, i. e.,* a Baptizing accompanied by, or conveying a reproduction, a second birth, a restoration of our decayed nature, by the new and fresh life, imparted by the Holy Ghost. The Apostle has been directed both to limit the imparting of the inward grace, by the mention of the outward washing, and to raise our conceptions of the greatness of this second birth, by the addition of the spiritual grace. The gift, moreover, is the gift of God in and by Baptism; everything but God's mercy is' excluded—'not by works of righteousness which we have done'— they only who believe will come to the washing of regeneration; yet not belief alone, but 'God, according to his mercy, saves them by the washing of regeneration;' by faith are we saved, not by works; and by Baptism we are saved, not by faith only; for so God hath said; not the necessity of preparation, but its efficiency in itself is excluded; baptism comes neither as 'grace of congruity,' nor as an outward seal of benefits before conveyed; we are saved neither by faith only, nor by Baptism only; but faith bringing us to Baptism, and 'by Baptism God saves us.' They are the words of God himself. As our Lord said negatively, without the birth of water and the Spirit, or Baptism, man 'could not see the kingdom of God,' so St. Paul, that 'by it we are saved;' saved out of the world, and brought into the ark, if we but abide there and become not reprobates."

Dr. Pusey quotes in confirmation the ancient Liturgies, among others the following: " Sanctify this water and this oil, that they may be a bath of regeneration (Amen) to eternal life (Amen); for a clothing of immortality (Amen), for the adoption of sons (Amen), for the renovation of the Holy Spirit (Amen), etc. Grant to it power to become life-giving water (Amen), sanctifying water (Amen), water cleansing sin (Amen), water of the bath of regeneration (Amen), water of the adoption of sons (Amen), etc." (p. 51).

BLOOMFIELD, *in loco: Through the washing of regeneration.* " All the most enlightened Interpreters have been long agreed that the opinion invariably supported by early Fathers is the true one, namely, that *baptismal regeneration* is here meant. . . . I will only add that the disputes upon baptismal and moral regeneration have too often degenerated into logomachies; whereas, if the disputants would take care to define the terms they employ, and have the patience to understand each other, they would be found to differ far less than they seem to do. Παλιγγενεσίας sometimes, in ancient writers, means *moral reformation.*"

BENGEL, *in loco:* " Two things are mentioned : *the washing of regeneration*, which is a periphrasis for baptism into Christ ; and the renewing of the Holy Spirit. This *regeneration* and *renewing* takes away all the death and the old state, under which we so wretchedly lay, and which is described, v. 3 ; 2 Cor. 5 : 17."

CALVIN, *in loco: He hath saved us.* " He speaks of faith, and shows that we have already obtained salvation, according to that saying—' He that beliveth in the Son of God hath passed from death unto life.'

" *By the washing of regeneration.* This alludes, at least, to baptism, and even I will not object to have this passage expounded as relating to baptism ; not that salvation is contained in the outward symbol of water, but because baptism seals to us the salvation obtained by Christ. Since a part of revelation consists in baptism, that is, so far as it is intended to confirm our faith, Paul properly makes mention of it. The strain of the passage runs thus : God hath saved us by his mercy, the symbol and pledge of which he gave in baptism, by admitting us into his church, and ingrafting us into the body of his Son.

" *And of the renewing of the Holy Spirit.* Though he mentioned the sign, that he might exhibit to our view the grace of God, yet, that we may not fix our whole attention on the sign, he immediately sends us to the Spirit, that we may know that we are washed by his power, and not by water. Paul, while he speaks directly of the Spirit, at the same time alludes to baptism. It is therefore the Spirit of God who regenerates us, and makes us new creatures ; but because his grace is invisible and hidden a visible symbol of it is beheld in baptism.

" *Through Jesus Christ.* It is he alone through whom we are made partakers of the Spirit. The Spirit of regeneration is bestowed on none but those who are the members of Christ."

ELLICOTT, *in loco:* " *By means of the laver of regeneration.* This is the *causa medians* of the saving grace of Christ; it is a *means* whereby we receive the same, and a pledge to assure us thereof. Less than this cannot be said by any candid Interpreter. The genitive παλιγγενεσίας apparently marks the attribute or inseparable accompaniments of the λουτρόν, the *possessive* genitive.

" *And renewing of the Holy Spirit, i. e.,* by the Holy Spirit, the second genitive being that of *the agent.* The construction of the first genitive ἀνακαινώσεως is somewhat doubtful. It may be regarded as dependent on διά or on λουτροῦ. The latter seems most simple and satisfactory. The exact genitival relation παλιγγενεσίας and ἀνακαινώσεως cannot be very certainly or very confidently defined. The genitive is most probably an obscured genitive of the *content*, representing that which the λουτρόν involves, comprises, brings with it, and of which it is the ordinary and appointed external vehicle: compare Mark 1 : 4, βάπτισμα μετανοίας, which, grammatically considered, is *somewhat* similar."

" *Which* (Holy Spirit) *he poured out.* The special reference is not to the Pentecostal effusion, nor to the communication to the church at large, but, as the tense and context seem rather to imply, to individuals in baptism. The next clause points out through whose mediation this effusion is bestowed."

DR. CARSON, p. 211: " Here baptism is called the bath or laver of regeneration. In the figure it is the place of birth. The baptized person is represented as born in the ordinance, and is supposed to be already born, or renewed by the Spirit. . . . None are represented in Scripture as born again, except through the belief of the truth. 'Being born again, not of corruptible seed, but of incorruptible, by the word of God, which liveth and abideth forever' (1 Peter 1 : 23)."

Λουτρόν.

Bishop Ellicott thinks that the meaning of λουτρόν as the instrumental object, the containing vessel, is not disproved by any cases of usage yet adduced.

This is certain, that λουτήρ and not λουτρόν is the favorite word used by the Septuagint and early Christian writers, to express the containing vessel.

Josephus (de Bel. VII, 6, 3) uses λουτρόν *not* to express " the containing vessel," but the water itself, to be used for bathing,— " hot and cold water mixed make a very pleasant (λουτρόν) bath."

President Beecher, p. 208, adduces evidence of the like character from Porphyry (*in libel. de antro Nympharum*) in which water brought from springs in a vessel carried by a boy, was used for purification, and was called λουτρόν, or λουτρά νυμφικά. Zonaras defines λουτρά thus : " τά εἰς λύσιν ἀγόντα τῆς ἀκαθαρσίας things which conduce to the removal of impurity." This usage seems to establish the same usage as that of Josephus, namely, this word was used to express *the water* used for purification (by sprinkling or pouring, in ceremonial cleansings, as well as by bathing), and not to denote "the containing vessel."

President Beecher adduces, also, the following from BASIL, *Letter* 386, " ' He washed away all the stains of his soul at the close of his life *by the washing of regeneration* λουτρῷ παλιγγενεσίας.' The case is that of the prætor Ariantheus, converted by his wife, and also baptized by her on his dying bed." This usage seems to exclude not only "the containing vessel," but, as well, the water itself (as a simple bath), and to reach over to *the effect* produced by the use ; *a washing* (purification) of regeneration. The containing vessel has disappeared ; the form of a bath has equally disappeared ; and the effect in the soul, as Basil believed (induced by sprinkling or pouring), only remains. A ceremonial sprinkling or pouring will effect a complete ceremonial washing = purification. Basil interpreted this text as a spiritual and not as a mere ritual water washing. In accordance with this usage is that in *Sirach* 34 : 30, " Baptized (= purified) from a dead body and touching it again, what is he profited by (λουτρῷ) his cleansing." Also, Clem. Alex., " Be pure not by washing (λουτρῷ) but by thinking (νόῳ) (I, 1352)." This evidence appears to be conclusive against the limitation of λουτρόν to "the containing vessel." Cremer (λούω, λουτρόν) says, the verb and noun are used for religious washings, purifications ; quoting Soph. Ant., 1186 λούσαντες 'αγνὸν λουτρώ, washing a pure washing.

The idea of *washing* (expressed by λούω and other verbs) in a purely spiritual sense, in religious applications, is common in the Scriptures : Ps. 26 : 6 : " I will wash (νίψομαι) my hands *in innocence.*" This is a different washing from that of Pilate when " he washed his hands in *water.*" Ps. 51 : 2 : " Wash (πλῦνον) me thoroughly from mine iniquity." Iniquities are not washed away by *water.* Is. 1 : 16 : " Wash you (λούσασθε) ; make you clean ; put away the evil of your doings from before my eyes ; cease to do evil; learn to do well; ... though your sins be as scarlet, they shall be as white as snow." Washing in " snow-water " will not accomplish such cleansing. Is. 4 : 4 : " When the Lord shall have washed away (ἐκπλυνεῖ) the filth of the daughters of Zion ... by the spirit of judgment, and by the spirit of burning." "Judgment " and " burning " do not wash physically.

Acts 22 : 16 : " Wash away (ἀπόλουσαι) thy sins calling upon the name of the Lord." *Prayer* will wash away sin ; *water* will not. 1 Cor. 6 : 11 : " But ye are washed (ἀπελούσασθε), but ye are sanctified, but ye are justified, in the name of the Lord Jesus, and by the Spirit of our God." The only thing we need to be washed from, under Christianity, is sin ; and the only means by which this can be done, is the blood of the Lord Jesus ; and the only Agent who can so wash, is " the Spirit of our God." Rev. 1 : 5 : " Unto him that loved us and washed us (λούσαντι) from our sins by his blood." This is not water washing. Rev. 7 : 14 : "And have washed (ἔπλυναν) their robes and made them white by the blood of the Lamb;" " Fine linen is the righteousness of Saints " (Rev. 19 : 8) ; and the righteousness of Saints is Jesus, " the Lord our righteousness ;" his people " put Him on " and are arrayed in robes made white by the blood of the Lamb. This is not water washing.

With such abounding use of " washing," wholly removed from the sphere of physical agencies and physical results, there is surely nothing to constrain us (if there be anything to warrant us) in finding physical elements in the washing spoken of in the passage under consideration. There are none.

The Genitive.

Bishop Ellicott thinks that there are special difficulties in determining the character of the genitives παλιγγενεσίας, ἀνακαινώσεως, but prefers their being connected together and placed in common relation with λουτροῦ, and expository of it. If this be done would it not be proper to make the entire phrase, the washing and its characteristics, directly dependent upon, Πνεύματος Ἁγίου? The sentiment being—Salvation through the washing effected by the Holy Ghost, the distinguishing features of which are—a regenerate nature and a renewed mind = the cleansed condition of the soul. If this phrase be broken, and considered in two distinct yet intimately related parts, must not παλιγγενεσίας and Πνεύματος Ἁγίου be made the governing words, and the sentiment be,—He saved us by a regenerative washing and a Divine renovation? We are saved by a washing such as *regeneration* effects, and a renovation such as *the Holy Ghost* effects. The regeneration being no less the work of the Holy Ghost than the renovation; just as we are " washed " *from sin*, and " sanctified " and "justified," all " by the Spirit of our God ;" and just as we are " saved by the Spirit through antitype baptism " (which is his work) and not through water, by which " the filth of the flesh " only, can be put away.

This very eminent Commentator also thinks, that βάπτισμα μετανοίας, grammatically considered, is *somewhat* similar to λουτροῦ παλιγγενεσίας. Is not the parallelism complete? Does not the first phrase express a baptism which is effected by *repentance* (a repentance baptism) whose nature is more explicitly stated as a βάπτισμα μετανοίας εἰς ἄφεσιν ἁμαρτιων = a thorough washing from sin by repentance ; while the second phrase expresses a washing effected by *regeneration* (= a regenerative washing), which necessarily implies the cleansing from sin. And is not βαπτισμῶν διδαχῆς equally parallel? Baptisms effected by doctrine (= washings, cleansings, purifyings by *repentance* and *faith*) as wrought by the Holy Spirit.

Is not such interpretation confirmed by the like relation in the phrase with which this is so intimately connected—ἀναχαινώσεως Πνεύματος Ἁγίου, the renewing which is effected by the Holy Ghost? Any reference even to ritual baptism in this passage is inadmissible. The work is that of the Holy Ghost and to him it is expressly and exclusively ascribed. To bring in rite or water on the ground of such a phrase as λουτροῦ παλιγγενεσίας is perfectly gratuitous.

HEART SPRINKLED—BODY WASHED.

HEBREWS 10 : 22.

'Ερραντ.σμένοι τὰς καρδίας ἀπὸ συνειδήσεως πονηρᾶς καὶ λελουμένοι τὸ σῶμα ὕδατι καθαρῷ.

" Let us draw near with a true heart in full assurance of faith, having our hearts sprinkled from an evil conscience and our bodies washed with pure water."

Interpretation.

" This refers to ritual baptism. To me it is evident that the whole body was covered with water. The heart is said to be sprinkled in allusion to the blood of the sacrifices; and the body, in allusion to bathings under the law, is said to be washed in pure water, referring to the ordinance of baptism. Now the pouring of a little water on the face is not a washing of the body. I admit that sprinkling a little water on any part of the body might be an emblem of purification; but this would not be called a washing of the body" (CARSON, p. 164). "'*Sprinkled.*' There is an allusion to the sacrificial rite by which the mind as well as the body of the worshipper was required to be pure. *Washed.* This designates the *external* purity which is wont to be conjoined with *internal* holiness. There is allusion to the daily washing of the priests. *Ernesti* says this washing cannot be taken *proprié,* unless understood of *baptism,* which *cannot here be meant"* (BLOOMFIELD, *in loco*). "'*Sprinkled, washed.*' There is reference to sacrificial rites by which the Law demanded purity in *mind* and *body, internal* and external sanctity. Some think there is reference to baptism" (ROSENM., *in loco*). "'*Sprinkled.*' A figure explained by sacrificial blood-sprinkling. *Washed,* as 'sprinkled,' is taken figuratively, so should 'washed,' and not be understood as the physical washing of the body with water by baptism. The meaning is: And if we are now thus washed from our sins" (EBRARD, *in loco*). "'*Hearts sprinkled.*' Both the *hearts* and the *body* are cleansed. *Body washed.* The allusion is to the Levitical washings. *Pure water.* 'I will sprinkle clean water upon you'" (BENGEL, *in loco*). "'*Sprinkled.*' The expression is borrowed from the rites of the law. Which was *external.* But when the writer says, 'Sprinkled as to our *hearts,*' he designates *spiritual, internal* purification, and shows that he is not speaking of *external* rites. *Bodies washed with pure water.* Another expression borrowed from Levitical washings for external purification. It seems to me, that there is here a plain allusion to the use of water in Christian baptism " (STUART, *in loco*). " The Jews cleansed themselves by various carnal washings. In Christ all these things are far superior. Away then with all the external washings of the flesh. The Apostle sets a true heart, a sure faith, and a cleansing from vice, in opposition to these external rites. *Our bodies washed with pure water.* This is generally understood of baptism; but the Apostle more probably alludes to the ceremonies of the Law; and so by water designates the Spirit of God, as in Ezekiel 36:25, 'I will sprinkle clean water upon you.' The meaning is, that we are sanctified in body and soul by faith, a pure conscience, and that cleanness of soul and body which flows from, and is effected by, the Spirit of God. So Paul, 2 Cor. 7:1, 'Let us cleanse ourselves from all filthiness of the flesh and spirit, perfecting holiness in the fear of God'" (CALVIN, *in loco*). " It is evident that baptism is not here referred to, because the Apostle is instructing the Hebrews, who had been baptized, how they were daily to draw nigh to God. . . . As sprinkling in the case of Christians is continually needed, so is washing, as the daily washing of the priests before they engaged in their duties. The sprinkling betokens forgiveness; and washing, sanctification or cleansing " (REV. JOHN OWEN, *transl.* and *annot.* of *Calvin*). " What is here meant by 'our bodies being washed'? Corporeal ablutions held an important place under the Old economy; and continually, as the priests entered the sanctuary, they had to wash their hands and their feet. But what corresponds to this in Christian times? We have no external sanctuary and no corporeal ablution to perform when drawing near to worship God. The Apostle must mean not formally the same thing as of old, but something corresponding to it in nature, which is simply a freedom from all manifest stains and blemishes in the conduct. Accepted worshippers of old, and now, must put away overt acts of iniquity. The symbol washing has dropped; the real obligation remains. It is of this reality that the language of the Apostle should be understood. With a purged conscience we must have an untarnished life " (FAIRBAIRN, *Herm. Man*, p. 130).

Result.

1. This passage is not grounded in Christian ritual baptism.

The "sprinkling of the heart" cannot be based *in a Jewish* rite, and the "washing of the body" be based *in a Christian* rite. While the use of water under Judaism and Christianity (and Heathenism as well) have an ultimate common ground in the physically purifying power of water, the immediate specific aspect of purifying in which water is used under the Old Testament and the New Testament is not the same. Jewish rites had efficient power to cleanse ceremonial defilement; Christian ritual baptism has nothing to do with such defilements. The defilements under Christianity are real, and its purification is real. Ritual baptism is not a purification at all. It is only the symbol of a purification. The heart is cleansed "by the blood of sprinkling" (Jewishly speaking); and by faith in the blood of the Lamb of God, Christianly speaking. The body is washed with pure water (Jewishly speaking); and it is washed by godly living, through the grace of the Holy Ghost, day by day, Christianly speaking—"Wash you, make you clean, *cease to do evil.*"

2. The washing of the body with water, *as a religious rite*, neither involves the covering of the body in water, nor the application of the water to the entire body, nor yet to a large part of the body. Dr. Carson (p. 493) admits that in a washing (λούω) the water may be applied "by sprinkling or pouring, or in any way, but the object must be covered."

Tertullian speaks of the *washing* (*lavacro*) of Jove "by showers of rain." And we speak of flowers, etc., being "*washed* by the rain" without any "covering" of the objects so washed. Carson (p. 271) says: "A purification by sprinkling, or pouring a few drops of water, would not be a *loutron*." This is a clear error, except as Dr. Carson should use this word in one sense (physical washing) while opposing it as used in another sense, namely, entire washing = cleansing, purification *religiously*, of the body, or the soul, or both, as the case may be. "Washing" is used to express (1.) A physical cleansing, where the cleansing is only coextensive with the application of the cleansing agency; (2.) A ceremonial cleansing, where the power of the agency, and the extent of its operation, is limited or extended not by the reality of things, but by ordinance; (3.) A spiritual cleansing, effected by spiritual agency, without any physical intervention. When Dr. Carson says, "A few drops of water sprinkled on the human body will not *physically* wash the entire body," he states a self-evident truth; but when he says a few drops of water or blood sprinkled on the human body will not *ceremonially wash* the entire body, or will not symbolize *the washing of the entire* body and soul *spiritually*, he states what is just as evidently untrue.

Chrysostom speaks of martyrs (λούονται) *washed* by their own blood. And Origen speaks of being *washed* (*loti*) by our own blood. Calvin (Harm. Pent., p. 186) truly says: " The washing of the hands and feet denoted that *all parts of the body* were infected with uncleanness, and it is very suitable to say, by synecdoche, that all impurity is purged away by *the washing of the hands and feet*." He also has the fullest vindication for saying (p. 210) "Moses, before he consecrates the priests, WASHES *them by the* SPRINKLING of water."

3. As this *heart*-sprinkling and *body*-washing expresses an internal and external purification, as comprising a complete purification (based on Jewish phraseology and made applicable to Christian truth), it throws light on other Scripture less clear. It confirms the interpretation given of the language addressed to the Jew, Nicodemus,—"born of *water* and of the *Spirit*," as expressing the necessity for *external* and *internal* = complete purification. It also illustrates and vindicates that broader Scriptural use of " washing " (separated from the mere physical element) to which we have had occasion to refer, denoting spiritual cleansing.

These passages—John 3 : 5; 1 Cor. 6 : 11; Eph. 5 : 26; Titus 3 : 5; Heb. 10 : 22—are the principal passages which are supposed to allude to ritual baptism and to teach : 1. That water, a physical element, is divinely appointed and is essential to wash away sin and to regenerate the soul; 2. That the terms used (λούω, λουτρόν) teach, that the mode of using this ritual water is by covering the body in the water by dipping; which is so essential that none of God's redeemed ones failing to observe such mode can rightly receive the Sacraments or constitute a church of the Lord Jesus Christ. If these texts be interpreted in subjection to Patristic sentiment and practice, much can be said in apparent favor of both these views; but if the interpretation be made by a just exegesis, under the teaching and usage of Holy Scripture, then, neither view will find the least support.

CHRISTIC BAPTISM: THE BAPTISM OF THE COMMISSION—WHAT IS IT?

ELEMENTS ENTERING INTO THE COMMISSION.

JOHN 20 : 21-23.

" Then said Jesus to them again, Peace be unto you : as my Father hath sent (ἀπέσταλκέν) me, even so send I you.

" And when he had said this, he breathed on them, and saith unto them, Receive ye the Holy Ghost:

" Whosesoever sins ye remit, they are remitted unto them ; and whosesoever sins ye retain, they are retained."

The Apostolical Commission.

Alford (*in loco*): " He confirms and grounds their Apostleship on the present glorification of himself, whose Apostleship (Heb. 3 : 1) on earth was now ended, but was to be continued by this sending forth of them."

To whatever immediate occasion or date these words may be assigned, they do unquestionably contain the Apostolical Commission, together with a statement of some of the endowments and powers entering into it.

The word βαπτίζω does not appear; but its very absence may be more instructive than its presence. The occasion and the time when these words were spoken may have been other than such as is indicated by the relations in which they stand recorded. There is no necessary connection from the form or the substance of vv. 19, 20, with the matter in vv. 21-23. The close of v. 20 is a natural close to the transaction to which it refers ; and the repetition, " Peace be unto you," in v. 21, is unnatural as considered in relation to an immediately preceding utterance (v. 19) of like character.

As John makes no other mention of the Commission, it is the more probable that this passage does either directly declare it or substantially embrace its elements. There is no uniformity of words among the Evangelists in recording the final Commission

25 (385)

of the Apostles, although there is an agreement as to the essentials which enter into it.

1. It is easy to see the harmony between this " Peace be unto you," and the " Lo! I am with you " of Matthew; 2. In the " as my Father hath sent me, even so send I you," there is more than mission and authority expressed; there is included, as well, the end of that mission and its bearing, through the Lord Jesus Christ, on the Father, and the Godhead represented by the Father, with whom this mission and its end originated. It stands related therefore to that other statement of Matthew, that those who are discipled to the Lord Jesus Christ are to be " baptized into the name of the Father, and of the Son, and of the Holy Ghost;" 3. " Receive ye the Holy Ghost," whether designed to express the bestowal of the Holy Ghost at Pentecost, or to announce the first fruits and pledge of that " promise of the Father," is in either case the bestowal of the pre-eminently essential requisite to the successful execution of the Commission; 4. " Whosoever sins ye remit they are remitted unto them; and whosoever sins ye retain, they are retained " is in equal harmony with Luke's " preach repentance and remission of sins, in his name, among all nations," and Mark's " Preach the gospel; he that believeth and is baptized shall be saved, he that believeth not shall be damned."

These are the elements in the Commission as stated by John. They accord with the like records of the other Evangelists.

THE PREACHING OF THE COMMISSION.

LUKE 24 : 44–50.

" And he said unto them, These are the words which I spake unto you, while I was yet with you, that all things must be fulfilled which were written in the law of Moses, and in the Prophets, and in the Psalms, concerning me.

" Then opened he their understanding, that they might understand the Scriptures,

" And said unto them, Thus it is written, and thus it behooved Christ to suffer, and to rise from the dead the third day:

" And that repentance and remission of sins should be preached in his name among all nations, beginning at Jerusalem.

" And ye are witnesses of these things.

" And behold I send ($\dot{\epsilon}\xi\alpha\pi o\sigma\tau\epsilon\lambda\lambda\omega$) the promise of my Father upon you: but tarry ye in the city of Jerusalem, until ye be endued with power from on high.

" And he led them out as far as Bethany, and he lifted up his hands and blessed them."

Stier.

STIER, VIII, Luke 24 : 44–49 : " Luke gives us a compendious selection of our Lord's words before his ascension, speaking further of it in the Acts of the Apostles. In this epitomizing the *when* and the *where* are lost sight of. This not being well under. stood by critics and expositors many particulars are misarranged. Although verse 44 appears to be a continuation of verse 43, yet verse 50 shows us the impossibility of so reading it. It involves too great a hiatus in the record, if we make the ' led them out ' follow immediately on the first evening. We must reject the reading of v. 44 as in strict historical connection. Lange would connect v. 44 with the preceding, and make v. 45 the beginning of what extends through the Forty days. But v. 46 seems to be connected with v. 44 in the strictest manner. The more common division made to begin at v. 49 is altogether forced ; for v. 49 continues the discourse and intimates a strict connection.

" *Schleiermacher :* ' v. 44 begins a summary postscript, which is independent of time and place, and reports only that which was essential in the conversations of the Redeemer. It appends a very summary notice of the departure and ascension of Christ.'

" *Grotius ;* v. 44 : ' The sum of the discourses follows, which occurred during the Forty days.'

" *Ebrard* decides also for such a résumé, and asks, whether on this *evening* there had been time to expound the Scriptures, and —to go out to Bethany.

" When and where did He thus speak ? *Bengel* thinks that the whole, including v. 44, was spoken on the day of the ascension But this would assign too late a period for the opening of the Scriptures to the disciples. *Lange* refers v. 45 seq. to the Ap- pearance on the mountain in Galilee ; and as spoken explana- torily *between* vv. 18, 19, of Matt. 28. But we must not consent to separate these verses."

The Elements of Harmony.

Luke (like John) makes no use of the word βαπτίζω in speaking of the Commission. Whether this fact necessitates the omission of any essential feature in the great work committed to the Apostles, we shall be able to determine better after an examination of the use of it as exhibited in the records of Mark and Matthew. The points of accord between this Summary of Luke and that of the other Evangelists as to the Commission is very clear:

1. Luke represents the Lord Jesus Christ as teaching that his atoning death and triumphant resurrection is the fulfilment of a Divine purpose incorporated in all Scripture—Moses, Prophets, and Psalms, whereby a scheme of redemption for a guilty world might be secured.

This truth, less fully developed, is the clear underlying basis of the Commission as stated by Matthew and Mark.

2. Luke is in literal accord with Matthew as to the field covered by the Commission—" all the nations," and differs from Mark—" all the world," only in the lack of pure literality.

3. The subject-matter of the Commission as stated by Luke is, " the preaching of repentance and remission of sins in His name;" which same duty is condensed by Matthew into the one word, μαθητεύσατε—" DISCIPLE," which could only be done by " preaching repentance and remission of sins in His name." Mark is more full. After the condensed statement of this truth in the command " Preach the *gospel*," he develops the necessity of faith —" he that *believeth* " (upon his name) " and is baptized " (into his name), with the result—" shall be saved," and also the reverse—" he that believeth not " (upon his name) " shall be damned." Faith and its result, and unbelief with its result are implied, not stated, in Luke by ἐπὶ τῷ ὀνόματι (v. 47 and again in Acts 2 : 38), resting by faith " UPON his name," as the foundation of Gospel salvation.

4. Luke indicates that Christ is not alone concerned in this Commission and its results, by the appeal to " Moses, and the Prophets, and the Psalms," where the reverse is shown, and the whole Deity is exhibited as indissolubly associated with the prosecution and completion of this great redemption. This is more expressly exhibited in the declaration, " I send the promise of *my* FATHER upon you;" which involves the active agency of the Holy Ghost, proceeding from the Father. Matthew brings out, with supreme distinctness, the relation of the Godhead to this

redemption by announcing a baptism (of those who are discipled to Christ) "into the name of the Father, and of the Son, and of the Holy Ghost." The special nature of which baptism and its relation to the scheme of redemption, will soon engage our attention.

It is evident, that the exhibit of the Commission as made by John and Luke presents no element of discord; while the more limited reference now made to that of Mark and Matthew, encourages us to look for a similar result, under somewhat greater verbal differences.

PAUL'S COMMISSION.

ACTS 26 : 17, 18.

'' Delivering thee from the people and from the Gentiles, unto whom now I send (ἀποστέλλω) thee; To open their eyes, and to turn them from darkness to light, and from the power of Satan unto God; that they may receive forgiveness of sins, and inheritance among them that are sanctified, by faith that is in me.''

This is Paul's Commission as an Apostle. It is the same as that of the twelve. Βαπτίζω is not in it. That which βαπτίζω is used to express—reconciliation with and subjection to the Father, Son, and Holy Ghost—is in it, = " turning them from the power of Satan *unto* God." "All nations " of Matthew, and "all the world " of Mark, are in it, = " delivering thee from *the people* (Jews) and *the Gentiles*." Salvation by discipleship of Matthew, and by faith of Mark, is in it, = " that they may receive forgiveness of sins and inheritance among the sanctified by faith that is in me." Paul understood his Commission to be (vv. 19, 20) Preach repentance, turning to God, and lead holy lives, = " teaching them to observe all things whatsoever I have commanded you." The Commission of Paul without βαπτίζω was the same as that of Matt. and Mark with their differently applied βαπτίζω. And as βαπτίζω is left out of the Commission as recorded by Luke and John, and as declared by Paul to be received from the Lord Jesus Christ, without detriment to the Commission, so, βαπτίζω might have been left out of the New Testament so far as *water* is concerned and been supplied by its *dry* New Testament equivalents "filled" (Acts 2 : 4), "put on" (Gal. 3 : 27), "endued" (Luke 24 : 49), "to trust" (1 Cor. 10 : 2 with Ex. 14 : 31) or that of the Syriac "to cause to stand" (*passim*).

Βαπτίζω has no control over water in the New Testament in a single instance.

BAPTISM THAT SAVES.

MARK 16 : 15, 16.

'Ο πιστεύσας καὶ βαπτισθεὶς σωθήσεται.

" And he said unto them, Go ye into all the world and preach the gospel to every creature.

" He that believeth and is baptized shall be saved; but he that believeth not shall be damned."

Salvation by Baptism—What does it Mean?

MARK agrees with John, and Luke, in making the sphere of the Commission "all the world" = "all the nations;" also, in making its subject "the Gospel" = the atonement, the death, and resurrection, of Christ—"thus it behooved Christ to suffer and to rise from the dead;" and also, that the end of the Commission was "salvation" = "the remission of sins."

But Mark has introduced the word βαπτίζω, which neither John nor Luke has done; has he thereby introduced an essentially new element into the Commission, to wit, a ritual ordinance, and made it a common basis with faith, for salvation?

This is the question which arises and claims consideration.

The simple mention in the New Testament of baptism, does not necessitate the conclusion that reference is made to *ritual* water baptism; because it is universally admitted, that the New Testament announces a *real* baptism, without water, by the Spirit, as well as a ritual baptism with water. Which of the two is meant, in any given case, must be determined by other considerations than the mere word.

In the present case, there are some (the larger number) who advocate a reference to ritual baptism, and others to real baptism. This diversity of opinion does not stop with the nature of the baptism, but reaches into its form and moral value : 1. Some say,

The baptism is ritual, *with* water, purely symbol in character, and without moral value except as the truth which it shadows (remission of sins by the blood of Christ applied by the Holy Ghost) is apprehended by faith in the divine promise, and obedience is rendered as to an ordinance of God. "The statement of Mark respecting faith and baptism, is an authoritative assurance that salvation was suspended on the faithful reception of the gospel, and submission to its initiatory ordinance. The faith of the professing Christian must be attested and sustained by submission to gospel requirement" (WILSON, *Prof. Sac. Lit., Gen. Assembly, Royal College, Belfast*). 2. Some say: The baptism is ritual by dipping the body into water, without which dipping there is no baptism. It is not said, Without which dipping there is no salvation; but saved and damned are placed in an *in terrorem* relation to the dipping so as to force into it. Thus Dr. Fuller begins his book—"The Act of Baptism. ' He that believeth and is baptized shall be saved ; but he that believeth not' (it was unnecessary to add, *and is not baptized*, for he that believeth not will, of course, not be baptized, or if he be baptized, it will avail him nothing), ' *shall be damned.*' Saved or damned! These are solemn thoughts, and solemnly should they be pondered by every man." 3. Some believe the baptism is ritual, without reference to mode, and not necessary to salvation, yet possessed of great spiritual efficacy. "There is an absolute necessity that every human being should be born again. The work of the Holy Spirit is absolutely essential to the production of this change. Baptism is one of the *ordinary* means by which the Holy Spirit works this change. This grace is *offered* whenever Baptism is administered, and is *actually conferred* by the Holy Spirit whenever the individual receiving it does not present in himself a conscious voluntary barrier to its efficacy. In Mark 16 : 16 something is mentioned as a MEAN, to wit, Baptism, and salvation is IN SOME SENSE conditioned upon it. When men read : ' He that believeth and is *not* baptized shall be saved,' they separate what God has joined and contradict our Lord. Faith is ABSOLUTELY essential to salvation, baptism ORDINARILY essential only " (PROF. KRAUTH, *Conserv. Reform.*, pp. 439, 441). " Baptismal regeneration is the distinguishing doctrine of the new covenant, but let us take care and know and bear in mind what ' Baptism ' means ; not the mere ecclesiastical act, not the mere fact of reception, by that act, among God's professing people, but that completed by the Divine act, manifested by the

operation of the Holy Ghost in the heart and through the life"
(ALFORD). 4. Some, who hold that Mark speaks of ritual baptism, believe it to be intimately related to and a condition of
salvation. "The view, then, here held of Baptism, following the
ancient church and our own, is that we be ingrafted into Christ,
and thereby receive a principle of life, afterwards to be developed
and enlarged by the fuller influxes of his grace; so that neither
is Baptism looked upon as an infusion of grace distinct from the
incorporation into Christ, nor is that incorporation conceived of
as separate from its attendant blessings" (DR. PUSEY, Holy Baptism, p. 24). "Baptism is a sort of embodiment of the gospel;
and a solemn expression of it in a single act. Hence the space
and the place assigned to it in the Commission. The Christian
Lawgiver and Saviour says: '*He that believeth and is baptized
shall be saved.*' . . . To associate faith and baptism as antecedents, whose consequent is salvation, no matter what the connection may be, will always impart to the institution a pre-eminence
above all other religious institutions in the world. The Lord does
not say, he that believeth and obeys this or that moral precept,
shall be saved; but 'He that believeth the Gospel and is baptized shall be saved.' . . . The baptisms of the New Testament,
both of John and Jesus, were for the true, real, and formal remission of sins, through faith in the Messiah and a genuine repentance toward God" (ALEXANDER CAMPBELL, *Pres. Bethany College, Christian Baptism*, pp. 257, 8). 5. There is a limited number who deny that Mark speaks of ritual baptism; also denying
that ritual baptism is to be perpetuated in the Christian church.
"As there is one Lord, and one faith, so there is one baptism.
And this baptism is a pure and spiritual thing, to wit, the baptism of the Spirit and fire, by which we are buried with Him, that
being washed and purged from our sins, we may walk in newness
of life: of which the baptism of John was a figure, which was
commanded for a time, and was not to continue forever" (BAR-
CLAY, *Apology*, p. 380).

True Interpretation.

All, so far as I am aware, who interpret the language of the
Evangelist as indicating a ritual baptism, do so without having
examined the question—"May not this be the *real* baptism by
the Holy Spirit and not *ritual* baptism with water?" This vital

issue has been assumed without investigation, and determined against the real baptism of the Scriptures, without a hearing. Such assumption is neither grounded in necessity, nor in the warrant of Scripture; whether regarded in its general teaching or in that of this particular passage. That there is no necessity for limiting the baptism of this passage to a rite is obvious, because the Scriptures furnish us with a real baptism by the Spirit, as well as with its symbol ritual baptism, from which to choose. There is no scriptural warrant in the general teaching of the Bible for identifying a *rite* with salvation; nor can such warrant be assumed in this particular passage (which does identify *baptism* and salvation), because there is no evidence on the face of the passage to show, that the baptism is ritual with water, rather than real by the Spirit. These points must be universally admitted: 1. The passage does not declare a ritual baptism by express statement; 2. It contains no statement which involves a ritual baptism as a necessary inference; 3. The Scriptures present a real and a ritual baptism, by the one or the other of which to meet the exigencies of any elliptically stated baptism; 4. That baptism which meets, in its scripturally defined nature and power, the requirements of any particular passage, must be the baptism designed by such passage.

We reject ritual baptism from all direct connection with this passage, in general, because, the passage treats of salvation and its conditions (belief and baptism). All out of the Papal church admit, that ritual baptism has not the same breadth with belief as a condition of salvation, and are, therefore, compelled to introduce exceptions for which no provision is made in the terms of this passage. We accept the real baptism by the Holy Spirit as the sole baptism directly contemplated by this passage, in general, because, it meets in the most absolute and unlimited manner *as a condition of salvation* the obvious requirement on the face of the passage, having the same breadth with belief, and universally present in every case of salvation.

We accept this view in particular: 1. Because it makes the use of "baptized" harmonious with the associate terms, "believeth" and "saved." The use of these terms, as well as "baptized," is elliptical. "Believe" has in the New Testament a double usage; the one limited to the action of the intellect, as, "the devils believe and tremble;" the other embraces and controls the affections of the heart, as, "with the heart we believe unto righteousness." It is the higher form of "belief" that is universally recognized as belonging to this passage. "Saved," also, is used in the New Testament, with a double application; as of the body, "all hope that we should be saved was taken away;" and of the soul, "He shall save his people from their sins." Again it is this higher salvation that is accepted without question. So, "baptized" is used in a lower and a higher meaning; applied in the one case to the body, as "I baptize you with water;" and in the other case applied to the soul, as "He shall baptize you with the Holy Ghost." By what just reasoning, now, can "believeth," and "saved," be taken in the highest sense, and "baptized," in the same sentence and in the same construction, be brought down to the lowest? We object to such diversity of interpretation as unnatural and without any just support. The only tenable supply of the ellipsis must be, "He that believeth" (with the heart upon Christ), "and is baptized" (by the Holy Ghost into Christ) "shall be saved" (by the redemption of Christ).

2. The construction allows and the case requires, that a relation of dependence and unity subsist between "believeth" and "baptized." There is evidently some *vinculum* binding these words and the ideas which they represent, together. MIDDLETON (Greek article, *in loco*) says: "In the *Complutens*. edit. the second participle has the article, which would materially alter the sense. It would imply, that he who believeth, as well as he who is baptized, shall be saved; whereas the reading of the MSS. insists on the fulfilment of both conditions in every individual." This is true; but it is not all the truth. This faith and this baptism must not only not be disjoined by being assigned to different persons, but they must not be disjoined by being assigned to different spheres, the one spiritual and the other physical; and being conjoined, in like spiritual nature, and meeting together in the same person, the whole truth requires, that they shall be recognized not as two distinct things existing harmoniously together, but as bearing to each other the intimate and essential relation of cause and effect, that is to say, the baptism is a consequence proceeding from the belief. As parallel in construction and in relation, we may take such phrases as "He that drinketh and is drunken;" "He that eateth and is filled;" "He that runneth and is wearied." In such passages it is evident that the relation of drinking, eating, running, to the associate members of their several phrases, is that of cause to effect. A parallelism of construction may be

found in such other phrases as this: " There fell on him a mist and a darkness " (Acts 13 : 11). " *Darkness* may denote the effect as distinguished from the cause " (*Prof. Alexander*). " *A mist and darkness.* Cause and effect " (*Prof. Hackett*). " A sort of Hendiadis " (*Bloomfield*). " Σκότος resulting from an affection of the eyes (ἀχλύς) " (Olshausen). A like relation, without the καί, is seen in the former part of this same verse, " thou shalt be blind, not seeing the sun ; " " μὴ βλέπων, states a consequence of the blindness, hence μὴ, not οὐ " (*Hackett*). And this phrase finds a parallel (with καί introduced) in Luke 1 : 20 : " Thou shalt be dumb and not able to speak." " The words ' not able to speak' are added in order to explain the preceding " (*Kuinoel*.) " 'Unable to speak' is merely an explanatory clause of σιωπῶν " (*Olshausen*).

A parallel construction, with contrast in sentiment and result, is seen in James 2 : 19, " The devils, also, believe and tremble." " The word *believe* is here used in a very wide sense ; for the devils perceive, and understand, and remember, that there is a God, *and tremble* in fearful expectation of eternal torments. So far is such a faith as that from justifying or saving its possessor ; and yet it has some efficacy, but in an opposite direction " (*Bengel*). This believing and trembling are not two independent facts, but they are connected as cause and effect : the believing causes the trembling. And this condition of trembling may, with the most absolute propriety, be termed *a baptism*, as this whole Inquiry demonstrates, and as is specially shown by Isaiah 21 : 4, " My heart panted, fearfulness affrighted me," translated by the Septuagint, " ἡ ἀνομία με βαπτίζει—Iniquity baptizes me, my soul is put into fear." Although there is no *word* in the Hebrew corresponding with βαπτίζω, yet the thought is represented by it with great accuracy and force. A consciousness of iniquity " affrights " = baptizes *into* FEAR. And belief in a holy God baptizes devils into trembling expectation of judgment and fiery indignation, because of conscious iniquity. The passage might be worded thus : Devils who believe and are so baptized shall perish. The belief, and the baptism, and the perishing, will, then, be interpreted by the character of the subjects—" devils." And the ellipsis will be supplied thus : " Devils who believe in a holy God, and are thereby *baptized into terror* because of their iniquities, shall perish with an everlasting destruction, under the divine justice."

Thus, on the authority of the Septuagint, and of all Greek usage, it is settled, that " belief" can *baptize*, and that it will baptize into a condition correspondent with the character of the believer and the subject-matter of the belief. While the belief of devils, directed toward a just and holy God, baptizes into present terror, issuing in everlasting destruction; the belief of the penitent sinner, directed toward a crucified Redeemer, baptizes into Christ (= into the remission of sins), and therefore into present "peace which the world cannot give," issuing in salvation and its everlasting redemption.

3. This interpretation is vindicated by other passages parallel in construction and sentiment. Matt. 13 : 15, " Lest at any time they should be converted and I should heal them." Here, the healing is dependent upon and is a consequence of the conversion. Mark 4 : 12, " Lest at any time they should be converted and their sins should be forgiven them." Here, more specifically, the forgiveness of sins is placed in a dependent relation on conversion. Acts 3 : 19, "Repent and be converted, that your sins may be blotted out." In this passage we have the phrase " be converted *and* be forgiven " resolved into the form, " be converted, *that* your sins may be blotted out," establishing the interpretation as a relation of cause and effect. But more; we have a like relation established between Repentance and Conversion— " Repent and be converted." Conversion is inseparable from and a consequence of repentance. It is a matter of indifference whether it is said : "Repent that your sins may be blotted out," or "Be converted that your sins may be blotted out," or " Repent *and* be converted that your sins may be blotted out." This last form no more presents two separate things as the ground of forgiveness than does either of the others. They all present one and the same thing. So, it is alike indifferent whether it is said : " Believe on the Lord Jesus Christ and thou shalt be saved," or, " Be baptized into Christ, putting on Christ, and thou shalt be saved," or, " Believe on Christ *and* be baptized into Christ, and thou shalt be saved." The latter form no more presents two diverse things as the ground of salvation than does either of the others ; they both present but one and the same thing ; an inseparable consequence implied in the one form being stated in the other. This view is confirmed by Acts 2 : 38, " Repent and be baptized (believing) upon the name of Jesus Christ, into the remission of sins." This passage does not differ, by jot or tittle, in

general construction or in sentiment, from Acts 3 : 19. The ruling element in both is, "Repent." On this depends alike "the blotting out of sins," and "the baptism into the remission of sins;" and between the resultant thought and value of these phrases there is not so much difference as the dust of the balance. These two phrases differing wholly as to the basis in which they are grounded, are yet equal in a supreme force and in absoluteness of result. Sins "blotted out" are absolutely extinguished ; and the guilty "baptized into the remission of sins" are most absolutely freed from sin = brought into a condition in which the remission of sins has its completest development.

4. This interpretation is vindicated by the most express statement of Scripture. Matthew (3 : 2) says, "John preached (Μετανοεῖτε) Repent ye!" He says, also, "He baptized those who repented (εἰς μετάνοιαν) into repentance," using water as a symbol of the purified condition consequent upon true repentance. But Matthew does not directly connect repentance and remission of sins, although he does so indirectly: (1.) By calling upon men to repent; (2.) By the statement (3 : 6) that the baptized "made confession of their sins ;" (3.) By refusing (3 : 7) to baptize those who had not shown repentance by a new life; (4.) By the symbol use of water, which in a baptism "into repentance" could only indicate (not repentance itself but) the purity consequent upon remitted sin granted to the penitent.

This gracious connection between Repentance and the remission of sin which Matthew only implies, Mark most expressly states. He does not, with Matthew merely say, "John preached, Repent!" but makes the fuller statement (1 : 4) "John preached (βάπτισμα μετανοίας εἰς ἄφεσιν ἁμαρτιῶν) the baptism of repentance into the remission of sins." This language, in view of the philological character and historical usage of βαπτίζω, and the verbal forms and doctrinal teaching of the New Testament, cannot possibly mean any other than that REPENTANCE *baptizes into the remission of sins.* And a "baptism into the remission of sins," cannot (in view of the same determining elements) possibly mean any other than the most complete, thorough, and absolute remission of sins. And the water which appears in a ritual service based in such baptism, cannot (in view of its use in all religious rites, heathen and Christian) possibly indicate other, than the purity consequent on the remission of sins as related to an antecedent repentance.

Now, as *Repentance* baptizes into the remission of sins, and as *Conversion* baptizes into the remission of sins, so does FAITH baptize into the remission of sins. This was taught by John, as interpreted by Paul (Acts 19:4): "John verily baptized the baptism of repentance, saying unto the people, that they should believe on Him which should come after him, that is on Christ Jesus." The phraseology used by Paul "(ἵνα πιστεύσωσι εἰς τὸν ἐρχόμενον) that they should believe (entering) *into* the Coming One," is grounded in the same conception as βαπτίζω εἰς, and the ellipsis necessarily implied, should be supplied thus—That they should believe *and be baptized* (εἰς τὸν ἐρχομενον, *i. e.,* εἰς τὸν Χριστὸν Ἰησοῦν) into the Coming One, *i. e.,* into Christ Jesus, there would not be between the statement as it stands, and the statement as thus completed, so much as an infinitesimal difference. Paul represents FAITH as immediately baptizing into Christ, who has now come, while John teaches, that REPENTANCE baptizes immediately into the remission of sins, through the coming Lamb of God who taketh away the sins of the world, to whom the faith of the repenting ones looks forward.

Repentance and Faith as baptizing agencies are exhibited in Luke 24:47 : "That repentance and remission of sins should be preached (ἐπὶ τῷ ὀνόματι αὐτοῦ) *upon* his name ;" where repentance is exhibited as causative of the remission of sins, and faith is implied in the preposition ἐπὶ, all resting "upon" that "only name given under heaven among men whereby we must be saved." And all this is confirmed by Luke's report of Peter's preaching under this commission in Acts 2:38 : "Repent and be baptized (ἐπὶ τῳ ὀνόματι) (believing) *upon* the name of Jesus Christ (εἰς), into the remission of sins." Here the addition of "baptized into" does not increase, or diminish, or modify in any way the *sentiment* in Luke 24:47; it merely introduces a form of expression which gives to it an additional and vivid force. The command of Christ to preach "Repentance and Remission of sins upon his name " was followed to the letter when Peter preached "Repent and be baptized into the remission of sins upon the name of Jesus Christ." Had he preached a ritual ordinance in answer to the despairing cry "What must we do ?" and announced Repentance and a ritual baptism as necessary for the remission of sins, he would have been utterly false to his trust and trampled the Commission of Jesus Christ into the dust.

The faith which is implied in the ἐπὶ of Luke and Peter is expressed by Paul in answer to the same anguished cry, "What must I do to be saved?" (Acts 16 : 31) "Believe (ἐπὶ) *upon* the name of the Lord Jesus Christ and thou shalt be saved?" There are not three distinct ways for the remission of sins and salvation —Repentance, and Conversion, and Faith ; but these three agree in one, uniting in Jesus Christ, the Lamb of God that taketh away sin and the only name of salvation, through whom they receive their power, while giving self-testimony to the regenerating work of the Holy Ghost in the soul.

May we not add that these things give to, and receive confirmation from, the interpretation of Heb. 6 : 2, as teaching that Repentance and Faith are "doctrines which baptize into the remission of sins, and into Christ," and should be so received as among the first "principles of the doctrine of Christ?"

5. This interpretation receives an interesting and forcible support from the Syriac Version. Dr. Murdock, translator of the Syriac New Testament into English, in an article on "The Syriac Words for Baptism," in the Biblotheca Sacra, Oct. 1850, says : "The declaration in Mark 16 : 15, 16, which in the Greek reads, 'Go ye into all the world, and preach the gospel to every creature: He that believeth and is *baptized* shall be saved ; but he that believeth not shall be damned' would in the Syriac read, 'He that believeth and *standeth fast* shall be saved ; but he that believeth not shall be damned.' According to the Greek our Lord seems to state *two* conditions of salvation, namely, *believing*, and being *immersed* or *washed* in the name of the Holy Trinity; but according to the Syriac he states in reality only *one* condition, namely, that of *believing* and *standing fast* in our confidence in the triune God. And therefore, very pertinently, the last part of the apostolic commission omits the clause respecting the *baptism*, and simply says, 'He that *believeth not* shall be damned.' Such views of these texts are in perfect harmony with the doctrine everywhere inculcated in the New Testament, that it is only the *steadfast*, *persevering* Christian that will be saved. . . . If the Jesuit missionaries had obtained their ideas of the nature and import of Christian baptism from the phraseology of the Syriac Bible, they could hardly have adopted the belief that by stealthily sprinkling water upon an ignorant Pagan, in the name of the Trinity, they converted him into a real Christian, and plucked him from perdition. Nor would some Protestants have been led to believe that the mere *rite* of baptism translated a person into

the Kingdom or Church of God, entitled him to divine grace, and
was necessary to a man's salvation. . . . The Apostles, when
writing or speaking in Syriac, did, probably, designate baptism
by a verb and its derivations, which properly signify *to stand up,
to be firm, erect,* and *stable,* like *pillars.* Of course both modes
of designating baptism rest on good authority; both are suitable,
and it is allowable to Christians to adopt either."

Dr. Murdock speaks with just reserve when he says, "The
Greek *seems* to state *two* conditions of salvation." If the baptism
spoken of was a ritual observance, there would indeed be *two*
conditions of salvation, because a spiritual faith and a physical
rite must of necessity be two things and not one thing; and if
they have been conjoined for salvation by the Lord Jesus Christ,
there is no power by which they can be disjoined. But Dr. Murdock shrinks from accepting for truth a *seeming* duality, because
of antagonism with the entire scope of Scripture teaching. His
embarrassment arises from supposing that the baptism spoken of
as a condition of salvation is a ritual baptism, and not that baptism "*into* CHRIST" which is by faith begotten by the Holy Ghost.
That Repentance baptizes "into the remission of sins" is a truth
of Scripture directly stated and as certain as any truth of Mathematics. That *Faith* baptizes "into Christ" is not as distinctly,
verbally, stated, and yet is clearly taught. It is involved in, and
in the relations of, ἐπὶ τῷ ὀνόματι of Luke (24 : 47), and ἐπὶ τῷ ὀνόματι
'Ιησοῦ Χριστοῦ of Peter (Acts 2 : 38), and the πιστεύσωσι εἰς τὸν ἐρχόμενον of Paul (Acts 19 : 4), compared with his baptism εἰς Χριστὸν
'Ιησοῦν (Rom. 6 : 3), εἰς Χριστὸν (Gal. 4 : 27), and his "baptisms of
doctrine " (βαπτισμῶν διδαχῆς) (= Repentance and Faith) (Heb. 6 :
1, 2), and all as bearing upon the declaration of Mark—"He that
believeth, and" so, by faith, "is baptized," εἰς Χριστὸν, "shall be
saved." Therefore the statement of CREMER (s. v. βαπτίζω) in his
New Testament Lexicon is well founded when he says : "As the
baptism of John was characterized as a βάπτισμα μετανοίας a baptism of repentance, so the baptism of Christ may be characterized
as a βάπτισμα πίστεως *a baptism by faith.*"

The Greek Testament is quite adequate to furnish, within itself,
evidence that Mark declares not two, but one only condition of
salvation; yet this evidence is, as uniquely as powerfully, sustained by the Syriac.

Dr. Murdock labors under a misconception when he supposes
that the baptism of Mark must be, as that of Matthew, "in (into)

the name of the Holy Trinity." There is as much, indeed much more, difference between the baptism εἰς Χριστὸν and the baptism εἰς τὸ ὄνομα τοῦ Πατρός, . . . as there is between the baptism εἰς μετάνοιαν and the baptism εἰς ἄφεσιν ἁμαρτιῶν. There is the greatest diversity as to the immediate and independent character of a baptism *into* REPENTANCE and a baptism *into* THE REMISSION OF SINS; and yet there is the greatest unity in their common and equal relation to salvation. So, considered independently, there is the greatest diversity between a baptism *into* CHRIST, the incarnate and crucified REDEEMER, and a baptism into the name of the Father, and of the Son, and of the Holy Ghost, the revealed TRIUNE GOD, as such, neither incarnate nor crucified. But in the scheme of redemption this diversity, in particular, embraces an ultimate unity; the baptism of the guilty *into* CHRIST being antecedent and in order to the baptism of the " washed by the blood of the Lamb " into the name of the Father, and of the Son, and of the Holy Ghost. But more of this when we consider the language of Matthew.

Finally: The interpretation which makes this baptism a ritual ordinance is full of embarrassment. (1.) It gives countenance to the Romish doctrine that ritual baptism is essential to salvation; (2.) To the doctrine, held outside of the Romish church, that if this rite is not absolutely and solely necessary and adequate to salvation, it only comes short of such character; (3.) To the doctrine that the rite does and must, of itself, effect some result accompanying salvation; (4.) To the doctrine of that class of Baptists who believe that the rite constitutes a condition of salvation in the same sense as Repentance and Faith, and especially is necessary in order to the remission of sins; (5.) To the doctrine of that class of Baptists who shrink from saying that a rite is essential to salvation, yet hold up (*in terrorem*) a dipping into water as essential to *a baptism;* (6.) It constrains those who do not believe that the rite is a condition of salvation, nor, in itself, efficient for spiritual good, but only a ritual symbolization by water of the real work of the Holy Ghost in the soul, to assume the task of *explaining away what is the apparent and natural interpretation* on the admission that the baptism spoken of is a ritual ordinance. On the other hand, under the interpretation that the baptism is *into* CHRIST by faith, the work of the Holy Ghost, every embarrassment disappears, and the doctrine is brought into direct and full harmony with the whole scope of Scripture teaching.

26

Βαπτίζω used elliptically.

How groundless is the idea, that βαπτίζω used elliptically or absolutely requires the introduction of *water* to expound the baptism will be manifest by glancing at a few cases of such usage taken from Classical writers.

" Ἐγὼ γνοὺς βαπτιζόμενον τὸ μειράκιον, I perceiving that the youth was baptized;" *Plato Euthydemus*, c. vii. A baptism *by* sophistical questions (*into* MENTAL BEWILDERMENT). There is no water.

" Ἐκπλήσσει τὴν ψυχήν, ἄφνω προσπεσόν καὶ κατεβάπτισε, Stuns the Soul, falling suddenly upon it, and baptizes it;" *Achilles Tat.*, I, 3. A baptism *by* profound emotion (*into* MENTAL APATHY). Here is no place for water.

" Καταβαπτισθήσεται μοι τὸ ζῆν μὴ βλέποντι Γλυκέραν, My life will be baptized, not seeing Glycera;" Alciphr., Epis. II, 3. A baptism *by* varied engagements (*into* DEATH). There is no water.

" Ὕστερον ἐβάπτισαν τὴν πόλιν, Afterward they baptized the city;" *Josephus, Jew. War*, IV, 3. A baptism *by* want of food (*into* FAMINE). Water can render no aid here.

" Ὁ βαπτιζόμενον εὑρὼν τὸν ἄθλιον Κίμωνα, Who found the miserable Cimon baptized;" *Libanius, Epist.* 962. A baptism *by* sorrow (*into* WRETCHEDNESS). Water can find no place here.

" Ἐβάπτισε ὅλην ἐκεῖ τὴν Ἀσίαν, He baptized there all Asia;" *Himerius*, XV, 3. A baptism by battle (*into* PROFOUND DISASTER). Water is not needed even in this naval-battle baptism.

" Ὀλίγον ὄν ἐβαπτίζετο, The number left being small were baptized;" *Libanius, Emp. Jul.*, c. 71. This was *by* excessive duties (*into* FAILURE OF ACCOMPLISHMENT). Water brings no help.

" Μήπω βεβαπτισμένον, Not yet baptized;" Plutarch Banq., III, 8. A baptism *by* wine (*into* DRUNKENNESS). *Water* will not do.

It is unnecessary to multiply cases. They prove two things: 1. Whenever a baptism is stated without an explanatory adjunct, there is no, of course, calling on *water* to fill the deficiency; 2. FAITH is as competent an agency for baptizing the soul *into* CHRIST, as any agency, for any baptism, ever used by Jew or Greek.

The evidence for a clear and harmonious scriptural interpretation of this passage seems to be complete.

THAT BAPTISM WHICH IS ULTIMATE AND ETERNAL INTO THE
NAME OF THE ONLY LIVING AND TRUE GOD,
FATHER, SON, AND HOLY GHOST.

MATTHEW 28 : 19, 20.

Ηορευθέντες οὖν μαθητεύσατε πάντα τὰ ἔθνη, βαπτίζοντες αὐτοὺς εἰς τὸ ὄνομα
τοῦ Πατρὸς, καὶ τοῦ Υἱοῦ, καὶ τοῦ ʻΑγίου Πνεύματος,

Διδάσκοντες αὐτοὺς τηρεῖν πάντα ὅσα ἐνετειλάμην ὑμῖν. καὶ ἰδοὺ, ἐγὼ μεθʼ ὑμῶν
εἰμὶ πάσας τὰς ἡμέρας ἕως τῆς συντελείας τοῦ αἰῶνος. ʼΑμήν.

"Go ye therefore, disciple all nations, baptizing them into the name of
the Father, and of the Son, and of the Holy Ghost;

"Teaching them to observe all things whatsoever I have commanded
you: and lo! I am with you alway, even unto the end of the world.
Amen."

The Redeemed reconciled and made subject to the Triune God.

The passage now about to be considered contains the last
words on earth of "God manifest in the flesh," who came into
our world "to fulfil all righteousness" by obedience to the Law
and by endurance of the penalty of the Law, in order to redeem
his people from all evil (*subduing their enmity, removing their
guilt, renewing them in the divine image, making them willingly
subject to the living and true God*), and so, "making peace." No
passage of Scripture has a higher value than this. No passage
of Scripture is richer in instruction or has a deeper reach into
eternity. And no passage of Scripture so develops in simple
grandeur the scheme of redemption as embracing all the world,
through all the ages, and terminating, where it began, in the one
living and true God. Its marvellous comprehension not only embraces the redemptive scenes of earth, but encircles the enthroned
Redeemer at the right hand of the Father where he reigns possessed of "all power in heaven and on earth" as Head over all
things to the Church, even until all enemies being subdued, he
shall give back this Messiah gift, and "God—the Father, Son,
and Holy Ghost"—"shall be all in all."

A passage of such unspeakable importance might be supposed to have an interpretation so clear and precise as to meet with universal acceptance. But it is not so. Few passages of Scripture have exhibited a more unsettled and varied interpretation. Such want of accord gives warning of a radical defect somewhere. It is our business to discover, if possible, where it is, and what it is. To this end any interpretation conceived in that spirit of deep reverence which the passage eminently demands, should be welcomed, and thoughtfully considered.

There is an interpretation, which comes commended as being the outgrowth of the radical meaning of βαπτίζω in its universal usage, and having been applied in an unswervingly uniform application through all the line of this Inquiry, whose worth may be finally tested by its fitness to elucidate these last, momentous words of our divine Redeemer.

But before making its direct application it will be profitable to examine some of the many translations and interpretations which have been offered without meeting with general acceptance.

Translation.

In the various translations of this passage there is no material difference except as to the words βαπτίζω εἰς. There is a very general assent to the translation which makes μαθητεύσατε mean *to make disciples, to disciple,* rather than " to teach." Some (Stuart) think, that βαπτίζω may be translated *to wash;* in its broad religious application, including *sprinkling,* and *pouring,* as methods for effecting the cleansing. Some (Williams, Beecher, Godwin) would translate *to purify;* leaving the method of purifying unlimited. The objection to such translations is not, that the word cannot, or does not, have such meanings; but when it has, it is the result of *absorbing a phrase* which was expressive of such idea; while here, the phrase is not absorbed, and consequently the verb must be received in its essential, and not in any acquired meaning. Patristic writers use this word superabundantly to express such acquired meaning; but it is very doubtful whether, in its absolute use, it is ever so used in the New Testament. It is more probable, that an ellipsis should always be supplied. Others (Carson, A. Campbell) insist, that the translation should be *to dip;* while others (Arnold) insist as absolutely that the translation should be *to plunge;* and yet others (Fuller) advocate *immerse.*

The objections to *dip* and to *plunge* are: 1. These words express severally a definite act, essentially different in nature and power, and therefore one word cannot express two essentially diverse conceptions; 2. Neither word can possibly express the force of the Greek word because definite action belongs to each, while definite action has no place in the essential nature of the word they claim to represent. The objections to *immerse* are: 1. It is used, by the friends of dipping into water as baptism, for the equivalent of *dip*, which is as far from the truth as darkness is from light; 2. The actual usage of this word by these writers is deceptive; sometimes it is used to express the momentary putting into and withdrawal of an object, and again, it is used to express an object being within an element without having ever been put *into* it, or ever taken out of it, which double meaning it is impossible for any one word to express; 3. If *immerse* were consistently used as the equivalent of *dip* there would be neither necessity nor advantage for using it at all; and it would be just as helpless to express the Greek word as the rejected *dip;* 4. If *immerse* should be used at its true value (putting into without limitation of time), it would become worthless on the hands of those who insist on putting men and women into water, for in such case (as they confess) they would have *to drown.* The simple remedy is to baptize, as God enjoins, without putting into water.

We understand this word here, as in every other like syntactic relation whether among Classic, Jewish, or Inspired writers, as demanding for its object withinness of position, without regard to the manner of introduction and without limitation of time for its withdrawal.

There is a very general agreement as to the translation of εἰς.

Among Baptist writers, Carson, Dagg, Wayland, Judson, as well as Alexander Campbell (in another branch) unite in saying, that this preposition should not be translated *in*, nor *unto*, nor *for*, nor *in order to*, nor *with reference to*, but by INTO.

Writers who differ from these as to the administration of the ordinance, such as Prof. Stuart, President Halley, Prof. Wilson, and critical Scholars generally, unite in the same translation, *into.*

Dr. Conant is an exception to this general agreement. He argues against the translation *into* and insists on that of *in*, in the sense *with reference to*. He admits that the literal translation is "*into* the name," but says: "Into the name is not an English phrase, and, though the literal form of the Greek, does not give the sense." In support of this view he says: "In the name is the proper English expression of εἰς τὸ ὄνομα; as in chapter 18 : 20, *are gathered together in my name*, and with the same ground idea, but with a different application of it, in chapter 10 : 41, *in the name of a prophet*, etc. The idea of *reference to* is the ground meaning of εἰς in these cases; and this with all it includes, is expressed by the English form, *in the name*."

Whatever may be the translation of εἰς in the passages cited, no light is thereby thrown on the passage before us, because the character of the verbs with which the preposition is in construction differs radically. In the phrase ἀναγω εἰς or δεχομαι εἰς, there is nothing in the verb to give a specific meaning to the preposition; but in the phrase βαπτίζω εἰς there is an essential power of the verb which fixes definitely the meaning of the preposition. The verb demands in such construction withinness for its object and necessitates εἰς to indicate the passage of such object *out of* one condition *into* another condition, without removal. There is no question as to the propriety of translating εἰς diversely, in diverse relations; but the question is this: Can εἰς be translated otherwise than by *into* when construed with βαπτίζω, or with any other verb of like character? Can this preposition in the phrase (1 Cor. 15 : 54) κατεπόθη εἰς νῖκος, have any other meaning than *into*? Does not the character of the verb (*swallow down*) necessitate such meaning? And in the phrase (1 Tim. 6 : 9) βυθίζουσι εἰς ὄλεθρον, is there not a like necessity for the translation *into*? Can a verb which carries its object into an *abyss*, be associated with εἰς in any other sense than *into*? The same necessity obtains in like usage of βαπτίζω. Dr. Conant does not object to the translation of βαπτίζω εἰς by *baptize* INTO, *per se*, for he uniformly gives such translation whenever this phrase appears in the Classics. Nor does he confine such translation to cases of literal and physical use, but extends it to the tropical and figurative, also. The same translation appears repeatedly in his version of the New Testament. It is only in connection with εἰς τὸ ὄνομα that this preposition is translated *in* (Acts 8 : 16 ; 19 : 5). But there is no reason in ὄνομα more than in ἀναισθησίαν, ὕπνον, or Χριστὸν, for modifying the preposition. It is a mistake to suppose, that the Greek εἰς τὸ ὄνομα corresponds with the English "in the name." The Greek form ἐν τῷ ὀνόματι corresponds both in form and in force with the English phrase. These two Greek forms are not equivalent and must not be confounded. When Peter commanded the lame man " *in the name* (ἐν τῷ ὀνόματι) of Jesus Christ to rise up and walk," the Greek phrase and the English are in entire correspondence. So, when Peter (Acts 10 : 48) commanded Cornelius and friends " *in the name* (ἐν τῷ ὀνόματι) of the Lord, to be baptized," there is the same correspondence; "in the name" being dependent on " command," and not on " baptize."

The active form of βαπτίζω does not in the New Testament, nor out of it, take ἐν after it to indicate the complementary idea of the verb. When, therefore, βαπτίζω is associated with εἰς τὸ ὄνομα it is not to be converted into ἐν τῷ ὀνόματι, but is to be interpreted in the same manner as every other like construction.

As Dr. Conant translates " βεβαπτισμένον εἰς ἀναισθησίαν *baptized* INTO *insensibility*," and " βαπτιζόμενος εἰς ὕπνον *baptized* INTO *sleep*," and " βαπτίζουσι εἰς πορνειαν *baptize* INTO *fornication*," and " ἐβαπτίσθητε εἰς Χριστὸν *baptized* INTO *Christ*," so, βεβαπτισμένοι εἰς τὸ ὄνομα τοῦ Κυρίου Ἰησοῦ must be translated *baptized* INTO THE NAME *of the Lord Jesus*, and βαπτίζοντες εἰς τὸ ὄνομα τοῦ Πατρὸς, . . . must be translated baptizing INTO THE NAME of the Father. . . . The phrases *baptize* εἰς τὸ ὄνομα INTO *the name* expressing the ideal element into which the baptized object passes, and *baptize* ἐν τῷ ὀνόματι *in* THE NAME declaring the authority by which the baptism is administered, are fundamentally diverse in conception and must be so exhibited in the translation.

Professor Schaff excepts to the translation of Dr. Conant (*in* the name) and to his vindicatory remark ("baptize *into* the name, is not English") by appealing to the fact, that the Authorized Version translates, "baptized *into* Jesus Christ" (Rom. 6 : 3); "baptism *into* death" (v. 4); "baptized *into* Christ" (Gal. 3 : 27); and asks, " Why not, then, say with equal propriety, 'to baptize *into* the name of Christ,' *i. e.*, into communion and fellowship with Him and the holy Trinity as revealed in the work of creation, redemption, and regeneration?" (Lange, Matt. 28 : 19, note).

Alford says : " It is unfortunate that our English Bible does not, here, give us the force of εἰς. It should have been *into* (as in Gal. 3 : 27) both here and in 1 Cor. 10 : 2, *and wherever the expression is used."*

A writer in the National Baptist (May 8, 1873) makes a plea for Dr. Conant's translation thus : "I have felt a serious objection to INTO *the name* after *baptize* or *immerse*, because that construction seems to me to indicate the element in or into which, literally or metaphorically, the person is placed by the act—Immersed *into* water, *into* (a state of) death, *into* suffering, *into* business. It appears to me that we cannot thus, either literally or metaphorically, be baptized, immersed, plunged, into the revealed character and relations ('name') of the Trinity; but rather we are immersed *in*, or, if you please, *into* water, WITH REFERENCE TO (unto?) the name, *i. e.*, the revealed character and work of the Father, Son, and Spirit. Hence I am not clear that we can improve upon the old familiar phrase ('*in* the name') unless we use several words, and say, *with reference to."*

It is not to be wondered at that those who seek to ground their theory of dipping into water in the Scriptures, should feel a serious objection to baptizing INTO *the name,* "because that construction *seems to indicate the element into which, metaphorically,* the person is placed by the act." This writer "seems to indicate" the dilemma in which he and his friends are placed, which is simply this—*change* OUR THEORY *or change the* WORD OF GOD. So long as the Bible teaches as its baptism, a baptism *into* REPENTANCE, *into* REMISSION, *into* CHRIST, *into* THE NAME of the Lord Jesus, *into* THE NAME of the Father, and of the Son, and of the Holy Ghost, and repudiates persistently and absolutely a baptism *into* WATER, just so long must that Bible "seem to indicate" an ideal element for its baptism, and a ritual symbolization of that baptism *with* water; and the theory must be discarded both as impossible in its nature (a dipping is not a baptism) and in contradiction to the most express, reiterated, and unvarying testimony of the word of God.

Various Views—Baptist.

"To disciple all nations, is to bring them by faith into the school of Christ. The persons whom this commission warrants to be baptized, are scholars of Christ, having believed in him for salvation, 'Baptizing them *into* the name of the Father, and of the Son, and of the Holy Ghost.' It is into the faith and sub jection of the Father, Son, and Holy Ghost that men are to be baptized" (*Carson*, 173). "'*Εἰς τὸ ὄνομα in the name*, intends *into the belief*, . . . instructed in, and brought over to the faith of Christ, which is the sense I contend for" (*Gale*, 272). " We must take the command, ' disciple all the nations' in the *best* sense, make true, genuine believers, bring sinners to Christ and make them his disciples. . . . The baptizing was to be coextensive with the discipling. . . . Grammarians teach that a participle following a verb, is frequently used in Greek like the gerund in *do* in Latin, signifying the means. This is not an invariable rule. The participle following the verb, in the Greek Testament, very seldom signifies the means. More frequently than not the action of the participle follows that of the verb. ' In those days *came* John the Baptist *preaching*' (Matt. 3 : 1). John did not come by means of preaching. ' There *came* a certain man *kneeling*' (Matt. 17 : 14). He kneeled when he had come. ' I *sat* daily with you *teaching*' (Matt. 26 : 55). Christ did not sit by means of teaching. ' The priests went into the temple accomplishing the service' (Heb. 9 : 6). The service was accomplished after entering the temple. Disciple all nations, baptizing them (that is the disciples) 'in the name of the Father, and of the Son, and of the Holy Ghost'" (*Morell*, 55 ; *Edinburgh*). " The Greek verb *baptizo* signifies *to immerse*. By *immersion*, we mean an *entire covering*, or a *complete surrounding* with some element. We maintain that the action alone (immersion) is enjoined, not the *mode* of immersion. The word *dip*, however unadvisedly, may have been used by some Baptist writers in the same sense in which we are now using the word *immerse*, although without any explanatory remark affirming this ; and certainly the assertion of Dr. Carson, that the Greek verb invariably means *to dip* has been animadverted upon with sufficient severity by those who have excluded from the English word every idea but that of *putting* the object *into* the element. In Matt. 28 : 19, this act is performed on the assenting believer *into* the name of Father, and of the Son, and of the Holy Spirit. This is the Christian rite " (*Ingham*, 26 ; *London*). " Go make disciples or Christians, baptizing them in the name of the Father, etc., *i. e.*, into subjection and obedience to the Father, the Son, and the Holy Ghost. This is the GRAND COMMISSION. We believe that the Scriptures represent the immersion of a professed believer in the name of the Trinity, and *that only*, to be Christian baptism. The *immersion* of the subject *in water* is ESSENTIAL to the ordinance " (*M. P. Jewett*, 12). " The ordinance of baptism is to be administered by the immersion of the body in water; baptizing the candidate ' INTO the name of the Father, and the Son, and the Holy Ghost.' We prefer *into* to *in*. Into is the proper translation. It expresses the meaning of the ordinance which the other (*in*) does not. *In the name* of any one means merely *by the authority* of, and nothing more. The NAME, here, has a totally different signification. To baptize into any one is, into a profession of faith of any one, and sincere obedience to him. This is the meaning of being baptized into the name of, or into the Father, and the Son, and the Holy Ghost. We could baptize anything *in* the name. . . . Romanists baptize bells, standards, or anything, in the name of . . . We cannot baptize into the Father, . . . anything but a *rational* being" (*President Wayland*, 89). " The form of expression is always baptizing *in* (ἐν) or *into* (εἰς) something. *In* water *in* Jordan, *in* Enon, *in* the Holy Spirit (ἐν); *into* the name of the Father, *into* the name of Paul, *into* my own name, *into* what were ye baptized, *into* John's baptism, *into* Moses, *into* Christ, *into* his death, *into* death. Baptism being *in* or *into* something must be immersion *into* water" (*Booth*, 260; *London*). " The use of εἰς in the New Testament, has a reference to the action performed by the person baptized. Thus the Jews were immersed *in* the cloud and sea while they were entering *into* Moses. It is not intimated that as many as were baptized *into* Christ, had not been baptized *in* water, but that they were baptized *in 'water* when they entered *into* Christ. They were immersed (entering) into Christ, and such persons must have entered 'into his death.' . . . To the same point must be referred the *into* in our Lord's commission. The words do not imply that the persons should be baptized *in the name* of the Father, etc., instead of *in water ;* nor are the words *into the name*, etc., intended to form the disciples' authority for baptizing the converts, for this is expressed in the imperative verb *go ;* but it is intended to describe those persons who are to be baptized. The whole meaning is expressed thus : *Go*, make disciples, baptizing in water those who enter *into* the name, or resign themselves to the authority, of the Father, the Son, and the Holy Spirit. *Enter into the name* is even stronger than the expression *resign themselves to the authority.* . . . The most vital parts of Christian duty have, in past time, been baptized in pollution and error, and in rising from this filthy submersion, it requires equal care, not to retain an adhesive wrong, and not to reject a Divine right" (*Stovel*, 500; *London*). "The commission, 'Go ye baptizing' gives no indication that the ordinance was thereby instituted. It regards the ordinance to be administered, as it does the gospel to be preached, as already known, a thing in existence. John's baptism and Christian baptism are in essentials identical. The time of the institution of baptism is thus fixed at the beginning of John's ministry" (*Prof. Pepper*, 27; *Bapt. Pub. Soc.*). "There is a phrase which no Christian can misunderstand, and have a just and true idea of his relation to God. I mean our baptismal formula: 'Into the name of the Father, and of the Son, and of the Holy Ghost.' . . . Our immersion is not merely immersion; it is *immersion* 'into the name of the Father, and of the Son, and of the Holy Ghost.' Bare immersion no more exhausts the idea of immersion into Christ, than the door of a temple exhausts the idea of the temple" (*Pres. Bruner, Oskaloosa College, Disciple Bapt.*). "This is the *law* of Christian baptism; the institution and origin of it. John's baptism was not Christ's baptism. ·John was not sent by the Lord Jesus Christ, but by his Father. It should be translated—'All *authority*' in heaven and in earth is given to me: go you, therefore, and *make disciples of all nations*, baptizing them *into* the name of the Father, and of the Son, and of the Holy Spirit, *teaching* them to observe, etc." (*Alexander Campbell, Baptism*, 220). "The immersion of a professing believer, into the name of the Father, and of the Son, and of the Holy Ghost, is the only Christian baptism" (*Adon. Judson, Sermon*, 55).

Unsatisfactory.

These views are very unsatisfactory. They are loose, confused, discordant, and untrue; both as expository of this particular passage, and of the general teaching of Scripture. There is a verbal acknowledgment of the vital relation between βαπτίζοντες and εἰς τὸ ὄνομα, together with a formal translation based on such relation, and, then, in the exposition there is an utter abandonment of such relation, and the establishment of another (with water) utterly diverse in nature, on which the interpretation of the passage is made to turn. To vindicate this separation of what God has joined together, and to justify this conjunction of what God has put widely apart, not one word is offered. It is like everything else under the theory, assumed without proof and in contradiction of the most express statements of inspiration, as well as of the uniform sentiment and practice of the friends of the theory in all like cases out of the word of God.

Dr. Conant stands almost, if not absolutely, alone as exempt from this condemnation. He denies (tacitly not expressly) any living relation between βαπτίζοντες and εἰς τὸ ὄνομα, and thus, is at liberty to translate the preposition uncontrolled ₊by the otherwise determining power of the verb, as also, to establish another and essentially diverse relation between the verb and water, elliptically introduced for the purpose. By this means Dr. Conant extricates himself from that absurd entanglement in which his friends involve themselves, by the admission of an organic relation in the phrase βαπτίζοντες εἰς τὸ ὄνομα on which they base their translation, and then, establishing another relation with water out of which they deduce their interpretation. But no attempt to dissolve the unity between this verb and its preposition can ever succeed. It is ingrained in the usage of Heathen, Jewish, and inspired Writers. We may therefore hope that it (together with its necessary translation) will be accepted by Dr. Conant, and that his eminent scholarship will, as a necessary consequence, reject the double and impossible relation of βαπτίζω with water. "Ulfilas," in the National Baptist, justly troubled by those portentous words —*baptizing* INTO THE NAME of the Triune God, pleads for a baptizing INTO *water*, *in* the name of the Trinity, to escape, what the words of inspiration "seem to indicate"—the ideal baptism of Christ's redeemed ones *into the* fully revealed DEITY. But it costs too much to maintain a theory at the expense of discarding the word of God. And when the unhappy theory of a dipping into water, as God's baptism, shall have been corrected and forgotten in the lapse of untold ages, then, will "the discipled of all nations" be found "baptized *into* THE NAME *of the* FATHER, *and of the* SON, *and of the* HOLY GHOST" therein to abide forever, even forever and ever. A correspondent ("J. W. James") of the Christian Standard (Disciple Baptist), is in trouble, as well as "Ulfilas," about this formula. He asks: "By what authority do we use these words, 'into the name of the Father,' . . . . when they nowhere appear in the baptisms by the Apostles in the Acts?" The Editor replies: "We have no right, from the mere silence of the historian in Acts, to suppose that the Apostles disregarded their instructions, but rather that the fact of baptism necessarily involved the use of the commanded formula. The fact generally stated in the Acts is—not that they were not baptized *into* the name of the Father, Son, and Holy Ghost, but—that they were baptized *in* or *upon* the name of Jesus Christ; the authority and saving power of Christ being the leading object in the mind of the narrator."

This answer is unsatisfactory: 1. Because it *assumes* that the Apostles were commanded to baptize (ritually) "into the name of the Father, ..." which is the point at issue; 2. Because it misinterprets Acts 2 : 38, " Repent and be baptized (*upon* (ἐπὶ) the name of Jesus Christ) *into* THE REMISSION OF SINS," and Acts 10 : 48, " He commanded them (*in* (ἐν) the name of Jesus Christ), to be baptized," as parallel and equivalent to baptism " *into* (εἰς) the name of the 'Father,'" . . . and, 3. Because he omits to state, that " the narrator " does expressly and explicitly declare, that baptism was administered (Acts 8 : 16; 19 : 5) " *into* (εἰς) THE NAME OF THE LORD JESUS." Now, unless " *the name* JESUS CHRIST' (a name obtained only by the incarnation of " the Son " and ex- pressive of that incarnation and of the redemption to be secured through that incarnation) be the same as *the Name of* THE FATHER (God unincarnate), *and of* THE SON (God essentially, as distinguished from the God-Man, = the Lord Jesus), *and of the* HOLY GHOST (God unincarnate), then, baptism " *into the Name of* THE LORD JESUS," is not the same as baptism " *into the Name of* THE FATHER, *and of* THE SON, *and of* THE HOLY GHOST," and the Apostles were, either, not commanded to baptize (ritually) into the Name of the Father, ... or they did not conform to such command in baptizing (ritually) into the Name of the Lord Jesus.

Other Views.

PUSEY, *Holy Baptism*, 62 : " St. Cyprian felt the ' Name of God ' to be God himself, and connected the indwelling of God with our baptism into his Name. The extreme reverence of the Jews, whereby they shrunk from uttering the incommunicable Name is far nearer the right feeling, than the careless way in which modern criticism treats the indications of a mystery lying concealed under that Name. When the Lord directs to ' baptize all nations into THE NAME of the Father, the Son, and the Holy Ghost,' a very little thoughtfulness would connect it with that Name, ' where- with the Father keeps those whom He hath given to the Son, that they may be one as the Father and the Son are one. The being ' baptized into the Name ' of the Three Persons of the undivided

Trinity, is no mere profession of obedience, sovereignty, belief, but (if one may so speak) a real appropriation of the person baptized to the Holy Trinity, a transfer of him from the dominion of Satan to Them, an insertion of him within Their blessed Name, and a casting the shield (to speak humanly) of that *Almighty* Name, over him; that Name, at which devils tremble and are cast out thereby, 'into which a man runneth and is safe.' . . . . It was not then mere glowing language, when the fathers spoke of the baptized being 'fenced round by the Trinity,' or the like; and in that they press the force of 'being baptized *into* the Name of the Father, Son, and Holy Ghost,' as something real, something efficient, an actual communion with the Blessed Trinity, they adhere more to the analogy of faith, and the usage of other Scripture, and the literal meaning of the text, than they who would interpret it of the mere commission given to the minister of baptism, and are withal at a loss to say what, 'to baptize into the Name of' can literally mean, or how they obtain the sense, which they vaguely attach to it."

BARCLAY, *Apology*, 402: "The Greek is εἰς τὸ ὄνομα, that is, *into the name;* now the name of the Lord is often taken in Scripture for his virtue and power. Now that the apostles were to baptize the nations into this name, virtue, and power, and that they did so, is evident by these testimonies, 'That as many as were baptized into Christ, have put on Christ;' this must have been a baptizing into the name, *i. e.*, power and virtue, and not a mere formal expression of words adjoined with baptism. . . . Perhaps it may stumble the unwary and inconsiderate, as if the very character of Christianity were abolished, to tell them plainly that this Scripture is not to be understood of baptizing with water, and that this form of 'baptizing in the name of the Father, Son, and Spirit,' hath no warrant from Matt. 28, etc. If it had been a form prescribed by Christ to his apostles, then surely they would have made use of that form in the administering of water baptism to such as they baptized with water; yet there is not a word of this form in any such case of baptism. But it is said of some, Acts 8:16, 19:5, 'they were baptized in (into) the name of the Lord Jesus;' by which it yet more appears, that either the author of this history hath been very defective, who having so often occasion to mention this, yet omitted so substantial a part of baptism (which were to accuse the Holy Ghost, by whose guidance Luke wrote it), or else that the apostles did in no ways understand that

Christ by his commission did enjoin them to such a form of water baptism, seeing they do not use it."

FAIRBAIRN, *Herm. Man.*, 314: "To be baptized into a person, into Christ, for example, or into his body, means, to be through baptism formally admitted into personal fellowship with Him, and participation in the cause or work associated with his name; that they were baptized into the faith of His person and salvation, or into the profession and hope of all that His name indicates for those who own His authority, and trust in His merits."

J. A. ALEXANDER, *Comm. Acts* 8 : 12, 16 : "The other subject of his preaching was *the name of Jesus Christ*, i. e., all denoted by these names, one of which means the Saviour of his people, and the other their Messiah, or Anointed Prophet, Priest, and King. Into this name, *i. e.*, into union with Christ, and subjection to him, in all these characters, the Samaritan believers were introduced by the initiatory rite of baptism, v. 16, *Into the name, i. e.*, into union with him, and subjection to him, as their Sovereign and their Saviour."

BEECHER, *Baptism*, 206 : "Why is there a commission given to baptize in Matthew and Mark, and none in Luke and John? The reply is, that a commission to baptize is in fact a commission to purify, that is, a commission to remit sins, and in Luke and John, the disciples do receive a commission to remit sins. . . . In short, Christ died as the Lamb of God to take away the sins of the world, and the great business of the apostles was to publish to the world the great doctrine of the remission of sins, through his death, and the terms on which it could be obtained, and to establish the rite by which this purgation from sin should be shadowed forth and commemorated in honor of the Trinity, and especially of that Spirit by whom this atonement was made effectual to purge the conscience from dead works to serve the living God. 'Go ye, therefore, teach all nations, purifying them (that is remitting to them that repent and believe, their sins) into the name of the Father, and of the Son, and of the Holy Ghost.'"

PROF. GODWIN, *Christian Baptism*, 151, *London:* "It has been supposed that in Matt. 28 : 19 we have the institution of the ordinance of Christian baptism, and also the form of words to be used in the administration of the rite. John 3 : 22, 4 : 1, clearly show that the rite of Christian baptism existed long before. There is nothing in this commission to make it more probable that they had not before baptized Jews, than that they had not before

taught Jews. Had this been a form of words for the administration of baptism, the expression would rather have been—Baptizing them, saying, I baptize thee, etc. There is no indication of
the use of this form in the Acts of the Apostles. The great object
of baptism is denoted by the terms, ' For the Father, and the Son,
and the Holy Ghost.' The *name* of a person, by a Hebrew idiom,
indicates the person himself."

CALVIN, *Instit. III*, 376 : " They err in this, that they derive
the first institution of baptism from Matt. 28 : 19, whereas Christ
had, from the commencement of his ministry, ordered it to be administered by his apostles. , . . The command here given by
Christ relates principally to the preaching of the gospel : to it
baptism is added as a kind of appendage. He speaks of baptism
in so far as the dispensation of it is subordinate to the function
of teaching. *Teach all nations* (Comm.). Here Christ makes the
Gentiles equal to the Jews. *Baptizing them.* Partly that their
baptism may be a pledge of eternal life before God, and partly
that it may be an outward sign of faith before men. *For we are
all baptized by one Spirit* (Comm. 1 Cor. 12 : 13). We are ingrafted by baptism into Christ's body. . . . Lest any one, however, should imagine that this is effected by the outward symbol,
he adds that it is the work of the Holy Spirit."

BENGEL, *Comm. Matt.* 28 : 19 : " The verb $\mu\alpha\theta\eta\tau\epsilon\dot{\upsilon}\epsilon\iota\nu$, signifies
to make disciples ; it includes *baptism and teaching ;* cf. John 4 :
1, with the present passage, $\epsilon\dot{\iota}\varsigma\ \tau\dot{o}\ \ddot{o}\nu o\mu\alpha$, *into the name.* This
formula of baptism is most solemn and important ; in fact it em-
braces the sum of all piety. . . . The Jews as being already in
covenant with *God (the Father)* by circumcision were to be bap-
tized *in the name* ($\dot{\epsilon}\pi\grave{\iota}\ \tau\tilde{\omega}\ \dot{o}\nu\dot{o}\mu\alpha\tau\iota$) *of Christ,* and to receive the
gift of *the Holy Spirit :* the Gentiles, as being wholly aliens from
God, were to be baptized ' into the name ($\epsilon\dot{\iota}\varsigma\ \tau\tilde{\omega}\ \ddot{o}\nu o\mu\alpha$) *of the
Father, Son,* and *Holy Ghost* ' (Acts 2 : 38)."

OLSHAUSEN, *Comm. Matt.* 28 : 19 : " Baptism was not now instituted for the first time, but was appointed by Christ for every
one who should afterwards enter the church, and at the same
time filled with power from on high. Some have misunderstood
this passage, as if the meaning of the words had been *first* in-
struct, and *then* baptize. But the two participles $\beta\alpha\pi\tau\dot{\iota}\zeta o\nu\tau\epsilon\varsigma$ and
$\delta\iota\delta\dot{\alpha}\sigma\varkappa o\nu\tau\epsilon\varsigma$ are precisely what constitute the $\mu\alpha\theta\eta\tau\epsilon\dot{\upsilon}\epsilon\iota\nu$. In the
apostolic practice instruction never preceded baptism. Baptism
followed upon the mere confession that Jesus was the Christ.

Afterward he participated in the progressive courses of instruction which prevailed in the church. *All the nations.* The whole human race is the object of Christ's reconciling agency. . . . The meaning of the words βαπτίζειν εἰς τὸ ὄνομα *to baptize into the name,* is best learned from baptism *into the name of Paul, into Moses. Baptizing into any one,* signifies baptism as involving a binding obligation ; a rite whereby one is pledged ; and the sublime object to which baptism binds, consists of Father, Son, and Holy Ghost. ' *Name* ' signifies the very essence of God himself. The Divine power is wedded to the human soul, which thus becomes itself the parent of a higher heavenly consciousness. . . . The question, ' Whether the Lord intended to establish a fixed formula of baptism ?' would not have arisen, had the other portions of the New Testament shown that the disciples, in administering baptism, employed these words. But, instead of this, we find that, as often as baptism is mentioned, it is performed only εἰς or ἐπὶ τὸ ὄνομα, ἐν τῷ ὀνόματι ᾽Ιησοῦ, or Χριστοῦ."

STIER, *VIII, Matt.* 28 : 18–20, " A sound exegesis demands that we rightly translate μαθητεύσατε, and establish its true connection with βαπτίζοντες. That exegesis is alone right which makes the two following participles subordinate to the one Imperative. It is more than, and different from, the *baptism of John.* ' *Name,*' ὄνομα, is never in the New Testament construed with a Genitive *rei, non personæ.* The unity of the three ' persons ' of the one Divine nature is held fast and witnessed by the τὸ ὄνομα. ' We regard it as saying—Into the name of *the Three, who are One,* into the Three-One God ' (Meyer). What means INTO or IN THE NAME ? Εἰς τὸ ὄνομα cannot be simply equivalent to ἐν τῷ ὀνόματι, which only occurs in Acts 10 : 48, where ἐν is for εἰς, or teaches that those Gentiles were baptized in the full and plenary authority and will of Christ. In the same depth of meaning as we so often find εἰς Θεόν, εἰς Χριστόν, ἐν Θεῷ, we are to be baptized into the Three-One. In connection with the dipping into *water,* there is the wonderful—Baptize ye (say—I baptize thee) *into the name* of God, the triune God ! There is a translation into communion of life with the Father, Son, and Spirit, in this dipping into their name ; the baptized become translated into the power and nature of God. . . . Did Christ intend by εἰς τὸ ὄνομα to give a form of words, which must necessarily be used, as a formula, in the administration of baptism ? Bengel thinks that the Jews were to be baptized into the name of *Jesus* alone. Another writer attempts

27

to prove that the Apostles baptized the Gentiles into the Father, the Jews into the Son, and John's disciples into the Holy Ghost! But how can this be a formula necessary to be used when we find from Acts 2 : 38 onwards only a baptizing in or into the name of Jesus Christ or the Lord Jesus, the perfect Trinitarian formula never being once mentioned ? *Zinzendorf's* marvellous device to reconcile the command of Christ and the practice of the Apostles is to make εἰς τὸ ὄνομα identical with ἐν τῷ ὀνόματι, meaning to baptize in the authority of the Triune God. He supposes that they baptized merely in the name of Jesus, and into Jesus ; and the revelation of the Trinity, and the mystery of the Holy Spirit, belonged to the *disciplina arcani* among *the Gentiles*, and therefore the Apostles never *uttered* the three names at once in baptizing. *Lange* says, the expression in the Acts is not the description of the apostolical act in baptism, but only a definition of *Christian* baptism, in contradistinction to the Jewish baptizing. *Thiersch*, ' That the sacred administration might be more dogmatically or more liturgically referred to in the several cases, with reference rather to its influence, or rather to its *rite*.' *Neander* says, ' It cannot, at least, be proved from these passages that the perfect formula was not in use, for there is no literal baptismal formula described, prominence being given only to the characteristic aim of baptism.' *Olshausen* adopts the same view and says, ' Acts 19 : 2, 5 ; Tit. 3 : 4, So mention the Son and the Holy Ghost in connection with baptism, that a reference to the FORMULA is highly probable.' *Storr* says, ' The expression in the Acts may be an *abbreviation*. For this the *first word* of the formula would not be so appropriate as the second, as not sufficiently distinguishing Christian baptism from that of the Jews.' In the four historical passages there is a close connection with the Holy Spirit ; while in the description of the baptism He is not directly named. In Acts 2 : 38, the entire formula on Peter's lips *at this time* would have been inappropriate and stiff, putting the letter harshly *first*. In Acts 10 : 48, the ἐν τῷ ὀνόματι τοῦ Κυρίου admits of another meaning, denoting the obligation and commission of the Apostle = He commanded them to be baptized precisely as the Lord commanded. But in Acts 19 : 5, the connection demands the most exact specification of the true baptism—of *that* baptism in which *the Holy Spirit* was named and offered as present and immediately operating; it is strange that this should be wanting *if* the full formula was always and essentially introduced. In Acts 8 : 16, it is not appropriate to interpret this as meaning that they were expressly baptized into the name of the Holy Ghost, whom, nevertheless, they had not received. The μόνον βεβαπτισμένοι appears to define the formula which was used, as not mentioning the Holy Ghost.

"*Voss* seeks to demonstrate by many of the fathers, and most of the schoolmen, that Christ did not bind the power and validity of baptism to the express *utterance* of these *three* names. He seems to be in a great measure right. But there is assuredly— and this remains absolutely fixed—no other real and essential baptism of Christ than that which is, according to its meaning, design, and power, into the name of the Three-One. This is the sure meaning of the word of institution, and must be maintained when heretics would change it, or when the full meaning of the faith is not understood. Otherwise, here as everywhere, the essential point is not the letter but the spirit. Hence we prefer to say with *Calvin:* 'We see that the complement of baptism is *in Christ*, whom therefore we may rightly call the proper object of baptism. Whatever benefits and gifts may be the result of baptism are all found in the name of Christ alone.' We agree, also, with the still plainer declaration of *Neander:* 'It is nevertheless probable that in the original apostolical formula only this one reference (to the name of Christ) was made prominent.' *Luther* rebukes those 'who with furious zeal pour out their condemnation upon those who should say—*I baptize thee in the name of Jesus Christ* (the form of the Apostles as we read in Acts), and would allow no validity in any other form than this—*I baptize thee in the name of the Father*,' etc. We would let the Greeks say as they do—'Let *this servant of Christ* be baptized;' we would not dishonor the sacrament by a superstitious adherence to names and words.

"*Baptizing* is followed by *teaching*, which is parallel with it. Both are included in the *discipling*. The first 'them' in our text singled out the individuals of 'the nations,' whether adults or children, for baptizing; the *second* 'them,' therefore *repeated*, means plainly the μαθητευθέντας, those who had *become disciples* and were *baptized*."

HALLEY, *Sacraments*, 290, *London:* "Are we bound by the terms of the Commission to administer baptism according to the form of words there prescribed? The command of our Lord seems to be so clear and absolute, as to admit of no exception. I do not see how any person can 'baptize into the name of the

Father, and of the Son, and of the Holy Ghost,' without mentioning the names of these Divine persons. I dare not assert
that baptism, in the name of Christ only, would require to be repeated in the full and complete formula. It is true that in the
Acts persons are said to have been 'baptized into the name of
Jesus,' but the expression may denote that they received Christian baptism. I do not assert that the precise words are essential, for if they were we must use a Greek formulary; but the
distinct recognition of the Persons is not external form, but the
great truth of the service. Athanasius and others declare such
baptism to be void as was performed without the mention of the
Trinity. This was not the general opinion, as in many instances,
heretics who had only been baptized in the name of Christ, were
admitted into the church without re-baptism. Trine immersion
became catholic, as an immersion before the name of each
Person.' . . . Our conclusion is, that the commission ought to
be expounded in its literal and unrestricted sense—disciple as
many as we can by baptizing and teaching them, admitting no
exceptions. 'The extent of our ability is the only limit of our
obedience.' "

BLOOMFIELD, *Comm. Matt.* 28 : 19: " *Μαθητεύσατε*, here, signifies
to *make a disciple of.* The sense is, make disciples of persons
of all nations. It is admitted by all (except Socinians and
Quakers) that baptism, as a token of *making any one a disciple,*
ought to be administered to all introduced into the number of
Christ's disciples. *To be baptized in the name of any one*, is, by
baptism, to be bound to observe the religious observances instituted by him. It has been debated whether the words of the
commission contain a formula of baptism prescribed by Christ,
or whether they indicate the *purpose* and *end* of baptism. Kuinoel states the arguments for the former view, thus: 1. In Acts
19 : 5, compared with v. 2, and Tit. 3 : 4, the subject is baptism,
and the Father, Son, and Holy Ghost, are mentioned; 2. Justin
Martyr speaks of baptism 'upon (ἐπὶ) the name of the Father of
all, and Lord God, and of our Saviour Jesus Christ, and of the
Holy Spirit;' 3. Baptism 'into the name of the Lord Jesus,' or
' in, upon the name of Jesus Christ,' *i. e.*, 'into Jesus Christ,' is
a shorter formula, with the same sense as that in Matt. 28 : 19.'
The arguments for the latter view (which he adopts) are these:
' 1. Christ did not command them to go and teach all nations,
saying, I baptize thee, etc., but only baptizing them, etc.; 2. No

passage is found in the Acts, or in the Epistles exhibiting a formula prescribed by Christ; 3. If Christ had prescribed a formula of baptism the Apostles would not have receded from it and used a shorter one.'

" To WHAT *formula the Apostles joined baptism may not clearly appear ;* but that at a very early period the *present* was introduced is *certain,* from the passage cited from Justin."

LANGE, *Comm. Matt.* 28 : 19 : " Μαθητεύσατε *make disciples of* The translation, *teach,* is incorrect. So, also, is the Baptist exegesis : In every case, first complete instruction, then baptism. To make disciples of, involves, in general, the preaching of the gospel, but pre-eminently the moment when the non-Christian has become through repentance and faith, a catechumen. This willingness in the case of children of Christian parents is presupposed and implied in the willingness of the parents. The Holy Scripture everywhere place the spiritual unity of the household in the believing father, or believing mother, representing this as the normal relation.

"*All nations.* Acts 10 : is the Spirit's exegesis of the already perfect commission. *Baptizing them.* But μαθητεύειν is not completed in baptism. There are two acts, the antecedent baptism, the subsequent instruction. *In* (or rather *with reference to, or into*) *the name of.* That is in the might of, and for, the name, as the badge and the symbol of the new church. Εἰς τό. 'Note,' says Meyer, 'that the liturgical formula, *In nomine, In the name,* rests entirely upon the incorrect translation of the Vulgate.' Yet not so *entirely,* because the expression ἐν τῷ ὀνόματι, is found in Acts 10 : 48. De Wette and Meyer explain εἰς τό, *with reference to* the name. But εἰς τό in other passages means either the element into which one is baptized (Mark 1 : 9, εἰς τὸν Ἰορδάνην; Rom. 6 : 3, εἰς τὸν θάνατον) ; or the object, εἰς μετάνοιαν, Matt. 3 : 11 ; Acts 2 : 38, εἰς ἄφεσιν; or the authority of the community, under which and for which one is baptized (εἰς τὸν Μωυσῆν, 1 Cor. 10 : 2). The last meaning is probably the prominent one in this passage ; a baptism under the authority of, and unto the authority of the triune God, as opposed to the baptism in and for the authority of Moses. But, as the context shows, we have expressed likewise the idea of being plunged into the name of the Three-One God, as the element, and the dedication of the baptized unto this name. The expression ἐπὶ τῷ ὀνόματι, Acts 2 : 38, brings out most fully the idea of authority, in virtue of which, or the foundation

upon which, baptism is administered. ' *The name*' refers to each
of the Persons of the Godhead, and brings out in the *one name*
the equality as well as the personality, of the three Divine Names
in one name.

"We must dissent from Meyer when he says that the passage is
'improperly termed the *baptismal formula*. No trace being found
of the employment of these words by the Apostolic church. It
was only at a later period that the baptismal formula was drawn
up according to these words.' But it is this development which
conducts us back to the germ, which we find here deposited in
the New Testament."

PROF. WILSON, *Baptism*, 307, *London :* "Baptism into Moses
clearly implied the acknowledgment of his claims as a leader
and lawgiver, and of the economy called by his name; baptism
into Christ implies the acknowledgment of our Lord in his personal and mediatorial character, and of the faith which he
founded; and the baptism of the Commission implies the acknowledgment of the Father, and of the Son, and of the Holy
Ghost. . . . The meaning of this baptism demands still closer
inquiry. This formula means more than the most ingenious interpreter of symbols can discover in the outward rite. Baptism
into Christ's death, according to Dr. Carson, comprehends *baptism into the faith of* his death ; and we may safely maintain that
the Commission enjoins *baptism into the faith of* Father, Son,
and Holy Ghost. In these connections our Baptist friends do
not obtrude their *dip* or *immerse*. Dipping into Moses, dipping
into the Father, dipping into Jesus Christ, are phrases which
they eschew. This substitution of baptism for dipping is a turning away from the boasted fruits of their philology.

"'Baptism into the name of the Father,' etc., viewed in its
isolated statement seems to be of a purely spiritual character.
Water is not mentioned ; it is implied. Had it been mentioned,
so long as Christian ministers are required to 'baptize into the
name of the Father,' we should contend that the ordinance possesses an essential character to which the use of water is merely
subservient. The latest leader of the Immersionists (Mr. Stovel
of London) assures us, that '$\beta\alpha\pi\tau\iota\zeta\epsilon\iota\nu$ $\epsilon\iota\varsigma$ means *to initiate*,' and
consequently neither dipping, nor affusion, nor sprinkling. When
Paul asked certain disciples, 'Into what were ye baptized?' they
said not, into Jordan, nor into the sea of Tiberias, but 'into
John's baptism.' Had these disciples understood Paul to inquire,

Into what were you plunged or dipped? and their views had been those of the modern Immersionists, the Apostle would have received a very different answer.

"Baptist writers labor to dispose of the structure of the Commission as a common and natural ellipsis. But this does not meet the difficulty. We read in Acts 16 : 15, 'Lydia was baptized,' and as no regimen is expressed after the verb, all parties supply *in water* or *with water*. The structure of the Commission is different; the participle *baptizing* is followed by εἰς with its appropriate case, thus presenting a form of expression complete both in sentiment and syntax. True, the preposition and its case do not refer to water; but this forms the very peculiarity of which the common ellipsis cannot give a satisfactory account. The Commission enjoins baptism *not into water*, but *into the name of the Father, Son, and Holy Spirit.* How shall we deal with this construction? The ordinary ellipsis is uncalled for, or inadmissible. If we inserted εἰς ὕδωρ after the participle we should have, 'Baptizing them *into water*, into the name,' etc., a collocation of words, we venture to say, without parallel either in sacred or profane literature. . . . If the verb denotes 'dip, and nothing but dip,' the Commission requires us to dip a disciple 'into the name of the Father,' etc. The force of the verb is expended on a spiritual act, and the construction does not touch the use of water in baptism. The Baptist may, on his own principles, *dip* 'into the name of the Father,' but he cannot dip *into water*, without inserting a clause to that effect in defiance of all precedent. Baptism *into the name* of the Father, and of the Son, and of the Holy Ghost, forms the substance of the ordinance.

"May it not be objected that our interpretation would pave the way for setting aside the use of water altogether, in baptism? We answer, no: for while the spiritual initiation constitutes, in our view, the essence of the ordinance, the examples of baptism in Scripture exhibit the use of water as a sanctioned and veritable fact.

"The real ellipsis of the Commission shown by 1 Cor. 10 : 2, corroborates our view. The fathers of the Jewish church 'were all baptized (εἰς) *into* MOSES (ἐν) in the cloud and in the sea.' The Israelites were *not dipped into the* CLOUD, and *into the* SEA. If in administering baptism *into* MOSES, sea and cloud could be used without immersion, may not water be used without immersion in administering baptism *into* CHRIST?"

Brief Examination of these Views.

Carson: "Scholars of Christ who have believed in him." All "scholars believing in Christ," must (normally) be ritually baptized into Christ, as they have really been so baptized by "believing in him." "When they heard that Jesus made and baptized more disciples than John" (John 4 : 1). "It is *into the faith and subjection they are baptized.*"

This is not interpretation, but naked substitution.

Gale: " εἰς τὸ ὄνομα = instructed in and brought over to the faith of Christ." Where is the proof that instruction and belief in *Christ* is baptism into the name of *the Father ?* . . .

Morell: "Baptizing is *not the means* of discipling." Very true ; but Alexander Campbell says it is, as much as repentance and faith.

Ingham: " Βαπτίζω does not mean *dip,* but *immerse,* covering in any way. This act is performed on the believer *into the name of the Father.*" Ingham as a Baptist, is good authority against Carson the Baptist, the one affirming, baptize does *not* mean *dip ;* the other affirming, " It means nothing but dip." Ingham is bad authority against the *truth,* when he omits *unlimited continuance,* as an essential element in immerse, which is thus disqualified from officiating in the *momentary* immersion of a dipping. Who can convert into English such language as, "this act is performed on the believer, into the name of the Father ?" . . .

Jewett: "Into subjection and obedience." This is blotting out "the name of the Father, and of the Son, and of the Holy Ghost," and substituting for it "subjection and obedience." "*The immersion of the subject in water* is essential to the ordinance." Prof. Milo P. Jewett speaks very positively on this point. It is not in the Commission. Did the Lord Jesus Christ forget to state this "essential" truth? Did Matthew forget to record it?

Wayland: "Immerse the body in water, baptizing the candidate 'into the name of the Father.'" . . . "Immerse the body in water" is Dr. Wayland's commission, not the Commission of the Lord Jesus Christ.

Booth: "The form of expression is baptizing *in* or *into* something, as 'in Jordan,' 'in Ænon,' 'in the Holy Spirit ;' 'into Jordan,' 'into Paul,' 'into my own name,' 'into what,' 'into John's baptism,' 'into Moses,' 'into Christ,' 'into his death,' 'into the name of the Father.' . . . The phrases βαπτίζω ἐν and βαπτίζω εἰς, are never used, in the New Testament or out of the New Testament, as equivalent expressions. The former phrase is never used, by inspired or uninspired writers, to express the passage of an object from without an element to a position within an element. Thus, βαπτίζων ἐν τῇ ἐρήμῳ (Mark 1 : 4), ἐν Βηθαβαρᾷ (John 1 : 28), ἐν Αἰνών (John 3 : 23), ἐν Ἰορδάνῃ (Matt. 3 : 6), the preposition ἐν has nothing whatever to do with the meaning of βαπτίζων; if this word meant *whittling sticks*, it would be all the same to the preposition, which simply points out the Wilderness, Bethabara, Ænon, Jordan, as *the places where* the baptizing took place. In the phrases, "He shall baptize you, ἐν Πνεύματι Ἁγίῳ" (Matt. 3 : 11); "I baptize you, ἐν ὕδατι" (Matt. 3 : 11); "He commanded them to be baptized, ἐν τῷ ὀνόματι τοῦ Κυρίου" (Acts 10 : 48); the preposition indicates the condition of the baptizer, and of the speaker, as invested (in the first case) with the divine power of the Holy Ghost, and therefore capable of baptizing = thoroughly changing the spiritual condition of the soul; in the second case, invested with the symbol power of water, and therefore capable of baptizing symbolly only = showing this spiritually purified condition of the soul by the application of water to the body; in the last case, invested with that divine authority which belongs to "the name of the Lord," and therefore empowered to give authoritative command for the ritual baptism of the Gentiles. Again, the preposition has nothing whatever to do with the meaning of βαπτίζω.

The phrase, "Jesus came from Nazareth of Galilee and was baptized by John" (having come) "εἰς Ἰορδάνην," is a case in which εἰς is as wholly disconnected from the meaning of βαπτίζω, as is ἐν in the previous phrases, and indicates *the place to which* Jesus came after departing from Nazareth. The proof of this is clear: "He came down to meet me εἰς τὸν Ἰορδάνην" (3 Kings 2 : 8), "The Lord hath sent me εἰς τὸν Ἰορδάνην" (2 Kings 2 : 6); "And they came εἰς Ἰορδανην;" in none of these cases does the preposition express the passing *into* the Jordan, but merely declares the place *toward* which the movement tended and *at* which it terminated. It is a mistake to suppose that this preposition takes its form from and is expository of βαπτίζω; it originates in and is expository of the movement which starts from Nazareth and terminates at the Jordan. This interpretation receives additional confirmation by the use of another preposition by Matthew in relating the same fact, which preposition can have no possible

relation to the meaning of $\beta a\pi\tau i\zeta\omega$. "Then cometh Jesus from
Galilee ($\dot{\epsilon}\pi\grave{\iota} \tau\grave{o}\nu \,{}^\prime I o\rho\delta\acute{a}\nu\eta\nu$) *upon* the Jordan, to be baptized by John."
There is no other statement in the New Testament of any move-
ment from one place to another in connection with baptism, and
there is no other statement in the New Testament where $\epsilon i\varsigma$ stands
in connection with $\beta a\pi\tau i\zeta\omega$ in regimen with what might be supposed
to represent a physical element. The evidence that it does not
here depend on $\beta a\pi\tau i\zeta\omega$, and connect it with a physical element,
but does depend on $\mathring{\eta}\lambda\theta\epsilon\nu$, and connects it with Jordan as a locality
and the place of arrival, is of the clearest and most conclusive
character. In all the other cases mentioned by Booth, "*into* ($\epsilon i\varsigma$)
what," "into ($\epsilon i\varsigma$) John's baptism," "*into* ($\epsilon i\varsigma$) the name of the
Lord Jesus" (Acts 19:3,5); "*into* ($\epsilon i\varsigma$) Jesus Christ," "into ($\epsilon i\varsigma$)
his death" (Rom. 6:3, 4); "into ($\epsilon i\varsigma$) Christ" (Gal. 3:27); "*into*
($\epsilon i\varsigma$) Moses" (1 Cor. 10:2); "*into* ($\epsilon i\varsigma$) the name of Paul," "*into*
($\epsilon i\varsigma$) my own name" (1 Cor. 1:13, 15); "into ($\epsilon i\varsigma$) one body"
(1 Cor. 12:13); "into ($\epsilon i\varsigma$) the Name of the Father, and of the
Son, and of the Holy Ghost" (Matt. 28:19); every phrase presents an organic unity, and the verb is organically and indissolubly related through the preposition to its regimen, which in every
case is of an ideal and not of a physical character. There is no
such thing in the New Testament as a "baptism *into*" a physical
element; nor is there any such thing as a "baptism *in*," expressive of an object *resting within* any physical element.

Stovel: "'Immersed in cloud and sea while entering into
Moses;' 'baptized in water when they entered into Christ;'
baptized in water those who enter into the name of the Father,
or *resign themselves to the authority* (= into the name)." Mr.
Stovel could not fail to see that his interpretation is the merest
caricature of the language of Scripture, if any one should substitute for the baptism of Scripture Mr. Stovel's "baptism in pollution and error" and, giving him measure for measure, should interpret it as "an immersion *in water, entering into* pollution and
error." (!)

Professor Pepper: "Baptism was not instituted by the Commission. The time of its institution was John's ministry." The
baptism of all who are made Christ's disciples into the name of
the Father, and of the Son, and of the Holy Ghost, was instituted
by, and will forever be the transcendent glory of, the Commission.
A ritual baptism by water was not instituted in the Commission,
nor at any other time by formal and public announcement. There

is no such record of John's authority to baptize. The time, and place, and manner of his investiture with such authority is not on record. He had such authority, for he says so (John 1:33); and his declaration and action under it is sustained by the question of our Lord (Matt. 21:23) "The baptism of John, whence was it? from heaven or of men?" But the Commission of John to baptize never gave any authority to the Apostles to baptize. John's Commission was exclusively personal and limited (without the power of self-perpetuation) to his own ministry. And unless a kindred commission had been enacted and committed to other hands ritual baptism would, of necessity, have perished with John. Such re-enactment and extension was made by the Lord Jesus Christ, as is shown by John 3:22; 4:1, 2. And this renewal and perpetuation of ritual baptism by divine authority was as private and informal and without record as to time, place, and language, as was the original institution under John. Our knowledge of such institution is derived solely from the historical reference to its administration. That this renewed institution of the rite was to extend into and be incorporated with Christianity is known only by the facts of a perpetuated administration, and the command by Peter, made "in the name of the Lord Jesus," that ritual baptism should be extended to the Gentiles. Such facts bear with condemning severity upon the disposition to magnify the form or the efficacy of a rite, the institution of which it has pleased God to leave without any formal verbal record. Dr. Pepper is right in saying ritual baptism was not instituted by the Commission; but not right in tracing Christian ritual baptism to John as its source.

President Brunner: "Immersion is not merely immersion; it is immersion 'into the name of the Father.' . . . Bare immersion no more exhausts the idea of immersion 'into Christ' than " . . . Any one who can so write, and yet say, Christian baptism is *a dipping into* WATER, must (if not technically, yet *pro hac vice*) be a deranged man.

Alexander Campbell: "Disciple, convert the nations baptizing them. The active participle, with the imperative mood, always expresses the agency for effecting the command." Morell (the friend of President Campbell, so far as dipping is concerned) disproves this position as a universal doctrine. And Acts 22:16, " *Baptize* thyself, and *wash* away thy sins ($\epsilon\pi\iota\kappa\alpha\lambda\epsilon\sigma\delta\mu\epsilon\nu\sigma\varsigma$) *calling upon the name of the Lord*," is a crushing, *ad hominem*, argument against the doctrine. "Calling on the name of the Lord" is a very effective means for "washing away sins," but a very ineffective means for dipping a man into water. "Enlist soldiers, making them patriots, training them to observe every commanded duty," is a parallel expression, and disproof of the doctrine.

Judson: "Immersion 'into the name of the Father' . . . is the only Christian baptism." Would that Dr. Judson had made the rule of his faith and practice the truth which he so unreservedly utters, then would he never have adopted and announced as truth the marvellous contradiction—*dipping into water* is the only Christian baptism.

Views of others, not Baptists.

Pusey: This writer must be acknowledged to be fully competent to report on the sentiments of the Fathers. He reports them as holding the opinion that the baptism of the Commission is a *bonâ fide* baptism "*into the* NAME," "insertion of the baptized *within* the Name," that "Name *into which* a man runneth and is safe." He also refers to "the embarrassment of those who say that baptism 'into the name' is a mere rite, to tell what baptism 'into the name' literally means, or how they get their meaning out of it." His testimony as to the sentiment of the Fathers is correct, and his reference to the embarrassment of those who make the baptism of the Commission a ritual service has a sharp point.

Barclay: "It may stumble to say, Baptism in water has no support in Matt. 28:19; but baptism 'into the name' is not baptism into water. 'Name' is *virtue, power*, and is baptism into virtue and power. 'Baptizing into the name of the Father' . . . is not a formula for baptism: 1. Because it is not so used by the Apostles; 2. Because they use another formula." Whatever was Barclay's error as to ritual baptism, his interpretation of this particular passage is not without merit.

Fairbairn: "Baptism into a person, *e. g.*, into Christ, means admitted into personal fellowship." This is a just exposition in principle, and in the right direction as to truth. But the farther statement: "It is baptism into the faith of his promises—into the profession and hope of all that his name indicates," has not equal accuracy. It is impossible to substitute "*into the faith* of promises," or "*into the profession* and *hope*," of anything, for a baptism "*into* CHRIST." The sentiment turns wholly and solely on

" Christ," and " baptism into " HIM, and not into _faith_, or _pro-fession_, or _hope_.   Take away " Christ," and you take away all.

J. A. Alexander: " Baptism ' into the name of Jesus Christ.' Jesus = *Saviour;* Christ = *Anointed;* = Prophet, Priest, and King.   Therefore, baptism into the name of Jesus Christ = baptism into union and subjection to him in these characters."   There is a verbal inaccuracy in the repetition of " *baptism into* " (the name) which develops " union and subjection."   We cannot repeat the " baptism into " which has been once used, by saying " *baptism into* union and subjection."   Baptism into the name of Jesus Christ = " union with and subjection to all that his name imports," is a good interpretation, and the literal truth.

President Beecher: " Purifying them into the name of the Father," . . . .   There is a difficulty in the way of translating, here, baptizing by " purifying."   The difficulty is not that baptize has not the meaning, *to purify;* it has, and that abundantly; but the difficulty arises out of the construction.   The meaning *to purify* arises out of a baptism into something which is possessed of a purifying quality, *e. g.,* into *repentance,* into *remission of sins,* into *Christ.*   Any one baptized into repentance, remission, Christ (= brought under the full influence of) is necessarily *purified;* but in reaching this result the form of the phrase is exhausted and perishes, leaving purification as its residuum.   By frequent and long-continued use of the phrase, the full form may be dropped, and the single word *baptize* may be used in proper relations, as representative of the full phrase, with the meaning *to purify.*   But this meaning cannot be substituted for " baptize " in the original or in any similarly constructed phrase; thus, you cannot say, *purify into* repentance, *purify into* remission of sins.   Saul's armor is not suited to David.   The construction which is suited to *baptize* is not suited to " purify."   *To dip into purple* effects a *dye,* and gives origin to *dye* as the meaning of " dip into purple;" but you cannot substitute *dye* for *dip* in such construction as originates the meaning, and say, " *dye into* purple."   The construction must be changed to dye *with* purple, and so we must say, purify *by* repentance, *by* the remission of sins.   We cannot, therefore, substitute an acquired meaning in a construction which belongs to a primary meaning.   The New Testament introduces $\beta\alpha\pi\tau i\zeta\omega$ to us in entirely new relations, but in precisely the same construction which the original nature of the word requires, and we must deduce the new ideas intended to be conveyed by a strict adherence to the construction and to the force of individual terms, and in doing this every difficulty will immediately be resolved. It must be borne in mind, that it is not *the word* βαπτίζω which is used in a novel sense in the New Testament; but the novelty is in its phraseological combinations. These combinations are organic and cannot be resolved into and be interpreted by disjunct words. Their interpretation must be as a whole. The combinations are not to be found in Classical use, and the ideas embodied in the phrases are limited to revealed truth. There is no such phrase in Classic literature as βάπτισμα μετανοίας; and no such conception as that contained in βάπτισμα μετανοίας εἰς ἄφεσιν ἁμαρτιων; consequently no heathen Greek could comprehend the conception in these phrases without instruction in the Scripture ideas of *repentance* and *remission;* but when such knowledge was secured there would be no farther difficulty; because the construction conforms to the laws of grammar and logic governing all such Greek phrases.

Prof. Godwin, London: " The words of our Lord mean: *Purifying* them *for* the Father." . . . Professor Godwin sees that if " purify " be the meaning of βαπτίζω, then there is a necessity for conforming εἰς to such meaning. " Purify *for* " is a proper combination, but not purify *into;* but, for reasons assigned, " purify " cannot be substituted in this construction, and the change of εἰς from "into " to *for*, is untenable, in view of the meaning of βαπτίζω, and the construction based on that meaning throughout Classic and inspired writings. Prof. Godwin agrees with Professor Pepper, of Crozer Baptist Theolog. Sem., in saying: " The Commission does not *institute* ritual baptism." He also says: " It does not announce *a formula* for ritual baptism."

Calvin: " Matt. 28 : 19 is not the institution of ritual baptism, which dates from Christ's ministry. Baptism is an appendage subordinate to the function of teaching. *Ritual baptism is a shadow of* the remission of sins through Christ, which remission is not effected by the outward symbol, but by the Holy Spirit." Calvin is right in dating Christian ritual baptism from the ministry and authority of Christ and not from that of John, even if they were entirely identical, which they are not. The baptism of John is Christian baptism *as far as it goes ;* but it is Christian baptism undeveloped in the blood-shedding of an atoning Redeemer, in which shedding of blood " for the remission of sins," ritual baptism has its exclusive ground.

Bengel: " *Μαθητεύειν* includes baptism and teaching. The Gentiles as being wholly aliens from God were to be baptized into the name of the Father." . . . Both these sentiments are of the first importance in the interpretation of this Commission: 1. The discipleship of Christ *includes ritual baptism;* 2. Alienation of Gentile idolaters from the living and true God is to be removed by baptism " into the NAME of the Father, and of the Son, and of the Holy Ghost," the Triune, and only true God. Of course such baptism must be real, not ritual.

Olshausen: " Baptism was not now instituted. Baptism into the name is to be understood by baptism into Paul, baptism into Moses. *'Επὶ τὸ ὄνομα, ἐν τῷ ὀνόματι,* equivalents of *εἰς τὸ ὄνομα.*" Olshausen agrees with Calvin, Godwin, Pepper, and others, that the Commission is not the institution of ritual baptism. He agrees with Bengel in including baptism and teaching in discipleship, but seems to base the sentiment on this passage, while Bengel grounds it more profoundly in John 4 : 1. He errs in making *ἐπὶ τὸ ὄνομα, ἐν τῷ ὀνόματι,* the equivalents or indeed as parallel (so far as baptism is concerned) with *εἰς τὸ ὄνομα.*

Stier: " *'Εν τῷ ὀνόματι* and *εἰς τὸ ὄνομα* are not equivalents. Baptized into the Three-One has the same depth of meaning as *εἰς Θεόν, εἰς Χριστόν, ἐν Θεῷ.*" Such views necessitate a real and not a ritual baptism " into the NAME." . . .

Lange: " In the name $=$ in the might and for the name, as badge and symbol. *Εἰς τὸ,* not *with reference to* (De Wette, Meyer), because elsewhere it means either the element into which one is baptized, as *εἰς 'Ιορδάνην, εἰς θάνατον*; or the object, *εἰς μετάνοιαν*; or the authority under which one is baptized." In every instance in the New Testament where *βαπτίζω εἰς* occurs, and the preposition is expository of the verb and points to the complement of its idea, there is but one meaning belonging to it. In the case cited, *εἰς Ιορδάνην* (Mark 1 : 9), the preposition is not dependent on *βαπτίζω*, nor is it expository of it. Its dependence is on *ἦλθεν* and is expository of the direction and termination of the movement. There is no standing-place for an attempt to prove that *a baptism* "into the Jordan " is *a dipping* $=$ a momentary putting into and taking out; and a putting into and remaining within *without limitation of time,* none will claim; and yet this element, to wit, *no limitation of time,* is essential to a baptism, *and exists in every baptism of the New Testament.*

Wilson: " Baptism ' into Moses ' $=$ the acknowledgment of his claims as leader and lawgiver. Baptism 'into Christ' = the acknowledgment of him as Lord in his personal and mediatorial character. Baptism 'into the name of the Father,' . . . . = the acknowledgment of 'the Father, Son, and Holy Ghost.'" This exposition is in the direction of the truth, but falls greatly short of it; because it is too feeble and inadequate. The after-statement: "The Commission enjoins baptism *into the faith of* the Father," . . . . is erroneous; because nothing can be a substitute for the divinely enjoined baptism *into the* NAME of the Father. . . . The additional statement: "The Commission enjoins baptism *not into* WATER, but '*into the* NAME of the Father, Son, and Holy Ghost,'" is entirely correct. And if our duty is to interpret that Scripture which the Holy Ghost has given to us and not to make Scripture to suit our fancy or our ignorance, then, our business is to interpret that command which has been given to us and not to substitute some other for it

Interpretation.

As the translation of this passage is unsettled so also is the interpretation. That this may appear I will present some of the various interpretations which have been given by those whose piety and scholarship give them a right to be heard as to the proper interpretation of any passage of Scripture. My object in doing this is not to present views which harmonize with my own, but that the manifold diversities may produce the profound conviction that the true meaning of the passage is yet an open question, and calls for renewed investigation.

CARSON, 169, 173: "It is well known that μαθητεύειν signifies to disciple, to make scholars. To disciple all nations, is to bring them, by faith, into the school of *Christ*, in which they are to learn his will. The persons whom Matthew calls disciples, Mark calls believers. It is into the faith and subjection of the Father, Son, and Holy Ghost, that men are to be baptized."

Little or no objection can be made to this interpretation on its face. It covers (vaguely) the general truth of the passage and does not exclude (by any necessity) the new-born babe.

STOVEL, 527: "The whole meaning is expressed thus: Go, make disciples, baptizing in water, those who enter into the name, or resign themselves to the authority of the Father, the Son, and the Holy Spirit."

Objection: Such interpretation breaks up the divinely established relation of βαπτίζω, and substitutes for it a phrase ("entering into the name of the Father," etc.) unknown to the Scriptures, thereby announcing a condition of baptism ("those that enter into the name of the Father," . . .) both unknown to the Scriptures and unsuited to the Scripture Rite.

RIPLEY, *Christian Baptism,* 118 : . . . "The Lord has commanded to baptize; but he has given no command about the circumstances of time, and place, etc. . . . The ACTION, whatever it be, expressed by the word *baptize,* is not a circumstance. . . . There was *an external act* enjoined. . . . It is on Paul's teaching, that the *manner* of the baptismal rite is regarded as significant. . . . The religious immersion of a believer in the name of the Father, and of the Son, and of the Holy Ghost is baptism, whether administered in a river, or a lake, or . . . The Hebrew word to which βαπτίζω corresponds, clearly means *to dip, to immerse.* . . . A particular act has; no particular body of water has been appointed, in which that act has been performed. . . . Baptists believe *only* the immersion of a professed believer in the name of the Father, etc., to be Christian baptism."

Objection: The command of the Lord is not a command simply "to baptize;" but it is a command specifically to baptize "*into* THE NAME *of the Father, and of the Son, and of the Holy Ghost.*" No external act is enjoined, nor is there any possibility for an external act *dipping, immersing, into* THE NAME *of the Father, etc. Immersion in a* RIVER, is no more *baptism into* THE NAME of the Father, Son, and Holy Ghost, than death is life. The Hebrew word טָבַל does not correspond with βαπτίζω. The usage of these words is irreconcilably diverse. The use of this Greek word by the Septuagint in translating 2 Kings 5 : 14, no more proves correspondence of meaning, than the word "wash" (used in the Syriac translation) proves a correspondence with this Hebrew word in the sense *to dip,* or than μολύνω *stain* (also used by the Septuagint (Gen. 37 : 31) in translating this same Hebrew word) means *to dip.* The whole scope of the usage and the essential power of βαπτίζω shows, that the meaning *to dip* is out of all question.

JUDSON, *Sermon,* 5 : "When our Lord commissioned his disciples to proselyte all nations, he *instituted* the sacred rite of baptism. The primitive word (βάπτω), from which the word denoting baptism is derived, signifies *immersion.* The word which

28

denotes the act of baptizing, according to the usage of Greek writers, uniformly signifies or implies *immersion*. The Septuagint expresses by it the action of Naaman when he *dipped* himself seven times in Jordan. Josephus uses it to convey the idea of immersion, in describing the death of one who was drowned in a pool, and in instances too numerous to be detailed. The words of the Commission are, 'Disciple all nations, baptizing them into ($\varepsilon i \varsigma$) the name of the Father, and of the Son, and of the Holy Ghost.'"

Objection : Judson differs from Pepper and Campbell as to the institution of baptism. One or the other is in error. Where error is obvious on related points there may be error on the main point. $B\acute{a}\pi\tau\omega$ does not signify "*immersion*," except with the profound and revolutionary qualification *momentary* (immersion). $Ba\pi\tau\acute{\iota}\zeta\omega$ does signify *mersion*, eliminating *definiteness* of action and *momentariness* of continuance. It does not express the *action* of Naaman in *dipping* himself. Its use by Josephus in the case of *drowning* is proof of this. Men are not drowned by *a dipping*. The translation of the Commission by Dr. Judson—"baptizing *into* THE NAME"—disproves his interpretation.

DR. CONANT, *New Version, notes :* "This Greek word, $\mu a\theta\eta\tau\varepsilon\acute{\upsilon}$-$\sigma a\tau\varepsilon$ is used in the New Testament with the accusative meaning *to make one a disciple. In the name* is the proper English expression of $\varepsilon i \varsigma \tau\grave{o}$ ὄ*νομα*. The idea of *reference to* is the ground meaning of $\varepsilon i \varsigma$ in such cases ; and this, with all it includes, is embraced by the English form *in the name. Into the name* is not an English phrase, and, though the literal form of the Greek, does not give the sense. The practice was adopted at an early period, of immersing at the utterance of each name. But this is clearly contrary to the terms of the command."

Objection : The English form "in the name" ($=$ *by the authority of*) has the same meaning as the Greek form $\varepsilon\nu \tau\tilde{\omega}$ ὀ*νόματι*, which differs essentially from $\beta a\pi\tau\acute{\iota}\zeta\omega \varepsilon i \varsigma$ ($\tau\grave{o}$ ὄ*νομα*) ; which is the form (both in the Classics and in the New Testament) for giving the utmost precision to any particular baptism. Beyond the precision of statement in $\beta a\pi\tau\acute{\iota}\zeta\varepsilon\iota\nu \varepsilon i \varsigma \theta\acute{a}\lambda a\sigma\sigma a\nu, \varepsilon i \varsigma o \tilde{\iota}\nu o \nu, \varepsilon i \varsigma \gamma\acute{a}\lambda a, \varepsilon i \varsigma \ddot{\upsilon}\pi\nu o \nu, \varepsilon i \varsigma \pi o \rho\nu\varepsilon\acute{\iota}a\nu, \varepsilon i \varsigma \mu\varepsilon\tau a\nu o\acute{\iota}a\nu, \varepsilon i \varsigma \ddot{a}\varphi\varepsilon\sigma\iota\nu, \varepsilon i \varsigma M\omega\upsilon\sigma\tilde{\eta}\nu, \varepsilon i \varsigma \Pi a\tilde{\upsilon}\lambda o \nu, \varepsilon i \varsigma X\rho\iota\sigma\tau\grave{o}\nu, \varepsilon i \varsigma \tau\grave{o}$ ὄ*νομα* $\tau o\tilde{\upsilon} \Pi a\tau\rho\grave{o}\varsigma, \varkappa a\grave{\iota} \tau o\tilde{\upsilon} \Upsilon\iota o\tilde{\upsilon}, \varkappa a\grave{\iota} \tau o\tilde{\upsilon} \Pi\nu\varepsilon\acute{\upsilon}\mu a\tau o\varsigma \text{'}A\gamma\acute{\iota}o\upsilon$, it is impossible for language to go. In every case the general force of $\beta a\pi\tau\acute{\iota}\zeta\varepsilon\iota\nu \varepsilon i \varsigma$ is the same, namely, placing the object of the verb under the controlling influence of the regimen of the preposition. The dipping of the head (of a person standing in the water) into the water, whether once or thrice, was not the baptism, but a means in order to the baptism, which was "into the Name," etc. This is shown, among other reasons, by the Nestorian ritual, which says, "and dips (*tabal*) him in water, and lays his hand upon his head, and says, such a one is *baptized* ('amad) 'in the name of the Father, etc.'" Here *tabal*, according to its definite meaning, expresses *the act* done in the dipping into water, while ('amad) expresses the *condition* effected by the act, namely, "into" (within all the influence which belongs to) the name of the Father, Son, and Holy Ghost.

BAPTIST MANUAL, *Bapt. Pub. Soc.:* "We believe that Christian baptism is the immersion in water of a believer, into the name of the Father, and Son, and Holy Ghost," Matt. 28:19.

Objection: A momentary "immersion in water" is *a dipping* for which there is no command in Scripture. An "immersion in water," *without limit of time*, is a baptism, and as Dr. Judson says, drowns men. A mersion into the name of the Father, and of the Son, and of the Holy Ghost, *without limitation of time*, is a baptism which places the soul under the controlling influence of the Triune God, *without withdrawal.*

An "immersion *in* water *into* the name of the Father," etc., is unintelligible. Are there two immersions, one "in *water*," and another "into *the Name*," etc.? If so, which is the baptism? Is the "immersion in water" causative of the "immersion into the Deity"? or what is the relation? If this immersion in water has relation, as is said, to *the Trinity*, how has it relation, as this "article of faith" farther says, to "our faith in *the crucified*, and *buried*, and *risen* SAVIOUR?" There is a vast difference between an immersion which relates to *the* TRINITY, and one that relates to the crucifixion, and burial, and resurrection of *the* LORD JESUS CHRIST. The crucifixion, and burial, and resurrection of *the Trinity* (!) is no doctrine of the Bible. If Christian baptism is "an immersion in water into the Name of the Father, Son, and Holy Ghost," then, Christian baptism cannot be an immersion in water bearing upon *the cross, the tomb,* and *the rolling away of its stone.* The two things are incongruous and impossible.

ALEXANDER CAMPBELL, *Christian Baptist*, 630: "Have you ever adverted to the import of the participle in the Commission, 'Disciple, or convert the nations, immersing them?' I need not tell you that this is the exact translation. Let me ask you then, does not the active participle, always, when connected with the imperative mood, express *the manner in which* the thing commanded is to be performed? Cleanse the floor, washing it; cleanse the floor, sweeping it; convert the nations, baptizing them; are exactly the same forms of speech. No person, I presume, will controvert this. If so, then, no man could be called a disciple . . . until he was immersed."

Objection: If it be not murder in the first degree to quote " Convert the nations, immersing them," as the command and means taught by Matt. 28 : 19, then, there never was murder committed in this fallen world. The doctrine of the active participle " always " with the imperative mood indicating the means for fulfilling the command, has been disproved by the Baptist scholar Morell of Scotland, as well as by Prof. Wilson of Ireland. Many heresies have been laid at the door of Campbellism, but none, perhaps, greater than that which the President of Bethany has laid there himself in teaching, that " the nations are to be converted by immersing them." The nations, once, were immersed, but there is no record of their conversion thereby, any more than by the preaching of Noah. There is, however, a very distinct account of their being drowned, which confirms the case of Dr. Judson's immersion drowning, as indeed will every case of *bona fide* immersion in water of a human being.

Interpreters, not Baptist.

STUART, 43 : " The noun ὄνομα is, no doubt, expletive. Baptized εἰς τὸ ὄνομα πατρὸς, etc., is the same as baptized εἰς τὸν πατερα, etc. Accordingly we find ὄνομα omitted in Rom. 6 : 3, 1 Cor. 10 : 2, Gal. 3 : 27; it is used in Acts 8 : 16, 19 : 5; 1 Cor. 1 : 13, 15. The sense of the whole formula is more difficult to be understood. Most commentators, after Vitringa (Obs. Sac.; iii, 22), explain εἰς as meaning *into the acknowledgment of;* with an implication of affiance, subjection, discipleship, etc. But the formula in 1 Cor. 12 : 13, seems not to accord with such an explanation. Here εἰς plainly means participation, *i. e.*, by baptism we come to belong to one body. In like manner, we may say, by baptism we come to belong (in a special and peculiar sense, no doubt) to Father, Son, and Holy Ghost; to Moses, 1 Cor. 10 : 2; to Paul, 1 Cor. 1 : 13. In this way all the passages may be construed alike, and the sense in all will be good. The idea is, for substance, that by

baptism we become consecrated to any person or thing, appropriated (as it were) to any person or thing, so as to belong to
him or it, in a manner peculiar and involving a special relation
and consequent special duties and obligations."

Remark: This view of a noble man and scholar (at whose feet
it was my privilege to sit as a pupil) is, I think, substantially
true, yet lacking in precision and confidence for two reasons: 1.
The ground on which (in physical applications) $\beta a\pi\tau i\zeta\omega$ $\epsilon i\varsigma$ must
be interpreted was not clearly in view; 2. The idea of a ritual
baptism entering into the statement confuses and precludes a
cleanly cut interpretation of the simple and explicit statement
of the Holy Spirit.

HALLEY, 414: "But admitting, as I do, that $\beta a\pi\tau i\zeta\epsilon\iota\nu$ construed
with $\epsilon i\varsigma$, is, to immerse into, let us apply this remark in expounding the Commission of our Lord.

"If to baptize is to immerse, in this passage, then, according to
the usual construction of the words, the name of the Holy Trinity
is the thing into which the nations are to be immersed. If the
words be taken literally, here is, certainly, no command to immerse *into water.*

"To immerse $\epsilon i\varsigma$ $\tau\grave{o}$ $\check{o}\nu o\mu a$, into the name of the person whose religion is professed, is the religious rite of making proselytes, as
to immerse into the name of the Father, and of the Son, and of
the Holy Ghost, is the appropriate act of the Apostles and of
ministers of the Gospel. The construction of the passage brings
the immersion of the passage, so far as it exists, not into the
element of baptizing into water, but into the object of baptizing,
into the name of the Father, and of the Son, and of the Holy
Ghost. So, Paul inquires of the disciples of Apollos, $\epsilon i\varsigma$ τi $\grave{\epsilon}\beta a\pi$-
$\tau\iota\sigma\theta\eta\tau\epsilon$; into what were ye baptized? And the answer is not, into
cold water, but, into John's baptism. Let it be observed, on the
other hand, that we have not the phrase, to baptize into water, to
baptize into the Holy Ghost; but to baptize with water, and to
baptize with the Holy Ghost; these being construed as the instruments with which the baptism was performed, not the substances into which the persons were baptized."

Remark: This interpretation is in harmony with the elegant
and accurate scholarship which is characteristic of President
Halley. The only disturbing element in it, is the supposed necessity for including and harmonizing the language with a ritual
observance, which has no place in the statement.

GODWIN, 151–162 : " There is nothing in this Commission to
show that the phrase here used, is a form of words for the administration of baptism. The great object of baptism and not
the language used at the observance of baptism by water, is denoted by the terms. The one incomprehensible and invisible God,
who manifests himself in the person of his Son and by the Spirit
which abides in believers, is the object of this Christian baptism.
The words of our Lord mean ' purifying them for the Father, the
Son, and the Holy Spirit.' This passage is not quoted as enjoining the rite of baptism, until the introduction of the doctrine of
Baptismal regeneration, which led to the supposition that every
baptism mentioned in Scripture was the one Baptism with water.

" The expression to immerse into God is objected to because the
figure is unnatural and unscriptural. It will hardly be supposed
that this command included nothing but what the Apostles, themselves, were able to effect. By their own power they could not
make one true disciple of Christ, any more than they could heal
the sick, cleanse the lepers, expel demons, and raise the dead.
The context, the occasion, and parallel passages, prove that the
purification of all nations for which the Apostles received this
great Commission, was not a ceremonial purification by water, but
a moral purification by the Gospel and the Spirit of Christ."

Remark: Professor Godwin very justly eliminates, largely if
not wholly, a ritual baptism from the direct command of this passage. Purification is in the baptism ; but rather as a prerequisite
for it (obtained through discipleship to Christ) than as a consequence of " baptism into the name," etc.; it is not derivable (as
here used) from the word βαπτίζω. Baptism into the Deity (rejecting all ritualism from the thought) cannot be " unnatural,"
seeing that it is so abundantly used, as in the phrases—baptism
into Moses, baptism into Joshua, baptism into Paul, baptism into
Christ; nor can it be " unscriptural " seeing that, *in* Christ, *in* the
Spirit, *in* God, are phrases which abound in Scripture, and exhibit *the condition in which* the soul abides, having entered into,
or having been *baptized into* Christ, *into* the Spirit, *into* God.

BEECHER, 206: " The Fathers regard the commission to remit
sins in Luke and John, as a commission to baptize, as really as
that in Matthew and Mark. They regarded it merely as another
mode of expressing the same idea. In short, Christ died as the
Lamb of God to take away the sins of the world, and the great
business of the Apostles was to publish to the world, the great

doctrine of the remission of sins through his death, and the
terms on which it could be obtained, and to establish the rite by
which this purgation from sin might be shadowed forth and commemorated in honor of the Trinity, and especially of that Spirit
by whom this atonement was made effectual to purge the conscience from dead works, to serve the living God."

Remark : President Beecher is entirely correct in saying, the
Fathers used the words *baptize* and *baptism* as the equivalents of
the phrases *to remit sins, the remission of sins.*   This usage was
derived, by abbreviation, from the Scripture phrases—"baptized
into CHRIST," baptism *into the* REMISSION OF SINS, which phrases
express a condition of purification, and hence the word "baptize,"
when used as the representative of such phrases, secures to itself
the meaning of the entire phrase.   But when the entire phrase is
used the single word "baptize" cannot have such meaning; but
it must be (distributed through the phrase, and) be received as
expressing the resultant change of condition in the object effected
by the interaction (upon it) of "baptize" and "Christ" or "the
remission of sins."   This condition of purification is the result
of baptism *into* CHRIST, the atoning Lamb of God, and not of
baptism *into the* TRINITY, which is quite another matter.   When
or where, in Scripture, is *a crucified* Redeemer and the Trinity
made equivalents or interchanged ?

BLOOMFIELD, *Crit. Comm. :* "The Commission embraces three
particulars—μαθητεύειν, βαπτίζειν, and διδάσκειν,—*i. e.*, 1. To disciple them, or to convert them to the faith; 2. To initiate them into
the church by baptism; 3. To instruct them, when baptized, in
the doctrines and duties of a Christian life.   We are baptized in
(or unto) the Father, Son, and Holy Ghost."

Olshausen : "The two participles go to compose the μαθητεύειν."

Lightfoot : "*Μαθητεύσατε* primum per baptismum, et deinde
διδάσκετε αυτοῦς."

Turretin : "It cannot be said that Christ (Matt. 28 : 19) instituted the baptism of doctrine and not of water, because he expressly distinguishes doctrine from baptism, saying, Teach and
Baptize."

Remark : The baptism enjoined by Christ is far nobler than
that of a "ritual initiation into the church."   The phraseology of
the text, and that of Turretin by the introduction of "and"
(Teach *and* Baptize), is essentially diverse as to the thought pre-

sented; still more, if he means to represent μαθητεύσατε by " Teach," as appears to be the case.

WILSON, 359–361 : " The import of the expression βαπτίζειν τινὰ εἰς τινα or εἰς τί, is still agitated among the most accomplished interpreters of Scripture. A thorough discussion of the entire question would be desirable ; but we can merely offer a few hints, at present, on the aspect of it with which we are immediately concerned. *Vitringa* in his Observ. Sacra., III, 22, understands εἰς as denoting '*into* the acknowledgment of;' a sense which is obviously too limited to meet all the occurrences, though it continues to command pretty general acceptance. Kuinöl, on our text and on Matt. 3 : 11, takes εἰς to be expressive of the design or end in view (*finem, consilium*): that is, ' Be baptized *that* you may receive pardon.' Dr. Halley does not like this exegesis, neither do I. It was adopted by *Fritsche* on Matt.; but in his more recent work on Rom. (6 : 3) he rejects it as not sufficiently comprehensive. His new theory assigns to the formula the general notion of directing the thoughts of the baptized to some person or object,—which he thus applies to our text—' *Ita lavari, ut* (futura) *peccatorum venia tibi monstretur.*' If an apostle in any instance baptized a true believer, it was a baptism εἰς ἄφεσιν ἁμαρτιῶν, not as a *future* blessing, but as one already conferred.

" *Krehl,* on Romans, explains the formula as meaning, ' To obtain (durch die Taufe) through, or by means of baptism, the forgiveness of sins,' an interpretation for which he deserves the best thanks of Dr. Pusey. Among the older critics, *Piscator* understands the words—' in testimonium atque confirmationem remissionis peccatorum.' *Poole* takes the same view, though its basis is scarcely broad enough. *Stuart* thinks that εἰς with the idea of *participation* will suit all the passages, and afford in all a good sense. *Olshausen* represents remission of sins as the *result* of baptism, though baptism he says, ' necessarily presupposes faith.' We find no such form as ' Be baptized *that* you may receive pardon ;' and βαπτίζειν εἰς has no such meaning. Whether we baptize *into* Christ's death, *into* repentance, *into* the remission of sins, etc., we do not *create*, we only *recognize* the relation presumed to subsist between the parties, and that into which they are baptized. Baptism *for* repentance, *for* the remission of sins, so far as we know, is an unauthorized rendering."

Remark: These views of Prof. Wilson give interest to and show the necessity for a re-examination of this profoundly interesting and deeply important passage. One thing seems to be clear,— *There is no fixed principle anywhere revealed in the interpretation of the phrase* βαπτίζειν εἰς. Until this is secured all interpretations must be fluctuating. When this shall have been determined, we will have a fixed element by which to test interpretations authoritatively, and not before.

NEANDER, 197: " We certainly cannot prove that, when Christ commanded his disciples to baptize in the name of the Father, the Son, and the Holy Ghost, He intended to establish a particular formula of baptism. . . . He wished to show the dependence of the whole life on the one God, who had revealed himself through his Son, as the Father of fallen man, and who imparts his Spirit to sanctify man, whom his Son has redeemed ; as well as to point to the true worship of God, as He had revealed himself through his Son, in a heart sanctified by the Divine life, which is shed forth from him."

Remark: The discrimination suggested by Neander between the peculiar work of THE SON *in redemption,* and THE TRINITY, *as the true* GOD *to whom* WORSHIP *is due,* is of the first importance to the right interpretation of this passage. Certainly there is the most radical difference in the relations of men to CHRIST *as a Redeemer,* and to the TRIUNE GOD *as the object of worship.*

SCHAAF, *History,* 566: " The full formula of baptism as prescribed by Christ (Matt. 28 : 19) is in the name of the Father, the Son, and the Holy Ghost; signifying the sinking of the subject into the revealed being of the Triune God, a coming into living communion with him, so as to be thenceforth consecrated to him, to live to him, and serve him, and to experience his blessed redeeming and sanctifying power. In practice, however, we find the Apostles always using the abbreviated form, ' into the name,' or ' in the name of Jesus Christ,' or ' of the Lord Jesus,' or simply ' into Christ.' Of course this included the other, binding the subject to receive the whole doctrine of Christ, and consequently what he had taught concerning the Father and the Holy Ghost."

Remark: Prof. Schaaf teaches, 1. The Apostles never used as a formula in ritual baptism the words of this passage; 2. The words βαπτίζοντες εἰς τὸ ὄνομα must be treated as an organic phrase presenting τὸ ὄνομα as the ideal element *into which* the subject, under the power of βαπτίζω, " sinks," and is thus introduced *into a new condition* = of communion, consecration, life, service, redemption, and sanctification, *without limitation of time;* all of which is the right opposite of *a dipping* (whether into water, or into τὸ ὄνομα), and is that which this baptism, and every other baptism of the New Testament, imperatively demands.

This interpretation may be elucidated, but it can hardly be essentially improved. Of course "sinks" is not to be understood as the expression of the definite meaning of βαπτίζω. But it does (in common with very many other words) express one form of action by which the demand of this verb (for inness of condition, without limitation of time, and without restriction in the form of the act) may be properly met. *Dipping* is not one of the forms of action which may meet the demanded condition of the verb, because it is essentially contradictory to one of the vital elements in this Greek word, namely, *without limitation of time.* A dipping being sharply limited to momentariness, is necessarily excluded from the class of words which like "sink" (not being limited in the time of continuance) can effect a baptism. While the soul can "sink" into the name of the Deity without withdrawal, and so be "baptized" into the Triune God, a living man cannot "sink" (without withdrawal) *into water*, and so be "baptized," without destruction of life; and THEREFORE it is that there is no such thing in the New Testament as a baptism *in or into* WATER; but a real baptism by the Holy Ghost "into repentance," "into the remission of sins," "into Christ," and a ritual baptism *with* or *by* water symbolizing the condition of purity induced in the soul by such real baptisms.

If *the dipping* into water, practiced by the friends of the theory, and called baptisms, were regarded as a valueless accident in the use of the water (the essential thing being in the quality of the element) then, while a very unwise way of using the water, and wholly without Scripture authority, it might still be accepted as a possible use of the element; but when *the* ACT *of* DIPPING is made the baptism, there is the most absolute nullification of the command βαπτίζοντες εἰς τὸ ὄνομα, and such a dipping must, in so far forth, be absolutely rejected as not being any *baptism* at all, much less Christian baptism. Alford (John 3:6), like Schaaf, uses "sink" as without limitation of time, and thereby securing inness of condition resulting in the penetrating, pervading, and controlling influence of the encompassing element over the sunk object, communicating to it its own quality. "The spirit of man is in the natural birth *dead*, SUNK IN *trespasses and sins*, and in *a state* of wrath." If *dip* be substituted for "sink," the sentiment ıs reversed, and the "state" of death and pollution is subverted. So, to substitute *dip* for BAPTIZE in the word of God is an absolute reversal and subversion of its teachings.

Proposed Interpretation.

General Structure. The ruling element in the passage is the command—*Μαθητεύσατε* : the relation of *βαπτίζοντες εἰς τὸ ὄνομα* to this command is that of an included and dependent result : the relation of *διδάσκοντες* to the command is that of means, covering both the immediate command—"disciple to Christ," and its included and dependent result—baptism "into the name of the Father, and of the Son, and of the Holy Ghost."

The relation between "baptizing into the Name of the Father," and "discipling to Christ," as proposed by Alexander Campbell, namely, that of cause to effect (as in "cleanse the room, sweeping it," sweeping being the cause of the cleansing), is a reversal of the truth here taught, and substitutes the effect for the cause. All who are made disciples to Christ by being "taught to observe all things whatsoever he has commanded," will, thereby, be "baptized into the name of the Father, and of the Son, and of the Holy Ghost;" but without this antecedent discipleship they cannot be so baptized. Gabriel, and Michael, and all the holy angels, are baptized into the name of the only living and Tri-Une God; but such baptism is not sin-cleansing, nor does it make them disciples to Christ. Holy angels can come unto the Father in other ways than by Christ; but no guilty man on earth can come unto the Father but by Christ—Redeemer, Mediator, and Advocate, with the Father. Every sinner must hear the call, "Be ye reconciled to God" (= Father, Son, and Holy Ghost) through Jesus Christ, the "merciful and faithful High Priest who maketh reconciliation for the sins of the people." This order can never, by any possibility, be changed. There is no such thing as "sweeping" sin from the soul by a baptism (ritual or real) into the name of the Trinity, and so "cleansing" it for discipleship to Christ. This is a scheme of redemption of which the Bible knows nothing. The relations of the several parts of the passage must continue (in harmony with all other Scripture) to declare, that the subjection and reconciliation of sinners with the living God—Father, Son, and Holy Ghost, must begin and end *with* JESUS CHRIST, "For it pleased the Father that in him should all fulness dwell; And *having made peace by the* BLOOD OF HIS CROSS, *by* HIM *to reconcile all things to* HIMSELF."

Disciple.

Μαθητεύσατε : The command is *to make disciples, to disciple.* The agreement on this point, so far as translation is concerned, is now so uniform, that nothing need be said upon it. There are, however, several points, not unimportant, embraced in this discipleship, which claim brief attention. Among these points are, 1. To whom are these persons to be discipled? A thoughtful answer to this question must be—They are to be made disciples of Christ. The New Testament speaks of disciples of Moses, of the Pharisees, and of John ; but to refer the disciples here spoken of to any of these, is out of all question. The only other disciples spoken of are disciples of the Lord Jesus. These are not only designated as " disciples " by common fame, but by the Evangelists, by Angels, and by the Lord Jesus Christ himself, who says, Matt. 26 : 18, " The Master saith, I will keep the Passover at thy house with my disciples." It would seem to be impossible to avoid the conclusion that this is a command *to make disciples to* CHRIST. This is farther confirmed by the declaration (subsequent to the command and action under it) in Acts 11 : 26, " They taught a great multitude, and *the disciples* were called CHRISTI*ans* first in Antioch," which clearly implies that they were made disciples by " teaching " as commanded by Christ, and that they were made and popularly recognized as disciples of CHRIST. The truth is of practical importance, because it shows that this discipling cannot depend upon or be expounded by " baptizing into the name of the Father, Son, and Holy Ghost ;" for disciples to *Christ*, obviously, can never be constituted by such a baptism ; and while a ritual baptism into the name of the Father, etc., would constitute all so baptized disciples of the Triune God, yet there are no such " disciples " recognized or recognizable under the teaching of the Scriptures. They who become related to the Triune God, become related to Him as redeemed and reconciled subjects and worshippers, and not as disciples. While, therefore, we recognize a vital and indissoluble relation between this discipling and this baptizing, we must as distinctly recognize a diversity which precludes the baptizing from being either causative or expository of the specific character of the discipleship.

2. A second question arises : What enters into discipling to

Christ? Among these elements are, 1. Repentance for sin; 2. Faith in order to the remission of sin; 3. Obedience as evidence of repentance and faith; 4. Ritual baptism, symbol of the remission of sin. We have seen from Acts 11 : 26, that "teaching" ($\delta\iota\delta\acute{a}\xi\alpha\iota$) enters into discipleship; and we learn the same, impliedly, from John 4 : 1, 2, and farther, that ritual baptism was an accompaniment of and consequent upon making disciples to Christ. John did not make or baptize disciples for himself, but for the Coming One. Paul indignantly rejects the idea, that he made disciples for himself, or "baptized into his own name," or apart from Christ crucified. But the Lord Jesus Christ did make disciples for himself; and they were in his presence (John 4 : 1, 2), and by his authority after his ascension (Acts 10 : 48), baptized ritually as his disciples. There is no other ritual baptism of disciples in the New Testament but "into the Name of the Lord Jesus." We must recognize, therefore, a ritual baptism of disciples *into* CHRIST, as essentially contained in the command to "disciple," which baptism is another and diverse from the additionally enjoined "baptizing into the name of the Father, and of the Son, and of the Holy Ghost," which is a real baptism without any attending rite. Discipling to Christ is that real baptism "into Christ" (so frequently spoken of in the Scriptures) which is effected by the truth blessed by the Holy Ghost, and makes such disciples partakers of all the fruits of Christ's redemption; among which is this all comprehending and never-ending baptism (= complete subjection and moral assimilation) into the living and true God. This real baptism into Christ is attended with a rite in which the cleansing of the soul from sin, by the blood of Christ received through faith, is symbolized by pure water.

The sinner *in all his guilt* may be, *must be* "baptized into Christ" (the Lamb of God that taketh away sin); but no sinner IN HIS GUILT *can be* "baptized into the name of the Father, and of the Son, and of the Holy Ghost;" nor is there *any quality in the* GODHEAD, as such, qualifying it to purge the sins of the guilty; *therefore*, the necessity for the Second Person of the Godhead to become incarnate, in order that as "JESUS," he might "save his people from their sins;" and so fit them for baptism (= subjection, assimilation, and gracious fellowship) into the Godhead in its holiness. The baptism (real) of sinners "into Christ" is an antecedent *sine qua non*, and an efficient cause of the baptism of *sinners* (not in their guilt, but) REDEEMED and PURGED and RE-

CONCILED into the absolute Deity. The ritual baptism of Christianity with its symbol water, belongs obviously to the former baptism, and not to the latter. And yet the Church, for many ages, has verbally separated the ritual symbol from the causative baptism "*into* CHRIST," and attached it to the resultant baptism " into the name of the Father, and of the Son, and of the Holy Ghost." These baptisms have an inseparable connection; and yet, they have as essential a difference as the SON *incarnate bleeding on the* CROSS, and the TRINITY *unincarnate reigning on the* THRONE.

All Nations.

Πάντα τὰ ἔθνη : The command to disciple all nations by preaching and teaching has evoked the sentiment, That none others are to be discipled to Christ but those who can understandingly hear the gospel and personally repent and believe. This sentiment cannot be true, 1. Because it destroys the command which it professes to expound. " All nations " is equivalent to *the human race.* Now, there never was a nation, nor was there ever a period in which the human race did not embrace a vastly numerous element (essential to the being of a nation and of the race) which was incapable of being discipled to Christ, by the intelligent hearing of the gospel and by personal repentance and faith. It follows, therefore, that all nations (= the human race) can never, thus, be discipled to Christ; but the command is so to disciple; therefore it is not true, that preaching and teaching are the only means for discipling to Christ, or making the nations participants in the blessings of his redemption. 2. Preaching and teaching can only be regarded as mentioned as being the obvious and outstanding, but not the exclusive, means for communicating Christ's blessings. Preaching and teaching are not of themselves sufficient to disciple the nations—" Paul may plant and Apollos may water, but God only gives the increase." Those who hold this sentiment do not use merely preaching and teaching for discipling to Christ; but use *prayer* as essential means to give them discipling power. But if God be not limited to preaching, and teaching, as a means for conveying the blessing of Christ, then, He may in answer to prayer or moved by the *direct intercession of Christ*, give that blessing through other channels. That this is true, not only as possible but as fact, is shown by the blessing of Christ bestowed upon the little children brought to him ; and also by the Holy Ghost bestowed upon John from his birth hour. As it is true, that countless millions of the nations cannot be brought to Christ by teaching and personal understanding of the truth, so also is it true, that these are not the only means for bringing the nations to Christ, else would he not have taught us *to pray*—"Thy kingdom come, thy will be done in earth as it is done in heaven." The ultimate and only essential agency in bringing the soul to Christ, is the Holy Spirit; and "the residue of the Spirit is with God." Discipling is not an ultimate end of the gospel, but a means to secure the blessings of redemption in Christ. But even this is not the ultimate end of the gospel; the work of Christ is not done until as Mediator and Advocate *he reconciles to the Father those washed by his blood*, making them subject to his authority and restoring the relation (disrupted by sin) which must rightfully subsist between the creature and the Creator.

Salvation is in Christ. Preaching and teaching are not exhaustive channel-ways for its outflowings; else, all infants dying in infancy must be excluded, not merely by their sin but by their infancy, from redemption. And inasmuch as infants are a grand, integral part of the nations, the elimination of which is destructive to the idea of a nation (*natus*), to exclude infants from the command "to disciple the nations" is to annul that command. But this command must stand; *therefore*, "disciple" must represent either a principal (not exclusive) means only, or it must have a breadth of meaning which will embrace every essential element entering into the being of "the nations" (= the human race) to wit, little children.

2. This sentiment is not true, because it overturns the divine economy under which the human race exists and by which it ever has been and still is governed.

The human race has been divinely established not on the basis of an absolute individual personality, but under a Family constitution. By this constitution we have the primal twain-unity of man and woman in the divine relation of marriage, issuing in offspring after their likeness "bone of their bone, flesh of their flesh," creating a Family unity in its most limited aspect, which develops under the divine law of marriage, through the multiplication of such Family unities, into tribal unity, national unity, and race unity. This Family unity, in its narrowest beginning to its broadest development, is under law; not law which elimi-

nates each individual from each other and lays its claims upon
each as an isolated personality whose responsibilities begin and
end within his own self-consciousness; but as a part of a whole,
and when self-consciousness begins it finds itself included within
law most absolute and in fullest operation. The individual exists
within and under all the responsibilities of this Family unity.
This economy which unites parent and child in a unity (physical
and moral) is invested with amazing powers, responsibilities, and
issues. As it is established by God, so it has been inflexibly
observed by Him in all his dealings with the human race, whether
in physics or in morals, in law or in grace.

Now, this economy is utterly subverted by the sentiment which
declares that the Lord Jesus Christ has established a kingdom
among men from which the divine corner-stone of human existence, Family unity, is stricken away, and a naked individualism
is substituted for it. But it is profoundly incredible that God
would abandon his chosen economy and substitute for it another
radically diverse; and, more, it is manifestly not true in fact.
This economy still exists in providence, still reigns under the
moral law, and the Lord Jesus Christ "did not come to destroy
the Law, but to fulfil," *therefore* "he was made of a woman,"
thus incorporated in the Family race unity, "made under the
law," from his birth-hour, "to redeem them that are under the
law," *provided*, they live long enough personally to understand
preaching and teaching! So, Dr. Carson (p. 173) says: "The
Gospel has to do with those that hear it. It is good news; but
to infants it is not news at all. They know nothing of it. The
Gospel has nothing to do with infants. Consequently, by the
Gospel no infant can be saved. . . . Infants are saved by the
death of Christ, but not by the Gospel." And, so (p. 215), in
capitals, "INFANTS ARE NOT SAVED BY THE NEW COVENANT." Dr.
Carson is honest and bold. He is honestly bold when he declares
that he will "order Gabriel to school" should he venture to differ
from him in Greek criticism; but there is something astounding
in the courage which dares to dash a human theory against the
divine economy of all ages. But it may be, that some potsherds
are thus best broken.

We reject that sentiment which rejects God's economy toward
our race. We claim, under that economy, the right and the duty
of parents (shadowed by Gospel promises—"the promise is to
you and your children"), to ask for their speechless, new-born

children, a place in the bleeding bosom of Jesus. And such parents need not fear his turning them away, saying—"Infants have nothing to do with the Gospel; it is not good news to them; it is no news at all; they are not saved by the new covenant; although they be 'bone of your bone, and flesh of your flesh,' yet, such unity does not bring them under the Gospel with you; you cannot, by any promise within the Gospel, pray to me to bless your children; when they get old enough to understand preaching then they will be brought within the range of the Gospel and you can pray for them, that they may be saved by the Gospel." This may have been the Gospel of those who forbade little children to be brought to Jesus; but we have his indignant rejection of it as another gospel and not his. We will not have it.

3. The sentiment which eliminates the infant children of the human race from a common redemption with their parents (dissolving the divine unity between parents and children under which the human race exists), is, on its face, absurd. The command to "disciple all nations," does not subvert the economy under which "all nations" exist.

Baptizing into the Name.

Βαπτίζοντες αὐτοὺς εἰς τὸ ὄνομα: The manifold diversities in the interpretation of these words and the entire lack of any one commanding acceptance above its fellows, while the prevalent translation "in the name" and its common understanding "by the authority of" has scarcely an advocate among scholars, seems to demand as a necessary conclusion, that there must be some essential error in the understanding of the words, or of their relations to each other. If these points are rightly settled on just and recognized principles, an interpretation should be developed such as must command general if not universal assent. Let us renewedly examine these points and see whether such an interpretation can be reached.

Βαπτίζω: 1. This word primarily makes demand for the intusposition of its object within a fluid element, by any competent act, moving indifferently the object or the element, without limitation of time as to the continuance in such intusposition, thus bringing the object into a new and thoroughly changed condition. 2. This word introduces its object verbally into an ideal element suggestive of a thorough change of condition in conformity with

29

the characteristic of the ideal element. 3. This word is used absolutely to express a thorough change of condition, the specific character of which is well understood by long and familiar use. The most important element in this word is *intusposition* WITH UNLIMITED CONTINUANCE.

While there are some objects which, by reason of their nature or that of the element into which they are introduced, may be materially influenced by a brief intusposition, such objects are few, especially when dyeing liquids are excepted from the elements to be used, as is true in this case, they being committed to βάπτω.

It is obvious, that any object which is capable of being influenced by a given element, will be so influenced most profoundly by being enveloped in it for an unlimited time. And there are but few objects indeed, which are not susceptible of such influence by some one or another element. For this reason baptizing into an element was practiced in order to secure the influence of the element by the communication of its quality to the baptized object. Thus human beings were baptized into water, in order to secure its destructive influence over life; a medical prescription was baptized into milk, in order to secure its emollient influence; the hand was baptized into blood, in order to secure its coloring influence for writing; and hot iron was baptized into water, in order to secure its heat-quenching influence.

4. While there are some elements which impart their characteristic qualities only when the object is enveloped within them for an indefinite period, there are others which will do this equally well without envelopment at all. Thus, water will quench heat equally well whether the heated object be enveloped in it, or the water be poured upon it. There are other elements which will not impart their characteristic quality by envelopment, but will do so, in other appropriate ways, without envelopment. Thus, *wine* will not impart its intoxicating quality to a man by envelopment within it, but will do so to a man who will *drink* it; and *a drug* will not impart its quality by envelopment within it, but it will do so when taken into the stomach; so also, sophistical questions and countless other things impart their characteristic qualities, through appropriate channels, without envelopment This result being identical in character (controlling influence by imparted quality) with that effected by envelopment, it would be natural and accordant with language development, to apply the

same word to all cases where the same generic result was effected (although by various methods) to designate such result, without regard to the method. And this, as a matter of fact, has been done and indicated by a change of syntax; the Dative (indicating the agency and controlling quality imparted) being substituted for εἰς and its regimen. Thus we have hot iron BAPTIZED (quenched) *by* water (ὕδατι); a man BAPTIZED (made drunk) *by* wine (οἴνῳ); a man BAPTIZED (stupefied) *by* a drug (φαρμάκῳ); a youth BAPTIZED (bewildered) *by* questions, *by* study, etc., etc. This usage of the Dative is more common than that of εἰς and the Accusative.

5. There is another class of elements, not physical, into which an object cannot pass, but, in fact, the association of βαπτίζω εἰς with which indicates the impartation of their qualities to the object of the verb. Thus we have a baptism (εἰς ἀναισθησίαν) *into* INSENSIBILITY; (εἰς ὕπνον) *into* SLEEP; (εἰς πορνείαν) *into* FORNICA-TION. This form of expression denotes (by a suggestive reference to physical elements) the subjection of the object to the controlling influence, respectively, of "insensibility," "sleep," "fornication," thereby thoroughly changing its condition.

This form for expressing a baptism, and this class of elements not susceptible of intusposition, is the only form and character of element to be met with in the baptisms of the New Testament. Thus we have a baptism (εἰς μετάνοιαν) into repentance; (εἰς ἄφεσιν ἁμαρτιῶν) into the remission of sins; (εἰς τὸ ὄνομα τοῦ Κυρίου Ἰησοῦ) into the name of the Lord Jesus; (εἰς Χριστὸν Ἰησοῦν) into Jesus Christ; (εἰς Χριστὸν) into Christ; (εἰς τὸν θάνατον αὐτοῦ) into his death; (εἰς ἓν σῶμα) into one body; (εἰς Μωσῆν) into Moses; (εἰς τὸ ὄνομα Παύλου) into the name of Paul; (εἰς τὸ ὄνομα τοῦ Πατρὸς καὶ τοῦ Υἱοῦ καὶ τοῦ Ἁγίου Πνεύματος) into the name of the Father and of the Son and of the Holy Ghost. All such baptisms do and can only indicate, *a thoroughly changed condition of the soul* CON-FORMED TO THE CHARACTERISTIC QUALITY OF THE IDEAL ELEMENT. This is an unvarying truth. In such of these baptisms as are associated with a symbol rite, as εἰς μετάνοιαν, εἰς ἄφεσιν ἁμαρτιῶν, εἰς τὸν Χριστὸν (varied forms for expressing the "one baptism" cleansing the soul from sin), the efficient agency (ἐν Πνεύματι Ἁγίῳ) effecting the real baptism, and the symbol agency (ἐν ὕδατι, ὕδατι) shadowing the nature of the baptism so effected, are stated in the Dative; thus giving the last degree of precision which the statement of any baptism can possess.

Into.

Εἰς: This preposition in organic relation with βαπτίζω can only (from the nature of the verb as established) be translated *into.* It cannot be divorced from the verb in order to express a *telic* sense. This would require a second preposition, thus: "Gedaliah was baptized by wine (εἰς) *into* insensibility (εἰς) *for, unto, in order to,* his murder." "Sinners are baptized (εἰς) *into* Christ (εἰς) *for, unto, in order to,* the remission of sins." "Eupolis was baptized (εἰς) *into* the sea (εἰς), *for, unto, in order to,* his being drowned." The verb in such form of expression can no more fulfil its function, deprived of its preposition, than the arm can act with its hand cut off.

The Name.

Τὸ ὄνομα: "The Name," applied to the Father, the Son, and the Holy Ghost, not severally and distinctively but jointly and in common, is indicative of union and communion in all that enters into "the Name," and especially of that supreme Sovereignty which belongs to the peculiar, divine Three-One existence of the Godhead in relation to all created beings.

A baptism into the Father distinctively, would differ from a baptism into the Son distinctively, and both such distinctive baptisms would differ from a baptism into the Holy Ghost distinctively, while each would differ from a baptism "into THE NAME of the Father, and of the Son, and of the Holy Ghost," because a baptism into the several persons of the Trinity would indicate subjection to the control of that which was *distinctive* of each Person, while a baptism "into the Name," etc., is indicative of subjection to the controlling influence of that which is *common* to their essential Deity.

The value of the several elements which enter into the phrase being determined, we are enabled to determine the value of the entire phrase.

Baptizing them into the Name of the Father, and of the Son, and of the Holy Ghost.

Βαπτίζοντες αὐτοὺς εἰς τὸ ὄνομα τοῦ Πατρὸς, καὶ τοῦ Υἱοῦ, καὶ τοῦ Ἁγίου Πνεύματος: This is an organic phrase whose parts cannot be separated without destruction to the sentiment. *Τὸ ὄνομα* is through εἰς in organic relation with βαπτίζοντες, on the one hand, and with τοῦ Πατρὸς, καὶ τοῦ Υἱου, καὶ τοῦ Ἁγίου Πνεύματος collectively, as a unity by nature, on the other hand.

The meaning of the phrase, according to the interpretation of every like phrase whether within or without the Scriptures, is, the subjection and reconciliation of the redeemed by Christ to the Triune God, from whom they had revolted and been alienated by sin.

The relation of this wonderful baptism to the baptism into Christ (which is only another form for expressing discipleship, as Paul rejecting Corinthian disciples, asks: "Were ye baptized into the name of Paul") is of like general character with the relation of the baptism (εἰς ἄφεσιν ἁμαρτιῶν) into the remission of sins, to the baptism (εἰς μετανοιαν) into repentance, namely, that of an effect to its cause. That such is the relation between these baptisms is expressly declared by Luke 3 : 3, " preaching (βάπτισμα μετανοίας εἰς ἄφεσιν ἁμαρτιῶν) baptism of (by) repentance into the remission of sins," which is illustrated by a like construction in Josephus (J. A. X., 9), " βεβαπτισμένον ὑπὸ μέθης εἰς ἀναισθησίαν Baptized by drunkenness into insensibility." Baptism into drunkenness precedes and is causative of baptism into insensibility, and is here expressed as a baptism by drunkenness into insensibility. In like manner, baptism into Christ precedes and is causative of the baptism into the Name of the Father, and of the Son, and of the Holy Ghost. It is not of accident, or as simply antecedent, that the soul is so related to Christ; but it is of essence, and in order to the baptism into the Name of the Father, etc. This relation is illustrated by the passage, "I am the way, the truth, and the life, no man cometh unto the Father but by me," and by suchlike passages; which teach that the sinner cannot come unto the unincarnate Deity, until he has come to the incarnate Son and been cleansed and reconciled through his atoning blood. This baptism of all who are Christ's into the Father, etc., is further illustrated by the Saviour's word—" all mine are thine, and thine are mine," . . . "that they all may be one; as thou Father art in me and I in thee, that they may be one in us." It is baptism into (= full subjection to) the Father, Son, and Holy Ghost, that gives final and eternal unity to all redeemed by the incarnate Son. And this subjection of all who are Christ's to the absolute Deity is intimately related to that other great truth: " Then cometh the end, when he shall have delivered up the kingdom to

God, even the Father; when he shall have put down all rule and all authority and power. For he must reign, till he hath put all enemies under his feet. . . . And when all things shall be subdued unto him, then shall the Son also himself be subject unto him that put all things under him, that God may be all in all."

If it should be objected—"That the Apostles could not baptize into (= subject to) the Father, Son, and Holy Ghost;" the answer is—Neither could they "make disciples to Christ" except by the power of him unto whom all power in heaven and on earth was given. If further vindication of such a command being given to the Apostles were needed, it may be found in the commission given to Paul (Acts 26 : 17, 18), "Delivering thee from the people, and from the Gentiles, unto whom I now make thee an apostle (ἀποστέλλω), to open their eyes, and to turn them from darkness to light, and from the power of Satan to God, that they may receive forgiveness of sins, and inheritance among them which are sanctified by faith which (εἰς ἐμέ)" = baptize into me. (?) The command to Paul "to turn men from the power of Satan to God" is substantially the same command as that given to the other Apostles and expressed in the words, "baptizing them into the name of the Father, and of the Son, and of the Holy Ghost." It is the power of Satan which keeps men from baptism into (= subjection to) God.

And Paul was no more able to turn the souls of men from the power of Satan than the other Apostles were to baptize them into the living and true God. The two commissions diverse in phraseology are the same in substance. Turning from subjection and assimilation to Satan unto God (= being made subject and assimilant to the Deity) is equivalent to and expository of, baptizing them into the Name of the Father, and of the Son, and of the Holy Ghost. There is a baptism out of Satan (1 John 5 : 19, Alford) the God of this world into the living and true God. The "forgiveness of sins," which Paul was to secure was bound up in "discipling to Christ" enjoined upon the other Apostles. We are justified in supplying *baptizes* to meet the demand of εἰς ἐμὲ, because of such use elsewhere in Scripture to express the source and attainment of the remission of sins. This brings into fullest harmony with the Commission in Mark 16 : 16, " He that believeth (upon Christ) and is (thus) baptized (into Christ) shall be saved." Paul's commission like that of his fellow-apostles teaches, that the forgiveness of sins and salvation ("inheritance among the sanctified ") is by faith, which brings the soul into Christ = baptizes εἰς ἐμὲ.

If a different solution of the baptism commanded in Matthew be attempted, by claiming, that baptism into the name of the Father, and of the Son, and of the Holy Ghost is equivalent to baptism into the name of the Lord Jesus, because of his divine nature as the Second Person of the Trinity, and therefore, the latter formula was constantly used (to the neglect of that formula used in the Commission) in ritual baptism by the Apostles, this answer may be given: 1. The language of inspiration announces a real baptism as distinctly as can be done by the use of words; 2. There is absolutely no evidence of a ritual baptism in connection with these words, either in this passage or anywhere else in Scripture; 3. A more violent improbability was never suggested than, that the Apostles having been commanded to baptize, ritually, into the Name of the Father, and of the Son, and of the Holy Ghost should never in a single instance so baptize, but should substitute another formula for it; 4. The ground by which this suggestion is sought to be sustained, namely, that baptism into the name of the Father, and of the Son, and of the Holy Ghost is equivalent to baptism into the Name of the Lord Jesus, is absolute error. It is nothing to the purpose to say, that the Second Person of the Trinity is equal in being and dignity with the first Person and the third Person and may, in this respect, represent the whole; because this is not the point at issue. There is no more a ritual baptism into the Son the second Person, than there is a baptism into the Father the first Person, or into the Holy Ghost the third Person of the Godhead. The baptism is into the Son *incarnate*, as exhibited in the person of "the LORD JESUS," "JESUS CHRIST," "CHRIST." Will any one say, that it is a matter of indifferent equivalence whether we say, *the* SON became the babe of Bethlehem, the Man of Nazareth, the Crucified of Calvary, or that *the* FATHER, SON, *and* HOLY GHOST were so born, so lived, and so died? But it is just because *the* SON was born of a woman, lived under the Law and died bearing the penalty of the Law, that his people are baptized *into* HIM, *and into* HIS DEATH. The New Testament knows nothing more of a baptism *into* THE SON simply, as a remission of sins, than it does of a baptism into the Trinity for the remission of sins; nor would there be any fitness or power in either of such baptisms to remit sins. Winer (N. T. G., p. 192) says: "Matt. 28 : 19 says nothing about the forgive-

ness of sins." It is into " God manifest in the flesh " and dying
as " the Lamb of God slain to take away the sins of the world,"
that a sin-remitting baptism must be secured. If a baptism into
the unincarnate Son or into the Name of the Father, Son, and
Holy Ghost, could have secured remission and reconciliation,
then, *the Son would never have become incarnate, and died upon
the Cross.* Until therefore it shall be affirmed, that a baptism
of disciples washed by the blood of the Lamb into the absolute Deity is the same or the equivalent to a baptism of sinners
unwashen of their guilt into the incarnate Redeemer slain for the
remission of sins, it must be an untenable error to say, that the
baptism in the Commission as recited by Matthew, is the same as
that baptism announced by the Apostles and their associates as
they went forth to execute that Commission preaching the remission of sins and reconciliation with the Father through the blood
of the Lamb.

Cause and effect while inseparably related can never be the
same, nor essential equivalents. They do reciprocally include
each other.

Teaching them to Observe.

"*Διδάσκοντες αὐτοὺς τηρεῖν*: Teaching them to observe all things
whatsoever I have commanded you." This teaching stands related both to the discipling and to the baptizing and yet, neither
to the making disciples nor originating the baptism. The teaching is clearly to be addressed to "them" who are already discipled, and out of this discipleship proceeds the baptizing into
the Name. Both the discipleship and the baptism are vital germs,
the vitalization of which is by the Holy Ghost; the development
of the vitality is under the nurture of truth (teaching them) fos-
tered by the same Divine Spirit. That this teaching does not
refer to the original making of disciples is further shown in the
statement, that it is not for enrolment as disciples, but for the
progressive development of discipleship already established, and
manifested by the observance of all that enters into it as from
time to time unfolded.

The Apostles while commanded to disciple, were not commanded so to do by any power inherent within themselves or in
their teaching; but on the clearly declared ground of the commit-
tal of all power to their Lord. With him the Holy Ghost abode,
and through the power of the Holy Ghost, under the ministry of

the Apostles, he made disciples. The ordinary means, in the case of adults, by which this was accomplished, was the preaching of fundamental truth pertaining to sin and Christ; the Holy Ghost opening the heart to receive the truth, while repentance for sin and faith in Christ were the manifestations of a new birth and a germinal discipleship. It is at this point that the "teaching" meets us and assumes the task of developing this initial discipleship by a perfected obedience. And it is to this condition of things reference is made in Heb. 6 : 1, 2, " Therefore leaving the principles of the doctrine of Christ, let us go on unto perfection; not laying again the foundation of *repentance* from dead works, and of *faith* toward God = Baptisms of DOCTRINE." The doctrine of repentance received by the power of the Holy Ghost, does baptize into the remission of sins; and the doctrine of faith received in like manner, does baptize into Christ as Lord and Saviour, bringing under the full influence of his power to protect and to redeem, to reconcile and to subject to the holy sovereignty of the Triune God, thus introducing into everlasting life.

And this discipleship effected by the Holy Ghost is germinal at whatever age effected, and in its germ is neither repentance, nor faith, nor obedience, nor love, but *regeneration*, which may as truly and as readily and as scripturally be imparted to a new-born babe in answer to a parent's believing pleadings, as to a sinner a hundred years old under the preaching of Paul; *unless* "all power in heaven and in earth" *is insufficient for it or has been given in vain.* The teaching commanded stands in a similar relation to the baptism as to the discipleship. They who are to be baptized into the Name of the Father, etc., are the disciples of Christ, and they are so baptized because they are and by consequence of being his disciples. And this baptism, like this discipleship, initiated by the power of the Holy Ghost, is capable of nurture and development through the truth. A baptism (= subjection to controlling influence) becomes more and more profound as the influence to which it is subjected does longer and more fully bear upon it, even until the power of the object to receive becomes exhausted. A striking illustration of the power of *teaching* to baptize is that furnished by Clemens Alex. (II, 1212), " Ἐχ σωφροσύνης εἰς πορνείαν βαπτίζουσι ταῖς ἡδοναις καὶ τοῖς πάθεσι χαρίζεσθαι δογματίζοντες TEACHING *indulgence in pleasures and passions* they BAPTIZE *out of chastity into* fornication." The disciples of these teachers being brought by their teachings under the controlling influence of licentiousness *pass out of a* CONDITION of purity and are *baptized into a* CONDITION of impurity. The teaching before us, as it is the opposite in moral character, so it effects a morally opposite baptism, namely, *out of the power of* SATAN *into the power of* GOD. The disciples of Christ delivered from the dominion of sin and taught the knowledge of God and holy obedience, are more and more baptized into the Name of the Father, and of the Son, and of the Holy Ghost.

Historical.

This wonderful baptism into the Trinity (dependent upon the baptism into the incarnate, atoning, and mediating Son) has no direct or designed relation to a ritual baptism. It was, however, very soon after the times of the Apostles, connected with the administration of the Christian rite, and continued to be used in common with the formula into the name of the Lord Jesus, until the third century, after which there was an enactment against the use of the Apostolic formula, and a declaration that baptism so administered was invalid. Such enactment, however, was in direct contradiction of the practice of the Apostles, and is rejected by both Luther and Calvin, who pronounce baptism into the Name of the Lord Jesus to be scriptural, while they observed, in their own practice, the formula which had been adopted by the church, and continued for many ages. The two formulæ have not equal fitness as applied to ritual baptism. The fitness of symbol water in a ritual baptism into the name of the Lord Jesus, is obvious. Its cleansing quality aptly expresses the cleansing power of the atoning blood of the Lord Jesus, into whose name the baptism ideally takes place. But what does the water represent in a baptism of *sinners* into the name of the Trinity? There is no atoning blood there. There is none in *the* SON *as the second Person of the Trinity.* And Christ the incarnate and the crucified, in whose atoning blood the rite originates, is excluded from the rite by lack of recognition and the use of a formula in which (as Winer says) there is no remission of sins. Baptism into the name of the Father, and of the Son, and of the Holy Ghost, is most scriptural; but the association of this baptism *with a ritual ordinance* is wholly wanting in scriptural authority, whether it be sought in command or in practice. The only scriptural interpretation that can be given of the conjunction of two things so diverse, yet each m itself so scriptural, is by regarding the two baptisms as condensed into one, which is true in fact, the water being taken from the baptism into Christ, with which it is so appropriately and scripturally conjoined, and united with that ulterior baptism into the Name of the Father, and of the Son, and of the Holy Ghost, which is dependent upon the antecedent baptism into Christ. The baptism EFFECTED would thus be substituted for the baptism *effecting;* that is to say, the cause would be expressed by its effect.

Whether it is, or ever will be, the will of God that the Church should return to the use of the original formula, is more than I can say. My own feeling is, that until such will shall be clearly made known, it cannot be displeasing to the incarnate Redeemer, as the Second Person of the Trinity, that every disciple of his should be ritually baptized into the Name of the Father, and of the Son, and of the Holy Ghost; it being taught, that the symbol water of the rite expresses the cleansing of his precious blood, by which alone this amazing, ultimate, and everlasting baptism is effected, and the guilty and the lost reconciled and made loving subjects to the living and true God. These two baptisms, while they differ in their immediate purport, are yet one, in so far as being inseparable and ever coexistent in the relation of cause and effect.

Patristic Writers.

The recognition by Patristic writers of the diversity between the baptism enjoined in the Commission and the baptism declared by the Apostles in the administration of ritual baptism to the disciples of the Lord Jesus, and the attempt (under the assumption that the baptism of the Commission was related to a rite) to make baptism into the Name of the Lord Jesus and baptism into the Name of the Father, and of the Son, and of the Holy Ghost, one and the same baptism, by diverse explanations, has been already mentioned, and may be referred to (p. 173). *Basil of Cæsarea* finds the unification in the word Christ (= the Anointed), because the Father *anoints*, the Son is *anointed*, and the Holy Ghost is the *anointing* influence. *Cyprian* seeks reconciliation in a supposed temporary distinction between the baptism of Jews and Gentiles. *Dionysius Alexandrinus* grounds the unity in the indivisible nature of the Trinity, and treats baptism into the name of *Christ* as though it were baptism " into the name of *the* SON " simply. *Hilary*, without giving any explanation of his own, makes the evident diversity between the baptism of the Commission and the baptism of ritual administration a ground for caution in the interpretation of passages of Scripture apparently contradictory or incongruous. Origen expounds the diverse phraseology on the ground of a wise fitness in the modification of the terms, because to baptize into Christ is to baptize "into his *death*," and " death" cannot be used in connection with " the Father, and the Son, and the Holy Ghost." This would be a very satisfactory reason to prove *the essential difference* btween these baptisms; it is a very unsatisfactory reason for proving their *essential sameness.*

These divergent attempts at explanation furnish proof within themselves that the true explanation has not been reached. The quotations given from modern Expositors show, that no progress whatever has been made toward an explanation of the commanded baptism and the administered baptism, on the supposition that the Lord Jesus Christ commanded a *ritual* baptism into the Name of the Father, and of the Son, and of the Holy Ghost, and that the Apostles administered a ritual baptism *into the Name of the Lord Jesus.* It is not too much to say, that if, after earnest endeavor through eighteen centuries, the most cultivated intellects have failed to shed one satisfactory ray of light upon the subject, from the standpoint which they have chosen, none can rationally be expected from that same point through eighteen thousand years to come? And more: Is it too much to say that the nature of the case peremptorily excludes any explanation on the basis of sameness in these baptisms? The sameness of these baptisms can never be proved. It can only be assumed on a precedent assumption (which can never be proved) that the baptism commanded in the Commission was a commanded ritual baptism; but, yielding this double impossibility, we still say that the mystery remains untouched, namely, that the Apostles being commanded to baptize ritually into the Name of the Father, and of the Son, and of the Holy Ghost, should baptize ritually into the Name of the Lord Jesus. The solution of such a marvel could only be obtained by another revelation.

These facts constitute an apology for rejecting the supposition on which these long and fruitless attempts at explanation have been made, as truly as the multiplied and fruitless cycles and epicycles of Ptolemy justified Copernicus in rejecting the supposition that the Earth was the centre of the Solar system.

We do, therefore, reject the hypothesis which makes the baptism of the Commission a ritual institution, as well as the further hypothesis that baptism into the Name of the Lord Jesus is the equivalent of baptism into the Name of the Father, and of the Son, and of the Holy Ghost; and deny, that the Lord Jesus Christ in enjoining the baptism of *his disciples* "into the Name of the Father, and of the Son, and of the Holy Ghost," had any idea of announcing a formula for a ritual ordinance. All disciples of Christ must as such receive a ritual baptism into Christ, and if after being discipled to Christ they are to be ritually baptized into the Name, etc., then there must be two ritual baptisms of Christianity. Standing on this ground, we immediately relieve the Apostles from the charge of flagrant disobedience by the substitution of a wholly diverse form of words for the most remarkable form of words contained in all the Scriptures, announced and enjoined under the most impressive circumstances, and by the highest authority.

This denial is sustained: 1. By the entire absence of all evidence in the Commission in connection with these words of a ritual injunction. *Βαπτίζοντες εἰς τὸ ὄνομα* is a complete phrase expressing a most positive sentiment in itself. Water (*ὕδατι*) cannot be introduced, elliptically, into it by any recognized law, because water nowhere appears in all Scripture with these very remarkable words. Again, these words cannot be converted into a ritual formula, because thereby the transcendent truth which they teach is destroyed. A rite is but a shadow. This baptism as it stands in the Commission is a reality. This reality is adequately secured by discipleship to Christ. Therefore, to convert it into a ritual shadow, is not only to give a stone instead of bread, but worse, it is to take away divine bread that has been given, and to replace it with a human stone. 2. By the absolute incredibility of the rejection by the Apostles of such a commanded formula, and the substitution of another. What amount of evidence could give probability to such rejection it is hard to say; but this is certain, *there is not a particle of real evidence* for it. 3. By the essential difference of the two formulæ as expressed in their terms. 4. *By the entire exclusion*, hereby induced, *of a* CRUCIFIED *Redeemer from the ritual entrance into that kingdom of which his* CROSS *is the door*. 4. By the want of significance in water ritually used in a baptism *into the* TRINITY, which, as such, *has no quality to remit sin ;* while it is demanded in a ritual baptism into Christ, whose great characteristic is "the Lamb of God that taketh away the sin of the world." 5. *By the absolute necessity for that real baptism into* CHRIST (everywhere taught in Scripture and ritually exhibited by the Apostles) *in order to that baptism into the sovereign and holy* THREE-ONE taught in the Commission.

Other reasons might be multiplied; but these if substantiated will be sufficient.

The only objection that I know of, that can be urged against this view, is the long-continued practice of the Church in using those great words of the Commission as a formula in ritual baptism. This usage is, in certain directions, a real embarrassment; yet, so far as touching the merits of the case is concerned, it has no place. *It is admitted,* both by ancient and modern expositors, *that the practice of the* CHURCH *is* NOT *the practice of the* APOSTLES. The only question therefore, on the merits of the case, is this: Have *the Apostles,* or has *the Church,* since the third century, more correctly interpreted the Commission? That the Apostles, in the administration of ritual baptism, differed in word or deed from that which was commanded (beyond the supposed substitution of another formula of words) is claimed by none; that the Church in the administration of ritual baptism did differ from that which was commanded, in wellnigh a score of ways, is admitted by all. Whether, then, this misunderstanding, or malpractice, or want of conformity to the Commission, be more rationally chargeable to the inspired Apostles, or to the Church (which through long centuries baptized men and women naked) let all men judge.

Vindication.

The interpretation given to the Commission as recorded by Matthew is vindicated by the statements and allusions to the same as furnished by Mark, Luke, John, and Paul. These have already received consideration. In them all appears, in one form or another, the statement, that *the remission of sins enters into that Commission* and through the Lord Jesus Christ. This remission of sins is stated, out of the Commission, as a *baptism* into repentance, into the remission of sins, into Christ, and into his death. Mark speaks of a baptism *which secures salvation,* and therefore is not ritual baptism but real baptism into Christ, effected, *as stated*, by believing. The real discipleship of Christ can only be effected by believing upon Christ, and the discipleship of Matthew is the same as the baptism into Christ of Mark. And since a ritual baptism belonged to the real discipleship and real baptism into Christ, it cannot be, that a second ritual baptism belonged to that real baptism into the Name of the Father. and of the Son, and of the Holy Ghost. This was an ulterior. real baptism due to the primary, real baptism into Christ, the Redeemer, Mediator, and Advocate with the Father.

Syriac Version.

This interpretation (especially as connected with βαπτίζω εἰς) is vindicated by the Syriac Version.

Dr. Murdock, translator of the Syriac New Testament, after adducing the definitions from the lexicons of *Buxtorf*, Chal. Talmud. et Rabbinicum, *Freytag*, Arabico-Latinum, *Castell*, Heptaglot., and *Schindler*, Pentaglotton, says (Bibliotheca Sacra, Oct. 1850): " This mass of evidence seems to prove, beyond all controversy, that the primary meaning of the Syriac word was, *to stand, stand up, stand firm*, etc. The Syrian Christians in appropriating this verb to denote the reception of baptism, did not change entirely the radical idea attached to it. They only transferred it from a physical to a metaphorical sense, or used it to denote a mental and not a bodily act. The proof lies in the fact, that they retained perfectly its grammatical character and its syntactical construction. . . . But what is the analogy between the physical act of standing, standing up, *standing firm*, etc., and the religious act of *receiving baptism?* This is the great problem which we must attempt to solve. . . . Our theory would be, that the early Syrian Christians,—in conformity, very probably, with Apostolic example and usage,—employed this word to denote *the reception of baptism*, because they associated with that act the idea of *coming to a stand*, or of *taking a public and decisive stand* on the side of Christianity. They considered all baptized persons as *established* in the Christian faith, and as having made a public *profession* of that faith, in and by their *baptism*, so that now they *stood up before the world* as professed or visible Christians. According to this idea of the latent or etymological meaning of the term, the Commission of our Lord to his Apostles, in Matt. 28 : 19. might be rendered,—not, ' Go ye and teach all nations, *immers*

ing (or *washing*) them in the name of the Father, and of the Son,
and of the Holy Ghost,' as in the Greek;—but, 'Go ye and
teach all nations, *making them to stand fast* in the name of the
Father,' etc. And the declaration in the parallel passage in
Mark 16 : 15, 16, which in the Greek reads, 'Go ye into all the
world, and preach the gospel to every creature : he that believeth
and is *immersed* shall be saved;' would in the Syriac read, 'He
that believeth and *standeth fast* shall be saved.' According to
the Greek, our Lord seems to state *two* conditions of salvation ;
namely, *believing*, and being *immersed* or *washed* in the name of
the Holy Trinity ; but according to the Syriac, he states in reality
only *one* condition, namely, that of *believing* and *standing fast* in
our confidence in the Triune God. Such views of these texts are
in perfect harmony with the doctrine everywhere inculcated in
the New Testament, that it is only the *steadfast* and *persevering*
Christian that will be saved.

"Comparing now this Syriac word for baptism with the Greek,
we shall see, that while the Greek word indicates the great *change*
of character and life requisite to salvation, by the figure of *a
moral purification ;* the Syriac word indicates the same great
change, by the figure or metaphor of *standing firm* in the faith,
or *standing up* before the world as one of those who follow Christ,
or who love and obey the Gospel."

Prof. Ewing, of Glasgow, says: "In this translation (Peshito
Syriac), all the words used for *baptizing, baptism,* and *Baptist,*
are taken from the Hebrew word which signifies *to stand, to cause*
or *make to stand, to support as by a pillar,* to establish, etc. It is
the same word, also, which is used in the Arabic version for baptism. This word is certainly worthy of particular attention in
the present inquiry, because in the Syro-Chaldaic dialect, it was
in all probability the very word used by John the Baptist ; the
very word used by Jesus when he gave the Apostolic Commission ; the very word used by the Apostles and Evangelists, as
long at least as they preached and baptized in Judea, Galilee, and
Samaria."

Prof. Stuart says: "This Version is the oldest of all the translations of the New Testament that are extant. It is admitted to
be one of the most faithful of all the ancient versions.

"How does this translate the word in question? Only and
always by a word which corresponds (in point of form) to the
Hebrew, Chaldee, and Arabic word, agreeing in sense with the

Latin, *stare, perstare, fulcire, roborare.* It is hardly credible that the Syriac could so far vary from all these languages as properly to mean, *immerse, dip,* etc.

"We come almost necessarily, then, to the conclusion, inasmuch as the Syriac has an appropriate word which signifies to dip, plunge, immerse, etc., and yet it is never employed in the Peshito, that the translator did not deem it important to designate any particular mode of baptism, but only to designate the rite by a term which evidently appears to mean, *confirm, establish,* etc."

The facts thus presented vindicate the results reached in this Inquiry.

1. The usage of the Syriac word which takes the place of βαπτίζω, and the usage of the Greek word is the same; that is to say, *neither of them is used in the New Testament with a physical application;* both are used in metaphorical relations.

Dr. Murdock says: "The Syrian Christians transferred this word from a physical to a metaphorical sense, or used it to denote a mental and not a bodily act."

In thus turning a word from the expression of a physical conception to express an analogous moral conception, the Syrian Christians only followed the example of the inspired writers in their use of βαπτίζω, which is never used by them in physical relations, but is invariably used in ideal relations for the purpose of developing moral conditions analogous to the condition resultant from physical use.

2. While the simple primary idea of the Syriac word (*to stand firm, to establish*) is as diverse from the simple, primary idea of the Greek word (*to envelop in a fluid without limitation of time*) as could well be, yet, in their results they are brought into the most intimate generic accord. An object which is made *to stand firm,* is thereby brought into a condition by which it is invested with a controlling power, changing its previous condition, and an object which is enveloped by a fluid without limitation of time, is, thereby, brought into a condition by which it is imbued with a controlling power changing its previous condition. When such words are used metaphorically, they harmonize in expressing (amid their variations) the same mental or moral conception,—thorough change of condition.

If I wish to describe a man truly and fully penitent or pardoned, it is a matter of indifference whether I say: He *stands*

firm or *established* in repentance—in the remission of sins; or
whether I say: He is *baptized. into* (= brought thoroughly under
the controlling influence of) repentance—remission of sins. The
idea expressed as to that man's relation to repentance, and remission of sins, is precisely the same, whatever may be the diversity
of medium through which the idea is reached.

So, if I wish to express the relation of a soul to Christ, or to
the Triune God, it is a matter of indifference whether I say, the
soul *stands firm* in Christ—is *established* in the Name of the
Father, and of the Son, and of the Holy Ghost; or, whether I
say, the soul is *baptized into* (= brought thoroughly under the
controlling influence of) Christ—the Name of the Father, and
of the Son, and of the Holy Ghost. The relation declared to
exist in the one case or in the other, is identically the same. The
form only, under which the conception is presented, differs. It
is then an unquestionable truth, that the *stand firm* of the Syriac,
and the *baptize into* of the Greek, are truly equivalent and justly
interchangeable expressions.

3. The idea, that βαπτίζω has any complementary relation *with
water* in the New Testament, or has any concern *in the mode of
using* the water in ritual baptism, is foundationless. The mode
of baptism (so far as this word is concerned) passes forever out
of, and should never have entered into, the field of theological
controversy. It never did *until yesterday* when the theory arose.

Confirmation.

The right and the accuracy of the Syriac translator in employing a word meaning *to stand firm, establish,* to represent βαπτίζω
εἰς, is strikingly indicated in the use of βαπτίζω εἰς, by the Apostle
Paul to represent the Hebrew אמן.

The meaning assigned to this word by Gesenius is, *to prop, to
stay, to support, to lean upon,* and, metaphorically, *to trust, to confide, to believe,* and *to stand firm.* A derivative from this Hebrew
word, as, also, a derivative from the Syriac word, means *a pillar.*
And this is equally natural as a derivative from the Hebrew *to
support,* and from the Syriac *to stand firm.* It is obvious, that a
very close relation exists between these words in their primary
use in physical applications, while in their development in metaphorical use and in their derivatives, they become still more
closely related, and even identical in meaning. If now, the

Syriac word could be properly used as an equivalent for the Greek, as is done in the Peshito, we might conclude that the *Hebrew* word could, with no less propriety in proper circumstances, be represented by the Greek, as its equivalent. And this will be found to be the case by a comparison of Exodus 14 : 31, in which the Hebrew declares, literally, "Israel *leaned upon* Moses," or metaphorically, "Israel *trusted in, believed in* Moses," and 1 Cor. 10 : 2, where Paul says of the same transaction, and very probably with a design to express *this very word by an equivalent phrase,* "Israel was *baptized into* (= brought under the controlling influence of) Moses."

Can any one possibly doubt, that the phraseology of Moses and of Paul (however diverse in their original primary application) does, as here used, express, with equal accuracy, the relation of Israel to Moses, in consequence of the miraculous power of Jehovah exerted in their behalf? Paul no more *dips* Israel into the Red Sea by βαπτίζω, than does Moses *dip* them by אׇמַן. But Paul and Moses, equally, bring Israel *under the controlling influence* of Moses.

This usage of Paul, and this usage of the Peshito, mutually expound and sustain each other. The Syriac translator employs a word (very diverse in its original use), as, in its outworkings, the just equivalent of βαπτίζω in its New Testament use; and Paul employs βαπτίζω εἰς as the just equivalent of a Hebrew word closely touching (in its original meaning and development) the Syriac word of the Peshito.

Dr. Murdock claims a divine authority for the Syriac word (as used by Christ and the Apostles) as well as for the Greek word; and here again, by Paul's translation (*ad sensum* if not *ad verbum*) or substitution, if it be preferred, we come upon INSPIRATION *as authorizing the interchange* of a related Hebrew word with the Greek βαπτίζω, where the Hebrew word (whether in primary, or in secondary, or in any other use) has not the remotest approach to a *dipping,* or a *plunging,* or an *immersing.* It is therefore demonstrably certain, *on divine authority,* that βαπτίζω in the New Testament does not mean to dip, or to plunge, or to immerse *in water.* This remarkable usage of the Peshito and of Paul unites with the grammatical construction of the Greek verb in the New Testament (which is always with an ideal element as its complement), as well as with the primary use of this Greek word (which envelops in a fluid *without taking out*), in establishing fully and firmly, that the baptism of the New Testament cannot be physical, and must be spiritual, with an attending rite wherein pure water symbolizes the purifying nature of the spiritual bap tism, which is verbally announced—"into the name of the Lord Jesus;" or its consequent, ultimate, and eternal baptism "into the Name of the Father, and of the Son, and of the Holy Ghost."

This conclusion rests on no specialty for its application to the cases in the New Testament. Its basis is of universal application to all cases of like construction, out of the New Testament as well as in it.

Whether I say: "He is baptized into (= under the controlling influence of) sleep;" or, "He *stands firm*, is *established, confirmed* in sleep," I say substantially the same thing. If I say: "He is, by wine, baptized into (under the controlling influence of) insensibility;" or, "He *stands firm*, is *established, confirmed*, in insensibility;" I say, substantially, the same thing. If I say: "He is, by a drug, baptized into (= under the controlling influence of) stupor;" or "He stands firm, is established, confirmed, in stupor;" I say, substantially, the same thing. If I say, "He is, by immoral teaching, baptized into (= under the controlling influence of) fornication;" or, "He *stands firm, established, confirmed* by immoral teaching, in fornication;" I change the word, but I do not change the sentiment.

And now, unless some essential evidence has been omitted, or unless some essential error has entered into that adduced, the conclusion is certain and imperative, that there is no baptism, or *quasi* baptism by dipping into water, known to the New Testament.

In Brief.

All the elements which enter into this great Commission and last words of our Divine Lord, as he is about to step from his footstool to his throne, have now (as I have been able to apprehend them) been considered.

This baptism has been considered last; because it is announced in the last words of our blessed Redeemer and is last in logical order, and must be in the nature of the case, the last in fact, as it is the baptism of *the redeemed* into the Name of the Father who gave his Son, and of the Son who became the incarnate Redeemer, and of the Holy Ghost who seals with atoning blood the soul-fruit of a Saviour's soul-travail, and thus baptizes into the absolute Tri-Une God *for all* ETERNITY!

This baptism will be the last, because it will have no end. No baptism is self-ending; THEREFORE *no baptism is a dipping.* This baptism is effected by Divine power as well as by Divine grace. As this baptism is not self-ending, so, *no enemy can take out of this baptism*—"I give unto them eternal life; and they shall never perish, neither shall any man pluck them out of my hand. My Father which gave them me, is greater than all; and no man is able to pluck them out of my Father's hand. I and my Father are one. . . . I pray for them. Holy Father, keep IN *thy Name* (ἐν τῷ ὀνόματι) those whom thou hast given me, that they may be one as we are." And who are IN *this Name* but they who are " baptized INTO *the Name* (εἰς τὸ ὄνομα) of the Father, and of the Son, and of the Holy Ghost "?

This is the last, consummating baptism of redemption. It is the amazing residual fruit of a Saviour's baptism into death. It is a baptism *forever*, even FOREVER *and* EVER.

And for this baptism, which is through the atoning death of the incarnate Son, Glory be unto *thy* NAME, O THOU TRIUNE GOD—the Father, the Son, and the Holy Ghost, world without end, *Amen* and AMEN.

PATRISTIC BAPTISM.

CHRISTIC BAPTISM AS EXHIBITED IN THE TRUTH AND ERROR OF PATRISTIC WRITERS.

MISINTERPRETATION OF MATTHEW 3:11 AND JOHN 3:5

PATRISTIC BAPTISM.

Agreement with the usage of other writings.

PATRISTIC writings furnish superabundant materials for determining the meaning of βαπτίζω within the range of their use of this word. The records are ample; the use of the word occurs times without number; the authors were Greeks by birth or training, or if of Roman birth and speech had the best opportunities for knowing the force and meaning of ecclesiastical terms derived from the Greek.

As Jewish writers employed this word in the ordinary Classic sense and applications, as well as to their distinctive religious rites, with a meaning modified by the nature of those rites, so, early Christian writers, in like manner, use this word in its ordinary Classic sense when employed within the same sphere, but in a modified sense when applied to express religious rites and doctrines which were diverse in conception alike from Classic and from Jewish thought.

This modified application and usage, however, whether Jewish or Christian, is in the most perfect harmony with the primary meaning of the word and the development of such meaning under the laws of language. Inasmuch as the Greek usage of these writers is of the highest authority, and in its breadth covers alike Classic, Jewish, and Inspired usage over which we have now passed, it may be well, in order to compare and to test the results reached with those about to be developed, to state briefly what those results are. We have found Classic writers employing this word, solely with a secular application, 1. To express a thoroughly changed condition of its object by causing it to occupy a covered condition within, commonly, a fluid or semi-fluid,

(473)

having no regard to the act by which such changed condition is effected, and without limitation of the time during which it is to continue. The primary result of such changed condition, namely, envelopment by a fluid without limitation of time, necessarily results in an ulterior change, namely, subjection to the fullest measure of influence which the inclosing fluid is capable of exerting over the inclosed object by penetrating and pervading it and thus assimilating it to its own characteristic whatever that may be. This secondary change of condition leads, under a well-recognized law of language development, to a modification of the primary use of the word so that it shall include cases in which the object undergoes a like change of condition, to wit, by an influence penetrating, pervading, and assimilating, which exerts its power to produce this condition by unlike means, that is to say, not by covering its object. This extended usage of βαπτίζω is abundantly illustrated in Classic writers. It is so in those frequent cases where it is used to express the thoroughly changed condition of a drunken man under the penetrating, pervading, and assimilating influence of the intoxicating principle of wine. This same use employs this word to express the thoroughly changed condition of a man in profound stupor effected by the penetrating, pervading, and assimilating influence proceeding from some τῷ φαρμάκῳ. These and many other changes of condition are effected by diverse modes of operation in the cause, but belonging to the same class of conditions, namely, as characterized by a thorough change assimilating to the characteristic of the operating influence they are designated by the same word,— βαπτίζω. This word is also used absolutely by the Classics to express a drunken condition.

Jewish writers, like the Classics, employ βαπτίζω to express a covered condition, by any act, without limitation of time ; a thoroughly changed condition effected otherwise than by covering, and absolutely, to express a thoroughly changed condition effected by religious rites without regard to the manner of using those rites.

Inspired writers never use βαπτίζω to express the physical covering of its object. Nor is it ever used by them except within a religious sphere and ordinarily relating to a thoroughly changed spiritual condition, the nature of which is commonly expressed by the conjunction of the verb with an ideal element into which the object is represented as passing by the preposition εἰς.

Sometimes, however, no ideal element is expressed, but the nature of the changed condition is expressed only by the agency in the Dative, as is often done by Classic writers. More rarely there is an absolute use of the word when (as designed) we are only informed that some thorough change of condition is to take place but its precise nature is not expressed. It is only by the adjunct ideal element in the Accusative with εἰς, or by the agency in the Dative, with or without a preposition, that we know the nature of the baptism of Inspiration.

Patristic writers will be found to present cases of all the varied forms of usage found among Classic, Jewish, and Inspired writers.

Disagreement.

While there is no difference between Patristic writers and others as to the essential nature and varied usage of βαπτίζω, there is essential difference from Inspired writers, in various aspects, in relation to Christian Baptism. Among these differences may be mentioned, 1. The confusion and unification of the diverse agencies Water and the Holy Spirit, by which they are made coactive in effecting an exclusively spiritual baptism, and the symbol baptism of Scripture by pure water is destroyed; 2. The introduction of a symbol burial into the use of the water, as ordinarily administered, of which the Scriptures know nothing; 3. The covering of the head three times in the water in correspondence with the three Persons in the Trinity, or with the three days and nights of Christ's burial; 4. The divesting of all candidates for baptism (male and female) of their entire clothing; 5. The practice of exorcism, the turning toward the west and the east, the use of oil, salt, spittle, etc. These departures from Scripture teaching and practice were vindicated as Scriptural by appeals to passages misinterpreted or misapplied, among which the most important were Matt. 3 : 11 ; John 3 : 5 ; and Rom. 6 : 3.

This agreement and disagreement will now be illustrated by the citation of passages reaching from the first into the fifth century, within which period the most authoritative writings are found. Our first inquiry will be as to the usage of the verb.

PATRISTIC USAGE OF βαπτίζω.

Intusposition without limitation of act or time.

It is in proof: That βαπτίζω demands for its object a condition of intusposition (usually within a fluid element) without regard to the act to be used in securing such intusposition, and without limitation to the time of continuing in such condition; never taking out what it puts in.

COROLLARY: 1. A baptized object is subjected to the fullest assimilative influence of the investing medium, by the interpenetration and communication of its characteristic.

2. An object which has received a pervading and assimilating influence, in any way, may be said to be baptized by such influence.

This truth, with its corollaries (proved from other writings) will now be shown to be accepted as truth by Patristic writers.

Classic and Patristic βαπτίζω the same.

1. Clemens Alex. (posterior): "By means of which the ship about to be baptized (βαπτιζομένη) is raised up."

2. Basil M., III, 432: "A ship while it bears its freight load, floats; but more than this (καταβαπτίζει) baptizes it."

3. Basil M., III, 452: "More wretched than they whom, in a sea storm, wave after wave, tossing and baptizing (ἐπιβαπτίζοντα), prevents deliverance from the flood."

This βαπτίζω of Clement and Basil is the identical primary and literal βαπτίζω of the Classics. It secures intusposition for its object in the depths of the sea or somewhere else, and leaves it there. The baptizing of the theory, which dips the head and shoulders taking them out in a moment, is not much like this shipwreck baptizing of Classics and Patrists which continues through a thousand years. The doctrine (maintained against all Lexicons) that this word has but one meaning, does not allow of any departure from this primary use; while its conversion into *a momentary into and out of water* eviscerates it of its entire life.

The βαπτίζω of Clement and Basil is the βαπτίζω of Josephus and Philo, and of Plutarch and Plato; always a word of power, thoroughly changing condition as grounded in intusposition within a fluid without limitation of time; yet, in development laying aside physical intusposition for ideal; and ideal for a direct expression of changed condition by the verb and influential agency without intusposition real or imaginary; and finally, by the absolute use of the word without adjunct directly expressing some complete, specific, change of condition.

Ideal Element.

Clemens Alex. (*prior*) 421: " ὑπὸ μέθης βαπτιζόμενος εἰς ὕπνον Baptized by drunkenness into sleep." This learned Christian Greek here uses βαπτίζω in all its Classic value and power expressing thorough change of condition; but substitutes an ideal element (εἰς ὕπνον) for the Classic physical element (εἰς θάλασσαν). There is no change in the value of the verb; the difference of value in the phrases is found solely in εἰς ὕπνον and εἰς θάλασσαν. An object which is really placed εἰς θάλασσαν *into the sea*, for an unlimited time, is thoroughly subjected to the influence of the sea; and a human being ideally passing *into sleep* is represented as being thoroughly subject to the influence of sleep. And this thoroughly changed condition of a profoundly sleeping man, Clement says, is a baptism. There is no actual or possible intusposition (much less a dipping); but merely a verbal form suggestive of the profoundest influence to which a specific character is given by the regimen of the preposition. A perfectly identical case is that of Josephus (Jew. Antiq., X, 9): " Βεβαπτισμένον εἰς ἀναισθησίαν καὶ ὕπνον ὑπὸ τῆς μέθης Baptized into insensibility and sleep by drunkenness." And a perfectly parallel case is that of Luke 3 : 3, " Βάπτισμα μετανοίας εἰς ἄφεσιν ἁμαρτιῶν The baptism of repentance into the remission of sins." In each case βαπτίζω and βάπτισμα present the same element of controlling influence changing condition, while the widely differing nature of the influences is presented in *drunkenness* on the one hand and *repentance* on the other. The resultant conditions (insensibility and remission of sins) being as diverse in nature as the influences (drunkenness and repentance) are diverse in character.

Analogous Words.

The usage of analogous words by Patristic writers confirms these views.

Clemens, Rom. I, 620: " Οὔτε γὰρ τον Νῶε κατέκλυσεν—He did not deluge Noah."

Basil M., III, 453: " Κατακλυζόμενον τῇ ἀμετρίᾳ τοῦ ὄινου—Deluged by wine without measure."

Clemens, Rom. I, 1464: " Μᾶλλον δὲ ὡς αὐτοὶ ληροῦσι βυθισθέντα— Or, as they madly say, he was drowned (abyssed)."

Marci Eremitæ, 1020 : "*Εἰς τὸν βυθόν τῆς ἀγνοίας καταπέπτωκεν—*
Fallen into the abyss of ignorance."

Origen, II, 1511 : "The tempest (*κατεπόντιζε*) has ingulfed me."

Matt. 18 : 6: "And (*καταποντισθῇ*) ingulfed in the depth of the
sea."

Καταχλύζω, βυθίζω, καταποντίζω, like *βαπτίζω,* demand intusposition
for their objects without limitation of time (do not take out what
they put in), and therefore, all such objects are of necessity exposed to the full influence of the investing element. Such verbs
are adapted to express the development of influence, of an analogous character, when such development does not take place by
the same form of influence ; that is to say, they drop entirely the
idea of a physical covering or only suggestively allude to it.

Thus we see, that influence of the most powerful character is
necessarily included in the case of Noah's cataclysm. Noah and
his family were not "deluged ;" therefore did not experience the
drowning influence of water. The rest of the human race were
"deluged," and by necessity of such intusposition, were drowned.
Now, this resultant effect (complete influence, not the intusposition causative of the influence) is expressed by Basil through
καταχλύζω in declaring the controlling influence of wine. He
neither means to say, that the wine bibber is within a deluge of
waters, nor within a deluge of wine ; but he uses a word (which
while not expressing influence in primary use, yet necessarily involves the highest influence) to express in secondary use the
highest influence of wine, which is developed not by intusposition
but by drinking; which does not drown but makes drunk. Noah
was not covered over (*καταχλύζω*) in the deluge ; but, alas, Noah
was made drunk (*καταχλύζω*) by wine. Who will question a diversity of meaning in this twofold usage of the same word? In
the first case we have inness with influence ; and in the second
case we have the influence (peculiar to wine when drunk) without
the inness ; which could not develop the intoxicating influence of
wine.

Clemens Romanus uses *βυθίζω,* in like manner, primarily, to
express the covering in water (which in the case of a human
being is necessarily attended with a destructive influence), while
Mark the Hermit uses its root ideally (*εἰς τὸν βυθόν*), not to express withinness but to suggest the profoundest influence of
"ignorance."

Origen uses *καταποντίζω,* which primarily covers in the sea without limit of time, to express not a covered condition in the sea, but the influence of overwhelming distress. The Lord Jesus Christ (Matt. 18 : 6) uses this same καταποντίζω to bring out the hopeless destruction which is inseparable from this word, applying it to the soul and the remediless influence of sin.

The general primary meaning of βαπτίζω (covering without limitation of act or time) is the same as that of κατακλύζω, βυθίζω, καταποντίζω; and, in the case of each, controlling influence is inseparable from such condition, and is directly expressed in secondary use.

Ideal Element and other Words.

As there is no characteristic of βαπτίζω so important as that of inness without limitation of time, so there is no usage of this word of such vital importance to this Inquiry as that which connects it with an ideal element, for the purpose of expressing controlling influence, while indicating by the form the origin of such meaning. It is important, therefore, to show that this usage is not singular, but common; that it is not obscure, but clear in meaning; that it is not difficult of interpretation, but facile and of universal consent. Let us, then, before entering upon that of βαπτίζω, look at the facts of Patristic usage in connection with other words.

CLEM. ROM. (op. dub.) 472 : " The disciples and hearers of an untaught and ignorant teacher overwhelmed by the darkness of ignorance (in interitum demergentur) will be demersed into DESTRUCTION."

S. CLEMENTIS (op. dub.) II, 332 : " Lest by much sudden joy she should come (εἰς ἔκστασιν φρενῶν) into DISTRACTION OF MIND."

TERTULLIAN I, 629 : " While the heathen (in voluptatibus immergunt) immerse themselves in PLEASURES."

TERTULLIAN I, 663 : " The worshipper of idols is an adulterer of the truth; (in stupro mergitur) he is mersed in ADULTERY." II, 1060 : " Peccati in gurgite mersis—mersed in the ABYSS OF SIN." 1063 : " In dementia mersos—mersed in FOLLY."

TERTULLIAN III, 234 : " Darkness having been scattered (de tenebrarum profundo in lucem sapientiæ et veritatis emergerem) I emerged out of the depth of darkness into the light of WISDOM and TRUTH."

CLEMENS ALEX. I, 417 : " Reason should preside lest the feast (παραπεσοῦσα εἰς μέθην) should glide into DRUNKENNESS."

CLEM. ALEX. I, 493: "The oppression of sleep is like to death (ὑποφερομένη εἰς ἀναισθησίαν) carrying us down *into* INSENSIBILITY."

CLEM. ALEX. II, 417: "Commanding the sinner (ἀναιρεῖσθαι καὶ μετατίθεσθαι ἐκ θανάτου εἰς ζωὴν) to be raised up out of death and transposed *into* LIFE."

AUGUSTIN IX, 186: "In quodlibet profundum malorum et in quamlibet horribilem voraginem peccatorum irruat. *Into* whatsoever DEPTH OF EVILS and *into* whatsoever horrible ABYSS OF SINS he may rush."

JEROME VI, 1349: "Qui in extremis peccatorum fæcibus habitant et in scelerum suorum ima demersi. Who live *in the extreme dregs of* SINS and demersed *into the lowest depths of their* CRIMES."

These passages are sufficient to illustrate the familiar employment by Patristic writers of an ideal element with verbally expressed withinness, in order to denote controlling influence. The ground of such usage evidently is: *The inseparable connection of the highest influence which a fluid can exert over an object, with its position within such fluid, for an unlimited time.* Such cases are the following:

TERTULLIAN II, 1071: "Hostes demersit in undis. He demersed (= *drowned*) his enemies in the waters."

Origen II, 844: "Mergatur in mare. Is mersed (= drowned) into the sea, flowing (in amaritudinem) into bitterness." The sweet water of a river flowing into the briny sea has its sweetness drowned in the bitter waters into which it flows.

HILARY I, 353: "Ut in profundum demergantur oratur—effectum cum illos diluvio submersos consumpsit profundum. He prays that they may be demersed (= drowned) into the deep—which was done when the deep destroyed them submerged (= drowned) in the flood."

AUGUSTIN V (prior) 382: "Unde tota navis mergatur. The whole ship is mersed (= swallowed up) by a leak."

Origen II, 875: "Ire in gehennam, mitti in ignem æternum, expelli in tenebras exteriores. To go *into* hell, to be sent *into* everlasting fire, to be driven *into* outer darkness." The complete influence of "hell," "fire," "darkness," is expressed by *going* INTO *them* for an unlimited time. Nothing is more obvious than the essential connection between position within a physical element and the completest influence; and nothing is more certain than that Patristic writers do use such intusposition not merely for the *intusposition*, but for the *influence resulting* therefrom. In like manner they do abundantly use a verbal form expressive of intusposition, in order to express the *controlling influence of the characteristic quality* of such ideal element over its object.

Βαπτίζω *is so used with an Ideal Element.*

The use of *βαπτίζω* is entirely harmonious, and largely identical, with that of numerous other words employed to express controlling influence through actual or ideal withinness. This has been already shown in connection with ships and men sinking into the sea; the ideal use is exemplified in the following quotation:

CLEMENS ALEX. II, 1212: "ʼΕχ σωφροσύνης εἰς πορνείαν βαπτίζουσι They baptize out of chastity into fornication, teaching to indulge in pleasures and passions."

Any attempt to take this passage out of the same category with those already considered (as establishing controlling influence through withinness) will rouse up in opposition not only the established usage of Patristic writers, but also a principle in nature, *i. e.*, that *withinness is causative of influence;* and the *primâ facie* demand of εἰς in association with ἐχ, as well as the essential requirement of *βαπτίζω*. The only interpretation of this passage which admits of defence, is that which makes vicious TEACHING to baptize *its disciples* = to cause them to pass *out of* a condition of chastity *into* a condition of fornication. To pass " into fornication " (baptize never takes out what it puts in) cannot possibly express anything short of or less than full subjection to the characteristic of this vice. This passage settles the all-important point *that βαπτίζω may* (like scores of other words) *be directly connected with an ideal element, and* THEREBY EXPRESS THE CONTROLLING INFLUENCE OF THE CHARACTERISTIC OF SUCH ELEMENT OVER THE OBJECT *which* (verbally) *is carried into it, and* NOT TAKEN OUT OF IT. If any further proof of this vital point were necessary, it could be readily furnished from this same writer. See the following:

I, 416: " Reason should preside at the feast lest it glide (εἰς μέθην) *into* drunkenness."

Will any one question that εἰς μέθην is the ideal element *into* which (and therefore under the influence of which) the convivial ists are passing?

I. 493 : "The oppression of sleep is like to death which carries us down (εἰς ἀναισθησίαν) *into* insensibility."

Is this condition, induced by ideal withinness, any less clear?

I, 421 : " *Βαπτιζόμενος ὑπὸ μέθης εἰς ὕπνον*, Baptized by drunkenness into sleep."

Here are the same elements (wine and drunkenness, sleep and insensibility) under the same grammatical form, and kindred ideal elements (εἰς μέθην, εἰς ἀναισθησίαν, εἰς ὕπνον), and are we to have a new principle of interpretation introduced and βαπτίζω put under ban, *so that* IT ALONE *must not introduce its object within an ideal element as suggestive of controlling influence?* This exclusion must be practiced or its common right must be acknowledged.

The seal is put to this evidence by the important testimony of Josephus in the passage often quoted : Jewish Antiq., X, 9, " *Βε-βαπτισμένον εἰς ἀναισθησίαν ὑπὸ τῆς μέθης* Baptized *into* insensibility by drunkenness ;" where complete influence is expressed by a verbal passing into an ideal element in a case of worldwide familiarity.

It is in proof : 1. That βαπτίζω is used in direct grammatical and complementary relation with an ideal element in order to develop the peculiar influence of such element over the object passing (ideally) into it ; 2. That in such ideal baptism the baptizing agency may be (in this case *wine*) a physical fluid element, and may be used in any way (in this case by *drinking*) appropriate to its nature, for the development of its baptizing power.

Βαπτίζω with the Agency and without Ideal Element.

The baptism into an ideal element, for the purpose of expressing the full development of the characteristic of such element over its object, finds a perfectly equivalent baptism in another verbal form in which the ideal element disappears, and the agency (without the statement of or any regard to the mode of application or influence) only appears and, by its association with βαπτίζω, expresses both the fact and the nature of the controlling influence exerted. Take the following quotation in illustration :

CLEMENS ALEX. I, 57 : " The man who is (βεβαπτισμένος ἀγνοίᾳ) baptized *by* ignorance is more stupid than a stone."

Clement gives the explanation of his own phrase, " baptized *by* ignorance," in the most unmistakable manner. He explains the phrase as indicating neither more nor less than the *most profound stupidity*. A man " baptized *by* IGNORANCE" is *more stupid than* A STONE. Has anything in nature less intelligence than " a stone"? No; but a man " baptized by ignorance" is not a thing of nature, but a *lusus naturæ*, and therefore, " *more* stupid than a stone." There is no figure (= ideal element) in this phrase. The idea may be expressed through an ideal element, thus :

MARCI EREMITÆ, 1020 : " The soul (εἰς τὸν βυθὸν τῆς ἀγνοίας κατα-πέπτωκεν) has *fallen into the* ABYSS *of* IGNORANCE or it would know by divine Scripture, etc." Here, precisely the same idea as ex-pressed in " baptized *by* ignorance" is expressed by the use of ignorance as an ideal element *into* which the soul is verbally rep-resented as " falling," and thus coming fully under its influence. The baptism " *into* ignorance" Mark expounds, as a condition of stupidity too profound to recognize the plainest teaching of Scrip-ture; while Clement expounds the baptism " *by* ignorance," as a condition of stupidity which outvies that of a senseless stone.

Clement uses βαπτίζω at the direct value which it has secured from primary and figurative use, viz., as expressive of a pervad-ing and assimilating controlling influence, separated from all modal form, for securing such influence.

This verbal form—" baptize by "—used by Patristic writers to express directly, without the intervention of figure, controlling influence, as a secondary meaning of βαπτίζω, is one of the most common forms of usage among Classic writers. Thus:

CONON L.: " "Οινῳ δὲ πολλῷ βαπτίσασα Having baptized him *by* much wine."

CLEM. ALEX. I, 416 : " Lest the feast glide (εἰς μέθην) *into* drunk-enness."

The first quotation from a Classic Greek, uses the verb in its secondary meaning and joined with wine expresses the fully de-veloped influence of wine without figure. The second quotation, from a Patristic Greek, expresses the same influence by the use of drunkenness as an element *into* which the wine-drinker is, verbally, represented as passing and so coming under the wine influence. The two forms present essentially diverse conceptions uniting in one common result.

CLEM. ALEX. I, 421 : " Βαπτιζόμενος ὑπὸ μέθης εἰς ὕπνον Baptized by drunkenness *into* sleep."

EVENUS XV : " Βαπτίζει δ' ὕπνῳ He baptizes *by* sleep."

Clement, here, uses sleep as an ideal element in connection

with the verb, to secure the idea of controlling influence by the suggested *withinness;* while the Classic Evenus drops the form of ideal element and adopts the equivalent, but more advanced, form of βαπτίζω with the *agency* to express directly the same idea, namely, a condition of profound sleep.

ACHILLES TATIUS II, 31: "*Τῷ αὐτῷ φαρμάκῳ καταβαπτίσας* Having baptized her by the same drug."

CLEM. ALEX. I, 285: "Sins are remitted (*παιωνίῳ φαρμάκῳ, λογικῷ βαπτίσματι*) by one perfect drug (medicine), spiritual baptism."

The Classic Greek and the Patristic Greek in these passages uses, each, the same grammatical form (βαπτίζω and the agency in the Dative) to express the controlling influence of a power designated by both as a "*φάρμακον.*" But this general term (taken from the *materia medica*) represents agencies very diverse in their characteristic qualities. The same term is applied, here, to cover agencies of very diverse qualities, and therefore effecting baptisms very diverse in nature. The *pharmakon* of Achilles effects a baptism whose characteristic condition is that of *profound stupor;* while the *pharmakon* of Clement effects a baptism whose characteristic condition is that of *absolute purity.*

The mode in which these baptizing influences operate is as diverse as that of an opiate taken into the stomach by drinking, and of a transforming spiritual influence received into the soul by divine power.

This baptizing *pharmakon* of the Classic Greek was a liquid; but not in the form of a river or a pool. It was contained in a wineglass. But *a wineglassful was enough thoroughly to* BAPTIZE *a fullgrown adult.*

This same form for expressing a baptism (the verb with the agency in the Dative) is a common form in the Scriptures and abounds among Patristic writers, as it is, also, the more common form among the Classics. It is grounded in withinness; but this it has wholly laid aside by entering into fellowship with agencies which exert a pervading, assimilating, and controlling influence without receiving their objects necessarily or possibly into withinness of relation. Neither wine nor drug baptizes by covering. It will, also, be noticed, that while all baptisms under all varieties of forms of expression have, in common, a condition characterized by controlling influence, the specific character of that condition must be learned from the receiving element (real or ideal) on the one hand, or from the agency on the other.

A fleshless skeleton will as soon declare the complexion of the skin or the color of the eyes of its once living possessor, as the naked βαπτίζω will declare the nature of a baptism without its complementary adjunct in the form of receiving element (real or ideal) or of the executive agency.

The importance of this statement will be appreciated in view of the fact, that in the Scriptures there is no baptism announced except through an ideal element or by a spiritual agency, with its associate symbol—Water, dove, or firelike tongue.

This has already been shown to be true of the Scriptures. It remains to be shown, that it is no less true, *that* CHRISTIAN *baptism is always represented by Patristic writers as a* SPIRITUAL *baptism whose nature is announced, exclusively, by an ideal element, or by an agency possessed of a correspondent spiritual power, which effects the* BAPTISM.

But while the baptism of the Scripture and the baptism of Patristic writers is alike spiritual in its nature, there is this very essential difference, *to wit:* the real baptism of the Scriptures is effected *solely* by the Holy Spirit, and is ritually represented (as to its purifying nature) by a symbol ordinance in which pure water is applied to the body; while the Christian baptism of the Patrists is effected *jointly* by the Holy Spirit *and water*, impregnated with a divine power. This baptism *has no symbol rite showing forth by water the nature of the baptism;* but uses the water (which, with the Holy Spirit, effects, as they believe, the real baptism of the soul) in such manner as to symbolize, not (their) *baptism* but, (their) *burial* with Christ in his rock sepulchre; an idea which has no place in the ritual baptism of Scripture, any more than oil, and spittle, and insufflation, etc.

That this is a just representation of Patristic baptism we now proceed to show. But before entering upon the discussion in detail, it may be well briefly to indicate the source of the Patristic error *by which water became essentially conjoined and coefficient with the Holy Spirit* in Christian baptism (= the remission of sins and the regeneration of the soul).

Judaic baptism was not a mere *symbol* baptism shadowing some other real baptism; but was a *type* baptism possessed of a real power, self-efficient for the purification of *ceremonial* defilement, and hence, the adequate type of an *antitype* baptism which did efficiently purify from *spiritual* defilement. This truth (the self-efficiency of the water, and blood, and heifer ashes in *Judaic* bap tism) was erroneously carried over into the water used in *John's* baptism (which was not a type but a symbol baptism) making it self-efficient for a *spiritual* cleansing (= *repentance* and foreshadowed remission of sin). This idea of spiritual efficiency (within limits) in John's baptism is seen everywhere in Patristic writings, and especially in frequent and explicit statements of Augustine, who declares John, as personally possessed of such power to baptize, to stand alone among men. The baptism of the Lord Jesus Christ as declared by John—" He shall baptize you with the Holy Ghost "—is made by these writers to differ from that of John himself not in nature, but only in measure. They were both spiritual; and thus both differed in nature from Judaic baptism, but agreed with each other, in kind, while differing in degree. The baptism of John was imperfect in its spiritual power; that of Christ was perfect. But while John excludes in the most pointed manner *water* from the personally administered baptism of Christ, these writers include it, saying—" *of course* John did not mean to exclude *water* from the baptism of Christ when he says, ' He shall baptize you with *the Holy Spirit.*' " They failed to discriminate between the baptism through the Holy Ghost personally administered by Christ and the rite, symbolizing that baptism, administered by his ministers with water. And this error of interpretation was the initial " letting out of water " which speedily became a flood, and would have swallowed up the Ark itself but for the conserving power and grace of God. This beginning of error received large accession from another misinterpretation of the words of our blessed Lord himself—(John 3 : 5) " Jesus answered, Verily, verily, I say unto thee, Except a man be born of water and of the Spirit, he cannot enter into the kingdom of God." These early writers forgetting (1) their own doctrine, that Jewish baptism was necessary for and had efficient power in order to cleansing from ceremonial defilement, and that these words were addressed to a Jew; and (2) forgetting also their own doctrine, that Christian baptism (= the copresence and coefficience of water and the Spirit) had yet no existence, and therefore any such doctrine for the instruction and personal benefit of the Jew Nicodemus was anachronistic; and (3) forgetting further, that such interpretation dashed itself against " the promise of the Father " (Luke 24 : 49) in which there was no wa'er, and against the fulfilment of that promise in the baptism of the Spirit at Pentecost in which there was no water, and

against the like fulfilment at Cæsarea in which there was no
water, and against the truth that "all" who are Christ's are
"baptized by one Spirit into one body" (1 Cor. 12:13) in which
there is no water; and forgetting still further, that the ingrafting
of a rite upon the baptism of the Spirit gives to the water neither
essential copresence (Cornelius the centurion) nor coefficience
(Simon the magician), they did yet magnify their first error in
the minisinterpretation of John's words (*adding* "water" to
them) by a kindred misinterpretation of Christ's words, transfer-
ring them from the sphere of Judaism in which they were spoken,
to that of Christianity which was yet future, thus perpetuating a
Jewish type (after its extinction in the presence of the antitype
—the poured out Spirit) by the origination of a coactive physical
element of which the Scriptures do not say one syllable.

This is the double-headed *fons et origo malorum* which has
been pouring its poisonous stream through the church for more
than a thousand years.   How unutterably important is the right
interpretation of one passage of Scripture.   What a millstone
has been hung about the neck of the church by *adding* one word
(*water*) to the baptism of the Holy Ghost.   What havoc is made
by *taking away* one word (*Christ*) from the "one baptism" into
CHRIST, and *adding to* it one word (*water*) transforming this divine baptism *into* CHRIST into the humanism of one *dipping* into
WATER, and thus disrupting the constitution of the church, reject
ing from it the living members of Christ's body, and writing upon
his holy sacraments—Baptism and Supper—"*Lie*," and upon the
brow of all (except the stolidly ignorant) who observe them according to divine appointment—LIAR.*

For all who so fearfully err (not an error against man but
against God in Christ) the prayer offered up on Calvary must live
in Heaven—"FATHER, *forgive them; they know not what they do.*"

---

* G. D. B. Pepper, Prof. of Theol., Crozer Theo. Sem.   (See pp. 21, 22.)

ΒΑΠΤΙΣΜΑ.

Βάπτισμα is not found in Classic Greek. It appears for the first time in the Scriptures. The interpretation of its Patristic use should be preceded by an examination of its probable value as deduced from its derivation and its Scriptural use. Both these elements admit of very definite determination.

All grammarians agree in saying: Substantives derived from verbs and ending in *μα* express *effect, product, result, state*. Thus, *Kühner:* "Substantives with the ending *μα* denote the *effect* or *result* of the transitive action of the verb;" *Buttman:* "The termination *μα* expresses the *effect* of the verb as a concrete;" *Sophocles:* "The termination *μα* denotes the *effect* of a verb;" *Crosby:* "Nouns formed from verbs denote the *effect* of the action, have *μα* added to the root of the verb;" *Jelf:* "Nouns ending in *μα* express the *effect* of the transitive notion of the verb;" *Winer:* "Formations in *μα*, as *βάπτισμα*, are used mostly in the sense of *product* or *state*." *Hermann Cremer (Bib. Theo. Lex.):* "*Βαπτισμός* denotes the act as a fact; *βάπτισμα* the *result* of the act; used *exclusively* by Biblical and Ecclesiastical writers."

It must therefore be regarded as settled, that *βάπτισμα* by derivation and form expresses the *effect, product, state, result*, of the act which is the executive of *βαπτίζω*. But whatever may be the specific act (among the legion that wait on *βαπτίζω*) the effect, product, result, state, accomplished is *withinness without removal* (involving of necessity all the influential issues consequent upon such withinness) when the verb is used in primary application.

The *effect, product, result, state*, of a ship with its crew sunk by a storm, or naval conflict, or excessive cargo, to the bottom of the ocean, might be described as a *βάπτισμα*; and such a *βάπτισμα* involves, of necessity, the utter loss of the ship, and the utter loss of life to the crew. But as a matter of fact *βάπτισμα* is never applied by Classic, or Inspired, or Ecclesiastical writers to any such physical effect, product, result, or state.

In the secondary use of *βαπτίζω* where withinness does not appear (but only a complete " effect, product, result, or state," as in " baptized by wine "), the *drunken* " effect, product, result, state," might be described as a *βάπτισμα*; but again, as a matter of fact, there is no such usage of this word by any class of writers. The use of *βαπτίζω* with an ideal element, expressed by *εἰς* and its regimen, does not appear in the Classics; this, like *βάπτισμα*, is found for the first time in the Scriptures, and is never found there with a physical receiving element.

Whenever *βαπτίζω* is used with a complementary ideal element, the " effect, product, result, state," of such use (indicated by the complete influence of the ideal element) will be properly expressed by *βάπτισμα*. And such, as a matter of fact, is and is the sole use of this word in the Scriptures. It is never there used to denote an " effect, product, result, state," within a physical element. The *βάπτισμα* of Scripture invariably expresses the changed condition " effect, product, result, state," of *the* SOUL passing "*into* REPENTANCE," *into the* REMISSION OF SINS, "*into the* NAME OF THE LORD JESUS," " *into* HIS DEATH," and not of *the body* passing *into* WATER. And this *βάπτισμα* is as invariably characterized by *Spiritual purification* as indicated by the ideal elements.

This, as has been already shown at large, is the unquestionable usage of *βάπτισμα* in the Scriptures. And it is in the most perfect accord with the laws of derivation regulating the import of all such words.

These points being established we proceed to inquire whether the usage of this word by Patristic writers is in harmony with them.

Patristic and Inspired Usage of βάπτισμα Harmonious.

It is certain, that Patristic like Classic writers while using *βαπτίζω* to effect the destruction of ships and of human life at the bottom of the sea, do never, in such cases, use *βάπτισμα* to express the consequent " effect, product, result, state." It is certain, that Patristic like Classic writers while using *βαπτίζω* to effect that drunken condition (without inness) consequent upon wine-drinking, do never use *βάπτισμα* to express such " effect, product, result.

state." It is certain, that Patristic writers do use βαπτίζω with an ideal element (εἰς and Accusative), and without an ideal element (Genitive and Dative with or without a preposition) to express physical, mental, and moral conditions (where no withinness is possible) *without using βάπτισμα* to denote the resultant effects; but in using identically the same grammatical forms to express a complete spiritual change in the condition of the soul, *they do employ and limit βάπτισμα to denote* THIS "effect, product, result, state." There is therefore, before any detailed examination is made, a violent presumption, that they use this word as Inspired writers use it in like relations, namely, to express not a physical but a spiritual "effect, product, result, state." With this antecedent presumption against a physical baptism (because unsupported by usage and destructive to life) and in favor of a spiritual baptism (because sustained by usage and in harmony with all Scripture teaching) we proceed to consider the direct evidence.

There is no small number of cases in which βάπτισμα appears without any feature in the construction or in the facts to determine the meaning of the word. This is true in all those cases where this word is used comprehensively to designate the whole rite; just as the widely differing term φώτισμα is used for the same purpose. The assumption, that βάπτισμα is used, under such circumstances, to denote the manner or the result of using the water is inadmissible: 1. Because as yet, if there should ever be, there is no evidence of the use of βάπτισμα to denote the effect of the verb where water is the complement to the idea of the verb; 2. Because there is evidence from derivation, that such use would involve the destruction of life; 3. Because there is evidence of the use of βάπτισμα where water has no place. These antecedent difficulties which bar the way against the use of this word to express the resultant state of an object put within water without limitation of time, must be met and overcome by indubitable facts before a step can be taken in the direction of a water covering, so far as this word is concerned. The presumption is heavily against such use. The burden must be lifted by those whose cause requires it.

The point at issue is this: Does βάπτισμα in Patristic writings indicate a physical "effect, product, result, state," over an object, from position within water, without limitation of time, or is it limited to express a thoroughly changed, spiritual condition, without limitation of time, effected with or without ideal withinness?

We proceed to adduce proof in support of the latter position.

THE PATRISTIC ΒΑΠΤΙΣΜΑ HAS A SPIRITUAL IMPORT.

General Idea: Definition.

The following question and answer presents an entirely accurate view of the purport of βάπτισμα as entertained by the Patrists.

BASIL the Great, III, 736: "Τίς ὁ λόγος ἢ ἡ δύναμις τοῦ βαπτίσματος; Τό ἀλλοιωθῆναι τὸν βαπτιζόμενον κατά τε νοῦν, καὶ λόγον, καὶ πρᾶξιν, καὶ γενέσθαι ἐκεῖνο κατὰ τὴν δοθεῖσαν δύναμιν, ὅπερ ἐστὶ τὸ ἐξ οὗ ἐγεννήθη.

" Quæ sit ratio aut vis baptismatis?

" Nempe ut baptizatus et mente et sermone et actione mutetur, atque per virtutem sibi datam fiat idipsum, quod est illud ex quo natus est.

" What is the purport and power of baptism?

" The baptized is thoroughly changed as to thought, and word, and deed, and becomes, according to the power bestowed, the same as that by which he was born."

This defining answer of Basil declares βάπτισμα to be the representative of a thoroughly changed spiritual condition assimilated to the characteristic of the power by which the change has been effected. And this view is in accord with all Classic, Jewish, and Inspired usage. It is identically the same conception as that which runs through all this Inquiry. The reason for the introduction of ἐγεννήθη is to be found, in general, in the equivalence (as these writers supposed) between regeneration and baptism; and, in particular, because this inquiry touching baptism is grounded in the immediately antecedent quotations of Matt. 28:19, " Go, disciple all nations, baptizing them into the Name of the Father, and of the Son, and of the Holy Ghost;" and John 3:3, 5, " Verily, verily, I say unto you, Except a man be born again he cannot see the kingdom of God." And again, " Verily, verily, I say unto you, Except a man be born of water and of the Spirit, he cannot enter into the kingdom of God." The conjunction of these passages strikes the keynote of Patristic views on Christian baptism. Their baptism (notwithstanding the presence of water and the manner of its ordinary use) does not belong to the sphere of physics; but is purely spiritual in its character.

Confirmatory of this view of Basil are the following references :
TERTULLIAN I, 1203 : "The Spirit of God borne above the waters
in the beginning, is a figure of baptism. The holy was borne
above the holy, or that which bore received sanctity from that
which was upborne. Since whatever substance is beneath receives, of necessity, character from that which is above, especially
is a physical substance pervaded by a spiritual, through the
subtlety of its nature. So the nature of the waters was sanctified
by the Holy and received the power to sanctify."

This was a baptism of the waters, according to the definition
of Basil, they having received a thorough change of character by
a communication of power from the Holy Spirit, whereby, also,
they are enabled to baptize others, which previously they could
not do. That is to say: SIMPLE *water* cannot effect *Christian*
baptism. It must have a special, divine power communicated to
it first. Therefore, DIDYMUS ALEX. (692) says, referring to this
same movement of the Spirit upon the waters and its effect in
changing their nature—" Ὅθεν ἀδιακρίτως παντὶ ὕδατι . . . βάπτισμα
γίνεται Whence baptism is effected by all water."

Does water require *a new power* to be divinely communicated
to it in order that it may be qualified for *a dipping?*

JEROME, II, 161 : "How can the soul, which has not the Holy
Spirit, be purged from old defilements ? For water does not wash
the soul unless it is first washed by the Holy Spirit, that it may
be able spiritually to wash others. ' The Spirit of the Lord,' says
Moses, ' was borne above the waters.' "

Jerome teaches : 1. Baptism is *soul* washing ; 2. Natural water
cannot wash the soul ; 3. Natural water is *washed* by the Holy
Spirit ; 4. This " washed" water has power spiritually to wash
the soul = to baptize it, thoroughly to change it, assimilating it
to the characteristic of the baptizing power ; 5, Patristic " washing" has no more to do with the sphere of physics than has Patristic baptism. What agent in physics can so wash water that
it can, then, wash the soul ? Jerome says : The Holy Spirit can
so " wash" water ; and Tertullian and Didymus say : He does
thus wash it by imparting to it his own quality ; and Basil says :
This is baptism—a thorough change and assimilation of condition.
All of which is, if possible, yet more expressly stated in Cyprian,
1057, 1082 : " For neither can the Spirit operate without water, nor
water without the Spirit. . . . But it is necessary that the water
be first purified and sanctified, that it may be able (τῷ ἰδίῳ βαπτισ-

ματι) by its own baptism to cleanse away the sins of the baptized man."

This teaches us: 1. Baptism is a changed condition in which appear "purification and sanctification;" 2. *Water* can be BAPTIZED; and is baptized when *purified* and *sanctified*. After water is thus baptized it has power to baptize the guilty soul = take away its sins; and without being itself so baptized, *it cannot baptize Christianly;* 3. Christian baptism is not a dipping into water.

These quotations exhibit ground elements running all through Patristic baptism, and any interpretation which does not accept them, and is not governed by them as first principles, must be worthless.

Assimilation.

Assimilation (that is to say, the characteristic of the baptism conformed to that of the baptizing power) is declared by Basil and Tertullian to be an essential feature of Christian baptism. This idea, so radical and so far removed from a water-dipping, may be further illustrated.

BASIL, III, 1551 : " The Lord himself declares what it is to be baptized by the Holy Spirit, when he says : ' That which is born of the flesh is flesh; and that which is born of the Spirit is spirit.' . . . Since we know and are fully convinced, that that which is born of the flesh of any one, is SUCH *as that of which it is born;* so, also, of necessity, we, born of the Spirit, are spirit; but not Spirit according to the great glory of the Holy Spirit; but according to the diversity of the gifts of God, through his Christ, to every one for profit. . . . 1564 : So, we are reckoned worthy to be baptized in the name of the only begotten Son of God, and deemed worthy of the great gift which the Apostle announces, saying : ' As many as have been baptized into Christ have put on Christ.' ' There is neither Greek nor Jew, circumcision nor uncircumcision, barbarian, Scythian, bond nor free, but Christ is all in all.' . . . 1565 : Having put on the Son of God, he is deemed worthy of the highest grade, and is baptized into the name of the Father of our Lord Jesus Christ, according to the testimony of John : ' He gave them power to become the sons of God.' . . 1571 : After we have put on the Son of God, who gives power to become the Sons of God, we are baptized in the name of the Father, and accounted the Sons of God, as says the prophet, ' I will be to you a Father, and ye shall be to me sons and daughters, saith the Lord Almighty.'"

We have here Basil's interpretation of baptism as a thorough change in thought, word, and deed, together with, of necessity, an assimilation to the baptizing power, just as "that which is born of the flesh is such as is the flesh of which it is born." How is such a baptism to be converted into "a dipping into water"?

JEROME VII, 456: "'In whom, also, having believed ye were sealed with the Holy Spirit of promise.' The seal is of God, that as the first man was made after the image and likeness of God, so, in regeneration, whosoever shall have received the Holy Spirit, he will be sealed by Him and receive the image of his Maker. But what is the meaning of the Holy Spirit of promise? I think, that as the Holy Spirit makes holy him in whom he is poured (eum cui fuerit infusus), and the spirit of wisdom makes wise, and the spirit of intelligence makes intelligent, and the spirit of counsel makes cautious and prudent, and the spirit of courage makes courageous, and the spirit of knowledge gives knowledge, the spirit of piety makes pious, the spirit of fear makes fearful and trembling through fear of God; so, also, the Spirit of promise or the Spirit of God makes him in whom he dwells Sponsor and God As, on the other hand, an unclean spirit makes unclean, and a filthy habitant makes for himself a filthy house; also, a spirit of fornication makes fornicators, and a vile spirit makes men vile and perverse, and a demon makes demoniacs, and as a liquor poured in a new earthen jar (novæ testæ infusus est) shall have been, the earthen jar long retains suchlike smell and taste."

1. The "seal" and the "regeneration" spoken of by Jerome represent baptism; 2. The Holy Spirit in sealing, regenerating, baptizing, makes like himself; 3. Like begets like, is variously illustrated, as baptisms are of endless variety; 4. The baptism of the soul by the Holy Spirit is represented by his being "poured" into it, as the wine is represented as "poured" into the earthen jar, baptizing it by communicating to it its own characteristics of odor and taste. Jerome agrees with Basil, and Tertullian, and Didymus, that baptism is enstamped with the characteristic of the baptizing power. None of them know anything of a water-dipping as entering into Christian baptism. Βάπτισμα is the resultant product assimilated to the baptizing power.

Baptism a New Life.

GREGORY NAZIANZEN II, 360: "The Word of God recognizes a threefold birth; the one of the body, the other of baptism, the other of the resurrection. Of these, the first is dark, servile, and impassionate; the second is bright, free, controlling the passions, exscinding every veil proceeding from birth, and conducting to the heavenly life; the third is more fearful and brief, collecting together in a moment every creature in the presence of the Creator to give account of their stewardship and manner of life. . . . Of the first and the last of these births we will not now speak, but will treat of the second.

"Baptism (φώτισμα) is the illumination of the soul, a change of life, 'the answer of the conscience toward God;' Baptism (φώτισμα) is the strengthening of our weakness; Baptism (φώτισμα) is the putting away of the flesh, the following of the Spirit, the partaking of the word, the rectification of our image, the purging of sin, the participation of light, the dissipation of darkness; Baptism (φώτισμα) is the chariot of God, the walking with Christ, the support of faith, the perfection of understanding, the key of the kingdom of heaven, the exchange of life, the abrogation of slavery, the loosening of bonds, the remodelling of our composition; Baptism (φώτισμα), what more is it necessary to enumerate? It is the noblest and the most magnificent of the gifts of God. For as some things are called the Holy of Holies, and the Song of Songs (because they are of wider compass and of greater dignity), so, also, is this Baptism (φώτισμα) more holy than all the other Baptisms (φωτισμῶν) which we possess."

This new life of the soul after the Divine likeness, the work of the Holy Ghost, is the Christian βάπτισμα according to the learned metropolitan archbishop of Constantinople. According to the theory it is a dip into water! Gregory N. interchanges βάπτισμα and φώτισμα; the former including the entirety of the changed spiritual condition, the latter pointing out one particular feature of it. How "Illumination" is to become the synonym for *dipping* I do not know. Φώτισμα is, like βάπτισμα, an "effect, product, result, state," and is a **water**-dipping as much (no more, no less) as is βάπτισμα.

HIERONYMUS GRÆCUS XL, 860: "I wish to learn how thou dost know that thou hast certainly been baptized. I know it (ἐκ τῆς ἐνεργείας) by its operation, as Isaiah says, 'Through thy fear, O

Lord, we have conceived and travailed and brought forth the Spirit of salvation.' It is evident that the Illuminated (οἱ φωτισ-θέντες διὰ τοῦ βαπτίσματος) through baptism, have received the Holy Spirit. For God again says through the prophet, concerning the baptized, 'I will dwell in them and walk in them;' and also, 'I will pour out (ἐκχεῶ) from my Spirit upon all flesh.' Therefore, as many as have received the Holy Spirit within them by the holy baptism (ἐν τῷ ἁγίῳ βαπτίσματι) do most assuredly know that they have been baptized by the boundings and prickings, and transports, and workings, and, so to speak, leapings of the grace of the Spirit, for no unbaptized man (ἀβάπτιστος) upon earth is possessed of such grace and power; it belongs only to those who have conceived (δι᾽ ὕδατος καὶ Πνεύματος) through water and the Spirit, and preserve this grace pure and unpolluted. For as ἡ γυνὴ ἔχουσα ἐν γαστρὶ αἰσθάνεται τῶν σκιρτημάτων τοῦ βρέφους ἔνδον αὐτῆς, so also they by the grace, and joy, and delight, begotten within them, do know that the Spirit of God, which they received (ἐν τῷ βαπτίσματι) by the baptism, does dwell in them. For concerning this grace (τοῦ ἁγίου βαπτίσματος) of the holy baptism, Christ said: 'The kingdom of heaven is within you.' And does every man, unlearned and learned, know that he has been baptized through this proof alone, and not through any other? Yes; this is the true and unerring proof of a Christian. As I have said: Ἡ ἐν γαστρὶ ἔχουσα οὐκ ἀπὸ ῥημάτων, ἀλλ᾽ ἀπὸ πραγμάτων καὶ τῶν τοῦ βρέφους σκιρτημάτων γινώσκει ἀκριβῶς ὅτι συνέλαβεν, so also the true Christian not by hearing from his parents, of those who baptized him, nor by any other means, but by his own heart, he ought to have the assurance that he had received the holy baptism, and that he was deemed worthy of the Holy Spirit. . . . This hidden grace and operation of the Holy Spirit in the heart no one upon earth ever receives except those who have been truly baptized into the Father, and Son, and Holy Ghost; concerning this our riches the Lord says: 'The kingdom of heaven is like to treasure hid in a field,' that is, the Holy Spirit which is hidden in us in the day of the divine baptism. . . . These things are adduced that the Christian may know that he has received the holy baptism, and that he is a true Christian. . . . The mark of a Christian is no external thing."

This Greek declares that the Christian βάπτισμα is, 1. A result effected; 2. That this result is *within* the soul; 3. That it is an abiding result; 4. That it is spiritual in its nature; 5. That it is assimilant to the power producing it; 6. That it is a matter of self-consciousness.

All which is absurd as applied to a water-dipping.

Diverse Names of Baptism.

CHRYSOSTOM II (*pars prior*), 225: "It is necessary to say something as to what (τὸ βάπτισμα) the Baptism is. But, if you please, we will first speak of the designation of this mystical (καθαρμοῦ) cleansing. For its name is not one, but many and diverse. For this purification is called (1) The washing of regeneration: 'For He saved us by the washing of regeneration and the renewing of the Holy Ghost.' It is also called (2) Illumination; Paul says, ' Remember the former days in which ye were illumined.' It is also called (3) Baptism; 'For as many as have been baptized into Christ have put on Christ.' It is called (4) Burial; 'For we are buried together with him by baptism into his death.' It is called (5) Circumcision; 'In whom we are circumcised by the circumcision made without hands, by the putting off of the body of the sins of the flesh.' It is called (6) Cross; 'For our old man was crucified that the body of sin might be destroyed.'"

These diverse names employed by Chrysostom to designate τὸ βάπτισμα, Christian baptism, are all spiritual or express a spiritual result: 1. "The washing of regeneration" is a washing by the power of the Holy Ghost which issued in τὸ βάπτισμα = a regenerate and renewed condition of the soul; 2. "Illumination" is the condition of the soul spiritually enlightened; 3. "Baptism" is the condition of the soul assimilated to Christ; 4. "Burial" is the spiritual unity with Christ in his death carried on to coburial in his sepulchre; 5. "Circumcision" is the application of the name of the type to its spiritual antitype, the excision of sin from the soul; 6. "Cross" is the application of the name of the instrument by which Christ was baptized into death, and the effect of that death in destroying the life of sin in the souls of his people.

These diverse titles are intelligible as expository of an " effect, product, result, state" accomplished in the soul; as expository of " dipping and nothing but dipping" they are worse than Babel echoings.

One of these titles Chrysostom, himself, explains; he says, " Many other names might be mentioned, but lest we consume all the time on the titles of this grace, let us return to the first title and explaiɴ that. . . . That washing which is through the baths (τὸ λουτρόν τὸ διὰ τῶν βαλανείων) cleansing the filth of the body is common to all men. There is a Jewish washing (λουτρόν Ἰουδαϊκὸν) which is much better than this, but much inferior to that of grace. . . . Jewish washing cleansed impurity which was ceremonial, not real, but the washing of grace (τὸ λουτρόν της Χάριτος) not only cleanses ceremonial but real impurity, which infects both body and soul. It cleanses not only from touching dead bodies, but from dead works. If any one should be an adulterer or an idolater, or should commit any other wrong, or should be full of all wickedness among men, having entered (εἰς τὴν κολυμβήθραν) into the pool of the waters, he would arise from the divine waters purer than the rays of the sun. . . . What can be more wonderful than this, when righteousness may be obtained without labor, or toil, or good works? . . . If a brief letter of a king can set free those who are guilty of ten thousand crimes and exalt others to the highest honor, much more may the Holy Spirit of God, possessed of all power, free from all wickedness, bestow abundant righteousness, and fill with all boldness. And as a spark falling into the midst of the sea, is immediately quenched, and becomes invisible (καταποντισθείς) swallowed up by the multitude of the waters, so also all human wickedness when it falls into the pool of the divine waters, is, more quickly and. more easily, than that spark (καταποντίζεται) swallowed up and becomes invisible. And why, if the washing (τὸ λουτρόν) takes away all sins from us, is it not called the washing of the remission of sins, or the washing of purification, but the washing of regeneration? Because it not ȯnly remits to us sins, and not only cleanses us from faults, but it does so as if we were *born again*."

Λουτρόν.

The important position occupied by λουτρόν in this passage and so frequently recurring in like important relations all through the Patristic writings, makes a clear and correct meaning of this word specially important.

Words of this termination do not receive as simple and single a meaning from Grammarians as words of some other terminations. *Crosby* includes under this termination: 1. Place; 2. Instrument; 3. Other means; *Buttman* makes it significant of "the names of instruments and other objects belonging to an action;" *Kühner,* "Substantives which denote an instrument or a means of accomplishing some object."

Liddell and Scott define—1. A bath, bathing-place; 2. Water for bathing or washing; 3. The equivalent of drink-offerings, libations; 4. Bathing; *Robinson,* "In N. T. a washing, ablution; spoken of religious ablutions or baptisms;" Sept. for רַחְצָה; which Gesenius defines "a washing. Cant. 4 : 2; 6 : 6." *Cremer* says, "Answering to the Biblical use of λούειν it denotes *baptism.* Eph. 5 : 26; Tit. 3 : 5; where we must bear in mind the close connection between regeneration and purification. In Classical Greek λουτρά in like manner denote propitiatory offerings and offerings for purification. Soph. El., 84, 434."

Bp. Ellicott (Eph. 5 : 26) thinks "the meaning of λουτρόν as *a laver* is indisputable. The peculiar force of the termination (instrumental object) may be distinctly traced, in all cases yet adduced."

The evidence in support of this position is not satisfactory. A laver is not the instrumental object for washing. A plough (ἄροτρον) is the instrumental object by which *ploughing* is effected; a currycomb (ξύστρον) is the instrumental object by which *currying* is effected; teaching-money (δίδακτρον) is the instrumental object by which payment for *teaching* is effected; and ransom-money (λύτρον) is the instrumental object by which *ransoming* is effected; but a laver (λουτρόν) is not the instrumental object by which a *washing* is effected. A "laver" stands in an essentially different relation to washing from that in which a plough stands to ploughing, or a currycomb to currying, or teaching-money to teaching, or ransom-money to ransoming; a "laver" does no washing. The Septuagint gives λουτήρ as the term for "laver," but the New Testament does not use the word; no doubt because no such instrument was known in New Testament baptism. We have, also (outside of the Scriptures), λουτήριον for the vessel containing the water, and not λουτρόν.

The instrumental object (including the means) in washing is the water; as the plough ploughs, and as the ransom-money ransoms, so the water washes. The water which makes up the bath is designated by Homer as θερμὰ λοετρά; and Josephus, de Bel. VII, 6, 3, calls the water from the hot and cold springs near Machærus, a very pleasant λουτρον. It would be remarkable if in usage a word used to designate the water used for washing, did not pass on to designate the washing itself. What else can such classic

phrases as λοῦσαι τίνα λουτρόν and Patristic phrases as λούσασθαι
τοῦτο τὸ λουτρὸν (Justin M., 516) mean, but to wash a *washing*?
And when this word passes out of mere physics into a religious
sphere, it would be natural for it to assume the broader idea of
purification where there was no physical washing; which Liddell,
Scott, and Cremer appear to recognize as a fact in heathen rites.
Cremer says: "λούειν is the term used by the Septuagint to
denote the theocratic washings on account of sin. And while
βαπτίζειν was used for the N. T. washing in order to purification
λούειν, λουτρόν, serve in some passages to give prominence *to the
full import of βαπτίζειν* which had become a *term. tech.*, or to denote purification generally. Heb. 10:22; Rev. 1:5; Eph. 5:26;
Tit. 3:5. See, also, Ecclesiasticus 31:25: 'What profits (τῷ
λουτρῷ) his washing to one baptized from the dead, when he
touches it again?' In classical Greek λουτρά denote offerings for
purification."

The intimate relation declared by Cremer to exist between
βαπτίζω and λούω, and βάπτισμα and λουτρόν, in relation to purification is abundantly justified by the passage before us, as, also,
everywhere throughout the Patristic literature.

Usage of λουτρόν in this passage.

Chrysostom is speaking in exposition of (τὸ βάπτισμα) the baptism. This he announces as a mystical purification (τοῦ μυστικοῦ
καθαρμοῦ). He adds: "This (τὸ καθάρσιον) purification is called
(λουτρόν παλιγγενεσίας) the washing of regeneration." This title of
Christian Baptism, "the mystical purification," can hardly be a
physical laver, or physical water constituting the material for a
bath, nor yet washing, as a process; the only appropriate interpretation seems to be the purification resultant from washing.
And this purification is shown to be spiritual in its nature by
reason of the qualifying παλιγγενεσίας—it is a regenerative purification; also, because what is here called by Chrysostom λουτρόν
παλιγγενεσίας is called by Origen (II, 850) βάπτισμα παλιγγενεσίας,
which, also, he calls "the second circumcision, purging the soul,"
showing its spiritual nature. This is farther confirmed by Justin
Martyr (500, 504): "Isaiah did not send you to the bath (βαλανεῖον)
there to wash away (ἀπολουσαμένους) murder and other sins, which
all the water of the sea is not able (καθαρίσαι) to cleanse; but, as

is reasonable, this was of old time (τὸ σωτήριον λουτρόν) that saving washing which he announced to the repenting, no longer seeking purification (καθαριζομένους) by the blood of goats and sheep, but by faith through the blood of Christ and his death. . . . Therefore (διὰ τοῦ λουτροῦ τῆς μετανοίας) through the washing of repentance and of the knowledge of God, we have believed and declare that that (βάπτισμα) which Isaiah foretold is the only baptism which is able (καθαρίσαι) to cleanse the repenting; this is that water of life. But ye have formed cisterns for yourselves which are broken and worthless. For what profit is there of that baptism which (φαιδρύνει) makes bright the flesh and the body only? Baptize (βαπτίσθητε) the soul from anger and covetousness, from envy and hate, and behold the body is clean!" Is not this testimony clear, full, and varied, showing that λουτρόν is neither " laver," nor " water for a bath," but is a spiritual washing of the soul effected according to Chrysostom by the " washing (λουτρόν) of regeneration," and according to Justin Martyr by " the washing (λουτρόν) of repentance?" Justin further says: " This washing (λουτρόν) is called Illumination (φωτισμὸς), since those learning these things are illumined as to their understanding. . . . And the dæmons having heard of this (λουτρόν) washing through the announcement of the prophet, required their worshippers (ῥαντίζειν) to sprinkle themselves." That this λουτρόν fulfilled its office of *washing, purifying,* by sprinkling and pouring, not only in the hands of heathen men but also of Christians, is not only inferable from the language of Justin, but is of direct testimony by Basil, Letter 386, " He (Ariantheus, baptized by his wife on his dying bed) washed away all the stains of his soul at the close of his life (λουτρῷ παλιγγενεσίας) by the washing of regeneration " (Beecher, p. 209). This λουτρόν washing, purifying, was not by covering in water for a bath, but by sprinkling or pouring. Farther proof of this is found in the additional statement by President Beecher: " Porphyry asserts, *in libel. de antro Nympharum,* that it was customary for married women to purify maidens by sprinkling or affusion, before marriages, with water taken from fountains and living springs. Photius tells us that the water used for this purpose at Athens, was brought in a pitcher from certain fountains which he specifies, by the oldest male boy of the family. The water thus used is called λουτρόν, or λουτρὰ νυμφικά, and Zonaras defines λουτρὰ thus, τὰ εἰς λύσιν ἀλόντα τῆς ἀκαθαρσίας. Those things which produce the removal of im-

purity = means of purification. The boy who brought the water
was called λουτροφόρος."

The proof is absolute: 1. That λουτρόν does not mean a laver;
2. It has no special limitation to water for a bath; 3. It is applied
to water in a pitcher; 4. It expresses the means for purification,
and also the purification effected; 5. The manner of using this
means to effect purification is a matter of the most absolute indifference; in religious rites, whether heathen or Christian,
sprinkling and pouring were common, lawful, and unquestionable
forms, in the most perfect harmony with the meaning and derivation of the word; other modes were exceptional.

The interchange and the equivalence of λουτρόν and βάπτισμα
appear everywhere in Patristic writings. Both terms are employed
to denote the means (and the same means) of purification. Both
terms are employed to denote the purification effected. Both
terms are employed to cover the entire, complex, rite. Both
terms are employed to denote the purifying element in a pitcher.
Both terms are applied to various purifying elements—water,
blood, tears, fire, etc. Both terms are employed in the same
combinations, λουτρόν μετανοίας, βάπτισμα μετανοιας; λουτρόν παλιγγενεσίας, βάπτισμα παλιγγενεσίας, λουτρὸν βαλανείων βάπτισμα λάκκων (Just.
M., 516). Both terms find their execution in sprinkling and
pouring. Both terms, throughout the Patristic writings in religious rites, relate to spiritual and not physical purification·
Neither term, as used, has any reference to a water covering.

Purification.

Chrysostom in the passage before us is treating of nothing but
purification and its varieties. He first speaks of "the washing
which is (διὰ) through the baths." It is impossible that this can
mean, the "laver" which is "through the baths." It is impossible
that it can rationally mean, "the water for a bath" which is
"through the baths." It is absurdly impossible that it can mean,
"the place which is through the baths." It must mean the washing = the purification which is effected "through the baths;" the
preposition requires this. This conclusion, forced upon us by
the terms, Chrysostom expressly declares to be his meaning by
saying, it is "the cleansing of the filth of the body" to which he
refers. This bath purification, he says, all men possess. He
then speaks of a purification which all men do not possess. It is

a Jewish purification (*λουτρόν Ἰουδαϊκόν*). This Jewish *λουτρόν* differs from the bath *λουτρόν*, in that it cleanses from legal impurity, which the other does not. That is to say, this Jewish *λουτρόν* is another thing entirely from that of the bath, in that the former is possessed of a *lutric* (purifying) power, of which the other has nothing. This ceremonially purifying power finds its ordinary development through the sprinkling and the pouring of the *λουτρόν* (as was daily done in the Grecian baths), but the purifying effect was wholly diverse; because there was a divinely appointed power in the *λουτρόν Ἰουδαϊκόν* which was not in the *λουτρόν διὰ τῶν βαλανείων*. Chrysostom introduces us to a third purification—*τὸ λουτρόν τῆς χαρίτος* the washing of grace. This *λουτρόν* is as essentially diverse from that belonging to "Judaism" as is that of Judaism diverse from that of "the baths." Each *λουτρόν* receives its distinctive character from the peculiar purification which it has power to effect. And the nature of this power is set forth by the adjunct to the general term; thus *λουτρόν βαλανείων* is a simple *physical bath* purification, the modus of which is no element of consideration; the *λουτρόν νυμφικόν* is a *bridal* purification essentially different in character from the bath purification as to its subject, as to its administrators, as to the bearer of the *λουτρόν*, and as to the nature of the purification effected, which was not physical but ritual; the *λουτρόν λάκκων* (the washing of cisterns) of Just. M., refers to ceremonial purification and is the same as the *λουτρόν Ἰουδαϊκόν* which was a *legal* purification cleansing from the ceremonial impurity caused by touching a dead body, etc.; the *λουτρόν χαρίτος* was a spiritual purification cleansing from the impurity, not of a dead body, but, of dead works. It is needless to say, how diverse is this purification from that of "the bath common to all men," and from that of ceremonialism restricted to "the Jew."

Patristic writers, generally, make the water used in baptism an efficient element in this Spiritual *λουτρόν*, not however as simple water but as possessed of a special power divinely communicated; but this is without any Scriptural basis. The word of God knows nothing but a *λουτρόν* of repentance, of faith, of regeneration, wrought by the Holy Ghost, and receiving all their *lutric* power from the atoning blood of "the Lamb of God who taketh away the sin of the world."

This usage of *λουτρόν* by Chrysostom and others as the equivalent of *βάπτισμα* is so abounding and so clear (therefore giving light to and receiving light from that word) that it could not be passed by without some special notice.

Dr. Carson.

Dr. Carson (p. 486) closes a "Dissertation on λούω" in the following words: "That the word does not necessarily express mode, I readily admit." And βαπτίζω expresses mode just as little as λούω. "Immersion is almost always the way of bathing." The common way of bathing among the Greeks was not by immersion, but by pouring water over the body. "All that I contend for from this word is, that the object to which it is applied is covered with the water, and that, without a regimen, it refers to the whole body." The bodies of Paul and Silas were washed (ἔλουσεν) but were not "covered with the water." The body of Dorcas was washed (λούσαντες) but not "covered with water." The bodies and the souls of the redeemed are washed (λούσαντι) but not "covered" with the blood of the Lamb. "The application of this word to baptism shows that the rite was a bathing of the whole body; and as immersion is the usual way of bathing, baptism must have been an immersion, because, when it is called a bathing, the reference would be to the common way of bathing: not to a merely possible way." The common way of Greek bathing was not by immersion but by pouring, therefore the use of λουτρόν in baptism does not imply that "baptism was an immersion." The application of λούω and λουτρόν to baptism shows nothing as to the manner of using the water in the rite, 1. Because it is admitted that the word "does not express mode;" 2. Because λούω and λουτρόν, as applied to baptism, have no reference to physics; but like βαπτίζω and βάπτισμα relate to a spiritual washing or purification—Eph. 5 : 26 (τῷ λουτρῷ) cleansing "by the word" spiritually, as perfectly as water cleanses physically; Titus 3 : 5 "διὰ λουτροῦ παλιγγενεσίας He saved us through regenerative cleansing;" Rev. 1 : 5 "λούσαντι Who washed us by his blood." Neither the "word of God," nor "regeneration by the Holy Spirit," nor "the blood of Christ," effects a physical washing. There is no more modal use in the symbol cleansing of water than there is in the cleansing by "the word," by regeneration, or by the blood of Christ. Heb. 10 : 22 "λελουμένοι, Our hearts (ἐρραντισμένοι) Sprinkled (v. 19 by the blood of Jesus) and our bodies washed with pure water, let us draw near." There is no reason why this washing of the body as originally applied to the " Hebrews " should not be a physical cleansing. Such was the universal requirement made of the Hebrews ; but we must not confound differences because of some common relation. This physical washing of the Hebrew is made the basis for inculcating a spiritual washing of the Christian. A physical washing was required of the Jew when he would present himself before God ; and to this Paul refers. A ceremonial washing, which was not a physical cleansing, was required of the Jew to remove an ideal, ceremonial, impurity, which might be effected by sprinkling. To this ceremonial use of water enjoined upon the Jew the Saviour refers (John 3 : 5) in his conversation with Nicodemus, addressing him as a Jew and teaching him that not only this cleansing was needed by him as a Jew, but a higher cleansing, even that of the Spirit, was needed by him as a Christian. Paul teaches us in Eph. 5 : 26, that the cleansing of the soul by the word is as perfect as the cleansing of the body by water ; and because the cleansing by " the word," by " regeneration," by " the blood of Jesus," is perfect, therefore, such cleansing is symbolized by the pure water used in ritual baptism. It is not true, however, that the water in John 3 : 5, Eph. 5 : 26, Rom. 10 : 22, has any direct reference to the water used in baptism.

Dr. Carson concludes thus : " I claim, then, the evidence of all those passages in the New Testament which by this word refer to the ordinance of baptism. I make a similar demand with regard to the use of the word by the Fathers. Justin Martyr not only always uses the word conformably to this distinction, but speaking of the pagan purifications invented by the dæmons in imitation of baptism, he showed that they used the washing of the whole body as the most complete purification. Baptism then is immersion and nothing but immersion is baptism."

This claim is foundationless alike as to the New Testament and the Fathers. The representation made as to the usage of Justin M. is specially inaccurate. This martyr to the truth speaks in the following distinct terms—" 492 : And when the dæmons had heard, through the preaching of the prophet, of this (λουτρόν) washing, they required their worshippers (ῥαντίζειν) to sprinkle themselves." Subsequently he speaks of a washing (λούεσθαι) ; but a washing in religious rites is effected by a sprinkling more frequently than in any other way. Paul speaks of the blood of Jesus being applied by "sprinkling" to the heart. Such sprink ling effects a washing = a thorough cleansing of the body and the soul from sin. It is this "sprinkling" which effects *the washing* (λούσαντι) in Rev. 1 : 5. Whatever has a power to wash, cleanse, is a λουτρόν; λουτρά are various in nature, and in the washings, cleansings, which they effect; and, also, in the manner of their operation. The λουτρόν νυμφικόν effected its bridal washing by the *sprinkling* of special waters. The washing (λουτροῦ) and the baptism (βάπτισαντος) of the victim on the altar of Carmel (Origen IV, 241) effected their ceremonial cleansing by the *pouring* of water upon it; just as the ordinary bath washing (λουτρόν) of the Greeks was effected. The washing (λουτρόν) of the blood of Jesus effects its cleansing of the soul from sin by an ideal *sprinkling* of the heart.

It is evident that every λουτρόν has a washing power; and the washing effected is (in kind) like to the washing power. Now, what is this but the βάπτισμα of Basil, to wit, a thoroughly changed condition, like, in nature, to the baptizing power which has effected the condition?

The usage of λούω and λουτρόν by Patristic writers is in entire conformity with this reasoning and its conclusion; they use these terms not only as capable of interchange with βαπτίζω and βάπτισμα, but as substantial equivalents, having no reference to modal action and in religious applications without reference to a physical covering element.

Therefore, all argument from the use of these words, in relation to baptism to prove a water covering, fails. The general usage and sentiment is well set forth by Clemens Alex. (*prior*) 620: " It is especially necessary to wash (λούειν) the soul (καθαρίῳ Λόγῳ) by the purifying Word. . . . 'Cleanse (καθάρισον) first that which is within the cup, that that which is without may also be made clean.' Therefore the best washing (λουτρόν) cleanses the defilement of the soul, and is (πνευματικόν) spiritual; concerning which washing the prophet clearly says: ' The Lord will cleanse ('εκπλυνεῖ) the defilement of the sons and daughters of Israel.' And the Word has added the manner of the (καθάρσεως) cleansing, saying: ' By the spirit of judgment and by the spirit of burning.' But the washing of the body, the fleshly washing, is accomplished (διὰ) by water only, as happens often in the country, where there is no (βαλανεῖον) bath." Clement here in (λουτρόν διὰ ὕδατος), like Chrysostom in (λουτρόν διὰ τῶν βαλανείων) distinguishes between λουτρόν *the washing* and βαλανεῖον *the bath;* the instrumental means (διὰ) by which "the washing" is effected. Clement, also, distinguishes between the λουτρόν διὰ μόνου ὕδατος, which is σαρχιχὸν, and the λουτρόν of Christianity χαθαρσίῳ Λόγῳ, which is πνευματιχον. This λουτρόν of Christianity was effected, Hilary says, "almost daily" (among the sick) by sprinkling, the only way in which the Scriptures ever say the blood of "the purifying Logos " is applied to the soul. And as this λουτρόν was identical with the βάπτισμα, the sprinkling which effected the one effected the other also.

Diverse Baptisms.

Chrysostom says: "The name of baptism is not one, but the names are many and diverse." Ambrose says: "Baptism itself (non unum est) is not one, but there are (multa genera) many diverse baptisms." This is the universal Patristic sentiment, and it is destructive to the nothing but water-dipping theory of Christian baptism.

GREGORY NAZIANZEN II, 353: "Let us discourse somewhat concerning the diversities of baptisms (περὶ διάφορας βαπτισμάτων)."
1. Moses baptized, yet with water only (ἀλλ' ἐν ὕδατι). . . . 2. And John baptized, yet not Judaically, for he baptized not only with water (οὐ ἐν ὕδατι μόνον), but also (εἰς μετάνοιαν) into repentance; still, he did not baptize altogether spiritually (πνευματιχῶς), for he does not add this (ἐν Πνεύματι) by the Spirit. 3. And Jesus baptizes, but (ἐν Πνεύματι) by the Spirit. This is perfection. And, that I may embolden some little, How is he not God by whom even thou mayest become God (ἐξ ὁυ χαὶ σὺ γίνῃ Θεός)? 4. And I know a fourth baptism, that (διὰ) by means of martyrdom and blood (with which, also, Christ himself was baptized), and, indeed, much more admirable than the others, because it is not polluted by after defilements. 5. And I know yet a fifth baptism, that by means of tears (τὸ τῶν δαχρύων); but more painful since, washing (λοὑων) nightly his bed with tears, the wounds of his transgression are a stench unto him. . . . 6. And there is a final baptism, hereafter, when they will be baptized (τῷ πυρὶ) by means of fire, both more painful and more protracted.

This last baptism by fire is made the last in a list of eight diverse baptisms by Athanasius. He says, IV, 759: "The eighth baptism is the final baptism, which is not saving, but burning and punishing sinners forever and ever."

These diverse baptisms are constantly met with through all the

Patristic writings. It is of essential importance to understand
what the diversities in these baptisms are, and to what they are
due.

A glance at the list of baptisms presented by Gregory N. will
show a diversity in the agencies by which the baptisms are severally effected. 1. Moses' baptism has as its agency *simple water
having a legal power* to cleanse ceremonially, but without any
spiritual power. The baptisma effected by this agency was a
condition thoroughly changed from ceremonial impurity to ceremonial purity. The more common mode enjoined in the using
of this water to effect this baptisma was sprinkling; dipping is
never enjoined. 2. John's baptism has as its agency *water neither
simple nor wholly spiritual.* The baptisma which it effects is an
imperfect spiritual condition (penitential in nature) preparative
for a perfect spiritual baptisma characterized by regeneration and
remission of sins. 3. Jesus' baptism has as its baptizing agency
the Divine Spirit (ἐν Πνεύματι). The presence of water as an element in this agency is not here mentioned : but such is the Patristic faith, and constitutes emphatically their error in relation
to Christian baptism. The Scriptures never associate water with
the agency by which (in contradistinction from his ministers) Jesus
baptizes. He never baptized with water. He does ever and only
baptize (ἐν Πνεύματι) by the Holy Spirit. His ministers personally
and directly do ever and only baptize with water, symbolizing the
pure nature and spiritually purifying effect of the baptism of their
Lord The baptisma effected by this Divine agency is a thoroughly changed spiritual condition, which (according to the somewhat startling language of Gregory N.) bears the divine likeness
of the Divine Agent. 4. Blood baptism does not (in the view of
the Patrists) present in its active agency any diversity as compared with the ordinary Christian baptism by water; there is
merely the substitution of blood for water, while the same divine
power of the Holy Spirit operates alike through the one and the
other, effecting the same perfect baptisma exhibited in regeneration and the remission of sins. 5. Tears' baptism occupies, as to
its agency, precisely the same relation to Christian baptism as
does " Blood baptism ;" penitential tears are the vehicle through
which the Divine Spirit operates in effecting that baptisma which
purifies the soul from all sin, and especially of sins committed
after baptism. 6. Fire baptism has as its agency "a *burning and
punishing* power." The baptisma effected by this agency (some-

times diversely explained) is a thoroughly changed condition, marked by the abiding woe proceeding from the execution of the penalty of a broken law and of rejected mercy.

Now it will be observed that in all these diverse baptisms the baptisma receives its character from and partakes of the nature (real or supposed) of the baptizing agency. And what is this but a necessity proceeding from the nature of things, as well as the verification of the definition given by Basil of a βάπτισμα? And what are all these facts but a ploughshare turning up the foundations of that remarkable theory which would convert the Christian baptisma into a water-dipping? There is no such thing. I know of no reason in the nature of things, or in the laws of language, why βάμμα might not be used to express a condition of *wetness*, the effect of dipping into water; but, in fact, it is never so used, but is limited to express a liquid having some definite quality with power to impart that quality; or the condition effected by this quality, as a condition of *color*, the effect of some agency having the power to color. So I know of no reason in the nature of things, or in the laws of language, why βάπτισμα might not be used to express the condition of *inness* (unlimited by time) within a fluid element, the effect of the action in βάπτιζω; but, in fact, it is never so used, but is limited to express a liquid possessed of a definite quality with power to impart that quality, or a condition the effect of such agency capable of thoroughly changing the condition by subjecting the object to its own quality. As a βάμμα may be secured by putting an object within a coloring element, or by putting the coloring element upon the object; so a βάπτισμα may be secured by putting an object within (really or ideally) an element which thus imparts its quality, or by putting the element upon or within the object, when the element does, in such way, impart its quality. And as it is an absolute indifference to the βάμμα whether there be a putting into or a putting upon, so to the βάπτισμα it is a matter of infinite unconcern whether the object be put within the agency, or the agency be put within or upon the object. That the Christian baptisma consists in a water-dipping, no Patristic writer ever thought of believing. That the Christian baptisma is effected in the most perfect manner and measure by sprinkling, no Patristic writer ever thought of questioning. In vindication of these positions, let us briefly glance at statements made of the diverse baptisms above referred to by Gregory N. and others.

Blood Baptisms.

TERTULLIAN I, 1217 : " We have a second washing (*lavacrum* [λουτρόν]) one and the same, to wit, of blood. These two baptisms (*hos duos baptismos*) he shed forth from the wound of his pierced side. It is this baptism which takes the place of the washing of water when it has not been received and restores it when it has been lost."

II, 135 : " God foresaw human infirmity and the imperilling of faith (*post lavacrum* = baptism) after the washing and established a final protection in martyrdom and (*lavacrum sanguinis*) the washing of blood. . . . To martyrs no sin can be imputed since life itself is laid down (*in lavacro*) in the washing (baptism)." 147 : " The martyrs rest under the altar. . . . ' These are they who have washed their robes and made them white by the blood of the Lamb.' The robe of the soul is the body. Defilements (*sordes*) are indeed washed away (*abluuntur*) by baptism (baptismate), but stains (*maculæ*) are whitened (*candiduntur*) by martyrdom."

Tertullian, like others, believed that while water effected a purifying baptisma or lavacrum (the terms are interchanged as equivalents), martyr blood effected a purifying baptisma or lavacrum, more desirable and more secure, because it had no after-defilement.

1028 : " Martyrium aliud erit baptismum, Martyrdom will be another *baptism*." For he says: Luke 12 : 50, ' I have, also, another baptism.' Whence from the wounded side of the Lord water and blood flowed forth, providing each washing— . . . first washing (*primo lavacro*) by water, second (*secundo*) by blood." Here washing = baptisma = martyrium.

CYPRIAN III, 1123 : " Can the power of baptism (*vis baptismi*) be greater or better than *confession*, than *martyrdom*, when one confesses Christ before men and is baptized by his own blood (*sanguine suo baptizetur*) ? And yet not even this baptism (*hoc baptisma*) profits the heretic. The baptism of a public confession and of blood (*baptisma publicæ confessionis et sanguinis*) cannot profit a heretic unto salvation." 1124 : " Catechumens not baptized in the church, but baptized by that most glorious and greatest baptism of blood (*baptizentur gloriosissimo et maximo sanguinis baptismo*) are not deprived of grace. The Lord declared (Luke 12 : 50) ' That he had another baptism to be baptized with ;' and he declares that those baptized with their own blood (*sanguine suo baptizatos*) obtain divine grace, when he says to the thief in his very passion that 'he should be with him in paradise.' 1198: Our God says: Luke 12:50, 'I have another baptism to be baptized with;' Mark 10:38, 'Can ye be baptized with the baptism that I am baptized with?' showing that he must be baptized not only by water but by his own blood . . . to be baptized by either mode (*utroque modo baptizare*) secures alike and equally ONE *baptism* of salvation and honor. When the Lord says, 'I have another baptism to be baptized with,' he does not mean a second baptism as if there were two baptisms, but he shows that baptism of the one kind or the other (*alterius speciei*) is given to us for salvation. Martyrs receiving *the baptism of* BLOOD experience no loss through lack of *the baptism of* WATER; and believers receiving the baptism of water experience no loss through lack of the baptism of their own blood."

CYPRIAN II, 654: " We who have given only the first baptism (of water) to believers, would prepare every one for that other (of blood) also, teaching that this Baptism is greater in grace, sublimer in power, richer in honor, a Baptism in which angels baptize, a Baptism in which God and his Christ exult, a Baptism which perfects the increase of our faith, a Baptism which unites us, leaving this world, immediately with God. The remission of sins is received by the Baptism of water, the crown of virtues is received by the Baptism of blood."

ORIGEN II, 980: " Our probation does not extend merely to scourging but reaches to the pouring out (*profusionem*) of blood: for Christ whom we follow poured out (*effudit*) his blood for our redemption, that we may go hence washed (*loti*) by our own blood. It is the baptism of blood only which makes us more pure than the baptism of water. The Lord says: ' I have a baptism to be baptized with, and how am I straitened until it be accomplished.' You see that he called the pouring out of his blood, baptism (*profusionem sanguinis sui*, BAPTISMA) . . . by the baptism of water past sins are remitted; by the baptism of blood future sins are prevented. . . . If God should grant unto me that I might be washed (*diluerer*) by my own blood, that I might receive this second baptism, enduring death for Christ, I would go safe out of this world."

Christ's Blood Baptism.

AUGUSTINE IX, 276 : " Petilianus says : The Saviour, having been baptized by John, declared that he must be baptized again ; not now by water or Spirit, but by the baptism of blood, by the cross of his passion (*sanguinis baptismo, cruce passionis*). . . . Blush, O persecutors! ye make martyrs like to Christ, whom, after the water of true baptism, baptizing-blood sprinkles (*sanguis baptista perfundit*)."

JEROME IV, 35 : " Isaiah 1 : 16, 'Wash you, make you clean.' Instead of ancient victims, and burnt offerings, and the fat of fed beasts, and the blood of bulls and goats ; and instead of incense, and new moons, and sabbaths, and festivals, and fasts, and kalends, and other solemnities, the religion of the Gospel pleases me; that ye should be baptized by my blood (*baptizemini in sanguine meo*) by the washing of regeneration (*per lavacrum regenerationis*) which alone can remit sin."

The personal baptism by blood of the Lord Jesus Christ does in its character stand unapproachably alone. That baptism was into penal death by blood substitutionally shed under the demands of a broken Law. This blood-shedding satisfied the Law, made an atonement, and hereby became invested with a power to remit sin unto all souls upon which it might, by the Holy Ghost, be " sprinkled." This baptism presents an infinite difference as it is related to Christ and to his people. He, sinless, sheds his blood unto death for sin, that that blood might secure the power to save sinners from death in sin, as a consequence of their sin. Therefore he declares (Mark 10 : 38), that in his personal baptism of blood (= fulfilling all righteousness and bearing the penalty of the Law) they could have no share. He trod the wine-press alone. Of the people there was none with him. And therefore, again, he declares (Mark 10 : 39), that in his personal blood baptism (as he is thereby made ' JESUS, *Saviour of his people from their sins*') they shall indeed share. This power to remit sin, secured to the atoning blood of the Redeemer (erroneously supposed to be communicated to and to become coefficient with the water of baptism, the blood of martyrs, and the tears of penitents) is the key by which Patristic language on the subject of Christian baptism must be resolved. Compare the above statement of Jerome IV, 35, " That ye should be baptized by my blood which alone can remit sin," with Jerome II, 161, " How can the soul which has not the Holy Spirit be purged from old defilements? For water does not wash (*lavat*) the soul, *unless it is itself first washed* (*lavatur*) by the Spirit, *that it* MAY BE ABLE SPIRITUALLY *to wash* (*lavare spiritualiter*) others. Moses says: 'The Spirit of the Lord was borne above the waters;' from which it appears that baptism is not without the Holy Spirit. Bethesda, a pool of Judæa, was not able to heal the enfeebled members of the body except through the coming of an Angel; and do you offer to me THE SOUL *washed with* SIMPLE *water* (AQUA SIMPLICI), as from a bath (BALNEO)? . . . The baptism of the Church without the Holy Spirit is nothing."

It is eminently the Patristic sentiment, that water, blood, tears, baptize (= remit sin) only through a divine power communicated from the blood of Christ through the Holy Spirit; and they do repudiate with scorn a *bath* (= " simple water ") baptism, or a *covering* with mere water, blood, or tears, as Christian baptism.

The blood of Christ is the agency (the power of God) to remit sin, which POWER has infinitely less than nothing to do with quantity, or covering, or form of application, and it was only as this *divine* POWER was (supposedly) communicated to simple water, martyr blood, penitential tears, that the Fathers of Christianity believed that Christian baptism could be effected. Without it all the oceans of earth could not baptize a babe; with it sprinkling drops are enough to baptize a world. In proof of this and in conclusion of these Blood baptisms I offer one other quotation.

CHRYSOSTOM II (*pars prior*), 408 : " Why did Christ suffer without the city on a high place and not under some roof? This did not take place without a reason, but that he might purify (καθάρη) the nature of the air; therefore he was offered on a high place, under no roof, but instead of a roof with the heavens stretched above him, that the whole heaven might be purified (καθαρθῇ) by the Lamb offered on a high place. Therefore the heaven was purified, and the earth was purified. For *blood from his side* DROPPED (ἔσταξε) *upon the earth*, and its defilement everywhere was cleansed away (ἐξεκάθηρεν). . . . Because the whole earth was defiled (ἀκάθαρτος) by the smoke, and the savor, and the blood of idol sacrifices, and of other pollutions, of the heathen, God commanded the Jews to sacrifice and pray in one place. But Christ having come and suffered without the city he purified the whole earth,

33

and fitted every place for prayer. . . . The whole earth was made holy (ἁγία)."

No one familiar with the Patristic writings will deny that Chrysostom does here represent the heavens and the earth as BAPTIZED (= purified) *by the uplifted body and the dropping blood* of the Lamb of God. If all the waters of the Jordan and of the whole earth were " baptized " (as we are told that they were) by the touch of the body of the Lord Jesus, then the whole heavens, into which the body of Jesus was lifted up, were baptized by that body; and if John the Baptist was " baptized" (as we are told that he was) by *touching with his hand* the head of Jesus, then, *the blood-*DROPS which fell from that thorn-pierced head had power to BAPTIZE *the whole earth;* and Chrysostom does teach, that blood-drops from the Cross did baptize a world.

These Blood baptisms, alone, are adequate to prove the theory (which makes a water dipping and nothing but a water dipping Christian baptism) to be utterly empty of truth and a supreme error with which no semblance of sympathy can be found in the Patristic writings.

Tears' Baptism.

CLEMENS ALEX. II, 649: "He wept bitterly. . . . Having been baptized a second time by his tears (τοῖς δάκρυσι βαπτιζόμενος ἐκ δευτέρου)."

ATHANASIUS IV, 644: "God has granted to the nature of man three baptisms (τρία βαπτίσματα) purifying from all sin whatsoever. I mean, 1. The baptism by water (ὕδατος); 2. The baptism by our own blood through (διὰ) martyrdom; 3. The baptism by tears (διὰ δακρύων) into which (εἰς ὅπερ baptism) the harlot was purified (ἐκαθαρίσθη). And likewise Peter, the chief of the Holy Apostles, after his denial, having wept, was received and saved. . . . . It is necessary to know that equally with the baptism (of water), the fountain of tears purifies (καθαρίζει) a man."

IV, 760: "A sixth baptism is that by (διὰ) tears, which is painful, as one washing nightly his couch, and repenting, and grieving, on account of sins committed."

Clemens Alex. speaks of the captain of a band of robbers (once a disciple of the Apostle John) as baptized, a second time, by tears. The case is spoken of absolutely as *a* BAPTISM, and the agency in effecting the baptism is said to be " tears." There is no such absurdity as that of making " tears " a receiving element into which the robber captain was *dipped*. It is not needful that one tear should moisten the cheek. Tears are worth nothing for this baptism except as exponential of the penitential sorrow of the soul. So in Blood baptism; it is neither necessary that the blood should touch the person of the martyr, or that one drop of blood should be shed in the martyrdom. The only value of the blood is its evidence of a love and faith stronger than death. Numbers without number have received the baptism of martyrdom in other ways than by the sword. But these "tears," and this "blood," *occupy the same identical relation to the* BAPTISM as that held by "the water" (however used) namely, *that of* AGENCY. Modal use has no more to do with effecting Christian baptism in the case of water (when there may be one, or three, or three hundred dippings) than in that of tears and blood, where there neither is in fact, nor can be by possibility, any dipping. The BAPTISM is identically the same in either case.

Athanasius teaches us, that the three baptisms—by water, by blood, and by tears—while they are diverse in their agencies, those agencies have a common power to effect one and the same baptism, whose characteristic is, as Athanasius says, "purification from all sin."

Βάπτισμα is applied both to the effect produced and to that which has the power to produce the effect. Therefore *water* itself is a Baptisma, a loutron, because it effects a baptism, a washing; and so are *blood* and *tears*, for the same reason. Tertullian says, the water, and the blood, flowing from the wounded side of the Redeemer were "two baptisms (*duos baptismos*)." Water is said, "to receive a washing in order that it may effect a washing " == to receive a baptism that it may effect a baptism. The same usage holds good of λουτρόν, and *lavacrum*.

The harlot is said to be baptized into the baptism which is effected by "tears." The phrase "into which she was purified " is mixed; fully stated it would be, baptized "into which " baptism (= purifying from all sin whatever εἰς ἄφεσιν ἁμαρτιων) "she was purified." The construction is analogous to "sprinkled" (by the blood of Jesus and so purified) "*from* (ἀπὸ) an evil conscience." Peter going out and weeping bitterly received the same baptism as did the woman that was "a sinner" and washed the Saviour's feet with her tears. It is hard for some persons to learn, even from Athanasius, that sprinkling tear-drops baptize equally with the billowy waves of Jordan.

In these three quotations we find the Dative without a preposition, the Genitive without a preposition, and the Genitive three times with *διά*; in every instance expressive of agency. If any dependence is to be put upon those two illustrious Grecians, Clement and Athanasius, *water*, *blood*, and *tears* hold the same identical relation to Christian baptism, namely, that of agencies and not of receptive elements, and must continue so to do until the theory shall succeed in dipping into their tears " the robber chieftain," " the woman that was a sinner," and " the chief of the holy Apostles." The Patristic baptisma is a spiritual condition and not a physical covering.

Fire Baptism.

TERTULLIAN I, 1212: " ' There cometh One who will baptize (*tingueret*) by the Spirit and fire ' (Luke 3 : 16). Because a true and firm faith is, by water, baptized into salvation (*vera et stabilis fides aqua tinguitur in salutem*); but a feigned and infirm faith is, by fire, baptized into condemnation (*simulata autem et infirma, igni tinguitur in judicium*)."

To this passage the following note by Thomas Corbin, a Benedictine monk, born A.D. 1694, is attached: " *Spiritu et igni.* For so John says Luke 3 : 16 : ' I indeed baptize you with water: but one mightier than I cometh, he shall baptize you with the Holy Ghost and fire (*baptizabit in* SPIRITU SANCTO ET IGNI).' John certainly did not exclude *water* from the baptism of Christ, but he means only this, that his washing (*ablutionem*) was only simple, that is outward, by simple water (*simplici aqua*); but that washing in the future by the Baptism of Christ, would be exalted to a higher mystery and also to an inner washing (*ablutionem*) of the soul, which cannot be without the grace of the Holy Spirit. But many have been exercised as to the meaning of ' by the Holy Spirit and *fire*,' and moreover it has furnished occasion to some greatly to err. For there were some of the old heretics who thought that that *fire* should be understood simply and of our real fire, and therefore that fire, equally with water, should be used in baptism. Clemens Alex. says: ' Some (as Heracleon says) burned the ears of the sealed (*baptizatorum*).' And another (Carm. in Marcion. I) relates concerning a fire baptism of the heresiarch Valentinus, that he taught a double baptism, the body taken through the fire—*Bis docuit tingi, traducto corpore flamma.*

Augustine, also (De Hæres. ad Quodvult. hær., 59) relates, that the Seleucian heretics administered baptism (*igne*) by fire. Whatever may be true of these, it is certain that fire was never used by the Apostles for baptism, and therefore it was never commanded by Christ. Some Catholic Interpreters think more correctly, that by 'Spirit and fire' is indicated the baptism of Christ himself, upon whom the Holy Spirit came in the likeness of a dove, and at the same time, as Justin M. relates: 'When Jesus had descended to the water a fire was kindled in the Jordan.' But in our baptism an invisible fire is kindled, when the grace of the Holy Spirit glides into our hearts, and, as Ambrose says, consumes our sins and purges the soul from their defilement. Some understand (metaphorically) that sufferings and persecutions are indicated by 'fire,' as gold is tried by the furnace of fire. Basil thinks that the fire should be understood of the *word of doctrine*, which brings both condemnation and justification. But Tertullian expounds it of the day of judgment, of the fire of hell.

"The opinion of those who understand it literally of the descent of the Holy Spirit *in the form of fire*, not only upon the Apostles, but also upon their disciples, freshly baptized, pleases me: an illustrious example of which is furnished in Acts 11:11. The best meaning, plain and literal, of the words of John the Baptist seems to be this: ' I, indeed, with water' (*a sterile element, having in itself no power of grace*) 'baptize you.' But ' He shall baptize you' (*not with mere water but*) 'with the Holy Spirit' (*impregnating the water of Baptism in order to generate grace*, aquam Baptismi ad progenerandam gratiam fœcundante) 'and fire,' to wit, with the gifts of the Holy Spirit about to come, with fire, by the imposition of hands. And this fiery baptism (*baptismus igneus*) is that which Christ himself foretold in Acts 1:5, 8, which was fulfilled ten days afterward when Pentecost was fully come."

This note presents the view very commonly held by Patristic writers by one who was in perfect sympathy with their sentiments. There is no attempt to introduce a covering in fire, or in the Holy Spirit, or in water, as Christian baptism. Such an idea can no more be found in this statement than a plenum can be found in a vacuum. Water baptism is an external ablution (*ablutio*); Spirit baptism is an internal ablution (*ablutio*); Fire baptism is the touch of the ear by hot iron, or the kindling of a

flame in Jordan, or firelike tongues resting upon the head at
Pentecost.

The water, the Spirit, and the fire, are all (equally and alike)
agencies changing the spiritual condition and not receiving elements covering the body.

There is one error of interpretation presented in this note which
pervades and vitiates all Patristic Baptism. I refer to the introduction of water into that baptism which John said should be
executed by Christ. There is no scriptural authority whatever
for conjoining water with that baptism which is distinctively (ἐν
Πνεύματι) effected by Christ. John the Forerunner expressly and
with the profoundest emphasis excludes it—" I ἐν ὕδατι (invested
only with that power which belongs to water as a symbol) do
symbolly baptize you ; He, ἐν Πνεύματι (invested with that power
which belongs to the Spirit) will really, spiritually, by Divine
power, baptize you." In this difference he establishes the incom-
parable superiority of "the Coming One." John the Apostle
(John 4 : 2) carefully guards against this error by an express
separation between the baptizing of the disciples and their Lord.
In the promised execution of this baptism (Acts 1 : 5) the Lord
himself does, by severe contrast, exclude water from his personal
baptizing and does limit it to the Holy Spirit. In the actual
execution of this baptism (Acts 2 : 4) not only has water no
place, but its absence is emphasized by the presence of a wholly
diverse symbol—firelike tongues. In the second, formally announced execution of this baptism (Acts 10 : 44), no symbol whatever appears. And in the universal execution of this baptism
(1 Cor. 12 : 13) whereby the redeemed of all ages are made living
members of the body of Christ, the Holy Spirit appears alone
baptizing by his sole baptism all who are Christ's into that one
body whose head is Christ.

The error which incorporates water in the distinctive baptizing
of Christ is the πρωτον Ψευδος of Patristic theology on the subject
of baptism, robbing them of the Scripture symbol-baptism by
water, by impregnating that water (through the associated Spirit)
with a divine power to regenerate souls. The symbol-baptism is
thus swallowed up. Correct this error, eliminate water from the
baptism of Christ (ἐν Πνεύματι), and restore it to its scriptural
relation to the real baptism by the Holy Spirit as a symbol, exhibiting its purifying nature, and you will give to Patristic theology (as to the nature and power of Christian baptism) a true

scriptural character. Their philology as to the usage of βαπτίζω and βάπτισμα needs no correction. The theory but dreams when it stakes its life upon the usage of these terms as importing a dipping into water or a water covering. There is, in the ordinary Patristic baptism, a dipping of the head into water, and therefore a momentary covering, but these Greeks knew well that no dipping or momentary covering could be exponential of the meaning or the power in βαπτίζω and βάπτισμα, and therefore they never used the one or the other for any such purpose. The exposition of this dipping-covering must be sought elsewhere. I now only repeat, that the Patristic *baptisma* was not a physical covering but a spiritual condition. In proof of which see further these other fire-baptisms.

BASIL M., III, 1436 : " The baptism by fire (τὸ βάπτισμα ἐν τῷ πυρί) condemns sin and accepts the Righteousness of Christ."

So, also, *de S. S. ad Amphil.*, XXXV : " The baptism of fire is the trial which is made in the Judgment."

TERTUL., III, 1202 : " When the Holy Spirit had descended upon the disciples that they might be baptized by Him (*ut in illo baptizarentur*), tongues as of fire (*quasi ignis*) were seen sitting upon (*insidentes super*) each one, that it might be evident that they were baptized by the Holy Spirit and by fire (*Spiritu Sancto et in igne*), that is, by the Spirit (*in Spiritu*) which is fire, or like fire. To-day the Spirit is invisible to men; but in the beginning of the mystery of faith and of Spiritual baptism, this same Spirit was clearly seen and sat upon the disciples like fire: likewise he descended upon the Lord like a dove. . . . By which it is evident that souls are cleansed by the Spirit (*Spiritu ablui*, ' which is fire or like fire') that bodies are washed by water (*per aquam lavari*), also, that by blood (*sanguine*) we come more speedily, by compend (*per compendium*), to the rewards of salvation."

IRENÆUS, 685 : " But others of them seal (*signant* baptize (?)) their disciples, cauterizing the hinder part of the right ear."

ORIGEN, II, 517 : " One of the Seraphim touched his lips with a live coal from off the altar and said: ' Behold I have taken away thine iniquities.' This has a mystical meaning, and signifies that every one, according to his sin, who is worthy of purification, has coals of fire applied to his members. The prophet says, ' I have unclean lips,' therefore the coal is only applied to his lips. But I doubt whether we can excuse any member of the body from needing the fire." 519 : " Those like Isaiah are purged by fire

from the altar, but others are purged by another fire. . . . The fire
of the altar is the fire of the Lord. The fire which is not of the
altar is not the fire of the Lord, but of the sinner, of which it is
said: 'The worm shall not die, and the fire shall not be quenched.'"

AMBROSE, II, 1227: "'He that toucheth the dead body of a man
shall be unclean.' Numb. 19:11. . . . We live among the dead.
Therefore, the Author of life says, 'Let the dead bury their dead.'
. . . Whoever lives among sinners needs to be purified. Therefore
when Isaiah said (6:5, 7), 'Woe is me, for I have unclean lips,
and dwell among a people of unclean lips.' One of the Seraphim immediately descended and touched his lips with a burning
coal, that he might cleanse his unclean lips. Baptism is not only
one (non unum est baptisma). That is one which the Church
administers by water and the Holy Spirit (per aquam et Spiritum
sanctum), with which it is necessary that catechumens be baptized. And there is another baptism (aliud baptisma) of which
the Lord Jesus says, Luke 12:10, 'I have a baptism to be baptized with that ye know not of,' when, certainly, he had already
been baptized in the Jordan; but this is the baptism of suffering
(baptismum passionis), with which, also, every one is cleansed by
his own blood. There is, also, a baptism (baptismum) at the entrance of Paradise which formerly did not exist. But after the
sinner was shut out the fiery sword began to be, which God placed
(Gen. 3:24); which formerly was not, when sin was not. Sin
began and baptism began (Culpa cœpit et baptismum cœpit),
whereby they might be purified (purificentur) who desired to
return into Paradise. That having returned they may say, 'We
have passed over by fire and water' (Ps. 65:12). Here by water
(per aquam), there by fire (per ignem). By water (per aquam),
that sins may be washed away (abluantur), by fire (per ignem),
that they may be burned away (exurantur).

"Who is it that baptizes with this fire? Not a Presbyter, not
a Bishop, not John, who says, Matt. 3:11, 'I baptize you into
repentance (in pænitentiam);' not an Angel, not an Archangel,
not Principalities, nor Powers; but He of whom John says, 'He
that cometh after me—He shall baptize you by the Holy Spirit
and fire. He has his fan in his hand, and he will thoroughly
purge his floor; and gather the wheat into his garner; but he
will burn the chaff with unquenchable fire.' It is not concerning
this baptism, which is administered by priests of the Church, that
the Lord himself testifies, Matt. 13:49, 50, 'So shall it be at the

end of the world : the angels shall come forth, and sever the wicked from among the just, and shall cast them into the furnace of fire ;' since this baptism shall take place after the end of the world, the angels having been sent forth who shall separate the good and the bad, when iniquity shall be burned up by a furnace of fire (*per caminum ignis*) ; that the righteous may shine as the sun in the kingdom of God. And if any one be holy as Peter, or John, he shall be baptized by this fire (*baptizatur hoc igne*). Therefore the great Baptist (*Baptista* Purifier) (for so I name him, as Gabriel named him (Luke 1 : 15), ' He shall be great '), shall come, and shall see many standing at the entrance of Paradise, and shall wave the sword turning every way, and say to them on the right, not having heinous sins, ' Enter ye who fear not the fire.' For I foretold you, Isaiah 66 : 15, ' Behold I come as fire ;' and Ezek. 22 : 21, ' I will blow upon you with the fire of mine anger that ye may melt away from lead and iron.' Therefore consuming fire must come and burn up in us the lead of iniquity, the iron of transgression, and make us pure gold. But because he having been purged (*purgatus*), needs there to be purified (*purificari*) again, he will there, also, purify us, because the Lord will say : ' Enter into my rest,' so that every one of us having been burned (*ustus*) by that flaming sword, but not burned up (*exustus*), having entered into the blessedness of Paradise, may give thanks unto our Lord. This is one fire by which involuntary sins are burned up, which the Lord Jesus has prepared for his servants, that he may cleanse them from their long sojourning among the dead : that is another fire which he has appointed for the devil and his angels, of which he says, ' Depart into everlasting fire (*in ignem in æternum*).' "

AMBROSE III, 173–175: " The fire of the temple altar is said to have been hidden in a pit by the Jews when about to go into captivity, and on their return when sought for was found to be changed into water. This water when sprinkled by the order of Nehemiah upon the altar (*Necmias, sacerdos, aspergere super ligna, jussit*) burst into flames and consumed the sacrifice." This is said to be a type of Christian baptism. Also the water poured on the sacrifice by Elias (*hostiam suam tertio ipse perfudit aqua*) and the fire coming down from heaven consuming the sacrifice, is said to be a type of Christian baptism. In vindication of these type-fire baptisms, appeal is made to the fact that Christ baptizes by the Holy Spirit *and fire;* also, to the actual baptism by the Holy Spirit and *firelike* tongues.

BASIL IV, 132: "'He shall baptize you by the Holy Spirit and fire.' He calls the trial which shall take place in the judgment (πυρὸς βάπτισμα) the baptism of fire, according to the saying of the Apostle, 'The fire shall try the work of every one what it is.'"

EPIPHANIUS I, 372: "The disciples of Carpocras affix a seal (ἐν καυτῆρι) by a red-hot iron to the right lobe of the ear of those deceived by them."

JEROME V, 730: "'He placed a fiery sword and Cherubim to guard the way of the tree of life.' This sword guarding Paradise produces double suffering, both burning and cutting. Take an illustration. Physicians say, in order to cure some diseases, both burning and cutting are necessary. To those who suffer from an old cancer they apply the sharpest knife, whitened by heat, that the roots of the cancer may be destroyed by burning, and the putrid flesh removed by cutting, and so the way be prepared for healing remedies. Sin is our cancer for which neither the simple sharpness of the knife, nor the mere burning of the fire, is sufficient; but both are required, so that it may be burned and cut. Hear the Saviour in two passages indicating the need of fire and knife. In one place (Matt. 10) he says, 'I have not come to send peace upon earth but a sword;' and in another (Luke 12), 'I am come to send fire upon the earth.' Therefore the Saviour brings fire and sword, and baptizes (*baptizat*) those sins which could not be purified by the purification of the Holy Spirit (*quæ non potuerunt Spiritus sancti purificatione purgari*)."

These quotations fairly present the "fire baptisms" of these early writers. And if language is capable of expressing the opinions of men, then the language of these writers does express as their opinion that fire baptisms, as related to Christian baptism, are neither dippings nor coverings, but spiritual conditions effected by fire or firelike agencies, applied by *touching* or *striking*, *sprinkling* or *pouring*, etc., etc. And what is thus true of *fire* baptisms, is equally true of *tears'* baptisms, and of *blood* baptisms, as proved both by positive statements and by the impossibilities of any physical dippings or coverings, and the absurdity of their attempted imagination. The same is no less true of *water* baptisms. This conclusion is not so compulsory and patent as in the other baptisms, because in them there neither were in fact, nor could be by possibility, any dippings or coverings of human beings, while there could be a dipping and thus a momentary covering in water; and, in fact, there was so in the ordinary administration of water baptisms. But this momentary covering, by dipping or pressing down the head, was neither Christian baptism nor any essential element in it. There is not a Patristic writer who does not repudiate the idea that Christian baptism is a dipping or covering in water. There is not a Patristic writer who does not declare that Christian baptism is a purely spiritual condition. There is not a writer (holding distinctively Patristic sentiments) who does not affirm *that the water effects no baptism within the range of its own natural powers or qualities,* but *effects a* SPIRITUAL BAPTISM *by reason of a divine power communicated to it for this end,* WHICH BAPTISM *consists in the* REMISSION OF SINS *and* REGENERATION OF THE SOUL. There is no evidence whatever to show that these writers regarded the momentary dipping of the head into mere water as any baptism at all, heathen any more than Christian. There is the most absolute evidence to show that they regarded a baptism as necessarily precluding any designed (momentary) limitation of time. That these positions are true will now be further shown by a reference to Clinic baptisms.

Clinic Baptisms.

The theory has no kind word to say for Clinic baptisms. As "baby sprinkling" is an offence which it abhors, so Clinic sprinkling is a sham which it detests. In both these respects it is admittedly and rejoicingly out of sympathy with these early Christians, as it is equally, though denyingly, out of sympathy with them in their estimate of water-dipping in relation to Christian baptism.

The theorists hold Clinic baptism by sprinkling or pouring to be worthless, because it effects no water-covering, which is, and which only is, they say, the baptism commanded by Christ. The Patrists hold Clinic baptism by sprinkling or pouring to be of matchless worth, because water-covering does not enter (as an element) into that Divine power by which alone water has power Christianly to baptize, never dreaming of any command from Christ *to cover in simple water* as his baptism.

The theory antagonizes Patrism (no less than the Bible) at all points, as much in the matter of water-dipping as in water-sprinkling, whether on "crying babies" or dying Clinics.

The evidence of this will be found in the following quotations, in which "Compend baptisms" (as another name for Clinic baptisms) will also receive attention.

TERTULLIAN I, 1213: "We do not find that any of the Apostles were baptized in the Lord, except Paul. . . . Some think, not naturally, that they were adequately baptized when in the ship they were sprinkled (*aspersi*) by the waves; and that Peter himself was adequately baptized (*mersum*) by entering the sea. But as I think, it is one thing to be sprinkled by the violence of the sea, and another thing to be baptized by religious requirement. . . . Whether the Apostles were washed (*tincti*) in any way whatever (*quoquo modo*) or remained (*illoti*) unwashed, it is rash to doubt concerning their salvation, for a first call and familiar intercourse with Christ could confer Compend baptism."

Tertullian makes no objection to baptism by sprinkling; but he thinks it objectionable to substitute the sprinkling from a sea storm for a religious ordinance, in "whatsoever way" administered.

CYPRIAN, 1147: "Thou hast asked (—'Are the sick not washed but sprinkled with the saving water, to be regarded as true Christians?'—) what is my view of those who have obtained the grace of God in sickness and debility, whether, since they have not been washed by the saving water, but sprinkled (aqua salutari non loti sint, sed perfusi), they should be regarded as true Christians. We think that divine benefits can in nothing be diminished or enfeebled, nor can anything less be there where what is said of divine benefits is received with a full and perfect faith of the giver and receiver. For the pollutions of sins are not washed away (*abluuntur*) by the saving sacrament, as defilements of the skin and body are washed away by a carnal and secular washing (*lavacro*), so that an alkali, and other helps, both tub and pool, are needed, with which a little body may be washed and cleansed (*ablui et mundari*). The heart (*pectus*) of the believer is washed in another way, the soul (*mens*) of man is cleansed in another way, by the merits of faith. In the saving sacraments, necessity urging and God granting favor, divine compends (*divina compendia*) confer full grace upon believers. Nor should it trouble any one that the sick are seen to be sprinkled or to be poured upon (*aspergi vel perfundi*) when they obtain divine grace, when the Holy Scripture says, Ezek. 36 : 25, 26: 'I will sprinkle clean water upon you, and ye shall be cleansed from all your unclean-

ness, and from all your idols will I cleanse you, and will give a
new heart to you and a new spirit within you;' likewise in Numb.
19 : 8, 12, 13 : . . . 'He shall not be clean and that soul shall be
cut off from Israel, because the water of sprinkling (*aqua asper-
sionis*) was not sprinkled upon him.' And again, Numb. 8 : 5, 7:
'The Lord spake to Moses saying, . . . Thus shalt thou purify
them ; thou shalt sprinkle (*circumsperges*) them with the water
of purification.' And again, Numb. 19 : 9 : 'The water of sprinkling is purification.' Whence it appears that the sprinkling of
water (*aspersionem aquæ*) possesses equal value with the saving
washing (*salutaris lavacri*), and when these things are done in
the Church, where there is true faith of the receiver and giver, all
things may be established, completed, and perfected by the majesty
of God and the truth of faith. But that some call those who have
obtained the grace of Christ by the salutary water and true faith,
not Christians but Clinics, I do not know whence they take the
name, unless, perchance, they who have read much and the more
secret things of Hippocrates and Soranus, have found these
Clinics. For I who am acquainted with a Clinic in the Gospel
know that to that paralytic, lying for long years on his bed, his
sickness was no hindrance to his obtaining, in the fullest measure,
a heavenly vigor, nor was he, by divine favor, merely raised up
from his bed, but with renewed and quickened strength, he took
up the bed itself. And therefore, this is my opinion, that whosoever shall have obtained in the Church lawfully and rightly divine
grace, by faith, should be adjudged a true Christian. Or, if any
one thinks that they have obtained nothing, because they have
only been sprinkled or poured upon with the saving water, but
are empty and void, let them not be deceived, so as to be baptized if they recover from their sickness. But if they cannot be
baptized who have already been sanctified by Ecclesiastical baptism (*ecclesiastico baptismo*), why should they be reproached for
their faith and the favor of the Lord ? . . . They who are baptized in sickness (*qui ægri baptizantur*) receive no less measure
of the Holy Spirit, nor are more exposed to the influence of evil
spirits. The power of the devil only extends to the saving water,
there the devil is overwhelmed and man is set free. . . . Finally,
experience shows, that those baptized in sickness (*in ægritudine
baptizati*) under pressing necessity, both obtain grace and live
worthily in the Church, daily growing in grace. And on the other
hand some of those baptized in health (*qui sani baptizantur*) fall-

ing into sin are troubled by the return of an unclean spirit, so
that it is manifest that the devil cast out by faith in baptism, if
faith afterward should fail, returns. Unless it seem right to ad-
judge them baptized who have been polluted by profane water
out of the Church by enemies and antichrists, but these who are
baptized in the Church (*in Ecclesia baptizantur*) may be regarded
as having obtained less of favor and divine grace; and so great
honor be attributed to heretics, that those coming thence may not
be asked whether they have been washed or sprinkled (*utrumne
loti sint an perfusi*), whether Clinics or peripatetics, while we de-
tract from a true faith, and rob ecclesiastical baptism of its majesty
and sanctity."

There are points in this passage from Cyprian which claim
special attention as throwing clear and valuable light on our Inquiry: 1. The question has not its origin in philology but in
theology. It has not βαπτίζω as its pivot on the ground that
" this word expresses a divine command, has but one meaning
through all Greek literature, and means a modal act to be done,
to wit : dip and nothing but dip." So far from this, the word βαπτίζω does not appear in the inquiry, and the word which does appear (*lavo, loti sunt*) is admitted not to express modal act, that on
which the life of the theory turns. If the question had turned on
βαπτίζω, and the Interrogator and Respondent had believed (as
we are told that they did believe) that this word expressed modal
act (dip), and embodied a divine command, then the question,
" Are sprinkled men dipped men ?" could never have been asked;
but neither of these parties believed that God had commanded a
modal act, or that βαπτίζω expressed a modal act, and therefore
they substitute for it a word (*lavo*) in which there is no modal act
of command, and philology becomes a vanishing quantity. The
question is purely theological. There is no reference to the meaning of a word, to dip or to cover ; but to the divine power of water
to change the spiritual condition of the soul. " Can baptizing
water, which when used for washing the whole body makes a true
Christian, also, make a true Christian when it is sprinkled or
poured upon the body?" this was the theological question ; 2.
The answer is as empty of philology and as full of theology as is
the question. It declares that baptizing water impregnated with
the Spirit washes spiritually, and not as the body is washed with
soap, and tub, and pool. It is not the water which washes, but a
divine power in the water. The impregnated water not by its

quantity, nor by its manner of use, but by its quality—*vis, virtus,* δύναμις—confers the full grace of the Spirit—remits sin, regenerates the soul, expels dæmons, drowns Satan, makes a "true Christian;" 3. The sprinkling of baptizing water has no more power to dip, or to cover than any other water; and Cyprian does not say that sprinkling dips or covers, for he was not a simpleton, but he does say again and again, that sprinkling baptizes. He applies this word alike to the sick and their mode of baptism and to the well and their mode of baptism—" qui *ægri* BAPTIZANTUR—qui *sani* BAPTIZANTUR." Sprinkling water does Cyprianly baptize; sprinkling water does under no condition dip; therefore, Cyprian's baptize is not *dip;* 4. As Cyprian calls baptism by sprinkling "Compend baptism," and "Ecclesiastical baptism," the theory talks wildly, in the use of words without knowledge, about the unrealness and worthlessness of such baptisms. All such might find it to their advantage to read, on this point, the gentle philippic of President Halley addressed to Dr. Carson, or better still to read the originals, and there learn that Compend baptism always includes the *baptism* whatever else may be absent, and that Ecclesiastical baptism includes that *sine qua non* (the Holy Spirit) without which the presence of all other things is worthless to effect Patristic baptism.

This answer of Cyprian declaring that sprinkling or pouring, equally with the washing of the whole body, effected Christian baptism was so convincing that a like question, so far as I know, never emerged for a thousand years. In these latter days a very different question (with some verbal similarities) has emerged for the first time since the origin of Christianity, in which by the invocation of philology (seen through a glass darkly) to prove that βαπτίζω means " dip and nothing but dip," that it represents a divine command to dip *into water,* and that early Greek Christian writers believed (?) these things, it is sought to establish the remarkable proposition, that "to sprinkle is not to dip," and therefore one sprinkled with water is not dipped into water, and therefore, living in disobedience to God, and therefore, is not a "true Christian," and therefore, must not come to the table of the Lord. Whenever the friends of this theory shall show outside of the Bible, that βαπτίζω means "to dip," or inside of the Bible that it means "to dip *into water,*" or anywhere in the Patristic writings that they believed either of these propositions, then, they will deserve an attentive audience. But until then the theory must be set down as among the latest and the chiefest of " the novelties in our theology " emerging for the first time in the history of Christianity after the lapse of a thousand and a half thousand years. Let it be understood, that the question of fact as to the customary covering of the body in water is not now at issue (any more than in the question propounded to Cyprian), but the ground and the value of that fact.

TERTUL. III, 1203: The passage about to be cited on " Compend baptism " is from an anonymous writer on Rebaptism in the same volume with that of the passage from Cyprian, and containing a portion of Tertullian's works. After referring to the forgiveness of sins granted by the Lord to the paralytic and to the woman that was "a sinner," he adds: " From all which it is shown, that hearts are purified by faith (*fide mundari*), but souls are cleansed by the Spirit (*Spiritu ablui*); but moreover bodies are washed by water (*per aquam lavari*), also, by blood (*sanguine*), we come more speedily to the rewards of salvation, by Compend (*per Compendium*)." Here are four baptisms *by* faith (*fide*) *by* the Spirit (*Spiritu*) *by* water (*per aquam*) and *by* blood (*sanguine*), in every one of which (faith, Spirit, water, blood) is declared to be an agency, and the mode of application in some instances (faith, Spirit), a vanishing quantity, and in others (water, blood), indifferent, or as diverse as any two modes could well be. While the Baptism of blood, especially referred to as a " Compend baptism," is here and everywhere referred to as the most perfect and glorious of all baptisms, instead of (as the theory would have it) a *non est*.

BASIL III, 436 : " Why dost thou delay that baptism (τὸ βάπτισμα) may be to thee the gift of a fever? When thou mayest be unable to speak the saving words, or, perhaps, to hear clearly, or to raise thy hands to heaven; or to stand upon thy feet, or to bend the knees for prayer." . . .

Was such a one, unable to speak or hear or stand or kneel, dipped into water? He received "the baptism (τὸ βάπτισμα), without an appended " Clinic," or " Compend," or " Ecclesiastic." Will this answer for a baptism by sprinkling, a baptism not physical, a spiritual baptism, effected by spiritual power given to the water? Basil the Great had some knowledge of Greek. He knew the meaning of the Patristic τὸ βάπτισμα.

AUGUSTIN VI, 469 : " Catechumens afflicted by disease or casualty, so that while they still live are yet unable to ask for baptism (*baptismum*) or to answer questions, should be baptized (*baptizentur*)."

AUGUSTIN IX, 121: "A man may wickedly hate his enemy, yet, alarmed by the sudden danger of death, he asks for baptism (*baptismum*), which he receives with so much haste, that the danger hardly admits the necessary asking of a few questions, so that that hatred may be driven from his heart, even if it be known to him who baptizes (*baptizanti*) him. Certainly these things do not cease to occur both among us and among them (Donatists)."

EUSEBIUS II, 621: "Novatian, relieved by the Exorcists, having fallen into a dangerous disease, and thinking that he was about to die, having been poured upon (περιχυθεὶς) in the bed where he lay, received (ἔλαβεν); if indeed it be proper to say that such a one received (τὸν τοιοῦτον εἰληφέναι). Nor, when he recovered, did he attain those other things which it is necessary to receive according to the rule of the church, and to be sealed (σφραγισθῆναι) by the Bishop. And not receiving this how could he receive the Holy Spirit? . . . Through the favor of the bishop, laying hands upon him, he was made a presbyter, when all the clergy and many of the laity opposed, because it was not lawful that one poured upon (περιχυθέντα), as he was, upon a sick-bed, should be received into the rank of the clergy."

An attempt has been made to discredit this Clinic baptism as unreal in itself and invalid in the judgment of those interested in it at the time. The attempt proceeds on misconception of the case. Parties interested in this transaction did file exceptions to it, but on no ground common with the theory. The first and main exception taken related to the moral character of Novatian. This is expressed by the derogatory phrase—"such a one τὸν τοιοῦτον." They believed him to be a bad man, under the influence of the devil both before and after his baptism, and therefore said, "Being poured upon *he received*, *if* SUCH A ONE *could receive*." Receive what? A dipping? So the theory must make them speak; but these men were not idiots, and knowing that he had received water by pouring, they did not express a doubt as to whether he had in *a pouring* received *a dipping*. The theory believes, that a bad man dipped into water by one of their ministers receives as perfect a baptism as the greatest saint. These early Christians had no such faith. They did not believe that Simon Magus, however the water was used, "received" any more than Novatian. The question with them was not whether a

pouring upon with water or a dipping into water had been "received;" but whether *the Holy Spirit* had been "received." This
was the *sine qua non* with their baptism; and it was just here
that a doubt whether "such a one could receive," was expressed.
This exception was intensified by another (in the same direction,
of bad character) namely: that he had not gone to the bishop
after his recovery, to be "sealed;" when, again, was pressed the
point of difficulty—"How could he receive *the Holy Spirit?*"
Exception, also, was taken to his being received into the ministry;
not because water had been *poured* upon and therefore he was
not baptized; but because this had been done "on a sick-bed,"
and the rule of the Church forbade any such from being inducted
into the ministry. But why? Because such were not *baptized?*
Such a reason would have been the most absolute self-stultifica-
tion of the Church, which declared, through a millenary of years,
that she did thus administer a perfect baptism; but the Church
objected to the postponement of baptism until death for various
reasons and, as a deterring penalty, denied to such access to the
ministry. The theory reverses this: men not dipped (only
poured upon) are received to all the rights of the ministry but
excluded from the rights of private members, at the communion
table. No exception was taken to Novatian's baptism because
the water was poured upon him. This is evident from the narrative and from the fact, that nowhere in the Patristic writings can
an objection be found to a Christian baptism grounded on the
fact, that the water used in it was by pouring. On the contrary,
Cyprian formally defends sprinkling and pouring upon the sick
as true and perfect baptism. Some objections to Clinic baptism,
not as to form and worth but as to time and circumstance, are
thus presented by

CHRYSOSTOM II (*pars prior*), 223: "I not only declare you
happy, but I praise your wisdom because you have come for baptism (φωτίσματι), not like more careless men at the last breathings
of life, but promptly as wise servants ready with good will to
obey the Lord, submitting the neck of the soul with gentleness
and desire to the yoke of Christ. For although the gifts of grace
τὰ τῆς χάριτος are the same to you and to them baptized (μυσταγω-
γουμένοις) at death, yet as to will and preparation the things are
not the same. For they receive (the gifts of grace τὰ τῆς χάριτος)
in the bed, but you in the bosom of the Church, the common
mother of us all; they grieving and weeping, but you joyous and

happy; they groaning but you praising; they stupefied by great fever, but you filled with great spiritual delight. Consequently, here, all things are harmonious with the gift (τῇ δωρεᾷ), but there all things are discordant with the gift (τῇ δωρεᾷ); for those about to be baptized (μυσταγωγουμένων), and children, and wife, and friends, and servants, are weeping and lamenting. . . . But I have not yet added the chiefest of the evils; for in the midst of the lamentations and preparations, oftentimes, the soul, leaving the body desolate, has fled away, and when present in many cases profits nothing. . . . For he who is about to be baptized (φωτίζεσθαι) lies like a log or a stone, knowing nothing, hearing nothing, answering nothing, differing nothing from a dead man: of what profit is the baptism (τῆς μυσταγωγίας) in such insensibility?"

It was in view of such a condition of things as here portrayed by Chrysostom that the Church urged prompt baptism in health and opposed its delay until death; but believing it necessary to salvation it was administered, in ordinary circumstances, to the sick and the dying in the full conviction of its reality and efficacy as a baptism. Whether the efficacy of the water reached to the souls of the dying who lay " as a log or a stone" was an unsettled point. But from the days of Cyprian it had been settled that the divinely impregnated water poured or sprinkled on the body, did in the truest and fullest manner initiate, illuminate, baptize, so that the Clinic, equally with the Peripatetic, did receive not a substitute for but identically the same *baptisma;* the same τὰ τῆς χάριτος (elsewhere (226) τὸ λουτρὸν τῆς χάριτος), which consisted in a spiritual renovation, = the forgiveness of sins and regeneration of the soul. A physical baptisma has no place in Patrism. Nor is it true, that a dipping (a designed momentary covering in water) is any more truly a physical βάπτισμα, than is a pouring or a sprinkling. The essential element of duration without limitation of time, is wanting, and consequently the element of power and controlling influence which inheres in βαπτίζω as compared with βάπτω is wanting, just as much as in pouring or sprinkling. But as βάπτω loses its feebleness and changes its nature amid liquids to which a power to dye, to color, has been imparted (which power may be developed through sprinkling or pouring, or dipping), so βαπτίζω, among liquids (water, tears, blood, etc.) to which is imparted a divine power assumes a new nature, and represents that power as developed by dipping (which in simple water does not baptize), pouring, or sprinkling, by either of which (according to Patrism) it is equally developed, but, according to the Scriptures, is equally *symbolized* by either pouring or sprinkling (dipping being excluded by unbroken silence), while the divine power to effect the βάπτισμα (always and solely spiritual) is limited in the most absolute manner to the Holy Spirit.

This passage of Chrysostom explains why Clinics were excluded from the ministry. It was not because such were not baptized or not fully baptized; but because they acted against the teachings of the Church by their delay, and it became questionable whether it was not the fear of death, rather than repentance and faith, which made them seek for baptism.

AMBROSE IV, 471: "There are not wanting sick persons who are baptized, almost daily *Non desint, qui prope quotidie baptizantur ægri.*"

This statement of Ambrose shows that baptisms by sprinkling and pouring (not *quasi* or *e gratia* baptisms but baptisms regarded as real and perfect in nature as baptisms under any form) were administered almost daily century after century. In none of these baptisms was there or could there be a physical water covering, and therefore in such Christian baptisms as a water covering was found the baptism could not be in this feature, otherwise where it had no existence there could be no baptism. These diverse cases to which, equally, the term baptism is applied is alone and is perfectly explained by the truth that the Patristic baptisma was no physical covering, but a spiritual condition effected by water (irrespective of modal use) impregnated with a divine power.

Sprinkling Baptisms.

As Clinic baptisms were by sprinkling I will adduce other cases of baptism by sprinkling to show that they are not limited to Clinics.

TERTULLIAN I, 1204: "But the nations without the knowledge of spiritual things, attribute the same efficacy to their idols, but with unmarried (*viduis* empty) waters, they deceive themselves. They everywhere purify villas, houses, temples, and whole cities by sprinkling water, and are washed (*tinguntur*) in the spectacles of Apollo and Eleusis. . . . Here we see the work of the devil emulating the things of God, since he practices even baptism among his own people."

These "unmarried, empty, waters" point to the all-controlling element in the interpretation of Patristic baptism, namely, *the impartation of a divine quality to the water by which it receives* POWER to baptize. If Patristic baptism were a water covering, the idea that water needed a new quality in order to have *power* TO COVER, would be lunacy; but without such superadded power, they declare, that water cannot Christianly baptize, therefore, if these writers are not lunatics, Patristic baptism is not a water covering. Tertullian announces this new quality as communicated to the waters in the following terms: "Supervenit enim statim Spiritus de cœlis, et aquis superest, sanctificans eas de semetipso, et ita sanctificatæ vim sanctificandi combibunt. For immediately the Spirit comes from heaven and brooding upon the waters, sanctifies them by Himself, and so having been sanctified they imbibe the power of sanctifying." The same thing is referred to in the following lines quoted in a note:

"Sanctus in hunc cœlo descendit Spiritus amnem,
Cœlestique sacras fonte maritat aquas."

If any object to the translation of "*tinguntur*" by washed, purified, they are referred to Ovid, "Ignibus et sparsâ *tingere* corpus aquâ." And for a new power being communicated to water, enabling it to exercise such power toward other objects, the same Classic says: "Et incerto fontem medicamine *tixit*." A dipping has nothing to do with *tingo* in either of these cases.

TERTULL. II, 736: "Where are those whom Menander has sprinkled (*perfudit*)? Or those whom he has mersed into his Styx (*in Stygam suam mersit*)?"

The Annotator remarks: "Mersion (*mersio*), perfusion (*perfusio*) or aspersion (*aspersio*) belong, equally, to Christian baptism. The one by rule (*ex ordine*) for the well; the other by necessity (*ex necessitate*) for the sick. . . . It should be observed, that it was usual in baptism both to sprinkle and to cover (*baptismo perfundi solitos simul et mergi*). Sprinkling or pouring (*perfusio*) indicated the washing from sins (*lavationem peccatorum*); covering (*mersio*) death and burial, codeath and coburial, with Christ."

IRENÆUS, 664: "But some of them say, to conduct to the water (ἐπὶ τὸ ὕδωρ) is unnecessary, and mixing together oil and water (with some words, such as we have mentioned), they sprinkle (ἐπιβάλλουσι) it upon the head of the baptized (τελειουμένων)."

These were heretics; but they were not charged with heresy because they baptized by sprinkling.

AMBROSE I, 875: "Sprinkle me with hyssop and I shall be clean; wash me and I shall be whiter than snow" (Ps. 51:10). "He asks to be cleansed by hyssop according to the Law; he desires to be washed according to the Gospel. He who wished to be cleansed by typical baptism (*typico baptismate*) was sprinkled with the blood of the lamb by a bunch of hyssop."

AMBROSE IV, 829: "He sprinkled the leper seven times, with cedar wood, and scarlet wool, and hyssop, and he was rightly cleansed. . . . By the cedar wood the Father, by the hyssop the Son, by the scarlet wool (which has the brightness of fire) the Holy Spirit is represented. He who wished to be rightly cleansed was sprinkled by these three; because no one can be cleansed from the leprosy of sin by the water of baptism, except by the invocation of the Father, and the Son, and the Holy Spirit. . . . We are represented by the leper."

HILARY I, 338: "Ziphæi in Hebrew signifies what we call sprinkling of the face (*oris adspersio*). But sprinkling according to the Law was the cleansing from sin (*emundatio peccatorum*). The sprinkling of blood purifying the people through faith. Of this sprinkling David speaks: 'Sprinkle me with hyssop and I shall be clean,' representing the sacrament of the future sprinkling of the blood of the Lord."

JEROME V, 341: "Ezek. 36:16, et seq. 'I will pour out or sprinkle (*effundam sive aspergam*) upon you clean water, and ye shall be cleansed from all your defilements. And I will give you a new heart and I will put a right spirit within you.' . . . I will pour out the clean water of saving baptism. . . . And it is to be considered, that a new heart and a new spirit may be given by the pouring out and sprinkling of water (*per effusionem et aspersionem aquæ*). . . . And I will no more pour out upon them the waters of saving baptism, but the waters of doctrine and of the word of God."

AUGUSTINE IX, 202: "In the Epistle which Cyprian wrote to Magnus when asked concerning the Baptism of the dipped and the sprinkled, whether there was any difference (*de Baptismo tinctorum et perfusorum, utrum aliquid interesset*) ?"

This form of stating the question addressed to Cyprian conclusively settles the point, that the mode of using the water as between dipping, or pouring, or sprinkling, was not involved. For to ask whether there was any difference between dipping, pouring, sprinkling, is absurd. It is no less conclusively settled, that "Baptismo" as used by Augustine does not mean *a dipping*. It is beyond all possibility that Augustine should say, "Cyprian was asked whether there was any difference in the dipping of the dipped and the sprinkled." And it is as certainly settled, that "Baptismo" expresses the spiritual effect of the impregnated water in the soul, and whether there is any difference in that effect when such water is used by dipping, or pouring, or sprinkling, is asked.

If Patristic writers wrote to be understood, they believed that sprinkling and pouring baptizing water did baptize; but sprinkling and pouring no kind of water can *dip*, therefore the Patristic "baptize" cannot be *dip*.

As there is an essential relation between Sprinkling baptisms and Pouring baptisms I will point out one of this latter class in further proof of the point before us, namely, that baptisms are not physical coverings.

Pouring Baptism.

In 3 KINGS 18 : 34 (*Sept.*): Elijah commands four water-pots of water to be taken and poured upon (ἐπιχέετε) the sacrifice laid upon the newly made altar. This command he repeats again and again, and it is done thrice. This water pouring without a water covering is declared by Origen, Basil M., Gregory N., and Ambrose, to be a Baptism, as shown by the following quotations:

ORIGEN IV, 241: "But why is it believed that the coming Elias will baptize (βαπτίσειν), when he did not baptize (βαπτισάντος) what needed cleansing (λουτροῦ) upon the wood of the altar, in the time of Ahab, that it might be burned when the Lord revealed himself by fire? For he commanded the priests to effect this baptism. How, then, is he coming to baptize (βαπτίζειν) who did not then baptize? Christ does not baptize with water, but his disciples; but he reserves for himself the baptizing by the Holy Spirit and fire."

The facts in this case are so simple, so clear, so unmixed with anything which could admit of " darkening counsel by words without knowledge," that it is a matter of universal admission, that here was a case of baptism (so declared by one of the most learned Christian Greeks that ever lived) and in this baptism there was no physical covering, although the baptism was by water.

In this transaction there was, also, a λουτρόν; but there was no "bathing-place," no "water for a bath," no "laver," but there was *a cleansing* from ceremonial impurity for the revelation of the Lord by fire. And it was this cleansing (λουτρόν) which was the baptism (βάπτισμα); the one word taken as the full equivalent of the other, here and times without number elsewhere, by these early writers.

BASIL M. III, 428: "Elias has shown the power of baptism (τὴν ἰσχὺν τοῦ βαπτίσματος) by burning the sacrifice upon the altar of burnt offerings, not by means of fire, but by means of water. For although the nature of fire is opposed to that of water, yet when the water is mystically poured, thrice, upon the altar, the fire begins and kindles a flame, as though it were oil."

The specialty of this passage of Basil as compared with that of Origen is, its bringing out a new quality given to the water enabling it to burn when mystically poured (μυστικῶς κατεχύθη) thrice. Does any one doubt that an effect is here ascribed to water beyond and inconsistent with its natural power, by reason of a new and diverse quality imparted to it? But it is just such a quality which is declared to be imparted to baptizing water, giving it a power, alien from its own nature, to baptize (not to cover, this it has by inherent quality, but) to cleanse from, "to burn up" sin in the soul. The "three mystical *pourings*" ally the transaction with the customary "three mystical *dippings*" which effect the "*one* Baptism" purifying the soul. A dipping is no more truly a baptism than is a pouring. And the Patrists no more imagined a dipping to be a baptism, or the three dippings to be the one Christian baptism, than Origen imagined the three pourings to be the Carmel baptism. The baptisma was a "result, condition, effect," of a power attributed to the water by special divine gift, developed in the one case by pouring and in the other case by dipping; but in neither case being the dipping or the pouring, nor in anywise dependent upon the one form or the other. The baptizing power was wholly and solely in the impregnated water.

GREGORY NAZ. II, 421: "I have three overflowings (ἐπικλύσεις) with which I will purify (καθιερώσω) the sacrifice, kindling fire by water (ὕδατι), which is most paradoxical; and casting down the prophets of shame using *the power* of the mystery."

Gregory is writing upon baptism, and especially magnifying, to those about to be baptized, the doctrine of the Trinity. In reference to this doctrine and its power he says: "I have three stones

which I will sling against the enemy. I have three breathings
with which I will give life to the dead. I have three overflowings
with which (αἶς) I will purify," etc. The "three stones," the
" three breathings," the " three overflowings," are identified with
the Trinity, from which they are represented as obtaining a power
not inherent in the nature of a stone, or a breathing, or an overflowing, and by which they are made divine agencies to accomplish
what otherwise they were incompetent or unadapted to accomplish. The stone, the breathing, the overflowing, were not receiving
elements into which Goliath, " the dead," the altar, were to pass,
but vehicles through which divine power was displayed. The
transaction on Carmel is identified by Gregory with Christian
baptism, and its water is made an agency, and not a passive
covering element.

AMBROSE I, 727 : "Baptism like a fire consumes sins, for Christ
baptizes by fire and the Spirit. You read this type in the Books
of the Kings (3 Kings 18:34), where Elias put wood upon the
altar, and said that they should throw (*mitterent*) over it water
from water-pots (*de hydriis*); and when the water flowed Elias
prayed, and fire came down from heaven. Thou, O man! art
upon the altar, who shalt be cleansed (*ablueris*) by water, whose
sin is burned up, that thy life may be renewed. . . . John baptized
into repentance (*in pœnitentiam*), and all Judea gathered together.
Christ baptizes by the Spirit (*in Spiritu*); Christ gives grace, and
men reluctantly assemble. Elias showed but a type of baptism
(*typum baptismatis*) and opened heaven, which had been shut for
three years and six months. How much greater blessings belong
to the real baptism (*veritatis*)."

Ambrose identifies the baptism of Elias, and the baptism of
Christ, as type and antitype. It is absurd to say that one thing
is the type of some other thing, when there is nothing in the
declared type correspondent with the essential characteristic of
the declared antitype. Now, the theory says, that the essential
characteristic of Christian baptism (that without which it is no
baptism) is the covering in water by dipping; but in the transaction on Carmel there is neither covering in water nor a dipping;
therefore it is absurd to say that that in which there is nothing,
answering to that which is the essence of some other thing, can
be the type of that thing. But Ambrose declares that there is a
typical relation between these things; and he further declares
that this typical relation is found in the baptism which is common

to both; that in both baptisms there was a victim, the bullock upon the altar corresponding with the man laid upon the altar of faith (*tu es homo super altare*); that the water and fire of Elias correspond with the "Spirit and fire" of Christ; and as the water invested with the power of fire burned up the victim, and stones, and wood, so the water of Christian baptism impregnated with the power of the Holy Spirit does as a fire burn up sin in the soul. The βάπτισμα on Carmel was no water-covering; it was a type-ceremonial purification, having its antitype in the βάπτισμα of Christianity, in which there is no water-covering, but a real spiritual purification. Thus Ambrose has his justification, and the theory has its condemnation.

There is another altar baptism very analogous to this, in which both sprinkling and pouring appear as the forms under which the baptism is effected. To this we will now briefly refer.

Sprinkling and Pouring Baptism.

2 Maccabees 1:20–36, "They found no fire but thick water. Then commanded he to take it up by dipping and bring it; and when the sacrifices were laid on, Nehemiah commanded the priests to sprinkle (ἐπιρῥάναι) with the water (τῷ ὕδατι) both the wood and that which lay upon it. When this was done, and the time came that the sun shone, which afore was hid in the cloud, there was a great fire kindled, so that every man marvelled. . . . Now, when the sacrifice was consumed, Nehemiah commanded the water that was left to be poured (κατασχεῖν) upon the great stones. When this was done there was kindled a flame; but it was consumed by the light which shone from the altar. . . . It was told the king of Persia that Nehemiah had purified (ἥγνισαν) the sacrifices therewith. And Nehemiah called this thing *Naphthar*, which interpreted is Purification (καθαρισμός)."

Ambrose III, 174: "The narrative of the preceding event" (see Levit. 9:24), "and especially the sacrifice offered by Nehemiah, betokens the Holy Spirit and Christian baptism (Christianorum baptisma). I think that we cannot be ignorant as to this fire, since we learn that the Lord Jesus baptizes by the Holy Spirit and fire. What, then, means the fire was made water, and the water kindling a fire, except that spiritual grace by fire burns, and by water cleanses our sins?

"Fire also in the times of Elias descended. . . . He

cleansed the victim (*hostiam suam perfudit*) thrice with water (*aqua*), and the water flowed around the altar, and they cry out, and fire fell from the Lord out of heaven and consumed the burnt offering. Thou art that victim (*hostia illa tu es*)."

Ambrose declares this sprinkling and pouring (not as simple forms of action, but forms of action conveying to the victim and the altar a fluid possessed of a power capable of purifying and consuming by fire the one and the other) to be a type baptism significant of Christian baptism, wherein the Holy Spirit, as fire, communicates to the water a power to burn up sin and to purify the soul.

In this transaction, as in that on Carmel, there is no appearance of a dipping or a covering; the appearance of either is excluded by the declared presence and action of sprinkling and pouring. How, in the presence of these baptized sacrifices and altars, any one can say that to baptize is to dip and nothing but dip, and baptism is a water-covering, is inconceivable. It must be set down as a marvel of marvels among all the marvellous workings of the human intellect. But, on the other hand, we point to these type baptisms as absolute demonstration that the βάπτισμα of the Patrists had nothing whatever to do with a physical covering; while it did ever express a thorough change of condition, and in connection with Christian baptism (whether in type or antitype) a thorough change of condition by a purifying agency, which therefore assimilated the condition of the object to its own characteristic.

While sprinkling and pouring appear in these baptisms, it must not be supposed that they are necessary to a baptism. A baptism has no exclusive dependence on sprinkling, pouring, or dipping. Because the theory (most erroneously) says, " To baptize is to dip, and to dip is to baptize," its friends conclude and argue (just as erroneously) that others say, to baptize is to sprinkle or to pour, and to sprinkle or to pour is to baptize. Such is not our faith. We do not believe that βαπτίζω means either to sprinkle or to pour. But we do believe that these are modes of action (among others) whereby the requirement of βαπτίζω (in its religious applications to which βάπτισμα is limited) is perfectly effected.

In proof that neither dipping, nor pouring, nor sprinkling, are necessary to a baptism, we will turn our attention to some cases in which neither of them appears.

Baptisms without Dipping, Pouring, or Sprinkling.

CLEMENS ROMANUS, 797 : " Thou, therefore, O Bishop, wilt anoint, after this manner, the head of the baptized, whether men or women, with the holy oil, as a type of the spiritual baptism (εἰς τύπον τοῦ πνευματικοῦ βαπτίσματος)."

In this type head-anointing baptism dipping cannot exist; pouring or sprinkling may have place but only of accident and not of necessity. This oil is not the type of any *action*, but of a result, effect, the new condition of the soul invested with spiritual endowments—the βάπτισμα resultant from the influence of the Holy Spirit. Of this result rich in gift and grace, a fragrant unguent applied to the head is a manifest type—a type baptism. As the type of an act—dipping, pouring, sprinkling, it is nonsense.

837 : " He that is reckoned worthy of martyrdom, let him rejoice in the Lord, as attaining such a crown and dying through confession, and if he should be but a Catechumen " (therefore unbaptized) " let him die without sorrow, for the suffering (τὸ πάθος) which is for Christ will be to him a truer baptism (γνησιώτερον βαπτισμα)."

In this baptism there is neither dipping, pouring, or sprinkling, and yet there is a baptism more real, genuine, legitimate, truer, than the baptism by water. Such a statement is absurdly false if βάπτισμα be a physical covering; it is patently true if it be a condition of soul resultant from the influence of the Holy Spirit.

Circumcision Baptism. JUSTIN MARTYR, 516 : " Wash you and be clean, and put away iniquities from your souls, as God commands you to wash this washing (λούσασθαι τοῦτο τὸ λουτρόν) and to circumcise the true circumcision. . . . This circumcision of the flesh is not necessary for all, but for you only. For we have not received that profitless baptism which is of cisterns (τῶν λάκκων), for it is worthless (οὐδὲν) compared with this baptism of life. Therefore God has exclaimed, because ye have left Him the living fountain and have hewn out for yourselves broken cisterns (λάκκους) which cannot hold water. And you, indeed, who have been circumcised as to the flesh need our circumcision ; but we, having this, have no need of that. . . . 537 : What need, then, have I of circumcision having received witness from God ? What need is there of that baptism (ἐκείνου τοῦ βαπτίσματος) for me, who have been baptized by the Holy Spirit (ἁγίῳ Πνεύματι βε βαπτισμένῳ)?"

Justin uses "broken cisterns" (λάκκους συντετιμμένους), as Isaiah does, to represent all worthless substitutes, for God and his life-giving blessing. Among these substitutes he places fleshly circumcision, which he calls a baptism because it was for typical purification, but being taken for real purification to the rejection of the true (that of the heart), Justin pronounces it (in this aspect) to be a "broken cistern"—a worthless baptism to them and one of which he has no need, being baptized by the Holy Spirit, which is the antitype circumcision.

It is unnecessary to say, that while in circumcision baptism there is the most impressive exhibition of the necessity for purification, there is no exhibition of a dipping, or pouring, or sprinkling.

Baptism of water as an element. TERTULL. III, 1082: "We judge that no one can be baptized (by heretics) out of the Catholic Church, baptism being one and existing only in the Catholic Church. For it is written: 'They have forsaken me the fountain of living waters and have hewn out for themselves broken cisterns which cannot hold water.' It is necessary, also, that the water be purified (καθαρίζεσθαι) and sanctified first by the priest, that it may be able by its own baptism (τῷ ἰδίῳ βαπτίσματι) to cleanse the sins of the baptized man (τοῦ βαπτιζομένου ἀνθρώπου). For the Lord says, through the prophet Ezekiel; 'And I will sprinkle you (ῥαντίσω) with *pure* water (καθαρῷ ὕδατι), and will purify you (καθαρῶ), and will give you a new heart, and will give a new spirit within you.' And how can a man being himself impure (ἀκάθαρτος) and the Holy Spirit not with him, purify (καθαρίσαι) and sanctify water? The Lord saying in Numbers: 'All things which the impure man shall touch shall be impure,' how then, can he by baptizing remit sins to another when he cannot out of the Church remit his own sins?"

This is the doctrine and argument of Cyprian and of the Council of Carthage represented by him, showing that water itself must be baptized before it can baptize, which baptism of water consists neither in its being dipped, nor poured, nor sprinkled, but in a thorough change of its condition by purification and sanctification, whereby it secures a new power by which it is able to baptize, *i. e.*, to purify and sanctify. This water with a new quality, now becomes ὕδωρ καθαρον, and its new power is developed (although not obtained) by sprinkling, and therefore (as Cyprian argues) The Lord says: " I will sprinkle (ῥαντίζω) you καθαρῷ ὕδατί with the purified, baptized and therefore baptizing, purifying water." This is Patristic doctrine on the subject of baptism (developed in a thousand ways) and it carries the theory away, as by a whirlwind, beyond their sympathy or recognition.

Painting Baptism. CHRYSOSTOM (*pars prior*, 2) 235. " Do as painters in painting the likenesses of kings. Before the true color is put on they remove and repaint without restraint, correcting errors, and taking away imperfections ; but after they have put on the proper color (τὴν βαφὴν) they are no longer masters to change and to repaint, lest the beauty of the likeness be injured. Thus do: regard your soul as a likeness. Therefore before the true color of the Spirit (τὴν ἀληθῆ τοῦ Πνεύματος βαφὴν) is laid upon it, blot out your evil practices, whether swearing, or lying, or rioting, or evil speaking, or any other unlawful practice, that you may not return to it again after baptism. The washing (τὸ λουτρὸν) makes sins disappear, do thou correct the practice, that the colors (τῶν χρωμάτων) being laid on, and the royal likeness shining forth, you may not afterward blot out and mar the beauty given to thee by God."

This comparison of baptism to a royal portrait, by Chrysostom, brings out the feature of assimilation which Basil says belongs to baptism. Baptism is not merely a thorough change of condition, but it is such a change stamped with the characteristic of that which baptizes—effects the change. The reason for this is obvious : βαπτίζω is derived from βάπτω and derives its characteristics from βάπτω *second*, TO DYE, TO COLOR, and not from βάπτω *first*, TO DIP. Now, an object whose color is changed by a dye has not merely its color changed, but changed so as to partake of the same color with that which effects the change. So it is with an object whose condition is changed by a baptism. These changes have nothing to do with colors ; that sphere is preoccupied ; but it has to do with a closely related sphere, namely, that of qualities without color. Thus, wine has an intoxicating quality, and it baptizes a man by thoroughly changing his condition, so that his condition is marked by the wine characteristic, intoxicating quality. Opiates have a soporific quality, and they baptize a man by thoroughly changing his condition, assimilating it to their characteristic, soporific quality. Water has, by nature, a deintoxicating quality, and it baptizes wine by taking away its intoxicating quality, thus thoroughly changing its condition by bringing it into assimilation with its own unintoxicating characteristic. But water has not, by nature, a quality which enables it Christianly to baptize, that is, thoroughly to change the condition of the soul so as to remit sin, to regenerate, and bring out the "Kingly likeness" of Christ; but water itself is capable (so Patrists believed) of being baptized (= thoroughly changed in its nature) by a divine power, so that it shall receive the purifying and sanctifying characteristics of that power, and not only so, but shall receive them in such fulness of power as to be able, in turn, to purify and sanctify. As this baptizing power is from the Holy Spirit, it follows, that in the baptized, thoroughly changed condition of the soul, a likeness to the divine Baptizer must be developed. It is on this basis, that the Royal likeness of Chrysostom is grounded. But if baptism be a dipping and a water covering, what then would be the picture in the soul?

The theory falls under every form of trial.

The evidence now presented showing that the βάπτισμα of early Christian writers was not a physical water covering, but a spiritual condition of the soul, and sometimes applied to the condition of the water as impregnated with a power making it capable of effecting such baptisma of the soul, is conclusive against the theory; but this evidence is capable of being indefinitely strengthened by other, independent, lines of argument. Among these is that which goes to show, that what the theory claims to be the receiving element within which the baptized object passes (which withinness constitutes the βάπτισμα) stands in no such relation to the baptism, but is (however used) the *agency* by which a spiritual βάπτισμα is effected.

The evidence for this is patent and abounding, and being adduced the foundation is taken from under the theory, and it falls out of sight.

The presentation of some of this evidence, already of necessity referred to, will now engage our attention.

ΥΔΑΤΙ καὶ ΠΝΕΥΜΑΤΙ.

WATER AND SPIRIT IN PATRISTIC BAPTISM ARE NOT RECEIVING ELEMENTS BUT CONJOINT AGENCY.

Water and Spirit Baptism.

FRIENDS of the theory seem to imagine that the admission, that the bodies of the baptized, when in health, were momentarily covered in water in ancient times, is a verdict in favor of the theory as affirming that such covering is Christian baptism, and that Patristic writers did so believe and therefore did so practice. We wish therefore distinctly to say, that in adducing evidence to show, that "the Water and the Spirit" appear in Patristic baptism as recognized agencies and not as receiving elements, we have no purpose to deny or to question or to shadow this fact; but on the contrary to give it unhesitating acknowledgment. In doing so, however, we mean to enter a peremptory denial of the conclusion drawn from this fact, that this momentary covering in water was believed to be Christian baptism or any baptism whatever.

With this acknowledgment of a historical fact, we ask the acknowledgment, in turn, of another, just as patent, historical fact, namely: that those not in health were "almost daily" for more than a thousand years baptized *without any water covering*, by pouring and sprinkling. We do not, however, append to this fact the conclusion—"and these acts were Christian baptism, and were so believed to be, and therefore were practiced." They believed no such thing. We believe no such thing. But they did believe, that baptizing water used by sprinkling or pouring did as absolutely and as literally effect the BAPTISMA of Christianity as was effected by the momentary covering of the body in water. The theory must confront this fact living through the history of a millenary of years. In attempting to do battle against it, resort should be had to something more effective than the cry—" *Clinic* baptism!" " *Compend* baptism!" " *Ecclesiastical* baptism!" Such tactics belong to China. They scatter no opposing ranks outside of the Celestial Empire. Others have learned, if the theory has not, that " Ecclesiastical baptism " is the only valid baptism ; that " Compend baptism " is " a most glorious baptism; " while old Cyprian tells the sneerer at " Clinic baptism," that he may have studied the mysteries of Clinicism *with Hippocrates*, but he has *yet to learn from Jesus Christ* as he blesses at the Clinic's bedside.

We accept the fact of a momentary covering in " ex ordine" baptism, and assume the responsibility of proving, that there was no baptism in said covering ; but that the water so used was employed as an agency to effect a baptism which was spiritual and not physical in its nature.

But there is another fact, likewise extending through more than ten centuries, which it is desirable for the theory to acknowledge and explain. I refer to the fact that all persons, male and female, through this long period were covered in water divested of all clothing.

For such a fact there must be a powerful reason. What was it? I know that some reasons can be presented in connection with a " new birth," a " new life," etc., which are all very inadequate to meet the case. But after some considerable examination I find none so satisfactory as that which is grounded in *the peculiar character of the water*, its wonderful power exercised over the body, and through the body upon the soul, and *therefore*, the desirableness of its being brought in contact with the *naked* body, and the *whole* body.

If any better reason can be given I will be pleased to receive it ; but until then I must say, that this naked water covering was a naked water washing, not grounded on the meaning of $\beta\alpha\pi\tau\acute{\iota}\zeta\omega$ *to dip*, but on the character attributed to the water, whose peculiar quality they sought *thus* to secure in the fullest manner possible.

This reason is enforced by another fact, to wit: that evidence disproving " dip " to be the meaning of $\beta\alpha\pi\tau\acute{\iota}\zeta\omega$ has been adduced so conclusive, that no attempt has been made to gainsay it. Therefore, a designed momentary covering of an object in water by dipping cannot be a baptism in any kind of water whatever. This reasoning receives additional strength from the baptizing

35

water not being simple water, but water *impregnated with a qual- ity* with which it parts to an object *dipped* (not baptized) into it, *sprinkled* with it, or *poured* upon by it. In this respect resem- bling a dyeing liquid into which when an object is *dipped* (for the sake of securing its dyeing quality) the dipping is no more the dyeing, than is the sprinkling or the pouring, when the same dye-- ing liquid parts with its quality under either of these processes. It would be an inexcusable error to convert βάπτω *second* into βάπτω *first*, because the former dyed a fleece through the action of dipping. *It is a like error* which seeks to convert the Patristic βαπτίζω into *dip*, because the baptizing water parts with its quality to an object dipped into it, the *effect* of which quality is declared to be a βάπτισμα; and more especially when this water *sprinkled* or *poured* is declared to effect *the same identical* βάπτισμα.

Another point which must be in present recollection in con- sidering this subject is, the Patristic inseparability of the water and the Spirit. The theory claims, that a momentary covering in *simple* water is Christian baptism. But there is no such water known to Patristic baptism. To say that this makes no difference is to talk as witlessly as to say: It makes no difference whether white linen be dipped into *simple* water, or into water *empurpled by murex.* There is difference; in the one case the color remains unchanged, *white;* and in the other case it is wholly changed, the *white* has become *purple.* The Patrists strenuously affirmed, that a dipping into simple water could by no possibility be Chris- tian baptism; for the soul came out of such a dipping just as it went in, unwashen of sin and unregenerate in soul; while one dipped into " our water" came out thoroughly changed in con- dition, sins remitted and soul regenerate, or, in other words, *bap- tized.* The theory is at war with this old baptism at every point. It can find aid and comfort nowhere. Even the dipping which appears in the two systems is as diverse in its origin as can be conceived, and as diverse in the βάπτισμα sought as in the case of spring-water dipping and dye-vat dipping. A man *dipped* into simple water is neither Patristically nor Classically baptized. A man put within simple water in any way, for an unlimited time, is Classically, *but not Patristically* baptized. A man cannot be *Patristically* baptized in *simple* water by any means, whether sprinkling, pouring, dipping, or (what is a very different thing) MERSING *through ten thousand years.* The reason for this is the same as that which makes it impossible for white linen to be *dyed* by being sprinkled, poured upon, dipped, or mersed in *simple* water whether for a moment or forever. Patristic baptism is due to a quality which simple water does not possess and therefore cannot give. Simple water becomes "baptized water" with the power to baptize, by means of a quality divinely communicated to it; which quality exerts its power, equally and perfectly, over an object dipped into it, poured upon by it, or sprinkled with it. That this is true, and that thus only can Patristic baptism receive any valuable interpretation, must now be proved.

Conjoined Agency.

A Benedictine monk commenting on Tertullian (III, 1175) says, with reference to John's statement of Jesus, "He shall baptize you with the Holy Spirit and fire." "Certainly he did not exclude *water* from the baptism of Christ; but John intends to signify only this, that his cleansing was only simple, that is, external, effected by simple water (*Suam ablutionem solum simplicem esse, simplici nimirum aqua exterius factam*); but the cleansing (*ablutionem*) of Christ by the future Baptism would be elevated to a higher mystery and also to the inner cleansing of the soul, which cannot be effected without the grace of the Holy Spirit (*quæ sine gratia Spiritus sancti nequit*)."

This is a correct representation of Patristic views, except that it does not give sufficient spirituality to John's baptism. It is their initial error on the subject of Christian baptism. This error did not consist in believing, that the use of water was to be perpetuated under Christianity; but that it was to have no distinct use and value as the ministration of men; its character as simple, symbol water in a distinct ritual use, disappearing by a mergement in the Holy Spirit, by whose influence it became thoroughly impregnated, and thus was made the vehicle through which his divine power was exerted to remit sin and to regenerate the soul.

For this destructive mersion of a symbol baptism with simple water by men, in the real baptism of the Holy Spirit by the Lord Jesus Christ, there is no scriptural warrant. John neither says nor implies, that water will enter into that baptism which is to be personally administered by Christ. When that baptism was administered at Jerusalem and at Cæsarea, no water entered into it. When its universal application to his people is spoken of—"We are all baptized by one Spirit into one body" (1 Cor. 12:

13), water is wholly eliminated. And when baptism by water is spoken of (John 4 : 2) as done in the presence and by the authority of Jesus, we are carefully guarded against the error of supposing that Jesus took any personal part in such baptism. Thus we are guarded both positively and negatively against the introduction of water into that baptism which was to be personally administered by Christ. He did baptize by the Holy Spirit. He did not baptize by water. There is a symbol baptism through simple water by men. There is no baptism through impregnated water by the Lord Jesus Christ.

No worthy estimate can be formed of the Christianity of these " Christian Fathers " without remembering, that they did most emphatically deny the power of " simple " water to remit sin and to regenerate the soul, and that their mixed agency of " water and Spirit " was, as to its power, nothing but the baptism of the Holy Spirit. The imagined conjunction of this divine agency with water administered by men necessarily led to other manifold errors, notwithstanding most sedulous efforts to guard against them, by teaching vital and antagonistic doctrines inculcating the necessity of personal repentance, faith, and godly living. But the adorable Head of the Church most effectually prevented this error from fruiting out in its worst forms by administering his own baptism of the Spirit (unmixed with water) from the skies, and girdling his people with the prison and the amphitheatre; the sword and the fire!

A few extracts will show the teaching of this conjoint and synchronously operating agency.

TERTULL. III, 1057 : " Except a man be born again of water and Spirit" (John 3 : 5). " This is that Spirit which in the beginning was borne above the waters. For *neither can the Spirit operate without the water, nor the water without the Spirit.*"

III, 1132, COUNCIL OF CARTHAGE : " *For water only, unless it have the Holy Spirit also,* cannot purge sins or sanctify man. Wherefore they must admit the Holy Spirit to be there where they say baptism is, or that baptism is not where the Holy Spirit is not: for baptism cannot be where the Holy Spirit is not."

AUGUSTINE IX, 206 : " It is true that every one who shall enter into the kingdom of God, is first born again of *water and the Spirit.*" VI, 255 : " For his baptism was not like that of John with water only ; but also by the Holy Spirit."

That this quality given to simple water by the Spirit has a

generic resemblance to water to which a dyeing quality has been communicated, is shown by the following extract.

AMBROSE I, 867 : " Have mercy upon me, O Lord, according to thy loving kindness and according to the multitude of thy tender mercies blot out my iniquity and cleanse me from my sin " (Ps. 51 : 1).   " David does not desire so much to be washed frequently as to be washed perfectly (*in multum lava*). He knew many means of cleansing according to the Law, but none was full and perfect. Therefore he eagerly hastens to that perfect one by which all righteousness is fulfilled, which is the sacrament of baptism, as the Lord teaches—' Thus it becometh us to fulfil all righteousness.' The divine word cleanses, our confession cleanses, right thinking cleanses, just working cleanses, also, a good conversation cleanses. Every one cleansed by these things more readily imbibes and as it were appropriates to himself a splendor of spiritual grace. In a word *it is not by one infusion of a fleece that a precious dye shines forth*, but first the fleece is tinged with an inferior color, afterwards by repeated dyeings the natural appearance is effaced and is changed by a different color, and thus a dye as of a fuller washing, is secured, so that a truer and better purple empurples the fleece. *As therefore in a purple dye* there are very many *murices, so in the washing of regeneration* there is a multitude of mercies that iniquity may be blotted out. Therefore he who is washed thoroughly is cleansed from unrighteousness and from sin, and lays aside the habit of sinning which has grown in the inclinations and the will, and loses the quality itself."

The most earnest friends of the theory admit that *dyeing* may be effected by sprinkling or pouring. The Patrists for like reason regarding " our water" as generically like a dye ; that is to say, simple water *with a superadded quality capable of communicating the characteristic of that quality in various ways*, therefore, believed that baptizing was by sprinkling or pouring, as truly as in any other conceivable way.

Special Quality and Power given to Waters.

TERTULL. II, 734 : " The madness of the heretic Menander is spit out declaring that death neither pertains to nor can reach his disciples. . . . They who put on his baptism are made immortal, and incorruptible, and immediately partakers of the resurrection.

We read, indeed, of many kinds of wonderful waters: those of Lyncesta which made drunk, of Colophon which made frantic, of Nonacris tinctured with poison. There was, also, a healing pool of Judæa before Christ. The poet tells of the Stygian pools wash- ing away death; but if Menander should merse into the Styx (*in Stygam mergit*) death must intervene to reach the Styx, for it is in the infernal regions. But what or where is that felicity of waters which John the Baptizer did not foreadminister, nor Christ himself make known? What is this bath of Menander? It must belong to magic art."

Tertullian recognizes the fact that various qualities are found superadded to those qualities which are inherent in simple water, whereby they are capable of exerting an influence which simple water cannot exert. He says, that Menander claimed a special quality for his baptizing water. And he claims, that there were special qualities belonging to the water used by John and Christ. But the several qualities of these waters was variously developed, some by drinking, some by stepping into, some by dipping, etc. And in like manner Tertullian and all his associates declare that the peculiar quality which they attributed to their water was vari- ously developed, by dipping, by pouring, and by sprinkling, or they declare nothing.

The theory hopelessly breaks down in treating Patristic water as simple water; as it does, indeed, in every other direction. The *quo modo* of communicating this quality is shown in the following passages.

Quality communicated to Baptizing Water.

By the Holy Spirit. TERTULL. I, 1203 : "A figure of baptism is presented by the Spirit of God which from the beginning was borne above the waters about to reform the imbued. The holy was borne above the holy; or that which bore was sanctified by that which was upborne. Since whatever substance underlies receives the quality of that which overlies, especially does a cor- poreal substance receive a spiritual quality being readily pene- trated and controlled by the subtilty of its nature. So, the nature of the waters having been sanctified by the Holy, it receives itself the power to sanctify. . . . All waters therefore have the power to effect the sacrament of sanctification, God being invoked. For immediately the Spirit from heaven comes and is above the waters sanctifying them by himself, and so, they being sanctified, *imbibe the power* of sanctifying. . . . Therefore the waters having received healing virtues (*medicatis*) through the intervention of the Angel, both the soul is corporeally purified by the waters and the body is spiritually cleansed by the same. The heathen, ignorant of spiritual things, ascribe the same power to their idols, but with unmarried waters (= unimpregnated with healing virtues, *viduis aquis*), they deceive themselves."

1205 : " If it should seem a strange thing that the holy Angel of God should intermeddle with the waters, we have an illustration in the troubling of the waters of the pool of Bethesda, into which whosoever first went down was healed after the washing. This figure of a corporeal medicine announced a spiritual medicine (*medicinam*) by such form as carnal things always precede, as a figure, spiritual things. The grace of God blessing men has added more to the waters of the Angel; what remedied the imperfections of the body, now heal the soul; what wrought temporal soundness, now effects eternal; what released once in the year, now profits the people every day; death being destroyed by the washing away of sins. Man is restored to the likeness of God."

DIDYMUS ALEXANDER, 692: " The indivisible and ineffable Trinity foreseeing the frailties of humanity, in creating a fluid substance out of nothing prepared for men the healing of the waters. Accordingly the Holy Spirit by his movement upon the waters, appears from that time to have sanctified them and made them life-giving. For it is evident to every one, that what overlies imparts of its own quality to that which underlies, and all underlying matter is accustomed to take of the peculiarity of that which overlies. Whence baptism belongs to all water indiscriminately, in necessity, as waters are of one nature and all are sanctified. Moses says: ' The Spirit of the Lord was borne above the waters.' . . . The pool of Bethesda is confessedly an image of baptism but not having the very truth; for an image is for the time, but the truth is forever. Therefore the water in it was moved once a year by an Angel, and one only, he that stepped first down, was healed of bodily disease but not of spiritual. But true (αὐθεντικὸν) baptism, after the appearing of the Son and of the Holy Spirit, every day, or every hour, or, to speak most truly, continually, frees forever all who step down from all sin. The

Angel who troubled the water was the Forerunner of the Holy Spirit."

JEROME II, 161: "How is the soul which has not the Holy Spirit purged from old defilements? For water does not wash (*lavat*) the soul unless it is first washed (*lavatur*) by the Holy Spirit that it may be able spiritually to wash others. 'The Spirit of the Lord, says Moses, was borne above the waters.' From which it appears that baptism is not without the Holy Spirit. Bethesda, a pool of Judæa, could not heal diseased bodies except through the coming of an Angel, and do you offer to me a soul washed by simple water (*simplici aqua*) as from a bath?"

The baptism of Tertullian, as well as that of Didymus and of Jerome, was a soul-washing through a special power medicating the waters, and they rejected with disdain the idea that " simple water" in the hands of an idolater or of a bath-keeper could baptize; not because of those who used it, but because they used " simple" and not divinely " medicated" waters. How long would it take the theory to get the *imprimatur* of such men to its dipping into " simple water "?

This medicated quality, by which and not by a dipping, baptism is effected, is, also, attributed to the Lord Jesus Christ.

Baptizing quality received through Christ. IGNATIUS, 660: " Jesus Christ was born and baptized that he might purify (καθαρίσῃ) the water by his passion."

TERTULL. II, 615: " Christ having been baptized, that is sanctifying (*sanctificante*) the waters by his baptism."

AMBROSE III, 627: " Perhaps some one may say, 'Why did he who was holy wish to be baptized?' Hear, then: Christ was therefore baptized, not that he might be sanctified by the waters, but that he might sanctify the waters, and by his own purity purify the stream which he touches; for the consecration of Christ is a greater consecration of the element. For when the Saviour is washed (*abluitur*) the whole water is cleansed (*mundatur*) for our baptism, and the fountain is purified (*purificatur*), that the grace of the washing may be supplied to the people coming after."

MARCÆ EREMITÆ, 927: " He indeed needed no washing, for it is written of him, ' He did no sin;' and where there is no sin there can be no remission. The waters for our washing were sanctified and purged by him."

EPIPHANIUS II, 880: " Christ baptized by John came to the

waters, not needing washing (λουτροῦ), to give rather than to receive ; giving them power for those who were to be perfected."

The proof is absolute that " simple water" could not patristically baptize (could it not cover ? " what is baptism in one case is
baptism in another" Carson), and that it might be qualified so to
do, a special quality was divinely conferred upon it, enabling it,
in turn, to confer like quality.

This office of efficient agency, not " to dip," not " to cover,"
but, to purify, to sanctify, to remit sin, and to regenerate, these
waters, thus qualified, did, according to Patristic faith, abundantly exercise. In evidence of which see these further quotations :

TERTULL. II, 720 : " When he comes to the faith formed anew
(*reformata*) by the second birth *by means of water* and power
from on high (*ex aqua et superna virtute*)."

CLEMENS ALEX. I, 279 : " If Christ was perfect, why was the
perfect one baptized ? To fulfil the human profession. He is
perfected by the washing only (τῷ λουτρῷ μόνῳ) and the coming
of the Spirit. This same thing happens to us of whom the Lord
was an exemplification. Being baptized we are illuminated ;
being illuminated we are made sons ; being made sons we are perfected ; being perfected we are made immortal. He says : ' I have
said ye are Gods ; and all of you sons of the Most High.' This
is variously designated as grace, and illumination, and perfection,
and washing (λουτρόν). It is called washing (λουτρόν) because we
are cleansed from our sins."

ORIGEN I, 601 : " We must remember that we have sinned
and that the remission of sins cannot be received without baptism ; and that according to the evangelical laws we cannot be
baptized again into the remission of sins *by water* and Spirit
(Ὕδατι καὶ Πνεύματι βαπτισάσθαι)."

CYRIL, 425 : " Rejoice, O Heavens, and be glad, O Earth, because
of those who are about to be sprinkled (ῥαντίζεσθαι) with hyssop
and to be purified (καθαρίζεσθαι) by the spiritual (τῷ νοητῷ) hyssop,
by the power of Him who drank at his passion from the hyssop
and the reed. . . . Prepare pure vessels and sincere faith of the
soul for the reception of the Holy Spirit. Begin to wash your
garments through repentance, that being called to the bride-
chamber ye may be found pure. . . . That the souls of you all
may be found not having spot, or wrinkle, or any such thing ; I
do not say before the receiving of the grace, for how could this

be, since you are called for the remission of sins, but that the grace being given, an uncondemning conscience may be found concurrent with the grace." 429: " *Do not regard this washing as by* SIMPLE *water, but as by the spiritual grace given with the water* (τῇ πνευματικῇ χάριτι μετὰ τοῦ ὕδατος). . . . For as sacrifices upon the altars are by nature pure, but become polluted by the invocation of idols, so, on the contrary, the *simple* water (τὸ λιτὸν ὕδωρ) receiving the invocation of the Holy Spirit, and of Christ, and of the Father, *acquires the* POWER of sanctification (δύναμιν ἁγιότητος). For, since man is twofold, constituted of soul and body, purification also is twofold, that which is incorporeal by that which is incorporeal, but that which is physical by that which is physical. The water indeed purifies the body, but the Spirit seals the soul, that having been sprinkled (ἐρῥαντισμένοι) as to the heart by the Spirit and washed as to the body with pure water (καθαρῷ ὕδατι), we may come unto God. Therefore being about to go down into the water do not regard the bareness of the water (τῷ ψιλῷ τοῦ ὕδατος), but expect salvation from the power (ἐνεργεία) of the Holy Spirit, for without both it is impossible to be perfected (τελειωθῆναι). It is not I that say this, but the Lord Jesus Christ has the power of the case; he says, ' Except a man be born again,' and adds, ' by water and the Spirit, he cannot enter into the kingdom of God.' Nor has one perfect grace who being baptized by the water (τῷ ὕδατι) has not received the Holy Spirit; nor if any one distinguished by good works should fail to receive the seal by water (δἰ ὕδατος) will he enter into the kingdom of heaven. This declaration is bold, but it is not mine; it is Jesus who declares it. Here is the proof: Cornelius a just man deemed worthy of the vision of angels, whose prayers and alms were as a monument before God in heaven, on whom with his fellow-believers the Spirit was poured out (ἐπεχύθη), after the grace of the Spirit, ' Peter commanded them, in the name of Jesus Christ, to be baptized.' In order that, the soul having been regenerated through faith (διὰ τῆς πίστεως), the body also might receive grace through the water (διὰ τοῦ ὕδατος). But if any one wishes to know why grace is given through water (διὰ ὕδατος) and not through some other element, reading the Scriptures he will find out. For water is some great thing, the best of the four great elements of the world; and before the six days' work ' the Spirit of God moved upon the water.' . . . The laver within the tabernacle was the symbol of baptism (σύμβολον τοῦ βαπτίσματος)."

AUGUSTINE VI, 255 : " Christ's baptism was not like that of John *with water only, but also by the Holy Spirit;* so that whosoever believes in Christ might be regenerated by that Spirit (*de illo Spiritu*) by whom (*de quo*) Christ was begotten (*generatus*)."

VI, 1209 : " You ought not to estimate these waters by the sight but by the mind. . . . God sanctified through which . . . by virtue of his power, secret sins which are not seen are washed away. The Holy Spirit works in that water, so that those who before baptism were guilty of many sins, and would have burned with the devil in eternal fire, merit, after baptism, to enter into the kingdom of heaven."

This is evidence enough to show that Patristic baptism cannot be effected without the joint presence and coaction of water and the Holy Spirit; and, consequently, that that baptism was something else than simple dipping into simple water which constitutes the solitaire gem of the theory. This truth, however, may be enforced by a few passages which make special mention of the power on which baptism depends, and without which no amount of water and no mode of using water could effect this baptism.

The Baptizing Power, Moral and Divine. TERTULL. II, 375 : " Christ cleanses the stains of the seven capital sins—idolatry, blasphemy, murder, adultery, fornication, false witness, fraud. Wherefore Naaman washed in the Jordan seven times, as if each one separately and that at the same time he might receive expiation of the whole seven, for *the power* (*vis*) and fulness *of one washing* belongs to Christ alone."

The " vis " ascribed to baptizing water is essentially diverse from that accompanying the Jordan water. No physical quality or power can cleanse the soul of " the seven capital sins."

EUSEBIUS II, 1212 : " When Constantine thought that the end of his life had come, and that this was the time for the purification (καθάρσεως) of all sins of his life, and believing that these would be thoroughly cleansed from the soul *by the power* (δυνάμει) of the mystical words and *the saving washing,* he expressed his desire for the rite 'for the salvation of God,' and 'for the seal of immortality.' "

GREGORY NAZ. II, 396 : " The image of the Emperor stamped in wax from a ring of iron or gold is the same, so is *the power* of baptism (βαπτίσματος δύναμις) the same, whether administered by presbyter or bishop, for the grace is of the Spirit."

II, 421 : " I have three overpourings upon the wood with which

I will purify the sacrifice, kindling a fire by water, that most wonderful thing! and will overthrow the prophets of idolatry, using
the power (δύναμις) of the mystery."

EPIPHANIUS II, 880: "Christ coming to the waters, giving
rather than receiving, illumining them, *investing them with power*
(ἐνδυναμῶν) for the sake of those afterward to be perfected,
. . . that they might receive *power* (τὴν δύναμιν) proceeding from
him."

This investiture of the waters with the power (δύναμις, *vis, virtus,
qualitas*) to baptize = to remit sin and to regenerate, has a like
generic character with the investiture of the Apostles with
"power" (δύναμις) by the Holy Spirit for the Apostolic office.
The nature of the power in the two cases differs; but the investiture with *a* power thoroughly changing the condition of the
recipient, with the ability to exercise that power to change the
condition of others, is common to both, and in both cases the
power conferred is said to baptize alike the waters and the Apostles.

The "power" (δύναμις) conferred upon the Apostles and their
baptism by the Holy Ghost through the conferring of such power
is thus presented by Cyril.

CYRIL, 985: "The Holy Spirit descended that he might endue
with power, and that he might baptize the Apostles (ἵνα ἐνδύσῃ
δύναμιν (καὶ) ἵνα βαπτίσῃ τοὺς ἀποστόλους). For the Lord says, 'Ye
shall be baptized by the Holy Spirit not many days hence.' The
grace (χάρις) is not limited, but the power (δύναμις) is complete.
For as one covered and baptized (ἐνδύνων καὶ βαπτιζόμενος) in the
waters is surrounded on all sides by the waters, so also they were
completely baptized by the Spirit. But the water is poured around
(περιχεῖται) externally, while the Spirit completely baptizes the
soul internally. And why wonder? Take a physical illustration,
trivial and simple, but useful to less cultivated persons. If fire
penetrating through the density of iron renders the whole fire,
and that which was cold becomes hot, and that which was black
becomes bright; if fire being matter works so readily, entering
within material iron, why do you wonder if the Holy Spirit enters
within the inmost parts of the soul? . . . 'And filled all the house
where they were sitting.' The house was made the receptacle of
the spiritual water. The disciples sat within, and the whole house
was filled; they were therefore completely baptized according to
the promise. They were invested (ἐνεδύσθησαν) both soul and body

with divine and saving vesture (ἔνδυσιν). 'And cloven tongues as of fire sat on each of them, and they were all filled of the Holy Spirit.' They received fire, not burning, but saving fire, destroying indeed the thorns of sins, but illumining the soul."

1. In this passage "to endue with power," and "to baptize," are equivalent expressions. The editor says he has introduced "and" between them—"that he might endue with power," *and* "that he might baptize." Whether with or without this connective the phrases are equivalent and mutually expository. They are so used in Scripture—"Ye shall be *baptized* with the Holy Ghost" (Acts 1:5); "Ye shall receive *power* (δύναμιν) from the Holy Ghost" (v. 8). It was the "power" (δύναμις) given to the waters which baptized them; it was the "power" (δύναμις) given to the Apostles which baptized them. Herein is renewed evidence that a thorough change of condition, assimilating to the characteristic of the power effecting such change, is a baptism.

2. The double illustration by an object perfectly encompassed in water, and a mass of iron penetrated and pervaded by fire, thoroughly changing the condition of the iron, and assimilating it to that of fire, converting coldness into hotness, blackness into brightness, sustains the results of this Inquiry into the nature of a baptism in the most absolute manner. It is also a perfect exemplification of the definition given by Basil. An object wholly within water, without limitation of mode in effecting such condition, or of time in abiding in such condition, has been insisted upon throughout this Inquiry as a physical baptism. Such is the baptism spoken of by Cyril. Such a condition is not a momentary dipping. A dipping is precluded by its very nature of momentariness from being a baptism. A dipping into BAPTIZING water may effect a baptism by reason of the nature of the water; but the dipping, in such case, is no more the baptism, than the dipping white linen into Tyrian purple is the resultant purple dye. Cyril had no idea of resting his illustration in the simple encompassing of an object with water for an indefinite period; that would by no means answer his purpose. He wants influence. Nothing can more fully develop influence than the enfolding of an object within the influential agency. And the consequent penetrating, pervading, and controlling influence, thoroughly changing the condition of an object, becomes the basis of the secondary use of βαπτίζω in Classic writers, and is its exclusive use in religious applications among all writers, Jewish, Inspired, and Patristic. Therefore it

is that a mass of iron not covered over in fire, but fully unde its influence, however that influence may have been brought to bear upon it, and made through all its substance fiery, hot, and bright, is baptized by fire. So, Cyril says, the soul is baptized by the Holy Spirit, not by an external surrounding, but by penetrating, pervading, and controlling the soul in its inner being.

3. The idea of the house being filled with "spiritual water," and the Apostles being baptized in it because they were sitting in the house, is, of course, neither founded in Scripture nor in fact. But if it were the theory would be ruined; for in such a baptism there would be lacking both the form of the act and the momentariness essential to the act. But again; such *encompassing* baptism would not suit Cyril's purpose any more than it would suit the teaching of the Scriptures. If the Apostles had remained sitting in the house encompassed by "spiritual water" until this hour, they would no more have received the scriptural baptism of the Spirit than if they had been sitting on the house-top, and no drop of "spiritual water" had ever come down from heaven.

The Apostles were not baptized by the Holy Ghost until his influence entered within their souls and left there his own divine light and grace as tokens of his "power." Neither here nor anywhere else do the Scriptures know anything of an outward encompassing baptism. And in this respect Patristic baptism is identical with that of the Scriptures. That baptism is a baptism of "power," the power of a divine influence, and the momentary encompassing of the naked body with the water in which this power was supposed to reside, was merely a mode for developing that power in "ex ordine" baptism, but was neither the baptism, nor in any wise essential to the baptism, as every page of Patristic writings through a thousand years clearly shows.

A few passages showing the development of this δύναμις as an agency will now be presented.

The δύναμις of baptizing water as an agency. GREGORY NAZ. III, 463: "The grace of baptism (λόετροῖο χάρις) is one of the helps given to men. For, as the children of the Hebrews escaped death by the christic blood (αἵματι χριστῷ) which purified the door-posts when the first born of the Egyptians perished in one night, so, also to me is this baptism (σφράγις) of God which delivers from evil; a seal indeed to infants (νηπιάχοις) but, also, a healing and the best seal to grown-up men, divinely flowing from Christ."

This metrical version is given:

> . . . . " Præsidium unum est lustrica lympha,
> Nam velut Hebræis perfusi sanguine postes
> A pueris olim arcebant pestemque necemque
> Una primigeni fetus cum nocte perirent
> Ægypte, signum nobis est haud secus unda
> Lustralis ; signum pueris tantum modo, verum
> Grandibus et signum simul et medicina salubris,
> Munifico a Christo manans." . . .

Such is the helpful agency residing in this baptizing δύναμις.

AUGUSTINE VI, 695 : " The devil rages when he sees us freed from his oppression *by* (per) *the water* of baptism. Cry to your Moses, the Lord Jesus Christ, that he may smite with the rod of his Cross the sea of baptism, so that the water may return and cover the Egyptians, so that as none of the Egyptians remained, none of your sins may remain."

Under the δύναμις of this water *sins* were baptized (Classically) in the pool and *left*, after the dipping of the subject, *at its bottom*, as were the Egyptians in like manner baptized and *left at the bottom of the sea.*

TERTULL. I, 1202 : " The waters were commanded in the beginning to bring forth living creatures. It is not to be wondered at therefore if the waters in baptism are able to give life. . . If I were to relate all the power (*vis*) of this element, or how great an instrument (*instrumentum*) it is, I am afraid that I should appear to rehearse the praises of water rather than the qualities of baptism."

Water has a " power " (*vis*, δύναμις) making it competent as an agency (*instrumentum*) " to give life." This is enough for our present purpose, the showing that baptizing water is not a mere receiving element, but is an agency whose δύναμις (patristically regarded) is divine.

Another line of proof showing the impossibility that water should be regarded as baptizing by inclosing its object, and not by its power exerted in thoroughly changing the condition of such object howsoever that power might be exerted, is seen in the use of Cases and **Prep**ositions, as in the following examples:

Cases and Prepositions reject receptivity and establish agency.
CYRIL, 930 : " Our bodies have received oneness through (*per*) that washing which is for incorruption; but our souls *through* (*per*) the Spirit. 1247 : As Naaman the Syrian leper baptized

himself seven times in the Jordan and was purified, so we lepers by sin are purified *through* the holy water (διὰ τοῦ ἁγίου ὕδατος) and the invocation of the Lord, from old sins; like new-born children, we are spiritually born again, as the Lord said: 'Except a man be born again *through* water and Spirit (δὶ ὕδατος καὶ Πνεύματος) he shall not enter into the kingdom of heaven.'"

CLEMENS ALEX. I, 285: "Our sins are remitted *by one perfect remedy* (Παιωνίῳ φαρμάκῳ) spiritual Baptism (Λογικῷ βαπτίσματι). For all our sins are immediately washed away and immediately we are no more sinful."

JUSTIN MARTYR, 793: "For Christ being the first born of every creature, became also the beginning of another race which was born again *by him, through* water (δὶ ὕδατος), and faith, and wood, which was the mystery of his Cross."

ORIGEN II, 100: "They who are regenerated *through* the divine baptism (διὰ τοῦ θείου Βαπτίσματος) are placed in Paradise, that is, in the church."

GREGORY NAZ. III, 960: "The washing of Christ was the purification of my waters. The water and the blood flowing together from his side was the twofold Baptism, *by* washing and *by* suffering (λούτρου καὶ πάθους)."

JEROME XI, 587: "There flowed out water and blood." "Remission is by (*per*) blood; Baptism is by (*per*) water." 593: "I baptize you with water, he shall baptize you with the Holy Spirit." "What difference is there between water and the Holy Spirit who was 'borne above the water?' Water is the agency of man (*ministerium hominis*), but the Spirit is the agency of God (*ministerium Dei*)."

If there is force in evidence this will suffice to take the water of baptism out of the category of a quiescent receiving element and place it among the most energetic of agencies.

Passing by other evidence I proceed to adduce, finally, on this aspect of the case, evidence from the manner in which the water is said to have been used, to show that it occupied in relation to the baptism the position of agency, and that the baptism was not a physical covering within simple water:

Sprinkling, washing, dipping, not baptism, but means. ALEXANDER I, Papa 1065: "We bless the water sprinkled with salt (*sale conspersam*) that all sprinkled (*aspersi*) by it may be sanctified and purified (*sanctificentur et purificentur*), which we command to be done by all priests. For if the ashes of a heifer sprinkled with blood sanctified and cleansed the people (*sanctifi-cabat atque mundabat*), much more water sprinkled with salt and consecrated by divine prayers, sanctifies and cleanses the people. And if by salt sprinkled by the prophet Elisha the sterility of water was healed, by how much more having been consecrated by divine prayers does it take away the sterility of human things, and sanctifies, and cleanses, and purges, and multiplies other blessings? For if we believe that the sick were healed by a touch of the hem of the Saviour's garment, by how much more are elements divinely consecrated by the power (*virtute*) of his sacred words, whereby human frailty receives healing of body and soul?"

This salt-sprinkled water was not the "baptizing water," but it did, like that, secure a "power" (*virtus*) to purify, to sanctify, to purge, and to bless, the body and the soul. And this power was developed, like that, by sprinkling. And as this purification, sanctification, purgation, and blessing of the body and the soul, was not the sprinkling, but was a result effected by the sprinkling, so, the remission of sins and the regeneration of the soul is not the sprinkling of baptizing water, but is the result produced by it. It is a patent error to suppose that salt sprinkled in a fountain, or heifer ashes sprinkled on masses of people, or consecrated salt water, or water impregnated with a divine δύναμις, has no controlling power beyond the spot upon which the drops may fall. The entire fountain is healed though the great body of the gushing waters has not been touched by the salt; the whole mass of the people is healed although individuals may not have been touched by one particle of the heifer ashes; and the whole "body and soul" is purified and sanctified by the consecrated and impregnated water through the falling of sprinkling drops. It is the wildest of errors to suppose that βαπτίζω and βάπτισμα have a physical representation in these water droppings; their representation is found exclusively in the result of this action, and the breadth of that result is to be measured not by the size of a drop, but by the far-reaching "virtus" of the consecrated water of Alexander, and of the δύναμις of the impregnated Patristic water. This breadth is said to be complete—to cover "body and soul," and it is to this completeness in their changed condition which originates and finds exposition in βαπτίζω and βάπτισμα.

If the theory asserts that Patristic writers in treating of Christian baptism use these terms to express physical relations and results, they must make their assertions in the ears of those unacquainted with these writings if an admiring auditory is expected.

TERTULLIAN I, 1169: "Our hands, which, with the whole body, we have once washed in Christ (*in Christo semel lavimus*), are clean. But the Jew daily washes all the members of his body, yet is never clean. Certainly his hands are always defiled with the blood of the prophets and are bloodied forever with that of the Lord himself."

This washing of "the hands" (not with gloves on) and of "the whole body" (not with clothes on) shows that the naked body was brought in contact through all its parts not to meet any demand of βαπτίζω but to secure the "VIRTUS" *in Christo* communicated to the waters. There was no physical washing contemplated; as the whole passage shows that it was a spiritual washing, once for all, cleansing spiritual defilements; there was no physical covering contemplated as a physical baptism: 1. Because a momentary covering is not a baptism; 2. Because it was a spiritual cleansing. The Annotator says: "Tertullian by this washing alludes to the rite of baptism in which men naked (*nudi*) were thrice covered in water." The water is used as an agency, however used, and for a spiritual and not a physical washing.

I, 1197: *De Baptismo.* "Happy sacrament of our water, by which having been washed (*abluti*) from sins of former blindness, we obtain eternal life."

These are the opening words of Tertullian's treatise of Baptism. They show: 1. "OUR water" to be water of a wholly diverse nature from the water of heathenism, Judaism, or heresy; 2. The washing effected by "*our* water" was not a physical washing; it did not depend upon any physical quality of water, and consequently the water could not be used for a physical covering (as an end) since this involves a purely physical quality inherent in all water; but the washing was purely spiritual through that divine quality singularly imparted to "our water" for this special purpose and for which it was alone adequate. Again, therefore, we are brought face to face with the truth that this water acted as an agency and that its function was spiritual and not physical.

I, 1201: *De Baptismo.* "There is nothing which so hardens the hearts of men as the simplicity which appears in the operation of the divine works and the magnificence revealed in the result; as here also, since with so much simplicity, without pomp, without novel means, and without cost, a man going down into the water and dipped (*tinctus*), during the utterance of a few words, arises not much or not at all cleaner (*mundior*), therefore, an eternal result is thought to be incredible. . . . Water first brought forth living creatures ; it is not wonderful, therefore, if water, in Baptism, produces life."

Tertullian in this passage repudiates a physical washing—"a man is not much or *not at all* CLEANER" physically after his baptism than he was before it. Nor did the Patrists know anything of a symbol washing in "our water." But there was a washing ; a washing of amazing power and compass. If this washing was neither physical nor symbol it must have been spiritual. If it was spiritual, then it depended upon a divine power. What depends on a divine power cannot depend upon quantity or mode. A spiritual washing may be represented by the sprinkling of that which takes away defilement of sin and thus washes the soul, as well as by any other means. The blood of Jesus Christ cleanses from all sin. Therefore we have "the blood of sprinkling ;" therefore "the heart is sprinkled from an evil conscience ;" and therefore "we are washed by the blood of Him that loved us." The Patristic washing is never physical, never symbolical, always real and spiritual, through "the *power* of the PASSION," developed by martyr blood, by penitential tears, and, equally, by sprinkling drops or covering pool.

AUGUSTINE IX, 379: "When we say that Christ baptizes, we do not say, with visible service, as Petilian thinks or wishes to think ; but with hidden grace, with hidden power by the Holy Spirit, as was said of him by John the Baptist, '*Hic est qui baptizat in Spiritu sancto.*' Nor as Petilian says, has he ceased to baptize ; but he does still, not with service of body, but by the invisible work of his divinity. For because we say, 'He baptizes,' we do not say, 'He holds and dips (*tingit*) the bodies of believers in water ;' but he invisibly cleanses, and that the whole Church . . . where ministers are seen to operate corporally, Christ washes (*abluit*), Christ cleanses (*mundat*). Therefore no one may arrogate to himself what belongs to God."

482: "Good men and bad men baptize so far as the visible ministry is concerned ; but He whose is both visible baptism and invisible grace, baptizes invisibly through them. Therefore both good and bad can dip (*tingere possunt*) ; but He only who is always good can wash (*abluere*) the conscience."

Augustine believed in a severe interpretation of the words
"This is HE that BAPTIZETH," limiting them absolutely to the
Lord Jesus Christ. While allowing men a visible ministry in
baptism, he peremptorily denied them the power to baptize. He
did not admit that men performed one baptism and the Lord
Jesus Christ performed another baptism. Neither Augustine nor
his associates believed in two baptisms. He did believe that men
had power to dip (*tingere*) men in water; but he did not believe
that this was baptism. He repudiates it as nothing but a "dipping." He believed in no baptism which did not wash the soul;
and he believed that the power to do this was not intrusted to
any man, but reserved solely to the Lord Jesus Christ. Augustine, then, was no believer in a water dipping as Christian baptism, while he did believe that (in *ex ordine* baptism) a man was
dipped into "our water" the Lord Jesus Christ baptizing, washing the conscience and the soul.

A more absolute discrimination between dipping and baptizing,
and between a water covering the result of dipping, and baptism
the result of baptizing, and the repudiation of the one as the other,
could not be made than has here been made by Augustine. The
theory affirms that dipping into water is the essence of Christian
baptism without which it cannot exist, and therefore sprinkling
with water cannot be Christian baptism, because the act of sprinkling is not the act of dipping, and sprinkling water does not cover.
To these erroneous *dicta* is usually added the additional and grievous error of Petilian, that "the Lord Jesus Christ has ceased to
baptize." We affirm with Augustine that dipping is not baptizing either heathenly or Christianly, that a water covering for a
moment or for eternity neither is nor has anything (*ex necessitate*)
to do with Christian baptism, and that the Lord Jesus Christ, by
the Holy Ghost, is the sole administrator of real Christian baptism, while men administer a symbol baptism in the use of water
by sprinkling, or pouring, or dipping; for these modal uses of
water sprinkling and pouring we have full scriptural warrant, while
dipping has absolutely none, being purely a usage and doctrine
of men. This error which identifies dipping into water with
Christian baptism is greatly to be deplored, because if not solely
originating in yet largely sustained by the error which attributed
a divine quality conferred upon the water, which it exercised in
the remission of sins and regenerating the soul, thus inducing (for
the fuller attainment of this blessing) the covering of the body

(and that naked) in this water of such miraculous " virtue ;" and further, because in these latter days it brings forth as its offspring: 1. A denial of the Churchhood of the great body of those who are confessedly temples of the Holy Ghost; 2. A denial of the Lord Jesus Christ as the sole, abiding Baptizer of his people ; 3. A steady looking toward the old error of a sin-remitting water dipping openly proclaimed by the followers of Alexander Campbell, and an occasional forthputting of word and hand by other friends of the theory, toward the same result.

Error is never sterile.

ΣΥΝΘΑΠΤΩ.

PATRISTIC DIPPING INTO WATER

WAS NEITHER PATRISTIC BAPTISM NOR CHRISTIAN BAPTISM BUT BURIAL OF SIN IN THE WATER AND SYMBOL BURIAL WITH CHRIST IN HIS " NEW SEPULCHRE."

" Symbol water burial not Christian Baptism."

THE theory attempts to enlist Rom. 6 : 4 ; Coloss. 2 : 12 ; as auxiliaries in maintaining that dipping into water is a burial; that this dipping burial is a burial now, with Christ in the Jordan, and now, with Christ in the sepulchre ; and that *this momentary burial in a water sepulchre is* CHRISTIAN BAPTISM. Patristic writers are also invited to enlist under this banner. But neither Paul nor Patrist will listen to such call for such end. Paul says: I believe that all who, by the Holy Ghost, are baptized into Jesus Christ, are, thereby, baptized into his sin-remitting death ; and that all who are baptized into his sin-remitting death are thereby united with him in his sepulchre burial in order that they may be united with him in his resurrection to newness of life ; thus receiving by true Christian baptism, the remission of sins and the regeneration of the soul. But I do not believe in any *baptism* of Christ by *burial* in the sepulchre ; nor in any dipping into water as an imaginary resemblance to a *rock-burial baptism*, which has no existence either in fact or in possibility. The Patrist says : I believe in a baptism of sin by which its life is destroyed and it is left drowned at the bottom of the pool ; and I believe in a momentary covering in water *(" ex ordine")* as *a symbol of the covering of Christ's body in the sepulchre;* but I do not believe that sin baptized and left drowned in the pool is Christian baptism, nor yet, that a momentary water covering, symbol of the sepulchre covering, is Christian baptism.

That the above statement truly represents the faith of Paul I have endeavored, heretofore, to show ; that the faith of the Chris-

tian Fathers is no less truly stated might be inferred from what
has been already adduced; but more direct evidence may be desirable and will, therefore, now be offered.

Dipping into Water is not Burial Baptism.

CLEMENS I, *Rom. Pont.*, 1044: " Then he comes to the water.
The priest giving thanks to him who underwent death through the
Cross for all, a type of which (οὖ τύπον) is the baptism of regeneration. . . . Let the priest say: Look down from heaven and
sanctify this water; and grant grace and power (χάριν καὶ δύναμιν)
so that, the baptized according to the command of Christ, *may
be crucified with him*, may die with him, may be buried with him,
and may rise with him to the adoption which is in him, dying to
sin and living to righteousness."

This passage teaches that baptism is effected by the δύναμις of
divine grace, that they who are so baptized receive a co-crucifixion, a co-death, a co-burial, and a co-resurrection with Christ, and
that "the baptism of regeneration" is a type of death through
the Cross (θάνατου διὰ τοῦ σταυροῦ). There is no dipping burial.

DIONYSIUS AREOP., 404: " *As the body is covered* (καλυπτόμενον)
in the earth, the complete covering (κάλυψις) by water, may naturally be received as a likeness (εἰκόνα) of death and burial. This
symbol teaching (συμβολικὴ διδασκαλία) initiates the sacredly baptized by the three coverings (καταδύσεσι) in the water to the imitation of the divine death and three days' and nights' burial of
Jesus the giver of life."

Observe: This covering in the water is based on the covering
of a dead body in the earth. Now, *the burial of the dead body
in the ground was never called a* BAPTISM by heathen, Jew, or
Christian; but *death upon* THE CROSS *is declared to be a* BAPTISM;
what, now, is the wit, to say nothing about the authority, for abandoning the baptism of the Cross, to conjure up one in the sepulchre
where is none by divine or human authority? Observe again:
There is nothing said about βαπτίζω in this earth-burial, it is καλύπτω; there is nothing said about βάπτισμα in this water-burial
likeness, it is καλύψις. Observe yet farther: There is no appearance of βάπτισμα in those threefold coverings, it is καταδύσις. Now,
bearing in mind that neither καλύπτω, nor καλύψις, nor καταδύσις, ever
expresses the Patristic βαπτίζω or βάπτισμα, what shall we say to
the attempt to introduce a baptism under this CALYPSIS?

There is declared to be a likeness between the covering in water and the covering in earth; but there is *no claim whatever for a* BAPTISM in the one or in the other. It is also true, that there is no more Scriptural ground for the one covering in water, than there is for the three.

484, 497: " Wherefore also the grace of baptism (for this is to be begotten of God) is perfected by the ointment poured out by the chief priest in the form of a cross upon the purifying baptistery, exhibiting spiritually the spiritual ointment—the Lord undergoing death, for the pool exhibits his death and the delivering by his triumphant descent into death (for he could not be overcome by death) those baptized into his death. This is called a hidden saying, because the reason of the baptism into Christ (τοῦ εἰς Χριστὸν βαπτίσματος) *is hard to be understood by many.*"

The view here presented of the water of baptism is not that of a grave but of the death of Christ through his crucifixion and seems to be grounded in an attempt to give visibility to the ideal baptism taught by Paul—" As many as have been baptized into Christ, have been baptized *into his* DEATH." This is a wholly different thing from burial and covering in a grave. If there had never been an attempt to give a physical vesture to the ideal baptism of Scripture there probably would not have been so many, even to this day, who find it " hard to understand the meaning of the baptism *into* CHRIST."

DION. AREOP. (*tom. post.*), 133: " Baptism is into the death of the Lord; the water being for the burial, the oil for the Holy Spirit, the Seal for the Cross, the ointment for the confirmation of the confession."

The declaration is express that the baptism is " into the *death* of Christ." A water covering as a likeness to a grave covering, can never be converted into a baptism into the death of Christ! The *burial* of Christ was a wholly distinct and diverse matter from the *baptism* of Christ.

TERTULL. II, 79: " We are thrice mersed (*mergitamur*) doing something more than the Lord commanded in the gospel."

We see, here, how mixed and self-refuting human conceits become. How impracticable to identify *three* coverings in water with the *one* burial in the sepulchre! What evident finger-marks of men is the going to and fro from one burial-covering likeness, to three coverings for the three days' and nights' interment! And then, without resting, passing on to three dippings for the three persons of the trinity! And then comes the theory with one dip-ping (entrance and outrance) for a baptism, which has no out-come to it!

TERTULL. II, 862: "An ignoratis, quod quicunque in Christum Jesum tincti sumus, in mortem ejus tincti sumus? Consepulti ergo illo sumus per baptisma in mortem."

This translation of Rom. 6:3, 4, by Tertullian is introduced because it may show more strikingly to some the distinction between baptism and burial, than it appears under the more familiar Greek form. And for a like reason I do not put it into an English dress.

No writer uses *tingo, tinguo*, as the representative of βαπτίζω so frequently as does Tertullian. This usage is very noticeable and claims attention. At present I only remark: a conclusion based on this usage that tingo *dip* is the equivalent representative of βαπτίζω, would be a great error. *Tingo* as used for dipping into water, and in ideal relations based on such use, is a very different word in its force and development, from *tingo* as used in relations with coloring liquids and in ideal relations based on such use. The same is true of βάπτω, as shown in the first volume of this Inquiry. It was there also stated, that there was an affinity in character and approach toward equality of power between βαπτίζω and βάπτω *to dye* (with development under that usage) as there was not between βαπτίζω and βάπτω *to dip*. The same re-mark holds good as to *tingo* in like relations. And it is only under this limitation that *tingo* can become in translation the proper substitute for βαπτίζω.

Try the truth of these statements on the passage before us. Suppose "tincti sumus" to represent tingo *dip*. The dipping is, from the necessity of the case, ideal. Every ideal use of dip, based in its relations to colorless liquids, is expressive of limita-tion and feebleness. Any one who has only " dipped into various studies," has devoted but limited time to their investigation and has reaped but trivial results. If this is the usage here, then, " all who have been *dipped* into Jesus Christ," have been in rela-tion with Him but for a brief period and have received no benefit worth mentioning from such relation. This beyond all question is the import of such a dipping. Is this the truth which Paul announces? Nothing could be a greater libel on the word of God. Then " tincti sumus" can by no possibility represent *tingo* DIP as related to colorless fluids. Try it as representing *tingo* TO

DYE. This meaning is secured by the use of the verb in relations with coloring liquids. And from such use this, in itself feeble, word secures power and develops a controlling and permanent influence. Thus while white linen dipped into water experiences an effect trivial and transient, the same linen dipped into a purple dye undergoes a profound and abiding change. And the same word in kindred ideal relations shows like development, thus : The man who " dips his hand in a brother's blood " incurs crimson guilt which no time, no tears can wash away. " Dipped in the rebellion " is a phrase used by Sir Walter Scott to express the abiding condition of a man as permanently colored or characterized by the *quality* of rebellion, so as to render liable to legal pains and penalties. So, " dipped in *infamy*." There must be some strong and readily communicated quality as the basis of such usage. Is there such quality in Jesus Christ ? " His name shall be called JESUS because he shall save his people from their sins." He is CHRIST because " anointed by the Holy Ghost," in whom is power to regenerate the soul. Does he part readily with these qualities ? "Ask and ye shall receive." The requisites, then, for the usage are fully met. What then is the purport of Paul's declaration— " Quicunque in CHRISTUM JESUM tincti sumus"? It is this: As many as have (ideally) been introduced into Jesus Christ have been brought under the influence of his distinguishing characteristics—power to remit sin ; power to regenerate the soul—and your condition is thereby thoroughly and abidingly changed, analogously to an object introduced into a strong and penetrating dye. And thus we vindicate and mirror the Greek—ὅσοι ἐβαπτίσθημεν εἰς Χριστόν Ἰησοῦν " as many as have been baptized into Jesus Christ " have been brought thoroughly under his sin-remitting power as JESUS, and under his regenerating power as the CHRIST anointed with and Baptizer by the Holy Ghost.

Need I say that in this baptism there is no water ? Alas ! that Patrist or theorist should ever (unwittingly) have taken away Jesus Christ and substituted for HIM *a pool of water*, hereby perplexing many so that they find it " hard to understand what baptism *into* JESUS CHRIST means," no less now than in the time of Dionysius.

Now, inasmuch as all baptized into Jesus Christ are, as Paul declares, " baptized into his death " (as that whereby he secures the power which belongs to him as " Jesus " and " Christ ") it follows, that " baptism into his death " is as diverse from lying

with him in the sepulchre, as regenerate life is from a shrouded
corpse; but, that unity which is established by baptism into him
as a crucified Redeemer making us participant in all the blessings
of redemption, gives us the right to union with him in his sepulchre also, that we may share in the new life of his resurrection.
If then, Patristic water covering be made a symbol of the *grave
covering* it is a thing wholly distinct (both in their eyes and in
Scripture teaching) from Christian *baptism*.

ORIGEN IV, 372: " As the physical body of Jesus was nailed
to the Cross, buried, and raised, so the body of Christ, the saints,
was nailed to the Cross with Christ. . . .   Therefore not only was
every saint nailed to the Cross with Christ, but also was buried
together with Christ, as Paul says, ' We were buried together
with Christ.' "

Whenever the theory can show, that *saints are buried in the
sepulchre* by the action of *nailing to the Cross*, they may proclaim
it as the exegesis of συνετάφημεν αὐτῷ διὰ τοῦ βαπτίσματος εἰς τὸν
θάνατον; until then we rest in the faith of Origen and of Paul,
namely: *because* the saints, who are the body of Christ, were
nailed with Him to the Cross, THEREFORE, they were, also, buried
with Him.   Any who can receive the nailing to the Cross as a
means of burial can substitute the theory for the Bible ; and any
who are disposed to reject the Patristic likeness between a covering in water and a covering in the grave, may follow the theory
and do what no Patrist ever did, to wit, convert a water dipping
into Christian baptism.

IV, 1038 : " ' Know ye not that so many of us as were baptized
into Christ were baptized into his death ? For we were buried
with him by baptism *into* HIS DEATH ;' teaching by these things
that if any one is first dead to sin, he is necessarily buried with
Christ by baptism ; but if any one is not first dead to sin, he
cannot be buried with Christ.   For no living person is ever
buried.   But if he is not buried with Christ neither is he lawfully
baptized.   If any one shall not have been *born from above*, he
cannot enter the kingdom of heaven, *for* THIS *is to be baptized by
the Holy Spirit.* . . .   But attend yet more closely to this mystical order.   It is necessary for thee first to die to sin, that thou
mayest be buried with Christ.   Burial belongs to the dead.   If
thou dost yet live to sin thou canst not be buried with Christ,
nor be placed *in his* NEW SEPULCHRE, because thy old man lives
and cannot walk in newness of life.   The Holy Spirit has carefully

taught that the sepulchre in which Jesus was buried must be new and that he was wrapped in clean linen, that every one who wishes to be buried with Christ bring nothing of oldness to the new sepulchre, nothing of uncleanness to the clean linen. . . . But some one may ask: Why does the Apostle in these passages, speaking of our baptism and of Jesus, say: ' We are buried with him by *baptism into death ;*' and again, ' If we die with him we shall also live with him;' and yet again, ' If we suffer with him we shall also reign with him ;' and never has said, We have been baptized with him ; since it appears, that as death is compared to death, and life to life, so, also, baptism should be compared to baptism. But observe how careful is the Apostle, for he says, ' Whosoever of us have been baptized *into* CHRIST.' Therefore our baptism is ' into Christ.' But Christ himself is said to have been baptized by John not with that baptism which is ' into Christ, but with that baptism which is into the Law. For so he says himself to John, ' Suffer it to be so now, for thus it becometh us to fulfil all righteousness.' By which he shows, that the baptism of John was the ending of the old, not the beginning of the new. Perhaps also you may inquire this: Since the Lord himself said to the disciples that they should baptize all nations into the name of the Father, and of the Son, and of the Holy Ghost, why does this Apostle use only the name of Christ in baptism, saying, ' Whosoever of us have been baptized into the name of Christ,' when clearly, it may not be regarded as lawful baptism except under the name of the Trinity. But notice the discretion of Paul since in the present passage he did not desire to discuss so much the character of baptism as that of the death of Christ, conformably with which he would persuade us that we should die to sin and be buried together with Christ. And clearly it was unsuitable when he spake of death, that he should mention either the Father or the Holy Spirit. For the word was made flesh and where the flesh is there death is properly spoken of. Nor was it suitable that he should say, ' Whosoever of us have been baptized into the name of the Father, or into the name of the Holy Spirit, have been baptized *into* HIS DEATH.' . . . Still further, this may be inquired: If we are dead to sin and have been buried together with Christ, and have risen together with him, it would seem necessary to show how, according to this form, we are buried with him three days and three nights in the heart of the earth. And see if we can make three days' burial with Christ, accepting the full knowledge of the Trinity: the Father is Light and in his Light, which is the Son, we see Light, the Holy Spirit. But we also make three nights, since we destroy the father of darkness and ignorance, together with lying, which is born of him, as he is both a liar and the father of it, and when he speaks a lie he speaks of his own, but also, in the third place, we destroy the spirit of error which inspires false prophets. . . . Which things are opposed to the Trinity as night is to day, and darkness to light, and falsehood to truth. These things are offered in explanation; but if any one perceives anything better, let him reject these and accept that."

This long extract is given to show how Origen treats that passage of Scripture which the theory makes the great pillar of its support. This treatment shows: 1. The baptism is spiritual and not physical. This is proved (1.) Because the baptism is "*into* CHRIST;" (2.) Because " to be born from above is to be baptized by the Holy Spirit;" (3.) Because baptism by the Holy Spirit is effected through the *agency* of baptizing water and is not a mere *covering* in it; (4.) Because neither Origen nor any other Patrist recognizes a physical baptism as entering into Christianity, nor any other spiritual baptism by the Holy Spirit as Christian baptism, save that only which is by baptizing water, or its equivalent, blood, tears, etc.

2. There is a radical discrimination between "*baptism* into the death of Christ " and *burial* "in the new sepulchre with Christ." Death must precede burial; " no living person is ever buried." Baptism into the death of Christ not merely precedes burial with Christ, but is causative of it as qualifying for and giving a right to such burial by the union which it establishes with Christ, by the cleansing from all sin, by the atoning blood shed in his death, thus fitting to lie in the " new sepulchre," and by the "clean linen," ready for the resurrection life. 3. The covering in the water is made a likeness to the covering in the sepulchre; but this had no more to do with a likeness to the " baptism *into* CHRIST'S DEATH," than it had to do with a likeness to piercing thorns and driven nails. Nor has the likeness established between a water covering and a sepulchre covering by a given mode of using water any more of Bible authority, than Origen's attempt to expound the three days' and the three nights' burial. 4. The plea of the theory, " Follow the example of Christ; be baptized as he was baptized," is repudiated by Origen as having

no truth to rest upon. He declares that Christ's baptism (however the water was used) was not a physical baptism but "into the Law," and was another baptism from that of his people, which is not "into the Law," but "into Christ." Origen never wrote anything truer or more Scriptural than this.

The baptism of Christ was not physical; the water was but a symbol of the nature of the baptism which was "into THE LAW" = "into THE FULFILMENT OF ALL RIGHTEOUSNESS." In this baptism, as meritoriously fulfilled in his life and death, none could share. It was a baptism such as none other had undertaken, and which never would be undertaken again. It was triumphantly "finished" in his death upon the Cross. And now his people are baptized *into* THAT DEATH which is replete with all the qualities of "fulfilled righteousness" and endured penalty, filling "the cup" which his Father held to his lips, and those qualities are all imparted to his people baptized into his wondrous death by the Holy Ghost, receiving the remission of sins, the regeneration of the soul, together with affiliation and everlasting subjection to the Father and the Son and the Holy Ghost. This is, and nothing else than this is, Christian baptism. Origen and his noble associates greatly and sadly erred when they associated this baptism with its divinely appointed symbol rite to be administered by men, merging the symbol character while retaining the symbol, making its presence an equal necessity with the presence and mighty energy of the Holy Ghost. But neither he nor they so erred as to mistake the real baptism of Christianity, and substitute for it a dipping into simple water. This supreme error was reserved for the theory.

AMBROSE IV, 100 : "Baptism is the death of sin that another birth may follow, which, the body remaining, renews the man in mind, all old sins having been buried. . . . It is celebrated by water (*per aquam*), that AS *water cleanses the filth* of the body, so also we may believe, that we are SPIRITUALLY *purged* and *renewed from all* SIN by baptism, and that what is incorporeal is invisibly cleansed."

Ambrose declares that baptism is "the death of sin," and that "sins are buried." This is a common statement. He refers to the *natural qualities* of water to cleanse bodily impurity. He says spiritual impurity is not cleansed by *such* water but "by baptism," which renews from all sin, the incorporeal being invisibly cleansed. Baptism, then, is not the work of "simple" water, nor is the burial in baptism that of men and women, but of sins.

This is the real burial; while the likeness to the sepulchre-burial is another thing entirely, and consists in the momentary covering by dipping.

429: "For there (in baptism) *the old man* is deposited (*deponitur* buried), and the new man is assumed."

GREGORY NAZ. II, 352: "John baptizes, Jesus approaches, perhaps that he may sanctify the Baptizer, but evidently that he may *bury in the water all the old Adam*, yet before these and through these sanctifying the Jordan, as he was Spirit and flesh, so perfecting by the Spirit and water. The Baptist did not receive him, saying ' I have need to be baptized by thee,' and add this, *for thee.* For he knew that he was about to be baptized by martyrdom (τῷ μαρτυρίῳ βαπτισθησόμενος). Jesus said, 'Suffer it to be so now.' For he knew that after a little while he would baptize the Baptist (αὐτὸς βαπτίσων Βαπτιστήν)."

Here is another real burial in baptism. The Saviour had no sins of his own to bury, so he is represented as burying the sins of his people—" all the old Adam "—in the Jordan. Let it be remembered that this, although an ideal, is still a real burial in its representation; while the " likeness " to a grave covering in the dipping is another thing altogether, and makes no claim to be really, ideally, or in any other way to be a burial, but by a momentary καλυψις to make *some resemblance to the covering* in a burial.

Observe the freedom with which βαπτίζω is used: 1. Of John's baptizing; 2. Of Jesus baptizing John, expressed in sanctify; 3. In baptizing the Jordan, expressed in the same manner; 4. In the baptizing of John by martyrdom; 5. In the baptizing of John by Jesus at some future time, without farther specification. And this is the word which means " dip and nothing but dip through all Greek literature."

GREGORY NAZ. II, 362: "As Christ the giver of this gift is called by many and diverse names, so also is the gift. . . . We call it gift, grace, baptism, ointment, illumination, the vesture of incorruption, the washing of regeneration (λουτρόν παλιγγενεσίας), the seal, and anything that is honorable. It is called *gift*, because it is given to those who **first** contribute nothing; *grace*, because it is given to debtors; BAPTISM, *because* SIN *is buried* (συνθαπτομένης) *in the waters;* ointment, because it is sacred and regal, for such things are anointed; *illumination*, because it is shining; *vesture.* because it is a covering of our shame; *washing* (λουτρόν), because it is a washing out (ἔκπλυσιν) ; *seal*, because it is a protection and mark of sovereignty."

This language of Gregory in expounding βάπτισμα, as grounded in the burial of sin in the water, is in harmony with other cases of sin-burial which have come under notice, but is worthy of special attention as showing the possible philological force and application of βάπτισμα. The use here, of course, is not physical; sin cannot have a physical burial; but this giving to sin a body and burying in the water, and calling it a βάπτισμα, is clearly predicated on its derivation from βαπτίζω, which buries things and persons in the depths of the sea. Such burial, without recovery, might properly be called a βάπτισμα; but I know of no such use of the word. It first appears in the New Testament as a derivative from the New Testament βαπτίζω, and is like it used solely in ideal relations, to express profound and abiding spiritual conditions, resultant from the operation of spiritually baptizing agencies. Its usage in this respect is, like that of the verb, in the most absolute accord with the demands of physical use. As sin buried in the water has no emergence therefrom, this condition of burial is with philological propriety called a βάπτισμα. So, if all sin be taken from the soul and buried for evermore, the soul becomes pure, washed, sins remitted, and soul regenerated; and to this condition, as thoroughly and abidingly changed by spiritual influence, βάπτισμα is with no less propriety applied; and this is its constant scriptural and Patristic use. In either aspect we see how far the theory is removed from any just conception as to the meaning of βάπτισμα. A dipping it never was, nor ever can be, by any philological possibility.

CYRIL, 444: "Jesus died bearing the sins of the world, that having slain sin he might raise thee in righteousness; and so thou descending into the water and *buried*, in a certain way (τρόπον τινά), in the water, as he was *buried in the rock*, that he might raise you up again walking in newness of life."

Again, this *covering* in the water is made neither a baptism nor like to a baptism, but like his "BURIAL *in rock*." To call this water covering Christian BAPTISM is as wild an utterance as to call sun-setting sun-rising.

1089: "And as Christ was *truly* (ἀληθῶς) crucified, and buried, and raised, you have been thought worthy, according to (κατὰ) the baptism in a *similitude* (ἐν ὁμοιώματι), to be co-crucified, co-buried, and co-raised with him."

In contradistinction from the actual crucifixion, burial, and resurrection of Christ, Cyril says, that the baptism-crucifixion, burial, and resurrection, were not realities but similitudes. Will any one acquainted with Patristic writings say that Christian baptism in their estimation was not a reality, but a similitude, a shadow? Surely, if there was anything in heaven or on earth which they believed to be a reality, it was Christian baptism. But they did not believe the crucifixion, or the burial, or the resurrection introduced into the administration of this ordinance to be reality, therefore they did not believe the one or the other, or all together, to be Christian baptism. And so they testify.

HILARY I, 977: "He is unworthy of Christ who does not take his cross, by which we suffer with him, die with him, are buried with him, rise with him, and follow him."

This use of crucifixion, death, burial, and resurrection (apart from baptism), shows that their introduction there is of accident and not of essence, and that the baptism is perfect without them, as is conclusively shown in the case of all baptisms of martyrs by their blood, of penitents by their tears, and of Clinics by sprinkled water, in none of which cases were these "similitudes" practiced, but in all of which cases real baptism was received. The theory may lament over the loss of a dipping-burial into blood, and tears, and sprinkled water (for in this loss she loses her all), but no Patrist sympathizes in her grief, for he retains still unharmed his perfect baptism.

AUGUSTINE II, 360: "If the Sacraments had no likeness to those things of which they are sacraments they would not be sacraments. From this likeness they receive their names. So, the Apostle says of baptism: 'We are buried together with Christ through baptism *into death.*' He does not say: We signify burial, but we are buried together."

Thus Augustine very explicitly teaches that the water covering which entered (among very many other things) into the *ex ordine* administration of baptism, was not the baptism (which was a reality), but was a "likeness" to quite another thing, to wit, the burial covering in the rock sepulchre. 1902: "What else is the sepulchre of Christ but the rest of the Christian? We are strangers in the world, and a sepulchre has been bought for us at the price of the Saviour's blood. 'We are buried together with him through baptism *into his death.*' Baptism, therefore, is to us the sepulchre of Christ, in which we die to sin, are buried to trans-

37

gressions, and the consciousness of the old man being dissolved
we are made anew by another birth with renewed infancy. Baptism, I say, is to us the sepulchre of the Saviour; because we there
lose our former life and receive a new life. Great, therefore, is the
grace of this sepulchre whereby we receive a useful death and a
more useful life. Geeat, I say, is the grace of this sepulchre,
which both purifies the sinner and vivifies the dead; he helping
who lives and reigns forever."

Augustine like other writers uses "baptism" to express sometimes the rite as a whole; sometimes to express a particular prominent feature of the administration, such as the water covering
as a likeness to the burial in the sepulchre; sometimes specifical!
the spiritual effect of the divinely impregnated water in changing
the condition of the soul, which is distinctively Patristic baptism;
and sometimes the intermixture and coaction of two distinct
elements, as in the above, where baptism is presented as "the
sepulchre of Christ," and the explanation has the doubleness, 1,
of a covering simply as a fluid, making the sepulchre likeness,
and 2, the δύναμις power of the impregnated fluid, by which "we
are made anew by another birth," this "power" being the channel
through which "he helps who lives and reigns forever."

In the following passages "baptism" is used in its distinctive
spiritual meaning.

VI, 693: "Let no one think because he is born again by water
and Spirit, having been imbued (*imbutus*) by these mysteries, that
he has securely fortified his soul by the sacrament of baptism. . . .
That water not only cleanses the body, but frees the soul from
sin. But you ought to know why the power (*virtus*) of that water
profits both soul and body. For all water does not cleanse; this
sanctifies through (*per*) the consecration of the word. Take away
the word and what is the water, but water? The word added to
the element and it becomes a Sacrament. The power (*virtus*) of
the Word has cleansed us through (*per*) the water, because He
walked upon the waters. See the power of the Word of God."
695: "The devil rages when he sees us by (*per*) the water of
baptism freed from his oppression. Cry to your Moses, the Lord
Jesus Christ, that he may smite with the rod of his Cross the sea
of baptism, so that the water may return and cover the Egyptians,
so that as none of the Egyptians remained, nothing may remain
of your sins." 775: "No man can obtain eternal life (except
those who are baptized by their own blood) but through the sac-

rament of repentance and faith, that is through Baptism." IX,
186 : " Baptism remains inseparably in the baptized person, for
into whatever depth of wickedness and into whatsoever abyss of
sins the baptized may rush, even to apostasy, he does not lose
baptism. . . . Wherefore as baptism is in him (*in illo*) who is
baptized by the Church, it is separated with him (*cum illo*) when
he is separated from the Church." 202 : " When inquiry was
made of Cyprian whether there was any difference between the
baptism of the dipped and the sprinkled (*de* BAPTISMO *tinctorum
et perfusorum*)." 67 : " If man baptizes when the baptizer is
evidently good, but when the baptizer is secretly bad, then God
or an Angel baptizes, and every such one is spiritually born such
as he may be by whom he is baptized, then, they who desire to be
baptized may wish that the men by whom they are baptized may
not be evidently good men but secretly bad men ; that thus God
or an Angel baptizing they may secure a more holy regeneration.
If they would escape this absurdity, let them confess that Christ
(of whom only it is said, ' This is he which baptizes with the Holy
Spirit ') baptizes by every man, whosoever he may be, who baptizes
with the baptism of Christ." III (*altera*), 1416 : " The baptism
which John received was called the baptism of John. He alone
received such a gift : no righteous person before him, none after
him, was so honored as to receive a baptism which should be
called his baptism. He indeed received it, because he could do
nothing of himself. . . . Since then John received a baptism
which should be properly called—of John, yet, the Lord Jesus
Christ was unwilling to give his baptism to any one, not that no
one should be baptized with the baptism of the Lord, but that
the Lord himself should always baptize : this was done that the
Lord should baptize through his ministers, that is, that those
whom the ministers of the Lord were about to baptize the Lord
would baptize, not they. For it is one thing to baptize by minis-
terial service, and another thing to baptize by power. For baptism is such as he is by whose power it is given ; not as he is by
whose service it is given. The baptism of John was such as was
John ; a righteous baptism as of a righteous man, yet of a man,
but one who had received this grace, and so great grace as to be
the Forerunner of the Lord. But the baptism of the Lord is such
as is the Lord ; therefore the baptism of the Lord is divine, because the Lord is God. But the Lord Jesus Christ could, if he
so wished, give power to any of his servants that he should be

stow his baptism as in his stead, and transfer from himself the power of baptizing and establish it in any servant, and give as great power to the baptism transferred to the servant, as the baptism given by the Lord should have. This, however, he was not willing to do, because the hope of the baptized would be in him by whom they would know that they were baptized. He was unwilling, therefore, that a servant should place his hope in a servant. . . . The Lord *retained for himself the* POWER *of baptizing*, and gave the ministration to servants."

These passages (a few among thousands) speak for themselves. They settle, 1. A dipping into water is not Christian baptism in the theology of Augustine, but a regenerate condition of the soul effected solely by the power of the Lord Jesus Christ through the agency of water under the ministry of men; 2. The error which makes a water covering Christian baptism, is (patristically) an absurdity; 3. Burial is used in connection with this rite, (1.) In reference to an ideal burial with Christ (as one of his body) in the rock sepulchre; (2.) In reference to the momentary covering in water by dipping into it, as a "likeness" to the covering in a grave burial; (3.) In reference to the ideal drowning and burial of sin in the pool, grounded in the actual drowning and burial of the Egyptians in the water of the Red Sea; (4.) Burial is not Christian baptism. Equivalence of burial and baptism is absurd.

This Patristic doctrine of baptism is not only erroneous in itself, but must, of necessity, produce error by its promulgation. Augustine was conscious of this tendency and doubtless saw such fruit in fact, so as to be constrained to utter the following warning: " Let us be very careful not to make men falsely secure, saying to them, that if they should have been baptized, howsoever they may live, they will obtain salvation ; lest thus we make Christians as the Jews made proselytes, of whom the Lord said : ' Wo unto you, Scribes and Pharisees! who compass land and sea to make one proselyte, but when ye have made him, you make him twofold more the child of hell than yourselves' (VI, 227)."

The following rebuke addressed to some heretics of his day is not without application in our own time : " Thou hast said, that BAPTISM *is thine*, that the Holy oil is thine, that *the* LORD'S TABLE *is thine*, that all those things *given by God to the faithful*, are THINE. What remains except that thou shalt impiously declare thyself to be God ?" (IX, 769).

ΒΑΠΤΙΖΩ

IN A RELIGIOUS APPLICATION DOES NOT EXPRESS A PHYSICAL
BAPTISM OR A MOMENTARY DIPPING.

General use.

IT has already been shown, that the general use of βαπτίζω by
Patristic writers corresponds perfectly with the use of that word
by Classic writers. This is true not only in primary but in secondary or figurative use. It is applied to express the condition
of vessels lost at sea and sunk beyond recovery to the bottom of
the sea. It is also applied to express the condition of drowned
persons. In such applications it is employed as the equivalent
of ποντίζω, βυθίζω, and suchlike words. And as these words are
used in ideal relations to express influence of the profoundest
character, so βαπτίζω is used in precisely similar relations to express the same idea. Ποντίζω and βυθίζω are never used with the
meaning *to dip* in physical relations, nor could any meaning derivable from "dip" expound their force in ideal relations. The
same is true of βαπτίζω. These views are sustained by quotations
already adduced.

Special Religious Application.

With such usage, which is beyond controversy, it is impossible
that this word could be used in a religious rite to express a dipping without a complete revolution in its meaning, and the most
absolute contradiction of all its previous history and contemporaneous Patristic usage.

We deny the existence of any such revolution or contradiction
We affirm the harmony of the use of this word in the religious
sphere with that of its use in every other sphere, whether by
Classic or Patristric writers. We deny its use to express the
dipping or momentary covering in water which took place in the
customary rite of baptism. We affirm its use in connection with
an ideal element into which it verbally introduces its object, but

(581)

out of which it does not withdraw it, thus subjecting it to the in
fluence of its characteristic quality in the highest degree; and,
also, its absolute use directly expressive of such influence without any attending ideal element.

Proof.

1. Philology forbids the use of this word to express a dipping
or a designed momentary covering. Such a meaning is already
provided for in βάπτω *first*. It is irrational to make a second
word the *ditto* of an already existing word. This feature (momentary covering) had already been eliminated by βάπτω *second*,
in assuming the meaning *to dye*. It is from this second stem
(substituting uncolored quality for colored quality) and not from
the first, that βαπτίζω is derived. As βάπτω *second*, is a stronger
word than βάπτω *first* (by reason of its dropping momentariness
and association with coloring qualities) so, βαπτίζω is a word of
power, because it introduces its object really or verbally into its
associated element and thus communicates the quality of such
element in the fullest measure. Hence it is used to express in
the highest degree the development of any quality where there
can be no intusposition, or where the quality, or the object, is
such that intusposition real or imaginary would not secure such
development. It is treason to philology to attribute to such a
word momentary withinness or trivial influence.

2. Language development forbids such meaning. There is
nothing more certain than that this word is used both by Classic
and Patristic writers to express a thoroughly changed condition
without the intervention of a covering—as by drinking wine to
drunkenness, or swallowing a drug inducing stupor. Such a
secondary use could not possibly originate in a momentary covering. It is the natural and unavoidable use (illustrated in many
other words) from a primary meaning which puts its object within
a fluid without limitation of time. Language development protests
against the monstrosity which allies the profoundest influence
with a dipping.

3. Theology unites in this protest. A momentary covering in
water can produce only a transient and trivial effect. The use of
a word of such primary meaning in figure or in secondary use can
only express a result which is limited in time and power. But
this word is used in Scripture in relations of supreme importance,

and which, by their nature, demand continuance and controlling power. Thus we have baptisms "into repentance," "into the remission of sins," "into Christ," "into the Name of the Father, and of the Son, and of the Holy Ghost." If, now, the leading word in these phrases is converted into *a dipping*, the sentiment is nullified and made the right opposite of that which is demanded by the teaching of Scripture and the nature of things. The theology of revelation is overturned by the doctrine that its great teachings through βαπτίζω and βάπτισμα are grounded in a dipping. But give to these terms their proper force—intusposition without limitation of time (=thorough change of condition specialized by the characteristic of the receiving element, whether real or ideal) and all the teachings of revelation are harmonized and vindicated.

4. Essential truth joins in this protest. There is no class of writings which so emphasizes *withinness* and bases its vital truths on this conception as do the Scriptures. The Father is *in* the Son, and the Son is *in* the Father; Jesus Christ is *in* the Holy Spirit, and the Holy Spirit is *in* the Name of Jesus Christ; the redeemed are *in* Christ, and Christ is *in* the redeemed, and therefore they are made temples *in* which the whole Deity dwells; inspired men speak *in* the Holy Ghost, and the Holy Ghost speaks *in* them; apostles being *in* the Name of Jesus Christ work miracles and issue commands with divine power; wrath and hate are exhausted by declaring that the Christ is *in* Beelzebub; and the charge is as exhaustively met by the declaration—"the prince of this world hath nothing *in* me." John came *in* the spirit and power of Elias; his Lord came *in* the Holy Spirit. Sinners are baptized *into* Christ that they may be without spot or wrinkle or any such thing. Sinners washed *in* the blood of the Lamb are baptized *into* the Name of the Father, and of the Son, and of the Holy Ghost. This use of WITHINNESS to express influence of the most absolute fulness, throughness, and completeness, is founded in the reality of things. Through all nature withinness and influence are twain-one. The God of nature as the God of revelation has carried this union into his holy Word, and no man may put asunder that which God has joined together. It is not true that Christian baptism is a dipping (= a momentary inness with a consequent outness), but is withinness without limitation of time, and *therefore* cannot be *within* WATER.

Καταδύνω, ἀναδύνω—demergo, emergo.

It is a very strong, if not wholly conclusive, argument against a momentary water covering being found in Scripture, in that no word expressive of such covering is to be found anywhere in connection with its baptisms, as announced by inspiration. And it is a very strong, if not wholly conclusive, argument in proof that such water covering was introduced independently of and in contradiction to inspiration, in that terms designating such covering and the necessary consequent uncovering are to be found everywhere in Patristic writings.

The most common Greek terms to express the water covering in "*ex ordine*" baptism were καταδύω, κατάδυσις. These terms do not of themselves limit the time of covering. It was necessary, therefore, in applying them to a water covering in a religious rite that there should be some evidence giving expression to such limitation. This is found in the equally extensive usage of the related words ἀναδύνω, ἀνάδυσις. What was covered in the water by καταδύνω was uncovered by ἀναδύνω. On this usage it may be observed, 1. There is no such usage in the Scriptures. The terms καταδύω, κατάδυσις, are not to be found as words of inspiration descriptive of or in anywise connected with the administration of ritual baptism. The overwhelming inference therefore is, that *what these terms were introduced to express in* PATRISTIC *baptism had no existence in* SCRIPTURE *baptism.* 2. There are no corresponding forms in Scripture such as καταβαπτίζω, ἀναβαπτίζω. And since the object which is covered by βαπτίζω can never be uncovered by that word, and the Scriptures furnish no word for such uncovering, we are, again, forced to the conclusion that the new words introduced by the Patrists, unknown to inspired nomenclature, were introduced to express new ideas equally unknown to the inspired writers. 3. Patristic writers no more introduce καταβαπτίζω, ἀναβαπτίζω, into the administration of the Christian rite to express a covering and uncovering than do inspired writers. There is no such thing to be found anywhere among numberless writers through long centuries as the interchange of καταβαπτίζω with καταδύνω, or of ἀναβαπτίζω with ἀναδύνω, expressive of a water covering and uncovering. And, thus, again, we are led to the conclusion that these writers use βαπτίζω just as the inspired writers use it, namely, *never expressive of a water covering,* introducing new terms to express the new facts of their own invention, to wit, *a water covering* and *uncovering*.

Demergo—Emergo.

The Latin terms *demergo, emergo,* correspondent with the Greek terms just considered, abound in Latin writers to express their accustomed covering and uncovering in water. Now these terms are like both in form and in force to the Greek καταδύνω, ἀναδύνω. They are used for identically the same purpose, namely, to express a water covering and uncovering. Can there be any rational doubt that these Latin words do and are designed to represent and duplicate those Greek words? But if they do, then these Latin words do no more represent the βαπτίζω of the Scriptures, or the βαπτίζω of the Greek Patrists in Christian baptism, than do those Greek words καταδύνω, ἀναδύνω. That this conclusion is made impregnably sure by the fact that the Greek βαπτίζω is transferred into the Latin language, and employed by the Latin like the Greek Fathers in relations and with meanings such as *demergo* and *emergo* are never employed in. If these words represented the usage and meaning of βαπτίζω, why transfer the foreign word into the Latin? Why, when transferred, use it in relations peculiar to the Greek, and to which the Latin could furnish no parallel usage in the history of *demergo, emergo?* Why preserve the same compound form with καταδύνω, αναδύνω, if they were not translations of and did not fulfil the same offices with these words? Why make them represent another word (βαπτίζω) to whose form they are unlike, and which is never in the Scriptures employed to fulfil that office which their form expresses, and which it is confessed, as a matter of fact, they do fill? That βαπτίζω is never used in Scripture to express a covering and uncovering of water, I hold to be as certain as any proposition in mathematics. That it is ever used in Patristic writings to express a covering and uncovering of water, I have never seen adequate evidence. That such use may be plausibly asserted, and that quotations may be made plausibly sustaining such assertion on a superficial examination, is certain.

1. Because βαπτίζω has a usage by which it covers its object in water, *without limitation of time*; 2. Because there is a facility in keeping out of view this vital point of unlimited time and metamorphosing the word into a limited, momentary covering—*a*

dipping; 3. Because there was, admittedly, a momentary water covering in the ordinary Patristic baptism, and by concealing (wittingly or unwittingly) the fact that another word was used to express this covering, the disguised βαπτίζω may be introduced to officiate at the dipping; 4. Because βαπτίζω is employed variously in connection with the rite and inclusive of the water: (1.) It is used to express comprehensively the rite, and consequently inclusive of the use of the water. This affords a very facile but a very groundless opportunity to say, βαπτίζω here expresses the manner of using the water; (2.) It is used more limitedly in connection with the use of the water, which being ordinarily by a momentary covering, there is opportunity to say that this is the work of βαπτίζω, while, in truth, it is the work of καταδύω (expressed or understood) while the effect of the impregnated water upon the soul is expressed by the verb in question; (3.) It is sometimes used to express the purifying effect in the soul, without any associate term or circumstance certainly to limit it to such application, and again there is opportunity to introduce the inevitable dipping. These are some of the reasons why plausibility is given to the claim that water covering in Patristic baptism is expressed by βαπτίζω. But if there be one passage or one fact which conclusively shows, that a mere water covering in the Christian rite was expressed by βαπτίζω I am not aware of it. Such a position can never be proved by the joint presence of βαπτίζω and momentary covering in the baptismal pool against the facts (1) that the baptizing water is impregnated water used as an agency to effect a Spiritual *baptisma;* (2.) That this *baptisma*, as declared in all ages, does not depend upon a covering in this impregnated water; (3.) That another word expresses the fact of a simple *covering*, which is never used to express the *effect* of such covering, nor interchanged with the Patristic βαπτίζω whose office it is to express the effect of this covering (or *the* EFFECT *of this water used in any other way*) and not to express simple covering.

If any one thinks that a simple momentary covering can be fastened on to βαπτίζω in any other way, the course is free for the attempt. But we give friendly notice that the course indicated is but a blind path and leads only to disappointment to any one setting out on such a mission.

Illustrative Quotations.

CLEMENS ROM. I, 1045 : " For this is the power of the imposition of hands; unless such invocation be made, he who is baptized (ὁ βαπτιζόμενος) only descends (καταβαίνει) into the water (εἰς ὕδωρ) as the Jews, and only removes the impurity of the body, not the impurity of the soul."

Will any one say, that βαπτίζω and καταβαίνω are here used as equivalents? Is it not certain that the latter refers to physical covering effected by descending into the water, while the former refers to the effect induced by the impregnated water, to wit, the removal of the impurity of the soul? But there are few if any cases stronger than this as a warrant for confounding βαπτίζω with water covering.

II, 760 : " This he says, because we go down (καταβαίνομεν) into the water (εἰς τὸ ὕδωρ) full of sins and impurity, and come up (ἀναβαίνομεν) bearing fruit, having spiritually the fear and hope toward Jesus."

Here καταβαίνω no more fills the place of βαπτίζω than does ἀναβαίνω, which the Baptist Quarterly acknowledges it cannot do. The representative of this unexpressed word is "the bearing fruit" as the effect of the impregnated water on the soul.

CYRIL, 444 : " For as Jesus bearing the sins of the whole world died, that having slain sin he might raise thee in righteousness; so, also, thou going down (καταβὰς) into the water (εἰς τὸ ὕδωρ) and after a manner buried (ταφεὶς) in the waters, as he in the rock (ἐν τῇ πέτρᾳ) might arise again walking in newness of life."

Here again, καταβὰς no more represents βαπτίζω than does ταφεὶς; and ταφεὶς " after a manner in the waters" no more represents βαπτίζω than does the body of the crucified Redeemer truly ταφεὶς ἐν τῇ πέτρᾳ. Who is bold enough to reject the Bible baptism of the Lord Jesus *on the* CROSS and substitute for it his BURIAL *in the rock?* The baptism in this passage is no *katabainism* in water, but the effect claimed for the impregnated water as shown in " walking in newness of life."

These passages are sufficient to show the gulf which separates the function of the water-covering καταβαίνω from the function of the soul-cleansing βαπτίζω.

Καλύπτω, κάλυψις. DIONYSIUS AREOPAGITÆ, 404 : " The sacred symbols (σύμβολα) have great fitness. . . . As the body is covered (καλυπτόμενον) in the earth, the complete covering (κάλυψις) by water may suitably be received as a likeness of death and burial. This symbol teaching (συμβολικὴ διδασκαλία) initiates the sacredly baptized (βαπτιζόμενον) by the three coverings (καταδύσεσι) in the water into the imitation of the divine death and three days' and nights' burial (ταφῆς) of Jesus the giver of life."

Is καλύπτω to be added to the list of words equivalents of βαπτίζω? Will any one say that the latter word in its Patristic (or Classic) use can be substituted for the former word, as here used, reading—"As the body is *baptized* in the EARTH"? Is there any such phrase in Christian Greek writers, or in heathen Greek writers, or is it possible to form such in accordance with Greek usage? If βαπτίζω cannot be applied to a "covering in the earth," it may not, here, be applied to a κάλυψις in the water.

Καλύπτω, κάλυψις, καταδύω, κατάδυσις, θάπτω, ταφή, are substantial equivalents, but neither of them has any equivalence with the Patristic βαπτίζω, βάπτισμα.

Καταδύνω. Gregory Thaum., 1185: "It is necessary that I should, now, be baptized with this baptism and hereafter bestow upon men the baptism of the coequal Trinity. . . . Cover (καταδυσόν) me with the waters of the Jordan as she who bare me wrapped me in swaddling clothes. Give me the baptism (τὸ βάπτισμα) as the Virgin gave me milk. Baptize me who am about to baptize them that believe through water and Spirit and fire (δι' ὕδατος καὶ Πνεύματος καὶ πυρὸς) by the water able (ὕδατι δυναμένῳ) to wash away the filth of sins, by the Spirit able (Πνεύματι δυναμένῳ) to make the earthly spiritual, by fire (πυρί) fit by nature to burn up the thorns of sin."

Καταδυσόν covering in the waters of Jordan may respond to wrapping in swaddling bands; will the Patristic βαπτίζω do so? Could Gregory say—"Give me the κατάδυσιν as the Virgin gave me milk?" Is there such a phrase to be found anywhere as "a κατάδυσις of the coequal Trinity?" or, "a κατάδυσις δι' ὕδατος καὶ Πνεύματος καὶ πυρὸς?" That this word is not the equivalent of βαπτίζω, and does not subserve the same office in the administration of baptism, is further shown by the adjunct δυναμένῳ with "water," and with "Spirit" when a baptism is spoken of. "Power" in water has nothing to do with a κατάδυσις; but it is the all-essential thing on which a Patristic baptism is suspended.

DIDYMUS ALEX., 720: "They who come into orthodoxy, although they may have been baptized, are baptized, I do not say rebaptized (ἀναβαπτίζονται) because they have not the true baptism. The Eunomians because they practice but one covering (κατάδυσιν), professing only to baptize (βαπτί'εσθαι) into the death of the Lord; the Phrygians, because they did not baptize into (εἰς) the three holy hypostases, but believed the Father, the Son, and the Holy Spirit to be the same." (Basil says (Epist. 188), they baptized into the Father, and Son, and Montanus, or Priscilla.)

Observe the marked discrimination, here and always, in the usage of κατάδύω and βαπτίζω, together with their derivatives. The Eunomian water covering is expressed by κατάδυσις, but when "the death of the Lord" is introduced, this word is promptly rejected and *baptism* is substituted. The same is true as to the Phrygians. Whether they used one κατάδυσις or three, in using the water, there was neither one nor three "into the hypostases," but this word is discarded and βαπτίζω is used. And when Basil speaks of their sentiments and practice, he does not speak of a κατάδυσις "into the Father, and Son, and Montanus, or Priscilla," but a *baptism*. This discrimination is uniform.

ATHANASIUS IV, 753: "As the Lord's body buried in the earth begat salvation for the world, so, also, our body buried in the baptism begat righteousness for us. The likeness is thus: As Christ died and on the third day arose, so, also, we dying in the baptism arise. For the thrice covering (καταδῦσαι) and uncovering (ἀναδῦσαι) the child in the pool signifies the death and third day resurrection of Christ."

The phrase ταφὲν ἐν τῷ βαπτίσματι affords very facile ground for serious error through hasty interpretation. It may, very plausibly, be said, βαπτίσματι here represents κατάδυσις, covering simply. But there are two objections to this: 1. The whole current of usage is against such a meaning; 2. The true representative of "covering" is ταφὲν, which we have already seen to be used as the equivalent of κατάδυσις. Unless these objections can be removed they are conclusive against this interpretation. A better one, harmonious with usage, may be found in either of two expositions: 1. Βάπτισμα is here used to denote the baptizing water characteristically, to wit, as water having the *power* (not to cover but) to baptize = to remit sin and to regenerate. This use of the word is shown (1) by its application to the water and the blood issuing from the wounded side of Christ, which (the blood, as well as the water) were called baptisms—"two baptisms." The reason for such appellation is found, not in their power to

cover, for the blood of Christ cannot cover his people, nor can
the blood of martyrdom cover the martyr, but in their power to
baptize = to remit sin, which is true in fact of the blood of
Christ, and was thought (erroneously) to be true of the blood of
martyrs; (2.) By its application to all water having this same
power, because " τῷ ἰδίῳ βαπτίσματι " it secured *the power* to baptize.   This designation of a liquid by a term denoting a quality
imparted to it and which in turn it is capable of imparting is illustrated in 2 Maccabees 1 : 36, where Nehemiah calls a liquid
which has secured the power of purifying, Napthar (καθαρισμός)
purification.   In like manner we call water to which a coloring
quality has been imparted *a dye*, because it has secured the power
of *dyeing*.   This truth must be recognized or Patristic writings
cannot be justly interpreted.   A covering in dye water is one
thing; a covering in simple water is another thing.   And no one
has a right to make them one thing by abstracting the differen-
tiating dyeing quality.   It is utter extinction to Patristic baptism
to take away from its water its impregnating quality.

When Athanasius speaks of a burial ἐν τῷ βαπτίσματι there is
no authority for converting his statement into a κατάδυσις within
a simple fluid.   That he does not contemplate a simple covering
he shows very clearly by the statement of the effect of the baptizing water in " begetting righteousness."   2. Βάπτισμα may not
be used here specifically, but comprehensively (like Φώτισμα)
which means *baptism* = the rite, just as does, very frequently,
βάπτισμα itself.   In such case the preposition (ἐν) in the phrase
under consideration is not local, within a space, but temporal,
during a time, *i. e.*, the burial takes place within the rite, during
the administration of the rite.   Either of these interpretations
finds adequate justification and is harmonious with the usage of
terms.   That κατάδυσις is to be found in ταφὲν and not in βαπτίσματι,
or is to be supplied by ellipsis, is evident from the subsequent
introduction of καταδῦσαι, ἀναδῦσαι in the triple covering of the
child to denote ˏ burial and resurrection, which βάπτισμα never
does nor can represent.

BASIL IV, 884 : " But I do not know why it should have occurred to you to inquire concerning the uncovering (ἀναδύσεως) in
the baptism, since you have received the covering (κατάδυσιν) as a
type exemplifying the three days.   For it is impossible to be
baptized thrice without being uncovered (ἀναδυντα) as often."

The use of the phrase ἐν τῷ βαπτίσματι in connection with ἀνα-

δεύσεως is confirmatory of the interpretation which makes it comprehensive of the whole rite, since if βαπτίσματι be understood to
mean *covering*, the phrase " uncovering in the covering " becomes
impossible and absurd.   We have, also, again the distinct statement that κατάδυσις is not the baptism, but a type of a wholly
different thing—the three days' burial.   The thrice baptizing will,
again, come up for consideration.

CLEMENT I, *Rom. Pont.*, 800 : " Baptism is given into the death
of Jesus.   The water is instead of a sepulchre.   The covering
(κατάδυσις) is the dying with Jesus.   The uncovering (ἀνάδυσις) is
the rising with Jesus."

Here is an express explanation of κατάδυσις and ἀνάδυσις.   It is
anything but the Patristic βάπτισμα.

The notions and utterance of these writers respecting baptism
are mixed and incongruous as might be anticipated in such wide
departures from Scripture teaching.   We are told that baptism
should be " into the death of Christ."   This is scriptural ; but it
is a purely ideal baptism and does not admit of any physical
representation.   And yet the manner of using water was constructed, not on the death, that was impossible, but on the
burial of Christ, which does not by one word of Scripture enter
into.his baptism which takes place upon the Cross, or with our
relation to that baptism.   Again, we are told that it is heresy to
baptize into the name or death of Christ, and the baptism should
be into the Name of the Father, Son, and Holy Ghost.   But in
that case what becomes of the κατάδυσις burial and the ἀνάδυσις
resurrection ?   Are there any such things in the Father, Son, and
Holy Ghost ?   And what becomes of the triple covering and uncovering—the typified three nights and three days ?   Converted
into the three Persons of the Trinity are they ?   But does this
shifting from the duplex-trine-type of days and nights to the
single trine Persons of the Deity exhibit divine wisdom and congruity, or human folly and inconsistency ?   Whatever may have
been the errors adopted by the Patrists they did not adopt the
error of confounding κατάδυσις and βάπτισμα.

DIONYSIUS AREOP. (*prior*) 396 : " The chief priest baptizes him
thrice, invoking the trine Hypostasis of the blessed Deity, at the
three coverings (καταδύσεσι) and uncoverings (ἀναδύσεσι) of the
candidate."

421 : " And since Jesus remained during three days and nights
in the heart of the earth, the three nights are represented by the

three coverings (καταδύσεων) and the three days by the three uncoverings (ἀναδύσεων).''

No one acquainted with the Patristic βάπτισμα can confound
these type burial-resurrection coverings and uncoverings with it.

President Beecher gives the following quotations: *Apostol.
Constitut. L.* "Three baptisms of one initiation." *Photius:*
"The three coverings and uncoverings of the baptism signify
death and resurrection." *Theophylact:* "As baptism through
the covering typifies death, so through the uncovering it typifies
the resurrection. . . . He gave one baptism with three coverings
of the body to his disciples."

Zonaras is quoted as expounding the τρία βαπτίσματα as the τρεῖς
καταδύσεις. President Beecher inclines to this view, but does not
think it necessary. Balsamon, also, is quoted as suggesting, not
without misgiving, the same interpretation, thus: "The βαπτίσματα
here seem to me instead of καταδύσεων." The doubt implied in
this language is well justified. The τρία βαπτίσματα can only be
referred to the several baptisms into the three Persons of the
Godhead. It is this explanation only which can constitute the
" ἐν βάπτισμα " into the Name of the Godhead in harmony with the
" τρία βαπτίσματα " into (severally) the Father, the Son, and the
Holy Ghost. This interpretation is required by the uniform usage
of βαπτίζω and βάπτισμα. Three physical coverings can in no sense
constitute one physical covering which they must be affirmed to
do if " one baptism " be *one covering;* but " three coverings "
may readily enter into something wholly diverse, to wit, " one
baptism." There is no difficulty in saying "three baptisms" into
the several Persons ("in Personas") of the Deity make "one baptism" into the Name common to each Person of the Deity.

Mergo—Mergito.

TERTULLIAN I, 1206: "Going out of the washing we are
anointed. . . . The ointment flows on us physically, but it profits
spiritually; as also the act of baptism itself is physical, because
we are covered (*mergimur*) in water, but the effect is spiritual,
because we are free from sins."

Here the physical water-covering is explicitly distinguished
from the effect of the water as impregnated with a spiritual
δύναμις, the operation of which reaching to the soul constitutes
the baptism, to wit, *the remission of sins.* The physical act by

which the body is covered in water, or otherwise made subject to the influence of the water, no more constitutes the baptism, than does the pouring or the flowing of the ointment on the body constitute the spiritual anointing (endowment) of the soul with the graces of the Holy Spirit. Neither has the covering in water anything essential to do with the baptism—this is simply "*ex ordine*,"—as is demonstrated by the "almost daily" baptism by pouring or sprinkling the water upon the sick. This was no mere *quasi* baptism. It was true, perfect, "most glorious" *baptism*, while it was no water-covering.

1209: "After the waters of the Deluge by which old sin was purged away—after the Baptism, as I might say, of the world—the Dove returning with the olive-branch announced peace."

Here was a water-covering beyond the craving of any friend to dipping; but as a water-covering it was no Patristic baptism (classical it was because it was no dipping), but as taking away sin it was a baptism. The covering form of the deluge is of no account; it is the *power* of the deluge waters, as an agency, to purge the earth from sin which constitutes the "baptism of the world."

II, 280: " He covers (*mergit*) the body destitute of salvation into this sacrament of salvation."

The simple covering of the body in this saving water is no more the baptism (= salvation), than is the simple covering of a fleece in a purple dye, the purple which the dye effects in the fleece. Mergo and βαπτίζω are never interchanged within the religious sphere by these writers. Mergo may be used in the process by which a dye may be effected, but mergo *never means* TO DYE; and mergo may be used in the process by which Patristic baptism was effected, but mergo *never means* Patristic baptism.

JEROME I, 661: "Micah 7 : 19 speaks of the grace of baptism—'He will cast all our sins into the depth of the sea.' How are all sins covered (merguntur) in the washing if one wife swims upon the surface?"

Jerome is speaking to the question—"Unius uxoris virum." Sins covered by God in the depths of the sea never emerge. The grace of baptism removes all sin from the sinner, and leaves them in the bottom of the pool forever classically baptized, while the sinner through *the remission of sins* lives a patristically baptized man. Water-covering is not Patristic baptism.

38

XI, 745: "When we pass over the sea of baptism then the devil and his army are drowned (demergitur) for us as was Pharaoh."

This is another case of water-covering classical baptism. The devil and his army may be drowned by being covered in the sea of baptism, but the sinner fleeing from him is not drowned but baptized—washed from sin and regenerated into a divine life. The baptism of the devil and his army is a simple water-covering; the baptism of Jerome and his associates is the remission of sins.

VII, 495: "'One Lord, one faith, one baptism.' It is said *one faith*, because we believe similarly upon the Father, and upon the Son, and upon the Holy Spirit. And *one baptism*, for in the same manner we are baptized into the Father, and into the Son, and into the Holy Spirit. And we are thrice covered (ter mergimur) that one sacrament of the Trinity may appear. And we are not baptized into the names of the Father, and the Son, and the Holy Spirit, but into one name, which expresses the Deity. . . . It may, also, be called *one baptism*, because although we may be thrice baptized on account of the mystery of the Trinity, still it must be considered *one .baptism*. That, also, is one baptism which is by water, by Spirit, and by fire."

Jerome like all others makes a broad discrimination in the use of *baptizo* and *mergo*. The latter is limited to the physical element, and the former is as strictly limited to an ideal element— Father, Son, and Holy Ghost, or of suchlike character. Besides, if these words were of like meaning and application, why introduce the foreign word into the Latin language and use it side by side with one of native origin? We, like the Latins, have adopted the Greek word on the declared ground that there is no word in the English language of the same meaning, with the same development, and the same peculiar application both as to form and subject. The same is true of the Latin; and when the theory borrows the Latin *im-mergo* (immerse) for its Bible as the square equivalent of βαπτίζω, they do what Jerome would not do for his Bible. But perhaps the friends of the theory understand Latin as well as Greek better than the translator of the Vulgate. Yet for all this there has not been a Baptist book ever framed on the idea, that "to translate βαπτίζω into English is the easiest thing in the world," for "baptism is dipping, and dipping is baptism," and "it means dip and nothing but dip through all Greek literature," but what superabundantly disproved itself.

Jerome satisfactorily explains the three baptisms, into the three several persons, Father, Son, and Holy Ghost, as one baptism into one Name, comprehending the Three-One. He does not undertake the task of explaining that three water-coverings may be one water-covering. The interpretation of Eph. 4 : 5, "one baptism," as one *dipping* into water (as against pouring or sprinkling the water), never entered into the mind of any Patrist any more than of Jerome.

II, 164: "There are many other things observed in the Churches through tradition which have assumed the authority of written law, such as to cover (mergitare) the head three times in the washing."

This declaration of Jerome, that there is no scriptural warrant for covering the head thrice in water, might as truly be extended to covering it once.

All Latin and Greek terms for covering in water in the rite are separate in use and meaning from βαπτίζω.

Evidence against the physical use of βαπτίζω in greater force.

That βαπτίζω and βάπτισμα, by long and frequent use in organic phrases expressive of purification, have acquired the power in absolute use to express directly the meanings *to purify, purification* in relation to spiritual things, is authoritatively established by the following quotations:

ORIGEN III, 704: "Physicians say, that to cure certain diseases not only is the cutting by a knife necessary, but burning, also. Cancers require to cut with the knife and to burn the roots with fire. Our sin is a cancer for which neither cutting nor burning, alone, is sufficient; both are needed. . . . Therefore the Saviour uses both sword and fire (*et baptizat quæ non potuerunt Spiritus Sancti purificatione purgari*), and baptizes those sins which could not be purged by the purification of the Holy Spirit."

The verb is here used absolutely, and the construction with *sins* (quæ) as its object constitutes an impassable gulf over which no friend of dipping can ever pass. Whoever may undertake the feat of dipping sins into "sword and fire" will have need to bear in mind the caution addressed to those who meddle with edged tools and burning coals. The only possible meaning which can be assigned to "baptizat" is *purifies, washes, cleanses.* "The Saviour *purifies* those sins which (or those things polluted by sin which) could not be *purified* by the *purification* of the Holy

Spirit." When the verb appears in an organic phrase with an ideal element possessed of a purifying power, as in baptized into repentance, into remission of sins, into Christ, etc., it has not in itself the idea of purification, but it develops this idea by bringing its object under the controlling influence of the associate member of the phrase. This is the aspect in which the verb is introduced to our attention in the New Testament. These phrases present a combination absolutely novel. Words never before presented such forms, or such verbal conceptions, as " *baptize* INTO REPENT- ANCE, *be baptized* INTO THE REMISSION OF SINS, *baptized* INTO CHRIST, *baptized* INTO THE DEATH OF CHRIST," *baptizing* INTO THE NAME *of the* FATHER, *and of the* SON, *and of the* HOLY GHOST. They are well calculated to arrest attention by their remarkable construction, their profound meaning, and the priceless worth of their sentiment. We might well conclude, that it was something of no ordinary character which thus induced the Holy Spirit to originate new forms of expression (almost constraining their preservation in all languages and their perpetuation through all ages in the same identical terms), taxing the power of language to the uttermost in order to its enunciation. This was true. The exigency arose in the wondrous death and purifying power of the atoning blood of God manifest in the flesh to cleanse a guilty race and restore redeemed souls to subjection and affiliation to the living God, Father, Son, and Holy Ghost. As the symbol and exponent of this marvellous work the wisdom of God has chosen above all other words, the word *ΒΑΠΤΙΖΩ.* This word in its com- binations exhausts, so far as human imagination can receive it, the depths of repentance, of remission of sin, of the bleeding wounds of the Crucified, of the duties of creatures, and of the sovereign rights of the fully revealed JEHOVAH. This word will endure and be diffused in all languages to bear witness to the profoundest SPIRITUAL PURIFICATION as essential to union and communion with the God of heaven and earth.

TERTULLIAN III, 1082: A letter from Cyprian to Jovian con- tains the following passage: " It is necessary that the water be first purified ($\varkappa\alpha\theta\alpha\rho'\zeta\varepsilon\sigma\theta\alpha\iota$) and sanctified ($\dot{\alpha}\gamma\iota\dot{\alpha}\zeta\varepsilon\sigma\theta\alpha\iota$) by the priest, that it may be able by its own baptism ($\delta\nu\nu\eta\theta\tilde{\eta}$ $\tau\tilde{\omega}$ $\dot{\iota}\delta\dot{\iota}\omega$ $\beta\alpha\pi\tau\dot{\iota}\sigma\mu\alpha\tau\iota$) to purge ($\dot{\alpha}\pi\sigma\sigma\mu\tilde{\nu}\zeta\alpha\iota$) the sins of the baptized ($\beta\alpha\pi\tau\dot{\iota}\zeta\sigma\mu\acute{\varepsilon}\nu\sigma\nu$) man."

It is impossible for evidence to be more complete in proof of the usage of $\beta\dot{\alpha}\pi\tau\iota\sigma\mu\alpha$ to express directly PURIFICATION. Does the priest purify and sanctify the water by dipping it into itself or into anything else? Is it possible to dip a pool of water into sprinkled oil and invocation any more than to dip the Homeric lake into frog's blood? Does not καθαρίζω mean purify? Does not ἁγιάζω mean sanctify? Is not βαπτίσματι the child of this parentage? Has the law, "Like begets like," been abrogated, so that purification and sanctification bring forth that *strangeling* —*a dipping*? But the force of the evidence cannot be increased by multiplying words. I only add, that expressions equivalent with that of this passage abound. They do not, however, usually employ the terms baptize, baptism, but the equivalents purify, purification, cleanse, cleansing. And hereby, namely, by the interchange of βαπτίζω with terms expressive of purification as equivalents, we have the argument from the refusal to interchange βαπτίζω with terms expressive of physical covering as equivalents, driven home and fastened as a nail in a sure place. There is no characteristic of Patristic writings more certain or more abounding than the equivalent interchange of βαπτίζω and words expressive of purification, such as καθαρίζω, λουω, *mundo*, *lavo*, and such like. It must be observed, however, that such interchange is not with βαπτίζω in organic phrases such as appear in the New Testament and in Patristic writings, namely, βαπτίζ. εἰς μετάνοιαν, εἰς ἄφεσιν, εἰς Χριστον, etc., but in its absolute use as having absorbed within itself and expressing by itself the import of the entire phrase. Such development is in the most absolute harmony with the laws of language, and the fact of such usage as that indicated establishing the development as a historical fact, is one of mathematical certainty. Some illustrative quotations will now be presented.

Καθαρίζω, λούω, mundo, lavo, etc. = *Βαπτίζω.*

CLEMENS ROM. I (*Const. Apost.*), 1081: "O thou, who hast said through the holy prophets, 'Wash (λούω) you, make you clean,' and hast established through Christ spiritual regeneration, look now upon these baptized (βαπτίζω) ones and bless them. Λούω = βαπτίζω.

1124: "O thou who givest water for drinking and for purification (κάθαρσιν) and oil to gladden the face, now, through Christ, sanctify this water and oil, and grant effectual power to heal, to expel diseases, and to put to flight dæmons." Κάθαρσιν = Βάπτισμα.

1460: "I am fully persuaded that the holy baptism (βάπτισμα) of Christ is spiritual purification ($\kappa \acute{a} \theta a \rho \sigma \iota \nu$) and regeneration both of soul and body." $K \acute{a} \theta a \rho \sigma \iota \nu = \beta a \pi \tau \iota \sigma \mu a.$

DIONYSIUS AREOPAGITÆ, 484: " Whence" (because Christ = anointed, sanctifies) " as I think, ointment is sprinkled upon the purifying baptistery ($\kappa a \theta a \rho \tau \iota \kappa \tilde{\omega} \beta a \pi \tau \iota \sigma \tau \eta \rho \acute{\iota} \omega$) in the form of a cross, showing that Jesus by his death through the cross delivered those baptized ($\beta a \pi \tau \iota \zeta o \mu \epsilon \nu o \iota \varsigma$) into his death, from death." The conjoint $\kappa a \theta a \rho \tau \iota \kappa \tilde{\omega}$ $B a \pi \tau \iota \sigma \tau \eta \rho \acute{\iota} \omega$ shows the intimate conjunction of $\kappa a \theta a \rho \acute{\iota} \zeta \omega$ and $\beta a \pi \tau \acute{\iota} \zeta \omega.$

JUSTIN MARTYR, 420, 500–516: " We will relate how, being re‑ newed through Christ, we consecrate ourselves to God. . . . Upon ($\grave{\epsilon} \pi \grave{\iota}$) the Name of the Father of all and Lord God, and of our Saviour Jesus Christ, and of the Holy Spirit, they are washed ($\lambda o \upsilon \tau \rho \acute{o} \nu \pi o \iota o \tilde{\upsilon} \nu \tau a \iota$) by the water. . . . This washing ($\lambda o \upsilon \tau \rho \acute{o} \nu$) is called illumination, because those learning these things are illuminated as to their understanding. The illuminated is washed ($\lambda o \acute{\upsilon} \epsilon \tau a \iota$) . . . Isaiah did not send you to the bath there to wash away ($\grave{a} \pi o \lambda o \upsilon \sigma a \mu \acute{\epsilon} \nu o \upsilon \varsigma$) murder and other sins, which not all the water of the sea is sufficient to purify ($\kappa a \theta a \rho \acute{\iota} \sigma a \iota$); but this saving wash‑ ing ($\lambda o \upsilon \tau \rho \acute{o} \nu$) was announced to the repenting no longer seeking purification ($\kappa a \theta a \rho \iota \zeta o \mu \acute{\epsilon} \nu o \upsilon \varsigma$) by the blood of goats and sheep, but by and through the blood of Christ. . . . Through the washing ($\lambda o \upsilon \tau \rho \acute{o} \nu$) of repentance and the knowledge of God, as Isaiah cries. . . . Be baptized ($\beta a \pi \tau \iota \sigma \theta \eta \tau \epsilon$) as to the soul from anger, and avarice, and envy, and hate, and behold the body is pure ($\kappa a \theta a \rho \acute{o} \nu$). . . . Wash ($\lambda o \acute{\upsilon} \sigma a \sigma \theta \epsilon$) and be pure ($\kappa a \theta a \rho o \grave{\iota}$), and put away the evil from your souls, as the Lord commands you to wash ($\lambda o \upsilon \sigma a \sigma \theta a \iota$) with this washing ($\lambda o \upsilon \tau \rho \acute{o} \nu$). For we have not received that worthless bap‑ tism ($\beta \acute{a} \pi \tau \iota \sigma \mu a$) of cisterns, for it is of no value compared with this baptism ($\beta \acute{a} \pi \tau \iota \sigma \mu a$) of life.

Justin M. continually interchanges $\lambda o \acute{\upsilon} \omega, \kappa a \theta a \rho \acute{\iota} \zeta \omega$ and $\beta a \pi \tau \acute{\iota} \zeta \omega$, as also, $\lambda o \upsilon \tau \rho \acute{o} \nu, \kappa a \theta a \rho \acute{o} \nu$, and $\beta \acute{a} \pi \tau \iota \sigma \mu a$, as alike expressive of the highest spiritual purification, and never for a simple water cover‑ ing or for a physical purification by simple water, however used.

IGNATIUS, 660: " Jesus Christ was born and baptized ($\beta a \pi \tau \acute{\iota} \zeta \omega$) that he might purify ($\kappa a \theta a \rho \acute{\iota} \zeta \omega$) the water." The changed condi‑ tion of water here expressed by $\kappa a \theta a \rho \acute{\iota} \zeta \omega$, is the same as that ex‑ pressed heretofore by $\beta a \pi \tau \acute{\iota} \sigma \mu a \tau \iota.$

TERTULLIAN I, 1216: " Heretics have not one baptism (baptis‑ mus) with us because they have not the same. . . . We receive washing (lavacrum) once. . . . We have indeed a second washing (lavacrum), one and the same, to wit, of blood, of which the Lord says, ' I have a baptism (baptismo) to be baptized with.' ... These two baptisms (baptismos) he shed from the wound of his pierced side, that they who believe in his blood might be washed (lavarentur) with water, and they who had been washed with water might drink the blood of martyrdom. This is that baptism (baptismus) which represents the washing (lavacrum) when not received and restores it when lost."

More absolute evidence for the interchange and equivalence of *baptismus* and *lavacrum*, and that neither is employed for a physical cleansing or covering, could not be furnished. How can a *lavacrum sanguinis* either physically cleanse or cover? And yet this "lavacrum sanguinis" is one and the same (*unum et ipsum*) with the "*baptismus aquæ.*" This is an absurd statement except as both *spiritually cleanse* from sin. And this was a universal faith. It is no less absurd to call the water and the blood flowing from the wounded side of Christ "duos baptismos," except as the water of Cyprian "τῷ ἰδίῳ βαπτίσματι" by its own baptism (purification) secures the power to baptize (to purify). To contend, that lavo, lavacrum, baptismus, relate to physical washings, and coverings, is to fight, with the eyes shut, against the wind when the battle has been all lost.

III, 1198 : "They who have been baptized (*baptizati*) by this baptism of blood alone, obtain a sound faith and worthy washing (*lavacri*), and to be baptized in either way (*utroque modo*) by water or blood, equally secures one baptism (*baptisma*) of salvation and honor." Was this lavacrum of blood and baptisma of salvation and honor, a thing of physics, crimsoning the body and brightening the flesh, or a common cleansing of the soul?

ORIGEN II, 980 : "Christ shed his blood that we may go hence *washed (loti)* by our blood. It is the *baptism (baptisma)* of blood, only, which makes us more clean than the baptism of water. . . . Christ called the shedding (*profusionem*) of his blood, baptism (*baptisma*). . . . If God should grant that I might be washed (*diluerer*) by my own blood, that I might receive this second baptism (*baptisma*) enduring death for Christ, I would go safe out of this world."

Here we have lavo, diluo, baptizo, baptisma, interchanged as equivalents where physical washings or cleansings are absurdly impossible. Origen, like Tertullian, calls *profusio sanguinis*, a BAPTISMA.

III, 280: "Jesus baptizes (βαπτίζω) by the Holy Ghost and fire . . . he *baptizes* the holy by the Holy Ghost. and him who sins again he WASHES (λούει) *with fire.* . . . Blessed is he who does not need that *baptism* which is from fire. . . . Most miserable is he who needs to be BAPTIZED *by fire.*"

Here, again, λούω and βαπτίζω are interchanged under circumstances which, rationally, exclude physics.

GREGORY NAZIANZEN III, 462: " He furnished a double *purification* (καθάρσιον) for men, through the eternal Spirit, and through our own blood." The translator says, " a double baptism (baptismum)." And Gregory does the same (960), " Baptism (βάπτισμα) is twofold, through washing (λούτρου) and suffering (πάθους)."

In this latter statement λουτρόν takes the place of the " eternal Spirit" in the former. It cannot take the place of *water*, simple, because no Patrist ever believed that simple water could effect the Christian baptisma. And πάθος takes the place of martyrdom.

NONNUS PANOP. 753, 756 : " And why dost thou *baptize* (βαπτίζεις)? Whence dost thou *purify* (καθαίρεις) man with water ? I have come *baptizing* with water of the *purifying washing.* . . . He that sent me before *to baptize* the body of regenerate men *by washing* (λοετροῖς) without fire and without spirit." Βαπτίζεις = καθαίρεις.

Heinsius, a commentator on the paraphrase of John by Nonnus, objects to the substitution of καθαρμοῦ for καθαρισμοῦ in John 3 : 25. He says καθαρμός denotes an expiatory victim, while καθαρισμός denotes the removal of uncleanness by washing. Of which purifications there were many kinds in use among the Jews. Different from both was ὁ ἁγνισμός expiation. For this John substituted *repentance.* Illam autem ὁ καθαρισμός sequebatur, quem et βαπτισμόν dixerunt Hellenistæ, quibus omnia ad unum fere nomina antiqui Christiani debent—The καθαρισμός (*purification*) which the Greeks also, called βαπτισμόν (*baptism*) followed." . . . Here is a competent witness who declares, not controversially but historically, that Jews, Greeks, and Christians, regarded " baptism " (βαπτισμόν) and "purification " (καθαρισμόν) as equivalent terms. Neither Jew nor Gentile ever believed καθαρισμός to express a dipping into water ; βάπτισμα has just as little to do with dipping as its meaning.

ATHANASIUS III, 1366: " 'He shall baptize (βαπτίσει) you by the Holy Ghost.' This means, that he will purify (καθαριεῖ) you

For the baptism of John is not able to do this, but the baptism of Christ has power to take away sins." IV, 228: "Through the side of the second Adam came redemption and purification (λύτρον καὶ καθάρσιον). For redemption is through the blood, and purification is through the water (διὰ τοῦ αἵματος, διὰ τοῦ ὕδατος)."

Athanasius here expressly says, βαπτίσει means καθαριεῖ. And the nature of this purification, no less when water is used than when it is not used, no less when water is used as a covering than when the Holy Ghost acts alone, is a spiritual purification, and the covering in the water or any other mode of using the water is no more expressed by βαπτίζω than it is expressed by καθαρίζω. The "redemption and the purification" coming from the side of the second Adam are the "two baptisms" of Tertullian, and Origen, and Gregory.

The evidence proving that καθαρίζω, λούω, mundo, lavo, and their derivatives are interchanged as equivalents with βαπτίζω and its derivatives as expressive of a condition of spiritual purification is varied in its nature and perfect in its value. And all the weight of this evidence is confirmatory of the previous evidence showing that βαπτίζω is not interchanged as an equivalent with καταδύνω, demergo, and other words constantly and exclusively used to express a physical water covering.

Κάθαρίζω, λούω, not used with Ideal Element.

An additional step in the evidence developing the nature and use of βαπτίζω is found in the fact, that while it may, classically, be interchanged as equivalent with καταδύνω, demergo (which καθαρίζω, λούω never can) and while it may, patristically, be interchanged as equivalent with καθαρίζω, λούω (which καταδύνω, demergo, never can), still, neither of these alien classes of words, between which βαπτίζω thus appears as a connecting link, is ever used as interchangeable equivalents with it in its usage with ideal elements. Thus, we never have καταδύνω, demergo (and just as little καθαρίζω, λούω), εἰς μετάνοιαν, εἰς ἄφεσιν, εἰς Χριστὸν. If the idea of βαπτίζω was exhausted by a simple covering, as is the case with καταδύνω, demergo, and if it is so freely and constantly interchanged with them as is claimed, then, it would be inexplicable that such interchange never took place in ideal relations. That no such interchange does take place is undeniable; that any such interchange, as is claimed, does take place, is denied

The reason for this diverse usage is found in the fact, that βαπτίζω is not exhausted by the expression of mere covering.

The whole current of the usage of this word, no less Classical than Jewish and Christian, shows, that its affinity is not with βάπτω (first) *to dip*, but with βάπτω (second) *to dye, to color in any way, to communicate quality, characteristic and abiding, like a color*. In this last sense βάπτω has an exceedingly limited use, as "βάπτεται ὑπὸ τῶν φαντασίων ἡ ψυχή The soul is imbued (colored) by the thoughts;" "Δικαιοσύνη βεβαμμένον εἰς βάθος Imbued (colored) by integrity through and through." This usage, of the greatest breadth and importance, βάπτω can hardly be said to enter. It but plants its foot upon the threshold, and introduces its offspring βαπτίζω to the work. That this task of developing and communicating characteristic quality is taken up by βαπτίζω where it is dropped by βάπτω (limiting itself to coloring quality) is shown by the adoption of the same grammatical forms, the Dative (δικαιοσύνῃ) and the Genitive (ὑπὸ τῶν φαντασίων) as agencies, and the Accusative with εἰς (εἰς βαθος) to denote entrance into and the *throughness* within which the quality is communicated. The usage of βαπτίζω can never receive just appreciation and intelligent discrimination from that of words related, in some respects, without this element derived from its origin is borne in mind.

It is this character which qualifies it for use in ideal relations where characteristic quality is to be developed and communicated to its object. And it is the entire lack of any power in καταδυνω, *demergo*, etc., etc., to develop and communicate quality which precludes their use in such phrases as εἰς μετάνοιαν, εἰς ἄφεσιν, εἰς Χριστὸν. In like manner, although for diverse reason, it is impracticable to use καθαρίζω, λούω, mundo, lavo, etc., etc., in such ideal relations. These words already express in themselves, generically, the idea which is intended to be developed by these phrases. The word baptize in the organic phrases, baptize into repentance, into remission, into Christ, does not mean *purify;* but it carries its object (ideally) "into repentance," so as to become thoroughly interpenetrated with it, and hence *purified* through the influence of godly sorrow for sin; so, its object becomes interpenetrated with remitted sin, and hence is *purified;* and so, its object becomes interpenetrated with all the virtues of the redeeming blood of Christ, and hence is *purified* from all sin. Now, while in any of these full phrases baptize can never mean "purify," yet when by long and frequent use these phrases become abbreviated and represented by the one word *baptize*, then the value of the entire phrase is transferred to and expressed by that word, and it secures the meaning *to purify*. And it is at this point, and only at this point, that it comes into relationship with καθαρίζω, λούω, mundo, lavo, purgo, purifico, and a host of like words, in whose equivalent fellowship we find it all through the Patristic writings. This is just what language development demands. Frequency of usage and length had abbreviated the ideal phrases of Scripture and conferred their idea upon a single word. But this Patristic development cannot be carried back to the New Testament. It may be used as proof, and that most conclusive, to show the value of its phrases, but the meaning acquired through one or more centuries cannot be applied to the word in its phrase relations, nor to its earliest abbreviations, when it would rather elliptically suggest the phrase than justly claim the right or power to express of itself what was yet the undivided thought of the whole.

These principles and facts indicate the double usage which excludes βαπτίζω from the water-covering function of καταδύνω, and includes it with καθαρίζω in expressing the spiritual purification which was believed to be effected by the impregnated water of Christian baptism however it might be used, whether by covering, pouring, sprinkling, or in any other becoming way.

Tingo.

There is another word which appears (especially in some of the Patristic writings) that is supposed to yield proof, that βαπτίζω means *to dip*. I refer to the use of *tingo*. This word is not of common use in early Christian writings, but appears with frequency in Tertullian, and, with less prominence, in Augustine. This usage it will be proper to consider in the present connection.

Tingo, as used in connection with Christian baptism, cannot be assumed to prove that βαπτίζω means *to dip*, without assuming that tingo, as so used, means to dip, and that, in this meaning, it squarely represents βαπτίζω. There are difficulties in the way of both of these assumptions. But the first might, limitedly, be true and the last remain untrue.

To dip is not the sole meaning of tingo, nor is it, according to the Lexicons, its leading meaning. Its various phases of mean-ing are exhibited in the related words of other languages, as in the Greek τέγγω, *to wet*, the English tinge, *to color*, and the German tünchen *to whiten*. The Latin tingo with the leading meanings *to dip, to dye*, has appropriate modifications of both these meanings, as is shown in Classic Baptism. *To wet* and *to wash*, are natural subordinate meanings of *dip*, when the act carries its object into pure water; as to dye, to color, to stain, are natural outgrowths of a dipping into coloring liquids. And *to whiten* (to take out stains or color) is a no less legitimate meaning from dipping into a liquid which has bleaching qualities—the power to make of a white color.

As tingo secures the meaning *to dye* (without reference to mode, dropping the action of dipping) from dipping into liquids having coloring qualities, expressing the communication of such quality, so, it secures as legitimately the meaning *to imbue* by dipping into a real or ideal element which has a quality other than that of color and which it imparts to the object placed within it. The specific character of *imbue* depending upon the specific quality with which it may be related. The meanings *to dye, to imbue*, are not dependent upon (although they may be connected with) the act of *dipping*. Their dependence is upon the coloring or other quality of the element by which the dyeing or imbuing is effected.

It is obvious from these general statements, that the simple use of tingo in connection with Christian baptism cannot justify a presumption much less the assumption that it must mean to dip. If it should be admitted that it may or does mean *to dip*, still there would remain that most vital inquiry—*Into what* does it dip? The answer to this inquiry rules in the most absolute manner the worth or worthlessness of the act of dipping as an element in the transaction.

If there be an element of peculiar quality with which tingo stands related in Christian baptism, then, in like relation, when such element is not expressed *tingo* must still have its determining *tinge* from that element, being *colored* or *imbued* with its quality whatever that may be.

1. The first point, then, to be determined in considering the meaning and value of *tingo* as used by Tertullian is this: Does this *tingo* stand related to simple water or to some element (physical or ideal) possessed of a quality communicable to the object dipped (really or ideally) into it?

To this question there can be but one reply   Tertullian and his associates with one voice deny that the water in their baptism is simple water. They affirm that it is impregnated with a divine influence by which it is itself purified and sanctified, and invested with a power to purify and sanctify spiritually those who are dipped into it, or who are otherwise brought under its influence. They declare that a man who goes down into this water "black" with sin, comes up out of it "whiter than snow." In view of such characteristic Tertullian says: The devil dips (*tingit*) his disciples into simple water under the lying promise of the removal of sin (*de lavacro*) by the washing.

It is unnecessary to adduce special quotations to indicate this point. Its evidence saturates the quotations already given, and is to be found everywhere.

Now, suppose that this *tingo* represents the act of dipping into this remarkable water, is it not a supreme blunder to make the value of the transaction turn upon such act? Is not the power of the rite concentrated in the quality of the water? Has *dip* any value beyond any other act which brings its object under the influence of this water? Does not *tingo* in the dye-house (where dipping is going on constantly) lose its dipping under the strong coloring of the dye-tub? Could the ecclesiastical *tingo* fare any better in dealing with such water in the baptistery? However much he may have gone into this water as a *dipper*, he could never tarry there a century without coming out a *tinctor* (not *dyer*, but analogously) *a purifier*. Whether *tingo* ever entered the baptistery *to dip* may be an open question, but that it comes out *to purify* is a concluded question.

Proof that this must be so from language development is found in the use of *tingo* in the religious rites of heathenism, as seen in Ovid, Fast. IV, 787–790:

> An, quia cunctarum contraria semina rerum
> Sunt duo, discordes ignis et unda Dei;
> Junxerunt elementa patres: aptumque putarunt
> Ignibus et sparsa tingere corpus aqua?

"Is it because the diverse seeds of all things are two, the discordant Gods fire and water, that our Fathers have joined those elements, and have thought proper TO PURIFY THE BODY *by fire and sprinkled water?*"

The whole current of this passage, as well as the forms and construction of the last line, preclude any other translation of "tingere" than *to purify*. It is a pure impossibility either *to dip* or *to dye* the body in "sprinkled water." Beside, " to purify " religiously is but the simplest and most legitimate extension of *to wash* on the one hand, and *to dye* on the other hand. Tingo unquestionably has both these meanings. Ovid gives conclusive proof of the first meaning in *Metamorph.* II, 459 : " *Nuda super-fusis tingamus corpora lymphis;* Let us *wash* our naked bodies by water *poured over* them." Now whether religious *purification* be ingrafted on to *tingo* through washing or through dyeing (an uncolored quality making pure as a colored quality imparts its dye) is of no consequence; it has it, and has it most legitimately. " These are they who have *washed* their robes and *made them* WHITE *in the* BLOOD of the Lamb." This statement in the ordinary sense of its terms is a contradiction; justly interpreted is a truth. The blood of the Lamb has a quality which *washes* out the stains of sin and *dyes* the soul *white.* Sprinkled water can neither *wash* nor *dye,* yet can do both; it can wash out *religious defilement* and make *white.* This washing and coloring meet together in *purification.* And it is through these channels, by means of impregnated purifying water, that Tertullian brings *tingo* into relation with βαπτίζω. If the interpretation of the passage from the Fasti needed confirmation, it could be found in another passage, IV, 725 :

> Certe ego transilui positas ter in ordine flammas
> Virgaque rorantes laurea misit aquas.

" I leaped thrice through the flames placed in order, and the laurel branch scattered the sprinkling waters."

Here the twofold purifying is seen in actual use without any dipping into the sprinkled water. This purification of heathenism we now transfer within, at least a heretical Christianity, under the authority of TERTULLIAN II, 1060 :

> Bis docuit *tingi* transducto corpore flamma.

" He, Valentinus, taught *to be purified* twice, the body being taken through the flame." The Annotator says Tertullian refers to some heretics who *purified (baptizarent)* twice, once with water, once with fire. *Tingo* and baptizo are interchanged by Tertullian and his Annotator. There is an adequate basis for so doing, but that basis is not found in *dip,* which is no meaning of baptizo. It is to be found in the fact that both these words secure the power to communicate quality to their object. We have met repeatedly with the statement of water being baptized, *i. e.*, a certain quality communicated to it, that it might be able to baptize, *i. e.*, to communicate the like quality in turn. Thus Tertullian calls the water and the blood coming from the wounded side of Christ " two baptisms " (*duos baptismos*), baptized that they might baptize. So Cyprian speaks of water baptized (impregnated with a purifying power), that " by its own baptism " (= purification) it might be able to purify. In precisely the same manner *tingo* is used to express the communication of a quality to water that the water may exercise, through *tingo*, that same quality. Thus OVID, *Metamorph*. IV, 388:

> Et incerto fontem medicamine *tinxit*.

"And *tincted* the fountain with a dubious drug." It is impossible for *tingo* here to mean either dip or dye. To dip "a fountain" in a drug is an absurdity. *To dye* a fountain with a drug which has no coloring quality is an impossibility. The fitness of *tingo* to officiate in such a case must be found in the analogy between the communication of a quality in both cases, extending the province of *tingo* to the communication of *quality* without color. An extended usage in this direction would necessitate (to escape confusion between colored and uncolored qualities) the introduction of a new word. This was done by the Greeks. When βάπτω passed from dipping into uncolored liquids to dipping into colored liquids, and secured the meaning to dye without dipping (as illustrated in ἐβάπτετο δ' αἵματι λίμνη, "the lake was dyed with blood"), there arose a necessity, in the exigencies of language, to advance still further, as shown by δικαιοσύνῃ βεβαμμένον, "IMBUED" (certainly neither *dipped* nor *dyed*) "in integrity." Yet just as certainly this usage comes through βάπτω to dye. As the necessity for expressing such conceptions must be of frequent occurrence, and βάπτω was already doubly weighted, the duty was handed over to βαπτίζω. And thus this word by its derivation has a hereditary right and facility to express the communication of *quality* to liquids, and through liquids to persons, which does not belong to other words with which it is related in other functions, as καταδύω for instance. Wine is baptized by pouring water into it. The condition of the wine is changed; the unintoxicating *quality of water* is communicated to it. The analogy of this *baptism* to that of the *tincted* water of the fountain is obvious. Yet more striking is the analogy with the wine baptized (changed in quality) by a drug, which in turn baptized the drinker of it. This is precisely parallel with the case of the baptizing water of Tertullian, which being baptized by a new quality communicated to it, did in turn, through its own baptism, baptize = communicate its purifying quality to those coming under its influence.

The effort of Tertullian to extend the sphere of *tingo* so as to embrace that of βαπτίζω was unsuccessful. It did not succeed with himself. His writings everywhere show the necessity which he felt, at times, to introduce the Greek word, and oftentimes in common with others to employ the Greek and Latin words in contrast; the first in a good sense, the last in a bad sense. This was especially done by using *tingo* to express the baptisms of heretics and baptizo to express those of the Church. The Latin, like the English, had no word corresponding in character with this Greek word, and the attempt, not to translate it by tingo, but to mould this word after the fashion of the Greek, did not succeed.

If Tertullian had believed that tingo *to dip* was the just representative of βαπτίζω what was to hinder his uniform translation of the latter word by the former? But he does not do it. His constant use of tingo shows that in his mind it was related to the *dyeing* side of that word and not to the *dipping*. Applied to the baptizing water of the Church it developed a purifying quality, and sins were washed, cleansed, purified; but applied to the baptizing water of heretics, it developed a defiling and polluting quality aggravating sin. The water of heretics was like a bad dye; it spoiled all that was put into it; it defiled and polluted. Therefore Tertullian says, "*tincti apud hæreticos, profana aqua, maculati—the tincted* by heretics are *stained* by their *profane water;*" those *tincted* in heresy (in hæresi tinctos) are made filthy (sordidatos); their *tinction* is an infection (tinctura infecta); it is a contagion (contagione tinctus); it is false, contagious, and profane (mendacio et contagione profanæ tinctionis). The same conception of heretical water as a *quasi* dye with a polluting quality, is presented by Cyprian, "those *tincted* outside of the Church are stained by the pollution of their profane water" (*foris Ecclesiam tincti, maculati*). So Augustine declares that such when *tincted* are infected (*tinctus et infectus*). And Ambrose in the same spirit declares that the twelve at Ephesus were commanded by Paul to be baptized (baptizari) "because they had not been *tincted* (*fuerant non tincti*) washed, made white, purified but had been defiled, polluted, stained (*sordidati*) by an adulterous (*adulterino*) baptism under the name of John."

That Tertullian uses *tingo* in a sense related to dyeing may be argued from his unquestionable use of the word for dyeing in I, 1305 : " *Si ab initio rerum Tyrii tinguerent* If from the beginning of things the Tyrians *dyed ;*" and II, 1094, " *Purpura nec Tyrio sic est intincta rubore* Such purple is not *dyed* with Tyrian purple." On this passage his Annotator quotes from Jamblichus, " *capillitio in fulvum aurum tincto.*" Now, translate this passage either—" with hair *dipped into* yellow gold," or, " with hair dyed (by passing) into yellow gold," *tinctus* expresses in itself (by antecedent usage), *dyed* and " *in fulvum aurum* " expresses the specific nature of the dye, or *tinctus* is used to develop the dyeing quality which belongs to "fulvum aurum," and *the phrase* means DYED *a golden-yellow.* There was no *dipping*, in fact, of the hair " into yellow gold " or into a yellow dye of any kind. If dipping be introduced it is wholly subordinate and ministrant to the effect. This is precisely the truth with reference to Tertullian's use of " tingo " in connection with baptizing water, and as a substitute for βαπτίζω in ideal relations. And it is a matter of concluding force that *tingo* is used in these ideal relations, and no other word. It is because of its power to develop quality and bring its object under the influence of such quality (*quasi* dye) that it is so used. Other words as καταδύνω, *demergo*, can cover as well or better than *tingo ;* but they have not its usage for extracting quality from the covering element, and therefore are never used to fill the place of βαπτίζω in relations where quality is to be communicated. Let us look at the evidence for this.

Tingo a Substitute for βαπτίζω in Ideal Relations.

There can be no doubt as to Tertullian's very frequent substitution of *tingo* for βαπτίζω. And it should be held just as certain that this was not on the ground that tingo *to dip* was the equivalent of this Greek word. Tertullian well knew that there was no such equivalence between these words, for he was a Greek scholar. When, therefore, he substitutes tingo in passages where the Greek word occurs it must be for other and better reasons than that of word equivalence. The fact of substitution is proved by the following passages.

TERTULLIAN I, 1212 : " John in preaching the baptism (baptismum) of repentance into the remission of sins, announced a future remission through Christ. . . . Likewise John only baptized in repentance; soon one would come who should baptize in spirit and fire; because a true and firm faith is baptized by water into salvation, but a pretended and feeble faith is by fire baptized into condemnation—Item in sola pænitentia *tinguere;* venturum mox qui tingueret in spiritu et igni. Scilicet, quia vera et stabilis fides aqua tinguitur in salutem; simulata autem et infirma, igni tinguitur in judicium."

It is evident that *tinguo* appears here as the substitute for the βαπτίζω of John and is intended to fulfil the office of that word whatever it was. Tertullian did not understand that office to be a dipping into water, for none appears in his statement and none belongs to the word. When he drops the phraseology of Scripture and speaks of " faith by water *tinguitur in salutem* " water is again absolutely excluded as the element of dipping as it is excluded in Scripture and we are shut up to the interpretation of tinguitur in salutem as an organic phrase from which " tinguitur," translate as you may, is inseparable, and the joint teaching of its parts is, that a firm faith is made fully participant of salvation. The same remarks may be made of the phrase *igni tinguitur in judicium.* " Fire " like water is excluded from being the receiving element, and the phrase teaches that a simulated faith is brought fully under the divine condemnation. Both which sentiments are eminently scriptural.

Cap. XI, *De Bapt.:* " But behold, they say, the Lord came and did not baptize (*tinxit*). For we read, 'Nevertheless he baptized not (*non tinguebat*) but his disciples,' as if John had announced that he would baptize (*tincturum*) by his own hands. . . . He will baptize (*tinguet*) you, that is, ye shall be baptized (*tinguemini*) by him or into him (*in ipsum*). But let it not trouble any one because he did not baptize (*tinguebat*). For into what should he baptize (*tingueret*)? into repentance? to what purpose, then, his Forerunner? into the remission of sins, which he gave by a word? into himself, whom he veiled with humility? into the Holy Spirit, who had not yet descended from the Father? into the Church, which the Apostles had not yet builded? Therefore his disciples baptized (*tinguebant*) with the same baptism (*baptismo*) as that of John."

It is certain, 1. That *tinguo* is substituted for βαπτίζω; 2. It is certain that *tinguo* is not used for a naked dipping " into repentance," " into the remission of sins," " into Himself," " into the

Holy Spirit," "into the Church;" 3. It is certain, that these phrases are saturated with influence.

1214: "Whether the Apostles were baptized (*tincti*) or remained unwashed (*illoti*)."

The contrast between "tincti" and "illoti" requires that "tincti" should express a condition effected and not a dipping.

1217: "We have a second washing (*lavacrum*), one and the same (with that of water) to wit, of blood; of which the Lord says, 'I have to be baptized (*tingui*) with a baptism (*baptismo*),' when he had already been baptized (*tinctus fuisset*). . . . This is Baptism (*Baptismus*) which realizes (*repræsentat*) the washing (*lavacrum*) of water when it has not been received and restores it when lost."

Here, 1. *Tinguo* fills the place of βαπτίζω in the Scripture text; 2. It is associated with *baptismo* in blood baptism; 3. It is called "washing of blood;" 4. It is said to be "one and the same" with the *washing* of water; 5. This *tinctio* (= *lavacrum*) of blood is expressly called "Baptismus." Any one who will undertake to hedge up this *tinguo* to a naked *dipping* will find a good deal of work on hand.

1222, *Cap.* XIX, *De Bapt.:* "The Passover furnishes a more solemn day for Baptism (*Baptismo*), the passion of the Lord in which we are baptized (*tinguimur*) having then been completed."

"The passion of the Lord" is here represented as the receiving element. If any one should say, Then we are dipped (*tinguimur*) in it, I ask, Has the passion of the Lord any quality belonging to it which is designed to be developed by this dipping over the object dipped? If so, then the dipping cannot be separated from the "passion," and it ceases to be a simple dipping and becomes part of a process in *quasi* dyeing, bringing its object under that peculiar coloring, quality or influence which belongs to the "passion of the Lord." I remark again: "Tinguimur" is merely another spelling for *baptizamur*, and if baptizamur does not mean a naked dipping, then, neither can Tertullian's substitute.

1239, *Cap.* VI, *De Pœnit.:* "Is there one Christ for the baptized (*intinctis*) another for the hearers (*audientibus*)? . . . That washing (*lavacrum*) is a seal to faith; which begins and is commended by the faith of repentance. We are not washed (*abluimur*) that we may cease to sin, for we have already been washed (*loti sumus*) in heart" by repentance. "For this first baptism (washing *intinctio*) is a just fear (*metus integer*). . . . If we cease to sin by the waters, we put on (*induimus*) innocence by necessity not by free will . . . bound by baptism (*intinctione alligatus*)."

Is this use of *intinctis, intinctio*, with the equivalents *lavacrum, loti sumus corde, metus integer, induimus innocentiam*, " cease to sin *by the waters*," a naked dipping?

II, 275 : " I know that the body is washed (*caro tinguitur*) (= *caro abluitur*, cap. 8, *De Resur.*); if sins are imputed to the body, the guilt of the soul precedes ;" compare with 147 : " ' These are they who have come out of great tribulation and have washed their robe and made it white in the blood of the Lamb ;' for the body (*caro*) is the robe of the soul. Impurities (*sordes*) are washed away (*abluuntur*) by baptism (*baptismate*), but stains (*maculæ*) are whitened by martyrdom."

Here *tingo* (used elsewhere as we have seen for the *lavacrum sanguinis*, martyrdom) is used for spiritual washing, cleansing, purification, to the absolute rejection of all modal action.

495: " To be baptized (*tingui*) for the dead." Whatever may be the meaning of " baptized " in this passage, that, no more no less, Tertullian meant should be the meaning of *tingui*.

862: " ' As many as have been baptized (*tincti sumus*) into Jesus Christ, have been baptized (*tincti sumus*) into his death.' " The same remark may be made of this as of the preceding quotation, with the additional evidence furnished by its fuller statement of the impossibility of a mere dipping.

991 : " Therefore if the condition is thereby changed, and having been baptized (*tincta*) into Christ puts on Christ, redeemed by the blood of the Lord and of the Lamb."

Here is an express statement that " in Christum tincta " effects *a thorough change of condition*, which can only arise from " in Christum " being possessed of a quality which is communicated (like a *quasi* dye) to the object brought under its influence. And this is precisely what has been proved to be the meaning of " *baptized* INTO CHRIST."

100 : " Commanding that they should baptize (*tinguerent*) into the Father, and Son, and Holy Spirit, not into one (*non in unum*). For we baptize (*tinguimur*) not once but thrice, at (*ad*) each name into each person (*in singulas personas*)."

Here the Father, the Son, and the Holy Spirit, are declared and expounded (*in singulas personas*) to be the ideal elements as plainly as language can express it. Is this a bare dipping?

Tertullian's tingo.

Nothing can be more obvious than the purpose of Tertullian to induct *tingo* into the place filled by the Bible βαπτίζω. In doing this it was not on the ground of believing that *tingo* was the equivalent of the Greek word in meaning and range of usage, but because he knew of no word in the Latin language which had an element in its meaning and a direction of usage so capable of being extended into the peculiar line of usage as that which characterized the Scriptural usage of βαπτίζω. In this judgment he showed scholarship and sagacity. Between *tingo* and βάπτω there is a very remarkable equivalence and identity of meaning and usage. And as it is out of a stem of βάπτω that βαπτίζω proceeds (dropping coloring quality and developing quality without color) it was natural for Tertullian to suppose that the functions of *tingo* could be extended so as to take in uncolored quality as well as colored quality *without forming a new word* for this duty. But his effort was unsuccessful. The Latin word was already burdened with a double duty (*dipping* and *dyeing*) and the attempt to introduce it into a third sphere of action broke down. There was an element in *tingo* which was susceptible of being wrought out in this direction, but the people would not undertake the task nor countenance it when undertaken by others. Neither would they form a new word for the exigency. This had been, already, done by the Greeks, and they preferred the adoption of that word sanctified by its appropriation to a phraseological combination such as had never before entered into the language of man. Nearly all languages into which the Bible has been translated have presented the same difficulty, and by almost unanimous consent it has been solved in the same way.

An attempt has been made to introduce into the Baptist Bible *immerse* as the equivalent of βαπτίζω. This word will answer well enough for a class of cases in Classic history; but it utterly breaks down when it is applied to the organic phrases of inspiration, with the spirit of which it has nothing in common, and has no element in itself or in its derivation to develop the quality of those wonderful elements of influence with which it is brought into the most anomalous combination. The friends of this word in such use claim that the *tingo* of Tertullian means *to dip ;* if this be so, then this is the word that they should have introduced into their Bible; that they have not done so, and have adopted a word of essentially different meaning, is proof that it could not be so used, and is proof that a scholar like Tertullian never meant to introduce *tingo*, in this sense, as the equivalent substitute for βαπτίζω.

The effort to introduce "immerse" into the English Bible will fail more disastrously than did the far more wisely considered effort of Tertullian to introduce "tingo" into the Latin Bible. Even Tertullian acknowledged the imperfection of his material by commingling *baptizo* with *tingo*, and the people accepted this judgment by dropping the imperfection out of their Bibles altogether.

This use of *tingo* is very conclusive proof that βαπτίζω is not used for simple water covering.

It is a fact, that no word expressive of mere passage into or covering in simple water was ever proposed by Patristic writers to fill the place of βαπτίζω in its New Testament phraseological combinations. It is a fact, that *tingo* (which is not expressive of mere passage into or covering in simple water, but which is used to carry its object into coloring water and medicated water for the purpose of bringing such object under such influence, and hence secures the power directly to express the communication of quality) is used as a substitute for βαπτίζω in all its peculiar ideal New Testament combinations. The conclusion from these facts is compulsory, that the reason for the use of this word and the rejection of those words, is to be found in that characteristic in which it differs from them. And this conclusion assumes a positive certainty in view of the additional fact, that βαπτίζω is derived from a word which has the same identical characteristics which thus distinguished *tingo*. When to this is added, that the ideal relations of βαπτίζω necessitate the development of those influences belonging to the several ideal elements, can evidence be more complete to prove, that the office of βαπτίζω is not that of a mere water coverer, but for the development of the noblest spiritual influence? This is its sole New Testament use.

Direct Proof that the Complementary Relations of βαπτίζω are Ideal.

In adducing final evidence in proof that the complementary relations of βαπτίζω in the New Testament, and as used in corresponding relations by Patristic writers, are ideal and not physical,

1 will offer modified statements of these relations strongly con-firmatory of this position.

CLEM. ROM., *Apost. Const.*, 1041: " Disciple first all the nations, and then he added this, ' And baptize them into the name of the Father, and of the Son, and of the Holy Ghost.' Therefore let the baptized in his renunciation say: ' I disjoin myself from Satan, and his works, and his pomps, and his service, and his angels, and his inventions, and all subject to him; and I conjoin myself with Christ, and believe, and am baptized into the one Unbegotten, the only true God Almighty, the Father of the Christ, Creator and former of all, of whom are all things; and into the Lord Jesus the Christ, his only begotten Son, the first born of every creature, begotten (not made) by the good pleasure of the Father, before the ages, through whom were all things which are in heaven and upon earth, visible and invisible; . . . and I am baptized into the Holy Ghost, that is the Paraclete, who hath wrought in all saints from the beginning of the world.' "

This passage furnishes conclusive evidence that the baptism is ideally "into the only true God," by reason of the contrasted relation with Satan in the past, and the relation to be established with the only true God in the future. The relation of the impeni-tent man toward Satan is one of complete subjection and con-formity. The absoluteness of this relation is described by the Bible as a baptism—" The whole world *lieth* IN *the* WICKED ONE (ἐν τῷ πονηρῷ)." And on the other hand the Bible describes (in op-position to this baptism inducing complete subjection and con-formity to Satan) the subjection and conformity of the Christian to the only true God as a baptism thus—" And WE *are* IN *the* TRUE ONE, IN *his* SON, JESUS CHRIST, *this is the* TRUE GOD." 1 John 5 : 19, 20. It would be difficult to construct more absolute evidence, that the baptism of the redeemed is a *passing* INTO and, as a consequence, the *abiding* IN the True God. The evidence is no less conclusive, that the import of this baptism is COMPLETE SUBJECTION AND CONFORMITY to the True God. This recovery *out of* subjection to Satan and introduction *into* subjection to the true God is the end of redemption and the ultimate prayer of the Redeemer—" I pray for them . . . keep IN *thy* Name those thou hast given me, that they may be one, as we are. While I was with them I kept them IN *thy* Name. . . . I pray that thou shouldst keep them OUT OF *the* EVIL ONE. . . . I pray that they all may be one as thou Father IN Me and I IN Thee, that they, also, may

be one IN US" (John 17). Therefore he sent Paul (Acts 26 : 18)
to the nations "to turn them from *the power of* SATAN *unto*
GOD;" and his fellow-Apostles (Matt. 28 : 19) " to baptize the discipled of the nations *into the* NAME of the Father, and of the Son,
and of the Holy Ghost."

948 : " Let one baptism only suffice, that which is given *into
the death* of the Lord; not by impious heretics, but by blameless
priests *into the* NAME of the Father, and of the Son, and of the
Holy Ghost. For as there is one God, one Christ, and one Paraclete, and also one death in the body of the Lord, so, also, let
there be one baptism given *into that* DEATH."

IGNATIUS, 921 : " There are not three Fathers, nor three Sons,
nor three Paracletes. Therefore the Lord sending the Apostles
to disciple all the nations commanded them to baptize *into the*
NAME of the Father, and of the Son, and of the Holy Ghost ; *not*
INTO *a three-named,* nor INTO *three incarnations,* but INTO *three of
equal honor.*"

TERTULLIAN II, 61 : " Menander, a magician and disciple of
Simon, held the same sentiments with his master, and whatever
Simon said that he was, Menander declared himself to be, denying that any one could be saved unless they should have been
baptized *in* HIS NAME."

II, 190 : " Commanding that they should baptize (*in Patrem
et Filium et Spiritum Sanctum, non in unum*) into the Father
and the Son and the Holy Spirit, not *into* ONE. For we are not
baptized once but thrice (*ad singula nomina in personas singulas*)
at each name *into* EACH PERSON."

II, 1177 : This is a note by an Annotator (Thomas Corbin, a
monk, born A.D. 1694) on a passage, I, 1212 : " ' He shall baptize you,' means ye shall be baptized (*per* ipsum vel *in* ipsum) *by*
him or *into* him." The Annotator remarks, "*per ipsum.* Ejus
nomine ac authoritate, by his name and authority. *In ipsum.*
In ejus virtutem ac nomen, ut scilicet transeatis in nomen *Christi,*
deinceps Christiani appellandi. *Into* his virtue and name, so as
if you pass *into the name of* CHRIST, and afterward be called
Christians. Thus St. Paul says, Gal. 3 : 27, As many as have
been baptized (*in Christo* [Vulgate]) in Christ (*Græce εἰς Χριστὸν,
in Christum*) have put on Christ."

I presume that this exposition of " in ipsum " as *into his* VIR-
TUE *and* NAME, and its further exposition as a *passing into the
name of* CHRIST (as into a *quasi* dye) giving the coloring of its

"virtue" so as to make *Christiani*, and the correction of the translation of Jerome (in accordance with this exposition) from " in Christo" to *in Christum*, will satisfy most persons that this Annotator, at least, did very thoroughly believe that the βαπτίζω of the Scriptures was organically related to ideal and not to physical elements; and that he believed Tertullian to be of the same faith.

IRENÆUS, 661 : " Others conduct to the water (ἐφ᾽ ὕδωρ) and baptizing speak thus: ' Into the name of the unknown Father of all, into truth mother of all, into him who descended into Jesus, into union, and redemption, and communion of the powers.'"

Whatever of heresy or folly there may be in such utterance, grammatical law, I suppose, applies to heresy and orthodoxy alike. Whether any one will undertake by its aid to secure " by the authority of" or " unto" or " in," or " in order to," or "with reference to," out of this "into unknown Father," and into truth, mother, etc., etc., I do not know. Some probably will conclude, that if these heretics could believe in one descending out of the Pleroma or somewhere else " *into* Jesus" (εἰς᾽ Ἰησοῦν) they could not have felt any special difficulty in baptizing "INTO the unknown Father, INTO the truth mother, INTO the descending one, INTO union, and redemption, and communion," and INTO any other imaginable thing. But sometimes folly and error may be made to pay tribute to grammatical truth.

657: " This heresy is sent by Satan for the denial of baptism, which is regeneration *into* God." . . . (929): " And giving tó the disciples the power of regeneration *into* God (*in Deum*), saying to them, 'Go teach all nations, baptizing them,' etc. The Holy Spirit descended *into* the Son of God (*in Filium Dei*) made Son of man, thus accustoming himself to dwell *in* the human race and to rest *in* men, and to dwell *in* the image of God, working *in* them the will of the Father, and renewing them from their old nature *into* the newness (in novitatem) of Christ."

Why not accept the ideal baptism *into the* DEITY which finds its counterpart (in the element of *withinness*) on almost every page of Scripture?

1074: " How can men be saved unless it be God who has wrought out salvation upon the earth? And how shall *man pass into* GOD (χωρήσει εἰς Θεὸν) except *God has* PASSED INTO *man* (εἰς ἄνθρωπον)?" The argument for man's " entering into God " is drawn from the incarnation, the Son of God entering into man. Without claiming

any parallelism, there is, surely, in the incarnation, a basis laid
for the ideal conception of a baptism of the redeemed into the
Name of the Deity.

CLEMENS ALEX., 693: "The man *baptized into* GOD has *entered
into* GOD (*εἰς Θεὸν βαπτισθεὶς εἰς Θεὸν ἐχώρησεν*), and has received
power over scorpions and to tread on serpents—the powers of
evil. And to the Apostles he commanded, 'Go, preach, and them
that believe baptize into the Name of the Father, and of the Son,
and of the Holy Ghost;' *into* WHOM (*εἰς οὓς*) we are born again,
having been made superior to all other powers." Could language
be more explicit than this?

ORIGEN III, 713: "*Non lavantur omnes in salutem;* All are
not washed *into salvation.*" This quotation is from Origen on
Ezekiel, which appears in a Latin translation by Jerome. In a
note on "lavantur," we have this Greek citation: "Catenæ MSS.
Τῶν βαπτιζομένων οἱ μὲν εἰς σωτηρίαν βαπτίζονται; Of the baptized some
are baptized into salvation." This is fresh proof of the equivalence of *βαπτίζω* and *lavo*. The " washing " not being due to a
dipping or covering in simple water, but a washing, cleansing,
purification *from sin*, a spiritual, saving washing (*in salutem*),
due to the divine influence impregnating the water. " Hear, O
catechumens, while you are catechumens, while you are not yet
baptized, and come to the washing that you may be washed into
salvation (*in salutem*), nor be washed as some have been washed,
but not into salvation (*in salutem*), as those who receive the water
but do not receive the Holy Spirit. He who is washed into salvation
(*in salutem*) receives both the water and the Holy Spirit. Simon
was not washed into salvation (*in salutem*); he received (*accepit*)
the water, but did not receive the Holy Spirit. Having obtained
baptisma (*baptisma*), he continued in fellowship with Philip; but
because he was not washed into salvation (*non erat lotus in salutem*), he was condemned by him who, in the Holy Spirit, said to
him—' Let thy money be *into perdition* with thee *Pecunia tua
tecum sit in perditionem.*' "

This passage furnishes conclusive evidence: 1. As to the ideal
use of *βαπτίζω* (*εἰς σωτηρίαν*); 2. As to its attaining the meaning
to wash, to cleanse, to purify spiritually, in absolute use, secured
through use with ideal elements, spiritually pure and purifying
in their nature; 3. As to the Accusative and its preposition representing an ideal element into which an object is represented as
passing, for the purpose of indicating that such object is brought

fully under such influence as belongs to the ideal element, whatever that may be (*in* SALUTEM, *in* PERDITIONEM).

BASIL M. III, 1429 : " He who is baptized (ὁ βαπτιζόμενος) is baptized *into the* TRINITY (εἰς Τριάδα βαπτίζεται), into the Father, Son, and Holy Ghost ; *not into* PRINCIPALITIES (εἰς ἀρχὰς), *nor into* POWERS (εἰς δυνάμεις), *nor into any* SUCH THINGS *among creatures* (εἰς τὰ ἑξῆς ἐν κτίσμασι)."

The redeemed are baptized into the fully revealed Deity = made subject and assimilated unto Him. They are not baptized into Principalities, or Powers, or any Creatures = made subject and assimilated to them.

GREGORY THAUM., 1180: "Then Jesus comes (ἀπὸ) from Galilee (εἰς) to Jordan (πρὸς) unto John to be baptized (βαπτισθῆναι) by him. . . . But John said, How shall I wash (λούσω) the spotless and the sinless ? . . . 1183: Baptizing others I baptize them into thy Name (εἰς τὸ σὸν ὄνομα), baptizing thee of whom shall I make mention ? Into whose Name (εἰς τίνος ὄνομα) shall I baptize thee ? Into that of the Father ? But thou hast the entire Father in thyself, and thou art entire in the Father. Or, into that of the Son ? But there is none other beside thee by nature the Son of God. Or, into that of the Holy Ghost ? But he is wholly with thee, as of the same nature, and the same will, and the same mind, and the same power, and the same honor, and with thee receives the same worship from all. Baptize, therefore, if thou wilt, O Lord, baptize me, the Baptist. . . . Crown by thy touch my head, that running before thy kingdom, crowned as a Forerunner, I may fitly cry, ' *Behold! the* LAMB OF GOD *that taketh away the sin of the world.*' " This passage is a remarkable testimony against the physical use of βαπτίζω : 1. It presents the interchange of βαπτίζω and λούω as equivalents, λούω being used for spiritual and not physical cleansing, as shown by the difficulty suggested in " washing the spotless and the sinless." There would be no more difficulty in dipping or covering in simple water a " spotless and sinless " one than in dipping or covering, in like manner, Simon Magus while " in the gall of bitterness and bonds of iniquity." 2. The answer of John to his own question, " Into whose Name shall I baptize thee ?" declaring the oneness of nature, equality in dignity, and likeness in character of the Son with the Father and the Holy Spirit, shows (1) that baptism *into the Name* was an ideal baptism, and that its import was *subjection* and *assimilation*, and *therefore* it was impossible to baptize the Lord Jesus

Christ into the Name of the Father, or into his own Name, or into the Name of the Holy Ghost. 3. Like proof is found in the baptism asked by John for himself, namely, by the touch of the Saviour's hand laid upon his head, communicating a baptism, making him " fit " to Herald " THE LAMB OF GOD WHO " (by his personal baptism into an atoning death, and its application to the souls of men by the power of the Holy Ghost) " TAKETH AWAY THE SINS OF THE WORLD."

Proof that the Patristic Βαπτίζω has no Physical Use ended.

We have now passed in review all the elements which enter into a determination of the question : Do Patristic writers use βαπτίζω and βάπτισμα in religious applications physically as meaning simply to dip or to cover for a moment in water? Or, do they use them in such applications, 1. In ideal phrases, to develop and to impart to the baptized object the characteristic of the ideal element? And 2. Absolutely to express pregnantly the idea of the entire phrase?

I do not say that all the evidence bearing on this question has been presented, for tens of thousands of pages written within the first five centuries after Christianity have come down to us, and in those pages few subjects occupy a more prominent position than that of Christian Baptism; it would not therefore be possible to present all that bears upon the subject within this limited period short of many volumes. But all that bears upon the subject (as diverse elements of evidence exercising a control in determining this question under consideration) has, I believe, been presented.

1. The evidence as to the use and meaning of βάπτισμα is of the most satisfactory character as showing, 1. That it has no usage, physical or ideal, in Classic writings; 2. That it has no physical use in Inspired writings; but is solely employed in ideal combinations to express the profoundest spiritual changes in the condition of the soul; 3. That this usage is perpetuated in Patristic writings, with the additional abundant absolute use of βάπτισμα to express directly the spiritual condition which was originally distributed through an organic phrase. The Patristic use of this word is in the most absolute accord with that of the New Testament so far as the meaning of the word is concerned;

while it is in as absolute discord so far as the agency in effecting
the βάπτισμα is concerned by the association of water with the
Holy Spirit in its efficient production. For this there is no just
New Testament authority and but little which has any such semblance. There is no statement of any inspired writer in which
βάπτισμα appears as the result of the conjoint use and influence of
water and the Holy Spirit. To say that there is a rare passage
in which water and the Holy Spirit appear (without the mention
of baptism and without the statement of their conjunct action)
which is supposed to refer to baptism and supposed to indicate
conjoint operation, is to say nothing against the absolute truth
of the above statement, nothing to overturn the whole scope of
inspired teaching, nothing which can furnish an adequate basis
for faith to rest upon.

Evidence from every direction points to the same conclusion,
namely, the βάπτισμα of Inspiration and of early Christian writers
has no physical usage, the baptizing water in Scripture being
used to symbolize the nature of the spiritual βάπτισμα effected
solely by the Holy Ghost whenever and however operating, while
the Patristic water is putatively impregnated with the influence of
the Holy Spirit and as a conjoint agency effects the spiritual
βάπτισμα; but in neither case is the βάπτισμα a physical covering
in the water.

2. The evidence that these early Christian writers use ὕδατι καὶ
Πνεύματι as a conjoint agency to effect Christian baptism, a
thorough change in the spiritual condition and not a physical
covering of the body in water, is so clear and so full as to admit
of no addition.

3. The evidence that the burial in water was not the Christian
βάπτισμα, but when practiced (for hardly a day passed in which
baptism did not take place without it) it was the symbol of a
wholly diverse thing, namely, of the burial of Christ in the sepulchre, is complete. No one, heathen or Christian, ever called a
burial in earth or in rock a baptism ; and if a covering in water
for a moment has been regarded as a likeness of Christ's burial
in the rock, it was not therefore a likeness of Christ's baptism on
the Cross. This likeness to Christ's *burial* in the manner of
using the water has nothing to do with Christ's baptism, does
not enter as an essential element into Christian baptism, Patrists
themselves being judges, and has no shadow of appearance in
the baptism of the Scriptures.

The evidence for the use of βαπτίζω as concurrent with that of other sources of evidence, now referred to, is as perfect as could be desired:

1. The Patristic and the Classic usage of βαπτίζω, where they meet together, is identically the same. (1.) Both employ it to express the loss of vessels and of human beings in the depths of the sea without recovery; (2.) Both employ it to express the thorough drunkenness and insensibility induced by excessive wine-drinking. This usage is entirely foreign from and inconsistent with the usage of this word to express a momentary dipping in water employed in a religious rite.

2. This conclusion is confirmed by the use of other words to express this momentary water covering, which words do not appear in the ideal relations of βαπτίζω.

3. Other words are used by Patristic writers in ideal relations to express controlling influence, and they use βαπτίζω in the same or in kindred ideal relations (outside of the religious sphere) to express in like manner controlling influence. Classical usage of the word shows that its primary meaning adapts it in the most perfect manner to such ideal use.

4. Independent of the same grammatical forms which appear in the religious use of βαπτίζω as in its use out of that sphere when employed ideally, going to show its ideal religious use, there are evidences in added explanatory phraseology which show that such was its use.

5. There are no such grammatical forms or explanatory terms which show a physical use of βαπτίζω.

6. This absence of all evidence of the merely physical use of βαπτίζω within the religious sphere receives a profoundly confirmatory seal as true, from the entire absence of any such usage in the New Testament.

ORIGIN OF INQUIRY.

This "INQUIRY *into the usage of βαπτίζω with a view to its appli-cation to Scripture baptism*," is now completed.

The apology for undertaking it is this,—my own personal in-struction. The treatment of the subject as heretofore conducted left the merits of the case, in some respects at least, clouded with uncertainty and embarrassed with perplexity. For my own satis-faction I sought to find out the reason for this unsatisfactory result. If any one should be disposed to say, " A country Pas-tor is not qualified for such work:" without admitting the cor-rectness of the remark as it applies to my brethren, I cheerfully accept it as it applies to myself, and only apologetically add, that I have supposed, the least endowed have a right to do the best they can for their own instruction.

The apology for publication is this: The usage of the word having been traced through Classic, Jewish, Inspired, and Patristic writ-ings, the results appeared to myself so clear, so certain, so harmoni-ous, so complete, so competent to solve every difficulty heretofore unsolvable, that it seemed to be not improper to submit those re-sults, not for the instruction, but for the consideration of others.

It seems to be proper to say, that the conclusions reached in Classic Baptism were not reached and published without having previously examined what was the usage of Jewish, Inspired, and Patristic writers, thereby originating the temptation to color the usage of those spheres, when afterward examined, to bring them into harmony with previously announced conclusions; but the conclusions in Classic Baptism were only adopted and announced after the entire field had been examined, and the results of each sphere of distinctive use had been brought into comparison, and an adjustment made so as to bring all into the most perfect har-mony, so far as I was competent to judge. With the conclusions reached, the materials on which those conclusions rest, are also submitted; so that each one can form an independent judgment for himself. No *dicta* are addressed to recipient masses; evi-dence and conclusion are submitted for the consideration of those who have equal right (and competency beyond my own) to form a personal and final judgment. I shall submit to that judgment

Results in brief.

1. The relation of βαπτίζω with βάπτω. It is of great importance to determine the relation of βαπτίζω with βάπτω; whether it is with that stem which signifies *to dip* or with that which signifies *to dye.*

Whether this relation be with the one or the other this is certain, it could neither mean " to dip," nor "to dye." Derived words are not simple *duplicates* of words from which they originate.

We say, that this word does not originate in βάπτω *to dip;* 1. Because it does not mean *to dip* nor any act which is a modification of dip, nor, yet, expressive immediately of any act whatever, but making demand for a certain condition, the act effecting which is left at will. 2. Because it does not mean *to wet,* or *to wash by dipping,* or any other effect dependent upon dipping.   When βαπτίζω is used in the sense *to wash, to cleanse, to purify* (as is done abundantly by Jewish and Patristic writers) such meaning does not originate in washing by dipping or in any other mode of physical washing, but it originates in its own usage with adjuncts expressive of ceremonial and spiritual power to wash, to cleanse, to purify.   *Βαπτίζω is never used for physical washing.*

The origin of this word is in βάπτω *to dye* (= THOROUGHLY TO CHANGE THE CONDITION of an object *as to color*). 1. Of course βαπτίζω does not mean " to dye;" this is already provided for; but it does mean *thoroughly to change the condition* of an object *by introducing it into* (not the dye-tub, but) *some new condition, other* than that of a *dyed* condition. This filiation in general conception is strong if not conclusive evidence of the intimate relation between these words.   This new condition is, primarily, intusposition within a fluid, by any competent act, without limitation of time. In all of these respects the likeness is with βάπτω *to dye,* and not with βάπτω *to dip.* 2. The result of intusposition within a fluid without limitation of time, is the exhaustion of the power of the enveloping fluid to influence its object or of the power of the enveloped object to receive such influence. Again, the accord is with the stem *to dye,* and not with that *to dip.* To dip is a feeble word; to dye is a strong word in its sphere; no word has more exhaustive power than has βαπτίζω. 3. Many liquids (vinegar, oil, melted wax, milk, etc.) which have no *coloring* quality are possessed of *characteristics* which they part with to objects intusposed without limitation of time within them: while other liquids (wine, opiates, fountain of Silenus, etc.) do not part with their characteristic qualities by intusposition, but do so in other ways as by drinking, etc. It is a fact in language, that words which originate in an effect produced by one mode of action are extended to embrace analogous effects produced by other modes of action. Thus βάπτω *to dye* having its origin in *dipping* into coloring liquids comes to include a changed condition of color induced in any way, by *sprinkling*, by *pouring*, by the *falling rays of the sun*, or by any act however diverse from the act of dipping. In like manner βαπτίζω is extended so as to include not merely a changed condition by *intusposition* with all its effects, but an analogous change of condition not effected by intusposition, but in any way however diverse from it, as by *drinking* wine, swallowing an opiate, answering sophistical questions, etc. Again, the close relation with the one stem and wide divergence from the other is manifest. 4. *Βάπτω to dye* comes to the threshold of a usage in which a change of condition is exhibited without any coloring in fact. Thus it is said, " The soul (βάπτεται) *receives its characteristic* from the thoughts;" and again, " Is (βεβαμμένον) *characterized* by righteousness." Into the broad sphere of *uncolored* characteristic, thus indicated, this word does not enter. It has already a double burden to carry (*to dip, to dye*) and refusing a third gives birth to βαπτίζω, and assigns this broad and noble sphere to it as its heritage. This word, therefore, has a legal right to develop and to communicate *uncolored* characteristics from any source, and thoroughly to change the condition of persons or things by communicating to them such characteristics.

The related features of βαπτίζω and βάπτω *to dye* are too many and too striking (while presenting all the differences suitable to a derived word) to allow of doubt as to its relationship with this stem rather than with βάπτω *to dip*, from which it is separated by the broadest diversities.

Special Results.

CLASSIC BAPTISM shows, 1. A thorough change of condition by intusposition within a fluid, by any competent act, without limitation of time; 2. A thorough change of condition without intusposition by any power or influence competent to control and to assimilate to its characteristic; the special characteristic of such changed condition being indicated by the adjunct; 3. A thorough change of condition indicated by the absolute use of βαπτίζω without adjunct, the result of long and frequent usage in a phrase, now dropped, the idea of which is embodied in the single word. This is exemplified in βαπτίζω *to make drunk* (= thoroughly to change condition by the controlling influence of the intoxicating characteristic of wine).

JUDAIC BAPTISM shows precisely the same physical use (vessels and crews baptized irrecoverably in the depths of the sea) with intusposition, and (men baptized by drinking wine) without intusposition. But besides this sameness of usage and application, there is another and quite new use of the word in connection with religious rites. This usage is traceable through one or more centuries. The result of this long and necessarily frequent use as connected with religious rites of daily recurrence, is precisely the same as in the case of this same word applied by the Classics to wine-drinking, namely, it came to be used absolutely to express that thoroughly changed condition which their religious rites were competent to effect, that is to say, *a complete* CEREMONIAL *purification*.

Βαπτίζω *to make drunk* among the Greeks, and βαπτίζω *to make ceremonially pure*, are certainly widely divergent meanings, but each is legitimately reached and under precisely the same laws of language.

A man baptized by drinking wine is a man whose condition is thoroughly changed by the characteristic of wine—a drunken man. A man who is baptized by heifer ashes steeped in water and sprinkled upon him, or by the sprinkling of mingled water and blood, or by pure water used in any way, is a man whose condition has been thoroughly changed by the purifying characteristic of heifer ashes, etc.—*a ceremonially pure* man.

JOHANNIC BAPTISM is a stranger alike to Classic baptisms by the intusposition of ships and men within the depths of the sea, and of men baptized, without any intusposition, by drinking wine. There is no physical use of βαπτίζω in the ministry of John. This word has nothing whatever to do *with originating the presence or in controlling the use* of the water in the rite connected with John's ministry. The presence of the water is due to the purifying nature of Repentance and the Remission of sins, and the function of βαπτίζω is to develop that characteristic in the fullest measure with the requirement, that the soul must be thoroughly changed in its condition by coming under the controlling power of this characteristic. This exhausts its office. It has no more to do with regulating the use of the water than the child unborn. Johannic Baptism is no less a stranger to the Jewish use of this word to express a condition of *ceremonial* purification. There is no such feature in John's ministry as a *ceremonial* purification. His baptism was exclusively *spiritual* symbolized in a rite by pure water. *Therefore* " a dispute arose between some Jews and the disciples of John respecting PURIFICATION."

CHRISTIC BAPTISM is like John's baptism purely spiritual in its nature with an accompanying symbol rite in which its purifying nature is visibly exhibited by pure water sprinkled, or poured, or otherwise suitably applied, there being no significance in the act, and βαπτίζω having no concern in the act whatever it may be; the command and the significance being exhausted by the use of water as an abstract element purifying in its nature.

CHRISTIC BAPTISM differs from Johannic Baptism in that it shows truth in its ultimate ground. John preached a baptism of the soul " εἰς μετάνοιαν, εἰς ἄφεσιν ἁμαρτιῶν, into repentance, into the remission of sins," with a rite shadowing this preaching; Christianity reveals the ground on which this preaching of repentance with its sin-remission rests, namely, " Christ crucified, the Lamb of God that taketh away the sin of the world." There-fore the baptism of Christianity is *into* CHRIST, and through him remission of sin (together with regeneration and reconciliation) having been secured, the further and ultimate baptism (changing the condition of the once rebellious and alien soul to one of sub-jection and affiliation) " into the Name of the Father, and of the Son, and of the Holy Ghost."

These baptisms of Scripture, while wholly diverse in their na-ture from the baptisms of Heathenism, have no diversity as to grammatical form or the principles of interpretation which ex-pound them. In the phrase εἰς τὴν λίμνην βαπτιζόντων the participle indicates intusposition and its essential controlling influence, in general, while the adjunct εἰς λίμνην points out, in particular, the specialty of influence, which to a human being is death by drowning.

In the phrase βαπτίζειν εἰς γάλα, the verb indicates intusposition together with the necessarily involved influence, in general, while εἰς γάλα shows the influence specifically, namely, emollient, over a medical application. In like manner the Scripture phrase βάπ-τισμα εἰς μετάνοιαν, the word βάπτισμα indicates an ideal intusposition with necessarily suggested influence, in general, while εἰς μετάνοισ·

declares the nature of the influence specifically. The soul is thoroughly changed in its condition by coming under the controlling influence of repentance = godly sorrow for sin. So, the phrase βεβαπτισμενοι εἰς τὸ ὄνομα τοῦ Κυρίου Ἰησοῦ indicates, by its participle, intusposition (ideal in this case) with involved influence, in general, while the preposition and its regimen, precisely as in classical cases of like grammatical form, indicate the specific nature of the influence, namely, that which belongs to "*the* LORD" and *to* JESUS, "Saviour of his people from their sins;" the condition of such baptized ones (not ritually but really) is a thoroughly changed condition by subjection to the Lordship of Jesus and a full participation in the influence of his power to save from sin.

These Bible baptisms stand on the same platform, precisely, as to grammatical form and the principles of interpretation as Classic Baptisms. The language in which they are expressed could not be more explicit or more forcible.

PATRISTIC BAPTISM. Early Christian writers being voluminous and varied in their compositions introduce the use of βαπτίζω into other relations than those which are religious. In such cases they employ the word in precisely the same meanings as do Classic and Jewish writers, namely, to express a thorough change of condition by intusposition within a fluid, by any competent act, without limitation of time. The word is applied to vessels sunk to the bottom of the sea, and to men drowned; also without intusposition to men made drunk by wine-drinking. It is obvious that such a word could never be used to express a momentary dipping. In application within the sphere of religion it is used as it is in the Scriptures only with an ideal element. Its use in connection with the water of the rite is to secure the divine quality with which they supposed it to be impregnated, and so to secure not a physical baptism in the water, but a spiritual baptism of the soul through the water, thoroughly changing its condition by regeneration and the remission of sins. The Patristic use of βαπτίζω is the same as that of the Scriptures (never physical in the religious sphere) with the exception of the union of water as a co-operating agency with the Holy Spirit in baptism. The covering in water which obtained in baptism was not due to βαπτίζω nor did it enter into the essence of the baptism, nor in fact was any part of the baptism proper, but was introduced as a symbol of another thing, namely, of the *burial* of Christ in the sepulchre. Baptism as a designed momentary covering in simple water is found nowhere.

This hasty glance over the entire field shows the same ground element running through the usage of a thousand years, and proving βαπτίζω to be always a word of power and never passing into the feebleness of a dipping.

Final Results.

1. THE BAPTISM OF INSPIRATION is a thoroughly changed spiritual condition of the soul, effected by the power of the Holy Ghost through the cleansing blood of the Lord Jesus Christ, and so making it meet for reconciliation, subjection, and assimilation to the one fully revealed living and true God, FATHER, SON, and HOLY GHOST.

2. This "ONE BAPTISM" OF INSPIRATION is, by divine appointment, ritually symbolized as to its soul-purification by pure water, poured or sprinkled or otherwise suitably applied to the person, together with a verbal announcement of the spiritual baptism thus symbolized.

3. DIPPING THE BODY INTO WATER *is not, nor* (by reason of a double impossibility found in the meaning of the word and in the divine requirement) *can it be* CHRISTIAN BAPTISM. That Christian baptism is a water dipping is a novelty unheard of in the history of the church for fifteen hundred years. This idea is not merely an error as to the mode of using the water (wnich would, comparatively, be a trifle), but it is an error which sweeps away the substance of the baptism without leaving a vestige behind. It is a sheer and absolute abandonment of the baptism of Inspiration, which is a baptism *into* CHRIST—*into the* NAME of the Father, and of the Son, and of the Holy Ghost, and the substitution for it of a *dipping into* WATER, which has no more place in the Scriptures than the English W has a place in the alphabet of the Greek Testament.

THIS RESULT (a nullification of the theory which says that "dipping into water is Christian baptism") has not been sought, nor is it announced with any feelings of triumph or gladness of heart as against the friends of this theory; but it is declared as a result demanded by the concurrent and unanimous testimony of Heathen writers, Jewish writers, Inspired writers, and early Christian writers, reaching through a continuous historic period of more than one thousand years.

CONCLUSION.

THIS CONCLUDED INQUIRY with its results is now adoringly laid at the feet of Him who is THE TRUTH for his approval and blessing.

Whatever of truth there may be in it is his, and as his is made by him the common heritage of all his people. This truth may he establish. And all error may he overturn, whether it be found in or out of this INQUIRY.

INDEX.

CHRISTIC BAPTISM.

ÆSOP:
baptism drowns, 46.

AGENCY :
blood, water, etc., the *agency* and not the receptive element, 40.

ALCIBIADES
baptism drowns, 46.

ALEXANDER, PROF. J. ADDISON:
Acts 22 : 16, 9 : 18, 104 ; Samaritans ritually baptized into the Name of the Lord Jesus (not as Matt. 28 : 19) purport of this formula, 180; correct, 180, 181 ; "unto" should be *into*, 212 ; 415 ; Acts 26 : 17, 18 ; Apostolic commission of Paul; the word βαπτίζω not used ; in accord with the commission of the twelve, 389, 390.

ALFORD :
John 20 : 21-23, 385.

AMBROSE :
baptism of Jesus, covenant to fulfil all righteousness, 31 ; 296 ; 312 ; uses "subjicio" as the equivalent of βαπτίζω εἰς, 313.

ANTITYPE BAPTISM :
I Peter 3 : 21, salvation by a purified conscience sanctified by the Spirit, sprinkled with the blood of Jesus Christ (I Peter 1 : 2) and through his resurrection, bursting the arresting seal of his enemies, and affixing his own seal of pardon and life to his people, 335-343 ; the type Ark saved all in it ; the antitype Ark, Christ, saved all in Christ, by baptism of the Holy Spirit, 338 ; patristic views of antitype baptism, 342, 343.

ARK, THE :
I Peter 3 : 21, type of saving baptism into Christ by the Spirit, ("wherein few were saved," v. 20), 337 ; error of Carson and Gill, 338-342.

ARNOLD, PROF.:
Eastern churches do not cover in baptizing, 190.

ATHANASIUS :
Three baptisms; by water, by blood, by tears, 42.

AUGUSTINE :
Baptism of blood, 42, 312.

BAPTISMAL, REGENERATION :
What is it ? Dr. Pusey, 356, 357; error, 358-365.

BAPTISMS :
Christic, what ? 1. Real, 2. Ritual, 17; fundamental char-

acteristic of baptism by the Holy Ghost, 18 ; received by Christ, 27-31 ; baptism by drinking from a cup, 34-44 ; blood baptism, 38 : causative of death, Æsop, Alcibiades, Heliodorus, Themistius, 46 ; baptism by drinking common, various in nature,—Achilles Tatius, Athenæus, Conon, Evenus, Lucian, Plato, Plutarch, 47 ; baptism by Christ with the Holy Ghost, in which he is, 52-58 ; baptism of the Apostles promised (Acts 1 : 5), 58 ; Carson's view of baptism of the Spirit, with criticism, 62-73 ; baptism by the Holy Ghost, varied in character, 78 ; Christian baptism, 94-130 ; Cæsarea, 95-98 ; Pentecost, Cæsarea, " only scenes in S. S. called baptism of Holy Spirit," 98 ; design of, Alex. Campbell, 109 ; at Samaria, 113 ; at Ephesus, 114 ; by touch of hand, 115, 116 ; at Corinth, by special gifts, 117 ; of all disciples " into one body," 117 ; baptism preached by Peter, 130-153 ; ritual, 163 ; physical, none in S. S., 167 ; of the Gentiles, 202 ; of John's disciples, 209-216 ; diverse baptism, 213 ; change of condition, 214 ; into the name of Paul, 216-218 ; household, 219-238 ; " into his death," 247 ; diversity and sameness, 294, 295 ; errors, 299 ; a state, 306 ; ideal, 310-313 ; diverse gifts and unity of body, 323 ; doctrine, 328 ; 332 ; 333 ; notion of covering cause of ludicrous errors, 343 ; Jewish, 348.

βάπτισμα:

not used in classics ; not used in Scriptures with physical element, 47 ; in New Testament always contemplates effect without covering, 125-128 ; relation with βαμμα, 214; other relations 215-322 ; rare use of βαπτισμῶν, 329 ; baptism of N. T. cannot be physical, 468.

βαπτίζω :

baptist meaning of, 18 ; act in baptizing " pouring," but the meaning of βαπτίζω is not to pour, 84 ; " immerse " (as a dipping) not exponential of βαπτίζω, 85 ; has the idea of power not of " abundance," 85, 86, 124 ; meaning, not, 100 ; " immerse " rejected, reasons, 120-122, 137, 138 ; " pour," relation to, 125 ; does not mean " to dip," 189, 190 ; not related to βάπτω through " dip," but through " dye," 215 ; force of " baptized into," 217 ; cannot alone prove ritual baptism, 283 ; double use of, 303-305 ; fitness to convey characteristic of complement to baptized object, 307 ; wholly under influence of, 314 ; nothing to do with manner of using water in N. T., 315, 466.

βαπτίζω εἰς–βαπτίζω ἐν–βαπτίζω ἐπί :

not to be confounded ; Baptist translator against Dr. Conant, 205-208 ; general agreement βαπτίζω ἐις means " baptized into," 294 ; passing into a new state, 302-304.

Ὁ βαπτίζων :

ἐν Πνεύματι Ἁγίῳ, the baptizer in, therefore under the influence of, and baptizing by the Holy Ghost, never baptizes with water, 321 ; 52, 126, 130.

"BAPTIZER, THE :"

As author, the Lord Jesus Christ, as executive agent, the Holy Ghost, 76, 84, 120, 123 ; universal, perpetual, 124, 128.

BAPTISM INTO CHRIST (Romans 6 : 2-4) :

Has an equivalent but more specific statement in baptism "into his death" (Rom. 6 : 3) ; " who, his own self, bare our sins on the tree, that we, dead to sin, might live to righteousness " (I Peter 2 : 24); Christ's death is his people's life ; baptized into that death they become dead to sin (Rom. 6 : 2), and receive a new, spiritual, life (6 : 4) ; Christ's death has this double power to kill and to make alive, and to this double end his people are, by the Holy Ghost, "baptized into his death." And this is real, not ritual baptism, 241-275 ; Carson, criticism, 245-253 ; Professors Ripley and Chase, 253-262; Errett, Fee, 262-264 ; Professor Wilson (Belfast), President Halley, Dr. Beecher, Stuart, Dr. Hodge, Dr. Pusey, 264-268 ; Patristic writers, 269-274 ; ritual baptism without slightest foundation, 275.

BAPTISM OF REPENTANCE :

this baptism (= heart sorrow for and turning from sin) John preached as introducing "into remission of sin " (Luke 3 : 3, Matt. 3 : 2), and in a rite by use of pure water symbolized this "remission" through the blood of "the coming Lamb of God " (Matt. 3 : 11, John 1 : 29, 31), 210, 213 ; two-one baptism, 330.

BAPTIST MANUAL

doctrine, "immersion in water into the Name," unintelligible, 435.

BAPTIST, JOHN THE :

was not ritually baptized ; for like reasons Saul may not have been, 100.

BAPTIST QUARTERLY :

on Acts 2 : 38, 146-148 ; criticism on, 149-153, 271.

BAPTIST TRANSLATORS :

not consistent, 56 ; Pentecost, Cæsarea, "only scenes in Holy Scripture called baptism of the Holy Spirit," 98 ; inconsistent, 132; right on Acts 10 : 48, 205, 206, 211.

BAPTIST VERSION :

use of ἐν, 54-57 ; personal Holy Ghost, 97, 98 ; essential difference in translation of I Cor. 12 : 13, and other like passages, 118 (Disciples version, 119, 120) ; 126, 127, 132 ; " by one Spirit," 318 ; water rite, antitype, 336.

BAPTIZINGS OF DOCTRINE :

difficulty of interpretation, 328-335.

BARROWS, PROFESSOR E. P. :

type and antitype, 337.

BASIL

Change in reading of I Cor. 12 : 13, 117, 297.

BEECHER, PRESIDENT EDWARD :

Rom. 6 : 3, 4, 265 ; I Cor. 10 : 2, 307, 439.

BENGEL :
Jesus did not receive "John's baptism," undertook "to fulfil all righteousness," did on the cross, 31, 332, 353 ; I Cor. 6 : 11, 366 ; Ephes. 5 : 25, 370 ; Titus 3 : 5, 376.

BIBLIOTHECA SACRA :
Syriac translation of βαπτίζω, 463.

BLOOMFIELD :
meaning of ' Anointed,' 34 ; "εἰς for ἐν" mistake, 310, 314 ; I Peter 3 : 21, 335, 353 ; I Cor. 6 : 11, 366 ; Ephes. 5 : 26, 369 ; Titus 3 : 5 "logomachy," 376.

BOOTH, ABRAHAM :
"wild talk" of Pentecost baptism, 87, 88.

BRENTIUS :
baptism of John is as his teaching, 333.

CÆSAREA, BAPTISM AT :
likeness with unlikeness of that at Pentecost, 95–98 ; views of Profs. Ripley and Hackett, and Baptist Bible, 96–98.

CALVIN :
why Paul baptized into the name of Christ and not as commanded, Matt. 28 : 19, 179 ; valuable, 180, 332 ; I Cor. 6 : 11, 366 ; water, outward symbol, 369 ; so, 376, visible symbol of invisible grace, 384, 416.

CAMPBELL, ALEXANDER :
baptize, means specific act, 19 : 99, 105 ; design of, 109, 135, 136, 158, 294, 302 ; new state, 304 ; "by one spirit," 318 ; ritual baptism related to remission as repentance and faith, 324 ; baptism for the remission of sins, 348, 392, 435, 436.

CARSON, ALEXANDER, LL.D. :
baptize implies immersion, 18 ; resurrection, 19 ; water a womb, 20 ; objects to connecting cup and baptism, 45 ; sources of power, 59, 60 ; views of baptism of the Spirit, 61 ; Saul immediately immersed, 99, 108 ; baptism of Eunuch, 182 ; views unsatisfactory, 184–188 ; his postulate, the rack, 200, 201 ; no difference in mode between baptism and baptism, baptism in one case is baptism in another, 213, 298 ; error in interpretation, 299–301 ; "by one Spirit," 318, 322 ; I Peter, 3 : 20, 21, 338, 345, 347 ; John 3 : 5 ; misinterpreted, 365 ; I Cor. 6 : 11, 367 ; Ephes. 5 : 25 ; water figure of washing by the word, 371 ; Titus 3 : 5, 377 ; Heb. 10 : 22 ; "sprinkling emblem of purification," 381.

CHASE, PROFESSOR :
Rom. 6 : 1–4, 261, 262.

CHRIST :
personal baptism of, what was it ? 27–30 ; personal baptism of by the Holy Ghost, 31 : 34 ; not the same as that of the Apostles, 33, 34 ; baptism into penal death under figure of drinking from a cup, 34–44 ; Christ's baptism by blood on the cross not the same as martyr baptism by blood, 43 ; personal baptism of, threefold, 50; Christ, the baptizer by the Holy Ghost, 52; being in therefore invested with and baptizing by, 58, 95, 208, 319, 320.

CHRISTIAN BAPTISM :

what it is not, what it is, 94 ; preached, 130–153 ; interpretation, 140 ; incorporated in a rite, 163 ; twofold manifestation, 167 ; not by conjoint agencies of water and Holy Ghost, 202 ; by the Holy Ghost alone and this symbolized by water, 203 ; express statement necessary at institution, 217.

CHRYSOSTOM :

112, 123.

CLEMENS ALEXANDRINUS :

quotes I Cor. 12 : 13, without 'εν, 118 ; full form expressing change of condition by baptism, 144 ; baptized *upon* a couch, 145 ; baptism by teaching, 333.

CODEX SINAITICUS :

Matt. 20 : 22, 44 ; I Peter, 3 : 21, 335, 352.

COMMISSION, APOSTOLIC :

what was its baptism ? real, of the soul through the truth by the Spirit, or ritual of the body through a symbol by water ? John 20 : 21–23 ; Apostolic commission, yet the word βαπτίζω not used, 385 ; no uniformity of words in recording the commission, 386 ; Luke 24 : 44–50 ; Apostolic commission, witnesses, enlightened in the Scriptures, preach repentance and remission, endued with power from on high—the word βαπτίζω not used, 386–389 ; Acts 26 : 17, 18 : Paul's apostolic commission ; βαπτίζω not used, and so far as the manner of using water is concerned this word might without harm have never been used in the N. T., 389, 390 ; Mark 16 : 15, 16 ; Apostolic commission, βαπτίζω appears but not with water, 390–402 ; Matt. 28 : 19, 20 ; Apostolic commission; βαπτίζω used, not into water but into the Name of the Triune God ; conclusion reached, 403–469.

CONANT, DR. :

Matt. 3 : 11—John 1 : 33—translation differs, 56 ; translation of 'εκ and εἰς, 195 ; not in accord with his fellow-translator of Baptist Bible, 205–208, 211 ; "unto," 294 ; baptize—"coming into new state" inconsistent with meaning *to dip*, 306 ; "in the Name" (commission) "not *into* the Name," wrong, 434.

COROLLARY :

purport of "baptism into Christ," 51.

COUNCIL OF CARTHAGE :

views as to baptism by the hand, 115 ; dipping into water not baptism, 350.

CREMER, PROF. HERMANN (BIB. THEO. LEX.) :

εἰς and its regimen denote the specialty of baptism ; εἰς invariably used in *ideal* sense, 335.

CRITICISM :

of Dr. Carson's view of baptism of the Spirit, 62–73 ; of Baptist views of the commission, 424–428 ; of others not Baptists, 428–432.

CUP :

baptism, by drinking, 34–44, 44–51 ; dipping does not belong to baptism, 80.

CURTIS, PROF. T. F. :
eulogy on dipping into water, 325, 326.

CYPRIAN :
"blood and public confession" baptism, 39.

CYRIL OF JERUSALEM :
martyr, blood baptism, 39 ; the baptizer with the Holy Ghost and fire, the baptizer with water, 91, 350.

DAGG, PROFESSOR J. L. :
Ephes. 4 : 5, " one baptism ;" failure to make *two* baptisms out of baptism by the Spirit and a rite symbolizing this baptism by water, 344, 348.

DIDYMUS ALEXANDRINUS :
change in reading of I Cor. 12 : 13, 117.

DIPPING INTO WATER .
in baptism, says Gale, and Roger Williams, and A. Barber, two hundred and fifty years ago ; and also more recently, Booth, and Carson, and Baptist Quarterly of 1871, but denied by the Quarterly of 1869, and both affirmed and denied by the Baptist Bible translators, 151–153 ; baptism = "passing into new state," says A. Campbell, 303, and Dr. Conant, most inconsistently, 306 ; Professors Pepper and Curtis say dipping into water is glorious, " a garment that fits all Christians, suits all ages," 325 ; evidence for dipping into water baptism is nothing, and multiplied a million times would remain nothing, 349 ; unknown to the New Testament, 468.

DONATUS :
baptism into, 312.

ΕΙΣ .
supreme importance of this proposition in relation to baptism ; uniformity of translation imperative, 210–212, 294, 295 ; indicates the receiving (*always ideal*) element, 310 ; Mark 1: 9, not exception, 311-

EK :
does not always mean " out of " (Carson), 190–200.

EN :
not always "in ;" meaning *by* results from " in," 52–58 ; 295–297 ; never indicates the receiving element, 310; Acts 10 : 48, no exception, 311 ; I Cor. 12 : 13, "by " five times, 318.

ELEMENT OF BAPTISM :
physical or ideal, 164, 165 ; indicated by ἐις invariably ideal, 310.

ELLIPSIS :
doctrine of, 217 ; elliptical quotations completed by assumption, 241, 298 ; treatment as ellipsis when none, 303, 304.

ELLICOTT, BISHOP :
52, 56, 294 ; Ephes. 5 : 25, 371 ; Titus 3 : 5, 377, 379.

EMBLEM :
" sound," " wind," " fire," not emblems, 80, 81.

Ἐν Πνεύματι Ἁγίῳ :
after this phrase, and ἐν Χριστῷ should supply ὤν, Olshausen, Stuart, Hodge, Winer, 52 ; parallelism with 'εν πνεύματι Ἡλίου, 77, 78; means in, therefore under influence of, so agency, 52–55, 293 ; " by one

Spirit," general agreement, 318 ; purport of, 319, 320, 322.

Ἐν τῷ Βεελζεβοὺλ :
parallel passage (in construction), 54 ; means *in*, therefore under influence of, so agency, 54.

ERRETT, REV. ISAAC :
baptism of Jesus different from that of a penitent sinner, 34 ; repentance and baptism both necessary *"for* the forgiveness of sins,"* 136, 262.

EQUIVALENT PHRASES :
baptized with the Holy Ghost (Acts 1 : 5) ; *filled with* the Holy Ghost (Acts 2 : 4), 76 ; *endued with* power from on high (Luke 24 : 49), *baptized with* the Holy Ghost ; shall *receive power* after the Holy Ghost is come upon you, Acts 1 : 4, 5 ; John 1 : 32 ; Luke 4 : 1, 14, 58 ; *baptized into* Christ = *put on* Christ, Gal. 3 : 26, 27, 282–293. While these phrases—baptized with, filled with, endued with, put on (very diverse in their literality), are used as New Testament equivalents, they are not nor can be used as equivalent with "dipping into water ;" but water (abstract) can be and in fact is used in a rite to symbolize the purifying nature of "baptized with, filled with, endued with, put on Christ by," the Holy Ghost, 293 ; Ambrose properly uses "subjici" as the equivalent of "baptized into " = subjected to, brought fully under influence of, 313–315 ; inspiration authorizes the use of βαπτίζω εἰς as the equivalent (I Cor. 10 : 2), of the Hebrew word (Exodus 14 : 31), meaning "to lean upon, to believe in," 467 : Dr. Murdoch claims divine authority for the Syriac word meaning "to stand firm " to represent the Greek βαπτίζω, 467.

EUNOMIANS :
rebaptized, heretical formula, 351.

EUNUCH, BAPTISM OF :
solitary case under Christianity of hope for dipping, 182–201 ; views of Carson, Ripley, Conant, Arnold, untenable, 185–200 ; only case of appeal lost, 201.

EWING, PROFESSOR GREVILLE (GLASGOW) :
connects cup and baptism, 45 ; Syriac version, 464.

FAIRBAIRN, PROFESSOR (SCOTLAND) :
baptized into a person, meaning of, 415.

FEE, PROFESSOR J. G. :
Rom. 6 : 1–4 ; Col. 2 : 12, 262, 263.

FIGURE :
baptism said to be a figure of burial, resurrection, womb, and birth (18–20), and this uno-multiple figure is said to be the figure of another figure (!), Carson, 292.

FIRMILIAN :
Paul baptized with spiritual baptism John's disciples, 115.

FORMULA :
"into the Name," meaning, Stier, Zinzendorf, Neander, Olshausen, Voss, Halley,

Bloomfield, Wilson, Lange, 417–423 ; first appearing in Christian ritual baptism, 164–166 ; changed from Matt. 28 : 19, 173–181 ; views of Patrists, 173–176 ; purport of formula, 181 ; true unification, 181 ; ʿεν τῷ ὀνόματι (Acts 10 : 48) not a formula of baptism, 204 ; formula, 216, 217 ; Schaaf, Matt. 28 : 19, not used by Apostles, 441, 459.

FRITSCHE :
Rom. 8 : 1, 56.

FLOOD, THE :
not a type of baptism, destroying (Ark saved), 337 ; Baptists illogically deduced a "dipping" from the saving (?) flood-water, and irrationally make *symbol* baptism the antitype of a claimed type flood, 337, 341.

FULLER, DR. RICHARD :
baptism, saved or damned, 19, 391.

FULL, TO MAKE, TO BE FILLED WITH (= BAPTIZED) :
is the equivalent of the New Testament "baptized ;" this is absolutely certain, Acts 1 : 5 (promise, " *baptism* "), Acts 2 : 4 (accomplishment, " filled "), 76 ; it is not the equivalent of all usage of baptize ; it cannot be interchanged with—the man, the ship, the axehead baptized in the sea ; it has equivalence and interchangeableness with—baptized by wine (Acts 2 : 13, 15), that is to say, it has equivalence with baptisms which are effected by pervading and assimilating power and not with baptisms depending on physical covering, *therefore* New Testament baptism is due to the assimilating power of the Holy Ghost, and not to a water covering, as all else testifies, 275–277, 280, 281, 313–315; Bloomfield, Robinson, Clemens Alex., Josephus, Pope, 314.

GABRIEL, THE ANGEL :
ordered to school, 347.

GESENIUS :
translation of Hebrew word related to Syriac word for baptize, 309 ; Dan. 4 : 14, 336.

GILL, DR. :
I Peter 3 : 20, 21, misinterpretation of, 339–342 ; Tertullian does not call the flood water a baptism or a "dipping" (?) because it covers, but because it purifies the world from its pollution, 338 ; "scorn of baptism," 340 ; Baptist doctrines of them lightly esteemed, 341 ; the Ark floating, a sorry example, like everything else, of a "dipping," 341; Baptists who (mistakenly) find a saving type baptism in the flood waters should find a saving antitype baptism in their rite water, but they leave this logical sequence to " Campbellites," and Puseyites, and Romanists, and content themselves with an illogical "dipping," 341.

GODWIN, PROF. (LONDON) :
Matt. 28 : 19, not institution of baptism, 415, 438.

GREGORY NAZIANZEN :
martyr and blood baptisms more

sacred, 42 ; destructive Baptists and Anabaptists, 351.

HACKETT, PROF. H. B. :
Acts 1 : 2, 2 : 6, 86, 87 ; Cæsarea baptism, 97 ; Middle Voice, 108 ; Acts 2 : 38, agreement and difference with Alex. Campbell and Dr. Pusey, 108–111 ; 'upon the Name,' 134.

HALLEY, PRESIDENT ROBERT (ENGLAND) :
Rom 6 . 2–4, 265 ; I Cor. 10 : 2, 307 ; Matt. 28 : 19, 437.

HARRISON, PROF. GESSNER :
"be baptized *upon* (ἐπὶ) the Name," 138, ἐκ, 191, 192, 195.

HELIODORUS :
baptism drowns, 47.

HILARY :
baptism of Jesus a covenant to fulfil all righteousness, 31.

HODGE, DR. CHARLES :
I Cor. 12 : 13 cannot mean immersed in the Spirit any more than Luke 3 : 16, Acts 1 : 5, can mean immersed in water, 122.

HOUSEHOLD BAPTISM :
Acts 16 : 15, Acts 16 : 33, I Cor. 1 : 16, 219–238 ; "As the soul of the father, so also the soul of the son is mine" (Ezek. 18 : 4), "*her* household," "all *his*," 220 ; Family a divine institution ; Family unity ; Family headship ; Household relation to God ; Family rejected from the Kingdom of God ; 220–230 ; Results ; Incredibilities ; Alex. Campbell ; National Baptist, 230–237 ; individualism has not supplanted the Family as an organic element in the constitution of our world, in the covenant of redemption and in the Kingdom of God, 237, 238.

IDEAL BAPTISM :
certain and concluding truth, no other baptism in N. T., 164, 310; *differentiæ* indicated, 311, 313–315 ; "by one spirit into one body," 319–323 ; Cremer, 335 ; I Peter 3 : 21, 336.

IGNATIUS :
"baptism into the death of the Lord," 350.

"INTO CHRIST :"
denotes the passing from a condition without Christ into a condition within Christ, 243, 244 ; so "into repentance ;" and *baptized* into Christ, into repentance, means precisely what it says—into *Christ*, into *repentance*, with that soul change of condition implied in "Christ," "repentance," and does not absurdly mean what it does not say—baptized into *water* with the bodily change of condition implied in "water," 257, 258 ; in the phrases dipped into *the dye*, dipped into *the wax*, you could as rationally substitute "the wax" for "the dye" as in the phrases baptized into *Christ*, baptized into *water* (if indeed there was any such phrase as "baptized into water " in the New Testament, which there is not), you could rationally substitute "water" for "Christ," 258–266, 284.

"IN CHRIST :"
is the complement of "into

Christ:" the soul which is baptized, *i. e.* a moral condition alien from Christ "into Christ," *i. e.* a moral condition assimilated to Christ remains abidingly in that condition—"in Christ." This is the profound and precious doctrine of New Testament baptism by the Holy Ghost uniting the soul to Christ, but what has the error of a water dipping to do with such profundity of power and grace? 275-282, 291, 292.

INGHAM, R. (LONDON):
death by drowning represented in baptism, 19; burial in tomb of Joseph, 19; I Cor. 12 : 13, 322 ; Ephes. 4 : 5, "not baptism of the Spirit ;" error, why? 345-347.

IRENÆUS:
baptism of Jesus and Apostles, 90 ; in Acts 9 : 17 substitutes "baptized" for filled with the Holy Ghost, 112, 377, 368.

JAMES, J. W.:
"by what authority do we baptize 'into the Name of the Father,' when the Apostles did not?" 412.

JELF:
meaning of ἐκ, 191.

JEROME:
297, 350.

JESUS:
could not receive "John's baptism," 27 ; baptism of, by the Holy Ghost, 31-34; baptism by a cup, 34-44.

JEWETT, PROF. M. P.:
baptize, an act, 18; entire immersion for entire depravity, 20.

JEWISH BAPTISM:
manner of using the water may have been the same as in Christian ritual baptism, while the baptisms were essentially diverse in nature, 348.

JOHN THE BAPTIST:
"baptism of," different from *baptism by*, 27 ; no certain evidence that John's baptism included females ; not an organizer, 168; his baptism preached and symbolized in rite by water a spiritual purification, 329 ; antagonistic to Jewish, 354.

JOHN OF DAMASCUS:
the Forerunner baptized by putting his hand on Christ's head, 115, 297.

JOHN'S DISCIPLES:
rebaptized, special case, 209 ; had been baptized ritually "into repentance ;" were taught, now, that repentance and remission and the Holy Ghost come through Christ Jesus, they believed and were baptized, ritually, "*into* the name of the Lord Jesus," and really *by* the extraordinary gifts of the Holy Ghost, 209-216.

JOHN 20 : 21-23 :
Apostolic commission ; no uniformity of words in the record by the Evangelists, 385, 386 ; but they are in accord, 386; the word βαπτίζω is not used, 385.

JOSEPHUS :
ritual baptism of John, symbolization of Spiritual purification preached, 354.

JOSHUA, A TYPE:
baptism into, 312; type of the antitype baptism into Christ (I Peter 3 : 21, I Cor. 10 : 2), 338.

JUDITH:
12 : 7, baptized herself upon the fountain, 145.

KNAPP:
I Peter 3 : 21, 335.

KRAUTH, PROF. C. P.:
relation of ritual baptism to salvation, 391.

KÜHNER:
meaning of ἐκ, 191.

LLOYD, J. T. (RELIGIOUS HERALD):
Pœdobaptists eat and drink damnation, 21.

λούω:
does not require covering, 367; Rev. 1: 5, 1 Peter 1 : 2, sprinkling of the blood of Christ can "wash" (= cleanse), 367, 368 (Calvin 366); faith "washes," Irenæus, 368; Ezek. 16 : 8, 374, 378, 379; covering not necessary (Tertullian), 383; Chrysostom, Calvin, 384.

λουτρόν:
containing vessel, laver (Ellicott), not tenable, 377, 378.

LUKE 24 : 44–50:
apostolic commission; Stier, Schleiermacher, Grotius, Ebrard, Bengel, Lange, 387; diversity of words accord in truth with other evangelists, 388; the word βαπτίζω not used, 388.

MANIFESTATION:
of the power of the Lamb of God to take away sin, therefore John used water in baptizing, 166.

MARK 16 : 15, 16:
apostolic commission; accord with John and Luke; differs, verbally, in the use of βαπτίζω; what is the baptism, real or ritual? It is "saving," therefore it is "real" baptism into Christ, through "believing," by the Spirit, 390; Wilson, Fuller, Krauth, Pusey, Barclay, 391, 392; interpretation, 392; Middleton, Alexander, Hackett, Bloomfield, Kuinoel, Olshausen, 394–399; Syriac, Murdock, 399, 400; ellipsis not necessarily water, 402.

MATTHEW 28 : 19, 20:
apostolic commission; its elements—1, the field = the world; 2, the duty = (1), disciple all nations (to Christ for the remission of sins); (2), baptize them (made disciples) into the Name of the Father, and of the Son, and of the Holy Ghost (reconciling them to the living and triune God); (3), teaching them (made disciples to Christ and reconciled to God) to observe whatsoever I have commanded, that they may adorn the doctrine of Christ their Saviour and glorify their Father in heaven, 403–469; last words of the Redeemer on earth; strict adherence to N. T. usage of βαπτίζω, 403, 404; various translations of Stuart, Williams, Beecher, Godwin, Carson, Arnold, Campbell, Fuller; objection, 405; translation of εἰς, Carson, Dagg,

Wayland, Judson, Campbell, *into;* Stuart, Halley, Wilson, *into*, 405 ; Conant *in;* Schaaf, Alford, object, 406, 408 ; Baptist views, Carson, Gale, Morell, Ingham, Jewett, Wayland, Booth, Stovel, Pepper, Bruner, Campbell, 408-411 ; unsatisfactory, 411-413 ; other views, Pusey, Barclay, Fairbairn, Prof. J. A. Alexander, Beecher, Godwin, Bengel, Olshausen, Stier, Calvin, Lange, Wilson, 428-432 ; objections to Baptist interpretations, 432-436 ; remarks on other views, 436-443 ; interpretation ; " disciples," " all nations," " baptizing into the Name," " of the Father, and of the Son, and of the Holy Ghost," " teaching them to observe," 443-458 ; history of use of formula, 458 ; Patristic writers reconciling the formula in Matt. 28 : 19 with the formula used by the Apostles in ritual baptism, not successful, 459-462 ; Syriac version (baptism = standing firm), 463-468 ; commission considered and result, 468, 469.

MATTHIES :
on the diversity between the formula in Matt. 28 : 19, and that used by the Apostles in ritual baptizing, 177 ; why unsatisfactory, 178.

MENANDER :
baptism into, 311.

MEYER :
into the Name not *in* the Name, 421 ; Matt. 28 : 19 " not baptismal formula, not found in Apostolical church," 422.

MIDDLETON, BISHOP :
overlooks the distinction between the prepositions in Luke 4 : 1, and Matt. 4 : 1, 53, 394.

MORRELL, THOS. (EDINBURGH) :
Pentecost baptism, " noise " not symbol, " tongues " more emblematic, 88.

MOSES, A TYPE :
baptized into, 294-309 ; the relation and the equivalence of the Hebrew (Exod. 14 : 31) and the Greek (I Cor. 10 : 2), 308-310 ; Israel baptized into = made fully subject to Moses, 310 ; into Joshua, 312 ; Noah saved in the ark, a type, 338.

MURDOCH, PROF. JAMES :
translation of Syriac Acts 22 : 16, 107, 126 ; Syriac word for baptism, 309 ; to baptize = *to stand fast*, 463 ; divine authority, 467 ; also, divine authority for parallel usage by Paul in I Cor. 10 : 2 for Hebrew word in Exodus 14 : 31, 466, 467.

NATIONAL BAPTIST :
" into," after baptize, indicates the element into which the baptized object passes—"into repentance,"—" into remission,"—"into the name of the Lord Jesus,"—" into the name of the Father, and of the Son, and of the Holy Ghost," —therefore would change the language of inspiration and remodel the Greek language to prevent the overthrow of a mistaken Baptist theory, 211, 212, 408.

NEANDER :
on the diverse formulæ " into

the name of Christ," "into
the name of the Father and
of the Holy Spirit;" 179;
defective, 179; Matt. 28 : 19,
441.

NESTORIAN RITUAL:
distinguishes between the act
(*tabal*) in using the water and
the baptism (*amad*) into the
Name, etc., 435.

NEWCOME, ARCHBISHOP;
I Cor. 10 : 2, typical baptism,
through miracle, 308.

OLSHAUSEN:
mistaken as to formulæ of baptism, 204, 353; I Cor. 6 : 11,
366; Ephes. 5 : 25, 370.

ONE BAPTISM:
into Christ; multunal, 242–245,
258–260, 271, 294, 295; triu-
nal, 273, 274; biunal, 330,
331; "Gospel and ordinances
the same thing in two forms"
(Prof. Pepper), then baptism
by the Spirit and baptism by
water (symbolizing that baptism in its purifying power)
cannot be two baptisms but
must be "one baptism" in
two forms, reality and symbol,
347; many diverse verbal
forms agreeing in "one baptism," 348, 349.

ORIGEN:
baptism of blood, perfect baptism, 41; "blood, water,
Spirit," agencies, 42; twofold significance of martyrdom, 44; baptism by Holy
Ghost and fire, 92; baptism
into Joshua, 312.

PATRISTIC WRITERS:
invariably regard water as
agency whether used by pouring or sprinkling, or covering,

171–173; water and Spirit
united in agency, 215; ritual
baptism (the Spirit with the
water cleanses from sin, and
regenerates the soul), 324.

PAUL:
baptized into name of, 310–315;
his view of the supremacy
of real baptism by the Spirit,
through the preaching of the
Gospel, over ritual symbol
baptism with water, 324; his
commission, no dipping into
water in it, 326, 327.

PENTECOST BAPTISM:
58–95; Baptism qualifying for
apostleship; Carson's view,
59–62; criticism of this view,
62–73; translation of (Acts
1 : 5), 73–76; the Baptizer,
use and disuse of ἐν, 76–78;
its emblem, 78–81; views of
Profs. Ripley and Hackett,
81–87; views of Booth and
Morell, 87–90; Irenæus,
Gregory, Cyril, Origen, 90–92;
its importance, 93–95.

PENGILLY:
baptism, figure of suffering, 21.

PEPPER, PROF. G. D. B.:
baptism, burial in Jordan, 19;
resurrection, 19; communion
before baptism, a lie, 21; I
Cor. 12 : 13, spiritual baptism,
322, 325, 326, 327; the Gospel
antecedent to symbols, symbols must be interpreted by
the Gospel, 328, 347; baptism
not instituted by the commission, 426.

PETER AT JERUSALEM:
first preached Christian baptism, 130; various views, 132;
true translation, 137; essence
of the Gospel, 146; repent-

ance and faith baptize into remission, 330.

PETILIANUS .
does not baptize twice, 40.

PHYSICAL BAPTISM :
unknown to Christianity, 167, 302, 306, 310, 311 ; differing from Greek, 313, 315, 345 ; cannot be that of the N. T., 466-468.

PEARCE, BISHOP :
I Cor. 10 : 2, *into* not "unto" Moses, 307.

PLACES OF BAPTISM :
upon the Jordan, Matt. 3 : 15 ; upon the Cross, Mark 10 : 38 ; in a house, Acts 1 : 5, 2 : 2-4 ; in a house, Acts 11 : 15, 16 ; in a house, Acts 9 : 17, 18 ; not stated, Acts 8 : 15, 16 ; in a house, probably, Acts 19 : 5; where Gospel preached, I Cor. 12 : 13 ; at a house, Acts 2 : 38-41 ; not stated, presumably at place of preaching, Acts 8 : 12, 13 ; at roadside, Acts 8 : 36.

Πνεῦμα Ἅγιον :
Matt. 3 : 11, "not the personal Spirit" (Baptist), 56 ; specific without article (Baptist translator), 57 ; not the receptive element of baptism, but the agent, 75, 84 ; baptizing at Pentecost the Apostles, 58 ; at Cæsarea, Cornelius, 95 ; at Damascus, Saul, 98 ; at Samaria, disciples ritually baptized, 113 ; at Ephesus, the twelve, 114 ; at Corinth (I Cor. 12 : 13, ἐν Πνεύματι translated, by Baptists, "*by* one Spirit,"and *five* times within a few verses similarly translated), "all" Christians, 119, 120 ; Agent

in baptism, 123 ; subjects of this baptism, "all," 127, 129 ; the one baptizing Agent effecting the "one baptism" of Christianity, 344-351.

PRIEST, ROMAN CATHOLIC :
"God the author of his error," 347.

PURIFYING, INVOLVING BAPTISM :
question about (John 3 : 25), 352 -355 ; Jewish baptism—ceremonial purification ; John's baptism (preached)—spiritual purification ; rite a spiritual purification symbolized, 354 ; "purification" can embrace generically that of the Jews and of John, 355.

PUSEY, DR. E. B. (OXFORD) :
I Cor. 12 : 13, 122 ; Acts 2 : 38, salvation by baptism, 136, 158, 267, 291 ; I Cor. 12 : 13, meaning, 321 ; one baptism into Christ and so into the Trinity, 351 ; baptismal regeneration, what, 356 ; Ephes. 5 : 26, 369 ; "miracle," 372 ; ancient liturgies, 375, 392.

"PUT ON CHRIST:"
Galat. 3 : 26, 27, expository and equivalent of "baptized into Christ," 285-291.

QUARTERLY, CHRISTIAN :
baptism, burial of old man, rising up of new man, 20.

QUARTERLY, BAPTIST :
Acts 2 : 38, 146-148 ; criticism on, 149-153, 211.

REAL, CHRISTIC BAPTISM :
meaning of, 17, 167 ; reference to in Rom. 6 : 2-4, 241-275 ; Gal. 3 : 26, 27, 282-293 ; I Cor.

12 : 13, 318-323; all "who call Jesus Lord" are ἐν Πνεί- ματι Ἁγίῳ and baptized by the Spirit into the name of the Lord Jesus and into one body, I Cor. 12 : 3. 13, 322, 323 ; real above ritual, 324.

RIPLEY, PROF. HENRY J. :
baptism, burial of old man, 19 ; moral loathsomeness left behind, 20, 81, 86 ; Cæsarea baptism, 97 ; the same Spirit baptizes all, 123, 133 ; wrong as to formnlæ of baptism, 204, 205, 253, 294, 301.

RITUAL, CHRISTIC BAPTISM:
meaning of, 17 ; adumbration of baptism by the Holy Ghost; water by its nature manifests purification, 164 ; in ritual baptism there is no baptism into the water, but the baptism "into the name of the Lord Jesus"—"into the name of the Father, and of the Son, and of the Holy Ghost," is announced and symbolized by water poured or sprinkled upon the subject of the rite, 164–181 ; perpetual obligation, 202, 206–216 ; value of, 218 ; all ritual baptisms examined (161–238); the results : 1, full formula; (1), the verb in the active voice ; (2), the agency in the dative, (3), the receiving element in the accusative ; 2, the complement of βαπτίζω in the New Testament is never water, but is always ideal element ; 3, to convert the New Testament baptism into a dipping into water is the most absolute abandonment con-

ceivable of that baptism which is taught by the Holy Ghost, 238–240, 324.

REGENERATION, BAPTISM :
John 3 : 5, supposed result of co-action of water and the Holy Spirit, 355-365; Patristic view, truth and error mixed, 355, 356 ; difficulty in explaining, Dr. Pusey, 356.

R. J. M. (WESTERN RECORDER):
to call Pœdobaptist bodies churches is logical insanity and idiocy, 21.

ROBINSON, PROF. EDWARD :
Rom. 1 : 29 (Lev.) 314.

SAMARIA, BAPTISM AT:
prayed for and character of, as that at Pentecost and Cæsarea, 113.

SAUL, BAPTISM OF :
98-112 ; what was it, a dipping into water ? 99 ; was Saul now called to be an Apostle ? 100 ; was this baptism to qualify for the Apostleship ? 101–105 ; filled with the Holy Ghost = baptized with the Holy Ghost, 103 ; "calling on the Name of the Lord" washes away sins, baptizes, 106.

SCHAAF, PROFESSOR P. :
"baptized in the Name, error, should be into," 310, 407 ; Matt. 28 : 19 not the formula used by the Apostles, 441.

STIER (WORDS OF LORD JESUS):
baptism of Jesus not " John's baptism " foreannounces baptism of the cross, 30 ; meaning of "into the Name," 417, 418.

STOVEL, REV. CHARLES (LON-
DON):

Matt. 28 : 19 shows immersion
in water, 19, 305.

SYMBOL:

why imperfect, 17 ; complexity
of Baptist symbolism, 18-22 ;
cloven tongues, symbol (Professor Hackett), 87 ; dove,
cup, tongue, water, 94 ; symbolization of " death, burial,
resurrection, womb, birth,
mother," foundationless in
inspiration, 275 ; what ? 337 ;
water in rite baptism a symbol of purification of the soul
by the atoning death of the
Lamb of God (John 1 : 29,
31), 339 ; (Calvin), 416, 430.

SCRIPTURE PASSAGES EXAM-
INED :

Matt. 3 : 15, (27); John 1 : 32,
(31); Mark 10 : 38, 39, (34);
Matt. 20 : 22, Luke 12 : 50,
(44); John 1 : 32, (52); Acts 1 :
5, (58); Acts 11 : 15, 16, (95);
Acts 9 : 17, 18 ; 22 : 13-16 ;
26 : 14-18, (98-112); Isaiah 1 :
16-18, (107); Ezek. 18 : 30, 31,
(108); I Peter 1 : 22, Acts 2 :
21, 38, (108); Acts 8 : 15, 16,
(113) ; Acts 19 : 6, (114-117);
I Cor. 12 : 13, (117) ; Acts 2 :
38, (130); Acts 8 : 12-16, (163);
Acts 8 : 35-38, (182); John 20 :
1, (198); Acts 10 : 47, 48, (202);
Acts 19 : 3-5, (209); I Cor. :
1 : 13, 15, (216); Acts 16 : 15,
33, I Cor. 1 : 16, (219); Rom.
6 : 2-4, (241); Colos. 2 : 9-13,
(275); Gal. 3 : 26, 27, (282); I
Cor. 10 : 2, (294); I Cor. 1 :
13, 15, (310); I Cor. 15 : 29,
(316); I Cor. 12 : 13, (318); I
Cor. 1 : 17, (324); Heb. 6 : 2,
(328); I Peter 3 : 21, (335);
Ephes. 4 : 5, (344-351); John
3 : 25, (350); John 3 : 5, (355);
I Cor. 6 : 11, (366); Ephes. 5 :
26, (369); Titus 3 : 5, (375);
Heb. 10 : 22, (381); John 20 :
21-23, (385); Luke 24 : 44-50,
(386).

SCRIPTURE PASSAGES REFERRED
TO :

Luke 12 : 50, I John 5 : 6, Matt.
3 : 15, John 19 : 30, (31); John
3 : 34, John 1 : 32, Luke 4 : 18,
21, Acts 10 . 38, Matt. 12 : 28,
Heb. 9 : 14, (32); Luke 4 : 1,
14, (33); Acts 10 : 38, (34);
Matt. 27 : 46, (35); Luke 12 :
50, Mark 10 : 33, 34, Matt. 20 :
28, Matt. 16 : 21, 17 : 21, 22,
Luke 9 : 22, 30, Matt. 26 : 39,
42, Luke 22 : 44, John 18 : 11,
(36); Ps. 42 : 7, 69 : 1, 2, 88 :
6, 7, (37); Matt. 5 : 10, (40);
Matt. 16 : 21, Luke 9 : 22, (46);
Rom. 6 : 4, (47); Jerem. 25 :
15-38, Ezek. 23 : 32-47, Matt.
26 : 39, 42, Luke 22 : 42, Mark
14 : 36, John 18 : 11, (49);
Luke 4 : 1, Matt. 4 : 1, (53);
Mark 3 : 23, Luke 11 : 20, (54);
Matt. 3 : 11, Luke 17, (55);
Ephes. 4 : 28, Matt. 27 : 40,
Gal. 1 : 23, (56); Acts 4 : 7, 9,
10, 12, 29, 30, (58); Gal. 3 :
27, 28, John 17 : 21, Joel 2 :
28, Matt. 3 : 11, John 1 : 33,
(127); Eph. 4 : 8, (128); Titus
3 : 5, 6, II Cor. 4 : 16, (129);
Matt. 3 : 13, (145); Matt. 10 :
14, John 6 : 37, Matt. 12 : 13,
Acts 27 : 32, (193); Acts 28 :
3-5, 12 : 7, (194); Matt. 3 : 11,
(208); Luke 24 : 49, Acts 1 : 5,
Gal. 3 : 27, (291); Exod. 14 :
11, 12, 31, (300); Jerem. 13 :

13, Rom. 15 : 24, Acts 5 : 3, Rom. 1 : 29, (314); John 3 : 34, Luke 4 : 18, Matt. 4 : 1, Luke 4 : 14, Matt. 12 : 28, Acts 2 : 33, Rom. 8 : 1, 9, Mark 12 : 36, (320); Dan. 4 : 14, (336).

SIMON MAGUS :
ritually baptized with water, not really baptized by the Holy Ghost, 170.

SPIRITUAL PURIFICATION :
how it originated as a conception belonging to and finally became the meaning of baptism, 307.

SPRINKLING, PURIFIES :
Heb. 10 : 22, Carson, Ernesti, Bloomfield, Rosenmüller, Ebrard, Bengel, Stuart, Calvin, Rev. John Owen, Fairbairn, 381, 382; interpretation, 383, 384; sprinkling washes (Calvin), 384.

STONE :
upon the grave of Lazarus—*upon* the lion's den—*upon* the sepulchre of the Lord Jesus, 198-200.

STOVEL, REV. C. (LONDON) :
I Cor. 10 : 2, 305.

STUART, PROFESSOR MOSES :
into the Name, 405, 436 ; Syriac version, 464.

SYRIAC VERSION .
baptize = " to stand firm," 463-468; correctness shown by Paul's use of βαπτίζω εἰς to express the Hebrew word in Exodus 14 : 31, which literally means "to lean upon," then, "to believe in," 466.

TEACHING, BAPTISM OF :
Heb. 6 : 2, 328, 332-334, 456, 457.

TERTULLIAN :
blood baptism, 38 ; disciples baptized again with spiritual baptism, 116.

THEMISTIUS :
baptism drowns, 47.

THEODORET ;
Ephes. 5 : 26, 369.

THEORY :
modern, of ritual Christian baptism, 18-22 ; outside of this theory, "no baptism, no Lord's supper, no Christian ministry," 21 ; objections to this theory, philological, chronological, symbological, exegetical, 22-26.

TRANSLATION :
the value of εἰς and ἐν and the simple Dative with βαπτίζω, 73-76 ; ἐπὶ, ἐν, εἰς τὸ ὄνομα, Baptist translation of, 132, 133 ; Prof. Hackett, 134 ; true translation of Acts 2 : 38, 137, 195, 205-208, 211, 294 ; commission, 434.

TYNDALE :
translation of Coloss. 2 : 9-13.

TYPE BAPTISM :
baptism "into Moses," type of baptism "into Christ," 294-310 ; I Peter 3 : 21, salvation in the Ark through the destroying water, type of salvation in Christ through his resurrection, triumphing over all enemies, 335-338 ; rite baptism cannot be the antitype of the waters of the flood or of the Ark, because the water of the rite is itself but a symbol, 337 ; salvation by the Ark is a type of the antitype salvation which is by the bap-

tism of the Holy Ghost "into the name of the Lord Jesus;" "into Joshua," 312.

WATER:

why universal symbol of purity, 18; what symbolized in baptism by the Holy Ghost, 18; necessary to ritual baptism; other than ritual baptisms in S. S., in which no water, 100; force of εἰς with Accusative of receiving element, *water* never so used, 118; used in ritual baptism to make manifest the power of the Lamb of God to take away sin, 166; invariably used in the Dative as symbol agency in S. S., never as receiving element, 170-171; only mentioned twice with baptism under Christianity; Acts 8 : 36, 10 : 47, 202; "water" in relation to baptism always spoken of abstractly, 203; quantity never named nor alluded to as entering into the administration of the rite, 209; baptism "into water" language absolutely unknown to the New Testament, 209; not a question as to "into what," *water*, *milk*, *or oil*, 212; essential requisite in ritual baptism, 217; not renewedly mentioned after John's baptism, 217, 218; must be supplied by ellipsis in that same form in which it appears when stated, 218.

WILSON, PROF. ROBERT (BELFAST):

translation of εἰς after βαπτίζω by *for*, wrong, 144, 264, 305, 332, 391, 422, 423; "the commission enjoins baptism" *not* "*into water*, but *into the Name of the Father, and of the Son, and of the Holy Ghost*," 423, 440.

WINER:

52, 53, 56, 104; meaning of ἐκ, 191; εἰς and ἐν not interchanged in doctrinal statements, 310; I Cor. 11 : 23, διὰ, κατὰ, ἐν, identical as respects the sense, 318, 319; Hebrews 6 : 2, 333.

VENEMA:

water of baptism denotes the punishing justice of God; this is the baptism in Matt. 20 : 22, 30.

ZINZENDORF:

view of formula of baptism, 418.

ZUINGLI:

Heb. 6 : 2, baptism of doctrine by both John and Christ, 333.

INDEX.

PATRISTIC BAPTISM.

AGENCY:

the water, the Spirit and the fire are agencies changing the spiritual condition and not receiving elements for a dipping, 518.

AMBROSE:

speaks of baptism by sprinkling, 534 ; baptism like a dye, 549 ; the burial of sins and new birth, 574.

ANNOTATOR:

in sympathy with Patristic views explains the difference between John's baptism by "simple" water and the baptism of Christ, not by "simple" water but by water impregnated with grace by the Holy Spirit, making the water an agency to change the spiritual condition of the soul, and not a receptacle into which the body was to be "dipped," 517 ; error in introducing *water* into the personal baptism of Christ and making water and the Holy Spirit joint agencies in Christian baptism, 518 ; John 4 : 2 ; mersion, perfusion, aspersion, equally belong to Christian baptism, 533 ; Benedictine Monk—water and Spirit effecting Christian baptism, 547 ; Annotator says, Tertullian alludes to men baptized naked, 562 : distinction between "per ipsum" and "in ipsum," the most explicit statement possible that the baptism is, ideally, into Christ, and not physically into water, 616.

AUGUSTINE:

Christian baptism is unlike that of John, which was by water only, being also by the Holy Spirit, 548 ; Moses a type of Christ ; the Egyptians types of sin and their drowning in the sea represents the destruction of sin by baptism and its being left behind in the water, 559 ; Christ still baptizes, he does not hold the body and dip it in water (that is not baptism), but he invisibly washes, cleanses, 563 ; men can dip (that is not baptism), Christ only can wash the conscience (that is baptism), 563 ; his view of Christian baptism ; the sepulchre of Christ is the Christians rest, "buried with him through baptism into his death," 577 ; the Lord Jesus Christ the baptizer and not

men, 578–580; his rebuke to
heretics of his day and its
application to the theorists of
this day, 580.

ASSIMILATION:
essential feature of Christian
baptism, the baptized object
assimilated to the characteristic of the baptizing agency,
493; assimilation belongs to
baptism, painting portrait,
542.

BAPTISM, CHRISTIC:
corrupted by Patristic writers,
471; not by simple water,
516–518.

BAPTISM, JOHN'S:
was a symbol and not a type
baptism, 486; simple water,
516.

BAPTISM, JUDAIC:
not a mere symbol baptism, 485.

BAPTISM, PATRISTIC:
general usage of βαπτίζω, 473;
agreement with other writers,
473; disagreement with inspired writers, 475; the heavens
baptized by the uplifted body
and the earth baptized by the
dropping blood of Christ on
the Cross; John baptized by
touching the head of Jesus,
514; Ambrose, 574; Nazi-
anzen, 575; various names
with the reasons for each
name of baptism, 575, 576;
baptism, crucifixion, burial,
and resurrection, 577, erroneous and leading .nto error,
580; never use baptism or
baptize to express a physical
covering or a momentary dipping, 581.

BAPTISM, SCRIPTURAL:
is ideal: 1, into an ideal element; 2, by a spiritual agency;
3, by a symbol physical agency, water, tongue, dove, cup,
485; real, effective, spiritual
baptism (thorough change of
its spiritual condition), by
the Holy Ghost, 486.

BAPTISM BY THE HOLY GHOST:
was the indwelling of, work by,
in the soul, not an outside
covering, 617.

βαπτίζω:
usage of by Patristic writers;
same meaning with Classic
writers used in the same
sphere; new meaning used
long in religious relations, a
new sphere, 473; Classic
meaning in secular relations,
473; used absolutely to express drunken condition, 474;
intusposition without limit of
act or time = complete influence, 475; physical element,
476; ideal element, 477, 481;
usage of analogous words,
477, 479; used with agency
only, the character of the
agency determining the character of the baptism, 482–484;
βαπτίζω alone cannot declare
the nature of any baptism,
whether physical or ideal,
with covering or without
covering, 485; used to express
the effect of touching the
Jordan by Christ, the waters
of the river were *baptized;*
the effect of John's being
beheaded—was "baptized,"
575; usage of, 581; its use in
legitimate meaning with an
ideal element affirmed, 581;
expresses *effect* and not merely
the fact of covering, as other

words in connection with baptizing, 584–586; affinity is with βάπτω *to dye, to color, to change condition through some quality,* and not with βάπτω *to dip,* to put into and take out of, 602; New Testament usage of, due to this relation, 613, 614; its relations are ideal, 614–622; Patristic and Classic use of, common and diverse, 620, 622; βαπτίζω is not used by inspired writers nor by uninspired Patristic writers to express (in the religious sphere), the passing of an object into a physical element, 622.

Βάπτισμα:

not in Classic Greek, meaning from philology Kühner, Buttman, Sophocles, Jelf, Crosby, Winer, Hermann Cremer, = *result, effect,* 488; only word used for John's or Christian baptism, and never used by Classic, Jewish, Patristic, or inspired writer to express a physical (mersion) baptism, 489; expresses the result, effect (changed condition), baptism of the soul consequent upon the ideal passing into repentance, into the remission of sins, into the Name of the Lord Jesus, into the Name of the Father, Son, and Holy Ghost, *never* used of the *body* passing *into water,* 489; while βαπτίζω is freely used by Patristic writers where a ship or a man passed, into river, lake, or sea, βάπτισμα is never used in such re'ation, nor to express the covered condition of the body in baptism, but

the changed spiritual condition of the soul, 490; the Patristic βάπτισμα expresses a spiritual result in the soul and not a covering in water of the body, 491–543; a new life, 495; diverse names, 497; λουτρόν equivalent of βάπτισμα, 502; diverse, 507; blood, 510; βάπτισμα is applied to the effect and to that producing the effect, therefore *water* is termed a *βάπτισμα,* and so, also, is *blood,* and *tears,* 515; fire baptism, 516–523; by fire and sword, 522; clinic, 523–532; sprinkling, 532; on Carmel, not water covering, 538; a painting, 542; not a physical water covering, 543; compend, Ecclesiastical, Naked, 545–562; like a dye, 549; into his death, 568; of the Jordan, of John the Baptist, 575; called by many names (Greg. Naz.), Why? 575; called baptism "because Sin is buried," 575; not interchanged with Κατάδυσις as equivalent 589–592; three baptisms one baptism, 594; in the passion of the Lord, 611; not physical, 615–619; 621.

Βαπτισμός:

"denotes the act as a fact," Bib. Theol. Lex., 488.

BAPTISM INTO CHRIST:

"into his death"—hidden saying; hard to be understood by many—because of misunderstanding its relation to baptism "into the Name of the Father, and of the Son, and of the Holy Ghost," 568; baptism "into Christ," "into his death," "into the death of the Lord," is a difference of phraseology but one and the same baptism and most scriptural, but *effected* only by the Holy Spirit *symbolized* (as to the purifying power of the blood of Christ), in the rite by water; water for *burial*, oil for Holy Spirit, seal for Cross, ointment for confirmation, all pure human invention, 568; Christ taken away by theory and pool of water substituted, 570; *quasi dye*, 612; a thorough change of spiritual condition assimilating to Christ, 612.

"BAPTISM INTO DEATH :"

what is death? view of Origen; "baptism into Christ," what? difference of "baptism into Law," 572; baptism into death secures and not merely *signifies* burial with Christ in his sepulchre (Augustine), 577.

BAPTISM INTO THE NAME OF THE FATHER, OF THE SON, AND OF THE HOLY GHOST :

" why when such command does the Apostle use only the name of Christian baptism?" view of Origen? 572; criticism of, 573, 574.

BAPTISM INTO THE LAW :

equivalent to baptism into "the fulfilment of all righteousness," 572, 574.

BAPTISM INTO CONDEMNATION :

by fire (Tertullian), 610.

BAPTIZER, THE GREAT :

the Lord Jesus Christ (Ambrose II, 1227); the only baptizer (Augustine); 576–578; did not baptize with his own hands, 610.

BAPTIST BIBLE :

has adopted a Latin word rather than transfer the Greek word as most other translations have done. In doing so they have reversed the action of the Latins themselves, who rejected "immerse" and transferred *baptize*, 613, 614.

BASIL THE GREAT :

definition of βάπτισμα, physical idea repudiated, "thoroughly changed spiritual condition," 491; baptism is an assimilation, the baptized becomes *such* as that of which it is born or baptized, 493, 494.

BATH, WATER OF :

will not wash away sins, the washing of repentance (Justin M.) will, 598; so will "our water" (Tertullian), 562.

BEECHER, PRESIDENT E. :
501.

BENEDICTINE MONK :

explanation of John's baptism by "simple water," and of Christian baptism by the Holy Spirit conjoined with the water, without which Christian baptism could not take place, 547, 516.

BLOOD BAPTISMS :

Tertullian calls " a second *washing*" (lavacrum = λουτρόν), showing that neither "washing" nor baptism required covering in the water or in the blood—cleansing by water or by blood was equally baptism, and both constituted "two baptisms," 510; Cyprian says *baptism* is by martyr-blood, and is superior to baptism by water, so

Origen, 510, 511 ; Christ's
blood baptism, another baptism, not by water nor by the
Spirit, but by blood, by the
blood of his crucifixion, views
of Augustine, Jerome, Chrysostom, 512–514.

BURIAL IN CONNECTION WITH
BAPTISM :

what is its true Patristic conception, 566–580 ; burial as
used in SS. in connection
with the words baptize, baptism (Rom. 6 : 3, 4 ; Coloss.
2 : 12), is not used as the
equivalent of these words,
nor to express a dipping or
a covering in water, nor to
intimate any resemblance
between a burial in earth or
in rock to a dipping into
water and its consequent
momentary covering ; but it
is used to express the co-
burial with Christ in his rock
sepulchre of all those who are
by the Holy Spirit baptized
into His death on the Cross,
566; the theory of modern
Baptists that the SS. use bury
as the equivalent of baptize
is untrue ; the notion that
the SS. speak of a baptism
into water is untrue ; the
notion that the SS. speak of
a baptism (dipping) into
water as an intended likeness
to the burial of Christ in the
rock is still more untrue ; the
notion that the SS. identify
baptism, burial, dipping into
water as equivalent or divinely related conceptions is untrue ; the assumption by
modern Baptists, that their
dipping into water appears in
SS., that it is a command of
God, that it is spoken of as a
burial, and that it constitutes
Christian baptism, is foundationless ; the assumption that
the dipping into water of
modern Baptists, is of the
same purport as the covering
in water by Patristic writers
and that they believed such
covering in simple water to
be Christian baptism, is
foundationless, 566 ; water
covering as likeness to grave
covering does not bring water
covering into any likeness to
Christian baptism, 570, 571 ;
"buried with Christ" means
co-burial in his sepulchre, just
as co-crucifixion means crucifixion with him on his cross ;
there is as much SS. authority
for converting co-crucifixion
into a wooden cross hung
around the neck as to convert
co-burial into a dipping into
water ; Patrists and theorists
make such conversion and
abandon the word of God,
571 ; the only burial of Christ
the SS. know anything about
is his burial in the rock
sepulchre, and the only "burial with him" that we can
have is co-burial in that
same sepulchre ; a dipping
into water cannot give any
such co-burial, but baptism
into his death on the cross
(co-crucifixion) by the Holy
Spirit does give such co-burial
(Rom. 6 : 3, 4), therefore the
teaching of SS. "baptism into
his death" by the Holy Spirit
must stand, and the teaching
of the theorists of a dipping

into *water* (of which the SS.
know nothing) must perish,
571–574; burial in baptism is
applied to the burial of sin
left at the bottom of the pool
—the death (drowning) of sin
in order to a new birth (Ambrose), 574; "the old man is
buried in the water," the new
man is received, 575; "the
old Adam buried in the
water;" this is an honest
baptism, never taken out of
the water, another affair from
a dipping burial, 575; called
baptism because sin is buried,
575; philological right to call
burial of sin in water to stay
there, a βάπτισμα, 576; burial
as used in connection with
the rite, 580; "burial in
water" not the Christian
βάπτισμα, but a symbol of
burial in the rock sepulchre,
621.

CALYPSIS:
    covering of dead body in earth
    like burial but not like Chris-
    tian baptism, 567.

CANCER LIKE SIN BAPTIZED:
    by cutting and burning, Jerome,
    522.

CARSON, ALEX., LL.D.:
    on λούω, 504.

CASE AND PREPOSITION:
    show that water was used as
    agency and not as a receptive
    element, 559, 560.

CHRYSOSTOM:
    gives six names for baptism,
    none a dipping, all of Spirit-
    ual significance, 497, 498;
    entering into the pool, arises
    purer than the rays of the
    sun, through the Holy Spirit,

therefore baptized (not because dipped), made regenerate, 498; baptism likened to
painting, 542.

CHRISTIAN BAPTISM:
    solely a Spiritual baptism by
    the Holy Ghost, and symbol-
    ized as to its purifying nature
    by water in a rite, 485.

CLASSIC AND PATRISTIC βαπτίζω:
    the same in same usage, 476;
    ideal element, 477.

CLEMENS I.
    co-crucifixion, co-death, co-
    burial, co-resurrection, 567;
    subjection to Satan renounced,
    to God avouched, interpreta-
    tion of baptismal formula,
    615.

CLINIC BAPTISM:
    523–532; the theory regards as
    a sham, Patrists regard it as
    of matchless worth, 523; tub
    and pool, and alkali, and
    covering in water not neces-
    sary to baptism, 524; sprink-
    ling of equal value with
    covering, 524–528; Tertul-
    lian, Basil, Eusebius (Nova-
    tian) 528, 529; Chrysostom,
    530, 532; "almost daily"
    baptized, 532, 545.

CONCLUSION:
    βαπτίζω has no physical use,
    inspired or Patristic, 630.

CONDITION:
    thorough change of, meaning of
    βαπτίζω, 474; effect of changed
    condition by covering in a
    fluid for unlimited time, 474;
    extension of the usage of
    βαπτίζω to express this effect
    induced without **covering**,
    474.

COMPEND BAPTISM :

sprinkling water, or familiar intercourse with Christ could confer "compend baptism," 524 ; by blood, saves more speedily, 528 ; a most glorious baptism, 545.

COROLLARY :

1. Assimilative influence ; 2, assimilating influence, in any way = baptism, 476.

COVERING :

baptism with and without covering, 474.

COUNCIL OF CARTHAGE :

water must be baptized itself before it can baptize, 541 ; water without the Holy Spirit cannot purge or sanctify, that is, cannot baptize, 548.

CREMER, HERMANN :

Bib. Theol. Lex. βαπτισμος denotes the act as a fact ; βάπτισμα denotes the result of the act, 488.

CROSS, OINTMENT IN FORM OF :

poured into the water to express grace given to the water and co-crucifixion, 568 ; "every saint nailed to the cross," 571.

CRUCIFIXION, CO- :

as essential an element in Christian baptism as co-burial, 567 ; Christ *really* crucified, buried and raised, others in a *similitude* are co-crucified, co-buried, co-raised, 576.

CYRIL :

explains baptism of the soul by the Holy Spirit ; like fire penetrating iron makes the whole fire, *i.e.* assimilates it to itself, makes the cold hot and the black bright, so the Holy Spirit penetrates the soul and assimilates it to itself, purifying the impure, 556–558 ; buried (in a certain way) in the water as he was buried *in the rock ;* this covering in water is neither Christian baptism nor like it, but like burial in a rock which is neither Christian baptism nor like it, 577.

DIPPING :

no Patristic writer ever affirmed that dipping into water was Christian baptism or was essential to it, 509 ; impossible to use βαπτίζω for momentary dipping in religious use without revolutionizing its secular use, 581 ; its use to express the momentary covering in baptizing denied, 581 ; dipping or momentary covering forbidden as meaning of βαπτίζω by philology, by laws of language, by theology, by essential truth, 582, 583 ; Greek and Latin words used for water covering and uncovering not found in Scripture, 584 : *tingo, intingo, lavo, induo,* not used for dipping (612), 603–614.

DIVERSE BAPTISMS :

of Moses, of John, of Jesus, of blood, of tears, of fire (six), mentioned by Gregory Nazianzen, eight mentioned by Athanasius, 507; their special diversities, 508, 509 ; without dipping, or pouring or sprinkling, 540 ; anointing the head with oil typical baptism ; suffering is eminently true baptism ; circumcision is a baptism ; sanctified water, by prayer, and is a baptism of the water and necessary to its power to baptize, 540, 541; like a dye after many washings, 549.

DOUBLE USAGE.
1, excluding βαπτίζω from the function of καταδύνω *covering in water;* 2, including it in the function of καθαρίζω expressing *spiritual purification,* 603.

DRUNKEN CONDITION:
βαπτίζω used to express, 474.

ECCLESIASTICAL BAPTISM:

EQUIVALENTS:
κάλύπτω, καλύψις, καταδύσις, never used as the equivalents of βαπτίζω, βάπτισμα; *to fill, to trust, to put on,* are so used, 567; Gift, Grace, Baptism, Ointment, Illumination, Vesture, Washing, Seal, 575, 576; words that are used as equivalents in secular application, 581; not used as equivalents with βαπτίζω in religious baptisms, 587–592; καθαρίζω, λόνω, are used as equivalents, 597–601; *tinguimur,* not dipping, 611; *abluo, lavo, tinguo,* καθαρίζω, λούω, are equivalents of βαπτίζω, 597-614; no word merely expressive of passing into or covered with water used by Patrists as the equivalent of βαπτίζω in religious use, 614.

EVIDENCE:
that covering and uncovering in the water originated after inspiration closed from words expressing such action abounding in Patristic writings but never found in inspired writings, 584.

EX NECESSITATE:
according to necessity; An Annotator on Tertullian thoroughly conversant with Patristic writings and sentiments says on II, 736: "Where are those whom Menander has sprinkled (*perfundo*)? Or those whom he has mersed (*mergo*) into his Styx?" Mersion or sprinkling equally belong to Christian baptism. "Mersion *by rule*" (not by the meaning of βαπτίζω and by command of God), "Sprinkling *by necessity*" (the "rule" not being capable of observance, but no departure from the meaning of βαπτίζω or from the command of God), 533.

EX ORDINE:
"according to rule," referring to the ordinary way in which by *a rule of the Church,* not by command of God, nor by the meaning of βαπτίζω, Christian baptism was usually administered, viz., pressing down the head into the water after the candidate has covered the rest of the body; sprinkling or pouring was no less the "rule" of the Church in case of sickness, 533; 545.

FACILITY FOR MISTAKE AND MISREPRESENTATION:
as to the usage of βαπτίζω, 585, 586.

FIGURE OF BAPTISM:
Spirit of God communicating his own quality to the waters when upborne by them in the beginning, 550; Tertullian, Didymus Alexandr, Jerome, Ambrose, 552.

FIRE BAPTISM:

Luke 3 : 16 ; fire applied to the lobe of the ear baptized ; if the ear was not covered by this baptism the whole man was hardly covered in fire, 516 ; Basil says the "fire" was the word of doctrine : Tertullian says the fire of hell; others "tongues as of fire" at Pentecost, 517 ; Basil, Tertullian, Irenæus cauterizing the ear, Origen touching the lips with a coal, Ambrose, Christ the administrator, the Great Baptist, Epiphanius, Jerome ("red-hot iron to the right lobe of the ear") "fiery sword," these fire baptisms boundlessly removed from a "dipping," 516–523.

FIRE AND SWORD BAPTISM:

Sins which could be baptized by neither fire alone, nor by the sword alone, baptized by their conjoint action, 522.

FORMULA, BAPTISMAL:

purport of, ideal passing into and dwelling in Jesus Christ = the true God, 615–620 ; so, Clemens Romanus, Tertullian, Irenæus, Clemens Alex., Origen, Basil M., Gregory Thaum., into the *Name*, into the *death*, into each *Person*, into *Christ*, into *God*, the man baptized *into God*, has *entered into God*, 615–618.

GREGORY NAZIANZEN:

baptism is a new life, an illumination, a thorough change of spiritual condition, "the remodelling of our composition" = *anything but a dip into water*, 495 ; on diverse baptisms, of John, of Moses, of Jesus, of blood, of tears, of fire, 507 ; image of the Emperor in wax does not depend upon iron or the gold nor the power of baptism on presbyter or bishop or water, but the Holy Spirit, 555 ; the Jordan baptized by the Saviour touching its waters ; John baptized by having his head cut off, 575.

HILARY:

baptism by sprinkling, 534 ; "it is the Cross by which we suffer with him, die with him, are buried with him, rise with him and follow him," 577 ; "similitudes" to these things supposed to exist in baptizing, have no scriptural existence, 577.

IDEAL ELEMENT:

in baptism, 477 ; in analogous Greek and Latin words, 479 ; usage of βαπτίζω, 481, 482 ; ideal baptism, the agency not the element expressed, 482 ; καταδύνω never used with ideal element as is βαπτίζω, reason, 601, 602 ; in like manner καθαρίζω, λούω, are not used with ideal element, why ? reason very diverse from the other case, 602, 603 ; *tingo* is used in ideal relations similarly with βαπτίζω ; shown an element which καταδύνω, καθαρίζω, λούω, have not, but which βαπτίζω has, 609–614 ; each person of the Trinity, the ideal element, 612 ; the N.T. use of βαπτίζω to develop the quality of the ideal element, 614–622 ; Annotator, 616 ; *pass into* God, 617, 619.

ILLUSTRATIVE :
of the power of water to baptize—to change the spiritual
condition of the soul ; shown
by power ascribed to water
sprinkled with salt, and power ascribed to ashes of heifer
sprinkled with blood, to purify
and sanctify, 560, 561.

IMPREGNATED WATER :
water, "simple" is said to be
"sterile," "empty," "un-
married," will not procreate
(= baptize), it must first be
fecundated by the Holy Spirit
in order to procreate grace
(= baptize), 516, 517, 532,
533, 549; such water is as
full of divine grace as a murex
dye is full of purple color,
and imparts grace to the soul
as the dye imparts its purple
to a fleece, 549 ; illustrated by
special quality and power of
waters, 550, 586.

IMBUED :
by these mysteries, the water of
baptism was supposed to have
a divine quality which like a
dye penetrated the soul and
gave its quality to it, 578.

INITIAL ERROR :
of Patrists that water and the
Holy Spirit were to be conjoined in Christian baptism,
547 ; destroys the Scripture
rite baptism, 547.

INSPIRED WRITERS :
never use βαπτίζω to cover an
object in water or in any
other physical element ; used
only in the religious sphere
(= thoroughly changed spiritual condition), εἰς indicating
the ideal element into which

the baptized object is represented as passing and which
gives specific character to the
baptism (= the thoroughly
changed spiritual condition),
474 ; never use words—
demergo, emergo, to express
covering and uncovering in
baptizing; such words abound-
ingly used by uninspired
writers ; βαπτίζω has no such
use or meaning, 584-586.

INNOCENCE :
put on innocence (612) ; "put on
Christ," 275-293.

IRENÆUS :
speaks of some heretics, "who
say to conduct to the water is
unnecessary, and mixing oil
and water sprinkle it on the
head." As Irenæus wrote in
the second century, any distinct statement of the manner
of using the water is of value,
533 ; Justin Martyr speaks of
"conducting to where there
was water" for "regenera-
ting," but he says nothing of
the manner of using the
water, 533.

JEROME, THE GREEK :
we know we have been baptized
not by any outward thing,
but by inward change wrought
in the soul by the Holy Spirit,
495, 496 ; not a water dipping,
497 ; baptism by sprinkling,
534.

JEROME :
water must first be washed
(cleansed, receive a spiritual
power from the Holy Spirit)
before it can baptize, 492 ;
water can be baptized, it cannot be dipped, 493 ; baptism

is an assimilation, as earthen jar becomes such like in smell and taste as the liquor poured in it, 494.

JEWISH WRITERS :

use βαπτίζω (like Classic writers) to express a covered condition without limit of time including effect, a thoroughly changed condition without covering, and a thoroughly changed ceremonial condition in religious rite, however the agency might be used, 474.

JORDAN :

baptized (sanctified) by touch of Jesus ; John baptized (sanctified) by touching with his hand the head of Jesus ; also, baptized by martyrdom, 575.

JUSTIN MARTYR :

we take them to where there is water and they are regenerated as we were, I, 240 ; some think "taking to where there is water" indicates a dipping into water ; but this interpretation is arrested by the statement of Irenæus (664), "some of them say, *conducting to the water is unnecessary*, and mixing together oil and water they *sprinkle it* on the head of the baptized." These were heretics, but this does not affect the use of language, 533.

Καλύπτω, κάλνψις :

will any one say that these words are used as of the same meaning as βαπτίζω, βάπτισμα ? They are used as of the same meaning as καταδύνω, κατάδυσις, 587, 588 ;

such terms make no appearance in Scripture in connection with baptism. They show conclusively that a new idea has been introduced into baptism by Patrists of which inspiration knows nothing, 587–592.

καθαρίζω :

is used as the equivalent of βαπτίζω ; so are kindred terms, λούω, *mundo, lavo* (but καταδύω, θάπτω, mergo, immergo, demergo, emergo, which are not kindred terms, 587, 595), 597–601.

LATIN WORDS .

demergo, emergo, are abundantly used to represent καταδύνω, αναδύνω, covering and uncovering in the water, but are not used to translate or express the idea of βαπτίζω, which word is transferred into the Latin and not translated except rarely when it is represented by *tingo, tinguo,* used in a derived sense and not in the primary meaning, 585.

LATIN AND GREEK TERMS :

expressing covering in water are in Patristic use markedly diverse from the use of βαπτίζω, 594–595.

LAVO :

illoti, lavacrum, tincti, baptismus, all used interchangeably —cleansing—without water covering, any more than a " *lavacrum* of blood" was a covering in blood, 611, 612.

Δουτρόν :

views of, by Crosby, Buttman, Kühner, Liddell, and Scott,

Cremer, and Ellicott; λούειν used in Septuagint "for theoretic washings for sins," denotes cleansing, purification, 498–500; not limited to laver, nor to water in laver, but means the washing, the spiritual cleansing, 501, 502; *lutric* power of bath washing, of Jewish washing, of bridal washing, of grace washing, *lutric* power of repentance, of faith, of regeneration through the Holy Ghost by the blood of the Lamb of God, 503; λουτρόν the equivalent of βάπτισμα, 503, 504; argument from λουτρόν to prove covering in water in baptism fails, 506; a cleansing by pouring, 535; not a "bathing place," not "water for a bath," not a "laver," but a *cleansing* (ceremonial), 536; wash this (λουτρόν) washing, impossible can mean laver or water for bath or bathing place, 540; so, = a washing, makes sins disappear, 542; washing, because it is a washing out, 575, 576,

Λούω :
no modal use in, no necessary immersion nor covering in any way, as none in βαπτίζω, in religious rites to cleanse the whole object not necessary to apply the cleansing agency to the whole of the object, sprinkling has a perfect washing (= cleansing) power not limited to the *spots* on which the drop may fall, 504–507; argument from λούω to prove water covering in baptism fails, 506.

MARTYRDOM :
John the Baptist baptized by martyrdom, 575.

MARITAT (*Sanctus Spiritus*) :
Cælestique sacras fonte *maritat* aquas used to express the union and conjoint action of the Holy Spirit and water in Christian baptism not to effect a dipping but to give birth to the soul, 533.

MENANDER :
virtue ascribed to his water in baptizing analogous to that claimed for "our water" by Patrists, 549, 550; this water of Menander Tertullian thinks belongs to "magic art," and no less does his own water, 549, 550

MERGO, MERGITO :
not used as the equivalents of βαπτίζω, 592–595.

MERSION (*mersio*) :
when practiced in baptizing indicated not the meaning of βαπτίζω nor obedience to any command of God, but a representation of "death and burial," co-death and co-burial with Christ, for which Patrism not the Bible is responsible, 533; three mersions not one mersion, 594, 595.

MISREPRESENTATION :
of Matthew 3 : 11; John 3 : 5.

MODE :
no modal limitation in λούω; none in symbol cleansing by water, any more than in cleansing by the word, by regeneration, or by the blood of Christ, 504; that Christian baptism consisted in a water dipping no Patristic

writer believed ; that sprinkling effected a perfect Christian baptism, no Patristic writer denied, 509 ; no more modality belongs to water baptism than to tears baptism or blood baptism, 515.

MOSES, YOUR :
the Lord Jesus Christ to destroy (drown) sin in the water of baptism as the Egyptians perished in the sea, 570.

NAKED BAPTISM
male and female so baptized through centuries, 545 ; Annotator on Tertullian says, he alludes to the rite of baptism in which men were baptized naked (*nudi*), 562 ; reference to naked baptism—"not much or not at all cleaner," 563.

NEW TESTAMENT USAGE :
of βαπτίζω is to develop the characteristic quality of the ideal element over the baptized object, assimilating it to that quality, as an object dyed is assimilated to the characteristic quality of the dye, 614 ; never has water or any other physical fluid as its complementary element, 614.

NOVATIAN :
baptized by pouring when sick ; attempt to discredit this baptism, 529, 530.

OINTMENT, FORM OF CROSS :
poured into the water—cross the instrument of Christ's death, water the symbol of death, covering in water a symbol of baptism "into his death"—of which symbol SS. know nothing, 568.

ORIGEN :
every saint is nailed to the Cross with Christ and is buried with him and raised with him, the one just as truly and in the same sense as the other ; crucifixion and death was intended to be embodied in the rite as much as burial and resurrection ; the word βαπτίζω was as much intended to express the act of nailing to the Cross as the act of covering in water, 571.

ORIGIN OF INQUIRY :
personal instruction, 623.

"OUR WATER :"
that used by Patrists had (as claimed) a special quality of grace which communicated grace as a purple dye communicates a purple color, and which no other water could do, any more than a liquid without color could make a purple color. This grace communicated to the soul was Patristic baptism, and no other water could baptize, any more than uncolored water could dye purple, 549 ; "our water" washes from sin and gives eternal life, 562.

OVID :
the use of *tingo* neither with the meaning "to dip" nor "to dye," but in the sense of changing condition in relation to some characteristic other than color and without the act of dipping. It is in this sense that Tertullian uses *tinguo* when he uses it to translate βαπτίζω, 533 ; uses it in religious rites of heathen-

ism in the sense to cleanse, to imbue with purifying qualities of "fire and sprinkled water," 605 ; this purification by sprinkled water, 606 ; tingo used to change condition of water by new quality imparted to it without any possibility of dipping, 607 ; analogy of baptisms with the *tincted* water of the fountain, 607 ; Tertullian used *tingo* with an eye to modify its secondary meaning, not to express its primary : failed to make it accepted to express βαπτίζω, 608, 609.

PATRISTIC BAPTISM :
    not accordant with Inspired, Christian, baptism, 475, 485 ; effected by joint action of water and Holy Spirit, 485 ; source of Patristic error, 485 -487 ; not physical nor symbol, but spiritual, 563.

PATRISTIC USAGE OF βαπτίζω :
    475-487 ; contrasted with Scripture usage, 584.

PATRISTIC WRITERS .
    exhibit the usage of βαπτίζω in all the varied forms presented by Classic, Jewish, and Inspired writers, 475 ; differ from inspired writers in various conceptions of Christian Baptism, 475 ; always represent Christian baptism as a spiritual and not as a physical baptism, 485 ; believed that sprinkling and pouring did baptize, 535.

PETILIAN :
    says Christ has ceased to baptize ; Augustine denies this, 563.

PHILOLOGY :
    with theology forbids the meaning " to dip" or to cover for a moment, 582.

PHYSICAL USE, NONE :
    proof ended, 614-620.

POWER OF BAPTISM :
    has the power of the Holy Spirit, which works in the water so that they who deserve hell being baptized mount to heaven, Augustine, 555 ; has power by one washing to take away the seven capital sins, Tertullian, 555-565 ; has the power of sanctification, 554.

PORPHYRY :
    marriage purification, 501.

πρωτον ψευδος :
    incorporating water with the distinctive baptizing of Christ, 518.

PURIFICATION, VARIETIES OF :
    of baths, of bridal, of Jewish, of grace (spiritual), 583.

POURING BAPTISM ;
    Origen, Basil, Gregory, Ambrose, 535-539 ; pouring and sprinkling, 538.

PROOF ENDED :
    showing that the Patristic βαπτίζω has no physical use,

PURIFIED (καθαρον) WATER :

PURIFY, TO :
    βαπτίζω secures this meaning beyond all rational controversy, 595-597 ; καθαρίζω, λούω, equivalents, 597-601.

PUT ON :
    "if we cease to sin by the waters we *put on* (*induimus*) *innocence*," 612 ; illustrates

baptized into Christ = *put on Christ*, 285-290.

QUALITY, THAT WATER MAY BE ABLE TO BAPTIZE

a new and divine quality necessary for water without which it cannot baptize (proof that baptizing is not dipping), 550, 552, 554 ; Augustine, 555.

QUARTERLY, CHRISTIAN (C. B.) :

baptism, burial of old man, rising up of new man, 20 ; Baptist Quarterly on Acts 2 : 38, 146-148 ; criticism on, 149-153, 211.

QUOTATIONS :

showing the diversity of function and meaning of βαπτίζω as compared with κατα βαίνω, ἀνα βαίνω, βάπτω, καλύπτω ; none of these words appear in Scripture to denote water covering in baptizing, nor was there any water covering known to Scripture, 587-592.

REBUKE :

by Augustine to some heretics of his day for claiming baptism and the Lord's table as theirs, 580.

REPENTANCE :

washes (= cleanses) the heart, 611 ; this heart washing by repentance is the equivalent of the "baptism of repentance," and of "I baptize into repentance" = that spiritual change of condition which repentance begets, 328-331.

RENUNCIATION OF SATAN :

by the candidate in baptism with declared subjection to Christ—to the Father, Son, and Holy Ghost, proves the baptism to be "into Christ," —"into the name of the Father, Son, and HolyGhost," and that such baptism was understood to mean breaking away from subjection to Satan and entering into subjection to the living and true God, 615.

RESULTS OF THE INQUIRY :

general, 624 ; special, 625 ; final, 629

SATAN, SUBJECTION TO :

renounced in baptism ; the sinner lives in subjection to and in the spirit of Satan ; a baptized condition=a thoroughly changed spiritual condition, changes this subjection and establishes subjection to the true God ; this is the purport of the formula " baptized into the Name," and therefore the candidate renounced subjection to Satan and avowed subjection to the Father, Son, and Holy Ghost, 615.

SCRIPTURE PASSAGES ILLUSTRATED :

Matt. 3 : 11; John 3 : 5, 471; Rom. 6 : 3, 475 ; Luke 24 : 49, 486 ; I Cor. 12 : 13, 487 ; Ephes. 5 : 26, 499 ; Heb. 10 : 22, Rev. 1 : 5, Ephes. 5 : 26, Tit. 3 : 5, 500 ; Ephes. 5 : 26, Titus 3 : 5, Rev. 1 : 5, Heb. 10 : 22, 504 ; John 3 : 5, Ephes. 5 : 26, Rom. 10 : 22, 505 ; Rev. 1 : 5, 506 ; Luke 12 : 50, 510 ; Luke 3 : 16, 516 ; John 4 : 2, Acts 1 : 5, Acts 2 : 4, 10 : 44, I Cor. 12 : 13, 518 ; Matt. 10 : 34, Luke 12 : 49, 522 ; Ezek. 36 : 25, 26, Numb. 8 : 5, 7, Numb. 19 : 8-13, 525 ; I Cor. 12 : 13, John 4 : 2, 3 : 5, 548.

SEPULCHRE, NEW :

all baptized by the Holy Spirit into Christ's death are co-crucified with him, are co-buried with him in his *new sepulchre;* dipping into water does not bury in the new rock sepulchre ; " death to sin," "born from above " does bury with Christ, 571, 574.

" SIMPLE " WATER :

cannot baptize, this is universal Patristic doctrine, 513 ; by "simple" water is meant ordinary water, water for the bath, water not impregnated with a special divine power, 517, 492, 546 ; Patristic the-ology knows no "simple" water in its baptism, no amount of dipping or immer-sing in "simple" water would effect Patristic baptism, 546, 547 ; baptism, the washing of sin, not by "simple" water, but by spiritual grace, 554.

SPRINKLING BAPTISMS :

Tertullian says the heathen think their idols can make baptism (by sprinkling, or otherwise) as efficacious as the true God ; they cannot, because the water they use is "unmarried," unimpregnated with divine grace, not for lack of dipping, 532 ; sprink-ling or pouring indicated the washing (*lavationem*) from sins, 533 ; Ambrose speaks of baptisms by sprinkling, 534 ; Augustine, 534, 535 ; sprink-ling and pouring, 538 ; sprink-ling has power to wash, cleanse, purify, sanctify, bap-tize, 561.

STYGIAN POOLS :

power of waters, illustrative of the peculiar power attributed to the waters of the baptis-mal pool, 550.

SYMBOL TEACHING .

" body covered in earth a like-ness to death and burial," but not to Christian baptism, 567.

TEARS' BAPTISM :

tears baptize equally with the baptism of water—Peter and the harlot baptized by tears, Athanasius ; robber baptized a second time by tears, Clemens Alex., tears (as is the water) the agency, 514–516.

TERTULLIAN :

views of baptism, not physical covering, but a change of character, condition, baptism of the waters, 492 ; uses *tinguo* frequently to translate βαπτίζω, but not in the sense *to dip,* but in its secondary sense, to change condition (as to color or other characteristic), 516 ; water cannot baptize without the Spirit nor the Spirit with-out the water, 548 ; water baptized, in the beginning, by the Holy Spirit, 550 ; cleanses the seven capital sins, 555 ; reference to *naked* baptism, 562 ; not much cleaner, 563 ; tingo not used in baptism in the meaning *to dip,* 569 ; relation to βάπτω *to dye,* 569 ; ideal use, passes from feebleness to power, 570 ; use of tingo as the equivalent of βαπτίζω (changing condi-tion by new quality), 603–613 ; abandoned, 614.

THEORY, VIEW OF BAPTISM BY :
water covering, a dipping, Lord
Jesus has ceased to baptize,
564 ; Augustine denies both,
563, 564 ; fruits of this theory,
565.

THREE BAPTISMS = ONE BAP-
TISM ·
may be rational that baptism
into the several persons of
the Trinity constitute one
baptism into the common
Name of the Trinity ; but
not rational that *three mersions in water* constitute *one
mersion in water !* 593, 594.

TINGUO, TINGO :
used by Tertullian frequently to
translate βαπτίζω, but not with
the meaning *to dip;* but extending the secondary meaning (to change condition as to
color) so as to change condition by some other characteristic than that of color, 516 ;
this usage noticeable, 569 ;
" to dip" is one meaning of
tingo but not sole meaning,
nor in this sense does it ever
represent βαπτίζω ; means *to
dye, to imbue,* and in this
latter meaning most nearly
represents the Greek word as
used, limitedly, by Patrists,
604 ; Patristic baptizing water
has a quality which no other
water has and which operates
assimilatingly upon the baptized as a dye does upon a
fleece, assimilating the wool
to its special color, 604-609 ;
tingo used in ideal relations
like βαπτίζω and for the same
reason, both are related to a
coloring element ; καταδύνω,

καθαρίζω, λούω, *mergo, demergo,*
are not so related, and have
no such usage ; conclusive as
to the essentially distinctive
character of these words,
609-614 ; Tertullian knew
Greek, he never could have
fallen into the error *tingo* (as
dip) expounded βαπτίζω, an
error from which the theory
is slowly and sadly emerging,
609, 610 ; equivalence between
tingo and βάπτω, 613 ; better
fitness of *tingo* above *mergo,*
καταδύνω, etc., 614.

TRANSFER OF βαπτίζω :
most languages have found
difficulty in translating βαπτίζω and have preferred to
transfer it from the Greek,
613 ; the Baptist Bible has
preferred to adopt a Latin
word (*immerse*) which the
Latins themselves rejected,
and are involved in its em-
barrassments and errors, 613,
614.

TRI-DIPPING :
something more than com-
manded by the Lord (Tertullian), 568 ; one dipping
into water is just as little
commanded by the Lord as
three, 569.

TYPE :
baptism of regeneration (namely, thorough change in the
spiritual condition of the soul
in removing sin and implant-
ing a new life), is a "type"
of Christ's death "through
the Cross for· all," that is,
makes sharers in his crucifixion, his death, his burial,

his resurrection, and recipients of all spiritual blessings secured by crucifixion, death, burial, and resurrection. Patrists believed these blessings efficiently conveyed through water imbued with divine power ; they believed covering in water gave a resemblance to burial in the rock, and they so say very abundantly, but they did not believe that this covering in water was Christian baptism, the baptism of Christ, "the baptism of regeneration," nor was necessary to it any more than a resemblance to crucifixion was Christian baptism, although they dropped oil into the water in the shape of a Cross. It is an utter error and perversion of Patristic sentiment to convert into Christian baptism the resemblance they trace between water covering and the rock burial. And this water covering and resemblance to burial is as unknown to the SS. as is the traced resemblance between the darkness under the water and the darkness of the night during the rock burial, 567–580 ; type or symbol burial with Christ by dipping for a moment the body into water is a very different thing (567 Clemens I), from the burial of sin, the old Adam, in the water, never to come out (575, 576, Greg. Naz.) ; type burial resurrection. coverings not Christian baptism, 592.

ὕδατι καὶ Πνεύματι :
"by water and the Spirit ;" Patristic baptism was a thorough change in the spiritual condition of the soul effected by the Holy Spirit operating through the water as a vehicle. The church rule for using the water was by covering the naked body in it ; but the covering (instead of constituting the baptism), had, as a covering, nothing to do with the baptism, but was observed for a wholly different purpose, namely, for the covering of the body of Christ ın the sepulchre. Patristic writings know absolutely nothing of a dipping—into and out of water—as constituting Christian baptism and a command from God expressed by βαπτίζω. The water covering is for a wholly different purpose and rests on an entirely different basis. The notion that Patristic baptism consisted in a dipping into simple watᴄr cannot be introduced into their theology without dislocating every tier of their system from top stone to foundation stone, 544–565 ; the use of water by sprinkling or pouring in Christian baptizing was an "almost daily" (Ambrose) fact, and by such sprinklings and pourings, all, through a thousand years, declared Christian baptism was effected ; that this united voice declared a "dipping" was effected by a sprinkling or a

pouring, men mad on a theory may believe, but others will decline while sanity bears rule, 544; water cannot baptize without the Spirit nor the Spirit without the water, 548.

VENEMA:
water of baptism denotes punishing justice of God; this is the baptism, Matt. 20 : 22, 30.

"WASH PERFECTLY :"
the divine word washes, confession washes, right thinking washes, just working washes, good conversation washes; so washed the soul imbibes spiritual grace from the impregnated water as a fleece of wool imbibes a purple color from a murex dye, 549; washing ("by blood") not used for covering in, 611; repentance washes the heart, 611.

WATER:
not used by Patrists as a symbol but as co-active and co-efficient through and with the Holy Spirit, 475, 486; this error *fons et origo malorum*, 487; baptism of the waters to give new quality fitting them to baptize, to give new quality, not to enable them to cover, 492; water can be baptized; before it is baptized itself it cannot baptize any one, 492, 493; water efficient element in spiritual λουτρον, cleansing, baptism, 503; water in John 3 : 5, Eph. 5 : 26, Rom. 10 : 22, no direct reference to water used in baptism, 505; "simple" water scornfully repudiated

as without power to baptize, 513; John's baptism was by "simple" water, Christ's was not, 516, 517; universal sentiment that water effects no baptism within the range of its natural qualities; dipping of the head into water regarded by no one as Christian baptism, 523; unmarried waters, not joined with divine grace and the power of the Holy Spirit, cannot baptize, 533; water itself baptized, 541; like a dye, 549; special quality and power given to waters, 549, 550, 556; a great power and agency (Tertullian), 559; power conferred upon water to purify and sanctify through salt sprinkled on, and prayer (Pope Alexander), 560; "our water" produces life, 562, 563; water used in baptism because as water cleanses the body from filth, so *baptism* cleanses the soul from sin (Ambrose), 574; *that* water cleanses the body and the soul, all water does not; take away the Word and the water is but water; the Word cleanses through the water because he walked upon the waters, 578; water of bath will not wash away sins, 598; water covering not the Christian βάπτισμα, but symbol of a very different thing, 621

WORDS ANALOGOUS TO βαπτίζω:
with like syntax, 477–479; also, used ideally, 479–481; like usage of βαπτίζω, 481, 482.

ZONARAS:
definition of λουτρὰ, 501.

AUTHORS QUOTED.

GENERALLY OF THE FIRST FIVE CENTURIES.

ALEXANDER I: 560.

AMBROSE: 507, 520, 521, 532, 534, 537, 538, 549, 552, 574, 608.

APOSTOLICAL CONSTITUTIONS: 592.

ATHANASIUS: 507, 514, 515, 516, 589, 600.

AUGUSTINE: 480, 486, 512, 517, 528, 529, 534, 548, 555, 559, 563, 564, 576, 608.

BASIL MAGNUS: 476, 477, 491, 493, 501, 519, 522, 528, 536, 590, 619.

CHRYSOSTOM: 497, 500, 501, 502, 503, 506, 507, 513, 514, 530, 542.

CLEMENS ALEXANDRINUS: 476, 477, 479, 480, 481, 482, 483, 484, 506, 514, 516, 553, 560, 618.

CLEMENS ROMANUS: 477, 478, 479, 540, 567, 587, 591, 597, 615.

COUNCIL OF CARTHAGE: 548.

CYPRIAN: 510, 511, 524, 527, 541, 607.

CYRIL: 553, 556, 558, 559, 576, 587.

DIDYMUS ALEXANDR: 551, 588.

DIONYSIUS AREOPAGITUS: 567, 568, 587, 591, 598.

EPIPHANIUS: 522, 552, 556.

EUSEBIUS: 529, 555.

GREGORY NAZIANZEN: 495, 507, 508, 536, 555, 558, 560, 575, 600.

GREGORY THAUM.: 588, 619.

HERACLEON: 516.

HIERONYMUS GRŒCUS: 495.

HILARY: 480, 507, 534, 576.

IGNATIUS: 598, 616.

IRENÆUS: 519, 533, 617.

JEROME: 480, 492, 494, 512, 522, 534, 552, 560, 593.

JOSEPHUS: 477, 482, 499.

JUSTIN MARTYR: 500, 501, 502, 503, 505, 517, 540, 560, 598.

MARCI EREMITÆ: 478, 483, 552.

MENANDER: 550.

NONNUS PANOP.: 600.

ORIGEN: 478, 480, 500, 506, 511, 519, 535, 553, 560, 571, 595, 599, 618.

PETILIAN: 563.

PHOTIUS: 501, 592.

TERTULLIAN: 479, 480, 492, 510, 516, 519, 524, 528, 532, 533, 541, 547, 548, 549, 550, 552, 553, 555, 559, 562, 568, 569, 592, 596, 598, 604, 605, 606, 608, 609–614, 616.

THEOPHYLACT: 592.

VALENTINUS: 516.

CLASSIC, AND OTHER AUTHORS.

ACHILLES TATIUS: 484.

CONON: 483.

EVENUS: 483.

HIPPOCRATES: 545.

HOMER: 499.

JAMBLICHUS: 609.

OVID: 533, 605, 606, 607.

PORPHYRY: 501.

GRAMMARIANS, LEXICOGRAPHERS, AND ANNOTATORS.

BALSAMON: 592.

BUTTMAN: 488, 498.

CORBIN, THOMAS: 516, 547.

CREMER, HERMANN: 488, 500.

CROSBY: 488, 498.

HEINSIUS: 600.

JELF: 488.

KUHNER: 488, 499.

LIDDELL & SCOTT: 499, 500.

ROBINSON: 499.

WINER: 488.

ZONARAS: 501, 592.